# DRAWING
# WRITING
## and the new literacy
### where verbal meets visual

## Susan Rich Sheridan

# Drawing/Writing Publications
68 Maplewood Drive
Amherst, MA 01002
(413) 549-1606
sheridan@k12.oit.umass.edu

Manufactured in the United States of America
**ISBN 0-9661422-0-9**

## Dedication

## To my mother

## ⅅ **Virginia Ruth Garberson Rich** ⅾ

*I would not be a writer nor a painter nor care as much as I do about people were it not for her influence.*

Virginia Ruth Garberson Rich
Jacket photo, *The Nantucket Diet Murders* by Virginia Rich
Author's photo copyright (c) 1985 by Brad Hess

# Acknowledgements:

Thanks to Cheryl Wright of Mystic Graphic Systems, designer of this book, for unflagging effort at the highest professional levels, and to Al Gismondi, a man of considerable generosity, President of Mystic Graphic Systems, Inc. in Woburn, MA, for printing and binding this book. Thanks to Doreen and Bob Daley of Dee Cee Graphics in Woburn, MA. Doreen provided much-appreciated product management support in the early stages and connected the author with Mystic Graphics.

Thanks to Kathryn Ann Graphics, Amherst, MA for promotional materials.

✦ ✦ ✦ ✦ ✦ ✦ ✦ ✦ ✦ ✦ ✦ ✦ ✦

As ever, I acknowledge my mother, Virginia Ruth Garberson Rich, writer and thinker. She taught me that I could do anything I wanted to, if I wanted to enough.

My father, Raymond Arthur Rich, who taught me perseverence and drive—invaluable skills when facing self-imposed challenges.

My three children, Jessica Rich Sheridan, Samuel Asa Sheridan, and Sarah Virginia Sheridan, whose names and lives are mentioned in this book. I thank them for their clear and courageous selves which have clarified and strengthened my life since each of them entered my life at their births. I also thank Sarah and Sam for their Drawing/Writing work included in this book, as well as for the extra illustrations which Sam provided. Jessica's business expertise was critical to this book's marketing and production, as has been her constant encouragement and support. To have your children believe in you as you believe in them is a humbling and moving experience.

My former husband, Michael Sheridan, who suggested I go back to graduate school in the late 1970's and who suggested I might think about becoming a teacher.

My sister-in-law, Gail Sheridan, who insisted on buying me the MacIntosh Performa 635CD on which I have finalized this book, and who called me weekly for several years to see how I was doing.

My brother, John Dayton Rich, and my cousins, Molly Bannister and John Dayton Garberson, for unconditional love. No one, especially someone trying to write and self-publish an innovative book, especially one in education, can survive a challenge like this without daily infusions of love. John Rich, Molly Heggen and John Garberson provided me with this love via e-mail from California, Shanghai, Calgary and Basel.

My cousins Whit and Jeff Garberson for their support via e-mail.

My second cousin, John Bannister, an undergraduate at Reed College in Oregon, whose letter of application to Columbia University's summer Physics internship program provided clarification and validation on the mutual interdependence of model making, practical research and theory. This letter is found at the end of the book in the section "Terms and Powerful Ideas" under the term "cross-modal."

Ronald C. Bechtle, who has undeviatingly lived his life through his art. A man with an extraordinarily lively mind, Charlie has been my life's mentor, believing in me as a painter and thinker since I was eleven. It was because of Charlie that I was allowed to paint a non-figurative mural featuring a male figure, a female figure and a lighthouse in primary colors and geometric forms over a pale, discreet Arcadian landscape featuring shepherdesses on the wall leading down to our formal dining room in Philadelphia. It is because of Charlie that I never stopped painting, even if the only time and space were in the middle of the night in the basement. Charlie stood me in front of Picasso's "Les Demoiselles D'Avignon" at MOMA and asked me why it was a poor painting. That's the kind of questions he asks.
Isabel Bechtle, my thanks to you, as ever, for support.

WHL, Jr. for unswerving belief across time and space. I hold the same for him.

The freelance editor, Ellen La Fleche of Northampton, MA for asking me for an entire year what I meant, demanding ever stronger verbs, and insisting on an active, non-apologetic voice.

Dr. Valerie Faith, teacher and author of "Illiteracy and Alienation"—my final editor. Valerie's experience in the field of literacy education made her invaluable as my editor, as was her ability to move me from inner speech to speech designed to reach my readers.

Priscilla Drucker, photographer, content and line editor.

Hoagland Keep, whose intellectual depth I respect and value and whose comments on the beginning of Part One were most helpful.

Dr. Barbara Keim, Chair of the Art Department at Westfield State College, for unflagging support.

Dr. Catherine Lilly, Dean of the Department of Continuing Education, Westfield State for supporting a lecture and a pilot course in Drawing/Writing.

Julian F. Fleron, Ph.D., Assistant Professor of Mathematics, Westfield State, for introducing me to Harvard Consortium's Rule of Four. Dr. Fleron has expanded the Rule of Four to the Rule of Five by adding three-dimensional manipulatables of his own construction from wood and wire to calculus instruction. (The Consortium's Four strategies include: words in sentences, graphs or pictures, algebraic notation, and numerical expression. See David Smith, "Trends in Calculus Reform," 1994 in Works Cited.) Photos of the "loaf," and the "deck" and the "cube on a curving wire"—Julian's calculus "toys"—are included in the text. As a teacher of elementary school-age children as well as of college level students, Julian understands that abstract thought requires concrete models at all levels of understanding. This appreciation for direct learning through touch is one of the tenets uniting Julian and me. In addition, our shared passion for ideas and for teaching join us.

I also thank Julian for connecting me through e-mail with the *Humanistic Mathematics Network Journal* and its editor Alvin White. I also thank him for casting a critical and informed eye on the mathematics and geometry sections in this book. Any remaining mistakes are mine. Julian's comments about the new literacy located on the back cover of this book indicate his understanding of my work as content and intent. I am most grateful for those comments.

Besides the importance of concrete models, Julian and I agree that the ability to speak more than one language is, if not critical to understanding, deeply useful to understanding.

Joan Arbeiter, New York painter and art teacher, for pushing me and networking for me since we presented at the CAA together in 1995 when 80 art educators asked me for this book.

Dr. William C. Wolf, Jr., former UMASS School of Education professor and member of my doctoral committee, 1991, for continuing support and advice.

Dr. Katherine Fite, Professor of Biology and Neurobiology, UMASS, Amherst, for serving as a member of my doctoral committee and for on-going support and information.

Dr. David Andrews, Professor of Psychology, Keene State, Keene, New Hampshire, for reading *Hitchhikers' Guide* with a critical eye and for sharing my interest in the relevance of brain science to education.

Dr. Anthony Burgess, University College, London, for confirming the fact that I had written a book that Breadloaf summer at Oxford in 1992 and for believing that, with work, it might make its way into the world.

Dr. Benoit Mandelbrot for generous permission to use images from his book *The Fractal Geometry of Nature*.

Dr. Cosimo Favaloro, archeologist and Northfield Mount Hermon School teacher, for enlightening conversations about paleolithic symbols.

Dr. Arthur Localio for support throughout the doctoral process, including arranging medical research support, and for connecting me with Dr. Rodolpho Llinas.

My former students who are taking Drawing/Writing into the field and who believe in me as much as I believe in them: Karen Whitney, Claus Kormannshaus, Anne Charron, Jean Whitlock, Joanne Quail, and Holly Tuttle.

Claus Kormannshaus (artist, art teacher, MAT student), Pamela Frigo (commercial graphic artist), Tim Lis (graphic artist), and Joanne Krawczyk (high school art teacher) in particular for their visual and verbal contributions to this book, as well as my deepest thanks to many former and current students from many schools and colleges for their contributions to this book.

Elizabeth Nyman of Skidmore College and Deerfield, Massachusetts for her two photographs—the sunflower and the chambered nautilus—which help to illustrate the section on fractal geometry.

Christopher Pennock of Dartmouth, and Ted Hsieh of Yale for interest in my thinking and in this book. I extend my belief and interest to them and their work in psychoacoustics, cell receptor sites, and the stock market.

Peter and Jeannine Lawall, owners and operators of Micro Research, Amherst, Mass., for patience beyond the bounds of professional service.

F.S. for the scanner, enabling me to take control of the images as well as the text for this book.

The Allen family of Deerfield, Shelburne and Buckland, MA for support and help with the data base, mailings, final editing, and book jacket photo.

As ever, for my students over the past seventeen years who have ranged in age from five to 80, pre-K through college level to the Elderhostel level, including art education, regular education, ESL education, special education, prison education, talented and gifted education, literacy education. Of these students, I especially thank Anne Charron of Westfield State who first used Drawing/Writing in her art ed. pre-practicum. I thank all of my students who have come away from my courses knowing they are more powerful thinkers.

For all teachers and other readers who work with this book, I send my thanks and my wishes for your success in this journey toward a humanistic literacy. The ways in which we touch each other's lives makes a difference. May you touch your students' lives, your children' s lives, your mothers' and fathers' and brothers' and sisters' and spouses' and colleagues' and friends' lives in ways that make a difference.

Aslan is on the move. Believe it.

**The author gratefully acknowledges the sources:**

Abelson, Harold and Andrea diSessa, **TURTLE GEOMETRY.**
Figure 2.23, page 93, Logo dragon. Copyright (c) 1980 Abelson and diSessa.
Reprinted by permission of MIT Press. All rights reserved.

Bloom, Lazerson, Hofstader, **BRAIN, MIND AND BEHAVIOR.** Chapter One opener, page 2 (c) 1985 by Educational Broadcasting Corporation. Reprinted by permission of W.H. Freeman and Company. All rights reserved.

**Dover Pictorial Archive Series** for permission to use ten images per publication free. Dover Publications. All rights reserved.

Escher, M.C., "Magic Mirror" (c) 1996 Cordon Art - Baarn - Holland. Permission by Cordon Art B.V. All rights reserved.

Freeman, Walter J., "The Physiology of Perception." *Scientific American* Feb. 1991, p. 78. Permission to sketch photo of phase portrait, p. 78 by Walter J. Freeman and Peter Broadhead.

**GARDNER'S ART THROUGH THE AGES,** tenth edition, (c) 1996. Naturhistorisches Museum for permission to reproduce b/w photo of "Venus of Willendorf," figure 1-8, p.31.

Gardner, Howard, **ARTFUL SCRIBBLES.** Figure 60, page 60, copyright (c) 1980 by Howard Gardner. Reprinted by permission of HarperCollins Publishers.

Gimbutas, Marija, **The Language of the Goddess.** Figures 5, 24, 25 , 160 264, 252, 236 216 (c) 1989 by Marija Gimbutas. Reprinted by permission of HarperCollins Publishers. All rights reserved.

Goodnow, Jacqueline, **CHILDREN'S DRAWING.** Tadpole figure copyright (c) 1977 by President and Fellows of Harvard College. Reprinted by permission of Harvard University Press.

Hall, James E., **Humanistic Mathematics Network Journal** #12 October 1995. Figures 10 & 27 copyright (c) 1995 by James E. Hall. Reprinted by permission of James E. Hall and Alvin White, editor of the HMNJ.

Heyman, Gene of Harvard University, permission to quote from his 1996 paper "Resolving the contradictions of addiction, *Behavioral and Brain Sciences,* 19, 561-610.

Korn, Hal for permission to scan his portrait with his wife, recently deceased, Amy Clampitt, as well as to include a snapshot I took of them in London.

Mandelbrot, Benoit C., **THE FRACTAL GEOMETRY OF NATURE.** (c) 1977. Dr. Mandelbrot generously gave permission to use images in his book. All rights reserved.

Martineau, Lavan, **THE ROCKS BEGIN TO SPEAK,** Figure 66, petroglyph from Rainy Lake, Ontario, Canada, page 132, copyright (c) 1973, KC Publications, Box 14883, Las Vegas, Nevada 89114. Permission to reproduce, Lavan Martineau.

Ornstein, Robert, Richard Thompson and David Macaulay, **THE AMAZING BRAIN.** Illustration pp.124-5 copyright (c) 1984 by David A. Macaulay. Reprinted by permission of Houghton Mifflin Co. All rights reserved.

# Table of Contents

# TABLE OF CONTENTS

# TABLE OF CONTENTS (Continued)

# TABLE OF CONTENTS (Continued)

## PART TWO: HOW TO DO IT: A USER'S GUIDE
Step by Step Instructions for Drawing/Writing

# TABLE OF CONTENTS (Continued)

# TABLE OF CONTENTS (Continued)

**PART THREE: HITCHHIKERS' GUIDE TO BRAIN SCIENCE**
A Thumbnail Sketch of Brain Structure and Process with Tips and Suggestions for WholeBrain Education

# TABLE OF CONTENTS (Continued)

# TABLE OF CONTENTS (Continued)

## PART FOUR: THE THINKING CHILD
A WholeBrain Curriculum Guide

# TABLE OF CONTENTS (Continued)

# TO THE READER

## DRAWING/WRITING and the new literacy
by Susan Rich Sheridan

### Literacy: verbal and visual

This book describes a drawing-based approach to writing. Literacy is a two-fold process and has been for thousands of years. Humans communicate through images and words. As we once relied on pictures, so we do, again, in an age of stunning visual technology. Literacy requires visual skills and verbal skills. Verbal skills have moved beyond familiar text to languages named for theologians and coffee.

### Humans as mark-makers

Marks distinguish us from other language-using creatures. We not only utter meaningful noises, posturing in significant ways: we draw and we write. Brain scans support what we have known or suspected: brain processes are connected. If our brains are connected, then the history of our mark-making must be connected, too. This book describes language's multi-layered connectiveness, and demonstrates an approach to language instruction which models and fosters these connections.

### Who this book is for:

This book is for children. Because children do not learn to speak, write or read without example and instruction, this book is designed for their language instructors: children's parents and teachers.

The scope of the book could be limited to very young, disenfranchised children, including the urban and rural poor. Currently, many children are short-changed in their language instruction. The book has a larger aim: to reach many mothers and fathers, teachers and other caregivers into whose keeping—by birth, accident or enrollment—children have been placed, and to give them the good news that a more natural, more comprehensive approach to language instruction is available.

This book was written by an artist, writer, parent and teacher. It is for artists, writers, parents and teachers. It is for first-time parents and experienced parents, for first-time teachers and seasoned teachers. It is for schools of education and for classroom practice. It is for teachers of English and teachers of the arts, and it is also for teachers of any language or content area, including mathematics and the sciences. Because this book provides a set of exercises designed to direct and enhance how we know the things we know, it is written for the philosopher in each of us who wonders about the connections between our brains and the world. Language is our responsibility and our major resource. We know and we are known by our pictures and our words. It is our responsibility to convey this resource in all its fullness to our children.

### What we can learn about brain function and education: bihemispheric processing and the new literacy. Is equal education possible?

Although most of us are non-specialists, we can learn more about brains and education. We can even hypothesize equal education for all students at least in connection with literacy. Literacy is not only our distinguishing human characteristic; currently, it is a survival skill. We can hypothesize an equitable education, but can we deliver it? Neurobiology, psychology, art history and the history of writing support a more natural approach to language instruction in which play, speech, drawing, writing and reading are accepted as a continuum. As our bodies and brains adapt to changing conditions, so educational theory and practice must adapt, too. Adaptation and survival go hand-in-hand. A society with maladaptive language skills can not be expected to produce nor to provide.

A method called Drawing/Writing preserves the connections between communication skills. By focusing on the considerable power of a universal skill—drawing—to bolster attention, confidence and engagement, all students are given a chance to develop a positive, self-directive attitude toward learning. When training in writing and thinking are tied closely to training in drawing, the result is the new literacy. With the new literacy as its goal, language *instruction* becomes adaptive, returning a full range to human communication. The ability to read and write combined image/text is as old as paleolithic drawings on cave walls, yet suited to an age of information and technology.

The practice called Drawing/Writing is supported by a theory of education called Neuroconstructivism and a curriculum called "The Thinking Child." The rationale for adopting this approach to literacy education is multi-layered, like the brain. Thus, a four-part book. Like the brain, the book is a unified system. The four parts work together.

### An almost-unified system:

It is natural for a unified system (this author's brain) to devise things like itself: a unified system of analysis, or proof (this book). This book unifies drawing and writing as logically and enduringly related steps in the evolution of human communication, constructing a drawing/writing system, and it shows that the distances between the maths, the sciences, the arts, and the humanities are not as great as we think. Each discipline is increasingly related: "An analogous explanation might be . . ."

Gödel's incompleteness theorem, Heisenberg's uncertainty principle, Hofstadter's strange loops show us that it is in the very nature of explanation systems to be incomplete. *There will be missing bits.* Each field fills in the missing bits from its point of view. The aggregate gives us a clearer picture.

A GUT (Grand Unified Theory) or a TOE (Theory of Everything) will include the fact of the missing bits. The cosmos, our brains, and our brains' explanation systems are the products of a law of Almost-Unified Systems. Seemingly irreconcilable items, like gravity, occur (with a periodicity related, perhaps, to $\pi$ or to Planck's constant). An irritant perturbs its system, changing it. Several transformations in thinking occasioned by incomplete explanations are discussed in Part Two, Step 2, Basic Shapes. Given the general applicability of chaos theory, this thinker's best guess is that our brains, the cosmos and our explanation systems share a law or principle that can be formally described as a spiraling or helical structure or operation which admits strange loops or blips or bulges.

Drawing and writing are two of the brain's ways to access and construct almost-unified systems. Because drawing and writing are also incomplete systems, they require each other—as the arts and mathematics and the sciences and the humanities require each other.

This book is a perturbation in the educational system. Its effect will depend upon the responsiveness of the system.

## How to read this book

This book can be read in several ways: a teacher may jump directly to Part Two, the how-to section, using the book as an instructional manual; the reader can start at the beginning, traveling from the persuasive, intertheoretic essay through the how-to section, moving on to the mini-guide to brain science, and concluding with the curriculum section, experiencing the book as a whole. Or a reader might dip into the lefthand pages of the section on Basic Shapes, exploring Euclidean and fractal geometry. A writing teacher or an art education teacher may focus on the detailed curricula offered at the end of the curriculum section. A curriculum designer, on the other hand, will find the general guidelines for cross-modal education that open the curriculum section useful. An undergraduate or a graduate student will identify research topics raised throughout the text. A detailed table of contents lets readers to pick and choose.

*For further information contact:*

Susan Rich Sheridan, Ed.D.
68 Maplewood Drive
Amherst, MA 01002
413-549-1606
sheridan@k12.oit.umass.edu
http://k12s.phast.umass.edu/~sheridan

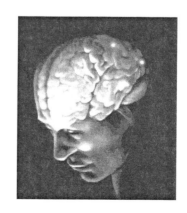

**PART ONE, "The Reasons Why,"** is a persuasive essay in four parts: The Drawing/Writing Experience, Brain Science Informs Education, New Classrooms, New Teachers, and The New Literacy. By including research from educational theory and practice, art history, and the history of writing, as well as from brain science, the essay provides both background and rationale for a drawing-based literacy program. Educators know that students actively construct knowledge. The fact that students actively construct their brains and invent their own optimum mental strategies is startling and exciting.

The Drawing/Writing program is timely and practical. Meeting the literacy challenge, Drawing/Writing proposes training in drawing—a universal language—as a springboard into writing and reading. Instead of relegating drawing to play for very young children, or sequestering drawing as an elite activity for a select group called artists, or isolating it as a legitimate but specialized tool for inquiry in the maths and sciences, it is far more useful to recognize drawing for what it is: a substantive mental activity useful across content areas.

Quality of learning and quality of brain construction are related; both depend upon practice and experience. The two hemispheres of the human brain have evolved not only to specialize but to cooperate. Visual and verbal information processes are unified mental activities. Learning to write apart from learning to draw, learning to read apart from learning to write, severs integrated mental processes. Effective educational strategies for language-learning deliberately connect visual and verbal approaches.

This book defines appropriate learning strategies as WholeBrain. This general term describes the complex yet unified quality of human thought. WholeBrain educational strategies are "cross modal": they deliberately encourage an exchange of information between systems of representation. This brain-based approach creates a new theory and practice of education called Neuroconstructivism. Neuroconstructivism extends the Piagetian/constructivist model: not only do children actively construct and scaffold knowledge and skills but they construct and scaffold their brains on a neural level through unified, complex processes. How children construct their neural networks—spatially and linguistically, or visually and verbally—affects how they think. A child deprived of visual training will be limited as a visual thinker. A child deprived of verbal training will be limited as a verbal thinker. The child as a combined visual/verbal thinker receives primary attention in a Neuroconstructivist curriculum.

Drawing/Writing proposes no age-based assumptions about readiness for writing, reading or abstract thinking, providing, instead, ample opportunities for these mental leaps. Students lay the groundwork for abstract thought by drawing, learning to ground their concrete thinking in accurate observations. Then the five-step Drawing/Writing program encourages a series of abstract constructions, both visually and verbally. Like brain processes, the effects of the Drawing/Writing program are layered and cumulative.

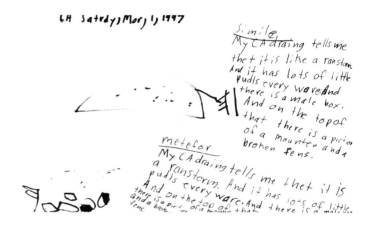

*Seven-year-old Elizabeth Wright's Composite Abstraction of a cow horn showing her grasp of metaphor*

Elizabeth Wright, a 7-year old student of Drawing/Writing wrote, "Simile: My CA drawing tells me that it is like a ranstorm and it has lots of little pudls every ware. And there is a mole box. And on the top of that there is a pictior of a mounten and a broken fens.

"Metefor: My CA drawings tells me that it is a rainstorm. And it has lots of little pudls every ware."

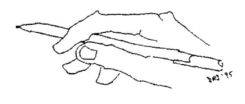

*Hand, SRS*

**PART TWO, "How To Do It,"** guides the reader through the five steps of the Drawing/Writing process. The Drawing/Writing approach is not just training in drawing in the context of writing exercises. Drawing/Writing is the deliberate connection of analytical drawing to reflective writing so that the writing accesses, expresses and transforms visual information in ways that move beyond description to other levels of analysis. The writing travels to places it could never have gone without the stimulus of drawing while the drawing is encouraged through verbal analysis to develop in new ways.

Drawing and writing are codes for representing and manipulating information. It is the combined effect of several codes that increases the possibilities for communication. It is precisely where verbal meets visual—where two information systems converge—that heightened understanding occurs.

*Hitchhiking on the Corpus Callosum, Sam Sheridan 1997*

**PART THREE, "Hitchhikers' Guide to Brain Science,"** provides background information from neurobiology useful for understanding Neuroconstructivism as a theory and Drawing/Writing as a practice. The most important piece of information is the active role the learner plays. This section includes thirteen tips to better teaching and learning. By demonstrating the centrality of attention to learning as well as the power of visual stimuli to direct and enhance attention, brain science clarifies good teaching: engage students' attention visually. By underscoring the intimate relationship between the hemispheres, and thus between spatial and linguistic modes of thought, brain science connects drawing as a visual attentional strategy with writing and reading. An understanding of the mutual influence between the two hemispheres clarifies the degree to which visual and verbal literacy are related. This intimate relationship provides the rationale for a larger concept of literacy as verbal *and* visual, or the new literacy.

The new literacy expresses the brain's ability to integrate, cross-reference and transform information. In the most general sense, the two major translation systems in the brain are the right and left hemispheres which

process information spatially and linguistically. Visual and verbal systems are sub-groups of these two larger systems. For instance, drawing and graphing are spatial systems for representing meaning. Written words and algebraic notation are linguistic systems. The brain "writes" and "reads" drawings and graphs as well as algebraic symbols and words.

The brain shunts information back and forth between two fundamental systems of representation: the spatial and the linguistic. The shunting is so continuous that the process is best described as inter-hemispheric. Human thought is a global enterprise in which myriad entities cooperate in a continuous exchange. The ability of the brain to devise a visual symbolic language, like drawing, precedes and undergirds the brain's ability to devise a linguistic system, like writing. These scaffolded systems characterize not only the history of human cognitive development phylogenetically, but each individual's mental development, ontogenetically. That is, children draw before they write or read. Logically, classroom strategies mirror and mine this relationship by introducing writing, reading and mathematics through training in drawing. Educational approaches which disconnect drawing from writing, or writing from reading—as has been the case in many schools—parse brain functions, interrupting the linguistic continuum. Drawing/Writing models the brain's complex yet unified approach to information, connecting and integrating these processes. An optimal brain-like strategy has optimal brain results: efficient networking on neural levels; rich syntheses on mental levels.

The brain is a bilateral yet unitary system. From birth, the integrative quality of the learning experience, particularly in connection with language, determines the quality and productivity of the system. Integrative brain exchanges are transformational: the output has the possibility of being phenomenally different from the input. The self-directed aspect of brain-based learning means that the learner rather than the teacher takes charge; when this happens, the outcome for learning may go far beyond curricular goals and expectations. Because brain activity is both naturally and optimally cross-modal, cross-modal language-learning strategies are both efficient and effective.

Within a prescribed period of years, or months, some neural networks, like the visual system, establish circuitry which persists as largely unmodifiable. The retinal neurons in kittens' eyes sutured closed from birth never develop properly. When these kittens' eyes are unsutured, the kitten is functionally blind. It cannot see and it will never see because its neural pathways for vision have never been properly stimulated. The same holds true for very young children's eyes, obscured by cataracts.

*Kitten with sutured eyes, Claus Kormannshaus, 1997*

Other neural networks, like those for learning, remain modifiable over a lifetime. Intervention by schools or by learners themselves will be effective at any time. The attitude and actions of the learner strongly influence the state of the neural networks and therefore the quality of learning and thinking. More than teachers or educational strategies or classroom environments, students themselves control their mental abilities. For students to take control of their mental growth, students must know something about brain development, and classrooms must provide exploratory learning experiences. This book provides the stimulus for both. Brain development, particularly as it relates to language, is a Moebius-like loop. Like the elements in other dynamic systems, teachers, curricula, classroom environments and students' attitudes are interconnected. The system flourishes or founders as a unit.

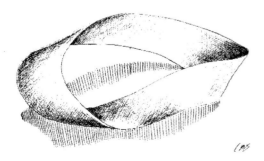

*Moebius strip, Claus Kormannshaus, 1997*

When brains operate at their optimum, a chain reaction of layered, refined and enhanced mental events is set in motion. The Drawing/Writing program provides a procedure for this chain of events. The visible results of the Drawing/Writing program are increased attention, self-direction, and visual and verbal skills. The invisible results are better brain connections.

*Thinking Children, Claus Kormannshaus, 1997*

**PART FOUR, "The Thinking Child,"** describes WholeBrain curricular guidelines and strategies and includes sample English and Fine Arts programs appropriate at the middle, high school and college levels.

The premise behind the "The Thinking Child" is that students are, first and foremost, thinkers, and that they can learn to construct effective mental strategies if they are given enough tools (including the applied and performing arts), enough opportunities, and enough time. These self-designed strategies will affect students' neural networks which, in turn, will determine how well their brains function. While genetics plays its part in determining intelligence, genetics is not all-determining. Early experience plays a major role, as does later experience. While encouraging the confidence necessary for learning, the Drawing/Writing program provides early and continuing enrichment for agile brains while compensating for gaps and delays in situations where the brain's natural agility may require more time and attention. This flexible approach encourages and allows the self-direction necessary to appropriate mental and emotional growth.

To grow intellectually—besides adequate food and emotional support or love—children's brains require rich, varied experiences with language, events, living beings, and ideas. To furnish the conditions useful to mental growth, students and teachers need to know how brains grow and function and encourage art-like, or highly engaged, expressive visual activities. Brains grow at different rates depending upon experience. Not all children will learn to speak or to write or read at the same time, anymore than babies roll over, crawl or walk at exactly the same time. The parameters for learning spoken language extend from birth to as late as twelve years of age. The windows for reading and writing stay open for a lifetime. Under such variable conditions, educational grace periods become a requirement. With the current overemphasis on visual stimulation and underemphasis on verbal stimulation—while the opposite is true in classrooms where text continues to dominate image—educational expectations for reading must remain flexible. In classrooms where primary languages differ, grace periods are necessary. A literacy curriculum which incorporates a universally accessible meaning-making activity, drawing, has considerable usefulness as readiness training for writing and reading in classrooms where the common denominator is diversity.

In a technological society, visual skills and verbal skills are equally important. If anything, visual skills are at a premium. It is increasingly apparent that the natural aptitudes and enthusiasms of children and the skills required by a technological society share common ground: the importance of pictures.

The closer to "natural" the learning environment becomes by valuing visual literacy as well as verbal literacy, the healthier the classroom will be. When "natural learning"—visual learning—translates to "brain-based learning," and when natural and brain-based equate with "technological," an intertheoretic integration becomes possible. Children, education and industry reap the rewards of an equation that produces an "intellectual capital"[1]—minds as visually acute as they are verbally able. With the primary focus on the child as a learning system, a strong visual component returns to the educational enterprise. The pressure for a dual literacy—the new literacy—is corrective, regulatory, and felicitous.

By educating children for the new literacy, we return a set of ancient skills evident on paleolithic cave walls: combined images and (proto) text. At the same time, we hand them the communication tools for the present and the future.

✦ ✦ ✦ ✦ ✦ ✦ ✦ ✦ ✦ ✦ ✦ ✦ ✦

---

[1]Steve Jobs, public radio, 7/6/97.

The Drawing/Writing program has been tested over the past ten years with a range of students and teachers from kindergarten through the college level in a variety of courses including English literature, English composition, English as a Second Language, prison literacy outreach programs, talented and gifted Native American middle school literacy programs, foreign languages, biology, studio arts, art education, special education, middle school science courses, and art history. Recently, a pilot program for pre-employment job skills training experimented with Drawing/Writing as its method of delivery. Drawing/Writing has provided positive classroom experiences for many students including those with attention deficits and learning disabilities. Its general effect is increased energy, attention, investment, confidence and intellectual excitement.

Benefits of the Drawing/Writing program include:

- training in thinking skills including description, analysis and inference
- training in self-regulatory attention
- training in listening and speaking
- training with abstract symbol systems
- readiness for writing and reading and mathematics
- remediation for attention and language deficits
- opportunities for peer mentoring and peer tutoring
- block scheduling opportunities
- core curricular status for the arts
- an innovative literacy program modeling brain function in which visual and verbal skills are interconnected, mutually reflective, and transformational.

Many children are talked to less, listened to less, and read to less than children of a generation ago. It should not be surprising if students speak less eloquently, read less avidly, and write less fluently. Language-related "delays" and "disabilities" are predictable in children who are bombarded with visual stimuli and deprived of verbal interaction. Writing and reading and thinking are like athletic skills; they are best learned young and require practice.

Children acquire language through language use. By experimenting with a range of symbolic languages, children are likely to discover several forms of expression suited to their needs. Some children think best visually, some think best verbally. All children's brains are organized to think visually and verbally in interconnected ways.

*Girl thinking, sketch, Claus Kormannshaus, 1997*

From the time I was a child, drawing and writing have been interconnected activities in my life. There is an organic unity to the way in which Drawing/Writing has unfolded in my life.

My years of teaching Drawing/Writing validate the five-step program as logical and comfortable. In the classroom, Drawing/Writing feels leisurely, yet directed. The easy-flowing rhythm between drawing and writing and the gentle progression from simple to complex analyses lend the program an inevitability. Students' drawings and writings often anticipate the next Drawing/Writing step. Drawing/Writing has been refined in diverse classrooms, sculpted to accommodate the learning pace and style of many students. May it fit your classroom needs, too.

Versions of the Drawing/Writing five-step with an accompanying language arts curriculum will be available in Spanish, as will an elementary school level Drawing/Writing curriculum emphasizing mathematics called "Rainbow Noodles and Zebra Trees."

### *A Drawing/Writing Curriculum for young children*

**Rainbow Noodles and Zebra Trees**, a book in progress for an elementary school literacy curriculum, is awaiting input from parents, teachers and other care-givers. At age three my son, Samuel, devised two metaphors. He called white birch trees "zebra trees," and he called elbow macaroni noodles "rainbow noodles." Now twenty-two, after a year in London studying at the Slade School of Art, he is returning to Harvard for his senior year. Sam was a normal little boy. What made him more verbal and visual than many of his peers was the absence of television and the abundance of conversation. Verbal stimulation and brain growth go hand in hand. Anyone can provide invested conversation. It does not need to be a parent, but few other people care about a child as much as a parent does and are willing to talk to a child in these ways.

As presented in this book, Drawing/Writing is appropriate pre-K on. A different, "younger" version of the Drawing/Writing five-step program is unnecessary. Tailor it to your requirements!

Students and teachers who wish to share Drawing/Writing experiences and to offer suggestions for this text or the projected elementary school text are encouraged to use e-mail, the Drawing/Writing worldwide web page or the regular postal service.

- sheridan@k12.oit.umass.edu
- http://k12s.phast.umass.edu/~sheridan
- Susan Rich Sheridan, Ed.D.
  DRAWING/WRITING
  68 Maplewood Drive
  Amherst, MA 01002

Amherst, November 1997

## RAINBOW NOODLES AND ZEBRA TREES

*Cover drawing, Sam Sheridan, 1997*

# THE REASONS WHY

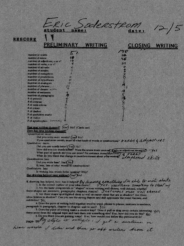

Eric Soderstrom, *Preliminary Drawing and Writing, Closing Drawing and Writing, & Rescore, Continuing Education, Westfield Sate College, 1996*

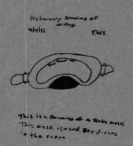

Tom Sheehan, *Preliminary Drawing and Writing, Closing Drawing and Writing, & Rescore, Continuing Education, Westfield Sate College, 1996*

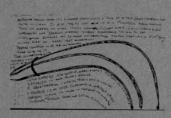

Paul Gagnon, *Preliminary Drawing and Writing, Closing Drawing and Writing, & Rescore, Continuing Education, Westfield Sate College, 1996*

**Note the changes in numbers of words and in the strength of the drawings from preliminary to closing drawing and writing.**

# The Reasons Why

*In the past, it was feasible to teach the visual arts apart from literacy. It is no longer feasible for several reasons:*

— *a student population less interested and practiced in reading and writing requires the highly visual, hands-on stimulus of the arts to bolster attention and to sustain interest.*

— *a technological society requires visual literacy skills as well as verbal skills*

*It is increasingly clear that teachers-across grade and content-must address literacy skills. Students always did require training in writing, reading and thinking. Now, even more of that training must occur in the classroom. Beyond providing specific bodies of information, this training is what schools are for. Literacy training becomes increasingly important in a technological society which places such a premium on these skills.*

*Drawing/Writing is a literacy strategy in which training in visual literacy precedes, by a heart beat, training in verbal literacy. Drawing/Writing has a fifteen-year proven track record for increasing levels of attention, commitment, self-direction and class cohesiveness as well as literacy skills in a broad range of students. Drawing/Writing meets the needs of under-funded, over-populated classrooms where the major characteristic shared by students is diversity— most especially in connection with the English language. Because Drawing/Writing includes an evaluation tool called Rescore, Drawing/Writing presents an abundance of data-quantitative, qualitative and anecdotal-useful to educational research. Drawing/Writing scores can be compared with standardized test scores to measure the effectiveness of this literacy program— not only on reading and writing skills, but on mathematical and science attitudes and aptitude, on learning disabilities, on ESL and TOEFL education, on foreign language education, on gifted education, and on the cognitive gains of homeschoolers who incorporate the Drawing/Writing method.*

*What does Drawing/Writing look like? What are some of the compelling reasons from child psychology, educational theory and practice, art history, the history of writing, and neurobiology for connecting drawing with writing? How does a Neuroconstructivist approach change teachers, students and classrooms? How does the new literacy work?*

*Gains in one area of endeavor, like drawing—a universal, easily developable skill—can be used to achieve gains in other areas of endeavor-like writing and reading. Small changes have big effects. This is a message of hope.*

# PART ONE

## *The Reasons Why:*
## *A persuasive essay in four sections*

The Drawing/Writing Experience

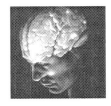 Brain Science Informs Education

New Classrooms, New Teachers

 The New Literacy

Conclusion

# THE DRAWING/WRITING EXPERIENCE

I happen to like the line drawings of very small children, better, in fact, than the work of anyone except masters. The closest thing to it, when children use pencils (colored or not), is the quill strokes of Rembrandt, the more spontaneous and less "spelled out" drawings by Picasso for *Guernica,* and a few stick drawings on paper by Pollock. If one assumes that a baby is born wholly integrated with its feelings and that separation from them is the result of intruding outside forces, for an adult to reintegrate himself with an equivalent lack of division and alienation in his expression is so rare that we call it, as well we might, "genius."

*The Collected Writings of Robert Motherwell*

*The Drawing/Writing program is leisurely and cumulative; it moves from the visual to the verbal, from the simple to the complex, and from the concrete to the abstract, modeling the development of intelligent thought.*

## 1.1 What Drawing/Writing Looks Like

A fifteen-year-old student from Thailand, Kanop Changtrakul, embarked on the Drawing/Writing program. He started with tentative English skills and minimal drawing skills, choosing to draw a cow horn. This is one of the most difficult objects to work with because of its subtle curves and bland colors. As he drew this object, Kanop gained confidence.

After several attempts, Kanop wrote three versions of the following poem. I include the version Kanop thought was best, the third one:

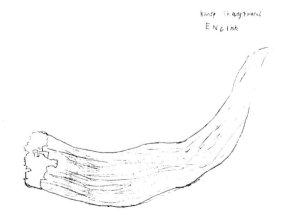

*Kanop Changtrakul's Preliminary Drawing and Writing, ninth grade, Eaglebrook School, 1987*

### The Cow Horn

*Smooth and no shape*
*But curved and twisted.*
*The shape is beauty.*
*The top is sharp.*
*The form is strong.*
*The color was white,*
*Now it's lined in brown.*
*Inside, dead body, cobweb's owner.*
*Strong gets weak*
*Beauty doesn't stay forever*
*It doesn't stay with any thing forever.*

Kanop now has his B.A. in Psychology from Boston University and will pursue his Masters in Psychology. At B.U. he studied English literature.

Another ninth-grade English student, Lawrence Chen from Taiwan, produced the following drawings and writings about a conch shell. Lawrence's balanced visual and

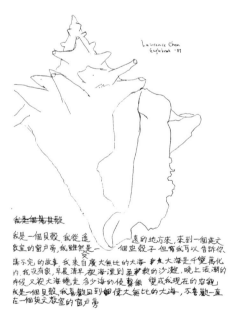

*Lawrence Chen's Preliminary Drawing and Writing, ninth grade, Eaglebrook School, 1987*

verbal capabilities are clear, even if we cannot read Chinese. The preliminary drawing and the writing show elegance, fluency and skill. After translating this work into prose in English, Lawrence wrote this poem:

Lawrence C

The shell is → The Shell

heavy
hard
unusual body
pink color
smell nothing lik salt
empty
but beautifuly
dumf and blind
indeed
sea's sculpture
ornament
sculpturesque

① It is a sculpture made of sea;
② In the summer every one like go to beach for swimming, the
③ They bent down to pick it up it from the sea best present;
④ My mother's buttons made of it this;
⑤

*The sea ever is my house.*
*The sand ever is my sleeping bed.*
*In the sea, the fish and the sea anemone are my friends.*
*The short seas and the rough sea made the noise [and]*
*    are my best music;*
*In the morning, I was on the beach taking a sun bath,*
*The people come to swim, the sea bird is flying*
*    around me;*
*Some shell collectors find me-*
*Now, I'm in the English classroom.*
*Grains of stone are my bed.*
*No friends and no wonderful music.*

Lawrence's English skills were more advanced than Kanop's; his aloneness was no less.

*Lawrence Chen's fishermen illustration showing the shell in the lower right hand corner, ninth grade, Eaglebrook School, 1987*

Lawrence received his B.A. in Chemical Engineering from the University of Rochester. Having worked for an international consulting firm, Lawrence is starting a three-year degree in business in Japan. Recently, he wrote, "You are my favorite teacher. I remember and admire the energy, passion and creativity you put into the class. You inspired me to write my first English essay which was quite a 'mission impossible' at that time. I remember that I had to spend all night flipping through the dictionary. I did it because you were so nice to me and I didn't want to let you down. I had a very good time in your class plus I got to draw stuff. Actually, I am still drawing 'stuff,' and I am into photography and Chinese painting, but am mostly sketching with a pencil" (February 27, 1997, Taipei, Taiwan).

## 1.2  What is a Drawing/Writing Teacher?

*Photo, Joanne Quail's Dr/Wr objects, second grade, Applewild School, Fitchburg, MA*

As a teacher, you may ask:
- How is this broader approach different from teaching writing or drawing in traditional ways?
- Why should I read this LONG lesson plan?
- How am I going to fit this program into my writing program or my drawing program?
- If it becomes clear that I am teaching drawing in a writing class, the conclusion may be I'm not teaching anything important. If it becomes clear that I am teaching writing in a drawing class, the conclusion may be that I've lost confidence in the arts. If my students are drawing, writing, and discussing, how am I going to get any *teaching* done?
- Most importantly, how will students react?

Art teachers may be dubious about their skills as teachers of writing. English teachers and other language teachers may be dubious about their drawing skills. The reader who intends to learn Drawing/Writing independently may be concerned about both. Drawing is a method for creating intelligible order. It is a universal language, and a natural one. Children draw on their own. Writing—as recorded speech—is another system for creating intelligible order. It must be learned.

The relationship of visual learning to verbal learning becomes reciprocal almost immediately. We see and we speak; we draw and read picture books. Then, we learn to write and read text. To eliminate or undervalue the visual aspects of the combined visual/verbal language acquisition process interrupts the dynamic, cutting its power in half. Drawing returns visual learning to the language acquisition process. Pictures speak to us.

Drawing is more than a resource for artists, designers, scientists and engineers. Drawing is a complex sensorimotor action requiring the selection, organization and communication of visual material. Drawing establishes a relationship between us and the world, providing us not only with content but with concrete evidence of the quality and characteristics of the relationship between us and the world. Our drawings show us not only what we see but how we see. The more accurately we draw, the more clearly we see, and the more we know. The more expressively we draw, the more persuasively we communicate. To paraphrase the Zen artist/writer Frederick Franck, drawing is the means by which we discover and rediscover the world (1973).

A visual approach to literacy in which the teacher fully participates allows teachers to share the frustrations and successes students experience. Joining students in the learning experience puts a different light on the enterprise: learning becomes a shared venture characterized by mutual respect. Drawing/Writing teachers do not demonstrate exercises and then stand apart as observers. They complete every step with their students, working on their language skills, too.

Joanne Quail, a second grade teacher at Applewild School, Fitchburg, MA, taught Drawing/Writing in January 1997. Her work and that of her students illuminate this book. Joanne wrote about her culminating drawing in the five-step series—the Composite Abstraction—in this way: "Sometimes shapes hold together and are tightly banded and defend each other with the force. Sometimes the shapes lie near each other and vibrate with energy to each other making the empty space between the shapes very powerful.

Other times, shapes are alone moving over or interacting with other shapes but keeping their own identity and oneness. Then, too, a line need not form or enclose or intersect but is on its own. It belongs to the whole but it is somehow free of form. Still a force is released, onto others, and other forms send vibrations out to the line where time has been taken to add depth and value to a space [where] it seems to have more stability within itself. The other shapes and lines are nearby but the influence of dynamics is less."

Eloquent, abstract, speculative writing often occurs at the end of the Drawing/Writing program.

*Joanne Quail, Composite Abstraction, second grade teacher, Applewild School, Fitchburg, MA, 1996*

## 1.3 A Cross-modal Strategy Defined

The brain has two hemispheres; they work together. A term to describe this integrated process is cross-modal. A cross-modal teaching strategy describes a dual process in which a deliberate transfer of information is achieved— from one mode of representation to another. Meaning occurs at the very confluence of the two modes and transformation is part of the process. The purpose behind the transfer is inter-influence: each mode of representation enhances and extends the other. For instance, in Drawing/Writing, a deliberate transfer of information is achieved from drawing to writing through the sentence, "My drawing tells me that my object is...because...." The explanatory words become part of the new expression. The work now includes image and text. The similes and metaphors routinely produced with each Drawing/Writing step as well as additional exercises with analogy, speculation, prediction and hypothesis train the bihemispheric brain to produce left/right, or verbal/visual messages where the *combined* information is what counts—not text, not image alone. By the end of the five-step program, students agree that the drawing and writing they have produced, particularly in

connection with the Composite Abstraction, could not have been achieved in any other way. The mutual influence established by Drawing/Writing is critical to the richness of the explanations, whether these explanations are visual or verbal.

Cross-modal creations abound. For instance, a cartoon is a cross-modal, image/text production. What varies is the degree to which a transfer of information is deliberately constructed between image and text. In the cartoon, the illustration and the text go hand in hand, and the image interprets the text or vice versa. The cartoonist probably did not spend hours drawing, then write the text from the image, nor spend hours extracting every verbal nuance from the text, translating that visually. In William Blake's illustrations of his poetry, the level of intent to translate between the two systems of representation is very high. The Drawing/Writing program structures a series of exchanges between drawing and writing with similar strong intent. The result is a different kind of drawing and a different kind of writing. In Drawing/Writing, each form of expression is deliberately informed by and directed by the other.

The slash between the words Drawing/Writing signals the following:

- a cross-modal, or interhemispheric relationship exists between these two mental activities
- the relationship is integrative and transformative
- an exchange of information is occurring between two closely related mental enterprises
- the results are both more precise and richer than those in which these mental enterprises are pursued apart from each other.

## 1.4 A Sketch of the Drawing/Writing Program

*A cross-modal, visual/verbal procedure for conducting an information search: a grammar for intelligent thought, or the Form of the form*

The goal of the Drawing/Writing program is training the brain to conduct information searches efficiently. It is efficient to start with a simpler, more accessible task and then to move to a more difficult one. For this reason, five drawing exercises introduce a series of concrete search strategies working from outside to inside and from there to a consideration of the whole. Each drawing exercise is accompanied by exercises in reflective writing.

The drawing steps provide training in observational, analytical and inferential visual thinking; the written exercises transfer this visual thinking into words. Drawing/Writing provides the following general strategy for acquiring and expressing information: work from the visual to the verbal, work from the specific to the general, work from the concrete to the abstract.

In the drawing exercises, the visual analysis begins with an outline drawing (Blind and Regular Contour drawings), and moves to internal form (Basic Shape drawings). Then, the drawings explore the ways in which light creates surface values and the illusion of three dimensions (Light-Medium-Dark drawing). By including details about texture as well as incidental surface markings, the next drawing becomes even more comprehensive and "realistic" (the "Perfect" Whole drawing). The culmination and heart of the visual analysis follows: by combining parts from the previous drawings, students produce an entirely new definition of the object—one which does not look like the object but which stands for it (the Composite Abstraction). This abstract drawing prepares the mind for other abstract symbol systems including writing, reading and mathematics. In Drawing/Writing, visual analyses precede and undergird verbal analyses, modeling cognitive development.

Because writing follows drawing in a program where drawing is initially targeted as the primary tool for gathering information, the organization of the five drawings set the conditions for the subsequent writing. The visual procedure for selecting, organizing and synthesizing information establishes a "grammar" for intelligent, communicable thought. Artists and writers routinely access and use this grammar. It can be practiced by any thinker who receives exposure to and training in visual strategies. A predisposition toward order is just that—a predisposition. The drive toward intelligible communication requires tools and practice. Drawing/Writing provides tools and practice.

Fully developed communications—visual or verbal, painting or poetry—exhibit parsimony, or restraint. Unless the brain is sick or damaged, its goal is the least, not the most expenditure of energy, as is true at atomic levels. The brain wishes to work well, not hard. The Drawing/Writing strategy described as "neither too much nor too little," encourages elegant communication. A parsimonious elegance describes all optimal mental processes—from neural networks to language. Efficient neural networks are—at once—as elaborate and as pruned as they need to be. Visual solutions in design,

verbal solutions in poetry or mathematics include all *necessary* elements. Students can learn to streamline the circuitry in their brains by practicing restraint and discrimination. The Composite Abstraction requires both.

### The Five Steps

Drawing/Writing requires the following supplies: pencils, magic markers, legal-size paper, legal-size folders, push pins or thumb tacks, and a box of objects including shoes, bones, kitchen utensils, carpentry tools and gardening tools.

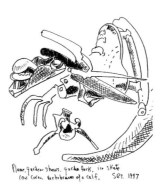

Plane, garden shears, garden fork, ice skate
(ice cores, vertebra arm of a calf.   SRP. 1997

*Sketch, bones and tools, author, 1997*

The integrated series of visual/verbal exercises is preceded by an informal pre-test called "Preliminary Drawing and Writing." This sample provides benchmarks for measuring changes in drawing, writing and thinking skills over the course of the Drawing/Writing program.

*Jennifer Welden, Preliminary Drawing and Writing of an immersion heater, Continuing Education, Westfield State College, 1996*

In the preliminary sample Jennifer wrote, "This is an immersion heater. It is useful when traveling to heat up some water for tea. It reminds me of early spring trips to the Maine coast. My mother and I take one along and drink tea by the window at the inn where we stay. Early spring can be very damp and cold up there so a hot cup of tea while we watch the cold waves crashing on the rocks and look forward to returning in summer [unfinished sentence]."

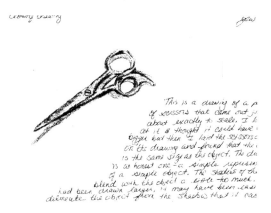

*Jennifer Welden, Closing Drawing and Writing of a pair of scissors, Westfield State College, Continuing Education, 1996*

In the closing sample Jennifer wrote, "This is a drawing of a pair of scissors that came out just about exactly to scale. I looked at it and thought it could have been bigger but than I laid the scissors down on the drawing and found that the drawing is the same size as the object. The drawing is an honest one—a simple representation of a simple object. The shadows of the object blend with the object a little too much. If it had been drawn larger, it may have been easier to delineate the object from the shadow that it casts." Both drawings show sensitivity and accuracy. Memory guides the first piece of writing. An analysis of scale, value and differentiation drives the second.

Step 1 includes two warm-up exercises and two drawings. The warm-up exercises include gesturing or tracing the shape of the object in the air with the arm and hand, and tracing the object on paper. The two drawings are the Blind Contour drawing and the Regular Contour drawing. In each instance, the writing exercise is structured in the same way: students write, "My Blind Contour drawing tells me that my object is...because...." This format is repeated throughout the program.

Step 2 includes three geometric drawings: Euclidean Basic Shapes, Fractal Basic Shapes, and Organic Basic Shapes. Students complete the sentence, "My Euclidean Basic Shape drawing tells me that my object is... because...." Students use the same sentence with the other

Basic Shape drawings, as they will with all subsequent drawings. Fractal geometry is so important to current understanding about mind and the world that an appreciable section in Step 2, Basic Shapes, is devoted to it.

*Jennifer Welden, Blind Contour drawing of the immersion heater, Westfield State College, Continuing Education, 1996*

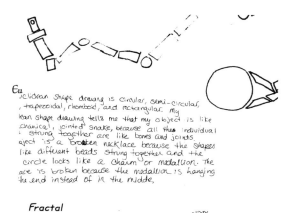

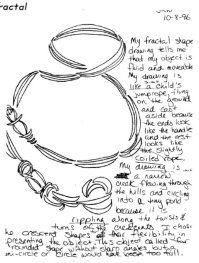

*Jennifer Welden, Euclidean and Fractal Basic Shape drawings of immersion heater, Westfield State College, Continuing Education, 1996*

Step 3 is a value drawing called Light-Medium-Dark, or LMD.

Step 4 is a fully rendered drawing called the "Perfect Whole."

Step 5 is a combined drawing called the Composite Abstraction.

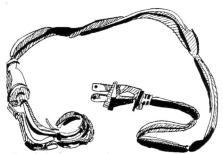

My LMD drawing has mostly medium values and even amounts of light and dark values. My LMD drawing is like an x-ray of an electric eel because the contrast between lights and darks are like the bones of an x-ray. It's an electric eel because it has a plug on one end. My drawing is an ink blot from a Rorschach Exam because it is nearly symmetrical and I keep looking at it and thinking "what doe

*Jennifer Welden, LMD drawing of immersion heater, Westfield State College, Continuing Education, 1996*

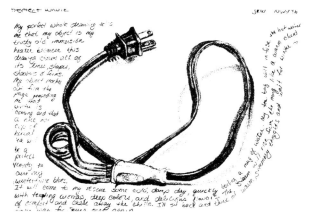

*Jennifer Welden, "Perfect" Whole drawing of immersion heater, Westfield State College, Continuing Education, 1996*

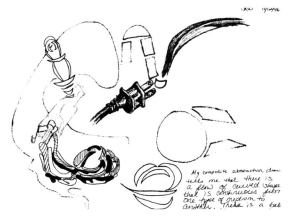

My composite abstraction draw tells me that there is a flow of curved shapes that is continuous from one type of medium to another. There is a bell

*Jennifer Welden, CA of the immersion heater, Westfield State College, Continuing Education, 1996*

The program is completed by an informal post-test called "Closing Drawing and Writing." This sample provides new benchmarks for drawing, writing and thinking skills. The students themselves quantitatively and qualitatively assess the preliminary and the closing drawing and writing samples using a tool called Rescore. Rescore is found at the end of Part 2. It includes counting numbers of words and parts of speech, as well as reflecting upon the meaning of these numbers. In this manner, grammar is built into the Drawing/Writing process. To assess progress, students require procedures and tools. Letter or number grades never replace a personal understanding of strengths and weaknesses. Even if teacher assessments are accurate, self-assessments are better. Learning to see oneself clearly is necessary to growth and change.

*The "Perfect" Whole, a comprehensive visual search, the Skate, Cedar Pruitt, Hampshire College, 1996*

### Procedure and results

Drawing/Writing takes certain "rules" or procedures for ordering information—what this book calls the grammar of intelligent thought—and makes these procedures overt, accessible and practicable. Drawing/Writing provides practice with:

- Conducting a comprehensive search for information.

- Selecting enough information from the steps in the search to create coherent, comprehensive statements, visually and verbally.

Eric wrote, "My Perfect Whole drawing shows the flexibility of my hack (hacky-sack). At the lower left corner it's pointed providing an imperfection. Easily I could have made a circle, but hacks are only like that in mid-flight or brand new. My object looks like a gigantic pea thrusting out of a pod."

*Eric Soderstrom's "Perfect" Whole of a "hack" (hacky sack), Westfield State College, Continuing Education, 1996.*

- Selecting one element from each drawing and combining these elements in a way that sums up the visual information in a pleasing or balanced or resolved manner; then analyzing and reflecting upon that innovative, unique, highly personal statement verbally.

*Bill Mattavi, Composite Abstraction of a wrench, Westfield State College, Continuing Eucation., 1996*

Bill wrote, "My CA tells me that the sealed ends of the object are dark, and the ends that are open are light. The shading indicates where the molecules are dense and where they are loosely connected."

- Including neither too much nor too little in both the visual and the verbal statements.

*Tim Lis, Composite Abstraction of the cow jaw bone, Westfield State College, Continuing Education, 1996*

Tim Lis, another Westfield State Continuing Education student who provided other drawings for this book, wrote, "My second CA drawing is sparse. It has a lot of open space. Few of the bits are filled in. My drawing is chaotic, almost like an explosion. My drawing has a slight 3-dimensional quality to it, as if expanding outward from slightly off-center of the page. It seems balanced on an axis at that same point. My drawing is curved and jagged. My drawing is like an explosion at a coat-hanger factory because mangled bits of wire and wiry shapes seem to be flying about. My drawing is a time-line for those who exist on a non-linear dimensions because the same events can be seen occurring more than once with only an unseen singularity near the middle for a reference point as it pulls and stretches events towards it."

- Incorporating the word "because" in each written statement for the sake of increasing the plausibility, reasonableness and logic of the writer's conclusions.

*Paul Gagnon, Light-Medium-Dark drawing of a sneaker, Westfield State College, Continuing Education, 1996*

Paul Gagnon wrote, "My LMD drawing is a ferry boat because it has a large front that opens to allow for the vehicles to enter and passengers to be onloaded and offloaded. This ferry is going to Block Island and leaves the port at Point Judith four times daily. The upper structure is the wheelhouse because it is raised up on top. I will ride my bicycle all day on the island and see all the sights."

In the Drawing/Writing exercises, information starts with the physical description of a line, moving to descriptions of shapes, to value studies, to fully rendered realistic drawings, and then to abstractions. The verbal descriptions move from concrete analysis to simile, metaphor, analogy, speculation, prediction and hypothesis. The accumulated visual/verbal information leads the thinker to a wealth of associations.

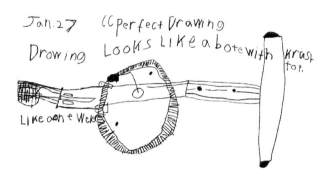

*Nicholas Joyce, Perfect Whole Drawing of an egg beater, Applewild School, second grade, 1997*

The following second-grade writing samples are reproduced verbatim. (Invented spelling is discussed at the end of Part 1.) Nicholas wrote, "My drawing looks like a bote with a krasht top. It looks like a one weler."

*Chad Daniels Euclidean Basic Shapes drawing of a bird's wing, Applewild School, second grade, 1997.*

Chad wrote,"It looks like a scell roting it looks like a wead gie walking it looks like a bird head."

*Kate Snyder, "Perfect" Whole drawing of a bracelet, Applewild School, second grade, 1997*

Kate wrote, " What I see in this object is flows with a blue senter. It kind of is jaged. My object is hade [hard]." If you look at her Closing Drawing and Writing, Kate's extraordinary drawing skills become even clearer.

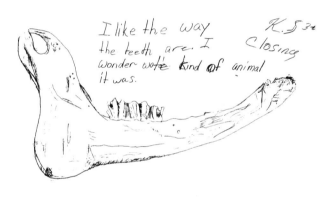

*Kate Snyder, Closing Drawing and Writing, jaw bone of a cow, Applewild School, second grade, 1997*

*Keith Palmer, "Perfect" Whole drawing of a bird's wing, Applewild School, second grade, 1997*

Keith wrote, "My 'Perfect' Whole drawing has lots of points and isicals shapes. it looks like a undersea place. It looks like a bird stachue. it looks like a rock climer climing it looks like grass growing on a hill. it looks like a under ground manchon. it looks like the workshop of Barbars Chrismas. a caterpiller climbing up a tree."

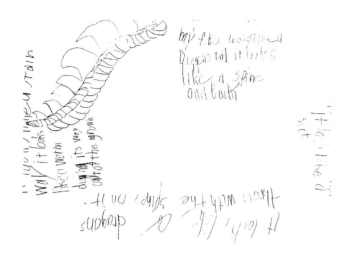

Keith Palmer, *Fractal Basic Shape drawing of a bird's wing, Applewild School, second grade, 1997*

Keith wrote, "My f.b.s. [fractal basic shape] looks like a dragons tail it looks like a spine and back it looks like an upside down catipler it looks like a seet.it looks like a dragons throan with spines on it."

## 1.5 A Personal History

In 1978-80, as a teaching assistant in Basic Drawing and Design at the University of Massachusetts, I developed the five-step drawing strategy described in this book. I tried to teach drawing logically. For me this meant incrementally. Visual information could be built up, step by step. The drawing exercises started with the outside and worked in. Most of my students were non-art majors. They all wanted to become convincing realists. I knew that if I taught observation skills, my students would reach their goal. Once they reached it, I faced another realization: I could not leave my students stranded on the bright shores of realism. This conviction was responsible for the fifth step called the Composite Abstraction. The fifth step has become the power house of the program.

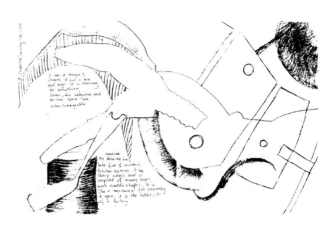

Teresa Mershon, *CA of garden shears, Hampshire College, 1996*

I designed writing steps to accompany the drawing steps, convinced that writing would allow students to construct a more extensive body of information and that this additional verbal information would encourage even more accurate drawing. Drawings carried information; how to access this information using writing? After experimenting for several years, I devised this sentence: "My Blind Contour drawing tells me that my object is...because...." The verb "tells" makes it clear that drawings carry accessible information, and the word "because" forced the writer to defend or explain the information.

Between the years 1980 and 1991, the five-step drawing program underwent a series of additions and refinements. Ease of use for other teachers and their students was imperative. If the program were not easy to use, it made no difference whether the Drawing/Writing approach worked for me and my students. I commenced clarifying and stream-lining the program.

Every student population has special needs. Every student is special. This being so, the program required flexibility. It had to appeal to students for whom writing and reading were troublesome as well as to students who found writing and reading easy. Research supported my own observations; dyslexic students often exhibited strong drawing skills. Convinced that a drawing-based literacy program would benefit dyslexic students, I approached a school for dyslexic students, proposing a pilot study for my doctorate. A one week session of Drawing/Writing improved students' writing skills. They wrote more words and, in some cases, their handwriting became more flowing. Most showed improvements in both their drawing and writing skills in three days.

of drawing changes the writing structurally—or grammatically—as well as motorically and aesthetically. The selection, evaluation and organization of visual information affects the selection, evaluation and organization of verbal information. These are startling and important results. Better drawing can bring about better writing—if the two activities are deliberately linked.

*Drawing/Writing, the lacrosse glove, Wally Shakun, eighth grade, Linden Hill School, 1987*

<u>Note:</u> *Writing scanned at same resolution as the drawing below: this Drawing/Writing sample shows tentative writing, and sure drawing. Pencil marks <u>are</u> lighter than marker drawings inherently, but the unevenness in <u>pressure</u> is key here.*

I documented cases where the initial drawing marks were dramatically more fluent than the same student's initial writing marks. After the one-week program of Drawing/Writing, the dyslexic students demonstrated increased ease in their writing marks, producing more words and richer content, too. A few years later as an English teacher, I observed similar motoric and cognitive improvements in the handwriting of dyslexic and attention deficit students at the middle and high school levels.

The shell drawing and writing and the small vertebra drawing and writing show more labored writing marks. The lacrosse glove and large vertebra show a quantity of writing, but, in both cases, the writing (scanned at the same resolution as the drawing) is less consistent in pressure. In all four cases, the drawing marks reveal more fluidity and pressure than the writing marks. Still, the act

*Drawing/Writing, the shell, Daniel Miller, eighth grade, Linden Hill School, 1987*

*Drawing/Writing, small vertebra, David Rheuble, eighth grade, Linden Hill School, 1987*

The first writing with the small vertebra follows: "this thing is boney and srage crved white, bran." The second writing, "I think It stings. I hate to dral. rouf, poine, smoth, inwad, squirr, reclang, this big and cred, skomey" (David Rheuble, 1987)

The first writing with the shell: "It look's like a cammle and a huorse. It is a sea shell too." Second writing: "I dyskover the shell can be ennething you went it to be. The shell has a lot of armoys and it is bumpe too." In both instances, an additional clause indicating the increased thoughtfulness of the writer is expressed grammatically, "I think"…. "I dyskover" (Daniel Miller, 1987).

The writing about the lacrosse glove is lighter in pressure and less well-formed than the drawings of the lacrosse glove. On the other hand, this writing is complex, it moves from description to metaphor and speculation. First writing: "its a pwde for a game called lacros you dont bert or a brus. its soft has a plustic shel and the reoset paret its smothe it also rofe." Second writing in response to the Basic Shape drawing: "B.S. looks like a robot hand or a sharp object it hole of difrant shapes to it its could be macanical the second is more corved." LMD writing: "it gets darker as you go along it has a lot of derent valy" (Wally Shakun, 1987).

In one instance, that of the large vertebra, well-formed drawing and careful writing go together. Still, the drawing has far greater authority and *panache*. Preliminary drawing: "It looks like a spas ship that has been traveling for a log time. It is a peese of a cow's bown." Contour: "It has a lot of angels and is jagged in a lot of plases." PW: "It has severl holes and craks all over the plas." BS and LMD: "There are more shapes in this picher then the last picher. It looks like a mape for a mall. It only has a fow darck plases and a lot of open light pases" (Christian Morrison, 1987). The "there is" sentence introduces distance. The writer moves from observation to comparison and generalization.

I made these notes teaching Drawing/Writing to ADD and LD students: "R's hand is more relaxed and I am not fooling. His drawing skills are good, he is able and powerful. J, who was a behavioral problem, is totally intent, quiet, involved, sitting still. Why? Why is drawing different? It must be different because these students are clearly good at drawing and clearly understand what they are doing. J. is so calm I cannot believe it. He is tracing the shoe—it seems to work wonderfully—he has seen the imprint of the toes" (1/15/87).

Encouraged by the improvements I observed motorically and cognitively in the writing skills of an identified

*Drawing/Writing, the vertebra, Christian Morrison, eighth grade, Linden Hill School, 1987*
<u>Note</u>: *More carefully controlled, uneven pressure in writing; more fluidity, and consistent, sure pressure in drawing.*

dyslexic population of schoolboys, I wondered whether Drawing/Writing could improve reading skills. Because drawing trains the brain to decode information as well as to encode it, training in drawing must also be training in reading. It stood to reason that drawing could be used to develop writing and reading skills. My continuing work bears out this double hypothesis: training in drawing facilitates writing *and* reading. Research and experience with Drawing/Writing support these basic assumptions:

- Children's early scribbling indicates a predisposition to make marks of significance. Scribbling is a motoric exercise demonstrating neural impulses toward expressed meaning. Scribbling eventually bifurcates into two sets of distinguishable marks: one set becomes drawing marks and another set becomes writing marks. How the child feels about the acceptability and intelligibility of the drawing marks contributes to the child's attitude about writing and reading—and even mathematics.

- Children's ability to draw is innate. Children are inherently interested in drawing and can learn to draw well with minimal instruction.

- Neurobiological research confirms the interconnections among drawing, writing and reading, identifying interhemispheric transfer as operative in the process. Neurobiology provides the structural and procedural reasons for the success of a cross-modal literacy program.

- Training students in a studio-like drawing course requiring group critiques encourages the acquisition not only of written language but also of spoken language.

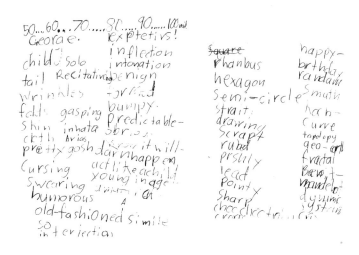

*Elizabeth Wright, Drawing/Writing journal, 2nd grade, Wildwood School, Amherst, and Santa Fe, NM, 1997.*

The challenge remained to create an easy-to-use program that connected the innate ability to draw with the innate predisposition to write. The five-step program met these requirements. To encourage oral language skills, including the ability to provide focused verbal analyses, I designed "Peer Share and Build" and "Group Critique." If designed properly, peer sharing and group critiques would allowed several things to happen in the classroom:

- First, in peer sharing and in group critiques students establish ownership. They talk about their drawings and their writings, actively presenting their own work. Ownership is one of the keys to learning.

- Second, by discussing their drawings and writings, students mentally revise their work, developing the ability to be self-critical.

- Third, by presenting their drawings and writings to their peers, and by discussing others' work in group critiques, students exercise the art of speech, learning how to use language effectively. Whether students are drawing, writing, or speaking, the goal in peer sharing and in group critiques is an increasingly precise use of oral and written language.

- Fourth, by writing down new words, students increase their vocabularies. The more extensive the vocabulary, the deeper and broader the thought.

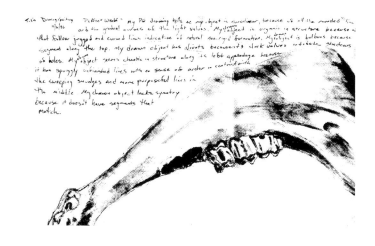

*Tim Lis, "Perfect" Whole drawing, jawbone of a cow, Westfield State, Continuing Education, 1996*

In my seventeen years of teaching, the Drawing/Writing work of Tim Lis, along with that of Joanne Krawzyck, show the most balanced, developed visual and verbal skills I have encountered. Tim's writing shows a great range in vocabulary. Tim came to the Continuing Education course with this vocabulary in place. Watch for the depth and logical precision of his writing and of Joanne's as you enjoy other examples of their work throughout the book. Joanne's work is featured in Step 4. In both of these cases, Drawing/Writing provided a vehicle for extending existing skills.

Tim wrote, "My PW drawing tells me my object is curvilinear because of all the rounded lines throughout the silhouette and the gradual curves of the light values. My drawn object is organic in structure because of its myriad abnormalities that follow jagged and curved lines indicative of natural, non-rigid formation. My drawn object is bulbous because it has a widened, rounded segment along the top. My drawn object has divots because its dark values indicate shadows like those cast along the walls of holes. My drawn object seems chaotic in structure along its left appendage because it has squiggley, unfinished lines with no sense of order in contrast with the sweeping smudges and more purposeful lines in the middle. My drawn object lacks symmetry because it does not have segments that match."

As a Drawing/Writing teacher, I continue to observe the phenomena predicted by my doctorate. Drawing/Writing increases attention. It elevates emotion. It encourages logical thinking within the context of an expanded vocabulary. Theoretically, the Drawing/Writing program is powerful because it models brain processes. Empirically, it is powerful because students like it. The growth they experience and the work they produce is extraordinary.

## How I use Drawing/Writing

I have used Drawing/Writing to teach middle school and high school writing courses, middle school English literature and art courses, high school interdisciplinary courses, and college art history and studio courses.

I first used Drawing/Writing as a middle school teacher in a boys' school with a high percentage of foreign students. I taught English to culturally diverse eighth and ninth graders, including students from Thailand, Japan, Honduras, Mexico, the Arab Emirates, Spain, and China. My school year began with a two-week session of Drawing/Writing. To start, each student selected an object from a box of tools and bones, drew that object, and then wrote about it in his own language (e.g., Lawrence Chen's work at the beginning of this chapter). Then the students showed their drawings to each other and read their writing aloud. It became clear, if it had not been so before, that students with fledgling English skills were literate in their own languages. Some were, in fact, trilingual. It is easy to make incorrect assumptions about the literacy levels of those who do not speak, write or read our own language. Allowing students to write in

their own languages, first, corrects these assumptions. American students also gain an appreciation for the aesthetic aspects of written languages like Chinese, Japanese and Arabic.

Drawing/Writing encouraged a tolerant, more relaxed atmosphere. Every student was able to draw, whatever his English language skills. The rest of the Drawing/Writing program continued in English. When I team-taught Spanish classes, Drawing/Writing was conducted in Spanish. Drawing/Writing can be used to build writing, reading and speaking skills in any language.

For instance, in a second-year Spanish class, Sam Sheridan wrote, "Está blanco y negro. Está a mismo de un avion nuevo. La debuja está maca. Está el mismo de un pezo. Está una cosa fuera del mundo. Yo pienso que el objectivo es de un gran animale."

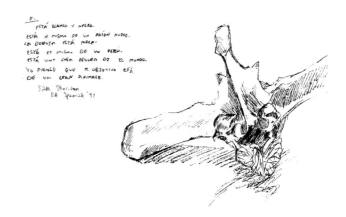

*Sam Sheridan's Preliminary Drawing and Writing of a vertebra, second-year Spanish, Deerfield Academy, 1991*

After students produced a preliminary piece of writing in their own language, I asked them to translate the writing into another language. The ESL students were required to translate theirs into English, producing a "pre-test" sample in English. English-speaking students were required to translate their writing in English into some other language, using foreign language dictionaries and grammar books or previous knowledge. These translation exercises sensitized native English speakers to the linguistic struggles their foreign classmates faced daily. These translation exercises encouraged useful social experiences, including empathy. The goal of every classroom, including the multicultural classroom, is the growth of the human mind and spirit in the context of language learning.

Through the years, a handful of disengaged students have come into my classrooms. Over and over again, I have seen the motivational wonders worked by drawing. Students make leaps in drawing skills and then they make gains in writing skills because they now care about what they are doing. Small, tentative pencil drawings are replaced by large, fully developed, high-contrast marker drawings. Sparse, disengaged writing becomes invested and rich. Rescore, the evaluation tool built into the Drawing/Writing program, often registers doubled or tripled word-use.

Changes become more subtle with successive Drawing/Writing sessions. Students may write less on the closing writing sample than on the first, but they write more precisely. One metaphor eliminates a paragraph. In a similar way, minimalist drawings signal a refinement, not a loss in drawing skills.

Football players have been among my successes. Most of them—like many of my students—take the art survey course as a core requirement. My highly interactive approach surprises them. The drawing component is an additional novelty. But there is more to it than that. Intellect and football correlate. Both require work. A football analogy is useful, too. The football player who runs for a ball thrown well ahead of him is like the avant-garde artist, reaching with all of his energy and skill to catch the drift of meaning. We all understand ideas better when they are defined in the context of our own experience.

*Rebecca Parco, Westfield State College art survey Drawing/Writing quiz, vocabulary, 1995*

It is becoming clear to teachers in disparate fields that drawing can be used to heal what my colleague Frances Jo Grossman of Georgia State University calls "wounded writing." The committed act of drawing acts like needle and thread, stitching writing back onto students' expressive lives.

*Football player reaching for ball, Claus Kormannshaus, 1997*

Drawing lets college students reclaim an activity they left behind in childhood. By drawing a work of art, even from a photograph in a textbook, students learn about the work in ways looking alone cannot provide. Because Drawing/Writing requires writing, students who enter college increasingly ill-equipped to write gain additional practice.

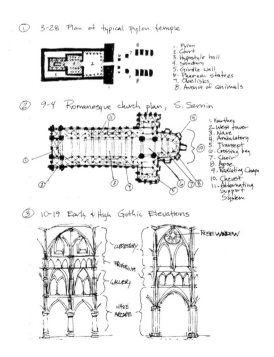

*Kendall Lamar, Drawing/Writing quiz, Westfield State College, art survey, 1993*

## 1.6 Eight Educational Benefits

The Fifth Step, the Composite Abstraction (CA), invites students to engage in inventive symbolic play. The purpose of the Composite Abstraction is to facilitate:

- the move from drawing to writing and reading
- the move from concrete to abstract thinking
- inventive solutions
- ethical sensibilities and behavior.

To achieve these skills and sensibilities, the mind must be alert and strategic. The idea of using parts of former solutions to create a new solution challenges students' inventiveness. As a personal, self-constructed symbol system that exists somewhere between drawing and writing, the CA readies students for understanding new symbol systems—like writing or mathematics.

The nickname for the CA is "the new hieroglyphics." Egyptian hieroglyphics evolved from the pictorial to the phonetic; a picture of a vulture came to stand for the initial sound of the word "vulture." In somewhat the same way, an optically accurate drawing changes its form in Drawing/Writing by becoming an abstraction, recapitulating the process of the invention of writing from drawing.

The eight educational benefits of the CA are:

(1) Each child learns a group of visual and verbal strategies, including the ability to examine, analyze, compare and contrast, evaluate, sequence, redefine, re-organize, balance, and integrate information.

Drawing/Writing returns children to direct experience with the construction of symbolic language, allowing them to re-create, as mini-experiences, the history of drawing and writing. Students are invited to regress to the beginning of recorded time, constructing a hands-on understanding of the development of symbolic language as drawing. Finding drawing natural and easy, children are freed to devise text experimentally, in bits and pieces, around their drawings. Drawing/Writing teaches students what it feels like to create pictographs, logograms, and phonograms, as well as the written word.

(2) Students who have completed a series of composite abstractions know how to create abstractions. They know they can make marks that do not look like an object but which describe it in new ways. They understand a very powerful idea: symbolic representation. The

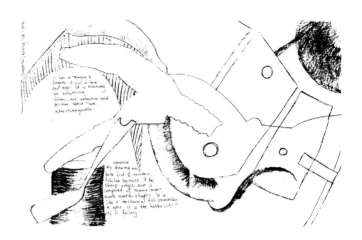

*Teresa Mershon, CA, Hampshire College, January term, 1996*

very young student who practices CA's is ready to believe that the abstract drawings he has created are like writing. If his CA carries meaning, writing will carry meaning. It is at this point that the child can be introduced to the idea that mathematical notation—whether arithmetic, algebra or calculus—or, for that matter, musical notation, will be meaningful, just as abstract paintings will be meaningful.

The gulf between symbol systems is not as wide as we imagine. Children can draw their way toward mathematical operations.

(3) Students who are not ready to write or read can create a series of meaningful Composite Abstractions, gaining an educational grace period in the language acquisition process. Because of differences in experiences as well as maturational rates, brains differ. Allowances must be made for differences. Some brains are ready to read in the first grade. Some make the breakthrough later.

On the other hand, children are born ready for symbol systems. Every representation children construct in their brains is an abstraction. Serious play with abstraction need not be withheld until a certain time or grade. Children demonstrate their readiness for meaning-making through spontaneous scribbling and drawing. Serious work with abstract symbols can be achieved through the CA before children are able to write or read. This work is not only preparatory. It is legitimate work in and of itself. The ability to make and use visual symbols is as important as being able to make and use verbal symbols, and a lifetime of confidence in verbal symbols may—for some children—depend upon it.

*Joshua Lucas, CA of a log, second grade, Applewild School, 1997*

Joshua Lucas wrote, "My CA tells me that it looks like the sun. It looks like a egg. It looks like a bote."

*Courtney Bergeron, CA of a toy horse, second grade, Applewild School, 1997*

Courtney Bergeron wrote, "My CA tells me mase, stret. Like a skate bord, a srkle."

A grace period for writing and reading is important for developmentally delayed children as well as for children at risk for language-related learning disabilities. The child who practices Composite Abstractions is more likely to accept the fact that marks like words or mathematical notations that mean nothing right now will mean something in the future. For this transfer to happen, teachers must make clear that the CA is an abstract symbol like letters, words, and numbers. CA's drawn by other students are initially unintelligible until they are explained in group critiques. Students who construct and discuss Composite Abstractions know they can work

with abstract symbols. These students may be less likely to adopt defeatist attitudes or mental blocks toward other abstract symbols systems like writing or mathematics, thereby avoiding "acquired" learning disabilities. Knowing their abstract drawings are important and intelligible, late-blooming readers sustain their natural exuberance and confidence as learners. If drawing is presented as a substantive mental activity in a literacy program, reassurance is also provided for anxious and embarrassed adult learners who have not yet learned to read or write.

Because of the brain's neural modifiability, Drawing/Writing—if it is implemented from pre-kindergarten on—may allow students who are at risk for learning disabilities to self-remediate before the onset of actual troubles with writing and reading. If a brain frames the act of writing the way it frames abstract drawing, that brain may be able to use its "drawing areas" to write and read. The drawing area of the brain may extend its neural influence into a less functional language area, reorganizing it for success the way the right hemisphere reorganizes or replaces language function following damage to the left hemisphere.

Beyond the recognized potential of the brain for self-healing, there is this to consider: what the brain thinks *is* going on is going on for that brain. The Drawing/Writing student who *believes* that writing and reading are more advanced forms of abstract drawing *knows* she will learn to write and read. If she can make meaning using drawings, she will be able to make meaning using letters and words. The CA allows the student to develop her symbolic skills at her own pace, while gaining confidence in the ability of abstract symbols to make meaning. Because the Drawing/Writing program is self-regulatory, all students have a chance to become literate.

The optically accurate fourth step in Drawing/Writing requires an exercise in abstraction. An optically accurate drawing is just another simulacrum. As convincing as it may be, it remains a partial representation; it is not the actual thing it depicts. It is a certain kind of drawing, no more or less real than a line or a dot on a page. By the same token, the abstract drawing, the CA, is no less descriptive than the optically accurate drawing.

Still, even to the student who created it, the CA is, to some degree, unintelligible as *content* at first. As balanced as it may be formally, the CA as narrative or content can only be understood inferentially. The student must scan the drawing for cues to meaning, constructing some written comment about them.

If the brain can construct a potentially infinite string of well-formed sentences from hearing spoken sentences (Chomsky, 1973), the brain is equipped for inference. Whether meaning-making strategies are called deep grammar or templates or schemata or innate predispositions or space phase sandwiches or the Form of the form (all of these terms will be covered), the brain is organized to extract and construct meaning. To extract meaning from minimal cues, the brain must be alert, it must be equipped with search strategies, and it must have a procedure for combining information in meaningful ways. Drawing/Writing provides a procedure for honing attention, for conducting informational searches, and for constructing meaning from minimal cues through drawing and writing.

(4) Students who receive training in the CA learn recombinant strategies.[2] Whether overt or covert, creativity is a system. Through the CA, Drawing/Writing teaches students one such system: how to construct a new whole out of old parts.

(5) Students trained in CA #1 and CA #2 learn to refine, re-evaluate, and redesign their inventions. "Going back to the drawing boards" is part of the process. The writing associated with several successive CA's undergoes similar revisions.

(6) Students practicing CA's are introduced to a powerful concept described as "right relationships." Right relationships exist in art when the formal elements of line, form, space and color are balanced in a harmonious whole. Aesthetic decision-making is often intuitive; still, aesthetic decisions can be discussed.

In group critiques there is usually agreement about what constitutes too much or too little in a drawing. Consensus about right relationships has implications for the relevance of art education to other levels of decision-making. The concept of right relationships in drawing is easily extended to include discussions about right relationships in human behavior. An approach to ethical behavior based on aesthetics becomes a possibility.

(7) Students who practice CA's learn another powerful idea: acceptable differences. When students learn to accept other students' initially unintelligible CA's, they're on their way to understanding this concept. By seeing

that there are many possible ways to draw a composite abstraction, even very young students learn flexibility. Experience with a range of drawing solutions prepares the mind to expect a range of solutions to any problem whether it is artistic, social or political. Rather than balking at new ideas, students learn to welcome them.

Training in the production of diverse solutions can be expanded through teacher-generated discussions to include tolerant and compassionate attitudes toward people, places, ideas, and customs. An arts-based approach to ethics, or right action, is especially compatible with classrooms where the one constant is diversity. A congenial classroom is one in which learning occurs. One of the hallmarks of a congenial learning environment is the expectation and acceptance of difference—in fact, taking pleasure in things just because they are different. The CA allows the teacher, the parent, and the child to understand that the "mind's best work" is different for every child. Not only will one child's best work vary from every other child's best work, but that individual child's best work will show itself in various ways, at various times. The importance of training young minds for variability cannot be overstated. Learning to accept what delights the mind makes literacy education pleasurable and useful.

(8) Group critiques teach students to speak precisely and critically. Gentle but relentless prodding by the teacher forces students to clarify vague or ambiguous statements. Eventually, the entire group becomes skilled in constructive criticism.

### Breaking the code

Visual and verbal codes are changing fast. New word processing programs, graphics programs and computer languages abound. Students need to learn to break codes. They need to be adept at new systems. Students who grow up with computers learn intuitive, exploratory behavior. Students who do not grow up with computers need to practice exploratory, code-cracking behavior, too.

In the context of this book and Drawing/Writing, reading first occurs when students create drawings they understand. Breaking the code starts with drawing and progresses to other symbol systems.

The Composite Abstraction prepares the mind to read what it cannot yet read. The CA allows the mind that is reading uneasily to read more easily through practice with abstract symbols. Drawing/Writing students at the "CA stage" literally "get the picture." Having broken the code of visual language, they know they can decode others.

---

[2] In *The Mind's Best Work* (1981), Harvard School of Education professor David Perkins defines creativity as learnable strategies. Like any other set of skills, creativity or inventiveness can be taught. In a similar vein, Seymour Papert's *Mind Storms* (1980) encourages procedural, step-by-step thinking through the computer language LOGO as a route to invention.

## 1.7 The Evaluation Tool Rescore

### Closing Drawing and Writing

After completing the Composite Abstraction, students choose a new object to draw and write about in a loosely timed, informal "post-test." The new object rekindles interest, challenging students' new skills. The student has learned how to extract information from one object and to express that information visually and verbally. The degree to which those skills transfer to a new object measures the effectiveness of the five-step program.

Like the Preliminary Drawing and Writing, the Closing Drawing and Writing is a timed exercise. Then, students evaluate quantitative and qualitative changes in their drawing and writing skills using a scoring tool called Rescore. The two sets of drawing and writing samples function as pre-test and post-test. Because the word "test" may provoke anxiety and inauthentic behavior, the words "pre-test" and "post-test" are not used. The terms "Preliminary Drawing and Writing" and "Closing Drawing and Writing" are clear and non-threatening.

### Rescore

Students learn to identify changes in their writing quantitatively first, and qualitatively second: first, the numbers; then, what the numbers mean. Students look for a change—say, in the number of adjectives in the writing—and then evaluate that change. What do more adjectives mean? A student who uses more adjectives might conclude that his writing is becoming more descriptive. A student who records fewer words may conclude that her writing is tighter, or more poetic. Elegant mathematical solutions are parsimonious. So is good writing.

To identify specific changes in her writing, a student must learn the parts of speech. To be able to use Rescore beyond the counting level requires an understanding of grammar.

### Grammar

The Rescore program provides a personal approach to grammar, introducing it in the context of students' writing. Students count not only the total number of words, but parts of speech, for instance, verbs. To use Rescore, students must understand what a verb is. A preliminary piece of writing may contain 40 words, and the closing writing may contain 60 words. Students may count 8 verbs in the preliminary writing, and 14 verbs in the closing writing. If students note an increase in active verbs, they may conclude their work is more forceful, less passive. Learning to distinguish between active and passive verbs allows students to fine-tune their use of language, moving them beyond content to a knowledgeable interest in the structure of their writing.

*Michael Cooper, Preliminary Drawing and Writing, corkscrew, Westfield State College, Continuing Education, 1996*

Michael Cooper wrote in his Preliminary Drawing and Writing about the corkscrew, "I wish I could give more on how it really is through my eyes. Not similar but good. If or when things progress, I might be more strong about my work. I think my ideas are good but my skills lack."

In his Closing Drawing and Writing, Michael wrote, "I don't know what to think? Closing that means the end, it is all over. My drawing is shaped like this because at first it started small at a point and grew. It is curved up and down. Like this class good times and overwhelming feelings at others. I see Euclidean shapes and beyond. I could use this horn and blow a loud earth shattering sound to let the world hear the new sounds of my poetic tongue. Tough and learned through time, class, life and man's evolution."

*Michael Cooper, Closing Drawing and Writing, cow horn, Westfield State College, Continuing Education, 1996*

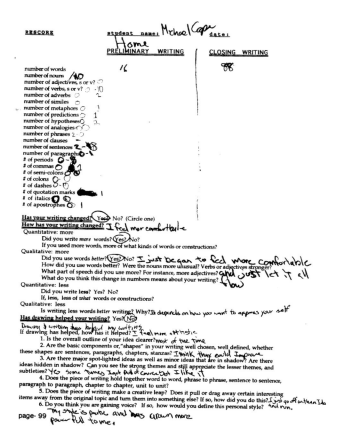

*Michael Cooper, Rescore, Westfield State College, Continuing Education, 1996*

Michael's Rescore shows that his word use went from 16 to 88; from 0 to 1 each for simile, prediction and hypothesis. Michael wrote, "I really felt more comfortable [with writing] and just let it all flow." He commented that his style is "poetic and more powerful." He felt that drawing helped him to express himself "in different ways" in writing and that his writing was "less scattered." He felt "more pleasure" drawing, and became aware of "a lot of negative space. dumb." In terms of his style in drawing, Michael wrote, "My overall style is more realistic and more expressive."

Drawing/Writing students recognize the relationship between structure and language through a knowledge of grammar and punctuation. Because grammar and punctuation provide tools for identifying changes in language use, Rescore provides a huge incentive to learn grammar and punctuation.

To write well, students must enjoy writing. Writing is a terrific amount of work, much more work, for instance, than painting. Spelling rules, punctuation and grammar rules taught as *preconditions* to good writing may discourage the early natural enthusiasm for this activity. Once writing takes root, rules of grammar and punctuation may be offered for consideration.[3] Ask young writers whether punctuation is necessary or not. Ask them to try reading their work aloud without it. Punctuation allows breathing if nothing else. As practitioners of writing, students are ready to care about commas and semicolons, adverbs and conjunctions.

We use a visual/spatial system to locate our bodies in space and to move around in the world. This earlier organizing system, or "grammar," this proprioception, undergirds the grammar of language. A visual/spatial grammar informs the natural act of drawing while providing a basis for the acquired activities of writing and reading. It is in this sense that this book accepts an innate grammar as the predisposition to order. "Grammar" as the names of the parts of speech must be learned.

The predisposition to drawing is innate. Children do not need to look at other drawings to draw. All they need is something to draw with and something to draw on. The predisposition to write and read is innate, too, but we need to look at books, be read to, and talked to, and see people around us writing and reading to learn how to read and write.

Drawing happens naturally. Writing and reading must be learned. No one has to teach children to scribble. The alphabet and some rudimentary ideas about spelling

---

[3] Two clever and hilarious handbooks for teaching grammar and punctuation at the middle, high school, college and adult levels are:

Karen Elizabeth Gordon, *The Well-Tempered Sentence: A Punctuation Handbook for the Innocent, the Eager, and the Doomed* (New York: Times Books, 1983).

Karen Elizabeth Gordon, *The Transitive Vampire: A Handbook of Grammar for the Innocent, the Eager, and the Doomed* (New York: Times Books, 1984).

must be learned before children can crack the language code. At this point in educational history, children's predisposition toward writing needs a boost. Training in drawing—a natural and accessible skill for all children—encourages children to write as part of a lifelong process.

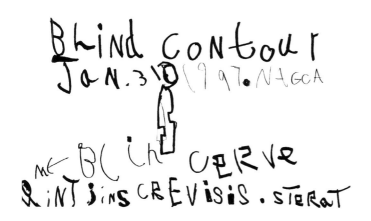

*Nate Gorlin Crenshaw's Blind Contour of a potato peeler, six years old, 1997.*

Nate wrote, "My blin cerve mintins crevisis.sterat [My blind curve mountains crevices. straight]."

### Grading

The Rescore grading sheet provides a personal approach to grading rather than an imposed approach. Students who get "A's" from teachers do not necessarily believe they are "A" students. On the other hand, many students howl in indignation over grades incommensurate with their estimation of their abilities. They equate time spent with the quality of the work. They lack an understanding that grades reflect product, not process. Both process and product have value. At this point in educational history, process is as valuable as product, if not more so. Students who use Rescore focus their energies first on product, and then on process. A second-year Spanish student produced these Rescore results and accompanying evaluation:

"Mi dibujo es un insecto con muchas piernas. Mi dibujo es como la cabeza de un perro. Mi dibujo es miedo porque él es una mano terrible de un gigante. Es como la mano de un lagarto. Yo puedo usar mi dibujo para guardar mis manos. Mi dibujo es una víbora porque tiene los dientes de un víbora. Mi dibujo es sencillo porque es una herramienta de lacrosse. Mi dibujo es corto y fuerte."

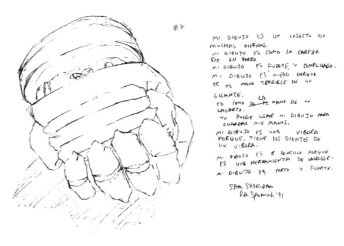

*Sam Sheridan's Closing Drawing and Writing of a lacrosse glove, second-year Spanish, Deerfield Academy, 1991*

When asked to reflect on how his writing in Spanish had changed after a session with Drawing/Writing, Sam wrote, "Miro un cambio grande, porque veo más palabras interesantes y realisticas. Miro un cambio de la calidad de mi escritura, porque ahora puedo espresar mis emocionentes." Gains in numbers of words, in the quality of the words, and in the expressiveness or emotional content of the words are common in Drawing/Writing. From his pre- to his post-test, Sam's word count went from 26 words to 73 words; from 4 adjectives to 12 adjectives, from one metaphor to 4 metaphors. It is not necessary to run a statistical analysis to evaluate changes like these.

Peter Chu, another student in that second year Spanish class, also produced Preliminary and Closing drawing and writing samples of interest.

Peter wrote, "Un mitod de patín—Cuando empezo, yo tengo un dificil tiempo. No me gusta esto projeto porque le patinar es un objeto malo debujar."

Peter wrote, "Mi dibujo es como un tiburón. Mi dibujo es un herramienta de romper nueces. Mi dibujo es muy interessante porque los aspectos son muy complicados. Por ejemplo, mi dibujo tiene los aspectos que aprendimos durante esto projeto. Ahora, me gusta esto projeto porque mis dibujos son más hermosos. Yo soy feliz. Aprendo mucho y yo sugero esto projeto para los estudiantes de todas las clases en el futuro. Ahora yo soy cansado y no hago escribo más. Yo creo que mi opinión está obvioso. Durante la projeto, yo aprendo muchas palabras nuevas también. Gracias Señor Taylor porque yo tiene muy divertido."

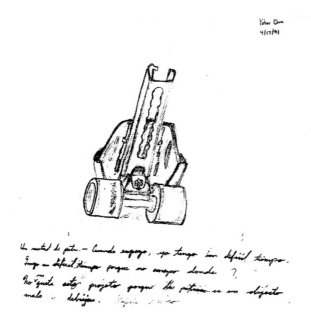

*Peter Chu, Preliminary Drawing and Writing, second year Spanish, Deerfield Academy, 1991*

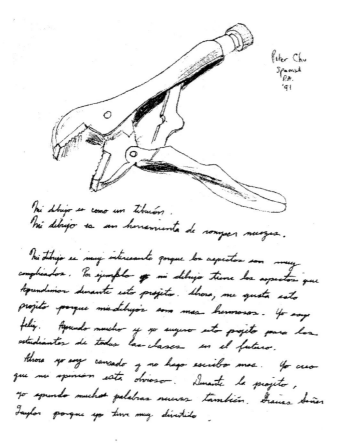

*Peter Chu, Closing Drawing and Writing, second year Spanish, Deerfield Academy, 1991*

*Peter Chu's Rescore, Deerfield Academy, 1991*

Peter Chu's Preliminary Writing had a total of 32 words; his Closing Writing had 90 words. From no similes, metaphors, predictions or hypotheses, Peter wrote one of each in the second writing sample. As Peter observed, "Mi vi un cambio grande porque ahora uso más similes, metáforas, y major adjetivos. Ahora mis escrituras son más comprendidas. Mi vi un cambio de números complemente tieno más calidad."

It is hard for students to argue with their own documentation of process and product, even if the results of both sets of evaluations do not match their perceptions of the quality and quantity of their work. Students cannot evaluate what they have not produced.

Rescore is an invaluable constructivist tool for parents and teachers, too. Parents receive an assessment of their child's reading, writing and thinking skills provided by the child. The detail and depth of the Rescore self-evaluation is impressive and reassuring to parents. Their child knows where she stands as a visual and verbal thinker. Because parents have received a letter from the teachers who include Drawing/Writing as a strategy, they appreciate that training in drawing is also training in visual literacy, allowing parents to look at drawings as evidence of growth. In fact, it is often easier to see a child's growth in terms of drawing than writing.

Teachers also need to know how their students' skills are growing. Students formally share their portfolios with the teacher, going over each piece of work. Using a check-list, they demonstrate the degree to which the portfolio is complete.[4] Together, students and teacher discuss the work as product and as process. For many teachers, it will seem strange to receive students' assessment of work instead of providing that assessment. Although Rescore displaces the teacher as portfolio grader, it does not remove the teacher from the evaluation process. Teachers may choose to include other criteria in a final grade like attendance, group critique participation, or work in other content areas.

Joanne Quail, teacher of second graders, provides this advice to prospective Drawing/Writing teachers: "You have to relax with this. My students loved the Euclidean drawings. There was not a sound in the room. I could have left the room and gone home. Students who move around all of the time were as still as rocks." Joanne adds, "Some students were locked when it came to similes. It was clear that they wanted to express themselves freely. Fear is the component. This block exists in kids. First-born children especially have so many rules. They can't float into new spaces easily." Joanne added this comment about "locked" children and Drawing/Writing: "I learned more from what did not come out [in their work]. I learned to be more sensitive to freeing them in their expression. It [Drawing/Writing's emphasis on simile and metaphor] is as freeing for the teacher as it is for the kids."

Holly C. Tuttle, twenty-five year veteran art teacher, Central High School in Springfield, MA, writes via e-mail, "I sent some Drawing/Writing monoprints to the MAEA convention. The writing is absolutely outstanding" (October 10, 1997).

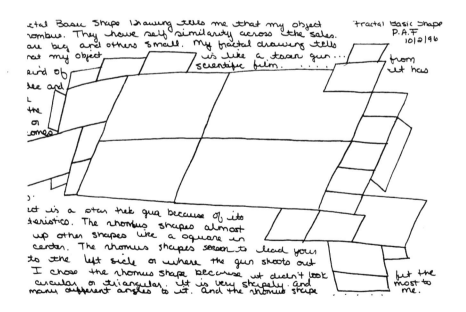

*Pamela Frigo, Fractal Basic Shape, skull, Continuing Education, Westfield State College, 1996*

---

[4] The portfolio check list is provided at the end of Part 2, along with Rescore.

# BRAIN SCIENCE INFORMS EDUCATION

My belief is that the explanations of "emergent" phenomena in our brains—for instance, ideas, hopes, images, analogies, and finally consciousness and free will—are based on a kind of Strange Loop, an interaction between levels in which the top level reaches back down towards the bottom level and influences it, while at the same time being itself determined by the bottom level.... The self comes into being at the moment it has the power to reflect itself.... In order to deal with the full richness of the brain/mind system, we will have to be able to slip between levels comfortably.... At the crux, then, of our understanding ourselves will come an understanding of the Tangled Hierarchy of levels inside our minds.

Douglas Hofstadter, *Gödel, Escher, Bach: The Eternal Golden Braid*

## 2.1 Neurobiological Processes and Language Learning: Brain Matters

Although the field of neurobiology is complex, it supplies accessible information which is useful to education. A more global, less lateralized approach to learning will not only be effective in the classroom but will produce the skills necessary to a global, information-based society.

### Clarification of right-brain and left-brain labeling

Betty Edwards' book, *Drawing on the Right Side of the Brain (1979)*, helped to popularize brain science, providing practical applications of drawing which she took successfully into the worlds of education and business. She offered two important observations:

- Everyone can draw.
- Drawing is thinking.

The theories in this book expand an appreciation for drawing:

- Training in drawing has general cognitive usefulness for teaching descriptive, analytical and inferential thinking skills. If training in drawing is combined with reflective writing, literacy becomes an integrative enterprise in which encoding and decoding skills extend well beyond words to all symbols including mathematics.
- Drawing is no more an exclusively right-brained activity than writing is an exclusively left-brained activity. Both activities involve global mental operations including interhemispheric transfer.

With this understanding, polarizations like "logical versus illogical," "creative versus critical," or "intuitive

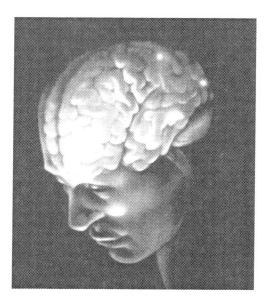

*The thinking brain*

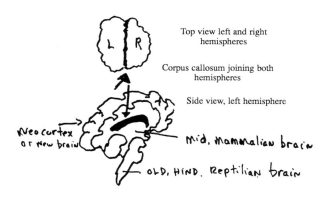

*Brain with arrow indicating corpus callosum, author, 97*
*The term WholeBrain is coined by this book to describe*
*a cross-modal, or interhemispheric approach to education.*

versus rational" lose their power. Brain science blurs or even eliminates such distinctions. WholeBrain (a term coined by this book) classrooms accept visual and verbal modes as equally viable approaches to learning and communication. The terms "visual" and "verbal" are descriptive, not evaluative; like the terms "spatial" and "linguistic," they define general categories of thought. Because the brain operates cross-modally, or interhemispherically, human thought is visual/verbal or, in more general terms, spatial/linguistic.

Some brains will excel at visual thinking and some brains will excel at verbal thinking. WholeBrain teaching avoids labels like "right-brain thinking" or "left-brain thinking," particularly as predictors of academic success. The goal in WholeBrain thinking is the growth of balanced, cooperative visual and verbal skills.

## 2.2 Cross-modal Processes

Visual and verbal information processing are linked in the human brain. The two hemispheres are connected by a nerve-rich strip of tissue called the corpus callosum, or "thick body." The corpus callosum works like a transformer. The exchange results in two kinds of information: visual and verbal. Since both hemispheres contribute energy to both kinds of information, the activity of thought is cooperative and transformational—like a good conversation in which neither person is sure who came up with the good idea.

The spatial and linguistic capabilities of the brain complement and cross-cue each other. In the same way, drawing and writing can be used to fertilize each other. In a literate mind, word and image can be equally eloquent.

### The M.C. Escher print

The brain-based relationship between image and word is illuminated by the M.C. Escher print *The Magic Mirror*. By passing through a mirror, two-dimensional griffins change into three-dimensional griffins. The mirror appears to be permeable, like a cell membrane. The path the griffins describe is a figure eight, like the Moebius strip. The magical aspect of the mirror is its ability to transform 2-D griffins into 3-D griffins, endlessly.

The salient aspect of the Moebius strip-like path of the griffins for our understanding of mental processes is an appreciation for the concept of infinity as ongoingness, rather than as unboundedness. If you run your finger over a piece of paper twisted into a figure eight, you will have a grasp of infinity as a single surface, or process without beginning or end, not as extending forever into space. Thinking is a continuous process like the symbol for infinity. A few minutes tracing the surface of a twisted piece of paper teaches a child from the fingertips out about the paradoxical nature of brain function; it is and it is not right or left. It is and it is not visual or verbal. The griffins walk right through a mirror, changing dimensions in the process. Thoughts do, too.

If we imagine that the mirror in the Escher print is the brain's corpus callosum, and that the two out-pouchings of the griffin/Moebius strip are the two hemispheres of the brain, we have a fairly accurate picture of the connected, reflective, transformative character of thought.

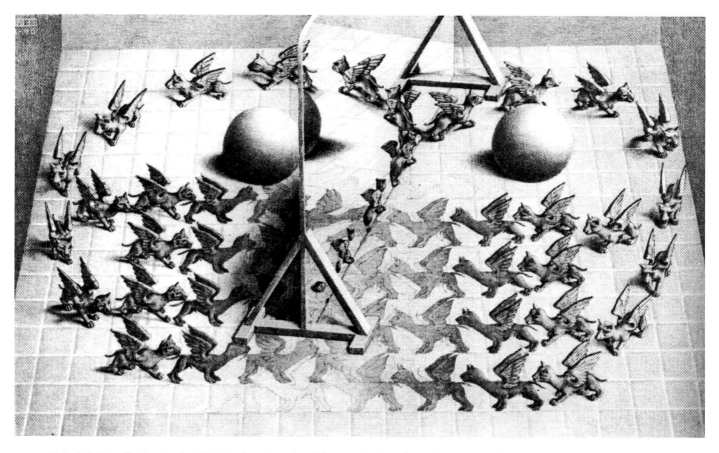

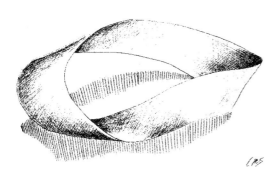

*Moebius strip, Claus Kormannshaus, 1997*

### A philosophical/scientific aside on duality

The implications of interhemispheric transfer for human thought are profound. Like the yin/yang symbol or the wave-particle theory of light, the relationship of energy to matter is so intimate that differentiating between waves and particles at the quantum level is difficult—if not impossible. The same is true of interhemispheric transfer.

At the quantum level, the word "embedded" describes the relationship between waves and particles. The dynamic is not simply reciprocal: it is nested. One state lies within and springs from the other. Experiments in physics distinguish one state from the other because it is the nature of experiments to select one aspect or another of some phenomenon for study. In fact, the design of any experiment influences the outcome. In addition, a quality of indeterminability touches every experiment.[5] We cannot know everything at the same time.

The term "wave-particleness" (Zajonc, 1993) more truly describes the equivocal relationship between energy and matter in light than the dichotomizing term "wave/particle duality." The term "wave-particleness" describes a complex unity. Brain activity is a complex unity, too.

---

[5] Heisenberg's Uncertainty Principle states that the more we know about one state, say, the position of a particle, the less we can know about its momentum. That is, we cannot be certain about every single aspect of any single thing or event.

The slash in Drawing/Writing reminds us that the left hemisphere and the right hemisphere are a complex unity. The slash between drawing and writing suggests that these two processes are analogous and indivisible. Drawing is not writing and writing is not drawing, yet the two skills remain related brain activities.

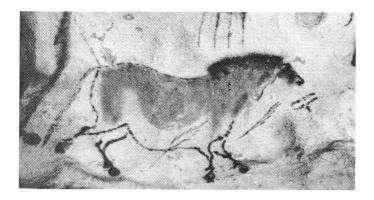

*"The Chinese Horse," Lascaux (c) by Jean Vertut*
*Reprinted by permission of Yvonne Vertut.*
*All rights reserved.*

An example of paleolithic cave art, "The Chinese Horse," shows a drawing of a horse accompanied by stylized, less accessible marks including, in the upper right, a tectiform. This cave painting suggests that interhemispheric transfer between visual and verbal information processing systems in the human brain was occurring at least 15,000 years ago. In fact, the ability to combine image and text as expressed by the the bicameral mind may date as far back as 50,000 years. Currently, images tagged with text resurface as a powerful form of human communication, with text once again subordinate to image.

### A spatial/linguistic sandwich

Information processing requires organizational systems. One description of these systems is "deep grammar." Noam Chomsky, MIT-based pioneer in language research, posits universal rules for language. He bases this innate grammar on the inborn predisposition of children to generalize a potentially infinite string of well-formed sentences from the sentences they hear. These sentences have a gross overall surface form. Children access reproductive syntactic rules embedded in this surface form to generate sentences (Chomsky, 1965, 1973, 1980).

Templates for images, like those for utterances, are coded neurally, too. The architecture of the brain includes parallel procedures. Arrays of neurons produce spatial matrices, or maps, which transfer and transform visual information in a mathematical manner. These matrices or maps or grammars—these ordering systems—generate language. Language has a spatial basis and may fairly be described as a "mapped map" (Llinas, Churchland, Pellionz, cited in Sheridan, 1991, 39).

Neurobiology describes brain networks as sandwich-like (Changeux, 1985 cited in Sheridan, 1991, 38). "Space phase sandwiches" (Churchland, 1986) describe brain mapping systems which layer information using mathematical-like procedures called tensor transformations. This layering eventually produces spoken and written language. These spatial/linguistic maps alternate in the

*Deli sandwich, Claus Kormannshaus, 1997*

brain like ham and Swiss cheese on rye. The layered maps produce pictures and words. Though useful, the sandwich metaphor is not exact because each layer in the brain's sandwich acts like a sieve or a fine-meshed screen rather than as a solid layer. It's as if each slice of bread, cheese and ham were permeable; information, like mayonnaise, mustard or pickle juice, seeps through one screen-like brain layer after another. At the level of language, the "seepage" produces images, words, and mathematical equations. Imagine a food mill. If you put cooked apples in a food mill and crank the handle, applesauce comes out, leaving the skin, seeds and core behind. Imagine an old-fashioned flour sifter: if you put flour in and turn the handle, a fine white powder mounds in the bowl. When apples become applesauce, the transformation is obvious. When one fineness of flour becomes another, the change is less obvious, but sifting has occurred nonetheless. Intelligent brain activity is like sifting flour; finely meshed spatial and linguistic analyses produce thought.

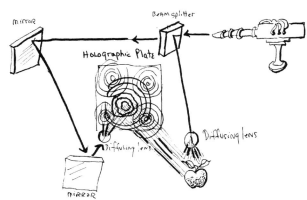

A hologram is when a single laser light is split into two separate beams. The first beam is bounced off the object to be photographed, in this case an apple. Then the second beam is allowed to collide with the reflected light of the first, and the resulting interference pattern is recorded on film. When another laser beam is shined through the film, an image of the original object re-appears. Planaria-like, any slice of a piece of holographic film generates an entire apple. Memories are stored in the brain in this overall way. Visual information is, too. Because of wave-like connectivity between branching nerve cells that send out ripple-like signals, brain function is holograph-like (Talbot, 1991, Sheridan, 1991).

*Diagram of a Holographic process, SRS*

*A flour sifter, Claus Kormannshaus, 1997*

### Three grammatical systems

The theory behind Drawing/Writing presupposes three grammatical systems for organizing meaning in the brain:

1. a meta or over-arching system described as spatial/linguistic
2. a visual system
3. a verbal system.

All three systems are linguistic in the sense that all three provide procedures or grammars for ordering stimuli and thus for selecting and organizing information. A spatial/linguistic system that uses spoken and written language as its basis is designated a verbal system. A spatial/linguistic system that uses images as its basis is a visual system. A set of syntactic rules organizes incoming stimuli in accordance with relationships recognized as coherent or well-balanced at deep neural levels, driving both sets of systems. The relationships are expressible mathematically and resemble, metaphorically if not actually, the relationships in holograms. This book identifies these relationships as the Form of the form.

Research in neurobiology supports the existence of innate syntactic rules which operate at levels well below verbal language. The fact that students in group critiques agree about "too much or too little" provides empirical support for the existence of innate sensibilities, or syntactic rules for rightness or pleasingness or balance.

Research with children's drawings shows that children begin drawing people as bristling, ovoid forms. These have been labeled "tadpole" drawings. These drawings demonstrate the existence of shared formal systems for representing meaning in very young children, as do the circular "mandalas" children create.

*Tadpole drawing, SR Sheridan, '97*

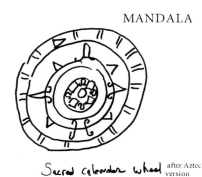

MANDALA

(A mandorla, on the other hand, is an almond-shaped lozenge-like, encircling or framing shape often used to enclose holy or otherwise important figures.)

Sacred calendar wheel <sup>after Aztec version</sup>

Mandala: concentric circles with radiating spokes; a deeply significant "innate schemata" and/or design pattern.

*Mandala, SRS*

Drawing/Writing operationalizes this grammar of intelligent thought or map for finding information in the following ways: work from the simple to the complex, from the concrete to the abstract, and from the visual to the verbal. More specifically, the three grammars or maps include these instructions:

- Select visual information and express it verbally.

- Combine visual information in one coherent presentation and express it verbally.

- Take the visual statement and break it back down into parts, expressing that new statement verbally.

- Take verbal statements about visual information presented as simile, metaphor, analogy, prediction and hypothesis, and translate them in visual terms.

- Do not include too much or too little in these visual and verbal translations.

- After every translation between visual and verbal modes, provide an explanation in words using "because."

In Drawing/Writing, visual information recorded in the Blind Contour drawing establishes the fundamental distinction between figure and ground. A decision has to be made about what is and what is not the subject under consideration. The informational search continues with an analysis of form—or the overall shape of the subject matter—and moves to a discussion of what information is more and less obvious, resolving the search by adding other pieces of information where necessary. This search creates a visual data base; this visual data base is translated into verbal data base. The process of selection,

accumulation, manipulation and translation of information models the overall shape or form or grammar of intelligent visual thought.

In Drawing/Writing, verbal information begins with physical description and works toward the metaphorical, analogical and hypothetical. These levels of analysis model the overall shape or form or grammar of intelligent verbal thought. Used in parallel mode, this visual/verbal approach to several related grammars enhance and extend intelligent thought.

## 2.3  A Model for Cognition: WholeBrain Education

### *The grammar of intelligent thought: Adaptive language instruction*

Drawing/Writing models the grammar of intelligent thought by deliberately shunting information back and forth between drawing and writing in ways that transform meaning. In neurobiological terms, the Drawing/Writing program "maps" writing exercises over drawing exercises. The resulting writing is a "mapped map" or a new mental orientation.

Just because the brain is predisposed to acquire languages does not guarantee that it will. The brain may adapt to the rapid presentation of visual information but it may not acquire the analytical skills to evaluate that visual information. Brain science provides cross-modal design cues for adaptive language instruction designed to cope with intense visual stimulation. Drawing/Writing incorporates these design cues, providing adaptive language education.

### *The self-correcting brain*

Unless the brain is sick or damaged, it has no intent of working against itself. An efficient expenditure of energy is what the brain desires. The brain's agenda is not to work as hard as possible, but to work as well as possible. The larger the number of useful connections, the deeper and faster the mental processes, including strange loops (explained below). The more finely tuned the system, the faster it self-corrects. A delicate responsiveness protects the dynamic system from serious perturbations. A newborn brain is mainly potential. Experience actualizes the system. To a large extent, the quality of experiences determine the quality of the system, including its ability to self-correct.

Intact brains function cooperatively. Discrete processes work together so intricately, so intimately and so densely, that it may be impossible not only to trace every interconnection, but to clearly distinguish one system from another. Besides the astronomical number of connections, what Douglas Hofstadter describes as "Strange Loops" characterize intelligent thought. Citing inconsistencies in music and in mathematics, he extrapolates inconsistencies in the processes of language and thought (1989, 10-27 & 691-692). As Hofstadter writes, "Without doubt, Strange Loops involving rules that change themselves, directly or indirectly, are at the core of intelligence" (27). Using the fugues of Bach and Gödel's mathematical theory of Incompleteness as models, he shows that not only are the loops in intelligent thought unpredictable, they are unexplainable, or, at least, unprovable. As with the tracks of particles too small and fast to see, it may be possible only to infer certain mental events, not to observe them. We tend to equate logic with reason and intuition with non-reason, supposing that reasonable thinking is trackable while intuitive thinking is not. The truth most probably is that neither is strictly trackable.

Still, mathematicians are able to provide *backward* proofs for intuitive solutions: intuition is reasonable. A combination of linear and non-linear strategies contribute to intelligent thought, particularly in highly inventive minds. A third category of reasoning beyond reason and intuition incorporates strange loops when mental processes operate via associative layerings, too fast for mapping.

The interplay between brain areas cannot, as yet, be exactly mapped, predicted or understood, but brain-imaging techniques are bringing us closer to understanding the interplay. Part of the mapping problem is the vastness of the system as well as its variability. Like the universe, the brain is a self-correcting system. The implications of a variable, self-regulating system are considerable: the constructivist classroom must accommodate children's brains as self-modifying. To do so, curricula must include exploration and choice and rich language-use, making room for Strange Loops.

## 2.4 Neuroconstructivism: Applying Brain Science to Education

The name of the theory supporting Drawing/Writing is Neuro (not neo) constructivism. The information about brain function relevant to the Drawing/Writing program is included in Part Three, "Hitchhikers' Guide to Brain Science." Children construct not only knowledge, but neural networks. For some time, psychology has informed educational theory and practice, but increasingly, the general public, including parents and teachers, appreciate the importance of brain science to education. Neurobiology in particular provides guidelines for learning environments and strategies appropriate for maximum brain development. When it comes to quality of mind, the child is the parent of the adult.

*Opening the black box, Sam Sheridan, 1997*

### Opening the Black Box

Like a black box, the brain has long remained closed, opaque and impenetrable. Neurobiology has opened the box. Several observations about the brain are of particular interest to parents and educators:

- Vision and attention are related.
- The quality of early, exploratory, interactive physical and linguistic experience in large part determines mental capacities.
- Multi-sensory, cross-modal storage of information results in stronger, more broadly retrievable "memories" or learning.
- Children find a variety of highly visual, open-ended problem-solving experiences rewarding. Because emotion and cognition are linked, an education that is fun or interesting will be more effective than education that is not. Complex tasks construct complex neural nets, cross-referencing information for fast storage and easy retrieval. Cross-referenced systems enhance the brain's processing capacities, allowing for a heavier work load as well as broader bases for reflective thought.

- Language is an embedded system. It continues to be informed by right-hemisphere input, or spatial information.
- Training in a variety of approaches to symbolic representation, including drawing and writing, stimulates orderly, yet adaptive or flexible thought.
- The relationship of concrete models to abstract thought is intimate, ongoing and of considerable use.
- Windows of opportunity for learning are wide open for a lifetime. Learning is a uniquely flexible, variable brain activity.
- Language learning deficits can be remediated through tactile, visual/spatial training.

These observations mean that to be effective, early language learning programs must be highly visual, highly verbal, challenging, and exploratory.

### Medical research

Medical research with brain-damaged patients provides additional information:

- The brain repairs itself. Two phenomena, neural drift and equipotentiality, allow one brain area to take over another's functions. Functional neural networks are able to grow dendrites or "drift" into dysfunctional brain areas, providing working circuitry. Or, several areas of the brain can perform the same function; if one area fails, another takes over.
- The brain is redundant. It makes more connections than it needs. Learning experiences cull connections which are no longer useful while creating useful, new connections.
- A mental task which raises attentional levels primes the brain for increased mental activity.
- There is evidence that gender differences exist: male brains are more specialized, more lateralized than female brains; the period of equipotentiality for the male brain is shorter and the degree to which the brain areas are equipotential is less.

### Bilateral processing

Cross-modal training enhances bilateral processing, providing two benefits: increased processing capabilities and faster and more complete recovery after trauma.

The thirteen years spanning the K-12 educational experience provide an appreciable period of time for training the brain. Whether or not thirteen years of bilateral brain training will affect eons of evolution, changing specialization and lateralization, is debatable. But cross-modal training, like any other kind of consistent, long-term training, will modify neural networks. Brain research documents the degree to which brains change in response to consistent, long-term experience. Research methods can be used to evaluate the neural effects of sustained cross-modal education. Statistics on academic and professional performance will shed additional light on the general usefulness of cross-modal teaching and learning and what could be called the balanced, bilateral brain.

### The Multilingual brain

Chameleon-like, the brain takes on the coloration of its surroundings, absorbing experience and language.

If the environment provides adequate linguistic stimulation, the brain will equip itself with languages appropriate to navigating in that environment. If there is a gulf between language systems—for instance, between the home, school, and the workplace—the learner will have to reach out for more languages.

Our brains have evolved over time. We think as we do via this evolved system. Structurally, we have inherited a bihemispheric brain. Notions of paradox attracts us, and we tend to describe some of our most fundamental experiences in forms of unified dualities. Procedurally, we've inherited a system which operates both discretely and globally, in linear and in parallel mode—in straight lines, in branchings, and in waves, via little leaps across spaces. The wave particle theory of light, the urge to take the road less travelled, a Kierkegaardian leap of faith—these phrases describe important ideas, and brain function as well. How we think and what we think relate. The question remains how our ingenuity with devising intelligent systems will modify the evolution of the human mind, structurally and procedurally, allowing us to sense and understand what we could not otherwise sense and understand. We may someday see like bees and hear like dogs, thinking in entirely new ways.

This book describes human language-use as various. Our brains have evolved to use several languages—most especially visual and verbal languages—syncretically, or co-creatively. Scholarly debates about the nature of language no longer hinge on innateness. The debate hinges on adaptability. MIT linguist Steven Pinker maintains with Chomsky that language is far too complex to be entirely learned. It must stem from innate brain programs. But Pinker adds that language most certainly is adaptive, too, and that its use conferred, for instance, certain advantages on early hominids, allowing them to share skills and to influence others. In addition, various modern languages share common features, suggesting that "natural selection favored certain syntactic structures" (Horgan on Pinker, 1994, 178, *The Language Instinct,* 1994: *How the Mind Works,* 1997). To acquire language in new ways, new methods are necessary.

Many Americans grow up with a language other than English, and then learn English in school. Many Americans learn two versions of their mother tongue: a home/neighborhood argot and the more formal language of the college-educated professional. For some, using one version of the language in the wrong setting may prejudice the listeners against them or even render them unintelligible.

The classroom can provide a place where languages intersect, enriching each other, creating a shared, extensive vocabulary. Nations and the tiny principalities we call human beings require negotiated settlements through discourse. If two nations speak two languages, translators are required. The corpus callosum in part fulfills this function for the brain. If we know that being able to use more than one language makes us better thinkers and communicators, we will acquire more languages.

# NEW CLASSROOMS, NEW TEACHERS

N ew brain scans will take almost instantaneous pictures of brain activity.... And new MRIs, hardly bigger than a salon-size hair-dryer, will tackle the most challenging question of all...: how the brain develops. The MRIs will safely image the brains of children, and show step by step how the most complicated information-processing device in the world becomes wired. Not far off: using the discoveries of neuroscience to retool education. Does musical training prime the synapses for learning math? How do some brains hold thousands more vocabulary words than others? The answers may point the way to new teaching techniques.

Sharon Begley, *"Uncovering Secrets, Big and Small"*

## 3.1 The Quandary for Contemporary Education: What's at Stake

### The challenge to language instruction

In the past, a relatively small number of children were required to be literate. Jobs for unskilled workers were available, providing money for a tolerable or even comfortable life. Now, to survive economically in the United States, adults must not only read and write but, in many instances, be computer literate. Most children with access to school learn to write and read, or they did until recently. Now schools face increasing numbers of "learning disabled" children. In addition, schools must teach every child to read and write *adaptively* with an eye toward future information systems for which no procedures or rules yet exist.

Traditional approaches to literacy education were effective for students who came from households where talking, reading, writing, singing, and game-playing were the norm. Many students no longer come from language-rich households. Children passively receive language from television. Television is not a conversational medium; research shows that infant brains respond to radio and television talk as sound, not as language. To acquire language, children's brains require a steady stream of emotionally charged, engaged adult language or "Parentese." Lacking adequate exposure to language learning at home, some second- and third-graders speak hesitantly, and are not ready to read or write. What is to be done?

### Replacing links

When children fail to crawl, a developmental processing link may be missing. Strategies for remediating learning disabilities include crawling, with the belief that recapitulating a step in motoric development will correct some deficit in cognition. Similarly, research suggests that an early education program featuring touch, regressing children back through the stages of language acquisition, provides them with an optimal language learning environment.

### The use of touch

We learn a mother tongue from our earliest caretakers; if our caretaker is a wolf, we learn how to howl. Stories about feral children raised in the wild by animals, as well as stories about children locked in closets, demonstrate the importance of early language-learning. Children who fail to acquire language normally have a very difficult time acquiring it later. If innate grammar is not triggered early, it will be hard if not impossible to lay language down, and the use of that specific language will never be as expressive as it would have been if it were acquired during early childhood. Intensive, highly tactile therapy is necessary to introduce language to a person who has been deprived of early language learning. Books like Harlan Lane's *The Wild Boy of Aveyron* (1976), Helen Keller's autobiography, *The Story of My Life* (1908), and Jill Paxton Walsh's *Knowledge of Angels* (1995), as well as the movie "Nell," describe the struggles of language-deprived children.

Harlan Lane taught the wild boy of Aveyron how to speak by placing his fingers on the wild boy's lips and by placing the boy's hand on his own throat while he was speaking. Annie Sullivan did the same highly tactile work with Helen Keller. Both teachers showed their pupils how spoken language felt. Annie drew words on Helen Keller's palm; Helen could feel the shapes of written words. Lane used touch/writing on the palm of the feral boy in this way, too. Maria Montessori also valued learning through touch. When teaching the alphabet to young children, she encouraged them to run their hands over large, beautiful wooden letters, or over the shapes of letters covered with sandpaper. The students felt the shapes of the letters intensely with their fingertips, learning all the more readily to know them with their eyes. Research with young children who have learned to play the violin before the age of eleven demonstrates that their fingertips are more sensitive to electric sensation than the fingertips of students who learn to play the violin when they are older. The area for the retinotopic map for the fingertips is larger in these children's brains than in the brains of children who learn to play the violin later. What registers at the fingertips as enhanced sensitivity registers in the brain as sensibilities.

Braille allows blind people to read by touch. A word projected in rays of light on the bare back helps the blind to read, too. Even though no information reaches the brain through the eyes, touch and light stimulate the visual cortex; the result is visualization or internal sight. Visually-impaired patients who receive corneal transplants discover that they still have to touch things to recognize them. The activity of seeing is so difficult for long-blind patients that some prefer navigating by touch, choosing to live in the dark even after the transplants (Zajonc, 1993, 4).

There are certain periods in children's lives when they are particularly receptive to learning certain skills. For instance, the critical period for verbal communication is somewhere between the ages of six and twelve. The 1797 study conducted by Jean-Marc Itard demonstrated that the approximately twelve-year-old "wild boy" was never able to master speech. Brain research suggests that hormonal changes in puberty terminate the brain's flexibility for language. Current research ("Your Child," *Newsweek*, Spring/Summer supplement, 1997) defines the critical period as birth through three years, with the first six months being crucial for the development of the neural nets responsible for *abstract* thinking. Intensive, child-centered early language learning programs, including an emphasis on touch, promote healthy brains.

## 3.2  Where Neurobiology and Classroom Practice Intersect

The neurobiologist's ability to monitor brain activity reveals information with significant implications for teaching and learning. The results of magnetic resonance imaging, or MRIs[6], can be computer-imaged and color-coded for brain activity. Highly-lit areas requiring more oxygenated blood may indicate normal activity or over activity. A lower level of activity may indicate a more efficient use of oxygen, rather than an understimulated area. Dyslexic brains struggling with language reveal hardworking, oxygen-depleted language areas.

In 1986, psychology professor David Andrews of Keene State College in Keene, New Hampshire, conducted a study with dyslexic teenage boys. Andrews reported that, after studying EKG-based computer images of their own brains at work, these boys were motivated to devise successful personal learning strategies. The potential value of brain-imaging to

---

[6] MRI: Magnetic Resonance Imaging. MRIs are non-invasive. They create fine-tuned, real-time maps of brain activity by tracking oxygenated hemoglobin in high magnetic fields. Oxygenated blood has not yet been depleted by the working brain. De-oxygenated hemoglobin has, and, like oxygenated blood, it exhibits specific magnetic properties. By mapping replete and depleted hemoglobin, MRIs show where the brain has expended energy and where it has not. Inferences about brain activity may be made from these maps (Fite, 1993).

PET: Positron Emission Tomography. PET is an invasive, expensive, problematic procedure that uses radioactive agents to describe rates of glucose metabolism. Glucose is the metabolic fuel used by active cells. By determining where glucose metabolism is highest, observations can be made about the amount of work done by that part of the brain (Fite, 1993).

student-designed curricula became apparent. When I visited Andrews in the late 1980's, I envisioned the future use of "thinking caps" in the classroom (Sheridan, 1991) currently predicted by *Newsweek* (Begley, 1997).

Because cross-modal thinking is natural, it is logical to assume that students will invent cross-modal curricula. At least at this time, most students are unable to observe EKGs and MRIs of their brain activity. Educators can, however, provide cross-modal guidelines and models as well as information from brain science, encouraging students toward self-directed learning.

### Neurobiology and reading deficits

Explanations for reading difficulties include visual problems (Geiger & Lettvin, 1987) and aural problems (Shaywitz, 1995, 1996)[7]. Solutions to visual problems range from parafoveal reading to colored glasses; aural solutions continue to include one-on-one tutoring in letter-to-sound correspondence, or phonics, as well as sound therapy (Gilmore on the Tomatis Method, 1989). The phonological deficit model describes the problem as the inability to break words into constituent sounds. Most children learn to break down the word "cat" into the letters "c" "a" "t" and to sound the word out: "kuh" "aah-tuh." Phonological processing at the level of speech is automatic for children. Dyslexic children do not usually have trouble with speaking.

Yale Medical School researcher Sally Shaywitz writes: "Speaking is natural, and reading is not. Reading is an invention and must be learned at a conscious level. The task for the reader is to transform the alphabet into sounds; dyslexia is difficulty with breaking words into their basic units, or phonemes" (Shaywitz, 1995).

In a study conducted by Sally and Bennett Shaywitz, a sounding-out activity revealed gender differences: "The men used a tiny area of their brain about a centimeter in size...near Broca's region," an area on the left side of the brain used in producing speech. Women used this region, too, but they also used the corresponding area on the right side of the brain. By identifying normal processing patterns, MRIs of children with abnormal patterns should allow parents and educators "to reliably detect young children who will have reading disabilities before they are faced with the daunting task of learning to read." The Shaywitzes concluded, "It may be possible to design ways to help these children overcome or even avoid the coming struggle" (Shaywitz, 1995).

---

[7] An overview of remedial strategies for dyslexia is included in the 1991 Sheridan dissertation.

Brains equipped with bilateral strategies burn brain fuel more efficiently and solve problems faster than brains working monolaterally. Female dyslexic brains not only over-metabolize glucose when reading, but may read in a more lateralized, less bihemispheric manner than non-dyslexic females. MRIs will help to clarify the degree to which significant differences in metabolic profiles exist in connection with gender and dyslexia.

### Mature reading and writing skills are visual

Mature reading skills do not depend upon phonetic linguistic analysis (Rubin, 1989) but involve skills more fairly described as visual or spatial. Research on the "psychogenetics" of writing suggests that early attempts at writing are not a transcription of spoken language but may more accurately be described as an offshoot of drawing (Ferreiro, 1979; Vygotsky, 1979). In fact, teaching writing as if it were a transcription of spoken language may be troublesome for many children, even creating learning disabilities (Ferreiro, 1979). This information provides further support for drawing as a bridge into writing and reading. In fact, drawing presents a range of benefits to pre-readers and pre-writers without (forgive the pun) drawbacks.

### A research proposal

1) If the two-week Drawing/Writing program is used at the beginning, middle and end of the academic year, accompanied by on-going drawing-based approaches to writing and reading throughout the rest of the year, dyslexic children will think about writing and reading either as extensions of drawing or as closely associated with drawing. This change in attitude about the nature of writing and reading places these activities within the Vygotskian continuum for the child, allowing him to write and read more easily as part of the natural unfolding of his mark-making process. Standardized tests, MRIs, and anecdotal evidence will demonstrate gains in writing, reading and thinking skills for these students. A comparison of pre- to post-Drawing/Writing brain scans will demonstrate changes in activity that may then be identified as indicators of improved brain function. There may or may not be a standard dyslexic brain pattern for students who think of writing as an advanced or more abstract form of drawing.

2) By using Drawing/Writing as described above, pre- and post-test writing and reading scores for experimental and control groups of pre-K, kindergarten, first, second and third graders recorded at one to five-year intervals will show a marked improvement in the experimental group. The brain scans of children who are encouraged to recognize writing, reading and mathematics as logical extensions of drawing will produce MRIs which differ from those of children who regard abstract symbol systems as discontinuous and non-related. This Drawing/Writing brain scan profile will be distinctive and characteristic. It may or may not be similar to scans of brains raised with calligraphic systems for writing.

## A testable hypothesis

If Drawing/Writing is used pre-K through third grade, there will be a lower incidence of "dyslexic" students than in traditional language programs. The prediction is verifiable through performance-testing and statistics. Brain scans may identify the neural changes characteristic of integrative thinking. The neural profiles of dyslexic Drawing/Writing students can be compared on a pre- and post-test basis individually and collectively across gender to identify which neural patterns correlate with gains in writing, reading and thinking. These classroom scores and brain research patterns can be compared with non-dyslexic scores and patterns, making it possible to draw conclusions about the Drawing/Writing method as a remedial approach to writing and reading for dyslexic boys and girls.

## *Pieces of the puzzle*

Several pieces of research support the drawing-based hypothesis outlined above:

1) Visual processing problems may occur due to the mis-organization of the retina; there may be too few visual cells in the macula, which is the area of greatest concentration of visual cells in the eye. Parafoveal vision, or reading off the center of gaze, is recommended for such students. Alternatively, the rods and cones in the retina may present information about wavelengths incorrectly. Words blur and dance on the page for some students. In some instances, colored glasses allow words to stand still for the reader; the supposition is that the

colored glass corrects wavelength distortion. Both pieces of research suggest that visual processing problems for dyslexic students are mechanical, not cognitive. Drawing/Writing suggests a modified position: whether mechanical or cognitive, a change in thinking may help. Anecdotally, a second grader for whom colored glasses[8] were prescribed for reading, writing and computer work, forgot his glasses on a day when he had Drawing/ Writing. He showed no difficulties with drawing or writing.

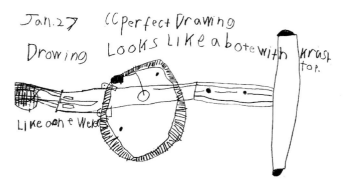

*Second grader, 1997.*

His mother reports that her son does not need the glasses to draw, nor were the glasses prescribed for drawing. When this student draws, or when he writes in close connection with drawing, apparently he does not experience troublesome wavelength distortion or interference.

2) The blind learn to read through touch using their fingers or through sensations of lighted words shone on their bare backs. Their eyes may not be receiving light, but their visual cortices are functional. The impairment is mechanical and not cognitive. Some phonological deficits are mechanical and relate to receptor/transmitter problems in the inner ear. With certain dyslexic students, sound therapy has proven effective. Tones "fed" into one ear or another or both have remediated phonological processing difficulties (Gilmore on the Tomatis Listening Program, 1989).

---

[8] The use of colored glasses for reading is described by Helen Irlen in *Reading by the Colors, The Irlen Method*, 1991, Avery Press: Calif.

3) The deaf learn to speak through touch, feeling vibrations in a speaker's throat, tongue and neck; they also learn to speak through gesture and vision, using sign language.

4) The blind can draw, and their drawings are like those of sighted people; they use foreshortening and converging lines to suggest depth (Kennedy, 1997). The innate templates for visualizing spatial relations are intact.

5) To learn to speak a language, children must hear language when they are very young. Yet the deaf can learn to speak through touch, even when they are older. Hearing must exert extremely powerful organizational pressure on the growing brain—even more so than sight. Or, the opposite may be true; the absence of child-directed, emotionally laden language may be more devastating to neural organization than the absence of optical information.

6) The brains of nuns whose written applications to religious orders included longer, more complicated sentences with emotional, evaluative, and speculative content were less likely to develop Alzheimer's disease than nuns who wrote more simply (Rogers, 1996). Writing more than simple sentences may structure brains for stronger neural networks which are less likely to fray and fragment. Language-use and mental health correlate at a structural/mechanical level.

7) By using bilateral strategies, female brains solve some mathematics tasks faster and more easily than male brains. Bilateral strategies may benefit all children.

8) Since drawing is innate and writing is not, and since speech is innate and reading is not, then drawing may furnish a bridge into reading as well as writing through sound. This bridge will be constructed by a drawing program in which writing and speech are emphasized.

Taking these pieces of the brain/language puzzle into account, guidelines emerge for remedial strategies for language deficits. Strategies for remediating difficulties with language will feature touch, gesture, and a continual language "bath" and will include drawing as a method of discovery informed by touch; this combined strategy should establish the necessary neural preconditions for writing and reading.

If this research is undertaken, the MRIs of brains engaged in drawing and writing will prove interesting in connection with gender and in connection with the incidence and effectiveness of bilateral processing. MRIs of brains doing Composite Abstractions should prove especially interesting. How does the metabolic profile of a brain drawing a CA differ from a brain that is writing or doing mathematics? Are there advantages to bilateral processing, in particular for the dyslexic student? If a combination of results—from standardized testing, statistics on dyslexia, and anecdotal reports—confirm the fact that training in Drawing/Writing raises students' verbal and quantitative scores while lowering the population of identified dyslexics, then encouraging brains to work in less specialized, more balanced, bilateral ways moves Drawing/Writing from a research topic to intelligent classroom practice.

Most good readers read visually, not phonetically. A deep memory of sound may remain but that memory is well below the level of conscious hearing. Fast readers rely on word recognition, or sight. If good readers process words visually, then training in drawing as visual decoding provides training in competent reading skills for all brains including those in which aural strategies are impaired.

Using MRIs as diagnostic tools, it will be increasingly possible to pinpoint, analyze and remediate language difficulties. Training in integrative coding should prove especially useful to brains in which language learning is delayed or dysfunctional.

### Training in decoding

Training in decoding one kind of marks provides training for decoding another kind of marks. If the skill for decoding a drawing requires attention and visual searches, then that same set of skills can be used for decoding other symbol systems, like written language or mathematical notation. A student does not need to know the sound of a contour drawing to read it. A contour drawing has no sound. It has a shape to recognize. The shape has a feel to it. Reading a drawing depends on touch, or the memory of touch. Direct touch, as well as the memory of touch captured in drawing and in writing is a particularly integrative activity. Of all the senses, touch may be the most integrative of all. We speak about the "healing power of touch." We observe the popularity of massage therapy, including a field described as therapeutic touch. This expanded appreciation for the integrative power of touch highlights the importance of drawing to a new field of inquiry described by this book as Neurocontructivism—a field in which education, medicine, brain science and psychology coverage. In the context of Neuroconstructivism, drawing becomes knowledge informed far more by touch than by vision, and vision becomes an extension of touch, allowing knowledge at a distance.

Light can be described as a unified wave/particle duality. So can the bihemispheric brain. Is there a connection between the physical natures of light and the brain? The visual brain is trained by light to apprehend the visible world. The act of sensing light organizes the brain to process light. A unified duality creates a unified duality. Sensations are felt, first, then seen or heard. Once seen or heard, all sensations are translated by the brain into one, identical electro-chemical signal. A forest of neural connections take that signal and make it into meaning. The extent of the translation is astounding. It is only slightly less astounding than the precision of the astronomically complex yet unitary system responsible for making meaning out of sunlight, the brain.

## Multi-modal training for reading and writing readiness

The skills developed in Drawing/Writing are useful to visual and auditory processing in general. To write and read, the brain must arrange sets of information coherently.

Peer sharing, ongoing discussions, and group critiques guarantee that the sound as well as the sight of language is practiced in the classroom. Greater emphasis could easily be placed on phonological decoding and encoding. For instance, every time a word is written on the board, students could pronounce it. Dyslexic students with phonological deficits could volunteer to read words on the board.

The hypothesis that drawing affects writing positively has been tested (Sheridan, 1991). The hypothesis that drawing remediates hearing deficits can also be tested. Because of the high spoken content of Drawing/Writing, as well as persistent training in multi-sensory, cross-modal transference, the possibility of learning to connect specific sounds to specific letters—that is, to read—becomes a likely benefit of this integrative process.

## A program for intelligent thought: Cues and stimuli

As Plato observed, wonder comes first; all else follows. The brain that attends, inquires. Brain research informs us that inquiry, or visual searches of interest, increase the brain's ability to attend. A dynamic circularity comes into play. The ability to pay attention increases the brain's

capacity for work. The ability to think intelligently depends on the brain's ability to work attentively and efficiently.

The Drawing/Writing program teaches a student how to wonder about, select, describe, analyze and record information. Then, the program teaches students to speculate and hypothesize about this information. The procedure models scientific inquiry. Drawing/Writing is, in fact, a program for inquiry, encouraging students as the artists/scientists championed by Goethe (Zajonc, 1993, 194) and exemplified by Leonardo da Vinci. The artist/scientist is a time-tested and accessible educational model.

Research suggests that one kind of attentional activity can "tune up" the brain for another more demanding activity. Empirical research with Drawing/Writing demonstrates that students who write after they draw transfer attention and processing power to their writing. Because the Drawing/Writing program requires writing about the knowledge encoded in drawings, students reap attentional and motivational benefits from the act of drawing and also gain confidence as writers; drawing shows students that they come to the classroom already equipped with knowledge and that they can communicate this knowledge to others.

It is important for all students, especially students who lack confidence, to know that their brains are not empty vessels. Just because they lack educational opportunities, under-educated students do not have to lag behind forever. The Drawing/Writing program assumes that students, even very young ones, come to the classroom equipped with knowledge and skills, and that interest and growing skills in drawing can be used to encourage other kinds of skills. Because practice with spatial information creates neural structures necessary for linguistic processing, drawing acts not only as an attentional and affective cue but as a neural net-weaver, too.

## Implications of brain science for early education and I.Q.

Early education has lasting neural consequences which profoundly affect the structure of the developing neuron system (Fite, 1993). Strategies like Drawing/Writing can be introduced as soon as a child can hold a crayon or a marker and continue at regular intervals from kindergarten through secondary school and beyond. It is as important at the most advanced educational levels to be able to visualize and verbalize as it is at the earliest levels. In fact, at highly abstract levels, visualization, including manipulation of three-dimensional models, is the most direct way to grasp certain concepts.[9] Minds trained in direct, physical manipulation of information are prepared to understand complex theoretical models; in addition, minds trained in the CA will expect to check their theories back against physical models and to modify solutions over time in response to new understandings. If children's literacy education teaches them to use visual and verbal languages not only adaptively but intelligently, those children's minds, or intelligence, will respond effectively to changing conditions.

### Modifying expectations: A whole mind approach

The Drawing/Writing program is based on a "whole mind" approach. Cross-modal strategies mirror the interhemispheric, integrative, global aspects of brain operations. The name of the philosophy supporting the WholeBrain program is "The Thinking Child." The Drawing/Writing program focuses on the child primarily as a thinker, tempering expectations about mental milestones with "periods of grace," or educational lag-time. Lag-time is required for several reasons:

- Some students trail behind because of developmental delays and
- Some trail behind because of deprivation.

It is far more important for students to learn to read and write and think effectively over a lifetime than for all students to learn to write and read in the first grade. As Harvard psychologist Robert Kegan so aptly wrote, those who teach "attend upon the child" (1982). The teacher who uses training in drawing to provide a grace period for writing and reading demonstrates attentive patience.

Sustained attention and information manipulation strategies are learned skills. Because children's brains require training in a range of basic skills including attention, language-use, and thinking, and because many children are not receiving this training at home for a variety of reasons, school language programs are under considerable strain. Students' brains consolidate specific neural networks within certain time periods. For example, the visual system consolidates by about age twelve. Educators have identified the middle school years as a

time when children's brains construct certain strategies like generalization and abstraction. If the first six months of language experience influence or even determine later abstract reasoning abilities—as news magazines attest—we may have to radically rethink cognitive parameters.

The Drawing/Writing program provides empirical, visual evidence that children of kindergarten age can construct fractal drawings and Composite Abstractions. It is safest to provide broad-gauge teaching and learning strategies which allow children to make their own mental breakthroughs into symbolic reasoning when they are ready to do so on their own visual and verbal terms. As parents and teachers, we must equip them with the visual and verbal tools for making these breakthroughs. Children cannot think about or know what they cannot express.

Students are ripe to learn about tolerance and right relationships at certain times, too. The emotional learning on which empathy and compassion rest occurs in the first three years of life (Begley, 1996, 1997). Still, one particular child's time for ethical understanding may not be another's, as one child's time for abstract similes may not be another's. My son, Samuel, invented his first metaphors—rainbow noodles and zebra trees—at the age of three. A language program which provides a range of approaches and time frames accommodates a range of learners. To be the most effective, the opportunities must be provided when children are very young. Currently, the optimum window of time for language stimulation in connection with neural bases for abstract reasoning skills is believed to be birth through six months (Begley, 1997). If correct, this information changes qualitatively the level of discourse with infants.

## 3.3 Literacy Education in Context

### A low-tech approach in a high-tech society

Modern technology poses serious problems for undereducated students and overstressed schools. How will barely literate students deal with information? How will minds ill-equipped with adaptive strategies respond to rapid change? How will students with little or no access to computers acquire technological skills?

To teach competent visual and verbal information processing skills, classrooms do not absolutely require computers nor do they absolutely require teachers with computer skills. High-tech skills can be learned through low-tech programs.

Although we cannot add one more teacher to every classroom, we can add a strategy that makes every student at least to some degree into a teacher. We can also

---

[9] Thanks to Hampshire College art and education student Emily Lavelle, Drawing/Writing now includes three-dimensional model-building. Emily is using the Drawing/Writing five-step as part of her senior project with sculpture, 1997.

provide a literacy program which teaches every student how to process information competently, providing, as a dividend, training in an approach that resembles scientific inquiry. Technical/vocational schools can add Drawing/Writing to their curricula, adding a hands-on approach to literacy, too.

*Photo from the Dr/Wr English class of Rusty Blossom, Franklin County Technical School, SR Sheridan, 1996*
*Group, from left to right, Jim Babij, Craig Riddell, Brandon Doyle. Single, Casey Miller, Gabe LaPollo [w. ring]. Brian Herzig ["fred" t-shirt]*

### A humanistic education

This book recognizes human beings as noble in reason. The terms cross-modal, WholeBrain, and Neuroconstructivist redefine humanistic education—the privilege of so few in the Renaissance—as a general requirement, now.

> *What a piece of work is man,*
> *How noble in reason,*
> *How infinite in faculty,*
> *In form and movement how express and admirable,*
> *In action how like an angel,*
> *In apprehension how like a god.*
> *The beauty of the world*
> *The paragon of animals*
>
>       *William Shakespeare, **Hamlet**, Act II, scene 2.*

During the Renaissance, a new emphasis was placed on the mind. Instead of being suspect or even the locus of

hubris, or overweening pride, reason and logic were acknowledged as positive attributes. The mind was recognized as a tool and an organ for knowing God and what is good. By placing an emphasis on knowledgeable humanity instead of on an all-knowing god, the Renaissance expressed a change in attitude toward the human mind.

It is challenging to accept something as elevated-sounding as a "humanistic education" as a practical necessity. Still, this is what is currently required. A humanistic education places the child as thinker at the center of its ethos and its strategies. "The Thinking Child"—the curricular design program introduced by this book—focusses on the importance of the child, emphasizing two points:

- The child is not a little adult equipped with full adult reasoning powers in a smaller body.
- On the other hand, the child is not a blank slate.

The brain of the child is like the Rosetta Stone: it is carved with codes. One code provides the key to others. Once the brain of the child cracks the visual/spatial code, it is prepared to crack verbal/linguistic codes. Through extensive practice with drawing as a visual code, the brain learns to write and calculate more easily.

*"Thinking Children" by Claus Kormannshaus, 1997*

The child mobilizes its primary spatial code through exploratory motion. Crackling and bubbling with exuberant synaptogenesis, the pure potential of the embryonic brain kicks and thrusts, gestures and reaches, creating neural templates for thinking and learning. Equipped with these organizational templates—this deep spatial grammar—the fetal child primes its brain for other codes, including language.

There are two aspects to the practicality of a humanistic education:

1) the more deeply engaged, successful, and happy students are, the happier and more successful schools, families and society will be. To be successful as well as happy, students must acquire skills necessary for economic and social survival. When activities that make students happy and also successful intersect, an opportunity for exciting educational design presents itself.

2) Many students are miserable, making schools miserable places to be. This misery is attributable in part to a lack of recognition or encouragement of students as thinkers. Brain science demonstrates that students' brains are destined to become artistic, literate, scientific, philosophical and aesthetic, at least, whatever else their brains may become. Something must be done about the fact that students, teachers, parents and employers are dissatisfied with the current state of affairs in schools. If classroom practice can meet the mental and emotional needs of students and bear on the larger requirements in students' lives, including successful family dynamics and job market viability, then some compromise will be achieved between the mind of the child, the needs of the family and the exigencies of society.

Because the brain is an organ for inquiry, the mind must be allowed and encouraged to question and to wonder. Because the brain is an organ for expression, the mind must be allowed and encouraged to express itself. To do so, the brain requires training and opportunity. To be a meaning-maker, the child must be allowed to make meaning.

As paradoxical as it may seem, a broad-gauge humanistic education in which logic, rhetoric, the arts, philosophy and aesthetics are combined with reading, writing, and mathematics allows students' natural mental and emotional predispositions and abilities to collide and merge with technological skills. A humanistic strategy like Drawing/Writing and curricular design plans like "The Thinking Child" designate the inquiring mind of the child as the heart of the educational endeavor. Neurobiological research places the bihemispheric, integrated and integrative brain of the child at the center of our mental gaze. Presto! the thrust of education becomes thinking skills and the method of delivery clarifies itself as cross-modal.

We cannot absolutely predict future cognitive demands and learning opportunities for the human brain. The future will probably hold less verbal stimulation and more visual stimulation; it will most probably offer less direct sensory learning experience, not more. In some instances computer-based learning may replace direct experiential learning. In many medical schools, practice with a range of diagnoses and recommendations is already provided through computer programs which train and aid medical students in comprehensive approaches to medical solutions.

The long-term neural effects of prolonged computer-use, including "virtual" or simulated reality, on the human peripheral and central nervous system are not yet known. To repeat: what the brain thinks is going on is going on for that brain. Those who design experiments in physics understand this mental/phenomenological truth. The people who design interactive computer programs understand this, too, taking into account the willingness of the brain to suspend disbelief for the sake of experiencing simulations as real. Computers and humanistic education are not mutually exclusive. What is in question is the neural effects of the computer and other electronic devices as the major delivery systems of information and stimulation to the brain, as well as how the brain will achieve its desired "highs" or peak experiences.

The "brain" is distributed neurally over the entire body (Pert, 1983, 188)[10]. "Mental" input from our bodies is necessary to our brains. If we did not need a peripheral nervous system, as well as a central nervous system (our brain), we would not have one. Without our bodies and our six senses (proprioception, or knowing where our bodies are in physical space, is the sixth sense—we could call the "sixth" sense the seventh), the brain would truly be a black box, closed off entirely from the world by the bony walls of the skull, the tough, protective meningeal membranes, and the cushioning cerebrospinal fluid. Without our bodies, we are shut-ins. A lack of direct stimulation to the body affects motor and mental development; stimulus deprivation registers as deficits not only at the emotional level but at the neural level.

---

[10] Candace Pert writes in "The Chemical Communicators" from *Healing and the Mind* by Bill Moyers, 1993: "You're still thinking it's your brain, but it's the wisdom of the body. Intelligence is in every cell of your body. The mind is not confined to the space above the neck. The mind is throughout the brain and body."

Neural nets become less connected through disuse and once-useful synapses lose length and weight and eventually disappear.

Sensory deficits affect neural pathways and therefore performance. From what we know about the effects of enriched and impoverished learning environments on children, as well as the effects of a lack of exercise on adult physical, mental and emotional well-being, predictions can be made about the neural effects of experiences increasingly removed from the physical, sensory world. The degree to which virtual reality experiences are also kinaesthetic will affect neural outcomes.

### Literacy issues: Computers

The trend toward image-heavy publications is clear. Computer technology facilitates the creation, modification, integration, and presentation of image as well as text. What it does not do is provide the direct experience of overheard, child-centered, engaged dialogue which very young children require for their brains to grow in connection with language learning. But, in other ways, as children mature, the computer provides a powerful thinking tool.

There is a tacit assumption that computers will solve our literacy problems. Because they are so visual, computers have enormous holding power. Children's brains thrive on visual stimulation. A lighted, colored screen exerts a very strong mental pull. Beyond this basic visual need and pull, computers provide extremely powerful tools for thinking on all symbolic levels, including writing.

Currently, the human brain is being asked to process visual and verbal information at a level of layeredness, speed and abstraction that requires training. Since much of the information has emotional content with a market-driven outcome, the reader must not only process the information but evaluate its effect. Brains trained to think clearly and analytically will be able to compete and survive in the marketplace.

The assumption that computer-use will automatically solve a host of classroom dilemmas springs from the following thinking:

- Students will eventually use computers for all of their writing.
- Students need keyboarding skills, not handwriting skills.
- Light pens and mouse-driven paint programs will replace pencils, charcoal, pastels, drawing pens and brushes.

Many schools of design, art and engineering continue to value and require traditional drawing skills as prerequisites to CAD or computer-assisted design programs. No computer program—no matter how sophisticated—is a substitute for intelligence.

Animal enrichment studies demonstrate that the brain tissue of rats engaged in physically active, challenging, purposeful activities differs at the synapse from underchallenged rats' brains. The richer the options, the longer and heavier the synapse. Children learn better in situations designed with their interests and abilities in mind, including their need to be physically active. Drawing and writing with pencils and pens differs qualitatively from using a computer mouse or a light pen as motoric stimulation and training, particularly with young children whose bodies require more extensive involvement. Until MRIs are used routinely in educational settings to map brain activity, we must extrapolate the most effective teaching strategies from research with animal brains and from our direct experience.

Computer users sit very still for long periods of time, seeing no other things, touching no other people. After hours of computer use, I, for one, become restless and irritable. Whatever our position on the usefulness of computers, there are two overriding reasons to use Drawing/Writing. One reason is cognitive, the other is practical and economic:

- **cognitive**: The lighted screen of the computer arouses the brain through the retina. This level of cognitive arousal is low. The programs displayed on the screen and their level of interactivity are what will determine the neural consequences of computer use for the student. Even if every child had a computer, existing tutoring programs are not responsive enough to allow the active construction of knowledge called for in this book. Computer-based literacy programs lack physical action beyond striking keys and clicking a mouse. These programs also lack the high level of verbal interaction provided by approaches like Drawing/Writing. Whether their skills and needs are widely divergent or not, students require mentoring provided best at this point in the history of technology and education by attentive, responsive human beings. Peer mentoring provides an adequate number of attentive, responsive human beings even in crowded classrooms.

Young students like to hold a pencil or pen or marker and apply it directly to a piece of paper as an act of exploration. For their brains to grow, they require visual stimulation beyond the low-level stimulation of the lighted computer screen. They need to develop fine motor skills beyond those provided by a light pen on a screen or a mouse on a pad. Brain science makes clear that direct bodily knowing helps brains to grow. Early infant stimulation programs support this finding. Early educational theory and practice corroborate this position. Drawing/Writing accommodates information on early mental growth provided by education, psychology, and neurobiology.

- <u>economic</u>: Paper, folders, pencils and markers are affordable. Computers for each student are not.

Not all students will have computers in school or at home. If students do not learn to write by hand, they will be unable to communicate through the written word. Computers alone will not solve the literacy dilemma. Computers facilitate writing and reading, and they return a powerful visual stimulus to the learning environment, but they do not, at least at this point, *create* verbal and visual skills. Nor, because of the necessity of direct, human voice input to children's brains, do they aurally stimulate the child's construction of the neural networks necessary for language development. It is the mental skills students bring to the computer that determine the quality of the visual and verbal work produced and, thus, the quality of the networks constructed in their brains.

If schools cannot afford enough computers for all their children, and if the children do not have access to computers outside of school, the question about computers as a literacy tool becomes moot.

### Drawing and kinaesthetic learning

Computer literacy is a technological application of Drawing/Writing and, as such, part of the language continuum that includes speech, play, drawing and writing. How students learn to use the computer or any other device for manipulating information will be positively influenced by direct learning experiences in the physical world. A technological society requires and validates direct, multi-modal, multi-sensory learning. Even in an age of technology, physical exploration and involvement provide important opportunities for emotional and intellectual growth.

The child who uses tools and strategies independently and creatively will become a competent adult. The point is not to put the cart before the horse: simple tools and strategies first, more complex tools and strategies second. As direct bodily learning, the act of drawing is qualitatively different from drawing or writing on a computer screen. It differs motorically; the hand is less

*Girl with computer thinking about pounds of feathers and lead, Claus Kormannshaus, '97*

constrained. If differs visually; dark strokes on white paper provide a less tiring retinal stimulus than dark pixels on a lighted screen. It differs at the level of touch; the drawing hand is able to explore the drawn object directly for information.

Seymour Papert, MIT researcher and educator, inventor of the computer language LOGO, put his finger on the nature of the connection between the child's brain and the computer; he described the computer as a tool to think with. For Papert, the computer provides training in procedural knowledge. The child needs to construct procedures that translate between codes. LOGO is a computer program which uses a lighted cursor or "turtle" to provide exploratory experiences with geometry useful to pre-kindergarten students as well as to sophisticated college students at MIT. Using a simple example: to draw a square, a child is invited to walk a square. She learns that drawing a square means walking in a straight line of equal length and making an abrupt turn, four times. After much experimenting, she types in the LOGO command: REPEAT 4 (FORWARD 10 RIGHT 90), hits the return key, and the cursor jerkily "walks" a square for her on the screen. If she stores the procedure as "TO SQUARE," she can experiment with this command: REPEAT 10 (SQUARE RIGHT 3). The turtle will start a process that will result in a circle. The child sees that a circle can be made from a rotated square. She can store this procedure as TO CIRCLE. Papert calls this approach a nested procedure. The child learns to break a problem into its steps, testing these steps until the desired effect is achieved. By doing so, she constructs an understanding of the problem and of the solution, and, if she nests procedures, she creates complex results. Because of the iterative, recursive aspects (see Part 2 for definitions of these terms), LOGO gives children direct practice with how their brain works neurally. LOGO teaches children to think, not to follow commands. Instantaneous code-to-code translation achieved by computers precludes the brain's construction of its own "translation" circuitry. The computer is an extremely powerful tool for thinking, but it does not replace cross-modal thought.

Drawing/Writing exercises lead students through the entire history of mark-making. This experience is very different from "Draw" and "Paint" programs. In addition, Drawing/Writing includes holding a palpable object, rich with mental and emotional associations. There is no such tangible object with Paint programs. Although computers allow the transformation from one mode of representation to another by hitting a return key, there is no automatic key in Drawing/Writing. The transfer is achieved by students' brains. Children roll over, crawl and pull up before they learn to walk and they babble before they learn to speak. Similarly, direct physical acts like scribbling, drawing and writing endure as active, exploratory developmental stages in children's language acquisition process. For many students, the process will include computer literacy. For some, it will not.

## The effects of enforced passivity

All of us have seen the effects of enforced passivity on animals and children. Think about the housebound dog at the end of a long day, or confined children who bounce off the walls. In 1978, it became clear to me that my television-mesmerized, ricocheting three-year-old son, Sam, should be outside playing. I was worried about the withdrawal period from television, and I was worried about depriving my children of highly engaging training in spelling, mathematics, artistic sensibilities and humane emotions provided by "Sesame Street," "The Electric Company" and "Mister Rogers." The withdrawal period for television for my children was approximately twenty minutes. All three children are well developed emotionally and mentally, and writing and reading are integral parts of their lives. They also speak well.

Adults who sit in front of a television or a computer too long become irritable, "spacey," and eye-weary. They develop low-level anxieties as well as physical problems in their wrists, shoulders, necks and backs. The phrases house-bound, stir-crazy and brain-fried describe real situations involving physical and emotional deprivation or overload. It is the visual holding power of both the television and the computer which allows us to spend more time in front of lighted screens than is useful to our bodies.

## Chemical assistance

Growing numbers of "attention deficit" children take Ritalin. These children's brains apparently require chemical stimulation. Given budget constraints, most classrooms have no choice but to increase control, resulting in even longer periods of enforced passivity. Passivity is not natural for children.

Two million American children (three to five percent) are diagnosed as having the attention disorder known as ADHD. Since 1990 the number of school-age youngsters taking Ritalin has increased 2.5 times. Among today's 38 million children ages five to fourteen, 1.3 million take Ritalin regularly (Hancock, *Newsweek,* March 18, 1996). The rate of Ritalin use is five times higher in the United States than in the rest of the world. The widespread ADHD diagnosis is an American phenomenon.

One theory for the increased use of Ritalin is rushed home lives ("Mother's Little Helper," *Newsweek,* March 18, 1996). The press of modern life requires fast moves from one activity to another. Because children can focus, involving themselves deeply in activities, it is hard for them to respond to rapid dislocation. In some cases, their understandable reluctance to be dragged from activity to activity may masquerade as impulsivity, inattention, or hyperactivity, resulting in a diagnosis and a prescription.

Some children benefit from drugs. For all of their apparent over-activity, the brains of attention-deficit students are actually under-stimulated, and need chemical revving up. It may be hard to distinguish between children whose attentional systems are deficient and children who are inattentive at school because of fragmented lives. Some children diagnosed as hyperactive are talented children reacting normally to understimulating educational environments. Feeling rushed and being overly controlled drives many people crazy. In such situations, adults have been known to act out and to take either stimulants or sedatives.

It's time to look at what is going on educationally. We cannot afford to wait until pediatricians, parents, psychologists, psychiatrists, school counselors and physical therapists announce that children have become mental, emotional and physical cripples. For the health of children's brains, kinaesthetic, multi-sensory, integrative stimulation must be factored into our educational programs. The applied and performing arts provide intelligent curricular choices for a humanistic education.

### A non-pharmacological approach

A drawing-based writing program provides a "natural" way to normalize certain aspects of neurochemistry relating to attention, motivation, cognition, and "highs" or peak experiences. This process of normalization has self-regulatory aspects. Students doing Drawing/Writing bring their own attentional, motivational and cognition systems to alertness, teaching themselves to focus, attend, examine, express, to initiate, sustain, and to regulate thought processes. Such self-regulation should decrease the need for classroom drugs like Ritalin.

Experimentation, the search for novelty, and the desire for peak experiences are built into the human exploratory and emotional learning system. The arts and the sciences provide opportunities for meeting these needs. Drawing, along with a more meaningful, cross-disciplinary approach to learning, may satisfy the needs for novelty and peak experiences that drive the human brain to experiment with drugs. These two hypotheses are testable:

- Drawing/Writing normalizes attentional systems through self-regulatory training in attention.

- Drawing/Writing helps to satisfy human cravings for novelty and peak experiences by providing deeply interactive visual/verbal learning experiences.

## 3.4 A New Understanding of Literacy

### Equalization in training: Making up for the deficits

Before they learn to read, children—even babies—are bombarded with electronic messages. Teenagers "surf" television channels, fast-forwarding programs at rates intolerable to viewers who grew up with the comparatively slow pace of reading. Like the televised messages, attention is trained to be short and fast. Many children and adults are more literate visually than verbally. The demands on their visual decoding skills are intense.

Visual ambiguities, subtexts and meta-messages on television and in magazine advertising may escape them because they lack the verbal skills to bring these complexities to consciousness. The ability to navigate successfully through a stream of visual stimuli demands strong verbal skills.

The place to start literacy training, laying the groundwork for powerful mathematical and scientific skills, is at the intersection of visual and verbal stimuli. Most media combine image and text. It is the relationship between the two that carries the sub-text, or the meta-message. These additional messages can be accessed and examined through training.

Discriminating among an assortment of complex stimuli, some of which—like ads for cigarettes and alcohol—are dangerous, is important not only to economic well-being, but to physical health. Assaulted by persuasive material, a mind lacking training in discrimination has several options:

- to become hypersensitive to minimalist cues using short bursts of intense attention geared to the "hype" and speed of incoming electronic stimuli, e.g., channel surfing;

- to "go with the flow," absorbing all of the information indiscriminately; or

- to become passive, assuming an attitude of over-assaulted blankness, shutting down and shutting off.

The outcome of strategies #2 and #3 is the degradation of discriminatory mental abilities. In connection with #1, an addiction to short bursts of intense stimuli may make sustained attention less attractive. Some "channel-surfing" minds may remain capable of sustained attention, but this outcome depends upon the rest of that mind's education, including training in literature and the arts.

### Time for a new literacy

Increasing problems with writing, reading, attention, critical thinking, and ethical behavior suggest that today's learning environments—the home, school, community, society—are failing to provide sufficient practice with these skills. It was not always true that people needed to be able to write and read to survive. Societal pressures change. When skills and attitudes appropriate to intelligent survival fail to develop, they can be taught. Drawing/Writing creates an environment where children learn skills relevant to their lives, as well as to a technological society.

Students need a new literacy. They need a tool to teach them to analyze information accurately and thoroughly. It is imperative that they "get" the real message; to do this, they have to work through, evaluate and reject or accept meta-messages and subtexts. For example, to make safe decisions, students need to be able to extract the salient information from drug education programs.

As well as being able to evaluate confusing or misleading messages, students themselves must learn to send clear, unambiguous messages. If they do not become adept at clear communication, they may be victimized or they may make poor choices with lifelong consequences.

Over 25 million American adults cannot read and write. Another 35 million cannot read above a ninth grade level and are described as functionally illiterate. The prison population represents the single highest concentration of adult illiterates. 85% of the juveniles who appear in court and over 1/3 of mothers receiving welfare are among the functionally illiterate. One out of 3 American adults cannot read a book. The United States ranks 49th in literacy among 158 member nations of the U.N.

Four to 6 million of the 8 million unemployed lack the basic skills to be trained for high-tech jobs. Functional illiteracy costs more than $22.5 billion annually in lost industrial productivity and unrealized tax revenues (National Coalition for Literacy, 1994 census). A child with functionally illiterate parents is twice as likely to grow up illiterate (Wolkomir, 1996, 82-91). Cross-generational as well as cross-cultural deficits challenge education.

The United States ranked 28th out of 41 nations for scores achieved by thirteen-year-olds in math and 17th in science, according to the 1997 Third International Maths and Science Study (TIMSS, *The London Economist*, March 29, 1997). Yet, except for Switzerland, the United States spends more money than any other nation on mathematics and science education. Neither teaching time nor money correlates with the highest scores, according to this study. Thirteen-year-olds from Singapore scored highest in both fields, followed by South Korea in the maths and The Czech Republic in the sciences. Even though the United States and Britain have had universal schooling much longer, Asian countries are pulling far ahead. The relationship of training in specific languages to brain structure and processing modes bears examination as does the relationship of literacy to achievement in the maths and sciences.

Massachusetts is a state with a reputation for doing well with literacy education. Still, according to the Massachusetts State Department of Education, of 41,400

adults seeking entrance to literacy classes, "just 27,500—two out of three—get a spot." Laura Papano in *The Boston Globe Sunday Magazine* (November 26, 1995), asks a critical question: "How can someone get off welfare and into a job if he or she can't read or write? Some experts say that many social and job programs fail because they leapfrog the fundamental problem of illiteracy."

A survey of Massachusetts employers conducted by The Massachusetts Coalition for Adult Education Network supports Papano's information: 19% of the state's adults are functionally illiterate; an additional 25% fall below the skills levels appropriate for high school graduates. One in three adults who seek assistance for literacy problems are turned away from state-offered remedial programs. Massachusetts businesses report that the most glaring training deficits they see in new employees relate to basic skills including mathematics, literacy, and English, and in the ability to learn new skills.

### The bogus bell curve

The de-skilling of the work force is a cause of concern, particularly as it relates to the urban poor. Some people conclude that populations with low skills are innately less intelligent. Not only is this position untrue but it is counterproductive. Devising educational strategies to increase skills is a productive approach. It is more likely that educational opportunities, not innate capabilities, have been unequally distributed

In their book *The Bell Curve*, authors J. Hernstein and Charles Murray use statistics to "prove" that "black" people are genetically less intelligent than "white" people. Comparing unequal skill levels in distinctly different populations using the bell curve is not statistically feasible. The probability theory behind *The Bell Curve* is questionable (Miriam Lipschutz-Yevick, 1995). Lipshutz-Yevick writes, "Hernstein and Murray's... conclusions...will not bring about a bellshaped distribution.... The authors cannot have it two ways; either the two population groups—black and white—are sufficiently homogeneous to generate a bellshaped curve with a common mean, or we are dealing with two distinct populations and the various statistical tests based on the model of the bellshaped curve simply do not apply" (22).

Hernstein and Murray use spurious statistics in prejudicial, pernicious, non-useful ways. The book *The Bell Curve* is a disservice to African Americans and to any under-educated group in our society.

### A position on the distribution of I.Q.

Unequal educational opportunities in society result in unequal skill levels. I.Q. tests measure qualitative and quantitative skills in the context of the English language and mathematics. An education that equalizes English language and mathematics training will close the gap in intelligence levels between groups. This hypothesis is testable and demonstrable through standardized test scores. Until we equalize the quality of instruction, the existing methods for testing intelligence are inappropriate. Furthermore, standardized I.Q. testing is a questionable approach to judging effective, flexible problem-solving skills, or the basic skills for intelligent thought.

Drawing provides teachers with a much-needed window on student intelligence. Weak drawing skills do not mean that students are unintelligent. Powerful drawing skills, on the other hand, are indicators of powerful visual intelligence. Because drawing and writing and thinking skills are highly developable, the educational challenge is to devise strategies for encouraging intelligence and then to test for intelligence with a humane yet precise, no-nonsense, student-driven evaluation system like Rescore, where desirable skills and the criteria for assessing them are clear.

Education in the twenty-first century is more than the liberal arts, more than a mathematics and science education, more than a technical vocational education. Education for the twenty-first century is grounded in language-based, analytical and inferential, transferable thinking skills requiring a humanistic scope.

### The tipping point: Applying epidemic theory to illiteracy

An analogy can be made between epidemiology and literacy education. A small change in healthcare can reverse an epidemic; a small change in teaching strategies can reverse illiteracy rates. To follow the analogy, we must make a detour through criminology.

In the June 3, 1996 *New Yorker*, Malcolm Gladwell writes, "Epidemic theory should change the way we think about whether and why social programs work." Gladwell continues, "Today, bringing epidemiological techniques to bear on violence is one of the hottest ideas in criminal research (38)."

The article describes a "tipping effect" in connection with crime rates in Manhattan. In the language of epidemiologists, the "tipping point"... is the point at which an ordinary and stable phenomenon—for instance, a low level flu outbreak—can turn into a public-health crisis. "Every epidemic has its tipping point, and to fight an epidemic you need to understand what that point is... But you don't really need to completely eliminate risk. If over time you can just cut the number of people capable of transmitting the AIDS virus, then our present behavior-change programs could potentially eradicate the disease in this country" (35).

Illiteracy has become an epidemic. Like crime and the AIDS virus, illiteracy reflects demographic and social trends. Social problems act like infectious agents. Bringing the number of AIDS infections down to thirty thousand from forty thousand has a "huge effect." This statistic provides hope; a small increase in literacy may reverse snowballing illiteracy.

Gladwell writes about the AIDS epidemic, "It all depends on when and how the changes are made.... Human beings prefer to think in linear terms.... Epidemics aren't linear. Improvement does not correspond directly to effort. All that matters is the tipping point, and because fifty thousand is still above the tipping point, all of these heroics will come to naught" (35-36).

There is a relationship between the number of employed adults in a neighborhood and the rate of teenage pregnancy in that neighborhood; if over five percent of the adults are employed, the teenage pregnancy rate goes down. A five percent change turns a dysfunctional neighborhood into a more functional one almost overnight.

The Gladwell article continues, "If reading problems are nonlinear, the failure of the program doesn't mean—as conservatives might argue—that spending extra money on inner-city kids is wasted. It may mean that we need to spend even more money on these kids so that we can hit their tipping point...tipping points give the lie to conservative policies of benign neglect" (37).

The goal of teaching five percent of all school children Drawing/Writing is not impossible. If a five percent change in one domain—like AIDS—brings about a vast change, it make sense to explore a five percent change in another domain—like illiteracy. If we must set aside hope for an infusion of money into our schools, we can still adopt more effective strategies. For the cost of this book and the teacher-hours it takes to implement Drawing/Writing, the five percent tipping point can be reached. Like the fluttering of the wings of a butterfly on one side of the world, small perturbations have large effects on the other side of the world. Chaos theory sheds light on current theories about epidemiology, criminology, sociology—and education.

One thing is clear: there is no more time. Jonathan Kozol's "savage inequalities" have arrived and persist. Knowing what we do about the power of small changes, teachers can reach the tipping point for literacy. If each of us, as teachers, home-schoolers, parents, day-care providers, grandparents, believes we can achieve this tipping point, we will continue to teach children to write and read with renewed hope and intentions informed by theories from other fields. We will go back into the classroom and open this book, take a deep breath, and say, "Put your names on your folders..."

Educational practice generally lags fifty years behind educational research. Information technology accelerates change at a rate of 7:1. In 1991, the first papers on Drawing/Writing were published. It is now 1997. It is time for Drawing/Writing.

# THE
# NEW LITERACY

Only one thing is certain—that the written language of children develops in this fashion, shifting from drawings of things to drawings of words. The entire secret of teaching written language is to prepare and organize this natural transition appropriately…. Make believe play, drawing and writing can be viewed as different moments in an essentially unified program of development of written language…. The discontinuities and jumps from one mode of activity to the other are too great for the relationship to seem evident.

Lev Vygotsky, *The Mind in Society*

This book coins the term the new literacy to describe the skills currently required by society. By educating children for this new literacy, we return an ancient set of skills. At the same time, we hand them the communication tools they need for the future. The new literacy is as old as picture writing on cave walls and as new as CD-ROMs.

The new literacy is the human brain's ability to integrate, cross-reference and transform information through a series of translation systems. In the most general sense, the two major translation systems are the right and left hemispheres of the brain. Visual and verbal systems are sub-groups of these two larger systems. For instance, drawing and graphing are spatial systems for representing meaning. Written words and algebraic notation are linguistic systems.

Joanne Quail, second grade teacher, defines the new literacy as "the freedom to see." As Joanne observes, Drawing/Writing frees student to see their objects on their own terms in new ways. Older "graduates" of the

Drawing/Writing program report that they experience newfound freedom through choice and action.

The new literacy has a long history. Its genealogy includes art history, the development of writing, linguistics, child psychology, and neurobiology. Each field provides information on the naturalness, usefulness and power of integrative visual and verbal thinking skills. Neurobiology provides the clearest, most cogent support for integrative teaching strategies like Drawing/Writing as well as for complex mental skills like the new literacy.

## 4.1 Art History

An intimate relationship has existed between drawing and writing for thousands of years. The Drawing/Writing program deliberately recreates this relationship. Neuroconstructivist theory supports the naturalness of this connection as well as its usefulness for learning.

The history of art demonstrates that drawing alone and writing alone do not suffice to tell the tale. From about 15,000 b.c.e.[11] until now, humankind has painted symbols on cave walls, carved inscriptions on stelae, or, most recently, painted flower-like frogs directly onto texts by Aristophanes (educator Tim Rollins' K.O.S., or Kids of Survival). A thoughtful discussion of the development of written language in the context of art history clarifies the genealogy of Drawing/Writing as a recapitulation of the history of human mark-making.

As recently as four million years ago, arboreal hominids left the forests and stood up. An enlarged brain pan accompanied bipedal locomotion. Climate changes and decreasing territory forced migrations. Hominids adapted to the hot, dry plains by lengthening their legs, slimming out and growing taller; then, according to the Single Origin theory, sometime between 150 and 100 million years ago, an ancestral African population began moving in successive waves into Europe and Asia.

By two million years ago, *homo habilis*—"handy man"—was using bones and stones as tools. Some tools were decorated. Many of the meaningful marks represent fertility.

Between 25,000 b.c.e. and 4,000 b.c.e. bits of clay and stone were crafted into hand-held sculptures. Sculpture preceded painting. Then, about 15,000 b.c.e. cave painting began. The subjects were mostly large animals, some of which were probably considered divine—horned cattle, woolly mammoths, sabre toothed tigers, bears, rhinoceros—along with horses and antelopes, and a few drawings and bas reliefs of shamanic, potent males and fecund females. Many of the hand-held statuettes were goddess figurines. These figurines were often monistic, clustering ovoid with elongated phallic forms in a unified expression of female/male generative power. Paleolithic grave goods suggest that this ancient society was egalitarian, gender-balanced, pacific and gynocentric. No man or woman had more or richer grave goods. While skeletons exhibited injury, the marks were not apparently made by weapons. Female statuettes were found in many graves. Underground holy places were constructed in the shape of a woman with large breasts and thighs, with a birth canal entryway, creating womb-tombs for another kind of birth. This design provides the prototype for the Western basilican "cruciform" church.

[11] "b.c.e" which stands for "before common era" provides a common but non-Christian dating system. The common era starts with the year 1 as identified with the birth of Christ, but, in deference to other world religions, no longer uses the descriptors "before Christ" or "after Christ." Instead, "b.c.e." and "c.e." are used.

*Elk's antler carving with female symbols, sketch, SR Sheridan, 1997*
*From: THE LANGUAGE OF THE GODDESS by Marija Gimbutas*
*Figure (c) 1989 by Marija Gimbutas*
*Reprinted by permission of HarperCollins Publishers*

*Ovoid male/female*

*Goddess figurines and the womb-tomb, 25,000 b.c.e.-4,000 b.c.e., sketches SR Sheridan, 1997.*
*From: THE LANGUAGE OF THE GODDESS by Marija Gimbutas*
*Figures (c) 1989 by Marija Gimbutas*
*Reprinted by permission of HarperCollins Publishers*

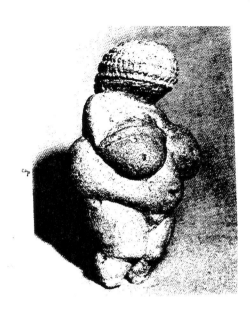

*The 4" high Venus of Willendorf, Gardner's*
*ART THROUGH THE AGES*
*Copyright (c) 1996, Gardner*
*Reprinted by permission of Naturhistorisches*
*Museum, Vienna*

As recently as 50,000 years ago, *Homo sapiens* produced speech. It is probable that humankind gestured with a stick in the dust before uttering a word. Speech captured and specified the gesture in the dust. Coinciding with the goddess sculptures, humankind began representing abstract thought in paintings and drawings on cave walls. Abstract thought eventually placed demands not only on speech, but on drawing. By about 2000 b.c.e.—about 4,000 years ago—in the ancient Near East, humankind's mark-making blossomed into systems of writing and calculation.

The exact relationship between drawing and writing varied depending on geography and chronology. In some instances drawing transformed itself into writing. In some instances, drawing and writing developed in parallel mode, demonstrating a syncretic, or mutually creative relationship. "Syncretic" comes from Greek roots and means "to join together in union." Highly schematic, abstract marks placed near optically convincing drawings of animals suggest this co-productive relationship. The cave painting from Lascaux called "The Chinese Horse" most probably demonstrates a syncretic relationship between drawing and writing.

Until recently, it appeared that "preliterate" cave artists developed drawing and writing 15,000 to 25,000 years ago in places like Lascaux, France. Now, it looks as if proto-writing goes back much further. In northwestern

Australia, on the face of a sandstone mountain and on the surrounding boulders, scientists discovered thousands of small, carved circles. These circles were also found on button-like stones which average 1.2 inches in diameter. All of these circles date from more than 60,000 years ago. Archaeologists calculate that it would have taken 900 days for a person working alone eight hours per day to carve the buttons. The circles must have been "of enormous cultural importance" to those who carved them (Wilford, 1996). Mandala-like circles comprise some the earliest images children continue to produce. Explanations from psychology and neurobiology suggest that the circle and the oval are innate schemata, or hard-wired mental images. These carved circles are symbolic and, as such, approach proto-writing.

By 3300 b.c.e. Sumerians were writing cuneiform on tablets; from 3100 b.c.e. Egyptians were carving and painting hieroglyphs on beetles' backs and plastered tomb walls. The Indus River script developed around 2500 b.c.e. Chinese characters developed in about 1200 b.c.e. Starting from about 250 b.c.e., Mayan glyphs codified astral anxieties using a calendrical system that took forecasting *backwards in time* 5 billion years (Robinson, 1995). The Runic alphabet developed in the 2nd century c.e. Japanese script flowered in the 5th century c.e. In all of these instances, writing included pictorial components.

### Art history and the history of language: Cave art

*"The Chinese Horse," Lascaux.*
*Permission Yvonne Vertut*
*Copyright Jean Vertut*

The histories of art and of writing show that from before recorded time (understood to be before the emergence of organized systems of writing like cuneiform and hieroglyphics), humankind combined representational drawings on cave walls with abstract drawings. These drawings can be classified as proto-writing or, in some cases, as proto-mathematics.[12] Whether the marks are identified as proto-writing or proto-mathematics, they constitute an order of symbolic representation distinct from optically accurate drawing. The cave painting from Lascaux called "The Chinese Horse" demonstrates the combined used of an optically accurate drawing (the horse) with pro-writing (the rectilinear "tectiform" to the right, hovering above the horse).

A pictograph is a "word-picture"; it is an optically accurate, if stylized, drawing of a person, place, or thing. A phonogram is a "sound-picture"; it is a drawing of a sound. This is usually achieved by drawing a picture of an object whose name includes the represented sound. The Sumerians and Egyptians created phonograms. The hieroglyph of a falcon evolved to represent the sound that starts the word "falcon" in Egyptian. Hieroglyphics employed homophonic cues. The picture sounded the same as the object it presented. For instance, the picture of an arm also stood for the sound for "arm" in Egyptian. Eventually, the picture of an arm was read as standing for the sound "a." A pictogram functions as a logogram or as a phonogram in Egyptian, depending upon the context.

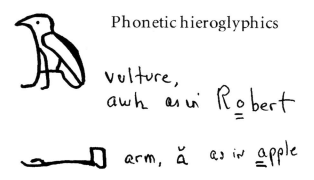

Phonetic hieroglyphics

vulture,
awh as in Robert

arm, ă as in apple

*Hieroglyphic of word vulture, the sound "a" as in the word "Roger," sketch by SR Sheridan, 1997.*
*Hieroglyphic of word "arm," the sound "a" as in "fat," sketch by SR Sheridan, 1997*

[12] The double dashes in front of the horse's muzzle in the cave painting in Lascaux called "The Chinese Horse" may mean several things: some scholars like Marija Gimbutas believe the double dashes stand for "the power of two" and signify pregnancy, conception, or increase. The power of two can be understood in a mathematical sense as well as in a biological sense. The power of two results from joining male and female: the unit is exponentially greater than either one.

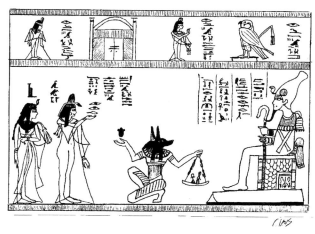

*Hieroglyphics after The Last Judgement of Hu-Nefer, Thebes. Dynasty XIX, Claus Kormannshaus, 1997*

Some written records—including hieroglyphics, cunieform, calligraphy, Navajo petroglyphs, and Mayan glyphs—demonstrate increasing stylization and simplification; a transition is made from a pictograph to a letter-like symbol. In some cases, the symbol becomes a phonograph, standing for a sound. During this evolutionary process, the pictorial content retreats and is eventually lost.

About 25,000 b.c.e., long before Sumerians developed cunieform (c.3,300 b.c.e.), paleolithic cave artists were creating both pictographs and logographs. We do not know if drawings of animals, hands, and cryptic symbols also stood for sounds, like consonants and vowels, or for quantities. We do accept that these drawings represented things and ideas with strong spiritual overtones. Because the drawings of animals and other marks were located deep in caves, away from the light, where people did not live on a daily basis—literally in the womb of the earth—many of the animal images probably related to the spiritual and physical rebirth of slain animals. Australian aboriginal people report that their marks on stone have important spiritual dimensions and are located in places with spiritual properties and energy. The fact that contemporary hunter/gatherers live an expressive life characterized by a ritual dimension may not mean that paleolithic rock painters lived the same kind of life, but conjectures can be made from communicating with aboriginal people, including the Lakota Indians, about the interconnected nature of the physical and spiritual world (Archeologist and Northfield Mount Hermon School teacher, Cosimo Favaloro, in conversation). The more abstract symbols accompanying these animals may have represented rebirth via the female principle. The earth was most probably understood as Mother, with life organized by a female principle. Whatever the exact meanings, the intent behind the marks was to communicate a serious idea, not just to decorate.

Paleolithic cave paintings reveal two distinct systems. One system is clearly drawing. The other is clearly not. Whether the second system is defined as full-blown writing, or pre-writing, proto-writing, or mathematical notation—or as highly stylized, minimalist drawing—this mark-making system is not the same as the optically accurate drawings of horses, bison, mammoths, reindeer, cattle and saber-toothed tigers. This book designates the second non-representational system of marks as the earliest examples of writing, or "proto-writing." This notation system is linguistic in the broadest sense, just as the drawing of the horse is a spatial representation in the broadest sense.

By 20,000 b.c.e., drawing and proto-writing coexisted. The relationship was syncretic and synchronic, that is, the two systems created each other more or less at the same time. The proto-writing accompanies certain animals—mostly horses and bison—in repeated patterns. Female signs often accompanied this animal dyad. Proto-writing and drawings evolved in tandem, undergoing parallel stylistic transformations. It is unlikely that proto-writing was slipped in among drawings of animals with no connection to them (Bonnefoy, 1993). We do not know for sure what paleolithic readers understood when they looked at grouped bison, horses and abstract signs but we can make inferences. The message may have been, "As horses and bison are fruitful and multiply, so may we and the whole earth be fruitful and multiply," or it may mean, "There are many horses and bison in our area." It may mean that the male principle as represented by horses and bison coexists with the female principle represented by the chevron. At least some of these symbols deep within the cave-womb of the earth signify rebirth.

The coexistence of two distinct systems clearly exists in "The Chinese Horse," a wall painting from 15,000 b.c.e. in Lascaux, France.

"The Chinese Horse," Lascaux. Permission Yvonne Vertut. Copyright Jean Vertut. All rights reserved, Jean Vertut, Yvonne Vertut.

"The Chinese Horse" looks like a Sung dynasty ink brush painting. Thus, the name. The drawing of the horse is optically convincing, clearly standing for "horse." Like most cave drawings, it shows the animal in strict profile, providing the most complete and characteristic representation. A frontal drawing of a horse would show two legs, a chest, no back, no tail, and no long muzzle. The distinctive shape of a horse's head and body would be indeterminable. Below the horse are some wheat-like or feathered arrow, or barbed, dart-like symbols. The scholars Abbe Breuil and Leroi Gourhan identify linear symbols, whether barbed, arrow-like or spear-like, as phallic and male. Female symbols, on the other hand, are curvilinear; some are vulvic, or oval with pointed ends, or "claviform" (key-shaped), representing the protuberant buttocks of a standing woman in profile. UCLA scholar and archeologist Marija Gimbutas maintains that the barbed, geometric shapes can as easily be recognized as female, containing the pubic triangle and bird-like angular wings, beaks and clawed feet—bird characteristics associated with the goddess in her owl-like, or death aspect. This point of view accepts the life-in-death, death-in-life duality of generative power.

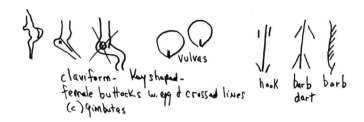

Barbs, claviforms: male and female symbols, sketches, SR Sheridan, 1997
After figures in LANGUAGE OF THE GODDESS by Marija Gimbutas

Above and to the right of the horse in the Lascaux painting is a hovering tarantula-like from called a tectiform or covered form. The drawing is linear and geometric. Sometimes the tectiform is rectilinear, as it is here, sometimes more pentagonal, constructed from interlocking chevrons or v's.

Some scholars believe that this symbol stands for a house, or for the number 13: the box represents 10 and the 3 legs add this number of items (Cosimo Favaloro, in conversation). Gimbutas conjectures that, like the curvilinear symbols, the geometric tectiform also represents the Goddess and her "life-giving body parts" (Gimbutas, 1989, 15). Whatever the exact meaning of the marks, two systems developed to provide mutual clarification as well as an extended message. In this case, the tectiform, the barbs or wheat, and the horse are meant most probably to be read together.

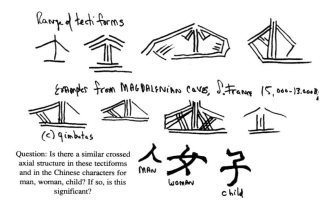

Question: Is there a similar crossed axial structure in these tectiforms and in the Chinese characters for man, woman, child? If so, is this significant?

*Tectiforms, sketches, SR Sheridan, 1997*
*After figures in LANGUAGE OF THE GODDESS by Marija*
*   Gimbutas*
*Copyright, (c) 1989 by Marija Gimbutas*
*Reprinted by permission of HarperCollins Publishers*

Cave artists apparently did not use the X-ray technique, a strategy in which invisible objects are shown as visible. If cave artists had used X-ray strategies, "The Chinese Horse" might have included a foal inside her belly. Still, a blade of feathered grass crosses the contour of the horse's abdomen. Cave artists did overlap images. The degree to which the overlaps (palimpsest) are intentional as debated. Pregnancy? Or a bounteous year for wild grasses? The proto-writing around "The Chinese Horse" to provide what Roland Barthes describes as the correct level of analysis (1985). The dilemma is that we

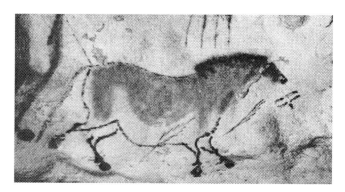

*"Chinese Horse" (c) Jean Vertut*
*Permission to reprint, Yvonne Vertut*
*All rights reserved.*

lack a Rosetta Stone for decoding tectiforms. An X-ray drawing of a foal would have clarified our reading of "The Chinese Horse." Without such clarification, the tectiform, the barbs, or feathered grass, extend the reading in several provocative directions.

Furthermore, a dashed line above the horse's tail points directly at the rump. By pointing to the point of sexual entry of a mare, that line may bear on the double dashes below the horse's nose reinforcing its meaning as "the power of two" in a generative sense. The combined message may be: "This mare is in estrus," or "This mare is pregnant," or, "May this mare be pregnant," or, "May the females in our clan be pregnant." Our contemporary symbol for women combines the oval, the tectiform, and the dash in a highly stylized form, carrying additional visual memories of the Egyptian ankh, or symbol for eternal life and happiness.

Symbols for female: paleo through present

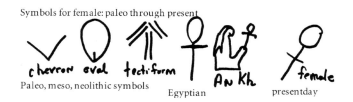

*Symbols for female, SR Sheridan, 1997*

Research with Australian aboriginal children supports the fact that preliterate peoples have astonishingly accurate eidetic memories. Paleolithic hunter/gatherers, including their artist/shamans, most probably shared this ability. These artists carried accurate mental images of animals into the caves. The close association of accurate drawings of animals and abstract marks depicts a world view where animals are sacred, and fertility, pregnancy, procreation and generation are focal concerns.

Whether the tectiform stood for a dwelling, water, nets, femaleness, the impregnated womb, fertility, or the earth goddess herself standing in a highly stylized pose, it does not constitute a "drawing" in the same way that the lines, colors and values used to represent the horse constitute a drawing. It is even possible that the tectiform stands for the sound paleolithic people used for mother. The sound for mother probably comes from appreciative noises made by babies during nursing. It is the easiest sound for babies to make. This appreciative sound may have become the initial consonant in the name of the Magna Mater herself. It is not beyond the range of possibility that the tectiform may represent the image, name and concept of the Mother/Mother-Home/Female-Male/Sex/Fertility/Abundance/Goddess/Mater/Mum.

However it may have been read, the tectiform stands as a pictogram, a picture of a complex idea. We cannot know for sure what original object gave rise to the tectiform. But we believe the drawing is an abstract symbol.

We do not know if the tectiform or the double dashes above the horse are concrete or abstract symbols. But we do know that these minimal, non-pictorial marks represent a "well constructed ideographic system" and an "elaborate ideology" (Honigsblum et al, 1993, 16).

The fact that cave artists developed two mark-making systems more or less simultaneously suggests that drawings alone would not suffice for the level of communication required by Stone Age lives. A cooperative approach to symbolic language-use has been a driving force in the human enterprise since humans embarked on speech. As Roland Barthes suggests, one system allows us to read another *at the proper level*. We may never know whether the tectiform is the goddess or the balloon frame for a dwelling. We do know that the tectiform allowed the Stone Age reader to interpret the drawing of the horse in specific ways. Whatever their marks on bone and stone were meant to communicate, paleolithic people used systems distinguished by different levels of schematization or abstraction. Experts agree that two distinct mark-making systems existed in the caves and grew in a mutual relationship. We must conclude that the two mark-making systems suggest considerable intellectual powers as well as an elaborate social system (Honigsblum et al, 1993, 16). The repertoire of written words may have been limited, but human beings were drawing words on cave walls as well as pictures at least 30,000 years ago.

## 4.2 The History of Writing

There are implications to writing systems which maintain visual clues to verbal meaning: the calligraphic model provides clues to the effectiveness of the Drawing/Writing strategy.

A language system organizes a brain in certain ways. The range of the language and its grammar constrain the brain's logic and thus the depth and breadth of that brain's thought. A language system that includes visual as well as verbal strategies for meaning-making, like drawing as well as writing, allows greater depth and breadth of expression than a language system which is entirely visual or entirely verbal.

There is evidence that people who speak more than one language score higher on some verbal intelligence tests. These people are identified as balanced bilingually. Cultures whose written language system retains visual cues may produce a certain kind of brain, too, identifiable as balanced bilaterally. A specific system for written language, say, Chinese calligraphy, may or may not be responsible for apparent aptitudes with mathematics and science. Whether culturally coded neural networks are suited to certain kinds of symbolic manipulations is investigatable.

Whatever the specific academic outcomes may be, dual systems for thinking encourage a broader range of possibilities for expression. It is probable that the "balanced bilateral" neurobiological profile describes bilingual brains as well as the brains of people who grow up writing calligraphy, or even drawing and writing. In a technological society, a brain organized for image and text is desirable and adaptive. If it becomes apparent that the balanced bilateral brain is desirable, to what degree can we educate brains for the challenge of a new literacy?

Whatever the pedagogical position on bilingual education, children can learn to use their whole brains. Balanced bilateral brains and cross-modal teaching and learning are logically related. As Drawing/Writing demonstrates, strategies for implementing WholeBrain education need not be costly or complicated.

Thought and language are reciprocal. Sixty years ago, researcher Count Alfred J. Korzybski observed that language-use determines mental flexibility.[13] According to Korzybski, if words are thought of as absolute, meaning turns rigid and agreement becomes difficult if not impossible. If words are intolerant, people are, too. On the other hand, if words are accepted as relative, tentative, responsive to adjustment and qualification, then a possibility remains for agreement through discourse.

Although the innate grammar for any language may not be modifiable, the language-learning environment is modifiable. *How* students use a culturally inherited code for organizing information is modifiable: students can learn to use language rigidly or flexibly.

The cross-modal Drawing/Writing approach teaches students that there is more than one way to express meaning. One way is universal and can be equally accessed: drawing. Other methods are culture-specific and carry with them certain approaches to codifying

---

[13] Count Alfred J. Korzybski founded an institute in Chicago in 1938 for linguistic, scientific and educational research. He developed a theory of semantics necessary to mental health, or sanity, which he developed in the book *Science and Sanity*, 1933.

information. Drawing/Writing students learn that meaning—visual or verbal, culturally coded or not—is cumulative, personal, and relative, requiring translation from inner speech to some form of adjusted expression that meets the other speaker halfway (Faith, 1989).

### A compulsion toward language

The changing relationship between the two hemispheres of the brain in paleolithic humankind resulted in image and text on cave walls. Humankind as mark-makers may have never been "pre-literate."

How many people crawled on their bellies into the caves to draw, write or read? Probably only a few, including those with shamanic power. Stencils of hand prints—some of very small hands belonging to children who were most probably lifted into place—as well as the imprints of bare feet, provide mute testimony to ritual gatherings. Who the artists, writers and viewers/readers were is not as important as the fact that Stone Age people were making marks of significance on walls in special places and gathering to read them.

Once humans stood up on their hind feet and looked out over the grasses, they were compelled to describe what they saw. They learned to scan the ground for clues. They scanned the middle and far ground, too, all the way to the horizon. They were not the only great apes to stand up on their hind feet and look out. But, once they did, they had to express what they saw. They were compelled to such a degree that their jaws and larynxes changed, their brains grew, and they invented language. They learned how to touch things at a distance with their eyes. They learned to translate touch with their eyes into touch at a greater distance by making marks. They learned to make marks for touching things no longer near them; finally, they learned to touch things that cannot be touched.

The compulsion to invent language endures. Children invent language over and over again. They babble and they scribble. Children experiment with drawings; they invent spellings; they devise fresh metaphors. Born with the compulsion to language, children arrive pre-programmed with certain schemata. As the art historian E.H. Gombrich comments, "The Egyptian or the child in us remains stubbornly there" (*The Story of Art*, 1989, 562). The ancient Egyptian convention of drawing combined profile/frontal views persists in children. Conceptual drawing—as opposed to optically correct drawing—persists. Conceptual representation, or drawing "in the Egyptian manner," is more natural for children than optically accurate drawing.

Gombrich describes another human impulse in connection with sculpture. He writes, "We must go back to our childhood, to a time when we still felt able to make things out of bricks or sand, when we turned a broomstick into a magic wand, and a few stones into an enchanted castle. Sometimes these self-made things acquired an immense significance for us,...an intense feeling for the uniqueness of a thing made by the magic of human hands" (585). Like cave artists and sculptors, when children make objects, they practice magic. With time, image and form become the incantation of writing.

Several stages exist in the history of writing. One is the development of pictographs, or pictures, like *The Chinese Horse;* another is the spontaneous invention of abstract signs, like the "power of two," and the tectiform; a third are specific instances of these abstract signs, like the logograph, or word-drawing like the tectiform; and a fourth, the creation of phonographic writing, or pictures of sounds like the letters "ph." Eventually, drawings were reduced to the barest essentials and abstracted, becoming the minimalist system we call writing. Some forms of writing retain visual clues to meaning. For example, pictorial content remains subtly embedded in Chinese characters. In English, it does not.

### Chinese and Japanese writing systems

In traditional Chinese writing, forming letters engages the writer in an aesthetic as well as intellectual exercise. In some instances, the characters retain enough visual clues to be accessible as pictographs. Calligraphy, or a "beautiful writing," is an aesthetic/cognitive activity.

*Chinese characters for man, woman, child, SR Sheridan, 1997*

In *The Story of Writing* (1995) Andrew Robinson writes, "Chinese students learn the technique early, beginning with the simplest characters and moving progressively to more and more complex ones. Following the teacher, a class of young students traces characters rhythmically in the air with broad gestures of arm and hand. As the students trace, they name each element— bar, leg, dot and so on—and at the end they pronounce the character. Then, when the gestures have been learned, the students write the character down, again broadly, rhythmically and collectively. In due course, they learn to write the character small and on their own" (194). This approach to writing is kinaesthetic and multi-modal; it starts with the body and includes the voice in naming. The Drawing/Writing program re-creates this process in a somewhat less dramatic fashion. As a warm-up exercise, students are invited to draw their objects in the air with broad gestures and then to trace them.

The current writing reform movement in China pursues a policy of "digraphia," or the use of two scripts, Pinyan and calligraphic characters. Pinyan is best suited for inputting Chinese into computers (197). Calligraphic characters are used for other traditional forms of written communication like newspapers and books and for simple signs and instructions. Speakers of Cantonese and Mandarin can read the same newspaper because of a shared pictorial writing system. In a similar way, students of Drawing/Writing can read each other's abstractions through training in a drawing system.

The Japanese base their writing system on the system of Chinese characters called Kanji. The embedded, pictorial aspects of Chinese characters are not accessible to the Japanese. This makes learning Kanji an incredible feat of memorization. For the Chinese, the semantic or embedded pictorial quality persists, easing the daunting task of memorization. The Navajos produced pictographs too, carving them in rocks.

Fig. 66. This panel from Rainy Lake, Ontario, Canada, tells of the capsizing of a canoe with three men in it (a). The upside-down man (b) indicates that one man drowned. Symbol (c) may be a second drowned man, but it is too faded to discern accurately. The bird track *going down* (d) clarifies *sinking* or *drowning*, and the bend in this track indicates *distance* (sinking to the bottom of the deep lake).
A third man (e) has the mouth of a bird, pointing upward (as some birds are required to do when drinking) to indicate *swallowing*. This man has a penis long enough to reach the ground, thus indicating *reaching shore*. His legs are also in the *arriving* position. This figure, with its *seeking safety* wings (arms) says, "This person swallowed water while seeking the safety of the shore, but succeeded in reaching it."
Symbol f (three dots) represents the position of the three nearby islands where the canoe capsized; symbol g represents the island reached by the survivor. The two *nothing there* lines indicate that it is *deserted*, or *barren*.
The remainder of the panel is too faded to venture any further attempts at reading.

*Navajo petroglyph.*
*THE ROCKS BEGIN TO SPEAK,*
 *(c) 1973 by LeVan Martineau*
*Figure 66 reprinted by permission of LeVan Martineau*
*All rights reserved.*

Even picture writing requires textural explanations for most contemporary readers. Still, an expressivity persists with pictures. Drawing/Writing returns expressivity to language. For students who find text empty of meaning, experience with drawing allows them to transfer expressivity to text.

### Implications of logographic and phonologic systems for science and mathematics

Approximately 50% of Chinese characters have a phonetic component (Shaywitz, 1997). Children reading Chinese access meaning visually and phonetically. Chinese characters train children in phonologic processing as well as in visual processing for "semantic" meaning. Chinese children acquire a system for language that is cross-modal, visual/verbal and balanced bilaterally in terms of interhemispheric exchange. If Chinese children excel with highly abstract symbol systems like mathematics and physics in which graphs, models, and computer simulations enrich understanding, design cues from Asian language systems combining visual and verbal elements could re-structure English language programs. By giving equal weight to visual literacy, image/text productions appropriate to cross-modal mental processes will become standard. It will not be enough cognitively to down-load images for text. If the intent is to structure neural nets appropriate to effective performance, say, in the maths and sciences, training in a combined visual/verbal system like Drawing/Writing will be necessary. This training allows early, ongoing and persistent participation in the creation of images and text.

## 4.3 Child Psychology and Drawing

Just as paleolithic people needed to express what they saw and felt and believed, so do children. If many children are not drawing and writing and reading naturally and easily, some fundamental instinct is being thwarted. By recapitulating the history of language-based thought, it should be possible to provide a natural return to the instinctual and emotional use of language.

At the scribbling stage, young children spontaneously devise two kinds of marks—drawing marks and, if they see people around them writing, writing marks. Children produce pre-writing as wavy scribbles but they do not spontaneously generate the alphabet. Writing has to be learned. On the other hand, children generate drawings without coaching or instruction.

Young children not only know more than they can show but more than they care to show. Young children use drawing more schematically than older children. The motives of the third grader are different from those of the kindergartner which, in turn, differ from those of the high school student for whom a realistically detailed drawing is the goal. Adults for whom optically accurate drawings are also desirable must temper their expectations about children's drawings by validating and appreciating children's intents as well as their skill levels.

### Respect for children's drawings

Children's brains require a constant stream of engaged adult speech to develop language skills including abstract reasoning skills. The fields of art history, the history of writing, the study of linguistics, child psychology, and neurobiology document humankind's impulse toward conceptual representation—the drawing of ideas rather than things. Many of these representations have had magical or holy properties. Children's utterances, including children's drawings, deserve the respect we accord other serious images.

Children not only produce conceptual drawings, they also produce drawings of astonishing truthfulness and accuracy. By providing children with traditional images, we may short circuit vision and expression. As Robert Kegan of Harvard suggests, as teachers we can "attend on the child," saying in an interested, gentle manner, "Tell me about your drawings." If adult drawings are passed along to the child, or if the adult offers to redraw the image, or if the adult defines the drawing, the child loses control, and may become confused or discouraged.

Very young children may not know what their drawings are about. They are simply doing them. The doing is all, and its intent is neural networking. Meaning emerges in the very act of telling.

My daughter, Sarah, drew a portrait of me when she was about five, feeling the first stirrings of one of her intellectual birthrights, the visual power of the Expressionist artist. She drew with a fearless disregard for symmetry, recording the differences she saw in eye size. Sarah skipped right past the conceptual tadpole stage, moving directly into realistic drawing.

Children's brains require exposure to images of power. The history of art is children's visual heritage.

### Profile, frontal and innate schemata

Children and Paleolithic artists share certain representational strategies. Early humankind and young children naturally invent and acquire and combine several symbol systems in their determination to express meaning.

Paleolithic artists generally drew animals in profile. The profile view provides a distinctive outline of an animal's head and identifies it more clearly than a view from the front. Grazing animals seen from afar are recognizable in profile. Approaching animals do not provide the best opportunities for storing mental images, especially if they are coming fast. Children also draw in profile, particularly animals. On the other hand, children's earliest drawings include the frontal "tadpole." Children see people's faces coming directly at them for the first few months of their lives. The frontal tadpole drawing may reflect this frontality and indicate the child's intent to draw on a "need to know" basis. Close up, the child needs to record certain kinds of information. At a distance, the child can afford to record other views, and other kinds of information.

No one teaches children to draw mandalas or tadpoles. On a mental level, tadpole drawings show what children need to know about themselves and other human beings; they are heads/bodies. These drawings represent that aspect most important for children to record: the face.

Tadpole drawings are described as conceptual, rather than optical. To distinguish between the two kinds of drawings from the point of view of the child's brain is probably spurious. The very young child may see human beings as heads/bodies, filtering out other aspects. The point is, children draw. They are drawing in ways that make sense to them. What very young children are intent on expressing through tadpole and mandala drawings goes deeper than words and may serve to construct neural nets necessary to abstract spatial thinking just as hearing language from the age of birth to six months is now said to build the baby's neural nets for abstract linguistic thought.

### X-ray art

Besides mandalas and tadpoles, children produce another kind of conceptual drawing, the X-ray drawing: an item which would be invisible is shown as if it were visible. Although a man's legs are invisible when he stands in a boat, a child will draw the legs. In a

Piagetian sense, legs are conserved. Eskimo art uses the X-ray technique; prey is shown inside the belly of the predator.

*X-ray drawing, man in boat, fish in fish*

Cave artists used a somewhat similar technique, the "palimpsest" or overlapped image. The overlapping may have been accidental, or intentional, indicating ritual relationships or time sequences; the animal placed in front may have been more important or one animal may have been more numerous at a certain time of year or one animal may have been painted simply at another time.

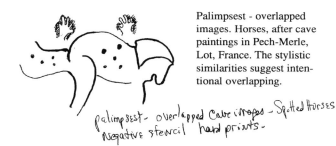

Palimpsest - overlapped images. Horses, after cave paintings in Pech-Merle, Lot, France. The stylistic similarities suggest intentional overlapping.

*Cave art palimpsest drawing, sketch, SR Sheridan, 1997*

### Blind artists

Recent studies with blind artists (Kennedy, 1997) show that the blind represent objects much as sighted artists do. They feel an object and then produce a contour line drawing from one point of view. Touch allows the blind to draw, just as touch allows them to read, using Braille. Whether we are sighted or blind, touch informs our mental images. Using touch, the blind may construct more accurate mental images than sighted people who assume they know how things look without confirming or modifying these notions through direct tactile and visual exploration. Drawing/Writing keeps us connected to touch as a source of seeing.

### The unfolding of language as conceptual and metaphorical first and optical and literal second

The unfolding of the human embryo recapitulates mammalian embryonic development. Similarly, children's drawings recapitulate the history of art, including both conceptual and optical phases; children's writings appear to parallel that progression. As schematic drawing is natural for young children, so simile and metaphor—a conceptual use of language—is natural, too. Young children often spontaneously generate metaphor and burst into poetry.

If we appreciate children's drawings as expressions of the human drive toward meaning, we will respond appropriately to them. We will value scribbles, dashes, dots, circles, tadpoles, cartoons, doodling in the margins, decorated text book covers and graffiti as expressions of the human impulse toward symbolic language and we will provide appropriate environments for expressing this pressing need. The more attentively children learn to draw, the more clearly they will express and communicate their ideas—optically or conceptually, literally or metaphorically.

Drawing/Writing recapitulates the history of drawing and of writing for children, allowing them to reclaim their powers of expression.

## 4.4  Language Education

### Invented spelling as a transitional symbol system

Invented spelling provides a transitional stage in children's writing. Similarly, each drawing step in the five-step program provides a transitional step in children's drawing. Still, each drawing step exists in and of itself as an authentic piece of word: invented spelling enjoys the same complex authentic/transitional status in connection with writing.

By providing practice with legitimate, serious, dignified abstract drawing (the CA), Drawing/Writing reassures children about transitional stages. The CA provides practice not only with abstraction but with transition. Because the Composite Abstraction is abstract, it prepares the mark-maker for writing, including both invented and standard spelling. Aligning invented spelling with abstract drawing allows invented spelling to take on an exploratory character. A drawing-based literacy program that accepts abstract drawing as preparatory training for written language preserves invented spelling as an authentic, exploratory and important activity.

### Acquisition of the alphabet and invented spelling

Unlike the mandala or the tadpole drawing which apparently exist in the brain as templates and appear spontaneously on paper, the alphabetic code does not appear spontaneously on paper. Still, with exposure to writing, children learn to write. Using a sound-to-letter correspondence, children crack the alphabetic code, recording what they hear. Like children's early drawings, this early writing deserves respect. As soon as "invented spelling" is read aloud, it is evident that children hear more complex sounds than traditional spelling accounts for. Remember how six year-old Nate Gorlin Crenshaw spelled the word "plastic": "pelasteck."

*Travis Clark, Euclidean Basic Shape, hose sprayer head with tube, second-grade Applewide School, 1997.*

*Travis Clark, CA#2, sprayer head, second-grade, Applewide School, 1997*

Travis' invented spelling produced this sentence: "It looks like a soard. It looks like a brege chrosing. It looks like a house because it has a dravy-a, barn and a tree haus." Travis wrote that his Composite Abstraction of the sprayer head "looks like a tellaskop." Travis' mother, Molly O'Shaughnessy, reports that Travis was drawing aerial views and complicated mazes from about the age of four. "He drew floor plans of houses and buildings when other kids were drawing the classic square with a triangle. In kindergarten, he drew a floor plan of my clinic very close to scale."

Children are able to sound out words. For confidence in this ability to develop, they need praise, support and leeway. Very young children may not know exactly what their writing-like marks mean. As with their drawings, an appropriate conversational gambit with young children's writing is: "My, this looks interesting. Tell me about this." This approach lets children decide what the marks are saying. A child's belief that his tentative marks are interesting and meaningful lays the foundation for the child's confidence in his writing and reading—as well as in the world as an intelligible place. Once children become confident as writers, spelling rules can be introduced.

Sometimes, there is an obvious difference between children's drawing and their writing marks. Some children use sure, strong, dark marks for drawing and then switch to tentative, sketchy marks when they are asked to write. This switch suggests that these children—like John Kozema—may think drawing and writing are two very different and distinct tasks.

*John Kozema's Preliminary Drawing and Writing, can opener, and Closing Drawing and Writing, Applewide School, 2nd grade.*

Second-grader John Kozema wrote about his "Perfect" whole drawing of a can opener, "It was easy to draw." For his CA, he wrote, "My CA tells me that it looks like an alien ship firing a gun. Looks like a robot. And I play and play with it."

With children who exhibit hesitancy with writing, spelling and reading, it is especially important to praise and encourage their drawing marks. Ideally, equal support is given from the beginning for all marks made by a child. The brain accords equipotentiality to both hemispheres, at least, initially. The classroom can accord the same equipotentiality to emerging mark-making systems. The common goal for the brain and the classroom is effective communication.

Children hear, see and think differently from adults. Their confidence in their ability to make sense of the world is fragile. I cannot underscore these points too strongly. For years, I have listened to the painful stories of adults whose confidence in their ability to draw, write, read or think was annihilated by one ill-considered adult judgment about their drawing. Children's drawings must be respected.

### Words seen and not heard

By looking carefully, we record images in our brains. For many of us, drawing "fixes" the image. In aboriginal, preliterate cultures, attentive visual study—unaccompanied by drawing—produces accurate mental images. Children from literate cultures lose this power. Drawing provides a way to retrain the brain to store accurate visual images. If children think of writing as a kind of drawing, they should be able to store words as accurate mental images, too, by copying them. When writing involves copying overheard sound, the writer's spelling may exhibit inaccuracies due to "overhearing" (like Nate's "pelasteck"), or to actual "phonological processing deficits," or mishearing. While recognizing the considerable usefulness of phonics to writing, Drawing/Writing focuses on writing as word-pictures. Because of the neural possibilities for self-remediation, training in drawing as careful seeing may remediate inaccurate hearing. Learning to draw accurately may not cure a tendency to confuse sounds and letters, but honing one sensory system hones another. If a child sees more accurately, he may hear more accurately.

In addition, spelling is not logical. For example, the "f" sound can also be represented by "p" and "h"—as in the word *phonograph*. Because the human mind is enthralled by uniqueness and weirdness, most students will accommodate additional spelling rules as a mental challenge, especially after flexibility training with the Composite Abstraction. Spelling anomalies are easiest to store as pictures.

Each experiment with drawing and writing constructs knowledge and scaffolds it on a preceding layer. The Regular Contour drawing constructs knowledge about the outline of an object and scaffolds itself upon the initial exploration in outline achieved by the Blind Contour drawing. In a sense, standard spelling imposes knowledge about letter-to-sound on the child's personally constructed knowledge expressed through invented spelling. Still, the child will be more willing to accept standard spelling if her own inventions have been honored.

No matter how flexible or willing the mind of the child, a sound-to-letter miscorrespondence may persist. As useful as phonics are to learning to spell, copying words as if they were pictures may make more sense for children with hearing problems than persisting in a sounding-out approach. For these children, writing and reading are best taught as visual rather than as aural coding tasks. Drawing/Writing provides this visual training automatically, as well as providing ample aural training through peer pair sharing and group critiques.

## 4.5 Drawing/Writing and Language Learning

Language learning consists of a progression from one mode to another. Drawing/Writing examines and recreates this progression for students.

The Russian scholar, psychologist and educational theorist Lev Vygotsky provides support for the progressive Drawing/Writing program in several ways. First, Vygotsky defines the linguistic progression as moving from speech to play to drawing to writing (1978). Vygotsky describes the move from drawing to writing in the following way: meaningful marks change from "pictographic to ideographic writing" (114), moving "from drawings of things to drawings of words." The goal of this continuum for Vygotsky is written language because it allows the mind to move into abstraction. In Vygotsky's continuum, writing enjoys a privileged position. Writing is not just a fine motor skill, but an entirely new way of thinking. As Vygotsky states, "Its mastery heralds a critical turning-point in the entire development of the child," because it allows abstract thinking (106).

In the Vygotskian scheme of things, drawing does not remain a co-equal participant in the linguistic continuum. Even though children's drawings "designate" (112) or gesture toward meaning, drawing—for Vygotsky—is not a tool for abstraction in the way writing is. Still, he appreciates the fact that drawing and writing exist as "different moments in an essentially unified program of development (116)."

According to Vygotsky, "jumps and discontinuities" occur between play, speech, drawing and writing. The child moves abruptly between these activities. The separate acts do not appear connected. As Vygotsky notes, "The discontinuities and jumps from one mode of activity to the other are too great for the relationship to seem evident" (116). It is easy to miss the continuity in the general meaning-making process. The connections between drawing and writing have been invisible. For this reason, it has been easy to exclude drawing from writing curricula.

According to Vygotsky, students will naturally move through the historical phases of mark-making, including the move from drawing to writing. To do so, they must be allowed to draw as well as to write. In addition, Vygotsky suggests that writing should enter children's lives by age three or four, and urges that once writing is acquired, it be taught as an activity that is "necessary and relevant to life" (118). According to this timetable, drawing should be encouraged by age two or three as serious preparation for writing and writing should become a relevant and possible activity soon thereafter. This moves literacy education firmly into the "preschool" period of education.

Vygotsky stresses an additional point of importance to the Drawing/Writing program. He maintains that teaching and learning strategies that prove effective with dysfunctional or delayed children work as well or better with "normal" children. The Italian educator, Maria Montessori, made the same observations (1912). Special education belongs in the regular classroom precisely because it provides optimal educational learning opportunities for all children. Remediation is enrichment; enrichment is remediation. Strategies like Drawing/Writing designed with this dual intent serve an entire student population.

Most importantly for Drawing/Writing, Vygotsky validates the role of drawing in the mental progression toward abstraction: "Only one thing is certain—that the written language of children develops in this fashion, shifting from drawings of things to drawings of words" (114). Young children's scribbled drawings are gestures toward meaning: "Children do not draw, they indicate, and the pencil merely fixes the indicatory gesture" (108). The indicatory gesture represents an intention toward meaning. Students' drawings are in fact "a particular kind of child speech" (112). There is substantial support for the part drawing plays in the prehistory of writing (Montessori, 1912/1964; Luria, 1979; Ferreiro, 1979; Scinto, 1987).

The Vygotskian legacy is this: the appropriate way to teach written language is to prepare and organize the natural transitions from speech through play to drawing and writing. Vygotsky would have recognized Drawing/Writing as a unified language program in which drawing re-introduces the organic unfolding of symbolic language, thereby reclaiming natural transitions between systems of abstraction. The fields of linguistics, psychology, education, and neurobiology share an appreciation for this continuum.

Drawing/Writing makes the Vygotskian progression visible and available to students who might not otherwise have the chance to construct this progression. Students of Drawing/Writing accept drawings as approximations, not replicas. As Alfred J. Korzybski observed in the 1930's, without corrective training, children grow up with the notion that words are *exact* replicas of things and, as such, are absolute and fixed. This attitude about language reinforces rigid thinking. Words are, in fact, approximate and variable, and, above all, *personal*. Through the ongoing experience of peer sharing and group critiques, as well as through the experience of a series of transitional and approximate drawings, Drawing/Writing students recognize the variability of words. They learn that shared understandings can only be achieved through discourse and the continual adjustment of meaning.

Drawing/Writing clarifies the Vygotskian progression from speech to play to drawing to writing as more lateral than hierarchical, more parallel than sequential. In neural terms, "embeddedness" is the most appropriate descriptor for linguistic development. One skill grows within the matrix of another and it remains part of that skill, requiring its neural and procedural contributions to function. Mental events occur globally and simultaneously, not in isolated, parallel strings. Instead of using the word "taxonomy" with its hierarchical overtones, the word "constellation" better describes how mental skills self-organize.

Children who learn to draw conceptually and optically, to write poetry, and prose, music and mathematics know that a variety of meaningful marks are natural and necessary. No system need be higher or lower, harder or easier, more abstract or less abstract than another. Usefulness to the child is the criterion.

The brain treats concrete and abstract ideas simply as mental objects (Minsky, 1985). It is the degree to which the mind is able to manipulate the object that matters. Systems for abstraction are, in the final analysis, only different. In and of itself, as a system for abstraction, drawing is no lower- or higher-order than writing, dance no higher or lower than music, music no higher or lower than poetry, mathematical understanding no higher or lower than poetry or prose. Levels of abstraction are ordinate, like numbers, not value-laden in a monetary sense. A number taken to the fourth power is no more valuable as an operation than a number taken to the first power. The ability to take numbers to powers is what matters.

The ability to recognize all marks as abstractions and to produce abstractions from abstractions is the skill Drawing/Writing teaches. It is a basic mental operation. By equipping students with a visual language before introducing a verbal language, abstract symbolic thinking is encouraged in brain-appropriate ways. The more visual and verbal languages children acquire, the more thoroughly they will be able to express themselves, increasing their chances of understanding and of being understood.

Training and exposure largely determine the mind's expressive modes. Educational theorist Howard Gardner describes these modes as "intelligences," or "frames of mind," and includes in his list: linguistic, musical, logical-mathematical, spatial, bodily-kinaesthetic, and personal intelligences (1983). Drawing/Writing takes as given that all children possess spatial and linguistic intelligence as the legacy of the human bicameral brain. These two categories include and subsume the other categories of intelligence listed by Gardner. This book adds that children's brains are designed to be scientific, artistic, literate, aesthetic and philosophical. Children's brains are designed to discover, express, evaluate and interpret meaning. Children's minds are "framed" for the development and application of these overarching intelligences.

Language development is personal and social, sequential and simultaneous, discrete and cumulative. There is no single blueprint for the development of language skills nor is there any absolute set of developmental milestones. Cooperative and reflective practice with at least two symbol systems encourages the unfolding of the expressive human mind.

## 4.6  Children's Representational Strategies

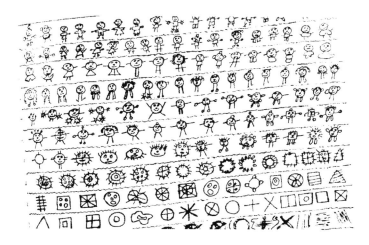

*Tadpoles and mandalas*
*From ARTFUL SCRIBBLES by Howard Gardner*
*Image 60, copyright (c) 1980 by Howard Gardner*
*Reprinted by permission of Basic Books, Inc., Publishers.*
*All rights reserved.*

### Sets of coordinates for physical and mental worlds

Getting around in the physical world requires coordinates for the body's proprioceptive system. Getting around in the mental world of ideas requires the acquisition of symbol systems, including written language.

This book suggests that the tadpole and the mandala are schematic manifestations of a deeper spatial location system designed to locate the human body in a physical universe determined by certain conditions expressible as coordinates (Changeux, 1985; Churchland, 1986). For this reason, a study of children's drawings illuminates the degree to which the human brain employs these spatial coordinates—as well as linguistic "coordinates"—to navigate meaningfully. The brain's spatial location system—*where is it?*—provides the framework for the brain's naming system—*what is it?*

The child's tadpole drawing is an expression of a mental template for creating intelligible order. By including all the child needs to know—in this case, about a human being—no more and no less, the tadpole drawing demonstrates the parsimony of this system for order. It is on this deep and conservative predisposition toward order that the child constructs language. The tadpole is not just a picture: it is a *procedure* for spatial order and, by translation, a system for linguistic order, too. Drawing/Writing is also a procedure for meaning, not just exercises in pictures and words.

# CONCLUSION

"Aslan is on the move."

C.S. Lewis, *The Lion, the Witch and the Wardrobe*

## Innate Behavior and Learned Skills

Like the behavior of animals, much of our behavior is innate, including the need to know and to express knowledge. To think and act effectively, we must activate or acquire certain behaviors. The quality of the learning environment determines the quality not only of the behaviors, but of the neural nets in the brain responsible for them—on which future learning and behavior depend. Recent brain research demonstrates that learning affects not only connectivity but the actual number of brain cells, making whole new sets of connections possible.[14] The optimum learning environment capitalizes on the brain's predisposition to know and to express knowledge, actualizing that predisposition in certain ways.

In the absence of rich natural learning environments, artificial environments must be invented. Artificial is a word we usually associate with unnatural, even frivolous situations. But if we take the word apart, we find that the word "artificial" means "made by art." It is possible to create rich learning environments by design, or artifice, in the absence of naturally rich learning environments. We now know that teaching environments where the arts play strong roles are neither frivolous nor unnatural learning situations but are filled with meaning and power because of direct sensory experience. This is a different "virtual reality," delivered not via electronics but through direct classroom experience with objects and people.

## The Intertheoretic Integration

An intertheoretic integration combines information from several fields for the sake of a richer explanation. In this book, information from neurobiology enriches educational theory and practice, redefining effective learning as cross-modal.

Neurobiology supports the existence of a genetically coded procedure for organizing spatial information

---

[14] Research with mice indicate that living in a miniature playground increases by 15% the number of brain cells in the hippocampus, the site for learning and memory reported in Gerd H. Kempermann, George Kuhn and Fred H. Gage (1997), "More hippocampal neurons in adult mice living in an enriched environment" (*Nature*, Vol. 386/Issue 6624, April 3, 1997, 493-95).

and demonstrates that this visual grammar provides the substructure for the verbal grammar we call language. Using both systems, visual and verbal, the human organism constructs its world.

If settling into states of minimal activity is desirable to the brain, as it is with other dynamic systems, then intelligible pictures and words must depend upon some level of neural resolution. Presumably, neural resolution occurs when information becomes orderly.

Drawing/Writing provides training in orderly searches for meaning. If the way in which stimuli are received affects brain organization, then an orderly, analytical whole-to-parts-to-whole approach will affect the brain's ability to categorize, organize and generalize information. If the search emphasizes relevant comparisons and logical relationships, the teaching strategy will prove challenging and rich.

The two hemispheres of the brain have evolved to specialize and to cooperate. The brain's predisposition to create orderly arrays from incoming stimuli exists at a level well below language. The whole brain cooperates to achieve spatial and linguistic meaning. In a literate mind, spatial and linguistic modes of thinking are differentiated and distinguishable, yet interdependent.

A painting is different from a book and a book is different from a painting, and yet many of the same mental skills are responsible for both modes of representation. Whether covertly or overtly, verbal thinking informs painting just as visualization informs verbal thought. What we observe on Paleolithic cave walls and on computer screens is the deliberate integration of pictures and words. This collaboration extends both modes of communication, revealing the transformational character of human symbolic thought. The combined results outstrip by light years what either mode could achieve alone. This is important information for education, design, the arts, the media and the marketplace.

## No Tidy Categories

This book falls into no tidy category. Research in neurobiology, physics, linguistics, psychology, art education, regular education, special education, art history, anthropology, computer science and artificial intelligence supports Drawing/Writing. The rationale for Drawing/Writing *is* this intertheoretic integration. Like brain processes, the rationale is layered. Each scholarly discipline provides an approximate explanation. Several explanations furnish richer understandings. Like the mirror in the Escher print, exchange is transformative. It

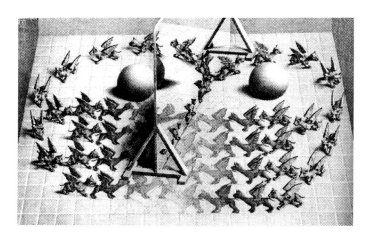

*"Magic Mirror" (c) 1966 by M.C. Escher. Reprinted by permission of Cordon Art - Baarn - Holland. All rights reserved.*

is in the aggregate that knowledge grows. As the transformational aspects of brain interrelationships come clear, a more literate and a more humane society becomes possible.

Reflecting brain development, the Drawing/Writing program unfolds organically and remains modifiable, meant to be shaped by teachers and students. Often, student input provides the catalyst for change. Like the relationship of intuition to invention, of parent to child, of teacher to student, the relationship between drawing and writing elicits a mutual exchange.

Teaching is a dynamic enterprise involving learners as well as teachers, and it calls for courage. Teachers most especially need to know that the outcome of their teaching—like chaos theory—is unstable and unpredictable, that learning happens on meandering paths as well as on highways, in little flickers as well as in crackling conflagrations. The only constant in teaching—as in the life of a healthy mind—is change and exchange. Classrooms are not meant to be static. Like the Drawing/Writing program, classrooms are meant to vibrate with energy.

✦ ✦ ✦ ✦ ✦ ✦ ✦ ✦ ✦ ✦ ✦ ✦ ✦ ✦

If you have read C.S. Lewis' book *The Lion, the Witch and the Wardrobe,* you will know what I mean when I say, "Aslan is on the move." If you have not read *The Narnia Chronicles,* understand that a movement for good is afoot where the intent is to benefit children.

Here and there, sequestered in unprepossessing locations and in obscure jobs, navigating largely alone, there are teachers who are determined to teach words so that they matter. There are teachers who are fighting—some with the last ounce of courage and strength—for literacy. In spite of nearly insuperable odds, there is a cadre of people who continue to care for the young. If these people join together in a concerted effort, it will be possible to avert the social tragedy of illiteracy. If we cannot avert this tragedy, there will be suffering the likes of which we have never seen. We cannot let this happen.

Aslan is on the move. *Believe it.*

*Aslan, silk screen, SR Sheridan, 1980*

# HOW TO DO IT

*Preliminary Drawing and Writing*

*Blind Contour*

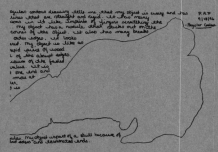

*Regular Contour*

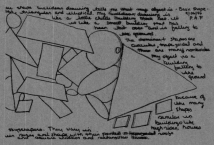

*Euclidean Basic Shapes*

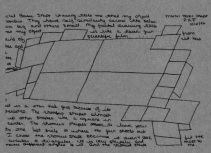

*Fractal Basic Shapes*

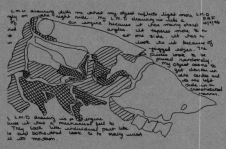

*LMD*

*"Perfect" Whole*

*CA #1*

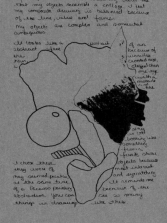

*CA #2*

*Closing Drawing and Writing*

*Pamela Frigo, Drawing/Writing, Jaw bone, Cow, Continuing Education, Westfield State College, 1996*

# PART TWO

*Step by Step Instructions*

# A User's Guide

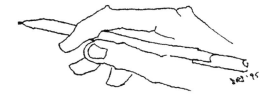

# HOW TO DO IT

The Dakota do not have a literal translation for the word art or artist.... *Wakahwayupike*, the word for artist, comes from wakaga, to make, form, cause to be or be the author of, to execute; and *wayupika*, to be expert, skillful, dexterous.

Yvonne Wynde, Sisseton-Wampetan art teacher, 1920-72
Museum of the American Indian, Battery Park, New York City

Drawing is the most universal human activity for organizing what we see. The visual grammar that allows simple marks to stand for complex visual information is already in our brain. It can be used to raise the level at which we can see and transcribe that experience.

Drawing is the principal means by which we organize the world visually. We use it to work out ideas of all sorts, collect information and analyse the way we see things in order to plan, instruct or speculate. Through drawing, we are led to 'see' and to understand.

Ron Bowen, *Drawing Master Class*

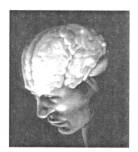

# Overview of the Five Steps

## Preliminary Drawing and Writing

To provide a pre-test sample for the evaluative tool Rescore, students draw their object for ten minutes and then write about it for ten minutes. They do this without any suggestions or instructions. In a multicultural classroom, students may do this preliminary writing in their own language with the understanding that they will have to translate this sample into English at their current skill level. After this preliminary step, all students must write in English. If skills in the target language are very weak, the student's mother tongue is used as a bridge into the new language. Starting with what students know is a cardinal constructivist rule. It is also sound neurobiology; the brain scaffolds new skills on existing structures.

In my experience, ten minutes is about the length of time most untrained students are productively able to draw or write about an object. Although students will be able to draw and write for longer periods of time after training in Drawing/Writing, the same ten minutes is allotted to the closing sample. The choice of a new object for the closing sample determines to what degree there has been a "transfer of skills." Skills learned by drawing a hammer, for instance, should transfer to a drawing of a geode. The goal of Drawing/Writing is the development

*Michael Cooper, Preliminary Drawing and Writing. corkscrew, Continuing Education, Westfield State College, 1996*

and transfer of thinking skills into other content areas and into life beyond the classroom.

Michael Cooper plays bass guitar in a rock band and teaches in a technical school. He wrote, " I wish I could give more on how it really is through my eyes. Not similar, but good! If or when things progress I might be more strong about my work. I think the ideas are good but my skills lack."

## Step One: Warm-up Exercises, Blind Contour and Regular Contour

The warm-up exercises are based on research with feral children and blind language learners, as well as on information about Chinese teaching methods for writing. Empirical observation with young Drawing/Writing students contributes to these warm-up exercises, too.

Touch helped children raised by animals in the wild—feral children—raised without early language learning, to speak. Touch helps the deaf to make spoken sounds and touch helps the blind to read. Young Chinese students first draw calligraphic figures in the air with their arms and bodies. They trace the broad gesture of the character. Then, they learn to write the character. This gestural exploration introduces the Drawing/Writing student to the shape of the object, too.

First, Drawing/Writing students close their eyes and touch the object. Next, students stand and gesture the shape of their objects in the air. Then, they trace the object on a piece of paper, literally feeling their way around the object, learning it by touch. Touch is a direct, early and natural way to know about things. As babies, our sight is highly informed by touch, but we lose track of touch when we enter school. Drawing/Writing reintroduces direct touch to knowledge.

The warm-up exercises are followed by the first drawing exercise. This outline drawing, called the "Blind Contour," establishes the critical distinction between "figure" and "ground." "Figure" stands for the subject in a work of art, and "ground" stands for the space around it. The Blind Contour drawing provides practice in this distinction, which is in itself practice for defining the scope of a subject, creating a boundary between what will be studied and what will not be studied. Making a Blind Contour drawing is analogous to defining a research topic.

This drawing is "blind" in the sense that the student looks at the object and not at the paper. In this way the student is forced to observe the object carefully, without assumptions. The line drawing and any subsequent writing about it will be based on direct observation, not on guessing, incomplete memories or vague associations.

moment in the life of the fruit, or time of day, or even the emotional life of the artist. An apple that is red at noon may be blue at dawn. In the case of the Blind Contour drawing, students focus on line quality alone. The outline of the object carries a tremendous amount of information. Depending upon how the student places the object, very different shapes and profiles emerge. Think about drawing a wood plane head on; you could be drawing a semi-circle, a series of tiny vertical lozenges, a very narrow, horizontal rectangular plate, two narrow, upright, elongated triangles sitting above a very small, central semi-circle, sitting on a slender horizontal rectangular plane.

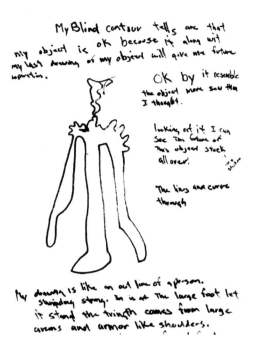

Michael Cooper, Blind Contour drawing of the cork-screw, Continuing Education, Westfield State College, 1996

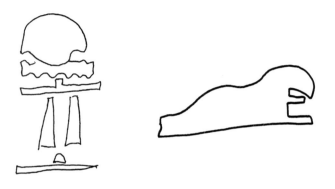

Sketch, plane, head on, profile, SRS

Michael wrote, "My Blind Contour tells me that my object is OK because along with my last drawing it will give me future information. It resembles the object more than I thought. I can see the future of this object stuck all over! The lines curve through. My drawing is like an outline of a person standing strong. The large foot lets it stand. The strength comes from the large arms and armor-like shoulders. The head of the object has facial features of hair, forehead, nose, lips and chin as in a side view."

A goal in Drawing/Writing is learning how to see accurately and thoroughly. Careful scrutiny of "what is there" is part of learning. Through careful seeing, the mind learns *not* to rely on old assumptions or irrelevant bits of information or guesses, but to explore a subject with full attention. For instance, it is inaccurate to assume that apples are red, bananas are yellow and trees are green. Color may be determined by time, or a

From the side, a wave-like shape sprouts a cobra-like hood which nearly touches a bottlecap-like section above a slender disk, screwed to a vertical trapezoid.

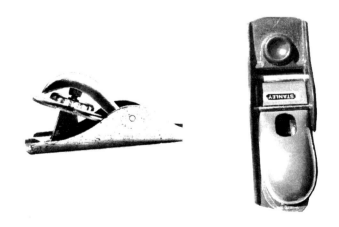

Photo of wood plane, in profile and from above, SR Sheridan, 1997

As students construct a clearer picture of their objects through the Drawing/Writing program, they make associations. Michael Cooper compares the outline of his object to an armored man with one large stabilizing foot. Associations are only as strong as the observations on which they are built. The Blind Contour drawing supports the future construction of the fully realized drawing just as framing supports a building. The ability to recognize what is and what is not the subject of an information search is an important skill.

The next Drawing/Writing step reinforces this skill by asking students to describe the physical characteristics of the Blind Contour line. From whatever angle the student chooses to draw the object, this Blind Contour line describes the object's exterior, providing information on the physical properties of that outer edge or surface. The student writes, "My Blind Contour drawing tells me that my object is straight, curving, bumpy, jumpy, jagged, smooth...." These words describe some of the characteristics of a drawn line.

After the student writes about the physical characteristics of the outline drawing, he or she is asked to look at the line drawing in a new way from any angle. A freely associated image will pop into the student's head. The teacher asks the student to write a simile based on that free association. Looking at his Blind Contour drawing, a student may see a pterodactyl. The student writes, "My Blind Contour drawing of garden shears looks like a pterodactyl because the blades of the shears are like long, skeletal wings." The word "because" forces students to explain the simile. The simple word "because" provides a cognitive nudge from the nest, encouraging fledgling logic systems.

From the beginning, the Drawing/Writing program encourages logical associations while teaching students to move from rigorous description of the physical world of tangible appearances to equally rigorous associations. Each additional step in the Drawing/Writing five-step adds new kinds and levels of analyses to the brain's mental repertoire, while structuring neural capabilities at the same time.

With every step, the Drawing/Writing teacher promotes student discussion through questioning. A Socratic approach continues throughout the program. In connection with the first step, the teacher asks: What is the purpose of the Blind Contour drawing? Students realize through discussion that the contour line creates a boundary between what is and what is not the subject of inquiry. Questions encourage the construction of knowledge.

The Blind Contour drawing is followed by the Regular Contour drawing; the student looks at both the object and the paper. Spatial relations become more accurate. The work continues to be done with markers, heightening the visual effect of the work. Psychologically, the use of markers encourages risk-taking behavior, commitment, and courage.

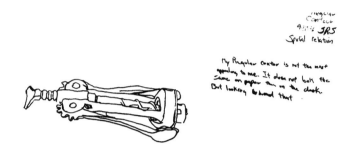

*Michael Cooper's Regular Contour drawing, corkscrew, 1997*
*(Michael did not yet understand contour drawing. He is anticipating basic shapes. The work shows accurate observational skills.)*

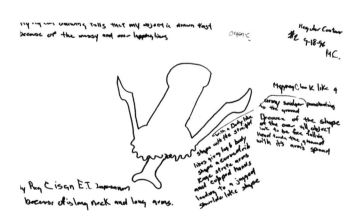

*Michael Cooper's second Regular Contour, extra, Continuing Education, Westfield State College, 1996*
*(Completed when he understood contour drawing)*

After his second attempt at the Regular Contour drawing, Michael wrote, "My Regular Contour drawings tells me that my object is drawn fast because of the messy and over-lapping lines. My Reg. C is an E.T. impersonation because of its long neck and long arms. It has a body-like shape with straight lines giving legs to body shape, a curved rib, huge straight arms and cupped hands leading to a jagged shoulder-like shape. My Reg c. looks like an army soldier parachuting to the ground because the shape of the overall object appears to be free-falling, head towards the ground with its arms spread."

Michael wrote, "My Regular contour is not the most appealing to me. It does not look the same on paper as on the desk. But looking beyond that...." Michael did not finish his sentence. The contour drawing is accurate. One wonders why Michael was dissatisfied with it. One thing is certain: his mind is growing in entirely self-directed ways.

Note that Drawing/Writing students will reflect on the process of drawing, as well as on the quality of their work. They may find the process challenging and their work inadequate. As students' observation skills and patience increase, negative comments turn into critical analyses.

### Step Two: Basic Shapes

Step Two of the Drawing/Writing program is called Basic Shapes. Students look at their objects and re-draw them as geometric shapes. While the Contour drawing provides practice in establishing outlines and boundaries, Basic Shapes drawings provide practice in form and structure. The word "basic" suggests "simple," or "fundamental." Students break the object into—or build the object from—a series of geometric shapes. First, they use Euclidean geometry, then fractal geometry. Squares and triangles are part of the language of Euclidean geometry. Self-similar shapes characterize fractal drawings; otherwise, there are no rules for the shapes employed.

Michael wrote, "My Euclidean BS drawing tells me that my object is full of semi-circles, circles, triangles, rhombuses, rectangles and trapezoids. The object is a shattered toy gun because of the overall shapes of where all the Euclidean shapes lie. The object looked shattered because the shapes do not touch and have no connection." Note Michael's jump into metaphor. Note also how the word "because" forces increasing precision with language.

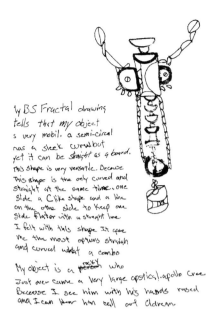

*Michael Cooper's Fractal Basic Shape drawing of a corkscrew, Continuing Education, Westfield State College, 1996*

Michael then wrote, "My Fractal BS drawing tells me that my object is very mobile. A semi-circle has a sleek curve but yet it can be straight as a board. This shape is very versatile because this shape is curved and straight at the same time. One side is a C-like shape with a line on the other side to keep one side flatter. I felt this shape gave me the most options: straight and curved, what a combo. My object is a person who just overcame a very large obstacle because I can see him with his hands raised and I can hear him call out a dream."

Inga Small wrote, "My fractal basic shape drawing tells me my object is very bat-like, because the shapes that I filled the inside with have horns and structures that

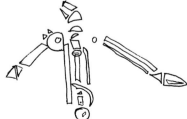

*Michael Cooper's Euclidean Basic Shape drawing of a corkscrew, Continuing Education, Westfield State College, 1996*

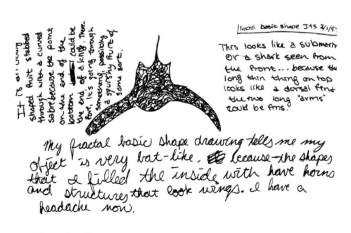

*Inga Small, Fractal Basic Shape drawing of a vertebra, 14 years old, Amherst Middle School, 1997*

look like wings. I have a headache now. It is an oddly shaped fruit stabbed through with a curved sabre because the point on the end of the bottom could be the end of a knife. Therefore, it's going through something, possibly a squishy fruit of some sort. This looks like a submarine or a shark seen from the front because the long thin thing on top looks like a dorsal fin and the two long 'arms' could be fins."

Part of the theory undergirding Drawing/Writing is that thought is naturally multi-modal: note how Michael hears and sees his metaphor. Another part of the theory is that concrete thinking and abstract thinking are related enterprises and that the move between them is not made in one direction only. The mind moves back and forth between concrete models and abstract theories: between a person and, in Michael's case, a dream. The ways in which we learn to construct and manipulate physical models—either two-dimensional models (drawing, painting, collage, print-making, graphing, photography, computer-simulation and manipulation) or three-dimensional models (sculpture, holographs, Fourier transformations, MRIs, dance, theater, snap-on chemical models, Julian Fleron's wood and wire models describing

calculus functions)—determine how we will be able to think about ideas. The ability to move between concrete models and abstract theories constitutes intelligent thought. Julian's three-dimensional models expand. The Harvard Consortium's Rule of Four (Smith, 1994) to a Rule of Five; not only do Fleron's students describe calculus problems using written language, algebra, graphs and numbers, they also explore calculus problems tactilely using physical models.

Evolutionary theorist Stephen Jay Gould observed that both artists and scientists use form and structure in problem-solving. For instance, the biologist Jim Watson, of Crick and Watson fame, extrapolated the formal structure of the genetic code by constructing a 3-D model of a double helix. Through a Tinker Toy-like model, Watson better understood the chemical sequence of DNA. Gould writes, "Watson succeeded by hard work and false starts, all guided, step by step, through an artist's central vision that we live, at all scales, in a universe of structure".[15] He quotes Jim Watson's comment about the physical model of the double helix, "A structure as pretty as this just has to exist." A "pretty" physical model guided an elegant theory. By combining an aesthetic intuition about a model with a theoretical conviction, Jim Watson was able to extend his thinking.

"The Deck"                          "The Loaf"

"The sliding cube on a wire"

Photo, Julian Fleron, Mathematics professor,
Westfield State College, with his models of calculus functions,
photo SR Sheridan, 1996

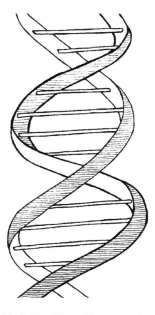

The double helix, Claus Kormannshaus, BA,
Westfield State, MAT candidate, 1997

---

[15] Stephen Jay Gould, "The Shape of Life," The Art Journal, Vol. 55, No. 1, pps. 44-46, 1996.

Basic Shape drawings provide practice in two-dimensional model-building, mobilizing the strategies of the artist/scientist. Compared to the spareness of the contour line drawings, Basic Shape drawings are complex and beautiful. They allow students to conduct formal inquiries using elegant forms.

Young students can be taught how to construct theoretical understandings in a variety of physical ways through drawing. They may wonder about the relationships among different systems of geometry as well as the connections between geometry, art and science. They may ponder the distinctions between the real and the ideal. For instance, does the idea of a triangle exist independent of actual triangles? These questions are not too sophisticated for young learners; speculations like these excite the mind. It is easy to open students' minds through geometry. A Euclidean triangle, for instance, when used in a Koch Curve (see figure below), is a step toward a circle. Once a triangle is rotated around a point or is used to decorate itself at intervals, the connections between circles and triangles becomes clear. These kinds of startling relationships attract children's attention and engage them in the overall enterprise of learning as well as in the specific fields of mathematics and geometry.

*The Triadic Koch curve, courtesy of the author Benoit C. Mandelbrot, from THE FRACTAL GEOMETRY OF NATURE, (c) 1977. All rights reserved*

A snowflake may not actually be made of triangles, and a curve may not actually consist of straight lines. But a curve may be approximated using straight lines, and a snowflake can be built from triangles. Using triangles to create a circle opens the mind to the interchangeability of forms, and, by extension, to the fluidity and plasticity of meaning. Shapes are malleable and transformational. So are words.

Practice with Euclidean and non-Euclidean geometry provides several ways of looking at structure—from snowflakes to brains. Fractal geometry expands our understanding of geometry, providing more descriptions of form. Euclidean geometry and fractal geometry are partial explanations. Instead of "rightness" and "wrongness," we can learn through the study of geometry to accept or reject explanations for their completeness, their elegance

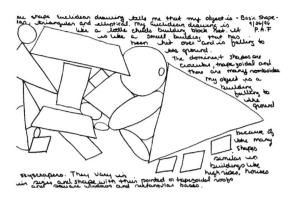

*Basic Shape Euclidean drawing, cow skull, Pamela Frigo, Continuing Education, Westfield State, 1996*

and for their applicability. The most powerful explanations often include several ways of looking at things.

Guidelines for exploring a series of explanation systems—like fractal geometry—are provided in this book. The journeys of discovery will differ from teacher to teacher and from student to student. One aspect of the journey will remain constant: the usefulness of drawing to thought. The art historian and critic E.H. Gombrich states that the tools we use to draw determine how we see; even if we use the same tools, our individual visions will vary. Each artist decides how much of his actual observations to layer over stored formulae. "The familiar will always remain the likely starting point for rendering the unfamiliar.... You cannot create a faithful image out of nothing".[16] The schemata we store and the models we use influence how we see and how we represent new information. By introducing students to several approaches to geometry, we broaden their range of tools and, thereby, their vision.

### Step Three: Light-Medium-Dark

In the LMD drawing, light, is the distinguishing element. To simplify an object in terms of one element without losing its identity is a challenging exercise.

The Basic Shape drawing paves the way for the Light-Medium-Dark, or LMD drawing. As students draw basic shapes, their minds, at least subliminally, are aware of the shapes created by lights and darks. Learning how to see lights and shadows and to reproduce them is one of the tricks of illusionary drawing. How to recognize the obvious while attending to the subtle is a useful transferable skill.

---

[16]E.H. Gombrich, *Art & Illusion, A Study in the Psychology of Pictorial Representation* pps. 113-114, 1956.

In art studio terms, light and dark have "value." The side of an apple on which the sun shines has a certain value of light; the side of the apple away from the sun has a certain value of shadow. The area in between is said to have "middle" value. These areas of light, dark and middle value are determined by the eye. A value drawing using markers is "hard-edged." The outline of each value is sharp and clear. A value drawing using pencil or charcoal can be soft-edged if the transitions between values are smudged. Because the LMD drawing is done with markers, it is hard-edged. It is a natural follow-up to the hard-edged, marker-drawn Basic Shape drawing.

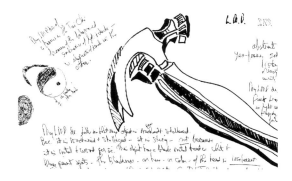

*SR Sheridan, LMD hammer drawing, 1996.*

For the LMD exercise—if possible—the teacher turns out the artificial lights. Students place their objects where the natural light strikes them. Then, using squinting as a filtering technique, students figure out exactly where an object is highlighted and where it is dark; the area in between is the middle value. The LMD drawing teaches students how to filter out extraneous information, recognizing strong contrasts and subtle distinctions.

The brain filters information constantly. Because we cannot pay attention to everything, our brains select and prioritize. If it did not, we would be overwhelmed. Culture and experience train our brains to "squint." Squinting is a filtering technique that blurs outlines, texture and form, making lights and darks obvious.

*Elizabeth Wright's LMD drawing of cow horn, 7 years old, Wildwood School, Amherst and Santa Fe, NM,1997*

Elizabeth wrote, "My LMD drawing tells me that my object is mostly dark when I squint my eyes because the lit is bonsing on the tip and it lands on the midel in an ovel shap. And the lit is shing down like it is coming from heven."

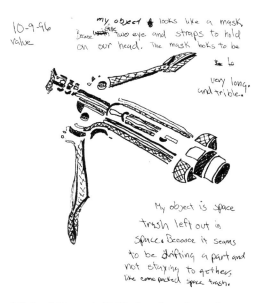

*Michael Cooper's LMD drawing of a corkscrew, Continuing Education, Westfield State College, 1996*

Continuing Education student, Michael Cooper, wrote, "My LMD drawing tells me that my object looks like a mask because of the two eyes and straps to hold it on our head. The mask looks to be very long and terrible. The LMD drawing is space trash because it seems to be drifting apart and not staying together like compacted space trash." Notice that Michael does not comment on light reflectivity and materials; he moves directly to simile.

*Leslie Arak, LMD, ice skate, 14 years old, Amherst home schooler, 1997*

Leslie Arak wrote, "My LMD drawing tells me that my object is smooth and shiny over most of the surface because there are large patches of light or medium over the curved bits. This looks like a mountain with snow and large patches of evergreens." Leslie connects the shapes and amounts of light with surface texture and materials.

Students learn to identify highlights and deep shadows and to reproduce a range of values. The Drawing/Writing rule for representing middle value is that all shapes with that value are represented by the same pattern; for instance, a student may choose parallel lines or cross-hatching to fill in the shape of the middle value. The student could choose to represent a range of middle values by adopting a range of intervals between dots or parallel lines.

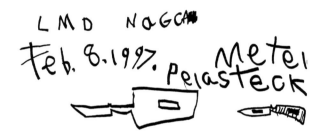

*Nathan Gorlin Crenshaw, LMD of a potato peeler, 6 years old, 1997*

Nate Gorlin Crenshaw wrote, "Metela, pelasteck."

*Maria Grigoryeva's LMD of a dried pomegranate, 14 years old, Amherst Middle School, 1997*

Maria Grigoryeva wrote, "My LMD tells me that my object is darkest on its bottom left side because that is where my darkest values are. It also tells me that my object is rather matte (using a new word, expanding my vocabulary; mom would be so proud)."

Students learn to value filtering. In addition to learning a drawing technique called chiaroscuro, or light/dark rendering, students are learning to distinguish the dramatic from the subtle. This analytical skill will prove useful in studying literature as well as in evaluating media events, like political speeches.

### Step Four: The "Perfect" Whole

For Step 4, the "Perfect" Whole, students switch from markers to pencils. Pencils have two special advantages besides erasability: the lead creates soft transitions between values, and erasers can be used for "lift-off," creating accents of light in the midst of a darkened area.

The quotation marks around the word "perfect" are ironic. Ten years' experience proves that even very young students know that no drawing is perfect. They easily understand that this drawing is "perfect" in terms of completeness, not flawlessness. The idea of perfection as flawlessness is daunting. Trying to create a perfect drawing is an unachievable goal. On the other hand, achieving a more or less complete drawing is possible. Drawing the "Perfect" Whole teaches students that they are responsible for deciding when a drawing or a piece of writing is complete. Step 4 encourages experiments with freedom and choice while avoiding the pitfalls of rigid expectations about excellence.

Students are urged to look carefully at the surface of their objects for details to add texture to their drawings. Step 4 brings together what students know about line, form, and value. Because it is both inclusive and accurate, the drawing looks "real." Students appreciate the fact that their "Perfect" Whole drawing will include elements another student might omit, and that every drawing, no matter how detailed, remains approximate.

Michael wrote, "My 'Perfect' Whole drawing tells me to slow down and check size, shape and angle of my object. My object could be used with a fine wine, served with chicken amaretto by candle light."

Kimberly Deverry, another Continuing Education student, wrote, "My PW tells me that my object has two parallel sides and that its form can be represented by Euclidean shapes. The lines are in varying thicknesses and spacing to produce tonal qualities. My PWD is like a family measuring rod because each line represents a hope, fear, creation, expiration, exhilaration, declamation, gift, rift etched into the surface."

*size, shape and angle of my object. Similar is basic size and shape but warped and stretch. My object could be involved in a fine wine to could be served with a surprise chicken amaretto sunset by candle light.*

*Michael Cooper's "Perfect" Whole drawing of a corkscrew, Continuing Education, Westfield State College, 1996*

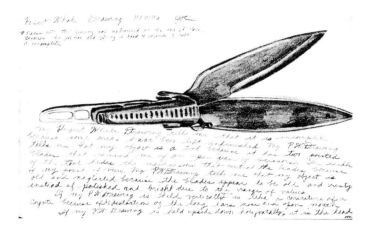

*Joanne Krawczyk, PW drawing of garden shears, Westfield State College, Cont. Ed., 1996*

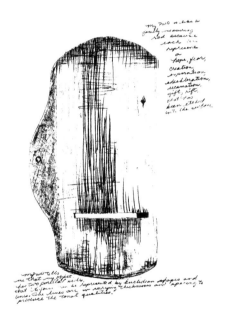

*Kimberly DeVerry, "Perfect" Whole drawing of a wood plane, bottom view, Continuing Education, Westfield State College, 1996*

Because no drawing is ever complete, students who draw the "Perfect" Whole learn that no drawing skills, even photographically accurate skills, record all available information. Drawing requires selection and therefore elimination, or editing skills. A drawing is as complete as the artist's skills and choices allow.

Joanne Krawczyk wrote, "My PWD tells me that it is incomplete because some areas have been left unfinished. My PWD tells me that my object is a tool because it has two pointed blades that remind me of an open pair of scissors. The handle of the tool hides the mechanisms that control the blades. My PWD tells me that my object is old and neglected because, due to their (low) range of

values, the blades appear to be rusty instead of polished and bright. If my PWD is held vertically, it is like a caricature of a coyote because of the distortion of the long ears, nose and open mouth. If my PWD is held upside down horizontally, it is the head of the famous pair of crows from the well-known Heckle and Jeckle cartoon series because of the exaggerated open beak and the misplaced, comical eyeball at the top end of the bill. There is also a pencil mark towards the tip which resembles an (air?) hole typically found on birds' beaks."

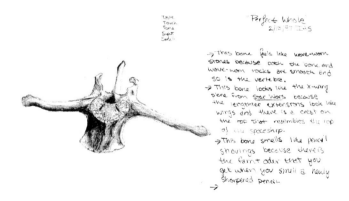

*Inga Small, age 14, Amherst Middle School, PW drawing of a vertebra, 1997*

Inga Small wrote, "This bone feels like wave-worn stones because both the bone and wave-worn rocks are smooth and so is the vertebra. This bone looks like the x-wing plane from *Star Wars* because the lengthier extensions look like wings and there is a crest on the top that resembles the top of the spaceship. This bone smells like pencil shavings because there is the faint odor that you get when you smell a newly sharpened pencil."

The goal in the "Perfect" Whole drawing is to include enough detail to suggest the illusion of the object as fully three-dimensional and *trompe l'oeil*, or "fool-the-eye"-real. By Step 4, students' drawing skills are equal to the challenge of optical realism just as their writing skills are equal to the challenge of the expository essay. At this stage of the program, increased drawing and writing skills fine-tune attention and boost confidence, making it possible to present a considerable number of writing exercises at this time. Some of these include similes, metaphors, analogies, predictions, and hypotheses constructed on concrete and abstract levels.

Equipped with a range of verbal strategies, students learn to construct increasingly rigorous explanations. Because these constructions are abstract as well as concrete and negative as well as positive, students' minds are stretched and challenged. When a student writes, "My object smells like dust because it reminds me of the choking dryness of the attic," the student has constructed a statement in a positive mode. When the student writes, "My object does not smell like dust because, although it reminds me of the dry, choking atmosphere in the attic, it also smells faintly like sand, which I associate with the dampness of the beach," the statement is negative, requiring more extensive justification. Forced to justify their verbal constructions, students may discover one apt explanation that edges out all the others.

By placing a premium on personal decision-making, the "Perfect" Whole encourages tolerance. It becomes clear in group critiques that each "Perfect" Whole drawing is different not only in content but in *emphasis* from other drawings. Each drawing is as complete *as it needs to be* to represent that object *for that student*. Because each student knows that all Drawing/Writing students go through the same comprehensive analyses, all Drawing/Writing solutions are respected.

Contemporary calculus education expects students to express problems using four explanation systems: words, arithmetic, algebra, and graphs. Drawing/Writing trains students to use two explanation systems—one visual (drawing) and one verbal system (writing)—to express meaning. Two is better than one. More are even better!

## Step Five: The Composite Abstraction

Step Five provides a procedure for abstraction. To create a Composite Abstraction, students examine all of their drawings from Steps 1-4. The floor may be the only surface large enough for these displays. Choosing one part from each drawing, students recombine them in any way they choose to, creating a new whole. The instructions for the CA are:

- choose one element from each drawing
- recombine these elements
- *at any scale*
- with or without overlappings
- using any media
- in a way that does not look like the original object.

The criteria for choice include aesthetics and accuracy. There are no instructions or constraints on the writing except that it must spring from the drawing.

While the optically accurate "Perfect" Whole drawing is like a descriptive essay or an instruction manual, the Composite Abstraction is like a poem or a theory—minimal, metaphorical and essential. This student-created transitional visual "language" has profound implications. The CA is the "cognitive kicker" of the Drawing/Writing program.

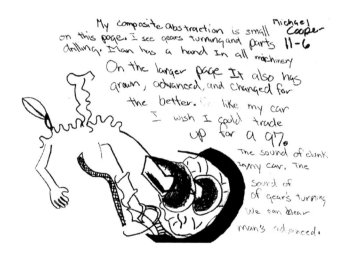

*Michael Cooper, CA of the corkscrew, Continuing Education, Westfield, State College, 1996*

Michael wrote, "My CA is small. I see gears turning and parts drilling. Man has a hand in all machinery. My object has grown, advanced and changed for the better. Like my car I wish I could trade up for a '97. The sound of clunk in my car. The sound of gears turning. We can hear man's advance."

Even though the CA is composed of parts of previous drawings, the CA does not look like the object any more. Students understand that the CA still *stands* for the object. As Eric Soderstrom's writing makes clear, this abstract drawing is fully intelligible to him.

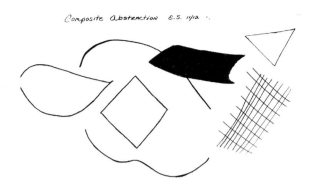

*Eric Soderstrom, CA of a hacky sack, 1996*

Eric wrote, "My CA is a collection of lines and shapes most appealing to me from my drawings. Every line and shape shows true meaning, such as the triangle in the corner that depicts how a hack is an inter-changeably-shaped object. My CA drawing tells me I'm in a maze because I'm walking around in my drawing. I lie in a field looking up at clouds as a skyscraper leaves its mark. I travel down a long and winding road, walking happily and peacefully. Taking in every little bit of nature as I go. The road ends...in the distance I see a tidal wave of water crashing towards me. I grab a surfboard and lie patiently waiting for the onslaught of wetness. Hitting me like a ton of bricks I fly towards the sky. Free-falling I watch birds soar by. Plunging into the deep dark waters my arms and legs get wrapped up in seaweed drowning me. Entrapped forever under the sea the creatures get a treat. My soul is beginning to see the light as I reach the stars." Eric is a songwriter. His CA's provided some lyrics.

The writing that accompanies the CA is different from other writing in the program. It tends toward the philosophical and lyrical. The visual recombination provides cues which may seem removed from the original object. Because the drawing is abstract, the writing that accompanies the CA is unpredictable. Still, as the drawing carries hints of the object, so does the writing. Exercises in Part Two in connection with the CA bring these persisting connections to the surface in an exercise called Referential Writing.

The compositional elements of color, line, form and space can be manipulated to achieve the "right relationships" which are the hallmarks of a successful design. In Drawing/Writing, instructions for creating right relationships are simple: "neither too much nor too little." These criteria make sense to students.

The CA is refined in the following way: Student #1, Jessica, holds up the Composite Abstraction of student #2, Sam, and then slowly rotates it. When a drawing is

rotated so that the top no longer remains the top, nor the bottom the bottom, nor the side the side, Sam sees his work in new ways. Jessica directs Sam to look for places in the drawing where there is too much or too little: too many lines, too little form, too much color. This can also mean too much or too little positive space or too much or too little negative space. She tells him to signal by nodding when he has decided what needs doing: at that signal, she stops rotating his drawing. After nodding, Sam takes a new piece of paper and starts the second CA, using the first for reference.

Sam is now free to achieve an even more successful design. He can add, he can subtract, he can distort or embellish. With his CA drawing turned upside down, Sam no longer sees a hint of his object. Neither a pair of garden shears nor a pterodactyl remain. Sam is free, now, to focus on pure design, engaging in new levels of analysis, working directly with the formal elements of composition. The work is abstract. There is no objective content—no horse, no child. Still, the eye can get stuck if the artist persists in seeing the work as solved just because it is "right side up." When turned upside down, the composition will most probably present additional problems. When working with objective art—images of horses, children—it is even more important to rotate an image to get away from narrative content in order to see how the formal elements are actually working together.

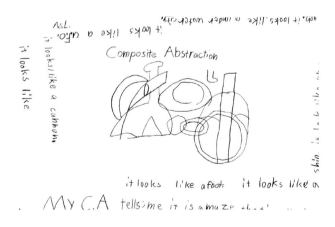

*Andrew Lai's CA#1 of glass bottle, second grade, Applewide School, 1997*

Andrew Lai wrote about CA#1, "My CA tells me it is a maze that is almost impossible. It is a fire hidrint. It looks like a sea dragon. It looks like a under water city. It looks like a UFO and it looks like a cannon."

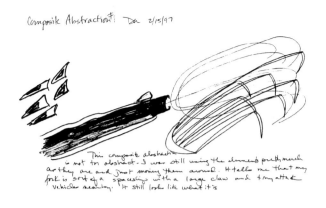

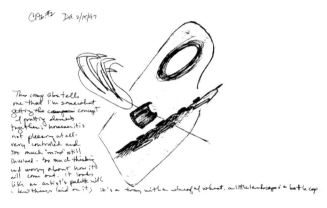

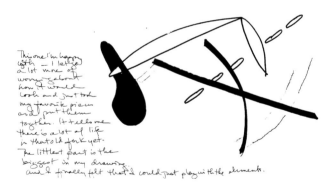

*Deborah Arak, CA#1, CA#2, CA#3, mother, businesswoman, Amherst, 1997*

Deborah Arak, my neighbor, a parent, gardener and co-owner with her husband of a telemarketing business, wrote:

#1 "This composite abstraction is not too abstract. I was still using the elements pretty much as they are and just moving them around. It tells me that my fork is sort of a spaceship with a large claw [with] my attack vehicles nearby. It still looks like what it is."

#2 "This CA tells me that I'm somewhat getting the concept of putting elements together; however, it is not pleasing at all—very controlled and too much mind still

involved—too much thinking and worrying about how it will come out. It looks like an artist's palette with a few things laid on it; it's a tray with a sheaf of wheat, a little landscape and a bottle cap."

#3 "This one I'm happy with—I let go a lot more of worry about how it would look and just took my favorite pieces and put them together. It tells me there's alot of life in that old fork yet. The littlest part is the biggest in my drawing, and I finally felt that I could just play in the elements."

Deborah's son, Jefferson, drew and wrote the following about a child's leather boot:

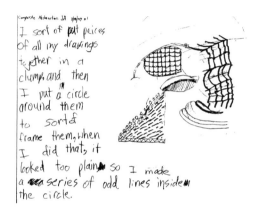

*Jefferson Arak, age 11, CA #1 and #2, Wildwood School, Amherst,1997*

About the CA#1, Jefferson wrote, "I sort of put pieces of all my drawings together in a clump, and then I put a circle around them to sort of frame them, when I did that, it looked too plain, so I made a series of odd lines inside the circle."

For his CA#2, Jefferson wrote, "I changed my abstraction to this because I thought that the (here Jefferson copies one of the wavy lines) sort of looked like water, and so I put it at the top and I put the other objects in the 'water,' like fish or something."

# Drawing/Writing: Before You Start

## LAYOUT

The layout for Part 2 differs from Parts 1, 3 and 4. In Part 2, the righthand and lefthand pages are both one-column rather than two. The righthand pages include "need to know" information and "need to do" instructions. The lefthand pages provide optional information, as well as a place for practicing the steps or taking notes.

The headings on the righthand pages include "BACKGROUND," "TIP" (useful in preventing misunderstandings), "DO," "SAY," "DEMONSTRATE," "ASK," "RECORD," "SET UP," "REHASH," "HOMEWORK," "DISCUSSION," "PEER SHARE AND BUILD," and "CRITIQUES." Each item has its own icon.

Terms on the lefthand pages include: "REMINDER/REMEMBER," "ADDITIONAL INFORMATION," and "ASIDES" (philosophical asides). Reminders provide encouragement while philosophical asides describe some of the deeper implications of the Drawing/Writing program.

The terms "SAY/DO" and "DEMONSTRATE/DO" identify the steps for the reader who is teaching him/herself Drawing/Writing as opposed to the longer list of steps provided for the classroom teacher.

There is space on the lefthand pages for teachers and other readers to try out Drawing/Writing exercises. There is also room to record comments about student work or one's own work. If you wish to share any of these comments, send them to one of the Drawing/Writing addresses.

The Drawing/Writing program includes five steps. Step 1 is outline drawing. Step 2 is shape drawing. Step 3 is shaded drawing. Step 4 is fully rendered, 3-D, shaded drawing. Step 5 is abstract drawing. The five steps take approximately two weeks to cover. As second grade teacher Joanne Quail observes, "Then, you're done."

Each step lasts as long as the time available. In most schools, this will mean between forty or fifty minutes. If your school has block scheduling, you are in an ideal position to teach Drawing/Writing. If you are home-schooling, allow 60 to 90 minutes per step, depending upon your students. If you are self-teaching, use whatever time you have.

It is important to follow the five steps in order. The five steps have been designed as a sequence. Seventeen years of teaching Drawing/Writing confirm the logical unfolding of these five steps. They are constructivist; in a Piagetian sense, each step builds upon the previous one, encouraging increasingly complex organization of visual and verbal information.

*Layout of Parts 1, 3, 4 and 2*

## THE SKILLS LEARNED:

Drawing/Writing trains students to see and to draw more accurately. Because the writing that follows each drawing step refers directly to the drawing, observational skills are transfered to writing, forcing it to be both descriptive and analytical. Because this writing requires simile, metaphor, analogy, prediction and hypothesis, this writing extends the information in the drawing. The more accurately and comprehensively students learn to see and to draw and to write, the more accurately and comprehendingly they will read. Encoding and decoding skills are connected.

Students who practice Drawing/Writing learn five specific drawing strategies. Each drawing strategy is a larger skill transferable to writing and other kinds of thinking like mathematics or design, journalism or marketing. The five steps build skills and information incrementally. Each drawing provides one way to represent the object visually and to think about the information that object carries. First, Drawing/Writing students draw an outline. Toward the end of the five-step process, students are able to produce a fully rendered or "realistic" drawing because they have the skills and the information to achieve a complex representation.

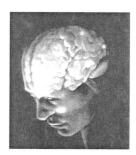

The writing that follows each drawing step depends upon it for information. Each piece of writing builds on the previous piece, too. As the Blind Contour is followed by the Regular Contour, so descriptive writing is followed by simile, metaphor, analogy and hypothesis. Both sets of work—the drawing and the reflective writing—are cumulative, increasingly complete and refined.

The skills learned through the drawing steps are general discrimination skills applicable to visual information or to verbal information. Information is unmanageable until it is categorized and named. Categories can be organized in a variety of ways. In Drawing/Writing, the eye learns to make discriminatory decisions in the context of certain visual categories: line weight, quality of line, direction and shape of line, overall shape of the object, how light strikes and defines an object, how surface texture defines an object. In Drawing/Writing, the discriminatory eye selects specfic details to construct a coherent, persuasive whole. By adding writing, the eye moves away from that unique, single representation to more general categories provided by the dynamics of simile and metaphor.

The five-step Drawing/Writing program teaches students to work with information, incrementally and globally, in brain-like ways. Students learn to:

- work from the visual to the verbal
- work from the simple to the complex
- work from the specific to the general
- work from the concrete to the abstract,

and to:

- describe
- analyze and
- infer.

The Drawing/Writing goal is establishing this procedure as a routine approach to managing information. Students are taught to work visually, then verbally, to proceed from simple observations to more complicated observations, to work with real physical objects before generating ideas and theories, and, above all, to tackle every available bit of information before coming to any conclusions.

## STEP BY STEP THINKING SKILLS:

- The Contour drawing teaches students to draw the outline of an object. By doing so, they create what is called a figure/ground distinction, learning to define the boundaries of a piece of information and to reproduce an accurate outline of the subject matter.

- The Basic Shapes drawing teaches students to describe the overall shape of an object using Euclidean and non-Euclidean geometry, applying a range of explanations to the overall structure of a piece of information.

- The Light-Medium-Dark (LMD) drawing teaches students to see shades, or values, and then to produce a chiaroscuro or light/dark drawing which is optically convincing because it looks three-dimensional. The student learns to identify obvious and subtle details and to select details relevant to a compelling presentation of information.

- The "Perfect" Whole drawing teaches students to draw an accurately outlined, accurately formed, fully detailed, shaded, optically convincing drawing. The general mental skill in this case is learning how to construct a coherent, cogent, fully developed knowledge base, including enough details to flesh out the knowledge base adequately and compellingly.

- The Composite Abstraction (CA) teaches students to create an abstract drawing by combining and reorganizing sections of the first four drawings. Students practice selecting, reorganizing and redefining information for the sake of producing a new solution. The new kind of thinking is described as "recombinant." Because the abstract drawing no longer looks like the object, students who practice the CA ready themselves for the abstract marks we call writing and mathematics.

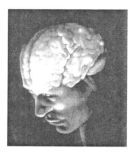

**First Philosophical Aside:** The Drawing/Writing process is Socratic. Socrates was a philosopher born in Athens in 469 b.c. e. His father was a sculptor and his mother was a midwife. Socrates' wisdom lay in the recognition of his ignorance. By convincing others of their ignorance, he encouraged them to seek knowledge and goodness. Socrates made an important contribution to logic. The word "adduction" comes from the Latin prefix ad meaning "to" or "toward" and the Latin verb duco meaning "to lead." Adduction leads the mind toward an answer in a certain way (Tredenick, 1959). This certain way for Socrates was through direct and persistent questioning. For instance, when a term like "courage" cropped up, Socrates asked what it meant; as the answers accumulated, each unsatisfactory in itself, Socrates proceeded to adduce certain shared characteristics from the various suggestions. This compilation of common characteristics became the definition of courage. This position on language and meaning is similar to that of Alfred J. Korzybski who felt that words are useful—and healthy—as layered, relative entities. Only through verbal negotiations does agreement about meaning become possible. For Korzybski, brain science provides the information necessary for promoting language as variable and modifiable (*Science and Sanity*, 1933).

Socrates protested that he was not a teacher but that he possessed a particular intellectual skill: the ability to ask provocative questions. Drawing/Writing encourages learners to develop questioning skills, too.

Teachers must remind themselves over and over that their responsibility is not primarily to impart knowledge but to encourage knowledge through questions, particularly about language-use.

In a skeptical age, Socrates identified moral goodness with knowledge. Students, too, require the knowledge that will allow right action or "good" behavior. Drawing/Writing encourages a relationship between aesthetics and ethics, presenting as a topic for discussion the possibility that a personal code of ethics may emerge from training in drawing. As will be seen in Step 5, strategies for balancing form, line and color can be used to make other decisions.

Drawing/Writing is an incremental procedure. The simplest drawing is followed by a more complicated drawings. The simplest writing is followed by more complicated writing. The Drawing/Writing student moves from descriptive thinking to analytical thinking and from analytical thinking to inferential thinking. Inference—the ability to come to conclusions from clues embedded in new information—is a necessary skill for mental, emotional, social and economic survival, particularly in an age of escalating information.

## REQUIREMENTS FOR TEACHING DRAWING/WRITING:

1) **A willingness to listen** to students and to ask questions instead of providing answers. This means open-mindedness—about yourself and your students as well as to what is possible in terms of thought and action. Overestimate students' abilities. Teach each Drawing/Writing exercise. Then, come to conclusions about students' capabilities. Over time, Drawing/Writing teachers may identify developmental parameters for specific visual and verbal thinking skills. Never underestimate the power of the child as a thinker.

2) **A willingness to question: the Socratic method** encourages thought. Drawing/Writing teachers ask two kinds of questions: "specfic" and "open-ended." When asking questions for which you have a specific answer in mind, signal this by saying, "This is a specific question." When asking open-ended questions, say "This is an open-ended question." Otherwise, students will assume you always have a specific answer in mind, forcing them into the position of mind-readers who ask themselves "What does the teacher want?" rather than "What do I think?" A string of rhetorical questions can be irritating. They also encourage passivity.

The Drawing/Writing process does have some specific goals. On the other hand, the process is designed to encourage free discussion and thought. Even when a line of questioning leads to a specific response, the answer can be achieved in many ways. For instance, the goal of the questions about magic marker-use is realizing that marker-use involves risks. The teacher probes until words like "courage" or "risk" surface. Words and terms like "mistakes," "slowing down," and "paying attention" may suggest themselves. Other lines of questioning may have no specific answers. For instance, when a teacher asks students about instances of risk-taking in their own lives, the responses depend upon student experience.

After asking a question, silence on the teacher's part, as well as moving physically away from the students, encourages student-driven discussion. Students have been trained to respond to teachers, not to each other, just as they have been trained to identify the answers sought by teachers. A teacher may actually have to move out of eye contact to encourage group discussions.

If children have learned by rote, their knowledge will be rote. However, if they learn by answering open-ended questions, they will develop inquiring minds capable of generating fresh, relevant solutions.

The Socratic method of asking questions instead of providing answers allows students to discover answers for themselves. This method has been developed as the "Paideia" approach by educator Theodore Sizer of Brown University. If the educational goal is self-directed learning, students must practice self-directed learning. Although the following drawing and writing exercises have specific goals—including how to take risks, make commitments and accept differences—much of the learning process is open-ended and exploratory.

The Socratic method may guide discussions toward known conclusions or, on occasion, deliver specific information. For instance, when I teach church architecture, I provide a series of specific architectural terms, and then I ask how the Romanesque Church S. Sernin is and is not like S. Etienne. How the churches are alike and different depends upon the individual student's application of the terms.

3) **A basic understanding of and appreciation for brain structure and function,** including how the brain learns and grows, provided by Part 3, "Hitchhikers' Guide to Brain Science."

4) **An appreciation for the mutual development of drawing and writing** provided in Part 1. Since Drawing/Writing recapitulates this relationship, the history of art and of writing as well as of children's drawings provided in Part 1 are important. By reproducing the intimate relationship between drawing and writing, this program sets itself apart from other English composition courses or drawing courses. The writing in a Drawing/Writing program is more precise and inventive in its descriptions, more thorough in its

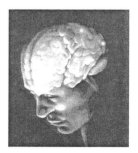

analysis, more far-reaching in its implications than other kinds of written work because the writing is generated by students' drawings and their intense examination of the process behind it, as well as the considerable input from peer responses to their drawing and writing. In a similar manner, drawings springing from writing differ from drawings produced without the benefit of reflective writing.

## PROMOTING A DRAWING-BASED WRITING PROGRAM

Past third grade, many students assume that drawing is for young children or for artists. A teacher who allows students to draw in the upper grades may be suspect. Students may feel they are being taught down to. Help students appreciate the substantive nature of the work they are involved with in Drawing/Writing. Students need to know why they are drawing, just as they need to know why they are doing any classroom exercise. Once students understand that training in drawing is training in careful seeing and that careful seeing is key to extracting information, they will be able to explain to other students, to their parents, and to other teachers why they are drawing as part of a regular writing course.

The most direct method of promoting a drawing-based writing program is to share the information in "Hitchhikers' Guide to Brain Science." Go over this information with students. Zerox the 13 points in Part 3 about brain development and read them aloud. Underscore the idea that what students do with and to their brains makes a difference. Stress that by using drawing and writing in integrated exercises, students are promoting intelligent brain activity; they are actually building brain connections. This shared information raises the level of intent and cooperation between teachers and learners.

It is important to reassure students that training in drawing is a "cutting edge," brain-based approach to teaching writing and thinking and to reassure them that the new literacy is a marketplace/workplace commodity. Explain the larger agenda behind each exercise in Drawing/Writing. Knowing the seriousness of each task enhances the process for students. Students will respect you for using scientific discoveries about the brain to develop their mental abilities, as well as for having their long-range life skills and job skills in focus.

As Harvard professor David Layzer writes "How we see the world depends on the visual apparatus with which evolution has endowed us. But individual developmental factors also play an important role. We *learn* to see in certain ways. A landscape painter doesn't see the same scene as a non-painter, even though the patterns of light impinging on their retinas may be nearly identical.... Finally, the language in which we grow up may influence our intuitive perceptions of space and time."[17] As Amherst physics professor Arthur Zajonc comments, the geologist looks at rocks in ways that Zajonc cannot. In effect, Professor Zajonc says he is "blind" to the rocks. When the geologist speaks, the rocks become visible to Zajonc (1993). How we learn to see transforms what we see.

## PRACTICAL POINTS:

**Marker-care:** Show students how to put tops back on markers firmly. Show students how to preserve the points by laying down parallel lines with a fat marker to fill large areas rather than "scrubbing" back and forth with a thinner marker. Tell students to throw away worn-out markers. Fresh, sharp lines from a new marker are encouraging and exciting.

**Classroom set-up:** Remove desks from your room if you can and replace them with cafeteria-like tables to provide enough space for students to sit beside each other as they form peer pairs. Set up individual cubbies for storage, for example, using stacked plastic milk crates. Clear one wall for group critiques.

**Economizing:** Reams of paper and boxes of folders, pencils and markers can be bought cheaply from office supply stores. Used tools and other objects for Drawing/Writing can be found at tag and garage sales. Butchers may give you some large bones to cook and dry.

---

[17] David Layzer, "Space, Time and Motion", course materials, p. 256,
Harvard College, 1995.

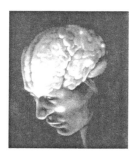

## MATERIALS:

A box of #2B (B is for black or dark) pencils with erasers

A box of #2 H or HB ( H is for hard) pencils with erasers

A set of new thin magic markers

A set of new fat magic markers

Paper; a ream (500 sheets) of white, unlined, legal size paper

A box of legal size manila folders to be used as portfolios

Scotch tape

A pencil sharpener

A carton of objects

A box of push pins

A dictionary. Drawing/Writing builds vocabulary. It is important to provide students with the correct spelling of words, as well as their roots and meanings.

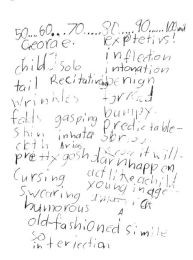

*Sketch of Materials, SRS*

**Portfolios:** Students need two legal-size folders or portfolios, one for school and one for home. In-class portfolios, like in-class objects, stay in the classroom. These portfolios hold all of the Drawing/Writing exercises.

**Drawing/Writing journals:** These journals can be made by folding legal-size paper in half and stapling the fold. Students record all new vocabulary and concepts here.

**Wish List:** A tackle box for each student which is carried to every classroom and subject. The tackle box contains: HB and B pencils, markers, drawing pens, watercolors, pastels, charcoal, a small can of no-smell hair spray to use as fixative, a kneaded eraser, a pencil sharpener or penknife, a tortillon (twisted cone of paper for smudging small places) , a small hand mirror for self-portraits, and whatever else is necessary to sustain the human spirit, including chocolate and poetry.

*Elizabeth Wright, age seven, Drawing/ Writing journal, Wildwood School, Amherst and Santa Fe, 1997*

## OBJECTS

There are no "good" or "bad" Drawing/Writing objects, but some objects are better than others. The best objects have clearly discernible structure and dignity, or *gravitas*, a Latin word for weighty seriousness. Seriousness is a "felt" characteristic. Bones, tools and utensils have dignity and are inherently interesting. Bones were tools, toys, religious objects for paleolithic people. Holding bones takes children back through time in the same way the Drawing/Writing process does. Home schoolers will need to designate one set of objects for the first time they tackle a Drawing/Writing exercise and a second set for the "at home" objects.

Common sense determines appropriate objects. Sharp or dangerous tools like rose clippers and gardening shears may not be appropriate with young children. This has not been my experience as a Drawing/Writing teacher, but this is a point to consider.

In school, avoid using objects from home. Students may ask to draw their own objects, including stuffed toys. Respond by saying that valuable personal objects could get lost at school, but that they can be drawn and written about for Drawing/Writing homework. Over time, students can decide for themselves which objects have lasting interest and power.

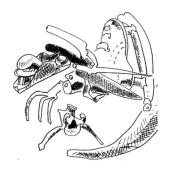

*Sketch, objects, SRS, 1997*

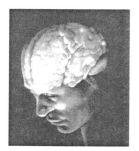

## KEEP THE OBJECTS CONSTANT

Choose objects that can be used over again during your teaching career. You may want to include spare or seldom-used tools.

If the same objects are drawn over the years, and if you keep a record of the work, successive waves of students will be able to compare their work with others'. Each Drawing/Writing student joins a community of students. Returning students are interested to see how current students work with the same process. Every time a student sees a Basic Shape drawing—whether in another classroom or in another school—the drawing triggers a mental review of the process of Basic Shape drawing and writing. A drawing of the *same* object arouses interest and curiosity to see how others solved the same problem.

Flexible expectations, along with a high tolerance for differences, are important mental attitudes in a fast-changing, multicultural society. Encouraging a community of like-minded students who are both literate and tolerant benefits society. Beyond shared experiences, object constancy underscores the possibility of a variety of viable solutions. Drawings of a hammer by three students may differ, but the differences are acceptable because each solution is the result of the same rigorous rules. In every group critique, students broaden their tolerance for differences.

## WHAT TO DO FIRST

**A letter home:** You might want to inform parents about the Drawing/Writing program via a letter at the beginning of the year explaining the rationale for the program. Parents, too, need education about the usefulness of drawing to the development of mental skills. Otherwise, parents may be confused by homework that emphasizes drawings, particularly once their children are beyond the third grade. Explaining a new type of homework to their parents may be too much, especially for young children. After an initial session of Drawing/Writing, students prove the best advocates for the program. Many students maintain that they had more fun and learned more and worked harder than in any other courses they have taken.

> **Dear Parents:**
>
> **We are experimenting with a new approach to teaching writing and reading and critical thinking skills.**
>
> **The program is called Drawing/Writing. The program has a successful ten-year record. It is based on research in brain science. Like the body, the brain requires training and exercise. Training in drawing—which teaches your child how to observe and analyze information carefully—can improve your child's writing, reading and thinking skills. Every time your child does a drawing, your child will be asked to write and to think in certain ways. In addition, your child will be honing visual skills. The ability to work with images as well as text is an important skill in a technological society.**
>
> **You will get to see your child's Drawing/Writing portfolio when we conference together. You will be interested to see your child's progress. Because this program includes an evaluation tool designed for students, you will also get to see your child's evaluation of his or her own progress.**
>
> **Your child will be repeating each day's Drawing/Writing exercises at home. Your interest and support are important. You may even want to do the work along with your child. Your child will be able to become your Drawing/Writing teacher. Thank you in advance for your support for this new approach.**
>
> **Sincerely,**

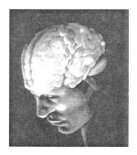

**Set up a peer pair system:** Depending upon age, gender and temperament, students may be able to pair up easily on their own, or you may have to devise some arbitrary but fair system relating, say, to even or odd numbered birthdays. The best route is letting students devise the system.

Once established, the peer unit remains constant for that Drawing/Writing session.

Peer sharing is efficient. Students get to show their drawing and their writing daily to someone who is interested in their work. Home-schoolers may want to pair up with other home-schooling families.

**How and Why to peer share and build:** Let students devise a pairing-up system to encourage social problem-solving skills. Because students show their drawings to each other and read their writing aloud to each other in pairs, revision is implied. Showing their drawings is the first step in the revision process. Reading their writings aloud is the second. Even though actual redrawing and rewriting do not occur, students identify areas for improvement. Do not let students give their papers to the other student. For the sake of building self-esteem and self-advocacy skills, each student keeps possession and thus control of his own drawing and writing and is the only one to present it. You will need to let students know at the outset that they will be sharing their writing.

**Each day:** At Drawing/Writing time, students will learn to get their portfolios, add more paper, retrieve their chosen object, choose markers and pencils, and take everything to their desks. They will know that every night's homework repeats the day's lesson.

## BENEFITS OF THE PROGRAM

**Learning to see:** Students will learn to see only through practice with seeing. They will learn to use language only through practice with language. To think abstractly, theoretically and philosophically, students' minds require tools and opportunity and practice.

**Training in a double three-step as a routine strategy for working with information:**

- work from the visual to the verbal
- work from the simple to the complex
- work from the concrete to the abstract,

and to:

- describe
- analyze and
- infer.

**Enrichment for everyone:** Drawing/Writing is a regular classroom enrichment strategy, beneficial to all skill levels, from the limited student to the talented and gifted student. It is a remedial strategy which doubles as enrichment, and it is an enrichment strategy which doubles as remediation. In addition, the program provides professional development for teachers by increasing drawing, writing, listening, communication and thinking skills.

**Portfolio assessment:** The five-step Drawing/Writing program produces a large body of material for assessing changes in visual and verbal thinking skills.

**Self-assessment:** A self-assessment tool called Rescore helps students quantitatively and qualitatively evaluate changes in their visual and verbal skills over the course of a Drawing/Writing session.

**Drawing/Writing journals:** Drawing/Writing journals are used with the five-step program to record vocabulary and concepts. In large art history lecture courses where it is impossible to teach the actual five-step program, Drawing/Writing journals provide opportunities for assignments in drawing as well as writing related to the content area. They also provide places for the teacher and student to interact on a personal basis.

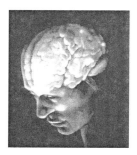

An architect, engineer, poet, and empirical scientist, Leonardo Da Vinci kept journals with exploratory drawings and text. The Drawing/Writing journals used in the five-step program teach children to develop curiosity and knowledge as Da Vinci did, directly, through mark-making. As suggested in the notes about the cover included at the end of this book, it is natural to be an artist/writer/scientist. The human mind is naturally scientific just as it naturally expresses itself through images and words.

**Prods for logic:** The word "because" incorporated in the writing exercises forces students to account for their comments; this accountability prods their logic systems. For instance, a student might write, "My Blind Contour drawing tells me that my object is curving because I note rounded rather than angular lines."

**Peer mentoring:** By listening to the probing approach of the teacher, peer pairs learn to nudge and probe each other's language-use. Student-to-student mentoring is especially useful in crowded classrooms.

**Peer teaching of the Drawing/Writing program:** By the end of an academic year in which three sessions of Drawing/Writing have been taught—once with the object, once with the self-portrait, and once with the figure—students will be able to take the five-step into other classrooms. The prospect of using students as teachers is exciting and practical. Programs in which older students tutor young ones are highly effective. Upper elementary, middle and high schoool Drawing/Writing graduates could also be used in adult literacy programs. When students become teachers, everyone benefits.

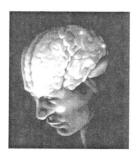

# Definition of terms

**OBJECTIVES:** Objectives are the concepts and skills learned in that particular step. These goals are bold-faced, and asterisked: *Commitment.* Class discussions target these goals and generalize them into everyday life.

**MATERIALS:** The physical items necessary to teach the step.

**PROCEDURE:** Step by step instructions for each step.

**BACKGROUND:** This information is located on the right and explains the purpose, procedure and goals for each step.

**ADDITIONAL INFORMATION:** This supplemental material is located on the left. For example, when you teach the Euclidean Basic Shape drawing, you will find information on the Greek mathematician Euclid as well as on the history of geometry.

**OPTIONAL:** Some of the exercises provided are optional. These are placed on the left. Time constraints or the age or skill level of students or your personal interests will guide the selection of these exercises.

**TIP:** These comments provide practical information and are placed on the right. Because I have taught Drawing/Writing for ten years, I can "troubleshoot" some situations. For instance, when students ask you how they are supposed to draw and write in connection with the Preliminary Drawing and Writing, I suggest the response, "Any way you want to." If you respond, "How about a story, or a haiku?" you have made the decision for the student. At first, some students and teachers are very uncomfortable without specific instructions. Discomfort often signals the stirrings of change.

**DEEP QUESTIONS, DEEP ANSWERS:** These items are located on the right. In the course of class discussions, serious questions and answers surface.

**POWERFUL IDEAS:** These items may occur on the left or the right. Startling, gripping ideas come up in the course of teaching—especially when teaching crosses content areas. For example, when the indeterminancy principle in physics is applied to neural explanations for thought, it becomes clear that there are strange loops in any complex system. Strange loops is a powerful idea. Using Douglas Hofstadter's term, Strange Loops are powerful ideas.

**PHILOSOPHICAL ASIDE:** These comments are located on the left and explore the larger implications of the exercises.

**REMEMBER/REMINDER:** These comments are located on the left and provide support and encouragement.

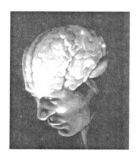

**SET UP:** Physical tasks connected with Drawing/Writing. For instance, how to lay objects out.

**REHASH:** Peer sharing of homework at the beginning of each class allows students to enjoy and review the night's work, providing a warm-up for the next exercise. Peer exchanges enhance attention and extend thought.

**HOMEWORK:** After peer sharing the previous night's homework, assign the next night's homework by reminding students that they will repeat this day's exercises with their at-home object. Because students do not take their in-class portfolios home, they must repeat the exercises from memory. This approach strengthens attention and memory and allows students to experience the work on their own terms.

Homework left undone deprives the peer of half the exchange. Let the peer pair sort this out, encouraging mutual responsibility.

**ASK:** "Ask" requests certain activities, as "ask students to draw using markers." "Ask" may also provide a provocative question.

**SAY:** What the teacher says to the students.

**DEMONSTRATE:** This describes what the Drawing/Writing teacher demonstrates for the class and completes as an exercise. The teacher's personal involvement sets the tone for the classroom. Involvement in Drawing/Writing also signals that the teacher is unavailable for other tasks. Being unavailable is a surprisingly effective way to get a roomful of students to settle down and to pay attention. Whenever possible, have a peer explain a step to a student who needs more explanations or who was not paying attention or who was absent. Resist doing this work yourself.

Working along with students also ensures that you, too, will be improving your drawing, writing and thinking skills. Because students conduct peer sharing and self-evaluation, you are released from those responsibilities. This lets you experience Drawing/Writing fully yourself. Students will find your engagement in the same work they are doing interesting and encouraging. Teachers tell me that this new relationship is both humbling and exciting. The one element you will lack as a teacher is a peer to share with, so, unless you bring another teacher with his or her students into your room to widen the Drawing/Writing influence in your school, you will be working alone. Because the constructivist teacher tips the balance of power toward students, she must not become a peer in a student pair. It is better to form a group of three peers if your numbers are uneven.

**DISCUSSION:** Suggestions for how to generate discussions are provided along with examples of student responses. A description of the desired results of a particular discussion is also provided. Remember to use these words to start a discussion: "This line of questioning has a specific goal," or, "This line of questioning is open-ended."

**DISCUSSION with a SPECIFIC GOAL:** The aim, for instance, of the marker discussion in connection with Step 1 is to teach students how to take risks and make commitments. Elicit the words "risk" and "commitment" from students by asking questions about magic markers and drawing. For instance, ask, "How are markers different from pencils? What can you do with a pencil that you cannot do with a marker? How does the ability to erase make a difference in your attitude toward pencils versus markers? If markers

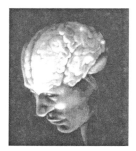

will not erase, what is your attitude about drawing with a marker?" Encourage students to talk about courage, risk, and commitment. By learning the words and practicing the actions, children learn to take risks, make commitments and show courage.

If students do not come up with the words "risk" and "commitment" because they do not know these words, teach them. Make the words personal by asking students to describe risks and commitments in their lives. List these responses on the board. Resist volunteering instances from your life because they are probably irrelevant and may discourage student response.

Appropriate language-use does not necessitate "teaching down." Precise, formal language can be used if the words and terms are defined. If students do not know a word, teach it. Use dictionaries to clarify usage. The goal in teaching language is not to mystify but to demystify.

**DISCUSSION, OPEN-ENDED:** A discussion with no specific term, concept, or lesson in mind. False Socratic discussions or rhetorical questions or apparent questions are demoralizing for students. If they think the teacher always has one specific answer in mind, they will stop thinking or only try to second-guess the teacher. This attitude is not conducive to mental growth.

**PEER SHARE AND BUILD:** The peer pair process builds vocabulary, critical thinking skills, listening skills and speaking skills. Each student shows her drawings to her peer and reads her writing aloud to the peer. Each student records all new terms and vocabulary from the peer's writing in her own Drawing/Writing journal as well as four new words provided by each peer pair in the group. The group builds a shared vocabulary. The depth and breadth of students' vocabulary bears on their ability to think and to communicate.

**GROUP CRITIQUES:** Informal group gatherings where student work is displayed and discussed provide opportunities for building communication skills. Critiques provide feedback and practice with speaking aloud using precise language.

**RECORD:** List all new vocabulary words and concepts on the board for students to copy into their Drawing/Writing journals.

**TIP:** If you record words and concepts on a large 24"×36" pad, rather than on the blackboard, and use the pad for all of the items listed under DEMONSTRATION, you will create a record of each session you teach of Drawing/Writing along with the vocabulary and ideas springing from that particular class. This record can be used to show other faculty and adminstrators what Drawing/Writing entails. The record can also be used in research when a comparison of language used by a series of groups may prove useful.

**SAY/DO, ASK/DO, DEMONSTRATE/DO:** These combined terms distinguish between what teachers say and do and what self-taught students do. The **/DO** cue allows self-teaching readers to skip certain items.

Comments on streamlining these Drawing/Writing instructions are appreciated. Use the Drawing/Writing addresses provided.

**TIP:** What to do with Drawing/Writing repeat students? If you should encounter students who have done Drawing/Writing in some other classroom who express boredom, remind them that minds as well as bodies require exercise. Many body- and health-conscious students work out with free weights, the StairMaster and the Nautilus; they jog for thousands of miles listening to their Walkman. A session with Drawing/Writing is equivalent to a good physical workout, and it is as necessary to a healthy mind as exercise is to the body.

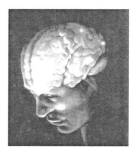

 **REMINDER:** Drawing/Writing students are learning to draw, but they are also practicing choice and commitment. Drawing/Writing students are learning to write, but they are also practicing discrimination and evaluation. The Drawing/Writing process is intended to equip students with skills and attitudes useful for a lifetime of thinking.

# Preliminary Drawing and Writing

<u>OBJECTIVES:</u>

**\*Commitment\***
**\*Benchmarks\***

<u>MATERIALS:</u> pencils, markers, objects, legal paper and legal-size file folders.

**BACKGROUND:**
"Preliminary Drawing and Writing" is the name for a sample of drawing and writing taken before the five-step program begins, providing benchmarks for skills at the beginning of the Drawing/Writing process. After completing a session of Drawing/Writing, students choose a new object to draw and write about in a sample called "Closing Drawing and Writing" which provides benchmarks for skills after the five-step process. Using a tool called Rescore, students evaluate changes over time based on these two samples or sets of benchmarks. A benchmark is a surveyor's mark made on something permanent, like a rock with a known position and altitude. The marks provide reference points for determining position. In Drawing/Writing, the benchmarks are visual and verbal skills and the understanding is that they are not made on a rock but with the brain which has no known position or altitude; therefore, these benchmarks will change over time. By comparing sets of benchmarks, students determine their current visual and verbal position.

No training precedes the Preliminary Drawing and Writing. This initial sample simply records a student's skills at a certain moment; the skill level does not define a student's mental capabilities. Students who understand pre- and post-tests as temporary markers in a lifetime of learning will regard tests as measuring devices—nothing more and nothing less. As the brain is variable and modifiable, so tests measuring brain function should be expected to show variation and modifiability.

Both the preliminary and the closing Drawing/Writing samples are timed in the same way: about 10 minutes is allowed for each drawing and each piece of writing, or 20 minutes per sample.

<u>PROCEDURE:</u>

**SET UP:** Lay out folders, paper, magic markers and pencils. Ask students to take a folder, five or so sheets of paper, and a pencil or a marker, and return to their desks or tables. You, too, choose a pencil or a marker, and gather the same materials.

Take the Drawing/Writing objects out of the box and lay them on a large table or the floor. Let the students look at the objects and handle them before making a choice. Ask students to devise how they will line up to choose the objects.

**HOMEWORK:** Homework is a repeat of the day's exercises. To explain this: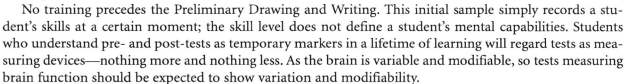

**SAY:** "Homework will be a repeat of each day's Drawing/Writing exercises. To do this work, choose a new object at home. You will leave your classroom object here. Draw your at-home object for ten minutes and then write about it for ten minutes, just as you will do in the classroom. Take a second folder right now and put some paper in it. Write your name on this second folder along with a label like 'Homework Drawing/Writing.' You will need to get your own markers and pencils for working at home.

"You will work with the same two objects—in class and at
*Drawing/Writing Objects*     home—for the full two-week Drawing/Writing session."

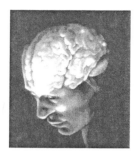

**TIP:** Before students make a choice, make it clear that the chosen object remains constant for the session. Resist saying any more lest you interrupt their decision-making. The skill of making decisions is learned over time and is based on experience. A student may choose to draw a small glass bottle because he thinks it will be simple. After a session with Drawing/Writing, he knows this object poses subtle and difficult drawing problems. A large, apparently more complex object like a pair of rose shears may be far simpler.

**TIPS:**

**Pencils:** Most students choose pencils for the Preliminary Drawing and Writing because pencils let them erase. The Drawing/Writing process strives to achieve two attitudinal changes. First, students become less fearful about mistakes. Second, they learn that mistakes are part of the learning process and that mistakes are inaccuracies which can be rectified. In fact, they learn that mistakes are opportunities.

**Scribbling:** Encourage scribbling. If we expect children to learn to write and read, we must encourage their mark-making. Scribbling is proto-drawing and/or proto-writing in a motoric, warm-up mode. Some scribbling produces rounded, bounded shapes, including mandala-like figures. Some scribbling looks like wavy lines or a series of dots and dashes. Whatever form scribbling takes, it is legitimate mark-making indicating the human predisposition to make marks of significance, and stands as early self-training in literacy.

**Doodling:** Doodling is the valiant attempt of the mind to stay alert.

**DISCUSSION with a Specific Goal:** This line of questioning has specific answers: For instance, you might ask, "Is there anything useful about sticking with one object for two weeks? What can we learn from choosing an object and sticking with it? What words could you use to describe this activity?" You are looking for the word "commitment," but you will accept a wide range of responses in the meantime, duly recording them on the board.

**DISCUSSION, open-ended:** Once you get the words "choice" and "commitment," or after you have taught the words "choice" and "commitment," ask, "Why is choice useful or important? Why is commitment useful or necessary?" Ask students where choice and commitment come into their lives, and where they anticipate choice and commitment coming into their lives in the future.

Some useful questions include, "Is it important to choose? Why is it important to choose? What can be learned from committed choice? Are there problems with choice and commitment?"

**SAY:** "Put your names on your folders. We are going to do an exercise called 'Preliminary Drawing and Writing.' Put your object where you can see it easily. We are going to draw the object for about ten minutes and then write about it for ten minutes. Put the drawing and writing on the same side of the page. You will be showing all of your drawings and reading all of your writings aloud to a peer. You will pair up later. So, just remember that all your Drawing/Writing work will be shared."

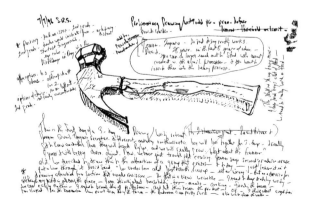

*Preliminary Drawing and Writing, Hammer, SRS*

*Preliminary Drawing and Writing, Lacrosse Glove, SRS*

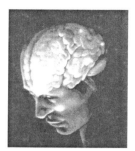

 **ASIDE:** "You are the boss" is a phrase I use with students to encourage them to take control. You may prefer to use other phrases like "Make your own decision," or "I trust your judgment about this, or "Only you can make this decision." The intent behind the phrases is returning power to students. Helplessness is a learned attitude; it is contagious and it can be crippling. Psychologists, brain researchers, and educators emphasize the importance of control to mental health. Students need to practice control.

**TIP:** Some students will ask you how to do Preliminary Drawing and Writing. Make clear that the students are to draw and write any way they choose to. Some students will be very uncomfortable, initially, with the prospect of such freedom. They will get used to it. Don't give this exercise too much weight; avoid using the terms "pre-test" and "post-test." If students ask you why they are doing this, tell them this preliminary drawing and writing provides "benchmarks " for their "visual and verbal skills." Although this answer may sound like gobbledygook to students at this point, you may have allayed test anxiety, insuring more or less authentic samples of work.

By making sure drawing and writing occur on the same side of the page, you reinforce the idea that drawing and writing belong together.

**SAY:** "Draw in any way you choose to. Write in any way you choose to."

**DEMONSTRATE:** Pick up your object, and write on the top of the board: "Preliminary Drawing and Writing." Add the date and your initials.

**SAY:** "Put these words at the top of a sheet of paper: 'Preliminary Drawing and Writing.' Add the date and your initials. Say, "These are my initials." If you do not say this, students may copy down your initials. (Many students have learned to copy mindlessly.)

**SAY:** "You may write in English or in whatever other language is easiest for you."

**TIP:** In a multicultural classroom, there will be several native languages, or mother tongues. To put all students at ease, ask them to write in any language that is comfortable for them, and then to translate that piece of preliminary writing into English. By the same token, ask the students who wrote in English to translate their writing into another language. If they do not know another language, give them some first year grammar books and foreign language dictionaries and let them struggle with a translation so that they will understand the plight of the student whose English skills are tenuous. In this way, every student in the classroom experiences comfort and discomfort with language and the group becomes a community in which language-learning is a shared enterprise. Because I am an English teacher, my goal is written English. If you teach French, your goal is written French.

**DEMONSTRATE/DO:** Loosely timing both activities, ask your students to draw their object for about ten minutes, and then write about the object for ten minutes. Ask them to write on the same side of the paper. Drawing/Writing includes display of work; it is impossible to look at two sides of a piece of paper at once.

**SAY:** "When I say, 'Write any way you choose to,' I am suggesting that you are the boss. It is your decision how you write."

**SAY:** "Let's start drawing." Remember, you will draw and write with students. After ten minutes, say, "We have to stop drawing now. The way you started to draw is the way you would have ended your drawing. I know it is hard to stop drawing. Now, let's start writing. Write in any way you choose to write." Be firm in using this non-directive approach. If students focus on this writing sample as a test, they may produce a writing sample that is larger or smaller than they would normally produce. After the Drawing/Writing program, you will ask for another sample of drawing and writing. The two sets of samples document changes in visual and verbal skills and are used for self-evaluation.

At the end of ten minutes, say, "Finish whatever you were writing." Let students finish the sentence they were writing. Stay quiet until this is done. In this way, you show respect for students and for the act of writing.

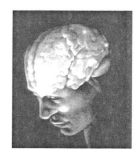

**TIP:** Some students will finish drawing and writing before ten minutes are up. Some will still be drawing and writing at the end of ten minutes. Both situations should be expected. If the whole class is done before ten minutes is up, stop the session. You do not want to make students uncomfortable. For students who are busily drawing and writing at the end of ten minutes, reassure them that they will have time to do more drawing and writing, and apologize for cutting them off in the midst of their work.

**SAY:** "We have to stop writing now. We will have time to do much more. This sample of drawing and writing gives us benchmarks, or measures, for your current skills."

**DO:** At this point, you will need to organize the room in pairs. You might simply count off the room by twos using the existing seating arrangement. Ask students for their ideas. Pairing can be thorny so it is best to use students' own solutions, practicing constructivism on this level, as on other levels in this program.

**SAY:** "Now show your drawing to your peer and read your writing aloud to your peer."

**PEER SHARE:** This will take about ten minutes. While students peer share, walk around the room, listening. Bring the class's attention to a particular pair. The reason for choosing one pair is teaching peer-mentoring behavior. How you choose this pair is up to you. You may overhear a particularly interesting exchange. Or, you may want to bolster the confidence of a certain pair. Or you may want to single out a pair who is having trouble engaging in the task. Rather than chide them, attend to their quandary by asking them to provide a model for class behavior.

**SAY:** (addressing one of the students in the pair directly) "Please read your writing aloud for us. How can we describe this writing?" (Address the other student and the rest of the class, too.) "Yes, that is descriptive writing. Yes, that other section of the writing tells a story."

**TIP:** Take whatever terms students provide and support them. Then, provide formal terms like "narrative," if necessary. At first, you will need to teach many new terms. Like other skills, language snowballs. Students' brains have been designed to absorb new words like thirsty sponges.

**TIP:** By starting at one side of the room with one peer pair and working your way around the room through every peer pair, you will do three things:
1) You will include every student immediately in the Drawing/Writing process.
2) Students will hear a broad range of student-produced writing and appreciate and start to learn the names for a broad range of genres, or kinds of writing.
3) By listening and asking questions about the writing where it is unclear, you will model the probing questions you want students to learn to ask each other. Make sure students understand that these questions are asked to teach students to use language more precisely, not to put them on the defensive.

**DO:** Make a chart of probing question, displaying it where it is easy for students to refer to. After going through several pairs, encourage the next peer to ask the questions.

**SAY:** As the partner responds with a better word, show your approval. "Yes, that word is much clearer, isn't it?" Some useful questions:

What exactly do you mean by that?
What does that mean?
That's too general for me. Could you be more specific?
Why did you use that particular word?
Can you be more precise?
Could you give me a simple example of that?
Could you give me a picture of that?
Could you give me an easy definition of that? Could we use a simile or a metaphor?
Could you make that clearer for me?

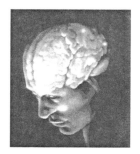

Is that the word you want to use? Is there a more accurate word?

I do not understand what you are saying. Can you help me?

What is your point, exactly? I am getting the idea, but I am not sure what you really mean.

Do you mean that " x" is like " y"? Would you say that "y" is a good example of what you are talking about?

If what you are saying is true, what does that mean? The logic of what you are saying suggests to me that.... Is this what you really mean to say?

**SAY:** "Remember, these questions are designed to help your peer speak, write, draw and think more clearly. You are not attacking your peer. But you are definitely pushing your peer to be more precise, especially in the use of language. Until you understand what is being said, keep asking questions. Do not be rough. Be kind. But be persistent. Keep pushing."

**TIP:** Show the class that there are a variety of ways to write. As suggested above, writing can tell a story and be called "narrative"; it can be loaded with adjectives and be called "descriptive"; it can be characterized by simile or metaphor and be called "poetic." This is a good time to introduce simile and metaphor. You will work with these constructions repeatedly.

**SAY:** Focus on a student and ask him to describe what kind of writing his peer did. If he cannot answer, ask the other student to read her work aloud again. Open a general discussion. "I hear many adjectives; what kind of writing uses many adjectives? I hear a story. What is this kind of writing called? I hear a simile. Do you know what a simile is? I hear a metaphor. Do you know what a metaphor is? A simile uses the words 'like' or 'as' to make a comparison. For instance, 'My Labrador dog is like a seal when she gets out of the water. Her coat is sleek and shiny. ' A metaphor is a direct comparison; for instance, 'My dog is a seal.'"

Start with what students know. Rather than imposing terms, provide them in response to students' comments. For instance, say, "Another word for the writing we call 'story telling' is 'narrative.'" Teach these terms. If you take the time to teach these terms incrementally, by the time students reach the third or fourth grade they will be able to recognize and name a variety of genres of writing.

**RECORD:** Write these terms on the board including:

Descriptive

Nostalgic

Emotional

Symbolic

Reflective

Evocative

Provocative

Spiritual

Sensual

Poetic

Metaphorical

Inferential

Representative

Analytical

Narrative

Expository

I have a possibly unfounded prejudice against using the word "expository." In Part 4, the sample English curriculum provides suggestions for introducing the expository essay to students in the context of previously generated writing without using this term, at first.

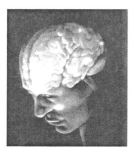

 **REMEMBER:** A Drawing/Writing classroom is characterized by a rhythm between noise and silence: peer pair exchanges, group discussions, and teacher instruction alternate with silent solitary application.

 **REMEMBER:** The preliminary and closing samples of writing must all be in the shared language of the classroom to encourage growth in that shared language and to allow an evaluation of changes in the use of that written language over time. As has been suggested at the outset in this user's guide, an initial translation of the Preliminary Writing from a mother tongue into the shared language of the classroom may be necessary.

**TIP:** Begin vocabulary-building. This process becomes routine. Ask each student to write down in his Drawing/Writing journal all words used by his peer that he does not know. Then, addressing each pair, ask each student to provide two new or interesting words used by the peer. Then, ask the peer to define each of the words. Then, ask other students for their definitions. Write down all of these words with their definitions, helping students appreciate the degree to which the meanings of words are personal and layered. In this way, individual vocabularies and a shared class vocabulary are built from student writing. I add more of my own words as we work. In this way, student vocabulary is enlarged by my vocabulary, too. Because you will use a dictionary to make sure you and students are using words precisely, more words are added to the mix from the dictionary.

**RECORD:** Write all of these words on the board. Make sure that students write down all words. This list becomes the shared class vocabulary.

**SAY:** "As you listen to your peer read, think about the new words or the interesting words or phrases being used. Write down in your Drawing/Writing notebook all of the words you do not know and some of the words or phrases you would like to use that you already know but forget to use.

"Now, I am going to go around the room and ask each student to call out two words used by her peer that she thinks the class would like to add to its vocabulary."

**GROUP CRITIQUE:** There is no group critique with Preliminary Drawing and Writing. The round-the-room sharing of work provides a general review of the work. Hereafter, a group critique follows each exercise. Remain sensitive to weak or shy students for whom group critiques will be, at first, painful. Still, these students, too, must learn to self-advocate and communicate in the world. Group critiques provide training in public speaking and in putting opinions "out there" and "on the line." The ability to speak up and speak out is necessary and requires training.

After the first formal Drawing/Writing exercise, the group critique becomes routine. Even at this early date, drawing and writing skills reflect an increased level of engagement, and students can better tolerate a public display of their drawing and writing. Differences in skill levels will be obvious, but growth in skills becomes clear, too. It has been my experience that the most exciting outcome for the group is the dramatic growth of the weakest student revealed in these critiques.

**SAY:** "Do the Preliminary Drawing and Writing exercise at home with an at-home object. Leave the class objects and folder here." You will not need to repeat these sentences again.

If you have a multicultural classroom, add these instructions: "Translate your writing into English as well as you can, on your own. For those students who wrote in English, you have a different task: translate your writing into some other language, as best you can on your own."

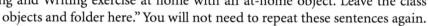

**TIP:** Buy some second-hand, first-year language texts and dictionaries. It does not matter how outdated these are. They will contain the vocabulary students need for this translation exercise. Lend these to students.

**RECORD:** Write on the board: "Homework: repeat Preliminary Drawing and Writing at home with a new object. Draw for ten minutes and write for ten minutes." You will not write this homework instruction down again. You will simply tell students to repeat the day's work at home at the beginning of each of the following steps.

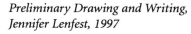

*Preliminary Drawing and Writing,*
*Jennifer Lenfest, 1997*

**SAY:** "Now, put your class object back in the box. Put your class folder away."

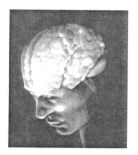

# Step One

# CONTOUR DRAWING

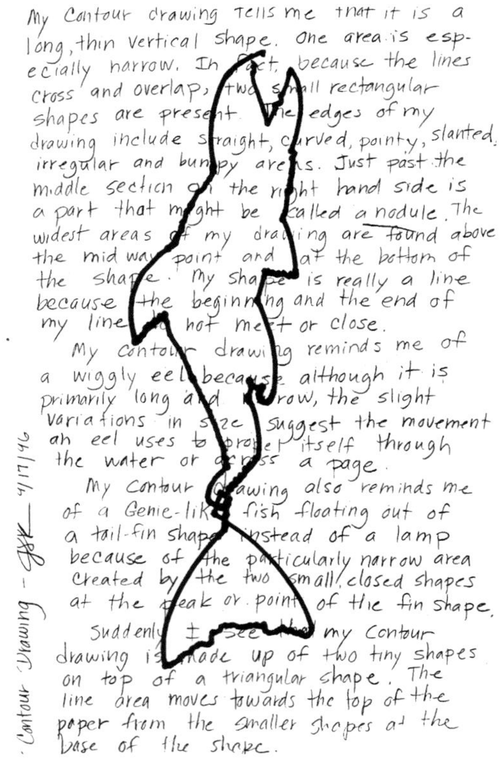


Blind Contour, writing, fish, Joanne Krawzyck

My (Blind) Contour drawing tells me that it is a long, thin, vertical shape. One area is especially narrow. In fact, because the lines cross and overlap, two small rectangular shapes are present. The edges of my drawing include straight, curved, pointy, slanted, irregular and bumpy areas. Just past the middle section on the right hand side is a part that might be called a nodule. The widest areas of my drawing are found above the mid way point and at the bottom of the shape. My shape is really a line because the beginning and the end of my line do not meet or close.

My contour drawing reminds me of a wiggly eel because although it is primarily long and narrow, the slight variations in size suggest the movement an eel uses to propel itself through the water or across a page.

My contour drawing also reminds me of a Genie-like fish floating out of a tail-fin shape instead of a lamp because of the particularly narrow area created by the two small, closed shapes at the peak or point of the fin shape.

Suddenly I see that my Contour drawing is made up of two tiny shapes on top of a triangular shape. The line area moves towards the top of the paper from the smaller shapes at the base of the shape.

*Blind Contour, Fish, Joanne Krawczyk, Continuing Education, Westfield State, 1996*

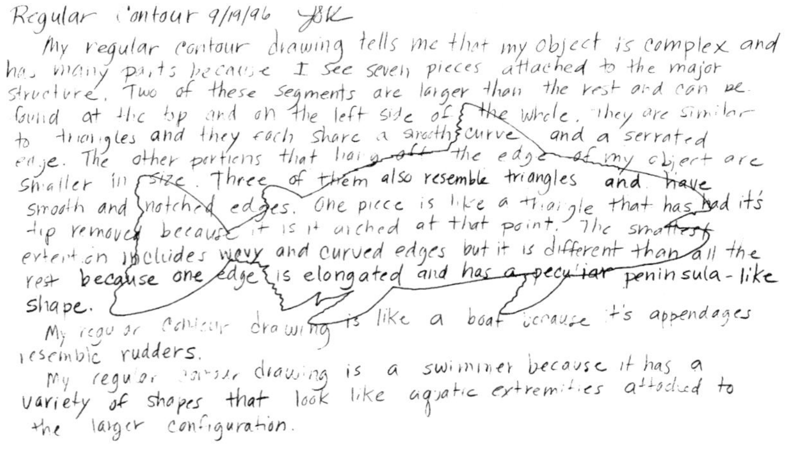


Regular Contour drawing, fish, Joanne Krawzyck

My regular contour drawing tells me that my object is complex and has many parts because I see seven pieces attached to the major structure. Two of these segments are larger than the rest and can be found at the top and on the left side of the whole. They are similar to triangles and they each share a smooth curve and a serrated edge. The other portions that hang off the edge of my object are smooth and notched edges. One piece is like a triangle that has had its tip removed because it is arched at that point. The smallest extension includes wavy and curved edges but it is different than all the rest because one edge is elongated and has a peculiar peninsula-like shape.

My regular contour drawing is like a boat becasue its appendages resemble rudders.

My regular contour dawing is a swimmer because it has a variety of shapes that look like aquatic extremities attached to the larger configuration.

*Regular Contour, Fish, Joanne Krawczyk, Continuing Education, Westfield State, 1996*

# STEP ONE

# Contour Drawing

### 1.1  Tactile and Gestural Warm-up Exercises

### 1.2  The Blind Contour Drawing

### 1.3  The Regular Contour Drawing

## 1.1  Tactile and Gestural Warm-up Exercises

OBJECTIVES:

**\*Direct sensory exploration\***

MATERIALS: the objects, pencils, markers, paper, folders

**BACKGROUND:**

We cannot always directly touch things we need to learn about, and so we must develop the ability to "touch at a distance." Drawing and writing are methods for touching at a distance.

As babies, our sight is highly informed by touch. As adults, we clearly remember things we have touched. We begin to rely less on touch when we enter school, devaluing touch as a mode for learning mistakenly relegating to the early elementary school years or placing touch "out of bounds" for a variety of reasons—many of which have been imposed by society. Drawing/Writing reintroduces the experience of knowledge directly informed by touch.

As a form of drawing, tracing is misunderstood as a "baby-ish" activity. Older students may even label tracing as "cheating." It takes time to train the hand to produce what the eye sees. Why not use a direct approach when we can? The impulse to trace is natural and useful. Because the eye follows the hand, tracing trains the eye for accuracy. Garments trace the shape of a body. Sewing patterns trace the shape of the garment. Police officers on the scene of a crime trace around the corpse to record its position. We trace the shape of the faces of the people we love with our hands. Touch helps the deaf to hear and the blind to see. Our brains may be pre-programmed to trace. The hand receives direct kinaesthetic experience while tracing, and the eye follows the hand, informing the brain. Tracing does not provide all the information about an object. It provides an accurate record of one profile, or outside edge or surface. How the draw-er feels about the object remains largely unrecorded. Tracing is an intelligent approach to direct bodily knowledge.

The following warm-up exercises with gesture and tracing are partly based on research: young Chinese students first draw calligraphic figures in the air with their arms and bodies and then trace the broad gesture of the character using a brush. Tactile and gestural exploration allows learners to feel the shape of their "alphabet." Italian educator Maria Montessori used this tactile approach, too, with her primary school students. According to a turn-of-the-century primer, Chinese children then receive instruction on spatial placement of characters using geometric guides indicating orientation of the character. It is also clear from

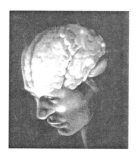

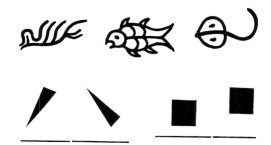

*Calligraphy: geometric guides to spatial relations from a 1900's primer plus schematic drawings indicating narrative content of ancient characters being practiced in a modern form.*

this primer that Chinese children learn that the characters they are drawing have strong narrative content: in this case, the content refers to a bird, a fish, a sting ray. The Drawing/Writing process begins with a gestural, tactile approach and includes geometry as a descriptive system. The procedure includes training the student to extract and reproduce narrative content (for example, by drawing a visually convincing hammer or jawbone) as well as to transform that visually freighted drawing or symbol (the "Perfect" Whole) into a far more abstract representation called the Composite Abstraction. This abstraction still carries cues to the original narrative content as Chinese characters do.

## PROCEDURE:

**DO/DEMONSTRATE:** Close your eyes and feel your object with both hands. Then, stand up and use your hands to draw the shape of your object in the air. Next, trace your object on a piece of paper, feeling your way around it, learning the object by touch.

*Tracing a hammer*

**SAY:** "Close your eyes and hold your objects. How do they feel? What do they look like in your mind's eye? What kinds of things do you see?

"Hold your object in one hand and trace its shape in the air with the other hand, keeping your eyes closed. Now, do the same thing with your eyes open. Is there a difference? What is the difference?"

**DISCUSSION:** Let students talk about what their objects feel like and look like in their mind's eye when they trace the shapes in the air with their eyes closed.

**SAY:** "Take a new sheet of paper. Write the word 'Tracing' at the top of the page. Add the date and your initials. Now, take your object and lay it down on the paper. Some objects will be so big they go off the paper. Do not worry about this. Place your object so that the most interesting parts lie on the paper. Now, trace around the edges. Do this slowly and carefully."

**DEMONSTRATE:** Write on the board "Tracing." Add the date and your initials. Take your object and lay it on the paper. Draw around it carefully.

**SAY:** "Now, let's write in a certain way."

**DEMONSTRATE:** On the board, write this sentence; "My tracing tells me that my object is...because...."

**SAY:** "Your tracing has information. For instance, my tracing of the hammer tells me that my hammer is long and smooth, has a block-like head which has a hook on one end, and a snub bulb on the other. When I write about what my drawing tells me about my object, I must add the word 'because' to explain my statement to myself. For instance, I have to add 'because the lines that enclose the handle are extended and flowing while the lines that enclose the head have abrupt corners and include a pointed, claw-like shape on one end as well as a curving, oval shape on the other.'"

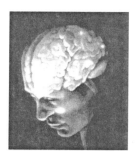

**PEER SHARE AND BUILD:** Repeat the vocabulary-building procedure until it becomes second nature for your Drawing/Writing students.

**TIP:** Peer sharing is a time to:
1) Build vocabulary by asking each peer to note down all the the unknown words used by the peer, as well as ones that are appealing.
2) Build a class vocabulary by going around the room, asking each student to provide two words from the peer's writing. Record these words on the board. Remind students to copy these words and use them in their own writing.
3) Show students how personal and idiosyncratic language-use can be by asking the student who used the word to define it. A good dictionary is critical to verify, correct or extend definitions. In the process, several new words are usually added to the group vocabulary. The definition process is fascinating because it reveals the degree to which we use language in personal, often approximate, even haphazard ways.

## 1.2  The Blind Contour Drawing

<u>OBJECTIVES:</u>

> **\*Practicing risk-taking\***
> **\*Understanding that drawings carry information\***
> **\*Accurate description requires attention\***
> **\*Figure/ground distinction: defining the boundaries\***
> **\*Learning to distinguish between simile and metaphor\***
> **\*Free association and inventive thinking\***
> **\*Invented spelling: valid and transitional\***

<u>MATERIALS:</u> markers, objects, paper, folders.

**BACKGROUND:**

Because students must use magic markers, and because students must stay with the object they chose, the Blind Contour drawing introduces exercises in risk-taking and commitment.

The rationale for Drawing/Writing in general and for the Blind Contour drawing in particular is this: until we look carefully at something and draw it, we do not have an accurate mental image of that object stored in our brain. Drawing is an extraordinarily efficient way to store precise visual information in long-term memory. The task of writing poses thornier issues in connection with eidetic storage. Is it likely that students will store their invented spelling as "the" way to spell? How many teenagers or adults do you know who have stored "fngrf" for "phonograph," or something analogous? Not many.

The Blind Contour drawing is a partially accurate representation. The Blind Contour drawing is a visual exploration. Invented spelling is an auditory exploration. Each sensory experiment constructs knowledge. Correct spelling can be scaffolded onto invented spelling. Teachers of young students need to point out that spelling is a complicated matter. The fact that the "f" sound can also be represented by the combination of letters, "p" and "h"—as it is in the word *phonograph*—will be startling at first. Because the human mind is drawn to unique instances, most students will accommodate additional spelling rules as a mental challenge, just as they will happily store eccentric words like "pterodactyl." Very young children love the complicated names of dinosaurs and learn them easily, dazzling their parents. Careful looking and painstaking representation may not cure phonologic non-correspondence between sound and letter, or problems with reading, but training in honing one sensory system cannot but help another sensory system, given the interconnectedness of the human mind. Rather than a sounding-out approach, children with

**ADDITIONAL INFORMATION:** Because of the high spoken content in Drawing/Writing as well as training in cross-modal transfer, the possibility of learning to connect specific sounds to specific letters becomes a likely natural benefit of the Drawing/Writing process. Literacy training that recognizes the intimate relationship between remediation and enrichment as well as the fact that all linguistic skills—speech, drawing, writing, and reading—are interconnected should prove effective for a range of students. Because Drawing/Writing includes the de- and reconstruction of so many words in reference to their Latin suffixes, prefixes and roots, it provides additional phonological training.

Phonological processing at the level of speech is automatic for most children. Dr. Sally Shaywitz, Yale Medical School professor and authority on dyslexia in children, comments: "Speaking is natural, and reading is not. Reading is an invention and must be learned at a conscious level. The task for the reader is to transform the visual percepts of alphabetic script into linguistic ones—that is, to recode graphemes (letters) into their corresponding phonemes. To accomplish this, the beginning reader must first come to a conscious awareness of the internal phonological structure of spoken words. Then he or she must realize that the orthography—the sequence of letters on the page—represents this phonology" (1996, 100).

One of the hypotheses supporting Drawing/Writing is that training in a cross-modal processing strategy for visual language remediates phonological deficits as well as visual deficits for language. This hypothesis is testable. Training for attention, recognition, transformation, recoding, information-storage in one realm may affect another. The hypothesis that drawing affects writing positively has been tested with statistically significant results (Sheridan, 1991). The hypothesis that training in drawing as it is presented in Drawing/Writing positively affects reading skills can also be tested.

### Invented spelling:

Spelling requires identifying "sound-to-letter correspondence." For instance, the sound "ssss" in "sister" corresponds to the letter "s." If we pronounce the word "sister" aloud, we clearly hear that hissing "s" sound. As a spelling strategy, sound-to-letter correspondence does not always work; consider the "silent p" in "pterodactyl." To spell this word correctly, you must memorize a picture of the word in your mind, not the sound.

"Invented spelling" happens when young children sound out words, writing down the letters that correspond to the sounds they hear. Generally, young children hear consonants clearly, omitting or confusing vowel sounds. For these reasons, what they write down differs from standard spelling. A flexible, supportive attitude toward invented spelling allows young children to build confidence in their abilities to "crack the code" of written language, as well as to help identify students with hearing-based learning disabilities. Examples of dyslexic writing provided in Part 1 may reveal some of these hearing-based differences. The spelling is clearly invented and appears to be phonological, representing what is heard in the writer's mind. Brain science supports the supposition that students who learn to draw accurately may learn to hear more accurately; they will also learn to store words as *pictures*—as many students do—circumventing imperfect auditory processes.

Invented spelling is commendable; it represents a faithful following of letter-to-sound correspondence rules—or the alphabetic code—we teach young children. Invented spelling is the result of scrupulous rule-following, and it depends on hearing and aural memory. An accurate visual, or eidetic, memory allows children to store pictures in their minds of spelled words that deviate from the basic alphabetic symbol-to-sound code like "pterodactyl."

By reading aloud the writing produced by language-disabled students, we may hear what they hear. Their spelling may provide sound-to-letter correspondence just like young children's invented spelling, or it may indicate sound-to-letter *non*-correspondence or "auditory processing problems." Encourage young children's invented spelling. As you urge them to adopt traditional spelling, acknowledge its lack of phonetic richness. A six-year-old of my acquaintance, Nate, spelled "plastic" "pelasteck."

Pronounce "pelasteck" aloud. "Pelasteck" actually provides a full alphabetic description of what the word "plastic" sounds like. Nate's sound-to letter correspondence is excellent.

*Nate Gorlin, drawing with word "pelasteck"*

Students with visual *and* aural processing problems may experience improvements in working with language through the repeated training in accuracy and in attention provided by a drawing-based literacy program like Drawing/Writing. Research with Drawing/Writing will help to clarify the relationships between visual and verbal processing as well as to identify those strategies useful for remediating visual and verbal processing deficits.

A question arises: if we encourage invented spelling, will students store incorrect spellings in long-term memory? Children who write and read are unlikely to store early invented spelling as standard English. Drawing/Writing improves visual memory through enhanced attention and increasingly accurate representations. Memory is a complex operation. The current understanding is that memories of specific events are distributed globally. Even though a precisely planted electrode may elicit a specific sound or smell, research suggests that memories are complex events

[CONTINUED ON THE NEXT LEFTHAND PAGE]

phonologic processing problems could draw a picture beside the word and then pronounce it. They could rely on the drawing as a mnemonic device and bypass the sounding-out step. Although this would mean that their writing would include a string of words and pictures, the child would be able to read. Since this is the way humankind has read for thousands of years, this combined approach has ample precedent.

As students move through the five-step Drawing/Writing program, they learn that drawing is a complex task, requiring many attempts at seeing. Students come to understand that words are complex constructs, too.

## PROCEDURE:

**SAY:** "Let's start by sharing homework with your peer pair. Show your drawing to your peer, and then read your own writing aloud. Do not pass your paper to your partner to read silently. When your peer finishes reading aloud, comment on her drawing and writing. Your peer can make comments, or ask questions, too, about your work. What questions might be useful? Yes, you're right; we can look back at our wall chart."

**REHASH:** In peer-pairs, students share their homework, the repeat of Preliminary Drawing and Writing done with an at-home object.

**HOMEWORK:** Remind students that they will repeat the following exercise for homework. Remind them that you will not be writing instructions on the board and that they will not be taking their in-class portfolios home. Students will need to remember what they did in class.

**SAY:** "Let's do Drawing/Writing. Get your class folders, your homework folders, your objects, paper, markers, pencils. Make sure you get a fat marker and a thin marker. Now, sit next to your peer. When I say let's do Drawing/Writing, this is what you will do from now on." Wait until students are ready. This may take some time the first time around.

**DISCUSSION: OPEN-ENDED:** Open this discussion by referring to the chart of supportive yet critical peer questions you drew up with students in connection with the Preliminary Drawing and Writing. Elicit probing questions. For instance, ask, "What questions could we ask to get the peer to choose more precise words?"

**SAY:** "We need to be supportive, but if a peer's writing does not make sense, you shouldn't fail to say it. What should you do if you do not understand a part of your peer's writing? What if a sentence is unclear, or the word-choice seems inaccurate? What could you say that would not hurt your peer's feelings, but would help get the point across?"

**DEMONSTRATE:** Add new questions to the chart. Refer students to the existing list of useful questions.

**SAY:** "Let's make sure we keep a positive tone to our comments about our own work. If we say, 'I don't like my drawing or my writing,' what do we really mean? We may mean that our drawing or writing really is not very good, or we may mean that it is good but we feel it would be bad form to praise our own work. Learning to praise our own work using objective standards requires practice. Let's agree to limit initial comments about our work to positive statements relating to accuracy or relevance, and to omit negative comments altogether."

**TIP:** The phrase "Here is my drawing" is declarative, not evaluative. The phrase, " My drawing is lousy..." is pejorative. Even when they know their drawings are good, many students will denigrate their work. Excellence remains unfashionable. Girls often say, "I hate my drawing," or even "This drawing sucks." A non-judgmental sentence like "This is my drawing" protects students from habitual self-criticism.

The phrase "My drawing is lousy" expresses at least two feelings: low self-esteem or reticence about accepting praise. The Drawing/Writing experience replaces low self-esteem with growing confidence and replaces reticence about accepting praise with honest self-appraisal. When students produce work according to self-determined levels for achievement, both praise and criticism become possible.

stored redundantly. Exactly how training in drawing improves memory may not be ascertainable, but those who draw know they can re-create images at will in the absence of the subject at the level of accuracy at which the image was stored. The storage of correct spellings as pictures should allow the retrieval of that word as an "accurate" image in the same manner.

At the very least, Drawing/Writing provides training in memory and attention useful to language learning. As part of that learning process, invented spelling provides a logical, useful, transitional spelling system.

The ability to spell has become progressively worse. One reason is that people are reading less. Another is that people receive little direct training in visual attention. If students receive rigorous training in identifying and recording visual information and if they write a good deal more, they will at least read a good deal more of their own writing, and, in the context of Drawing/Writing, of their peer's writing. The exercise of building a class vocabulary by writing words on the board also encourages correct spelling as well as a larger vocabulary. A multi-modal approach to writing in grades K-12 and at the college and graduate school levels will train students as spellers as well as thinkers. After that, there is no better way to learn to spell than reading.

You can emphasize the usefulness of invented spelling with its high phonetic content as a powerful transitional system not only for spelling but for reading. The Blind Contour drawing and the drawings that follow are all, in a sense, transitional drawings on the way to achieving the "Perfect" Whole—a fully developed drawing. The "Perfect" Whole drawing itself is a transitional statement on the way to the Composite Abstraction, which is also a transitional work existing somewhere between optically accurate drawing and the completely abstract symbol system we call "writing." Like the CA, invented spelling provides a substantive transitional symbol system on the way to writing and reading.

**REMEMBER:** The Blind Contour drawing is simple but important; it not only records physical characteristics of the object, but it defines the boundary between what the student will draw and will not draw. Everything inside the outline will be examined. Everything outside the outline is eliminated as subject matter. In art, this distinction is called figure/ground. Artists must work with ground as much as they work with figure. In fact, figure and ground are equally important; this point becomes especially clear in abstract art. For Steps 1-4, Drawing/Writing students, like many beginning art students, work only with the figure, or the object under consideration. Then, like maturing artists, Drawing/Writing students move on to the Composite Abstraction (CA), learning to work with negative and positive space, or both figure and ground. The Blind Contour drawing is the first step in learning to limit an information search to one aspect of the figure, or subject: the outline. This step teaches students quite literally to define the boundaries of a topic.

*Hammer, Figure/Ground, Negative/Positive Space drawing*

**DISCUSSION: SPECIFIC:** Encourage students to talk about the non-usefulness of saying, "I don't like my drawing." It is fine to be critical, but you want students to discover that "not liking" something is too general as a judgment to encourage improvement. For this reason, probing questions are critical to increasingly precise thinking skills.

**SAY:** "Now, we are going to do a Blind Contour drawing. The drawing is an outline only. It is deceptively simple. An accurate drawing like this is actually challenging. It requires control."

**TIP:** The Blind Contour drawing allows the students to look at their objects while they draw, but not at the paper. During the Blind Contour drawing, some students hold their object up high so that they will look only at it and not down at the paper. Some students lay a piece of paper over their drawing hand to prevent themselves from seeing the paper and "cheating." If their paper is un-anchored, it may skitter around, requiring a book or a piece of tape.

**SAY:** "Take a new piece of paper. Put your initials and the date at the top. Now, take a magic marker, any color, any size. We are not going to use pencils for awhile. If you have drawn small, this time try to fill the page with your drawing. A larger drawing holds better from a distance in group critiques and allows you more room to record information."

**ASK:** "Why do you think we are going to start with markers and not pencils? If we use pencils to draw with, what does it mean? If we use markers to draw with, what does it mean?"

**DISCUSSION: SPECIFIC:** Ask students to think about pencils. What makes pencils different from markers? Pencils have erasers. Erasers correct mistakes. Pencils are safe because they allow tentative marks and correction.

Markers set up different expectations; markers require risks and commitment because the lines they make are strong and indelible. Because the goal of Drawing/Writing is information, not perfection, marker-use helps students appreciate mistakes as inaccurate information. Students also learn that no matter how careful they are, they will make mistakes. Even masterful drawings have inaccuracies. Students begin to see the connections between attention and accuracy. Because drawing is thought made visible, the move from inaccuracy to accuracy is particularly easy to follow with markers.

The goals connected with marker-use include:

- enhanced attention
- increasing clarity and accuracy
- experience with commitment and risk-taking
- an appreciation for mistakes as inaccuracies or incompleteness
- an acceptance that no drawing is perfect because no representation is ever complete.

Focus on the benefits and problems of pencils versus markers until the students come up with the idea that marker-use provides training in risk-taking, commitment, and attention. Show students that attention and quality of action are related. Lead the discussion around to issues involving clarity. Although mistakes made with markers are obvious, by the same token, a well-drawn line made by a marker is very clear.

**SAY:** "Because we cannot erase, markers encourage us to pay attention, while letting us relax about mistakes. Because we cannot erase, we practice risk-taking and commitment."

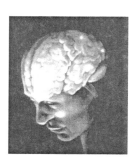

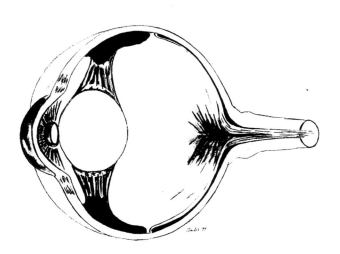

*Eyeball, Tim Lis, 1997*

**DO:** Copy the labeled drawing below of the eyeball. Ask students to copy it.

EYE BALL

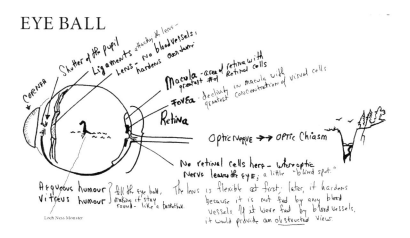

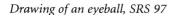

*Drawing of an eyeball, SRS 97*

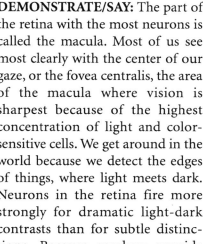

**DEMONSTRATE/SAY:** The part of the retina with the most neurons is called the macula. Most of us see most clearly with the center of our gaze, or the fovea centralis, the area of the macula where vision is sharpest because of the highest concentration of light and color-sensitive cells. We get around in the world because we detect the edges of things, where light meets dark. Neurons in the retina fire more strongly for dramatic light-dark contrasts than for subtle distinctions. Because markers provide strong lines, and thus strong light-dark contrast, neurons in our retinas fire strongly for marker drawings. By using magic markers, we make sure that the retina receives strong signals. What does that mean about a pencil drawing versus a marker drawing? Right, more neurons in the eye will fire more strongly for the marker drawing. At a basic neural level of excitation, the effect on the brain will be greater.

Have you ever wondered why certain images grab your attention more than others? Strong light-dark contrast is one of the reasons. So markers provide more visual power."

Using "'Hitchhikers' Guide" for reference, copy additional drawings of the eyeball, if you wish, asking students to copy them into their journals, too.

**DISCUSSION: OPEN-ENDED:** Encourage students to describe powerful images. They may describe the jackets of CD's, clothing or shoe advertisements, MTV videos, certain movies, computer graphics, TV programs. Ask students whether these images are powerful because of strong outlines or strong light-dark contrast, or because of content? Does strong content demand strong lines? Does strong emotional/narrative content come across despite the visual method of delivery? On the other hand, can strong visual appeal mislead us about the message? Could there be strong visual appeal and a weak message? Can we be manipulated by visual images? Ask students to provide specific examples. The literacy developed by this book allows students to discriminate among messages. These skills may protect them from being manipulated, visually or verbally. To encourage the protective benefits of the new literacy, the transfer of skills from Drawing/Writing into life must be made obvious. Keep asking for examples of messages with compelling and conflicting effects.

**TIP: Dyslexia:** The following information about vision is useful for all students, including dyslexic students. Showing students how teaching relates to their own learning is crucial. One of the major benefits of Drawing/Writing is that it incorporates strategies appropriate to cross-modal learning, optimizing learning for a range of students including dyslexic students. If dyslexic students know that for many learning disabled, or LD students, drawing is a strength and that drawing may help them to write and read better, their personal interest in Drawing/Writing will be aroused, Additional theories on dyslexia will interest them, too, making them more knowledgeable about their brains, including their visual systems.

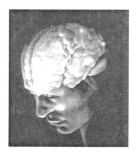

**SAY:** "One theory proposed several years ago by MIT researchers (Geiger, Gad and Lettvin, 1987) is that dyslexic students have fewer neurons in the macula, the area of the retina with the largest concentration of cells where most of us locate our center of gaze. According to the MIT research, these students should use peripheral vision to read. If they stare directly at a word, they will see it less well than if they read parafoveally, or, off to the side. Try looking right at a word. Now, put a piece of paper with one large black dot on it over the middle of a sentence. Look at the dot. Can you read the words on either side more clearly than you can see the dot? If you can, you may be a candidate for parafoveal reading.

"Reading difficulties may also be due to hearing problems. Experts at Yale pinpoint "phonologic" deficits or letter-to-sound non-correspondence as a major part of the problem for dyslexic students. (Sally Shaywitz, *Scientific American*, November, 1996, p. 98-104). A poor reader looks at a word but cannot break the word into constituent sounds. Most children learn to read by pronouncing the letters in the word "cat" as "kuh" "aah-tuh." Some cannot. Do any of us have this difficulty?

"It's possible that learning to connect lines and shapes into drawings may help with reading. Learning to see more clearly, listen more carefully, draw, write and speak more precisely can only improve writing and reading skills."

**DISCUSSION:** Ask students to think about Drawing/Writing in connection with strategies useful for reading from their point of view. They are becoming increasingly aware of individual items like line, shape, shadow, highlight. They are learning to examine structure. Every time they draw, they write, translating one mode of expression into another. These same skills are necessary for successful auditory processing in reading. In addition, the sounds of language are constantly being practiced in the Drawing/Writing classroom through peer pair sharing, discussions and group critiques, heightening awareness of words as sounds.

**SAY:** "Now, we are going to do a Blind Contour Drawing."

**ASK:** "What do you think a Blind Contour drawing is? Focus on the word 'blind.' What do you think the word 'blind' means?"

**DISCUSSION: SPECIFIC:** Let the students respond until you get a range of responses, including these in connection with a "blind" drawing:

- closing the eyes while drawing—that is, blind to the object and the paper. An accurate drawing would presuppose a very accurate mental image and the ability to transfer that by touch alone.

- looking only at the paper—that is, blind to the object. Again, this drawing would assume that the mind held an accurate mental image.

- looking only at the object—that is, blind to the paper. This is the answer you are looking for.

**ASK:** "Is it possible to draw something with our eyes closed if we don't have a mental picture of it? Think of a person. We can draw a stick figure, but how much farther can we get if we have not done drawings of the human figure? We have stock images in our heads. Think about the houses we draw. Do these really look like houses? We draw an idea of a certain kind of a house with a chimney, a door, some windows, and a pointed roof. This is a stock, or standard image. It is not a drawing of an actual house. A drawing of an actual house includes more information, and drawings of other very different houses are possible with walls of windows, for instance, and flat roofs.

*Stock house, sun, grass, tree*

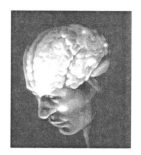

"What else might the word 'blind' mean? We could draw with our eyes closed, or we could not look at the object. What good would that do? That would be like drawing with our eyes closed. Or, we could draw by being blind to, or not looking at, the paper. Which do you think we will do in connection with the Blind Contour? Which is logical, given the goals in Drawing/Writing? Right, looking hard at the object but not at the paper so that we make sure we are learning about the object."

**SAY**: "We need to look hard at objects if we are are going to learn anything specific and individual about them. After we stare hard and do an accurate drawing, we start to store an accurate specific image of that object in our heads instead of a generic drawing. Let's use our objects to practice careful seeing as the way to store accurate mental images."

**ASK**: "What does an outline drawing do?"

**DISCUSSION: SPECIFIC:** The contour drawing establishes the boundaries between figure and ground, or between what is under consideration and what is not under consideration. Encourage students to see that the contour line marks where the object begins and ends. This understanding can be transfered to other tasks like determining where the topic for a paper begins and ends.

**SAY:** "It is easy to understand the difference between figure and ground in a drawing when we can recognize the subject matter. Let me show you this by doing a blind contour drawing of my object. In this case, the figure, or the subject matter, is a hammer. All the space around it is called 'ground.' In art, both the fig-  ure and the ground are equally important and work together. In fact, in some art work, the ground is as important as the figure and sometimes cannot be clearly distinguished from it.

*Hammer, Figure/Ground, Negative/Positive Space drawing*

"In this case, we are going to think about the figure as our main subject. It is the thing we are focusing on, paying attention to and learning about. So, a contour drawing is going to show us where our subject begins and ends. The contour drawing will show us the overall shape of the subject, and it will give us specific information about the outside edge of our subject. The outside edge provides a good deal of information."

**DEMONSTRATE:** Do an outline drawing of your object on the blackboard. Do <u>not</u> look at the board; <u>do</u> look hard at your hammer.
    Now focus on the word "contour."

**ASK:** "What do you think the word 'contour' means?"

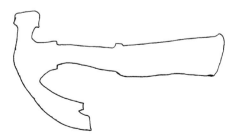

*Outline of hammer with blank ground around it.*

**DEMONSTRATE:** On the board, deconstruct the word "contour" into *con* meaning "with" or "together" and *tour* meaning around. Talk about world tours. Or tourism. Help students get the idea that a contour drawing is like an exploratory trip with a continuous line that goes around an object. This kind of contour drawing is not "topographic," a

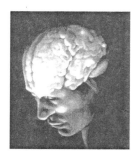

 **POWERFUL IDEA:** Choice of angle is a powerful idea.

Blind Contour drawing, hammer

type of contour drawing that registers the ups and downs of the surface of the object like topographic maps of mountains. Clarify the distinction between the two kinds of contour drawing.

SAY: "Our contour drawing just follows the exact outline of the object. It does not enter into the form, tracing across the inner surface. Let me show you what I mean."

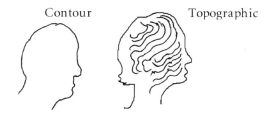

Topographic versus outline contour drawing.

DEMONSTRATE: Hold the hammer in several positions before you start to draw. Then, draw the outline of the hammer on the board. Start at one spot and go entirely around the outside of your object until you feel you have come back to where you started. Only then, lift the chalk off the board. Make sure you look at the object only, not at the board as you do this. Make clear that a blind contour drawing involves looking hard at the object and not at the paper. Your drawing will depend on the angle you choose.

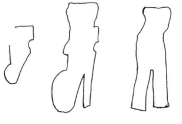

Drawing of a hammer head-on and from
directly below and directly above

Photo, plane, profile and top view

SAY: "It certainly makes a difference how I hold the hammer. If I hold it straight on, I could draw a circle on top of a rectangle and that could be a hammer, wouldn't it?" You will return to this point again.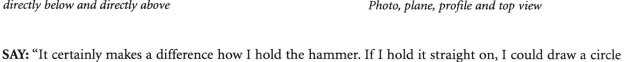

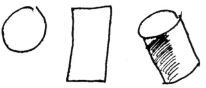

A circle, a rectangle, and a Coke can seen from
above, from the side, and from a three-quarter view.

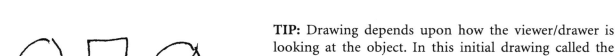

TIP: Drawing depends upon how the viewer/drawer is looking at the object. In this initial drawing called the Blind Contour, the student must suppress everything but what appears to be the outline of the thing being drawn.

SAY: "Suppose I am drawing a Coke can. Depending on how I hold the can, the drawing may 'look like' a Coke can, or it may 'not look like' a Coke can. For instance, a

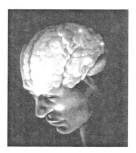

 **REMINDER:** Your Blind Contour drawing will not close exactly where it should. This imperfect or inaccurate result is desirable because it shows you have not cheated by looking away from the object to the board. Even if your drawing is wildly inaccurate and distorted, it still registers information.

 **POWERFUL IDEA:** The idea of defining an information search is a powerful idea. The ability to decide what one wants to know and then to figure out where in general that idea or body of knowledge begins and ends is a useful skill.

bird's eye view of a Coke can is a circle; a direct, frontal view of a coke can is a rectangle. A Coke can seen from above, but at an angle, looks like this. Any object can be seen and therefore drawn from many angles."

**DEMONSTRATE:** Draw a circle and a rectangle, and then a Coke can seen from directly above, and at an angle.

Pick up your object again. Rotate it in your hands. Do another Blind Contour drawing, from another angle. Try to find an angle that results in a contour drawing that is not typical of the object. For instance, the drawing below does not look like a hammer, yet it is a contour drawing of a hammer if the hammer is held directly before your eyes, head on.

*Hammer , head on, SRS '97.*

**SAY:** "Artists are rarely bored. Some artists live to a ripe old age, fully engaged in their art. They always have something to do because they can always see things in new ways."

**TIP:** Stress artists' ability to entertain themselves. Students need skills for work and outlets for emotion. One of your goals is to convince students that it is natural and desirable to be artists and writers and that both sets of skills will benefit them in the workplace, marketplace and in everyday life, including solitary periods, over a lifetime.

**SAY:** After bringing up the fact that artists are rarely bored because they have strategies for seeing the world around them in new ways, I bring up the topic of self-sufficiency.

"The brain is encased in a bony skull, protected by tough membranes called the meninges, or envelopes, which contain a cushioning layer of fluid. When we are born, the skull has not quite grown closed. It has a little flexible leeway to make the skull compressible so that the baby's head can pass down the birth canal. This flexible area where the plates of the brain meet, like sections of an orange, is called the 'fontanelle,' or 'soft spot.' The fontanelle closes sometime after birth. Once the fontanelle closes—were it not for our five senses—we would become shut-ins, locked away inside our skulls. Our senses connect us to the world. Still, sometimes we feel alone. At these times, drawing and writing are especially important."

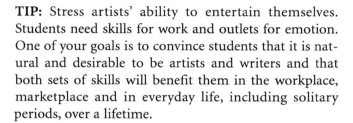

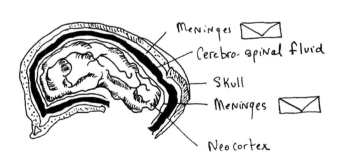

*Cross section of the brain with skull, meminges, cerebro-spinal fluid, SRS 97*

**SAY:** "The kind of contour drawing I am talking about goes around the outside of the object only. By going around the outside of the object, what have we done?" You are leading the students to ideas about where the object begins and ends and thus, for instance, where a research topic begins and ends. Younger children may associate the outline of an object with the subject of a story. As young children continue with the Drawing/Writing five-step, their ideas will become clearer about how they will write a story. Drawing/Writing is a clarification process. Drawings clarify the picture. Writing makes the picture more explicit by using language.

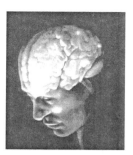

**REMEMBER:** After a few minutes, students will finish the Blind Contour. The first Blind Contour drawing is often unsatisfactory because it is rushed. Students tend to rush the Blind Contour because they think it is simple and because they are unused to sustained control. Tell students to take their time. A clean, accurate line drawing demands concentration and control. Reassure students that once they complete these two Blind Contour drawings, the hardest drawings will be over.

Do not be discouraged if students tell you that this drawing is easy or stupid. You have told them up front that this drawing is deceptively simple, and that it is hard to do, and that it is important. Because it is so difficult to produce an accurate contour drawing, students are often frustrated by this first exercise. Once you have completed the Regular Contour and started the Basic Shapes drawings, students will be more confident and into "the swing" of the process.

**SAY:** "Yes, you are right. This drawing is like saying, 'I am going to write a paper on the pyramids. I am not going to write about castles. I am also not going to find out how and why the Egyptians mummified the dead. I am not going to figure out why they used the lotus motif on the capitals of columns. I am only going to explore the construction of pyramids.' "

**TIP:** Eventually, you will gain skill with the Blind Contour drawing. For students' sakes, make your Blind Contour drawing *not* come out perfectly. Many students' first Blind Contour drawings are inaccurate and therefore frustrating—largely due to rushing. Initially, many students lack patience and are unused to sustained concentration. If you do draw an accurate blind contour drawing, have the grace to act surprised, and say something like:

**SAY:** "I am very surprised; this is pretty good. Blind Contour drawings are hard to do. You may find this first drawing frustrating, but if you go slowly enough, you will still be recording useful information about your object."

Add, "Do you see how the line tells us something about the object? For instance, this line tells me that my object is smooth here, bumpy here, sharp over here."

**TIP:** As you describe your line quality, you increase students' vocabulary. Similes will occur naturally: "Bumpy like a dirt road." Then, you can search for a better word than "bumpy." "Rutted" might be better because it emphasizes the down parts rather than the up parts in more graphic ways.

**SAY/DO:** "Let's do a Blind Contour drawing. Put your object where you can see it easily, and remember not to look at your paper. Remember to use a marker. And try to fill the whole paper with your drawing. Try to draw big."

**SAY:** "As soon as you finish the Blind Contour drawing, you are going to write about this drawing . You will write on the same side of the paper. Write this: 'My Blind Contour drawing tells me that my object is...because....'

"Your drawing tells you something. It tells you that you already know something about your object. For instance, I could write, 'My Blind Contour drawing tells me that my object is ....'(substitute the appropriate adjectives to describe the quality of the contour line you used to draw the outline of your object). For instance, after drawing a Blind Contour of my hammer, I could write 'smooth, straight, rounded, curving, angular.' Remember to include the word 'because' which will make you explain why you chose those adjectives."

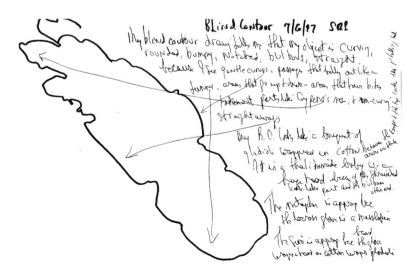

*Blind Contour of a lacrosse glove, SRS*

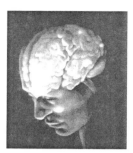

 **REMEMBER:** Ask the student who wrote the word to define it. Write that definition and all other class suggestions for defining that word on the board.

"Show your drawing and read your writing aloud to your peer. Then, look at your peer's drawing and listen to your peer read aloud. Now, record in your Journal all of the words your peer used that you do not know. Also, record words you like. When something appeals to our senses, we use the word 'aesthetics;' you might already know the word 'crackling' but because it appeals to you aesthetically (that is, to your sense of sound) you might want to write it down to remind yourself to use it in your writing."

## SHARE AND BUILD IN PEER PAIRS:

**DEMONSTRATE:** Go around the room, asking all students for words used by their peers which are new or desirable to add to their vocabularies. Write all of these words on the board. Have all students take down all other students' words shared in this way. Build up a class vocabulary with **Share and Build in Peer Pairs** with every Drawing/Writing step. Vocabulary building is as relevant at the college level as it is at the kindergarten level.

**ASK:** "Besides pleasing words, are there particular parts of your peer's drawing that you find pleasing? Lines have aesthetic qualities, just like words."

**PEER PAIRS:** Discuss aesthetically pleasing elements in their writings and drawings.

**SAY**: "Let's make up some similes to go with these Blind Contour drawings. Could someone define a simile?"

**TIP:** Introduce and define new terms rather than assuming students understand or remember them. Even adults may be unsure what similes are—or they may have a different understanding of the term than others in the group.

The goals of a Drawing/Writing teacher are multiple. At this point, you are interested in teaching students to:

- pay attention
- describe their object accurately in terms of line
- describe their object by reflecting in words what the line tells them they know about the object
- understand that aesthetics plays a huge role in how words and images are crafted and used
- understand that drawing and writing can be used in straightforward description, as well as in more poetic or metaphoric ways, when associations may shed light on the item being described or may serve as a springboard for inventive thought. By teaching students to draw accurately, to write descriptively, and THEN to write metaphorically, you establish an effective rhythm for their mental lives. They learn a procedure for fact-finding that encourages apt similes and metaphors as well as sound conclusions and theories.

**ASK:** "What does the word 'simile' remind you of?"

**DEMONSTRATE:** Write the word 'simile' on the board. Add whatever words students come up with. Among them should be the word 'similar.' Add the words 'like' and 'as.'

**SAY**: "Let me make up a simile about my Blind Contour drawing. Remember, one of the basic questions that drives intelligent thought is how things are alike and different. I am going to try to figure out what this outline drawing is like. The simile I come up with does not have to have anything to do with my hammer. I am going to do what is called 'free associating.' Here is how I do it."

**ASIDE:** Free association allows students to generate similes from their drawings in fast, intuitive ways, making connections between two apparently disparate items. The ability to link dissimilar items encourages inventive thinking. At first, many students have trouble generating similes about the Blind Contour drawing. Practice with a line drawing and free association trains students to be inventive on a fast, intuitive level. "Off-the-wall" associations are causes for celebration.

Once the connection is made between the Blind Contour drawing and some item the line drawing resembles, the student has created the connection that supports a simile. Like other mental skills, free association can be taught. Like intuition, free association generates ideas. It is non-linear in the sense of employing "dog-leg logic," or thinking that makes an apparently illogical, abrupt turn like a dog's hind leg. Students learn to use similes to stimulate unusual comparisons.

**ASIDE:** Explanatory writing encourages students to reflect about their free associations, and to defend them and to refine them. For instance, if a student writes, "My Blind Contour drawing of a pair of pliers looks like a bird's beak because the two blades are open in a beak-like way," the student may notice that the shape of the blades is like the beak of a particular bird, the Toucan. The student can then write, "My Blind Contour drawing looks like the beak of a toucan because...." Additional writing may reflect on similarities in function—and differences in function—between beaks and scissor-like blades. Comparisons and contrasts deepen an information base, broadening its usefulness.

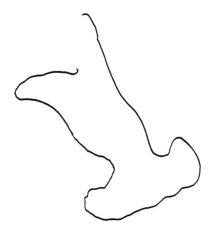

*Hammerhead shark Blind Contour of a hammer*

**DEMONSTRATE:** Rotate your drawing, turning it all around. Make some thoughtful noises like "hmmmm" and "I wonder if....."

**SAY:** "I've got it. 'My Blind Contour drawing of a hammer looks like a shark because....' Don't forget to use the word 'because' every time you make a simile. We have to explain the simile to ourselves. Once we explain the simile to ourselves, we will know whether the 'likeness link' really fits. For instance, the word 'because' forces me to write this: 'My Blind Contour drawing of a hammer is like a shark because certain sharks' heads have snub yet flaring profiles just like the squat, flanged snout of a hammer. Sharks use their heads like battering rams to stun prey, then they tear it apart with their teeth.' Do you see how I now understand more about sharks' methods of feeding through my own simile? The hammer as a tool *is* relevant to the way hammerhead sharks feed."

**ASK/DO:** "Even though I could have written anything I wanted to, I saw a shark in the Blind Contour outline of my hammer. The interesting question is this: What is the connection between your simile and your object? Write about that."

**DEMONSTRATE:** Write on the board, "The connection between my shark simile and a hammer is that some sharks knock their prey senseless in a hammering way and then eat them."

**ASK:** "What did you come up with?"

**PEER SHARE**

**SAY:** "Now, let's make that simile into a metaphor. What's a metaphor?" (Never assume a term is known.)

   "A simile creates a link between two items using the words 'like' and 'as'; 'My drawing is like a shark's head.' A metaphor is a comparison between two items made without using the words 'like' or 'as': 'My drawing is a shark's head.' We know that the drawing is not really a shark's head; it is a drawing. But the similarities are so powerful that it is possible not only to compare but to *identify* the two items."

**SAY/DO:** "Right, just take away the word 'like' or 'as' from your simile. Then, you have an instant metaphor. For instance, 'My Blind Contour drawing of a hammer is like a shark's head' turns into 'My Blind Contour drawing of a hammer is a shark's head.'"

**SAY:** "Share what you have drawn and written, including your similes and metaphors."

**PEER-SHARE AND BUILD**

**DEEP QUESTION:** "Do you think it is harder to write a simile or a metaphor? Which seems more powerful to you?"

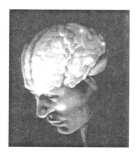

**DISCUSSION: OPEN-ENDED:** Most students agree that metaphor is more powerful and harder to construct because it is so direct: My hammer is a shark. By talking about the differences between similes and metaphors in terms of power and difficulty, students increase their appreciation for language as an exciting, useful system about which they can make personal decisions. They do not have to accept language as a culturally imposed structure designed to constrain and control them. Quite the contrary; they can use language to expand their lives.

**SAY:** "I tend to agree with you; metaphor is harder. A metaphor is more than a comparison, isn't it? If I say that a drawing is a shark, that's a lot more direct than saying a drawing is like a shark. In fact, what does the metaphor say about the relationship between the drawing of a hammer and a shark?

"Let's think about the word 'metaphor.' The prefix *meta* means 'over, above, beyond.' The root word *phor* comes from the verb *pherein* and means 'to carry.' Thus a metaphor is a way to carry meaning over from one thing to another thing in a way that goes beyond, or further.

"A prefix is a word fragment that qualifies the word it joins. The prefix *pre-* means before. For instance, prehistoric means before the dawn of recorded history. Metaphysical means beyond the physical in the sense of the spiritual or philosophical. So a metaphor must carry meaning a long way, and *up*—that is, to an elevated understanding. It seems to me that a comparison made without the helping words "like" or "as" elevates understanding because of its directness. If we probe for the abstract quality behind the comparison, we may achieve a more general understanding. For instance, I might write that the contour drawing of the hammer is a hammerhead shark, or our metaphor might be, 'My contour drawing of a hammer is brute power.'"

**RECORD:** Write the words "simile" and "metaphor" and their definitions and derivations on the board. Write the words "prefix" and "suffix."

**TIP:** If students learn prefixes and suffixes, they can figure out what many words mean without using a dictionary. This skill is useful when reading, or for the verbal sections of standardized intelligence tests. Because so many of our words derive from Latin, teaching Latin prefixes, suffixes and roots is part of literacy education, as training in drawing is part of literacy education. By equalizing literacy education for all cultural groups, test scores for language-based intelligence tests should come closer together.

**TIP:** If time allows, teach prefixes and suffixes. Although many students no longer study Greek and Latin, they can learn Latin and Greek prefixes and suffixes. This information in and of itself will increase their vocabulary skills.

**DEMONSTRATE:** Instruct students to do this Blind Contour drawing and writing a second time.

**SAY/DO:** "Let's try a second Blind Contour drawing. Take your time. Really look at the object and draw slowly. Write in the same way about this drawing; ' My second blind contour drawing tells me that my object is....because...' Now, make a new simile and turn that into a metaphor. Then, Peer-Share and Build as usual."

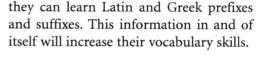

*Lists of prefixes and suffixes*          **PEER SHARE AND BUILD**

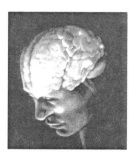

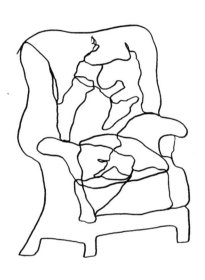

For some a chair is just something you sit in but for me a chair is much more. It has many characteristics. It is rich in color and texture. And stands statuesque like a human figure with its long curvy arms and legs. It looks like it is posing with all of its charm and grace. The chair has a meltingly soft veiled modeling of its features. It shares the same silky feel and texture as a human figures skin. It's back is broad and sturdy and its seat is round and shapely.

With its many tonal values it is an artists canvas filled with a variety of colors, lines and planes.

Next time you sit in your favorite chair feel the warm embrace, real or imaginary.

*Blind Contour drawing, Chair, Pamela Frigo, Drawing/Writing, Continuing Education, Westfield State College, 1997*

*Note: This Blind Contour includes "topographic" contour lines; these lines are __not__ required in the Blind Contour as it is usually taught. Pam chose to include them at this point as part of her early exploration of this object.*

**ASIDE:** By introducing students to aesthetics, you are preparing them for Step 5 when you will introduce a very powerful idea: pleasing or right-seeming relationships among line, form and space. These relationships in a drawing provide bases for decisions about pleasing or right-seeming relationships with people, places, and things.

Shapes and lines can be in balance—or not. So can relationships between people. Aesthetic and ethical resolution depend upon the balance or imbalance of certain properties. In Plato's time, when Beauty, Goodness and Truth were related concepts, it was taken for granted that aesthetics provided a basis for moral decision-making. A relationship between aesthetics and behavior is less accessible now, probably because neither ethics nor aesthetics are standard academic subjects. Although venerable precedents exist for connecting aesthetics and ethics, the idea that training in drawing provides criteria for behavior is startling. In a world of multiple values, a reliable, personal basis for ethical decisions is useful.

Training in aesthetics can transfer into ethics. This transfer is encouraged in Drawing/Writing.

**GROUP CRITIQUE:** Ask students to display their Blind Contour drawing and writing. Gather the students around. Set the guidelines for discussion. By setting guidelines for critiques, you will teach students how to praise and criticize each other in constructive ways.

**TIP:** Unless they are directly called on, many students tend to take a mental rest. When you call on them, they ask you to repeat your question. This is not efficient. Train all of students to pay attention all of the time. In my large art survey lectures at Westfield State College where I use seating charts so that I can call on students by name, I repeatedly tell my students that *each* of them must think about the questions I am asking. No one is to assume that I will call on someone else. Recognizing and knowing students by name is critical to their positive classroom performance.

Make your criteria for critiques clear:

- only positive comments about accuracy and pleasingness are acceptable. Silence has its implications.
- every student must participate.

In this way, you train all students to pay attention and you train all of them to speak intelligently. Students will learn to formulate answers to every question you raise, whether you call on them or not. Knowing that they may be called on at any time, students will stop "spacing out."

**SAY:** "Let's have positive comments about the quality of these line drawings. If you look at a drawing and it seems entirely inaccurate, what might you still find to say that is supportive?"

This question encourages students to think about other qualities than accuracy, including aesthetics, as explored below.

**RECORD/SAY:** "Lines have qualities. Let's write some of these on the board:

- fluency (the degree to which the line flows smoothly)
- direction (lines may go up or down or diagonally, vertically or horizontally, and appear to do so at a certain speed depending upon how they are drawn)
- line weight (the thickness or thinness of a line)
- line as expressive (depending on fluency and weight, certain lines will appear to express certain emotions or ideas).

**SAY:** "Lines have direction, weight and rhythm. A line may not be entirely accurate, but that inaccuracy may increase its emotional power. If we think about a line as pleasing or displeasing, we move into what realm? Correct, aesthetics. Our comments in group critiques can refer to accuracy or to pleasingness. When a drawing is accurate, let's mention it. When a drawing has emotional power, let's try to explain why the drawing has power. When it's pleasing, let's try to analyze why it is pleasing."

**SAY:** "Put your Drawing/Writing papers away in your portfolio. Put your object back in the box, put your pencils and markers in their boxes. Put your portfolios.... (you decide where in the classroom)."

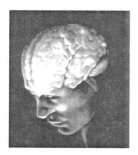

## 1.3  The Regular Contour Drawing

<u>OBJECTIVES:</u>

*Accuracy through adjustments*

<u>MATERIALS:</u> objects, markers, paper, folders

**BACKGROUND:**

The terms "blind" and "regular" are used in studio art courses. This Contour drawing could be called a Looking Contour to distinguish it from a Blind Contour, but the term would be like teaching students to use baby-talk—an alternative, unnecessary language. The terms Blind Contour and Regular Contour are the accepted terms for these drawings. Blind Contour means the student may only look at the object while drawing; the purpose for this limitation is to force the student to look at the subject under consideration. The Regular Contour, on the other hand, allows students to look both at the object and at the paper as they draw, learning to judge "spatial relations." Spatial relations are the distances between certain points on the object and corresponding points on the paper. These distances can be judged by looking at the object, and then away from the object, down at the paper, making ongoing decisions about relationships between points, lines and distances. Training in judging spatial relations teaches students how to measure distances through estimation by observing relationships.

<u>PROCEDURE:</u>

**SAY/DO:** "You know the procedure. Get your folders, objects, and materials, and sit in peer pairs. Remember, no pencils."

**REHASH HOMEWORK**

**HOMEWORK:** Remind students that they will repeat the following exercise for homework. Remind them that you will not be writing instructions on the board and that they will not be taking their in-class portfolios home. Students will need to remember what they did in class.

**SAY/DO:** "Take a new piece of paper. Write the date and your initials at the top and add the words 'Regular Contour drawing.' Artists and writers sign and date their work. Make sure you are using markers, and make sure your drawing fills the page."

**DEMONSTRATE:** Write the date and your initials on the board. Add the words "Regular Contour Drawing."

**ASK:** "What do you think a regular contour drawing is? We know what a Blind Contour drawing is. What would a 'regular' contour drawing be?"

**DISCUSSION: SPECIFIC:** Ask students what the word "regular" means as opposed to the word "blind." Students will eventually come up with the idea that "regular" means that they can look at the object and at the paper.

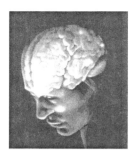

**SAY/DO:** "When we look back and forth from the paper to the object and back again, we are judging spatial relations. Spatial relations measure the distance between one point and another point on your object. Because you are using markers, you cannot erase. So draw slowly enough to allow yourself to get this contour drawing as accurate as you can by judging spatial relations."

**DEMONSTRATE:** Hold up your object and start a contour drawing. Keep looking back and forth from the object to the board as you draw.

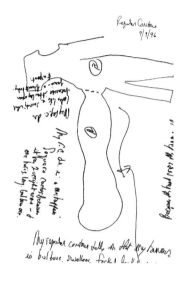

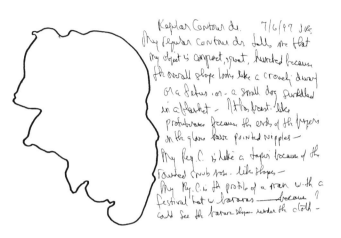

*Regular Contour drawing, hammer SRS*              *Regular Contour drawing, lacrosse glove, SRS*

**SAY:** "Take your time. This drawing takes several minutes. A longer time means you are being extremely attentive and are probably drawing an object with a complicated outline."

**SAY/DO:** "Now, write, 'My Regular Contour drawing tells me that my object is...because....'"

**DEMONSTRATE:** Write on the board, "My Regular Contour drawing tells me that my object is rounded, elongated, curving, blunt, smooth because the contour line is sensitive to these characteristics of the rectangular hammer head and the long, straight shaft." The contour drawing records these characteristics of my hammer.

**SAY/DO:** "Now, generate one simile and turn that simile into a metaphor."

**DEMONSTRATE:** Write, "My Regular Contour drawing of the hammer is like a candy cane because it has the same long shaft and hooked end."

**SAY:** "This is the simile. Now, for the metaphor: 'My Regular Contour drawing of the hammer is a candy cane.' Or, I could generate an entirely new metaphor: 'My Regular Contour drawing of a hammer is a long-necked bird with an open beak.'"

**PEER SHARE AND BUILD**

**ASIDE:** Besides accurate multi-sensory physical description, Drawing/Writing teaches students to make comparisons. Douglas Hofstadter maintains in his book *Gödel, Escher, Bach* that the basic questions of intelligence focus on likenesses and differences.

**REMEMBER:** Once students have completed the Blind Contour drawing and the Regular Contour drawing, you are in a sense "home free." Students have learned to focus, they have learned to accept at least one wildly inaccurate drawing, the Blind Contour, and they understand from direct experience how quickly drawing skills improve. They are ready, now, for more sustained, more complicated drawing.

**RECORD:** Write all class vocabulary on the board, reminding students to take down all words and ideas recorded on the board.

**DEEP QUESTIONS:** "Which is harder to draw, the Blind Contour or the Regular Contour? Why? How are they alike? How are they different?"

**DEEP QUESTIONS:** Thinking about how things are alike and different provokes questions. A blue heron and a pterodactyl are alike because of the extreme length of their wings and hollow bones. In other ways, blue herons and pterodactyls are very different. What is a major difference?

**SAY:** "Contour drawings have to be done slowly to be accurate. It is hard to slow down, isn't it, especially when the object seems so simple? What about an angular object ? Does it take longer to draw? Some drawings feel pleasing because the lines flow. Is an angular drawing pleasing even though the lines do not flow? When a drawing registers information in pleasing ways, it exhibits aesthetic properties."

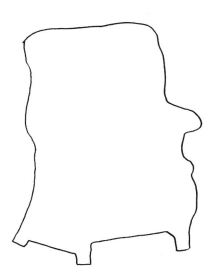

My regular contour drawing tells me that my object has many smooth edges and contains fluid movement. My drawing is like a paperdoll cut out because it looks like the object has been severed from the whole. It is exceedingly dignified in form and style. The object has numerations sticking out so that they may be creased and folded over. My regular contour drawing is a chair because of the easy comfortable feel of the small arches at the top and two apperdages at the bottom. It has a bulkiness to it. The heavy black outline shows my object is ample, extensive, and has a sturdy body. It contains a certain softness with its curvaceous lines, making it esthetically pleasing to the eye.

*Pamela Frigo, Regular Contour drawing, Chair, Continuing Education, Westfield State College, 1996*

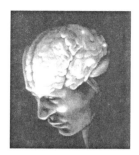

ʆ

# Step Two

# BASIC GEOMETRIC SHAPES

*— Tom Sawyer painting a fence on the surface of the earth which is a spinning ball, by Claus Kormannshaus, 1997. A picture of a Euclidean fence on the surface of a non-Euclidean world.*

Surfaces that appear flat locally and are useful as flat locally—for instance, pouring a flat slab and building a house—may be curved, globally or cosmically, and be far more usefully described as curving at such a scale. Such is the case with the Earth. Now that we are able to fly above the surface of the Earth and look back at a green and blue sphere, several geometries are necessary to describe our experience.

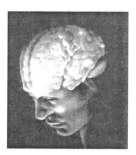

 **ASIDE:** Mathematician Rudy Rucker describes the number-space distinction as "extremely basic." Together the pair make up what the Greeks called a "dyad," or pair of opposing concepts... What takes intellectual priority, Rucker asks, number or space? His answer is neither. "Smooth-seeming matter is said to be made up of atoms, scattered about like little spots, but the chunky little atoms can be thought of as bumps in the smooth fabric of space. Pushing still further, we find some thinkers breaking smooth space into distinct quanta, which are in turn represented as smooth mathematical functions. The smooth underlies the spotty, and the spotty underlies the smooth."[18] Rucker cites Quantum physicist Niels Bohr's term "complementarity", commenting, "Reality is one, and language introduces impossible distinctions that need not be made" (7).

Rucker adds, "It is more likely that the number-space split is a fundamental feature of reality, and that our brains have evolved so as to be able to deal with both modes of existence" (9). "Two complementarity world views seem to be built into our brains—the human brain has allocated different functions to its two halves." (9). Rucker adds, "The ideas of mathematics reflect certain facts about the world as human beings experience it. Just as our bodies have evolved in response to objective conditions imposed by the environment, our ideas have evolved in response to certain fundamental features of reality" (14). Fractal geometry is one such feature to which our bi-hemispheric brains respond.

 **ADDITIONAL INFORMATION:** Geometry is the study of shapes and the study of space. Space affects objects; objects affect space.

---

[18] Rudy Rucker, *Mind Tools,* Boston: Houghton Mifflin, 1987.

# STEP TWO

# Basic Geometric Shapes

### 2.1 Euclidean and Non-Euclidean Basic Shapes: Background

### 2.2 Euclidean Basic Shape Drawing

### 2.3 Fractal Basic Shape Drawing

### 2.4 Organic Basic Shape Drawing

Drawing/Writing students practice breaking down their objects into Euclidean and Non-Euclidean shapes. Of the four categories listed under Non-Euclidean shapes, students will practice two: fractal shapes and organic shapes. In the process of working through Step 2, students refresh and extend their understanding of Euclidean geometry. They also learn about spherical geometry and "rubber sheet" geometry, discovering that there are systems for representing curved lines as well as straight lines, for representing round or bulging surfaces as well as flat surfaces, and for representing irregular shapes as well as regular shapes.

By experimenting with five different geometries, students expand their thinking about shapes in particular and about explanation systems in general. Explanation systems, like words, are approximate. More than one provides a fuller description. It is as important to teach students many words as it is to expose them to several geometries. The word "peach" does not communicate the experience of eating a peach. Other words and phrases are necessary: "pink and rose, fragrant, fuzzy, juicy, containing a large corrugated pit, sweet as a summer morning."

OBJECTIVES:

      *Mathematics is larger than arithmetic and includes geometry*
      *Geometry is the study of shapes*
      *There are Euclidean and non-Euclidean geometries*
      *One system builds on another*
      *More than one system is necessary for a comprehensive description*

MATERIALS: objects, markers, paper, folders

## 2.1 Euclidean and Non-Euclidean Basic Shapes: Background

To most of us, the word "math" means arithmetic while geometry refers to Euclidean shapes like circles, squares and triangles drawn with protractors and rulers on flat surfaces. However, geometry includes more than this. Curving and bulging shapes, curved planes and spaces require exploration, too. Geometry is the study of both shapes and space, a unified duality. Space is recognized and described in relation to the behavior or presentation of shapes, and vice versa.

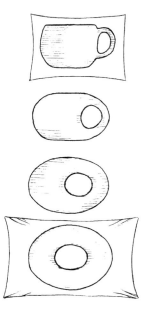

*Doughnut and tea cup transformation,*
*Claus Kormannshaus, 1997*

**ADDITIONAL INFORMATION:** Shapes defined by holes are called "torus" in the singular and "tori" in the plural. The word "genus" denotes quantity or level of holes in a torus, as in a torus of genus zero, one, two and so on. For instance, a doughnut is a torus of genus 1: it has one hole. Dark glasses are a torus of genus 2: there are two holes in the frames. No matter how much you stretch a rubber doughnut, a hole remains a hole. In the world of rubber sheet geometry, a tea cup and a doughnut are the same; they both have only one hole. They are tori of genus 1. Although the tea cup appears to have two holes, one for the liquid and one in the handle, when a tea cup is stretched out flat, as it could be it if were made of rubber, the declivity which holds the liquid turns into a flat surface, while the hole in the tea cup handle remains a true hole. No matter how far you stretch the rubber, even so far that the hole appears to become a line, this is not so. The hole remains. A pretzel is a torus of what genus? Right, three. Several languages for shapes—several geometries—expand students' appreciation for shapes. By learning to read other geometries, Drawing/Writing students gain additional confidence in the power of language to describe the shape of thought.

Several systems of geometry are required to describe our increasingly complex understandings of the world. Our sensory apparati, like those of other organisms, evolved adaptively; currently, because our technology takes us to cosmic macro levels and atomic micro levels previously unavailable to our senses, we perceive a world both flat and curved, planar and spherical, rigid and flexible. Our sense perceptions make it possible for us to navigate in the world effectively, physically and mentally. As our mathematical and geometric understandings grow, so must our understandings of language. Language is not a straight jacket. Like geometry, language, too, is malleable and approximate. Like several systems of geometry, words provide insight in the aggregate.

New geometries replace old geometries. An "old" geometry like Euclidean geometry still holds true in certain circumstances. Geometrical facts are "conventions... one geometry cannot be more true than another; it can only be more convenient (Poincaré in Layzer, 345). The Euclidean geometry of our childhood—triangles, circles, squares—works well for flat surfaces, and can be used as an entry into the larger study of shapes. The constructivist approach begins with what students know and builds from there, adding additional levels of classification. The Drawing/Writing program begins its Basic Shapes section with Euclidean geometry, moving on to spherical and fractal geometry. Largely because of computers, geometries other than Euclidean, including fractal geometry, are reaching the popular imagination.

In Step 2, students examine their ideas about geometry. When they draw a triangle on the curved surface of a balloon, the lines are not straight and the angles do not add up to 180 degrees. When students draw a triangle on a rubber sheet and stretch the sheet, the shape of the triangle changes, too. Shapes like triangles which were once so well known become unfamiliar. In fact, a triangle drawn on a rubber sheet can be stretched to form a circle. The behavior of shapes and space are variable and interrelated.

*A triangle drawn on a stretched rubber sheet becoming a circle*

Rubber sheet geometry takes invariant or non-changing properties like straightness, length, and angle-size and makes them variant or changeable. Three sides no longer distinguish a triangle drawn on a rubber sheet; insideness and outsideness do, including what we call holes. The question becomes: does the continuous line drawn on the rubber sheet enclose a hole or delineate an unbroken surface? A doughnut has one hole no matter how the thickness of the coil surrounding it is distorted by stretching. A tea cup has only one hole, too. If a doughnut is drawn on a rubber sheet and stretched every which way, one hole remains: the hole in the center of the doughnut. Number of holes becomes the invariant or unchanging property. Topology is the name for the study of shapes in which invariance involves considerations other than angle size and number of sides.

While recognizing that sense perceptions may lead them astray in situations where masses and forces are huge or very small or when events occur in a vacuum, students first need to trust their sense perceptions. Students know from direct experience that the world feels flat. When they walk down a sidewalk, their first impression is not "I am walking on a curved surface and my path, if I continued it, would eventually describe a huge circle." In a similar manner, students know from experience that a body in motion will not stay in motion forever. If they throw a ball, the ball will eventually fall. If they roll a croquet ball across a shag carpet, the ball will stop rolling. In the second case, the Newtonian "outside

*A croquet ball rolling over a shag carpet*

force" of friction is obvious. Air as material substance and air resistance are less obvious. A space station keeps orbiting because once it is set in motion it will continue in motion in the airless vacuum of outer space until it is acted upon by an outside force. An outside force, such as molecules of oxygen, will not influence the space ship; meteors and space debris might. Students who live in a space age are more able to accept Newton's laws than those who lived before objects orbited in space. Once students understand that

**i**

**ADDITIONAL INFORMATION:**

Newtonian physics and Euclidean geometry provide appropriate descriptions for some aspects of our world. Many students are introduced to Newtonian physics as if the rules were directly applicable to the physical world we inhabit. The conflict between our empirical knowledge and Newtonian rules creates confusion. Confusion leads to befuddlement, and befuddlement encourages a conviction that physics and mathematics are impossible to understand or are even irrelevant. The opposite could not be more true. Mathematics and physics provide explanations especially relevant to understanding the world, including our brains.

"Pre-prims" is a term used to describe the empirical understandings that make it hard to grasp certain concepts in mathematics and physics. "Pre-prims" stand for preliminary and primitive; they are intuitive guesses based on experience. For instance, most of us would guess that lead falls faster than feathers. In fact, we would swear that a pound of feathers and a pound of lead would fall at different rates. But, in a vacuum, where there is no air resistance, any amount of lead and feathers will fall at the same rate if dropped from the same height. Time, velocity and height are the controlling factors in a vacuum, not mass or weight. It is the extensive surface area of a feather that makes it fall through resistant air in a meandering, leisurely way. It is the compactness of a block of iron that makes it fall more directly to the ground when dropped through air.

*A pound of lead and a pound of feathers being dropped off a tower, Sam Sheridan, 1996*

*A meandering feather, SRS, 97*

Even experiments with lead and feathers conducted in a theoretical, computer-modeled vacuum or through mathematical equations may not change our thinking. A computer game like the Bill Budge Pinball Machine allows the player to experiment with the speed and direction of objects in a vacuum. Experience with this game does not convince children that Newtonian laws for feathers and lead hold true—even in a vacuum ("The Bill Budge Pinball Machine and Douglas MacLeod: an Empirical Study," with video, Sheridan, 1990).

*Girl with computer thinking about equal weights of lead and feathers, Claus Kormannshaus, 1997*

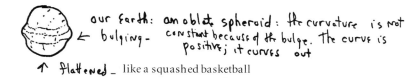

our earth: an oblate spheroid: the curvature is not constant because of the bulge. The curve is positive; it curves out

← bulging—

↑ flattened — like a squashed basketball

*Lines drawn on the ball of*                              *Oblate spheroid*
*the Earth*

Newton's laws apply to the vacuum of outer space, earth-related intuitions about air resistance and friction and Newtonian physics are no longer in conflict. When students look at photos of the Earth as a shining ball in space, they can see that lines drawn on the surface would in fact describe great circles. They may not be able to detect the bulges signaling that our earthly sphere is actually an oblate spheroid, but once they know about the bulges, and learn the words "oblate" and "spheroid," they can accurately describe in geometric terms a sphere that is flattened at the poles and "thrusts forward," or bulges in the middle, at the equator. New geometric terms help them modify their understanding of the shape of the Earth and its geometric properties.

One of these new terms is fractal geometry. Fractal geometry—a term which will be explored in depth in this section—describes the process and structure of the natural world as well as other events on vast and on minute scales more accurately than Euclidean geometry. Fractal dimensions and processes are not beyond our sensory apparati; in fact, we appear to carry fractal pattern memories into the arts and crafts. The fact that these patterns—for instance, Paisley patterns—look like computer-generated fractal images is arresting. Equally intriguing is the fact that fractal patterns painted by migraine sufferers may actually be pictures of brain activity (Sacks, 1992).[19] Many dynamic systems including our brains and the universe share a fractal geometry.

A neuroconstructivist epistemology encourages an adaptive use of language. Adaptive brains are structured by adaptive language-use.[20]

Euclidean geometry describes a flat land. The word "geometry" includes the Greek words *ge* for earth and *metron* for measure. To pre-Galilean sailors, the earth was the center of the

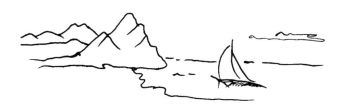

*Mountains, the sea, a sailboat, SRS 97*

*Paisley patterns. Courtesy of Dover*
*Pictorial Archive Series*

---

[19] Fractal processes at deeper levels may generate as well as describe brain activity (Sheridan, 1991).

[20] Maladaptive language-use structures maladaptive brains (Alfred Korzybski, *Science and Sanity*, 1933). Literacy statistics suggest that our maladaptivity as a nation, if not as a species, turns on language education. Because language-use correlates with social, educational, and economic success or failure, language instruction is a primary social responsibility. Students who graduate after twelve years of language education uncomfortable with writing, reading and analytical thinking lack the means for self-examination, self-reflection and communication necessary to an effective existence. Linguistics, physics and neurobiology demonstrate that adaptive language instruction will stress the approximate, negotiated aspects of a shared language. Experience with several geometries prepares students' minds for this appreciation for language as non-absolute and non-rigid.

**ADDITIONAL INFORMATION:** Euclidean geometry maintains that one and only one line parallel to another can be drawn through a point. In 1829, the Russian mathematician Nicolai Lobachevsky disproved several Euclidean axioms. The Lobachevskian Parallel Postulate proves that more than one line parallel to another line can be drawn through a point if the lines are drawn on a curved surface. Surfaces that curve can be either positive or negative—they can curve out or in. Lobachevsky worked with surfaces that curve in; Riemann worked with surfaces that curved out.

In 1851, the German mathematician Riemann wrote a thesis on the geometry of the surface of the sphere, demonstrating that all "straight" lines are great circles; there are no parallel lines on a curved surface. Riemann offered these non-Euclidean premises:

- a line is not infinite but finite; on a curved surface it returns on itself; still, it is unbounded in the sense that it can traverse endlessly around the sphere (Burton, 1985, 565; Poincaré in Layzer, 339).
- every pair of lines on a curved surface meets at some finitely distant point; there are <u>no</u> lines parallel to a line through a point on the line.
- an arc of a circle, not a straight line, will be the shortest distance between two points.

These three tenets of spherical geometry redefine the word "line." Line does not necessarily mean a straight line. With this definition of lines on spheres, the idea of "unbounded but finite" space becomes possible. Think about walking on a ball. You can walk forever yet a complete tour can be made.

The book *Flatland* by the Victorian writer, scholar, educator and theologian Edwin A. Abbott helps students make leaps in their thinking about points, lines, surfaces, and dimensions. *Flatland* is a satirical tale about social and gender stratification designed to expand understandings about geometry—and society. Students who read this book appreciate how hard it is to live in a world of two dimensions and still grasp the idea of three-dimensions—or, to live in a three-dimensional world and grasp the idea of four or more dimensions. The study of geometry raises epistemological questions about what we know and how we know it. We know about triangles, but how do we know about triangles? Do we observe triangles in the external world, or are triangles innate schemata in our brains?

The neuroconstructivist position on how we know what we know is this: human beings are born with responsive, modifiable, variable sensory/mental apparati which are *potentially* appropriate to apprehending the world in which we find ourselves. Practically speaking, it is less important to determine the exact nature of the world—that is to pinpoint "truth" as Platonist, rationalist, or empiricist— and more important to determine how best to respond to the world. The post-industrial information age places new demands on brain organization. Farms and factories no longer organize brains. Image and text do. Still, the intense, hands-on, empirical problem-solving skills of the farmer and the tradesman, craftsman and mechanic remain valuable, analytical skills. Students who have never built or repaired, never cooked or sewn, never planted or harvested or cared for animals find themselves increasingly at a loss in an age which requires speculative thinking.

The degree to which reality is objective or subjective, extrinsic or intrinsic is less important than the degree to which we respond accurately to the information we receive. We can optimize perception and action by using several well-developed language systems like drawing, writing, physics and mathematics, geometry and biology, music, painting and photography. The quality and scope of our inquiries determine the quality and scope of our actions and perceptions. The slash between Drawing/Writing signals a fusion and an equivocation between images and words; the relationship between the objective and the subjective worlds of our experience is fused, too, by the attentive, well-tuned mind.

Each of us constructs the world in personal ways. Differences in construction do not mean that one world is right while another is wrong. Exercises in "Right Relationships" and in "Acceptable Differences" introduced in Step 5 encourage students to respect and to share each others' worlds. The health and survival of society depend upon shared visions.

*Balloon with triangle and ruler,*
*Claus Kormannshaus, 1997*

universe, and the land and the water were flat. Our everyday experience still tells us that the earth is flat. It may have bumps—like mountains—but we do not normally think of the earth on which we walk as curved, nor of the waters on which we sail as curved, nor of the sky covering us as curved. Locally, the earth is Euclidean. You can draw a straight line on a small area of its surface. Globally, the earth is not Euclidean. It is curved. You cannot place a ruler on the surface of a ballon and draw a straight line. The ruler will not lie flat. You cannot place a hypothetical ruler on the spinning ball of the earth and draw a straight line, either. Drawings in atlases show us that lines on the sphere of the earth are really great circles. The word used to describe a curved surface is Riemannian, named for the mathematician who developed a two-dimensional geometry for describing positively curved surfaces. To express our experience of outer space, as well as of our earth seen from outer space, we require a curvilinear or Reimannian geometry. In fact, the surface of the earth is curved non-spherically, or hyperbolically. The bulges exist on such huge scales that they are hard to detect, even from outer space.

**TIP:** Complicated drawings encourage interest and confidence. After the difficult task of achieving accurate outline drawings, students are ready for the more complicated Basic Shapes drawings.

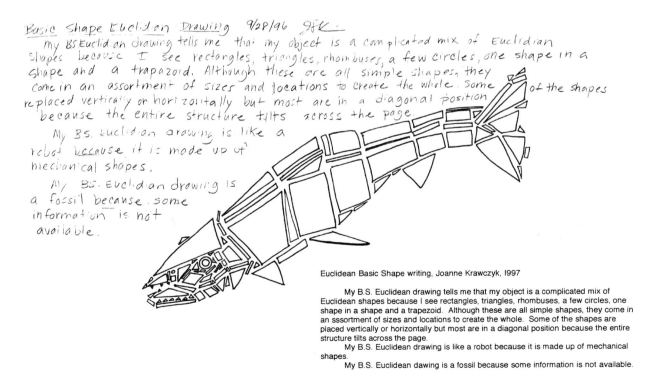

Euclidean Basic Shape writing, Joanne Krawczyk, 1997

My B.S. Euclidean drawing tells me that my object is a complicated mix of Euclidean shapes because I see rectangles, triangles, rhombuses, a few circles, one shape in a shape and a trapezoid. Although these are all simple shapes, they come in an sssortment of sizes and locations to create the whole. Some of the shapes are placed vertically or horizontally but most are in a diagonal position because the entire structure tilts across the page.

My B.S. Euclidean drawing is like a robot because it is made up of mechanical shapes.

My B.S. Euclidean dawing is a fossil because some information is not available.

*Euclidean Basic Shape drawing, fish, Joanne Krawczyk, Continuing Education, Westfield State College, 1996*

**i**    **ADDITIONAL INFORMATION:** As we like to think about the surface of the earth as flat, we like to think about time as absolute; a minute is a minute, an hour is an hour. Normally, we do not think about time as relative nor about time as a function of the curvature of space. But once we begin to think in this way, our thinking about time and other absolutes changes.

One measurable phenomenon—the speed of light—is absolute. Light travels at the rate of 186,000 miles per second. Time and motion, on the other hand, are relative and depend upon the position of the observer as well as on the nature of the experiment. Measurements of time and motion are determined by space; space is defined by the curvature that results when huge celestial masses—like stars—interact. Big planets and stars curve the space around them, bringing objects nearer. Gravity is a phenomenon of the behavior of large masses.

The Euclidean geometry pertaining to flat surfaces proved so useful that it took two millenia before alternative geometries surfaced. Using a pole, the sun, a well, and straight lines between the cities of Alexandria and Syene (present day Aswan), the geometrician Eratosthenes devised in 230 b.c.e. a practical method for measuring the circumference of the earth. Well before humans got off the earth in airplanes and rocket ships, mathematicians and geometricians knew that the surface of the earth was curved. Now that we travel above that curved surface, we appreciate other descriptive geometries.

*A space ship on a curved trajectory, Tim Lis, 1997*

## 2.2 Euclidean Basic Shape Drawing

OBJECTIVES:

⋆**Geometry as a familiar system: childhood shapes**⋆
⋆**Straight lines at the local level: curved lines at the global level**⋆
⋆**Certain kinds of invariance: length and angle**⋆
⋆**New kinds of invariance with "rubber sheet"geometry**⋆

MATERIALS: markers, objects, paper, folders. Examples of paintings by the artists Paul Cezanne and Fernand Leger.

**BACKGROUND:**
   There are two points to remember: Students construct knowledge and knowledge builds on itself. Work from what students know; lead them toward their own new understanding through questions. The Basic Shapes exercises put these two cardinal constructivist rules into practice.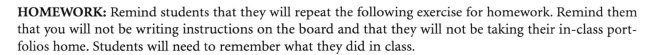
   The history of mathematics and geometry provides a model for teaching and learning: when one answer no longer suffices, another way of looking at a problem presents itself. The old and the new solutions provide a more complete explanation. The new theory answers questions left unresolved by the old solution, posing new questions, and engendering new solutions. For instance, Euclid was famous for codifying rules for planar, or flat, geometry. The fact that Euclidean geometry fails to describe relativistic or curved space does not cancel out Euclid's contribution.

PROCEDURE:

**REHASH HOMEWORK IN PEER PAIRS. (Regular Contour homework)**

**HOMEWORK:** Remind students that they will repeat the following exercise for homework. Remind them that you will not be writing instructions on the board and that they will not be taking their in-class portfolios home. Students will need to remember what they did in class.

**SAY/DO:** "Take a new piece of paper. Write your initials and the date at the top. Add the words 'Euclidean Basic Shape drawing.' What does the word 'shape' mean?"

**DISCUSSION:** Make sure students appreciate that the drawing and writing exercises have moved from exploring the profile or outside edge of the object as a line drawing to the volume or mass enclosed by a line, or shape.

**SAY:** "What does the word 'basic' mean?"

**DISCUSSION:** Students understand that certain shapes are basic, or fundamental. Triangles, for instance, are part of the stock vocabulary of geometric shapes children inherit. When you ask students to name "basic" shapes, they will call out, "Triangle, circle, square, rectangle." You will not need to define the word "basic."

**SAY:** "What does the word 'Euclidean' mean?"

**TIP:** Kindergartners spell Euclid "Ukld."

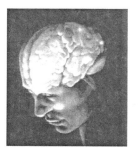

**DISCUSSION:** Most students know very little about Euclid as an historical figure. Even if they know nothing about the man Euclid, students possess a rich understanding of Euclidean geometry, including a vocabulary of shapes learned in early childhood.

**SAY:** Euclid lived in the 3rd century b.c.e., about 2,300 years ago. His drawing tools were the straight-edge and the compass. These tools are useful for drawing shapes on flat surfaces. What is the shape of our earth? Our earth is round. Its primary characteristic is curvature. Can we use a ruler to measure a line drawn on a ball?

Locally, close to the surface of the Earth, Euclidean geometry provides useful straight-line measurements. However, globally and astronomically, Euclidean geometry provides an inadequate description. If we shoot a laser beam from New York City to Helsinki to New Delhi and back, we create a huge triangle. The laser beams are actually describing segments of great circles over the face of the globe of the earth. A drawing of this 'triangle' would reveal sides that curved outward, just like the sides of a triangle drawn on a balloon. A ruler cannot measure these curving lines.

Still, Euclidean geometry is a useful and familiar way to start exploring our objects as shapes."

*Balloon with triangle and ruler, Claus Kormannshaus, 1997*

**ASK:** Help students see their objects in terms of Euclidian Basic Shapes. Ask them to discuss the shapes they see in their own objects. "How about this hammer? What Basic Shapes do you see? What shapes do you see in your own objects?"

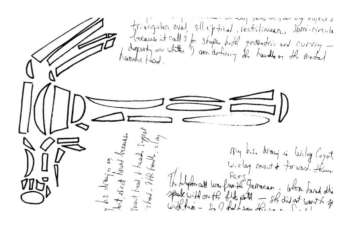

**RECORD:** List the basic shapes students identify, adding a sketch of each shape beside the word. Add the adjective. For instance, write the word "triangle," draw a triangle, and write the word "triangular."

*Hammer, Euclidean Basic Shapes, SRS, 97*

*"Triangle," drawing of a triangle, "triangular"*

**SAY:** "The word 'poly' means 'many' and 'gon' means 'side.' A polygon is a shape with several sides and angles, usually over four. In a regular polygon, the opposite sides and angles are equal."

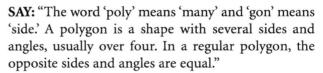

*Rectangle, square, rhombus. Label opposite and equal sides and angles*

**DEMONSTRATE:** Draw regular polygons on the board—squares, rectangles, rhombuses. Show that shapes fall into general categories: for instance, rectangles, squares and rhombuses are all parallelograms because their opposite sides are equal and parallel.

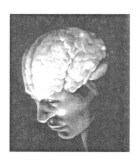

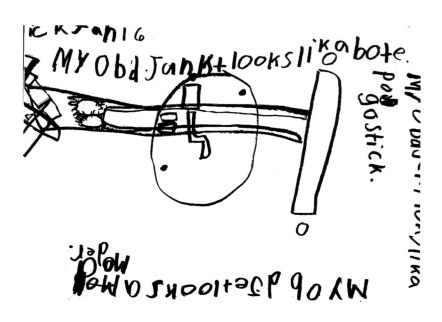

*Euclidean Basic Shape, Nicholas Joyce, Second grade, Applewide School, 1997*

**TIP:** Drawing/Writing students learn to categorize shapes according to shared characteristics: in this case, equal sides and angles. When students compared their Blind Contour drawing to something it reminded them of by using simile and metaphor, they began identifying shared characteristics. Basic Shapes exercises teach students to make geometric comparisons, sharpening and extending their abilities to identify shared characteristics.

**DEMONSTRATE:** Draw a square and write these words:

1)  *poly* means "many"
2)  *gon* means "side"; *quad* means "four"
3)  *latus* means "side"
4)  parallel describes two lines equidistant from each other, like railroad tracks; they never come together.
5)  a *polygon* (a several-sided shape)
6)  a *quad*rilateral (a four-sided figure)
7)  a *quad*ri*latus* *poly*gon which is regular (only if it is a square!)
8)  a special kind of *parallel*ogram where all sides are parallel and equal. (A rectangle is also a parallelogram: the opposite sides are equal and parallel.)

**ASK:** "A square is a polygon. So is a triangle. How are squares and triangles alike and different?

"Is a triangle an idea invented by human minds—did we invent it and then see it in things around us?—or does a triangle exist outside of our minds? If mankind disappeared, would triangles still exist? And, if so, how would they exist? A Greek philosopher named Plato reasoned that if chairs exist, then the quality of 'chairness' must also exist, giving rise to individual chairs. This quality of "chairness" was realer than individual chairs. What do you think?"

**DISCUSSION: OPEN-ENDED:** Great minds do not agree on these issues. Why should students agree? And why should students not grapple with them? Young minds have made many of the breakthroughs in mathematics. Allowing students free rein in provocative discussions *conducted by them at their level of understanding* prepares their minds for confident and audacious thinking.

**SAY:** "The word geometry comes from the Greek word *ge* for earth, and *metron* for measure. The Egyptians were the first practical geometers: they needed to measure the earth for N/S and E/W alignment of their temples for religious as well as for mathematical reasons. Perfect alignment, perfect symmetry and divinity were related. The pyramid as a structure embodies all three, thereby providing a fitting tomb for pharoahs. In addition, the equilateral triangle symbolized the rays of the sun god, Re. The pharoah was the son of the sun.

"The Egyptians also had to figure out how to measure tracts of land. Taxes were levied according to the surface area flooded by the silt-laden Nile. The higher and farther the Nile flooded, the richer the layer of alluvial soil washed down from the African highlands, and the more valuable the land. The more valuable the land, the higher the taxes. Thus, for practical reasons, the Ancient Egyptians invented geometry 4000 years ago to measure land flooded by the Nile.

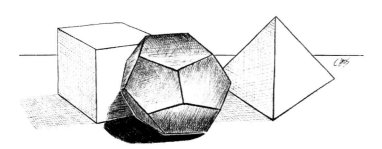

*Cube, pyramid, dodecahedron, Claus Kormannshaus, 1997*

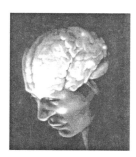

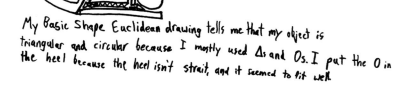

My Basic Shape Euclidean drawing tells me that my object is triangular and circular because I mostly used Δs and Os. I put the O in the heel because the heel isn't strait, and it seemed to fit well.

*Euclidean Basic Shape, Jefferson Arak, Shoe, sixth grade, 1997*

"Egyptians used addition in a multiplication-like operation. There was no symbol for the operation of multiplication like our *times* or x as in 4x2=8. Pictographs were used for each new power and were used expressively. For instance, the number 1,000,000 was represented by a man holding up his hands as if in great astonishment. Two men in this position stood for 2,000,000."

*Man with raised arms*

**SAY/DO:** "Let's try drawing a big triangle with a washable marker on the surface of a bowl or a basketball or a large balloon."

**DEMONSTRATE:** Now that you have raised some provocative ideas about mathematics and geometry, teach a mini lesson on "rubber sheet" geometry. Invite students, including preschoolers, to draw triangles on a flat sheet of paper and then on a big ball. Try using a ruler on the surface of a ball. You can't. The lines used to draw a triangle on a curved surface have to curve, and the three angles will add up to more than 180 degrees. This very simple demonstration immediately shows students the difference between flat and curved surfaces and linear and non-linear geometry.

Now, draw a triangle on a bathing cap and stretch the cap. By pulling in various ways, the triangle becomes a square, a rectangle, even a circle. With "rubber sheet" geometry, certain kinds of lines and angles no longer distinguish a triangle. Other considerations, like holes, do. A doughnut has one hole. So does a tea cup. Tea cups and doughnuts are the same kind of shape according to rubber sheet geometry. Non-Euclidean geometry provides greater precision than the Euclidean approach when it comes to items like holes rather than sides or angles.

*Triangles drawn on a piece of flat paper, and then on a bowl or basketball*

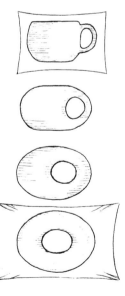

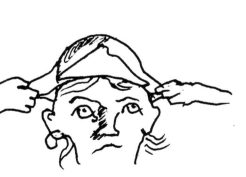

*A stretched bathing cap with a distorted triangle*

*Tea cup to doughnut transformation by Claus Kormannshaus, 1997*

**SAY:** "Drawings let us distort and change things. Words allow us to do the same thing. Geometry shows us that distortions reveal things in new ways. So do words. Now, let's go back to our Euclidean Basic Shape drawing."

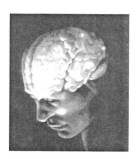

Blind Contour Drawing 6-5-96 B.A.D.

*similes*
my object is
like a jungle
gym that little
kids could play
jump around and
go ~~their~~
through the
holes. Because
it looks
like a jungle
gym. It has
circles and
things
that people
jump off
of.

my blind contour tells me that my object is
very weid looking it has circlar parts, zigg zags in it
and it also is sort of Rectangler and straight
it looks sort of cool. it looks nothing like the
object. maybe just a little. I looks more like
a Block on the left side that you can jumboffand
jump on to a circle. it looks like a jungle gym
that kids could have fun on if their was
a such thing looking like this.

*metaphor*
my ~~object~~ is a jungle
gym.

*Euclidean Basic Shapes, plane, Bobbie Jo Dunn,*
*Student of Peggy Redister and Brenda Ewing, GED instructors, June 1996*

**DEMONSTRATE:** Now that students have a store of Euclidean shapes and the words for them as well as some interesting ideas about shapes, you can return to the Euclidean exercise. Remind students that they are still using markers and that they can use both fat and thin markers. Remind them that as soon as they finish drawing, they will write as before: "My Euclidean Basic Shape drawing tells me that...because...."

Take time to really look at your object. Turn it around. Show that you are thinking about how you are going to draw it. Talk out loud about this. Remind students that as artists and writers they exercise choice and control.

Draw your object, using Euclidean shapes. Do this by constructing it from a combination of Euclidean shapes—circles, triangles, squares, rectangles—working from shape to shape, as if they were separate, floating building blocks.

*Euclidean Basic Shape drawing, lacrosse glove, SRS*

Draw your object a second time, creating Euclidean Basic Shape #2. Show students that you do not need to record both sides of an object in the same way even if your object is symmetrical.

**SAY:** "As I started to construct my lacrosse glove out of basic shapes, I realized that I did not have to solve both sides of the glove in the same way. Look at a friend's eyes, nostrils, flanges of the lips. Isn't each item—right eye and left eye, right nostril and left nostril—slightly different?"

**SAY/DO:** "Copy these Euclidean geometric shapes with their names and adjectives at the top of your piece of paper. Don't forget to write 'Euclidean Basic Shape' and add your initials and the date. Keep using markers. Make sure your Euclidean Basic Shape drawing fills the page."

"After you finish your Euclidean Basic Shape drawing, write, as usual, 'My Euclidean Basic Shape drawing tells me that my object is...because....' Then, as usual, generate a simile: 'My Euclidean Basic Shape drawing looks like a...because....' Then, turn that simile into a metaphor: 'My Euclidean Basic Shape drawing is a...because....'"

**PEER SHARE AND BUILD**

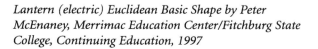

*Euclidean Basic Shapes: the circle, semi-circle, oval, ellipse, square, rectangle, triangle, rhombus, trapezoid, a few other regular polygons like the pentagon and hexagon.*

*Lantern (electric) Euclidean Basic Shape by Peter McEnaney, Merrimac Education Center/Fitchburg State College, Continuing Education, 1997*

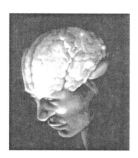

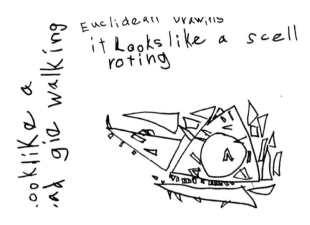

*Euclidean Basic Shape, Chad Daniels, second grade, Applewide
School, 1997*

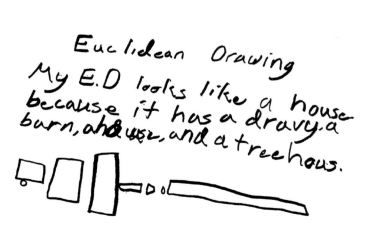

*Euclidean Basic Shape, sprayer, Travis Clark, second grade,
Applewide School, 1997*

**GROUP CRITIQUE:** By asking leading questions, encourage students to discuss each other's drawings and writings. Urge every student to speak.

**SAY:** "The post-Impressionist/Cubist artist Paul Cezanne was interested in 'great primary forms.' Can you find geometric shapes in "The Still-life with Peppermint Bottle?' Hold up this image or another painting by Cezanne.

   "What about the painting by Fernand Leger called 'Three Women' painted in 1921? Identify the primary shapes." Hold up this image or another like it.

**DISCUSSION:** Encourage students to see great primary forms in architecture and art work, transferring their ability to see Euclidean shapes in their objects to other areas.

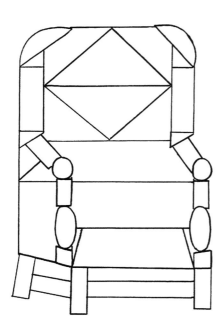

My basic Euclidean drawing tells me that my object is rectangular, triangular, trapezoidal, elliptical, oval, and circular. My Euclidean drawing is like a pinball machine because the upper portion of the drawing has triangular, rectangular and semicircular. Also because of the base of the pinball machine which is square and rhombus. And the legs at the bottom are rectangular. The sides are like the arms that you hold on to and pull the lever to shoot the ball and start to play. My object is a pinball machine because many of the shapes are similar. The dominent shapes are triangular, square, and rectangular.

*Euclidean Basic Shapes, Chair, Pamela Frigo, Continuing Education, Westfield State College, 1996*

*Art nouveau tendrils. Courtesy of Dover Pictorial Archive Series*

My fractal b.s. drawing tells me that my object can be recreated using triangular shapes because I see a patchwork of triangles in assorted sizes that are organized in a way that represents my item. I choose triangles because my object's appendages are triangular and the torso could be drawn by arranging various triangular shapes. My memory tells me that my object is symmetical because both sides are equally balanced but my drawing tells me that my object is missing a limb near the top right side and the bottom of my object takes a peculiar turn instead of following the pattern dictated above.

My object is like a kite Picasso might have designed when he was inspired by African art because the top is large and diamond-like and the decreasing size at the bottom reminds me of a tail. The geometric pattern at the top of the kite is like a primitive mask due to its economy of shapes.

My fractal b.s. drawing is a foreign insect racing across the water in an attempt to sting me in a bad memory because of the severity and repetition of the triangular segments assembed like a legless crustacean.

*Fractal Basic Shape, Fish, Joanne Krawczyk, Continuing Education,*
*Westfield State College, 1996*

## 2.3 Fractal Basic Shape Drawing

OBJECTIVES:

> *Mathematical images are beautiful and "resonant"*
> *Isomorphisms and intuition: the significant spiral*
> *Tiling, tessellation and intimations of fractal dimensions*
> *Repetitive geometry: recursion and iteration*
> *Self-reference, self-construction and self-correction*
> · *Fractals, the brain, Drawing/Writing and other flexible, transformational systems*

MATERIALS: markers, objects, paper, folders, and fractal images from books, postcards, computer programs, and videos of fractals like "Nothing but Zooms." Your local university mathematics department is a resource, as is your library.

*Aubrey Beardsley "fleurs du mal", SRS*

*Celtic spirals and animal interlace.*
*Courtesy of Dover Pictorial Archive Series*

OUROBOROS: serpent or dragon devouring itself; the eternal circle of disintegration and re-integration, a world-wide symbol. It begets, weds, impregnates and slays itself. The All was from the beginning like an egg with a serpent (pneuma) as a tight band or circle around it. Common in medieval animal interlace style artwork.

*The self-biting oroboros or eternal circle of*
*disintegration and re-integration, SRS 1997*

*Photo, Chambered Nautilus, Elisabeth Nyman,*
*Skidmore College and Deerfield, MA, 1997*

*The ladybug in the computer-generated*
*Mandelbrot set "Paisley-like" pattern from*
*THE FRACTAL GEOMETRY OF NATURE*
*by Dr. Benoit B. Mandelbrot. Copyright (c)*
*1977, Benoit B. Mandelbrot*
*Reprinted by permission of Dr. Mandelbrot*

*Photo, sunflower, Elisabeth Nyman,*
*Skidmore College and Deerfield, MA, 1997*

 **ADDITIONAL INFORMATION:** Fractal objects and procedures describe complicated systems which we used to call chaotic, meaning indescribably messy and disorderly, or having no pattern. Fractals provide the pattern and the explanation and the order for heretofore chaotic situations, thereby changing the way we use the word chaos; chaos now means vast, complex systems whose orderly patterns repeat so infrequently that only a vast string of computations with their attendant images can reveal the pattern or order, like the Mandelbrot set.

Euclidean geometry works for one, two and three dimensions. Fractal geometry works for the fourth dimension, if the fourth is shapes unfolding over time.

Fractal objects, procedures and dimensions are appropriate for describing brain and mind, the physical nature and physics of the brain, including the shape of thoughts. Both dynamic systems—brain and mind—operate in time and space.

 **POWERFUL IDEA:** "A fractal is a structure and process whose mathematical properties are uniquely related to chaos, which in turn is defined as unpredictable in detail but possessing an order in its overall behavior" (Bevlin, 1963, 1991, 314).

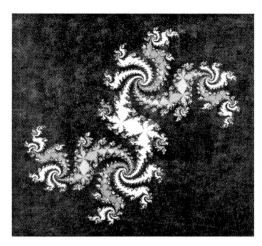

*The fractal dragon/cover of the book*
*THE FRACTAL GEOMETRY OF NATURE by*
*Dr. Benoit B. Mandelbrot. Copyright (c) 1977,*
*Benoit B. Mandelbrot*
*Reprinted by permission of Dr. Mandelbrot*

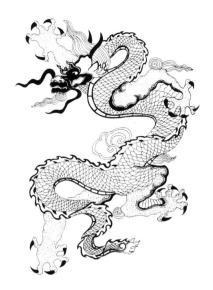

*Qing and Ming dynasty dragon. Courtesy of*
*Dover Pictorial Archive Series*

## BACKGROUND:

A principle of fractal geometry is that one set of instructions—in this case—the same piece of a draw-ing, repeats over and over. This makes the tree drawing especially useful in demonstrating a fractal process, a fractal object, and fractal dimensions.

I have taught this Fractal Basic Shapes lesson for the past ten years to teachers with little or no mathematics background as well as to students, including kindergarteners, who know nothing about fractals. Because fractal images are beautiful, they provide emotional entry for very young students into the world of mathematics and geometry. As soon as students connect a mathematical process with a shimmering, transmogrifying fractal image, they better understand the descriptive power of mathematics and geometry.

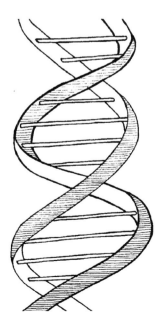

*Double Helix, Claus Kormannshaus,*
*1997*

In general, the Geometric Basic Shape drawings encourage all three of the "R's"—reading, writing and 'rithmetic. As noted above, the word "arithmetic" describes a discipline within the larger field of mathematics which also includes geometry. It is not enough for children to study numbers. The study of geometry is more directly useful to children's understanding of mind and experience than numbers because it provides provocative and exciting ideas about form. Logically the teaching of geometry should precede the teaching of arithmetic at the elementary levels of education.

As Watson said about the model of a double helix, "Something so pretty must exist." The same is true of fractal images.

Students who are computer literate already appreciate fractal processes as image-compression. It is much more efficient for a computer hard drive to store the instructions for one frond on one branch of a pine tree than, say, a Quark Express TIFF image of the whole tree; the memory on your drive is put to efficient use if the whole tree can be generated from one set of instructions for a branch. The Microsoft program Encarta Encyclopedia (on-line) includes images using fractal compression. Adobe Photo Shop lets you download actual fractal images. In my time, my only hands-on approach to fractal images was through LOGO programs.

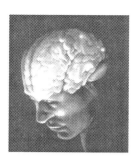

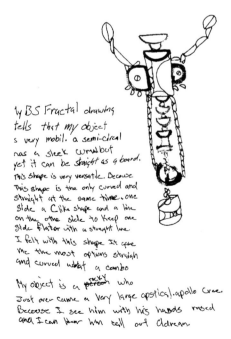

My BS Fractal drawing
tells that my object
is very mobil. a semi-circal
has a sleek curvs but
yet it can be straight as a board.
This shape is very versatile. Because
This shape is the only curved and
straight at the same time. one
side a C like shape and a line
on the other side to keep one
side flator with a straight line.
I felt with this shape It gave
me the most options straigh
and curved what a combo

My object is a rocky person who
Just over came a very large opstical. apollo Cree.
Because I see him with his hands rased
and I can hear him call out Adrean.

*Fractal Basic Shapes, Michael Cooper, Continuing*
*Education, Westfield State, 1997*

Fractal geometry provides a yardstick for measuring and exploring Non-Euclidean surfaces and shapes. The word fractal comes from the Latin verb *frango, frangere,* "to break." The term was coined nearly thirty years ago by Dr. Benoit Mandelbrot. Dr. Mandelbrot, a scientist born in Poland, educated in France, and working in the United States, developed a mathematics and geometry called fractal. The word "fractal" was meant to suggest "pieces of" as in "fraction" or "fractured." Fractal geometry describes a class of objects, procedures, systems and dimensions, which share several characteristics: repetition, self-similarity and potentially infinite variety, or irregularity. Paisley scarves, Persian carpets, the drawings of Aubrey Beardsley, the organic swirls of Art Nouveau, the curling tails of sea horses, the fronds of ferns, the shapes of leafy or needled trees, the rockiness of coastlines, the layers of mountain chains, banks of clouds—all of these known patterns, objects and phenomena—can be reproduced by fractal mathematics. In fact, many fractal motifs in arts and crafts may be fractal pattern memories in our brains. Even more interesting, fractal patterns are useful to describe brain wiring and function (Sacks, 1992; Sheridan, 1991).

*Sea horse by Claus Kormannshaus, 1997*

*Paisley patterns. Courtesy of Dover Pictorial Archive Series*

A tree provides an easy-to-draw example of this repeating, or fractal, geometry—in structure, process, and dimension. A tree starts with a shoot which branches; that branch branches in turn, until a tree is produced. A whole tree may look disorderly and its growth is unpredictable *in detail,* but it meets the requirements of a fractal system, helping us to expand and modify our understanding of "chaotic" behavior.

At a major junction or at the most minor intersection of a branch and a twig we can see the same forking structure. The important observation is that the fork looks the same across scales. Branch, twig, trunk; whether middle-sized, tiny, or huge, the fork structure looks the same. Fractal processes demonstrate self-similarity across scales.

*Forkings in the branching process, circled at different scales.*

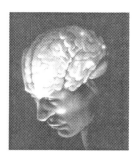

A tree is a self-decorated procedure, generating itself from forkings or branchings. One little procedure—grow a little and fork—is all it takes besides a leafing procedure to make a tree. Fractal processes demonstrate parsimony; one simple set of instructions repeated over and over again with minute variations produces a vast system.

Although the tree contains large and small copies of itself—the forking structure—the entire tree reveals variety, even infinite variety. This suggestion of infinite variety within which one design motif insists on  reappearing describes fractal dimensions.

*A tree as copies of itself*

Minute variations to the branch and grow instructions produce an asymmetrical tree: one side of a tree and the other are not the same. If tree growth were strictly linear, a tree would be a pole with identical branches at identical intervals at identical angles. Instead, a tree has an irregular, complex shape.

Two operations characterize fractal shapes like trees: iteration and recursion. Iteration is repetition. Recursion literally means "running back." In a fractal process, a simple set of instructions is repeated by calling itself back. In the case of a tree, the branching procedure calls itself back over and over again. Powerful computers make it easy to repeat procedures so many times that the visual results give the impression of being infinite. Videos of fractal images generated by computers demonstrate potentially infinite variety while revealing a self-repeating "seed."

By mathematically manipulating one set of instructions like "grow a little and branch," or the "seed," the seed "sprouts," producing an increasingly irregular form. Two of the words used to describe this irregularity are "tangled" and "wrinkled." Within a nearly bewildering, rich pattern, the seed figure reappears, over and over again, no matter how complicated the pattern becomes. Zooming in or panning out makes no difference with fractal patterns; the seed emerges at all scales. In the image below, the coastline of the island chains is equally complicated from high up, or, if the computer program zoomed in, at the level of a millimicron of the surface of a rock on that coastline.

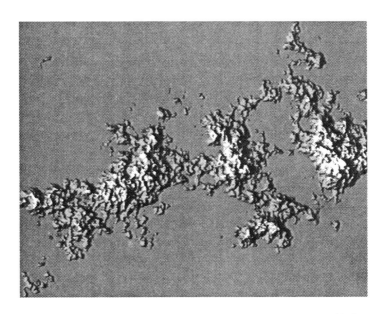

*Fractal coastlines and island chains as irregular or wrinkled*
*from THE FRACTAL GEOMETRY OF NATURE by Dr. Benoit B. Mandelbrot.*
*Copyright (c) 1977, Benoit B. Mandelbrot. Reprinted by permission of Dr. Mandelbrot.*

**ADDITIONAL INFORMATION:** A second-grade teacher successfully taught fractals to her students. The problem she came across was that students used the same shape she chose to construct her object for their object. Still, they got the principle that one motif can be used over and over at different scales to construct an entire object.

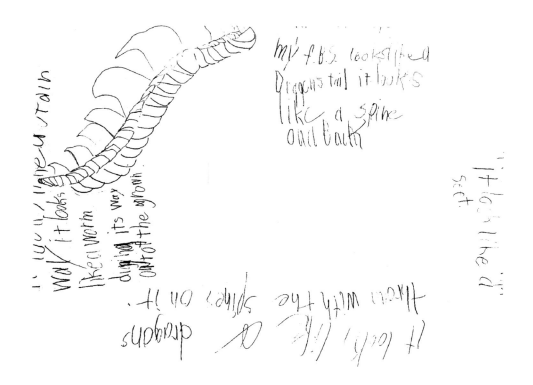

*Fractal Basic Shape, Keith Palmer, second grade, Applewild School, 1997*

Fractal geometry, brain processes, Drawing/Writing, and the Neuroconstructivist classroom share certain characteristics. These include self-reference, self-organization, and self-correction. In dynamic processes, the output is greater than the input, and the output is largely unpredictable. Slight variations in simple instructions produce startling results. This unpredictability—or non-linear quality— can be described as a "strange loop".[21] Strange loops characterize constructivist classrooms as well as brain process.

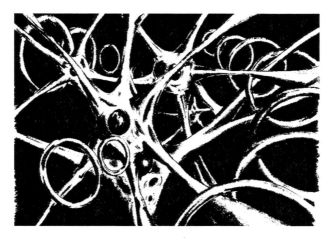

*Strange Loops, Tim Lis, 1997*

Practice with Fractal Basic Shape drawings provides:

- a realization that mathematics, including geometry, is more than a string of abstruse symbols; mathematics and geometry produce stunning images. Familiar fractal patterns demystify mathematics and geometry, encouraging students to explore both fields as relevant and compelling disciplines
- direct practice with a geometry that differs radically from Euclidean geometry in process and form
- preparation for the idea that powerful systems—like their brains—are self-generating and self-modifying.

You can reach young students and older students with the grow-and-branch drawing described above. Then, add a stockpile of provocative fractal images. Fractal videos like "Nothing but Zooms,"[22] are especially useful, because they reveal the actual unfolding of a mathematical procedure.

Students who have accepted non-Euclidean geometries like rubber sheet geometry and fractal geometry are ready to think about their brains in sophisticated ways. From understanding that the brain has two hemispheres which communicate via the corpus callosum, students are now prepared to explore the idea that the brain is iterative and recursive in structure and process. The Fractal Basic Shape drawing provides a useful point of departure for thinking about thought as well as about the natural world.

*[THE RIGHTHAND PAGES CONTINUE ON PAGE 207]*

---

[21] Strange Loops is a phrase used by Douglas Hofstadter in *Gödel, Escher, Bach* (1980) to explain the logical inconsistencies in any powerful explanation system like mathematics, physics or brain processes.

[22] Homer Wilson Smith and Jane Elizabeth Staller at Cornell University produced some of the earliest commercially available fractal videos and slide sets in the late 1980's through a company called Art Matrix 1-800-PAX-DUTY or (607) 277-0959. The video "Frontiers of Chaos" was available through Mapart, P.O. Box 2039, Mill Valley, CA 94942, (413) 381-4224. The video "Chaos, Fractals & Dynamics" produced by Dr. Robert Devaney through Science Television was available through Dr. Devaney, Boston University, Math Department. The video "Chaotic 1" was available through Dr. James P. Crutchfield, Physics Dept., University of California, Berkeley, CA 94720.

**ASIDE:** Most recently, I realized that the similarity in the spirals in arts, crafts, nature and mathematics must mean something. Growing or dynamic systems look alike. I concluded that the Golden Mean and the Fibonacci sequence must be related, and that both of these ratios or procedures must relate to fractal processes and dimensions.

A medieval scholar, Fibonacci (Leonardo da Pisa), discovered a series of numbers with a close relationship to the structure of natural growth. The Fibonocci sequence describes how seeds spiral in the head of a sun flower. The sequence is 1, 2, 3, 5, 8, 13, 22, 35, 57 and so forth. Any number in the series after the second is the sum of the two previous numbers. For instance, 1+2=3; 2+3=5. The series is verifiable by experience by looking at the spiral of packed seeds in a sunflower head or in a pine cone. Leaves in Fibonacci sequences provide shade or light for newer leaves, depending upon the arrangement.

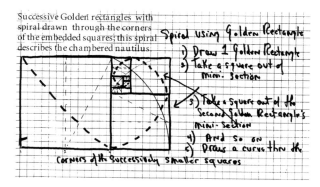

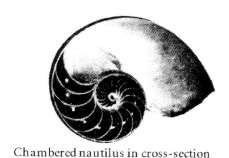

Chambered nautilus in cross-section

*Successive golden rectangles creating a spiral by drawing through the corners of the embedded squares, drawing, SRS.*

*Chambered nautilus*

If you divide any number in the Fibonacci sequence by the next highest number, the result will be nearly 0.618, and almost exactly 0.618 after the 14th number in the series. That is, it is almost true, or true "in the limit," that the ratios get closer and closer to the Golden Ratio the farther out you take the numbers in the Fibonacci sequence.

The Golden Mean and the Fibonacci sequence are related. I found this out leafing through a book on organic motifs for designs in weaving (Dendel, 1978). To the Ancient Greeks, the Golden Mean expressed an especially beautiful or pleasing relationship between parts. For instance, the longer side of a golden rectangle, like the length of the Parthenon, is 1.618 times the length of the front of the Parthenon; the front is 0.618 of the longer side. Both the Golden Mean and the Fibonacci series demonstrate a "dynamic symmetry" (Hambridge, in Bevlin, 167)—a relationship appealing to studio artists, too.

If a series of golden rectangles are drawn and then a curve is drawn touching the corners of successively smaller squares embedded in the rectangles, a spiral is generated. "The major and minor parts of a parent golden rectangle are generative: their offspring whirl around them. The golden rectangle is a whirling rectangle" (Dendel, 1978, 45). It is the whirling rectangle generating a spiral that reminds me of the fractal video called "Nothing but Zooms" in which the Paisley-ish profusion of the Mandelbrot set unfolds in all its spiraling, ruffled complexity. I do not know how the Mandelbrot set (f (z) =z tan z+c) and the Golden ratio and the Fibonacci sequence relate mathematically, but I do know that they relate aesthetically, that they all generate spirals, and that they must therefore relate mathematically in some way.

The recent challenge has been figuring out how the verse form called the sestina, described as a "spiraling" form, fits in. The sestina has been an extremely successful verse form to teach in connection with Drawing/Writing. You will encounter it at the end of Step 4, the "Perfect" Whole, and again, in Part 4, the curriculum guide. As I continue to learn about mathematics, geometry, and poetry,

*The Parthenon, Desiree Dubois, Hampshire College, 1996*

[CONTINUED ON THE NEXT LEFTHAND PAGE]

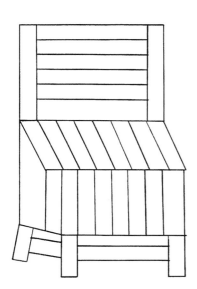

My fractal basic shape drawing tells me that my object is rectangular. The shapes are recursive throughout. Some are larger in size than others. My fractal drawing tells me that my object is like an outdoor grilling system because of the open lid at the top and base of the grill. Also because of the protruding arms and appendages at the bottom. My object is an outdoor grill because of all of its characteristics. The shapes are clutched tightly together and have sharp defined angles. It stands tall and contains a certain rigidness.

*Fractal Basic Shapes, Pamela Frigo, chair, Continuing Education, Westfield State College, 1996*

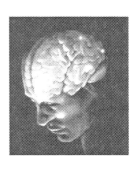

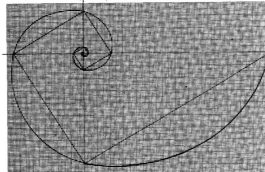

*The Fibonacci spiral, drawing, SRS*

*Fibonacci pine cones*

it seems to me that certain properties attract the mind; the spiral is one such property. The sestina is a 39-line poem organized mathematically into six stanzas of six lines each. The same six words end the lines, rotating in a prescribed manner. The poem ends with a triplet in which all six words are used in a certain order.

| 1 | 6 | 3 | 5 | 4 | 2 | 2—5 |
|---|---|---|---|---|---|-----|
| 2 | 1 | 6 | 3 | 5 | 4 | 4—3 |
| 3 | 5 | 4 | 2 | 1 | 6 | 6—1 |
| 4 | 2 | 1 | 6 | 3 | 5 | |
| 5 | 4 | 2 | 1 | 6 | 3 | |
| 6 | 3 | 5 | 4 | 2 | 1 | |

After writing the first stanza, using a predetermined set of six words to end the lines, the second stanza is written in this way: the word ending the sixth line moves to the end of the first line, the word ending the fifth line moves to the end of the third line, the word ending the fourth line moves to the end of the fifth line, the word ending the second line moves to the end of the fourth line, and the word ending the first line moves to the end of the second line. The verse pattern twists around and around itself in a vortex aimed at the triplet, or the last three lines in which the six words are concentrated. In nature, the spiral moves outward, to accommodate growth. The creature inside the chambered nautilus grows. For poems to grow and to coalesce toward some core, thought processes twist and spiral, too. In this case, the spiral seems to move inward.

If fractal processes and dimensions characterize brain patterns on the surface (Sacks, 1992) and deeper (Sheridan, 1991), and if the Golden Mean and the Fibonacci sequence can be used to describe spiraling dimensions, then the Golden Mean and the Fibonacci sequence must be part of the brain's computations. The sestina may be attractive to students because its pattern is familiar to them on some deep neural level. The spirals in nature, art, mathematics, language and thought are isomorphic and resonant.

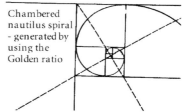

*Chambered nautilus, schematic drawing, SRS 97*

The sestina is a permutation of the numbers 1 through 6. It is a finite pattern with elements that repeat. The poem, after all, does not go on forever. It ends after 39 lines. The pattern repeats but it is not recursive. It calls backs the same six words but they are not embedded as fractal "seeds" are embedded. The Fibonacci sequence, on the other hand, is defined recursively; each number is derived from the previous two and the series is infinite. The Koch snowflake is recursive, too. Its elaboration is infinitely complex, whether going out or going into the pattern.

Were it not for this element of infinite complexity across scales, the Koch snowflake would be just another regular geometric object. A sestina does not exhibit fractal dimension, nor does it reveal or express the Fibonacci sequence, nor is it based on the Golden ratio. Still, the sestina is engaging. Even though it is a poem made up of words, the sestina is also a visual game, attracting the brain at something like the level of a paradoxically dimensional (up/down, down/up, inside/outside, outside/inside) M.C. Escher print.

**P.S.** I have discovered that the Julia set on the Mandelbrot set provides a sufficiently complex fractal to be appropriate to holography, confirming my 1991 speculations about the connections between fractals and holographs. As Douglas Windsand writes in "Fractal Holograms" (*Fractal Horizons*, edited by Clifford A Pickover, 1996, 186), "A Julia set generated from a point closer to the boundary of the Mandelbrot set...has a fine structure along its boundary and would be a candidate for a fractal hologram."

[CONTINUED ON THE NEXT LEFTHAND PAGE]

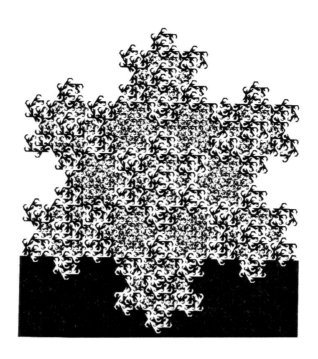

*Koch Snowflake*
*from THE FRACTAL GEOMETRY OF NATURE by Dr. Benoit B. Mandelbrot.*
*Copyright (c) 1977, Benoit B. Mandelbrot*
*Reprinted by permission of Dr. Mandelbrot*

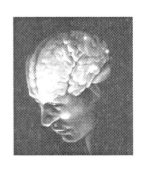

The Neuroconstructivist viewpoint presented in this book on repeating spirals is this: artists, including migrainous and schizophrenic artists, mathematicians, craftspeople, saints, poets, designers, philosophers, musicians, and engineers access "pattern memories" which are fundamentally neural events, and express them so that we can see them. These expressions often have religious or philosophical dimensions.

This book suggests that neural circuitry and firing patterns provide templates or schemata on which symbolic, abstract thought patterns itself, thereby arriving at notions, ideas, concepts, theories, rules, tenets, postulates, beliefs and images. These include the goddess, the cosmic egg, Shiva, the dying vegetal god, the mandala, the mandorla, the Moebius strip, feedback loops, recursion, iteration, self-similarity, self-construction, dynamic systems, the Golden Ratio, the Fibonacci sequence, the sestina, Paul Tillich's Ground and Abyss of Being, Martin Buber's I/Thou relationship, the tao of physics, and fractal dragons.

*M.C. Escher's "Magic Mirror" (c) 1996 Cordon Art - Baarn - Holland. All rights reserved*

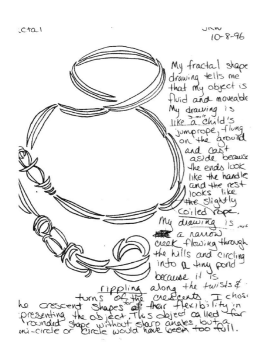

.cta.1                         URW
                              10-8-96

My fractal shape drawing tells me that my object is fluid and moveable My drawing is like a child's jumprope, flung on the ground and cast aside because the ends look like the handle and the rest looks like the slightly coiled rope. My drawing is not a narrow creek flowing through the hills and circling into a tiny pond because it is rippling along the twists & turns of the crescents. I chose the crescent shapes for their flexibility in presenting the object. This object called for a rounded shape without sharp angles, but a semi-circle or circle would have been too full.

*Fractal Basic Shapes, Jennifer Welden, Continuing
Education, Westfield State College, 1996*

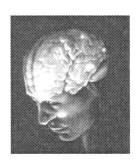

**ASIDE:** Tree growth is non-linear; small changes to the input yield a nearly bewildering output. The growth of the human zygote—another fractal process—is non-linear, too.. The fertilized egg becomes a small clump of cells which proliferate into a vast differentiated mass identifiable as a human body. The zygote is a self-constructing fractal system which uses a parsimonious set of instructions coded in genetic material. Because of minute adjustments to these instructions, the output—the growth of a human body and of the brain—is phenomenally different from the economical input. Forests of neural networks are generated, like trees, by a "grow a little bit and branch" procedure, producing a tremendously complicated, system in which input from sensory experience provides the impetus for mental output. As structure is to process, so neural nets are to the complex non-linear nature of thought. Fractal processes and structures describe brain function accurately—and probably literally.

One of the fascinating aspects of fractals is self-repeating similarity, despite considerable variety or irregularity. The significant aspect of this repetitious self-similarity is its power for self-construction. A fractal object generates itself.

The mathematical instructions known as the Mandelbrot set are:

$$f(z) = z \tan z + c$$

By repeating this set of instructions, or seed, over and over, a sprawling, dragonish pattern unfolds on a computer screen. The seed, variously described as a "ladybug" or as an "apple," reappears at all scales. It is easy to see that this ladybug or apple is decorated with itself at increasingly smaller scales. Color coding in fractal computer images indicates the speed with which numbers are heading away from or toward infinity. All of the numbers contained within the black ladybug are heading toward zero or one or some other number or are bumping about randomly. All of the numbers outside the ladybug are heading toward infinity. The viewer needs to understand that the swirling colored forms and the black reappearing bug stand for numbers which are being manipulated mathematically, in this case, by the Mandelbrot set.

**ADDITIONAL INFORMATION, BIOGRAPHICAL:** Let me share my journey toward understanding fractal geometry. Then, you will better understand this section on Fractal Basic Shape drawings.

In the late 1970's, I fell in love with fractals. I saw one photo, and I was smitten. The object in the photo was a curving, pastel, translucent, fluted, flaring funnel-like object. I had no idea what it was, but it was visually compelling. The caption under the photo was, too: this object was an "infinite but minimal surface" and it was "a model for the universe," as well. The more I learned, the more convinced I became that fractals were relevant educationally. The question was how to include them in the Drawing/Writing five-step.

To understand the caption, I had to relearn two words. Mathematically, the word "infinite" describes an endless process—not an unbounded expanse as I had thought. The word "minimal" describes the least surface area necessary to cover a space: a skin—not, as I had thought, the littlest quantity of stuff. Water filling a glass to the brim has a miniscus. Because of surface tension, the water swells up in a convex dome. This humped-up surface is more than minimal. If you tightly stretch a membrane of Saran wrap across the top of a glass, you create something like a minimal surface. The Saran wrap is stretched flat and taut like the skin of a drum. The fractal and its caption expanded my understanding of the universe. The universe is something like a translucent, curving, tubular, taut shape, infinite as a continuous, no-inside-no-outside Moebius strip, minimal as a skin of Saran wrap over the mouth of a glass.

With time I learned that fractals and chaos theory are connected. Chaos theory does not provide, as I first thought, explanations of indescribably messy systems. Chaos theory describes orderly systems so complex that at first, or for a very long time, such systems of behavior seem messy and unpredictable, like the weather. Chaos theory describes the complex order that exists at the boundaries of orderly and disorderly behavior, like the place where the orderly pattern of a roostertail wake touches the more random behavior of the surrounding water. Chaotic systems are self-organizing and they are responsive to minute changes.

*U. Mass. School of Engineering
magazine fractal image*

[CONTINUED ON THE NEXT LEFTHAND PAGE]

*The "ladybug" or "apple" in the Mandelbrot Set*
*from THE FRACTAL GEOMETRY OF NATURE*
*by Dr. Benoit B. Mandelbrot. Copyright (c) 1977, Benoit B. Mandelbrot*
*Reprinted by permission of Dr. Mandelbrot*

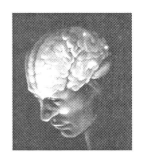

Perception is a good example: waves of neural excitation passing through the brain intersect, creating spiraling EEGs. Very small changes in firing patterns achieve and modify these spirals (Freeman, 1991). Think of a school of fish swimming one way—and then—presto! swimming another. Spirals express not only the actual patterns of thought, but the growth of snail shells, tips of ferns, elephant tusks, rams' horns, and cats' claws—"anything that grows by increasing size at the outer edge so it does not change its shape" (Bevlin, 1963, 1991, 165). It is useful for students to learn that there is a very fine line between disorderly and orderly behavior, including the thoughts in their own brains. It is useful to notice repeating patterns like sprials and to think about the implications of similar shapes that characterize an assortment of phenomena.[23]

I needed to figure out a practical approach to understanding fractal process and dimensions. Ideas about beauty, or visual resonance, and about similarity, or isomorphism, might be useful. To respond to fractals, students would need to see a range of fractal-generated images that resonated for them. The fact that many beautiful, familiar objects share fractal dimensions meant that I could use a wide range of beautiful objects to introduce fractals to students. We could think about how these things were alike, ferreting out repeating motifs or pattern, and then devise our own repeating motifs to construct our objects, as we did with Euclidean shapes.

In the early 80s, few fractal programs for computers were available. Students could generate fractal dragons with the computer language LOGO invented by MIT professor Seymour Papert. These students were rare. In any event, in Drawing/Writing students, would have to stick with pencils and markers. I suddenly remembered the woodcuts of the Norwegian artist M.C. Escher. His work could help us.

Escher's prints are compelling because of repetition and because of illusionary, often conflicting visual dimensions. A high level of paradox does not hurt: when up is down and down is up, students pay attention. Recognizable motifs like birds and fishes help students grasp repeating patterns and processes. When M.C. Escher uses angels over and over again in a design, creating devils from their negative spaces, and when these angels and devils go from large to tiny, an infinite progression of self-similar shapes emerges. Prints by Escher help students understand repetition and self-similar processes. If students practice tiling and tessellation—the methods Escher used to produce his images—they participate in intimations, at least, of fractal dimensions. For these reasons, it has made sense to me to design warm-up exercises in tiling and tessellation to prepare students for fractal dimensions.

Motifs that interlock without gaps or overlaps "tile." A bathroom floor, for instance, "tiles;" one small, identical shape is combined over and over again to provide the flooring. Tessellation is another plane-filling approach. Tesserae are the small blocks used in mosaics, like Roman and Byzantine mosaics. Tiling and tessellation fill areas without gaps or overlaps. Several strategies can be used to tile the plane: one unit can be repeated over and over again. Or one unit can be manipulated so that the negative spaces it creates are identical and also tile. The positive and/or negative units can be rotated around a point, or mirror imaged, or slid at specified intervals along a diagonal and then mirrored in a maneuver described as a "glide elision."

After creating their objects using one self-repeating motif, students begin to understand recursion and iteration, fractal "seeds," and self-generative, and self-correcting processes. With the dawn of these understandings, we can talk about fractal geometry. Eventually, we are able to generalize from fractal geometry to the brain as a fractal process. As important as grasping fractal geometry, students learn that images which resonate strongly, and elements which reappear in a variety of beautiful, complicated objects, are significant. They have meaning—at the very least, for them, and most probably for many others.

*Rotation around a point, mirror imaging, sliding along a diagonal and mirroring (glide elision)*

[23] The book *The Curves of Life* by Theodore Andrea Cook, originally published in London by Constable & Co., 1914, recently published by Dover Publications, Inc., New York, 1979, provides a fascinating and exhaustive description of spirals in shells and plants, including ferns, pinecones and sunflowers. Cook writes, "Chinese philosophy had adopted the logarithmic spiral as a symbol of growth as long ago as the twelfth century.... The Formula for Growth now suggested in this book is here called the $\phi$ (theta) spiral, or Spiral of Pheidias, a new mathematical conception worked out from an ancient principle.... There is a very significant characteristic of the application of the spiral to organic forms...nothing which is alive is ever simply mathematical.... The nautilus is perhaps the natural object which most closely approximates to a logarithmic spiral; but it is only an approximation" (xi).

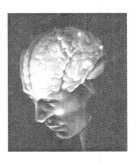

f

**ADDITIONAL INFORMATION:** Dr. Mandelbrot has taught at Caltech, Harvard, Yale, Albert Einstein College and MIT in the U. S. as well as at universities in Paris and Geneva. He has conducted research at the Watson IBM labs. Currently, he is at Yale University. His fields include aeronautics, mathematics, economics, engineering, and physiology. His insights and mathematical skills coincided with powerful computer technology. A new geometry for entirely new surfaces—neither uniformly flat nor uniformly curved—revealed itself; Dr. Mandelbrot named this geometry "fractal." In 1977, Dr. Mandelbrot published *The Fractal Geometry of Nature*. Because of his work, the descriptive power of fractal geometry is accepted, especially for dynamic, self-organizing systems—like the natural world, including us and our brains. Readily available, easily operable fractal programs are popularizing this once recondite mathematics and geometry. By working with fractal procedures and images, we learn more about geometry and about ourselves.

## PROCEDURE:

### REHASH HOMEWORK IN PEER PAIRS

**HOMEWORK:** Remind students that they will repeat the following exercise for homework. Remind them that you will not be writing instructions on the board and that they will not be taking their in-class portfolios home. Students will need to remember what they did in class.

*The fractal dragon/cover of the book*
*THE FRACTAL GEOMETRY OF NATURE by*
*Dr. Benoit B. Mandelbrot. Copyright (c) 1977,*
*Benoit B. Mandelbrot*
*Reprinted by permission of Dr. Mandelbrot*

**SAY:** "Let's look at some images from art history and from the natural world. What do you see?" Use the images provided at the beginning of this section.

"Let's think about another kind of geometry called fractal, or repeating geometry. One shape it takes is dragon-like.

"Before this shape was called 'fractal,' shapes like it were called monsters, or 'pathological' because they did not fit within the framework of Euclidean shapes. Benoit Mandelbrot recognized the relevance of these "monsters" for describing irregular, apparently disorderly or patternless aspects of the natural world. A man of broad interests and disciplines, Mandelbrot saw new connections between an existing mathematics and a strange but relevant geometry.

**SAY:** "The natural world is filled with examples of fractals. We see them in the fern, the pine tree, clouds, coastlines and mountains. From close up or from far away, from a mile or an inch, a rocky coastline looks very much the same in terms of roughness or complexity.

"Generated intuitively, through aesthetic sensibilities, quite apart from formal mathematical reasoning, fractal images abound in art history. Fractal designs appear in Islamic textiles and oriental carpets, in Paisley shawls, neckties and scarves, in Aubrey Beardsley's art nouveau prints, as well as in the borders and initial letters of illuminated manuscripts and in Celtic and medieval animal interlace designs. At some deep level we know, recognize and replicate these images, most probably because our brains utilize these patterns neurally.

"The artist M.C. Escher provides a good example of a combined artistic/mathematical intelligence striving toward a fractal understanding of the world through decorative design in which one motif is used over and over again. Escher was exploring self-repeating geometry. By using birds and fishes rather than abstract Islamic images, Escher made 'filling the plane,' or 'tiling' understandable to the viewer. Long before computer technology, Escher's woodcuts provide a stunning intuition of fractal processes."

**SAY:** "Deep within our brains, we preserve pattern memories—some Euclidean, some fractal—which surface when we create artistic work. These pattern memories connect art, mathematics and neurobiology. Paintings by migraine sufferers looks like fractals. British psychologist and writer Oliver Sacks concludes that at least as surface pattern, neural firings during migraines operate fractally (Sacks, 1992)."

**SAY:** "Clouds, coastlines, trees, the tips of ferns, the seeds of a sunflower, the spiraling structure of a sea shell, these objects are familiar to us. The fact that these phenomena can be expresssed mathematically is interesting. Sharing mathematically expressible characteristics with those phenomena, particularly in connection with the structure and process of our brains or thought processes is more than interesting—it's fascinating. Even though we may have suspected all along that we had something in common with Paisley patterns and sunflowers, it is still exciting to see mathematical proof.

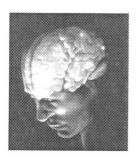

**ASK:** "If complex patterns produced by nature, art, crafts and architecture are alike, including spirals with curling tendrils, or exhibit other isomorphic elements, what does this mean? How do the alveoli in lungs, tree branches and Chinese dragons relate to each other? Let's agree that a range of objects and phenomena share beautiful and complex patterns and look alike, especially in the spiraling or coiling sections. The coils are often decorated with a ruffle or fringe or mane or scalloped crest. The spiraling curve of the Chinese tidal wave or tsunami is decorated with a foaming ruffled edge, as are Chinese drawings of dragons' tails.

*"The Great Wave" by Katsushoka Hokusai (1760-1849), with permission of Dover Pictorial Archives*

*Qing and Ming dynasty dragon, Courtesy of Dover Pictorial Archive Series*

There is an element of elaborate, irregular decoration to the repeating curves.

"Once we agree that many fractal objects exhibit similar coils and ruffles, we can start looking for other things as beautiful and compelling as these objects. We can think about the idea that isomorphisms provide strong cues to meaning, and require our attention. The meaning may be personal only, or general. We may have come upon a larger truth.

"The artist M.C. Escher designed tiled images. Because his motifs were often self-similar across scales, his work helps us understand fractal processes and dimensions. Because Escher used recognizable motifs like birds and fishes rather than abstract designs like the ones he studied at the Alhambra in Spain, it is possible for the viewer to easily notice two items:

- the motif tiles; to "tile" means to fill a plane without gaps or overlaps

- the tiling units are birds and fishes; it is hard to tell which is figure and which is ground; each motif provides the negative space for the other, and also tiles

- the pattern suggests an infinite process; the motifs could tile the plane forever, no matter how far the plane were extended.

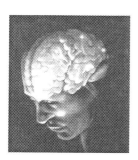

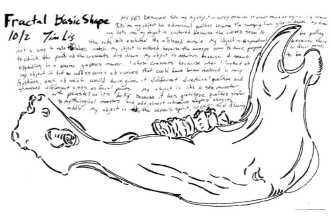

*Fractal Basic Shapes, Timothy Lis, Continuing Education,*
*Westfield State College, 1996*

"A variety of shapes tile:

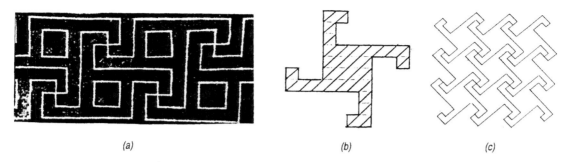

(a)                                (b)                        (c)

Figure 10: Ravenna mosaic (a), underlying figure of Ravenna mosaic (b), and tiling of the plane using Ravenna underlying figure (c).

*Figure 10 "Tilings in Art and Science," by James Hall.  Copyright (c) James Hall, 1995.*
*Reprinted by permission of the Humanistic Mathematics Network*
*Journal #12, October, 1995, Alvin White, editor.  All rights reserved.*

"A good approach to tessellation is called the 'nibble' technique. If students cut a shape from one side of a square and tape it to the opposite side, they will create a new shape that will fill the plane without gaps or overlaps.

*A nibbled square that tiles*

"One of the easiest fractals to recreate was discovered at the turn of the century by a man named Koch. The fractal is called Koch's Snowflake or the Koch curve."

*The Triadic Koch Snowflake or Curve*
*From THE FRACTAL GEOMETRY OF NATURE by Dr. Benoit B. Mandelbrot*
*Copyright (c) 1977, Benoit B. Mandelbrot*
*Reprinted by permission of Dr. Mandelbrot*

**TIP:** After showing students the tree branching drawing, the Koch curve is the next best way to teach a fractal process. A Koch curve is a mathematical entity which starts with a triangle and ends with a "snowflake" by decorating the triangle with itself, repeatedly, at smaller and smaller intervals and scales. The fact that repeated straight lines create a curve, and that repeated triangles create a circle is exciting in the way rubber sheet geometry is exciting. What has been understood in only one way—that triangles and circles are very different things—is now understood in another; straight lines and angular forms can be used to create curves and circles. With the Koch curve, as with rubber sheet geometry, the intent of the Drawing/Writing teacher is to open students' minds to thinking in entirely new ways, building confidence in their ability to think.

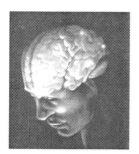

**SAY/DO:** "Let me show you a Triadic Koch curve. Tri stands for three. Do you see how repeating triangles create a star, and, then, a snowflake, and ultimately, a circle? Straight lines can create curves."

**SAY:** "Like a branching tree, a Koch curve decorates itself with itself. Instead of using the 'branch and grow a little' instructions and the fork image—as a tree does—the Koch Curve starts with a triangle and, by 'triangling' itself at increasingly smaller scales, transmogrifies its angular linearity into a circle. The intricate result shares some of the delicacy of a snowflake—hence, the alternative name, the Koch Snowflake. In nature, fractal geometry takes less regularized forms. Consider a coastline; the edge is increasingly complicated as we zoom in on its structure, but that edge does not reveal a series of nested triangles. It reveals consistent irregularity or roughness.[24] A self-sustainable process without beginning or end which exhibits consistent levels of complexity or irregularity or roughness is described as fractal in dimension. Fractal dimensions are infinite in the sense of being endlessly complex at micro and at macro scales. Because its inside is the same as its outside, the Moebius strip—as a continuous loop—provides direct tactile experience with infinity. The Moebius strip/fractal understanding of infinity is different from the common understanding of the word infinite as a surface or a space that extends forever over limitless distances. The Moebius strip provides tactile understanding of infinity as on-going—without beginning or end. Tiling is a procedure for organizing a plane. It may also refer to "lattices" in polymer science and in nature, but this is a highly specialized use. The difference between tiling as a process and fractals as a process hinges on an expanded understanding of the word "infinite" as a self-sustaining process. Tiling could go onward and outward forever, filling a hypothetically infinite plane of infinite extension. A fractal process is self-contained, far more like the Moebius strip than an endless plane. A new understanding of chaos as orderly if unpredictable behavior is necessary, too, to appreciate fractals as visually complex systems.

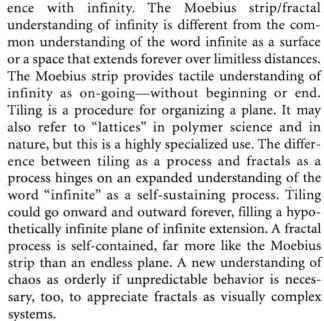

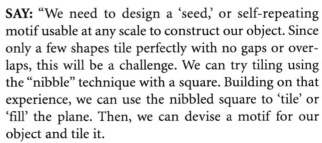

*Moebius strip, Claus Kormannshaus, 1997*

"Using the simple branch-and-grow drawing, we can practice the basic principles of fractal geometry.

**SAY:** "We need to design a 'seed,' or self-repeating motif usable at any scale to construct our object. Since only a few shapes tile perfectly with no gaps or overlaps, this will be a challenge. We can try tiling using the "nibble" technique with a square. Building on that experience, we can use the nibbled square to 'tile' or 'fill' the plane. Then, we can devise a motif for our object and tile it.

"Our Fractal Shape drawings will only approximate a fractal process. We have pencils and markers, but no other tools: no rulers, protractors, compasses, no graphing calculators or computers."

*Branch and grow, tree*

---

[24] From exhibit notes written by Robert Oserman of Stanford University for "Frontiers of Chaos," Boston Museum of Science, late 1980's.

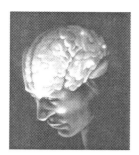

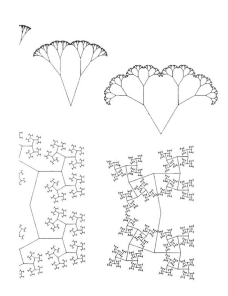

*Fractal tree*
*From THE FRACTAL GEOMETRY OF*
*NATURE by Dr. Benoit B. Mandelbrot*
*copyright (c) 1977, Benoit B. Mandelbrot*
*Reprinted by permission of Dr. Mandelbrot*

**ASK:** "What does the word 'fractal' remind you of?"

**DISCUSSION:** Students will probably say, "fraction," or "fractured."

**ASK:** "What is a fraction? What happens when something fractures?" Keep asking questions until students produce "parts of" and "pieces."

**SAY:** "Fractions are parts of things. In fractal mathematics, one tiny part is repeated over and over to make a whole. The 'whole' in this case is potentially infinite.

"One set of instructions, like 'to branch, ' can make a tree. "Here's a drawing showing how 'to branch' makes a whole tree. Now, you are going to try a fractal drawing with your object. You will need to figure out one shape—it might be the overall shape of your object as is the case with a tree and a branch or it might not—and clone it, using it in different sizes to construct your entire object. The clones will have to fit tightly together with no leftover spaces like pieces of a puzzle."

**DEMONSTRATE/DO:** Draw the trunk of a tree growing up and forking off to its first major branch. Then draw another branch forking off from that, and another off that, and so on. Circle the places where the forking happens. The circle identifies the single set of instructions.

**ASK/DO:** "Do you see how each forking is really a little instruction from the tree to itself about how to grow? The piece of instruction is: 'TO BRANCH: Grow a bit and then fork.'"

**TIP:** To demonstrate this procedure, you do not need to draw a whole tree. You need to draw one small piece of information—grow a little and then branch—repeating itself over and over at varying scales until it creates a huge, complex entity like a tree. You can show students the fractal branching tree above. Because the forking is so easy to see at large and small scales on a tree and because it looks identical, this drawing makes it easy to understand a fractal process. This tree drawing is the easiest way I've found to introduce students to fractals.

*Tree branching drawing with circled forkings*
*labeled "self-similarity across scales"*

**SAY:** "Do you see that the 'forking piece of information'—the instruction 'To Branch'—looks the same whether we are near the trunk or out at the tips of branches? The message 'grow by forking' is the same.

"Have you seen science fiction movies where the landscape is computer-generated? Some of those landscapes are produced by fractal mathematics. Increasingly, films use fractal-generated images because of the economic practicality of image compression. The costs are in the programming, not in shooting on location."

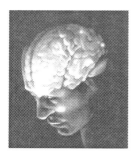

**DEMONSTRATE:** Show students a range of fractal-generated images. As long ago as the late '70's or early 80's, IBM ads included fractal-generated images of misty, smoky mountains rising above wide lakes.

*Fractal-generated landscape*
*From THE FRACTAL GEOMETRY OF NATURE by*
*Dr. Benoit B. Mandelbrot*
*copyright (c) 1977, Benoit B. Mandelbrot*
*Reprinted by permission of Dr. Mandelbrot*

**SAY:** "Think about a fern. The overall shape of the fern, and one section of the fern and any section of a section of the fern looks the same. Think about a coastline. At a mile up, or at one inch from the water, a piece of coastline and the irregular surface of a rock look a lot alike. Self-similarity across scales is a fractal property."

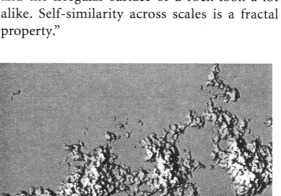

*Island chain from Mandelbrot book*

*Ferns, courtesy of Dover Pictorial Archive Series*

**RECORD/DO:** Write "self similar across scales" on the board, drawing arrows connecting the words to the circled "Y" or branching sections of your tree.

**SAY:** "A fractal process is efficient. To create a tree, all you need is to take one set of instructions and repeat them, introducing a small change each time: 'grow a little.' Brain processes most probably use fractal procedures, too. Neural networks look like tree branches. The word 'dendrite' means branch."

**ASK:** "Besides ferns and coastlines, what other things might be fractal? Think about repeating processes or about repeating patterns or intricate, lacey patterns like the crest of a crashing wave."

*Neural networks, Strange Loops, Tim Lis, 1997*

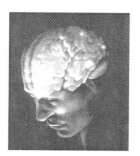

**DISCUSSION: OPEN-ENDED:** Students may suggests pine trees because the shape of the tree and the shape of a branch and the shape of a section of a branch look the same. Or a snowflake. Or wallpaper designs.

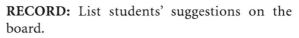

**RECORD:** List students' suggestions on the board.

**SAY/DO:** "Let's talk about repeating processes in connection with two words: iteration and recursion."

**RECORD:** Write "iteration" and "recursion" on the board.

**SAY/DO**: "Take a new piece of paper. Write your initials, the date and the words 'Fractal Basic Shape' at the top. Now, let's come up with a shape we can use over and over again, in different sizes, to create our whole object, just the way the little fork or branching drawing can be used

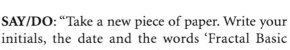

*"The Great Wave" by Katsushoka Hokusai (1760-1849) with permission of Dover Pictorial Archives*

over and over to make a whole tree—the way MC Escher used interlocking knights on horseback arranged positively and negatively to create a design. It is hard to find a shape that will fit together without gaps or overlapping. Look at your object. Figure out one shape that may work. It might be the overall outline of the object. It might not. Think about the Euclidean Basic Shapes drawing. Are there any clues there? Draw the shape you think will work at the top of the page. Remember, you can only use that shape, in different sizes, to construct your whole object. That's the rule for fractals we learned with trees and with the Koch curve."

**TIP:** Some students will solve this problem with an outline drawing of the object, using it, at different scales, to "fill up" a larger contour drawing. This is an intelligent if obvious solution.

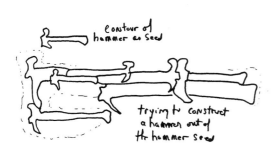

*Fractal drawing of hammer using contour drawing of the hammer as the "seed," SRS*

My fractal drawing tells me that my object is floating in space. It is an object meant to hypnotise me and pull me in. It looks like platforms floating in space, and I could just jump weightlessly from one to the next. These platforms get further and further from my origion, but it doesn't matter because the boundries are limitless.

Poetic
Descriptive

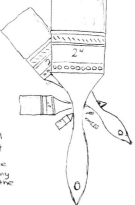

*Paint brush, fractal drawing as a series of the same object, getting smaller, Brian Stone, Central High School honors art program, Springfield, MA, 1996. Dr/Wr teacher, Holly Tuttle.*

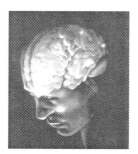

Most of students' fractal drawings will not actually tile. That is, the shape students choose to re-draw over and over will not completely fill in the shape of their object with no empty spaces and no overlaps. Still, by attempting to tile using a shape that is self-similar across scales, students will begin to understand fractal geometry in principle. A true fractal unfolds—while tiling or tessellation repeats. There is a huge difference mathematically—and thus visually—between a kitchen floor made up of identical units that stay the same size and a fern which unfolds from a basic set of instructions creating self-similar units which vary in scale.

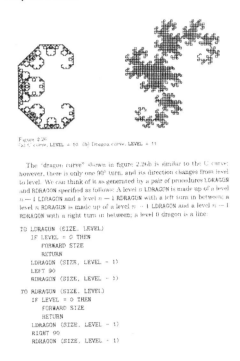

Figure 2.26
(a) C curve, LEVEL = 10. (b) Dragon curve, LEVEL = 11

The "dragon curve" shown in figure 2.26b is similar to the C curve; however, there is only one 90° turn, and its direction changes from level to level. We can think of it as generated by a pair of procedures LDRAGON and RDRAGON specified as follows: A level *n* LDRAGON is made up of a level *n* — 1 LDRAGON and a level *n* — 1 RDRAGON with a left turn in between; a level *n* RDRAGON is made up of a level *n* — 1 LDRAGON and a level *n* — 1 RDRAGON with a right turn in between; a level 0 dragon is a line:

```
TO LDRAGON (SIZE, LEVEL)
    IF LEVEL = 0 THEN
        FORWARD SIZE
        RETURN
    LDRAGON (SIZE, LEVEL - 1)
    LEFT 90
    RDRAGON (SIZE, LEVEL - 1)

TO RDRAGON (SIZE, LEVEL)
    IF LEVEL = 0 THEN
        FORWARD SIZE
        RETURN
    LDRAGON (SIZE, LEVEL - 1)
    RIGHT 90
    RDRAGON (SIZE, LEVEL - 1)
```

*LOGO dracon curve from Turtle Geometry by Harold A. Belson and Andrea diSessa Copyright (c) 1980, the Massachusetts Institute of Technology. Reprinted by permission of MIT Press.*

Students who have studied LOGO or who have used other computer programs for generating fractals may be able to generate bona fide fractal images including the Mandelbrot "dragon."

These students should still construct a grassroots, hands-on knowledge of fractals in the Drawing/Writing way. This low-tech approach enriches the high-tech approach. The tree-branch sketch is accessible to all students from kindergarten up. An easy approach to a complicated process is a mainstay of constructivist education. By working from what most students can access through a simple drawing of plant growth, all students can work toward a more sophisticated understanding of dynamic growth as fractal.

**SAY:** "We can create a drawing with a fractal feel without a computer by exploring ways to "tile the plane" with no gaps or overlaps. Some regular polygons tile, including equilateral triangles, squares and regular hexagons. Any triangle can be used and any quadrilateral can be used to tile the plane."

Draw some of these shapes on the board for students referring to:

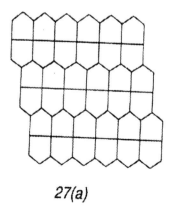

### 27(a)

*Figure 27 from the **Humanistic Mathematics Network Journal**, #12, October 95 "Tiling in Art and Science" by James Hall (c) 1995 reprinted by permission of Alvin White, editor*

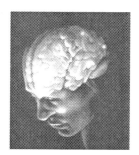

"Let's try the nibble technique: draw a square, cut off a section from one side and paste that to the opposite side. This irregular shape will tile.

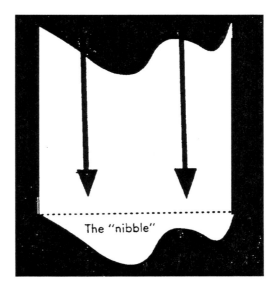

*The nibble technique*

"It will be a challenge to generate a shape that will tile my object. I'll try. I could just repeat the contour of the hammer, working from little to big, and hope they lock together. Or, I could devise a different shape altogether."

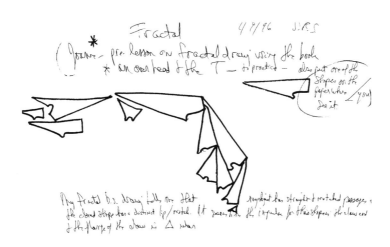

*Another approach to the fractal drawing of a hammer SRS.*

**DEMONSTRATE/DO:** Look at your object. Try out several shapes on the board. Let the students watch you struggle.

**ASIDE:** "The Ah-Ha Principle" describes a flash of understanding like the one experienced by Archimedes when he jumped out of the bathtub and ran into the street, suddenly understanding that body volume could be calculated by water displacement. When students achieve a fractal drawing, the experience may be like Archimedes' breakthrough. "Ah-Ha!" they will say, "I see what fractal geometry involves now."

**POWERFUL IDEA:** Learning how to tile the plane or do a fractal drawing raises a more general problem: how to construct a self-replicating system. The relevance of the problem to the Drawing/Writing process is the self-replicating nature of brain processes. By practicing fractal drawings students experience brain processes metaphorically and actually, forging neural self-replicating systems at the same time as they construct a drawing of an object using a self-replicating system. They learn that fractal geometry has practical applications for their actual mental processes.

**ADDITIONAL INFORMATION:** Fractals and tiling provide parsimonious, or spare instructions for self-replication like those responsible for transforming a zygote into a human being or for growing a brain or for solving problems in mathematics, biology or physics. The natural world employs self-assembling systems; wood, bone, shells, and human skin are examples of self-assembling chemistry. The brain can learn to optimize its self-actualizing properties by studying other self-organizing systems.

There are medical applications for self-assembling systems. Sheets of skin for burn victims are being generated from foreskins of circumcised babies. Self-assembling systems pose challenges for polymer science. The natural world creates skin and bark. How can chemical engineers achieve a "super lattice" that grows? Most polymers are dominated by entropy; they tend to lose, not gain, order. It is extremely interesting that a lattice made of mushroom-like, or broccoli-like shapes, with gaps between the bushy heads (filled by solvents) creates lattices better than layers do. The fact that a self-assembling polymer sets up a lattice with gaps suggests that self-assembling systems may include Strange Loops, too. By building on information about self-assembling systems including fractals, it may be possible to generate new organs from pieces of organs through mathematically organized quasi-lattices. (Manfred Shroeder, in Pickover, 1996, 219.)

Histopathology is the branch of pathology concerned with the study of changes in shapes in cells and tissues. Pattern matching between "monstrous" or aberrant, irregular pre-cancerous and cancerous tissue is possible using fractal geometry. Ironically, a geometry no longer thought of as pathological has applications for pathology (Gabriel Landini, in Pickover, 1996, 252).

**SAY:** "Every time we try to see in a new way, it's hard, isn't it? I am having a hard time filling the plane without any gaps."

**DISCUSSION:** Some students will figure out how to fill the plane without gaps. Many students will struggle. To avoid discouragement, mention that gaps and inconsistencies are inherent in life, too. Keep touching on the parallels between mathematics, geometry, life and art.

**SAY/DO:** "Keep using markers. Fill the page. Create a fractal drawing of your object. After you complete the fractal drawing, write 'My Fractal Basic Shape drawing tells me that my object is...because....' As usual, follow this descriptive writing with a simile and then turn that simile into a metaphor. For instance, 'My fractal drawing looks like a court jester because of the tasseled cap with bells.' 'My fractal drawing is a court jester with a tasseled cap with bells.'"

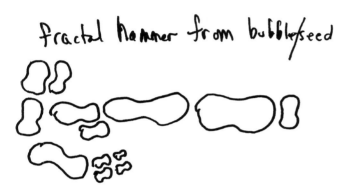

*Fractal drawing of hammer, bubbles, SRS.*

**SAY/DO:** "We are going to generate two positive similes and two positive metaphors. Then, we are going to write one negative simile and one negative metaphor. For instance, I could write, 'My Fractal Basic Shape drawing of a hammer looks like frog spawn because of repeating clusters of circles.' 'My Fractal Basic Shape drawing of a hammer is frog spawn.' For the negative simile, I could write, 'My Fractal Basic Shape drawing of a hammer does not look like the crystals in a geode because the repeating shapes are curving, not straight-edged.' In the same manner, my negative metaphor would be, 'My Fractal Basic Shape drawing of a hammer is not a geode.' Furthermore, it is possible to qualify both comments; in other words, I could write that my hammer is circular at the striking end, and in this part is round and thus like frog spawn, and I could write that at the claw part, the hammer is sharp and angular and could be compared with the crystalline forms at the heart of a geode.

"Do you see how drawing and reflective writing clarify your object?"

**POWERFUL IDEA:** Being able to refine understanding through sameness and difference is an important skill. Understandings become less approximate, more specific and more complete.

"We need the proper analytical tools to think with and we need to know how to use them. In this case, we are using two tools in two different ways. What are they? Correct, we are using simile and metaphor and we are using them in positive and in negative modes. Are the similes and metaphors about the hammer concrete or abstract?"

**SAY/DO:** "A concrete simile is like concrete; one thing named by a noun is compared with another thing named by another noun which stands for a physical thing which can be touched. It is tangible. An abstract simile compares something to an idea which cannot be touched. It is intangible. If you jump up and down on a sidewalk, you can feel it under your feet. It is concrete. Geodes and frogs' spawn can be touched and felt. An abstraction is not touchable in the same way. If I compared the head of the hammer to fertility or the claw of the hammer to cruelty, I would be using abstract nouns to describe my object. I can touch the idea of fertility or cruelty with my mind, but not with my body. Let's name some more abstract ideas."

**POWERFUL IDEA:** Gaps in powerful explanation systems generalize to life's paradoxes, logical contradictions and inconsistencies. Gödel's Incompleteness Theorem, Hofstadter's Strange Loops, and Heisenberg's Uncertainty Principle provide caveats and comforts for students who want answers. Answers cannot always be provided. Many if not all explanations will be metaphorical, at best. Still, it is possible that fractals provide not just a metaphor for dynamic processes but are the dynamic processes responsible for the universe and us.

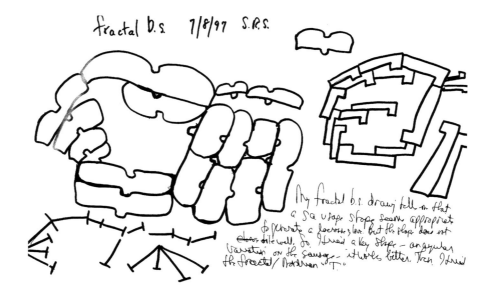

*Fractal drawing, lacrosse glove, SRS*

**RECORD:** List students' abstract ideas on the board; "freedom, pain, hunger, thirst" and so forth.

**SAY:** "My Fractal drawing of the hammer suggests this abstract simile: 'My Fractal Basic Shape drawing is like joy because I see clusters of bubble-like sensations in my stomach.' Or, 'My Fractal Basic Shape drawing is like joy because the shapes express an understanding of clustered wholeness.' The second one is a little too abstract, isn't it?

"I note that my explanation of the abstract feeling is expressed abstractly rather than concretely. Clustered wholeness is an idea; 'wholeness' is an abstract noun, like joy; bubbles are touchable things; 'bubble' is a concrete noun. When you have finished writing your abstract similes, let's see if your explanations include abstract nouns, too."

**SHARE AND BUILD IN PEER PAIRS**

**GROUP CRITIQUE**

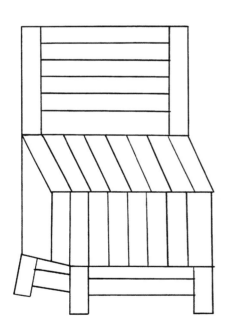

My fractal basic shape drawing tells me that my object is rectangular. The shapes are recursive throughout. Some are larger in size than others. My fractal drawing tells me that my object is like an outdoor grilling system because of the open lid at the top and base of the grill. Also because of the protruding arms and appendages at the bottom. My object is an outdoor grill because of all of its characteristics. The shapes are clutched tightly together and have sharp defined angles. It stands tall and contains a certain rigidness.

*Fractal Basic Shape drawing, Chair, Pamela Frigo, Continuing Education, Westfield State College, 1996*

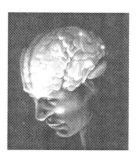

Organic Basic Shape drawing, fish, Joanne Krawzyck

[note addition of negative similes and negative metaphors]

        My organic basic shape drawing tells me that my plastic fish is round because all of its boundaries are curved.  My organic b.s. drawing tells me that even my object's triangular limbs have smooth corners because there is an absence of points.
        My organic b.s. drawing is like a cartographer's description of land because the pieces are divided into irregular sizes and shapes dependent on each landowner's wealth.  My organic b.s. drawing is not like a map because it doesn't have the lables or symbols that make a map useful.
        My organic b.s. drawing is a steam, cluttered with flat slices of rock, meandering through an imaginery wooded lot.  My organic b.s. drawing is not a stream because it doesn't have any of the necessary ingredients: water, rocks and sand.

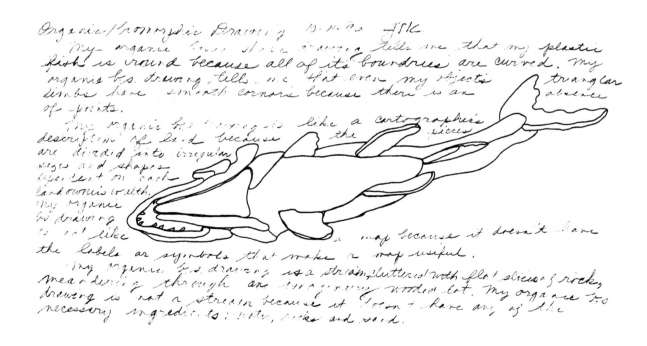

*Organic Basic Shape drawing, Joanne Krawzyck, Continuing Education, Westfield State College, 1996*

## 2.4  Organic Basic Shape Drawing

OBJECTIVES:

**\*Free-form shapes\***

MATERIALS: objects, markers, paper, folders

**BACKGROUND:**

Organic shapes provide another geometry or visual vocabulary. Since the intent in Drawing/Writing is to develop and extend visual skills, the Organic Shape drawing is included in this Basic Shape section. Organic shapes are biomorphic, or "life form-like." *Bios* means "life"; *morphos* means "shape". Biologists and artists use the term. Artists use the term "organic" to distinguish curvilinear, free-flowing shapes from the straight lines and sharp angles of "geometric" forms.

Organisms grow in response to biological processes. These biological processes are constraining—like Euclidean postulates. However, when we draw organic shapes, we do not need to follow rules. Drawings of organic shapes are free-hand and free-form.

Straight-edged geometric shapes are associated with man-made objects; organic shapes are associated with living things. This rule of thumb does not always hold: a crystal contains facetted, geometric shapes— yet crystals grow. They may not grow in a strictly biological sense—but they self-organize.

By drawing organic shapes, students get a *feel* for the bulging surfaces of hyperbolic geometry; they get a *feel* for the curvature of Reimannian space. They get a feel for the spiraling thrust of dynamic processes, like fractals. They also add another term to their vocabulary of shapes, extending the tadpole schemata of their babyhood to the study of living form.

PROCEDURE:

**REHASH HOMEWORK IN PEER PAIRS**

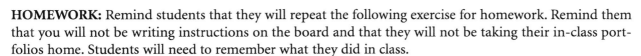

**HOMEWORK:** Remind students that they will repeat the following exercise for homework. Remind them that you will not be writing instructions on the board and that they will not be taking their in-class port- folios home. Students will need to remember what they did in class.

**SAY/DO:** "Take a new piece of paper. Write 'Organic Basic Shape' at the top. Add your initials and the date."

**ASK:** "What do you think the word 'organic' means?"

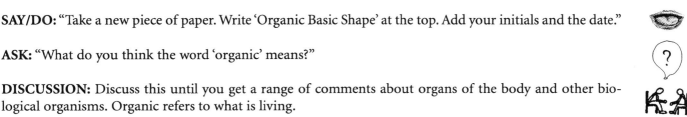

**DISCUSSION:** Discuss this until you get a range of comments about organs of the body and other bio- logical organisms. Organic refers to what is living.

**SAY:** "When we drew blind and regular contour drawings, we learned what a line could tell us about an object. We did the same with Euclidean Basic Shapes and Fractal Basic Shapes. These shapes follow certain rules and give us information about an object. Sometimes Euclidean shapes seem more appropriate to dis- cuss our objects, sometimes fractal do. The shape you will now use to describe your object will be blob-like. Later, we will see whether geometric, organic or fractal shapes best define our particular object, or whether a combination serves it best."

**DEMONSTRATE/DO:** Take your Drawing/Writing object and demonstrate an Organic Basic Shapes draw- ing. Construct your object using organic shapes just as you did with Euclidean shapes. Look at the object, then at the board. Then, construct your object using biomorphic shapes. Draw the shapes thoughtfully.

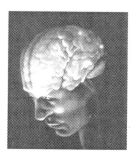

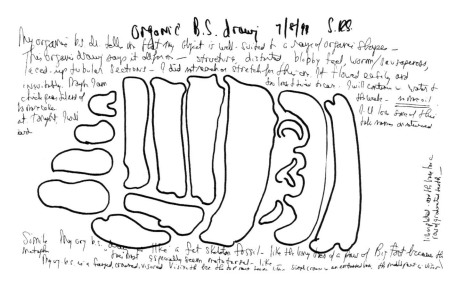

Organic B.S. draw 7/8/11 S.RS.

*Organic Basic Shape, Lacrosse glove, SRS*

7/10/96   S.R.S.

*Organic Basic Shapes, hammer, SRS*

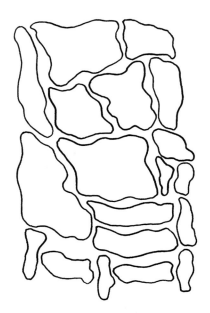

My organic/biomorphic shape drawing is free-formed. My object is like a group of jellyfish because they are clustered together and their boundaries are curved and smooth. There is an economy of shapes of assorted sizes. Some look to be expanding and multiplying. It looks like they are getting ready to sting because they are swelling in a curving way. My object is a multitude of water droplets because they are distorted and bloblike. Not one is the same, each is unique in its own way. They seem to be taking on personalities of their own.

*Pamela Frigo, Organic Basic Shape, Chair, Continuing Education, Westfield State College, 1996*

**SAY/DO:** "In the fractal drawing, one shape had to be used over and over to construct the whole object. Here, we can use a series of different shapes. Each shape must be blob-like. An organic drawing of my hammer is very different looking from my Euclidean drawing or my fractal drawing. See how soft it is, round and puffy? My writing is as follows: 'My Organic Basic Shape drawing tells me that my hammer is round as well as straight because the head of the hammer swells out in a curving way.'

"When you have finished the organic drawing and writing, construct one concrete simile and change that into a metaphor. Construct an abstract simile and turn that into a metaphor. Construct one negative concrete simile and make this into a negative concrete metaphor. Construct one negative abstract simile and turn that into a negative abstract metaphor.' Keep using magic markers and fill the page with your drawing.

"For example, after looking at my organic drawing, I wrote, 'My Organic Basic Shape drawing of a hammer looks like a lizard with warts because it is elongated and covered with bumps.' Then, I wrote, 'My Organic Basic Shape drawing is a lizard with warts,' following that with 'My Organic Basic Shape drawing is not like a lizard with leprosy because it has no eyes, no long tail, it is not colored green, and it does not have four legs.' Next, I wrote, 'My Organic Basic Shape drawing is like despair, because it is long and knobby, ugly and without strong shape,' adding, 'My Organic Basic Shape drawing is despair.'

"Moving on to negative comparisons, I wrote, 'My Organic Basic Shape drawing is not like despair because the repeating nodules suggest embryonic growth and growth signals hope,' and I will add, 'My Organic Basic Shape drawing is not despair.'"

**PEER SHARE AND BUILD:** Remind students to put all new vocabulary from their peers in their Drawing/Writing journals.

**SAY/DO:** "Remember to note down all new vocabulary in your journal. Use these new words."

**ASK/DO:** "Which geometric drawing—Euclidean, fractal or organic—do you think best suits your object? Make a decision and write about this on theê bottom of your Organic Basic Shape drawing."

**ASIDE:** Students benefit by experimenting with several systems. They make discoveries and they make decisions.

**SAY:** "Don't forget to use the word 'because.' For instance, 'It is clear to me that the Euclidean Basic Shape drawing suits my object best because....' Or, 'It seems to me that a mixture of Euclidean and organic shapes describes my object because....'"

**TIP:** It's best not to complete this sentence because students may parrot it back. Let students figure out their own reasons.

**ASK/DO:** "Could all three kinds of shapes be useful? Why? Is one kind of geometry more useful to describe one part of your object, and is another kind of geometry more appropriate to describe another part?"

**GROUP CRITIQUE:** Have students put up all of the Basic Shape drawings—Euclidean, fractal and organic—clustering them so that they can evaluate and comment on them in mini-groups, identifying the shapes that work best for certain parts of their objects.

**DISCUSSION:** Find out what other kinds of situations students have experienced where several solutions have proved useful.

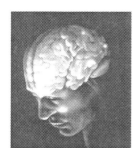

# Step Three

# LIGHT MEDIUM DARK

## A Value Drawing

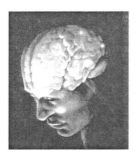

LMD writing, Joanne Krawczyk, 1996

My LMD Drawing tells me that my object is ruled by darkness because the majority of the drawing is completely or nearly black. My LMD Drawing has a sxant amount of gray and light areas near the left bottom section of my object because I see a minor amount of gray and an almost non-existant measure of high lights.

My LMD Drawing is like a monster emerging from the sea to serve its time on medieval shores as a mythical dragon because its fins are evolving into wings and the fire in its belly has reached its throat.

My LMD Drawing is the lurking shadow of the sea's equilvalent of the Grim Reaper because the murkey darkness that lies on my creature resembles the Reaper's ominous cloak.

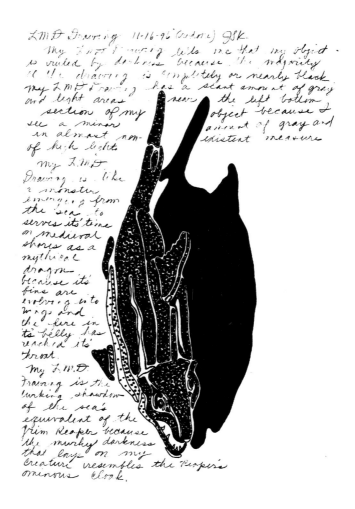

*LMD, Fish, Joanne Krawczyk, Continuing Education, Westfield State, 1996*

# STEP THREE

# Light Medium Dark

## A Value Drawing

OBJECTIVES:

   *Training in discrimination*
   *Light defines objects*
   *Chiaroscuro*
   *Hard-edged transitions between values*
   *Squinting as a filtering technique*
   *Distinguishing the dramatic from the subtle*
   *Simplification produces strong visual patterns*

MATERIALS: markers, objects, paper, folders, a shiny spoon and some other object with a dull or non-shiny surface like a piece of driftwood. Some pictures with a range of values (drawings, photos, magazine ads). Some prints by Fauve artists Derain, Vlaminck, Matisse, Gauguin, Marc.

BACKGROUND:
   Besides teaching students to set the boundaries for an information search and to determine its shape or scope, Drawing/Writing teaches students to distinguish the obvious from the less obvious in the context of a drawing called Light-Medium-Dark. Students learn to filter out all elements except one: light. The transferable skill students learn from the LMD drawing is how to discriminate, distinguish and select certain bits of information in the midst of a barrage of information.
   At first, it is difficult to distinguish lights from darks. We are used to seeing a thing and calling it an apple. Unless we are trained to see with the artist's eye, we are less likely to say, "Oh, there is a strong highlight on the top left side of that apple, and, because of a bruise, there is a discoloration below it that is still highly lit because the light hits the bruised spot strongly." Dramatic differences between lights and darks may not be apparent at first, and subtle differences may be undetectable or confusing. For instance, as the curve of the apple moves away from direct light, there is a transition area, partially light and partially dark. In addition, color complicates the issue; a shiny black shoe may be brightly lit and could best be represented by a glaring white—and yet we will insist on coloring it black.
   In the LMD drawing, the L stands for light and indicates the area with the greatest amount of light; the M stands for medium and indicates the transitional area between the lightest lights and the darkest darks; and D stands for dark, the area in shadow. This exercise teaches a fundamental illusionary drawing trick called chiaroscuro. Skill with chiaroscuro or "light/dark" drawings lets students create startlingly realistic work. Drawings with strong contrasts engage the eye on several levels. The first is retinal and neural. Neurons in the retina fire more strongly for strong contrasts. The second is "mental." Because they seem so real, so touchable, so three-dimensional, the LMD drawings also engage the mind.

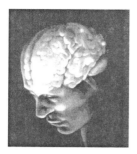

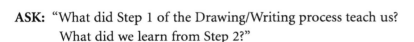

*Cow Skull, LMD drawing, Cecily Howell, 1997*

## PROCEDURE:

### REHASH

**HOMEWORK:** Remind students that they will repeat the following exercise for homework. Remind them that you will not be writing instructions on the board and that they will not be taking their in-class portfolios home. Students will need to remember what they did in class.

**ASK:** "What did Step 1 of the Drawing/Writing process teach us?
What did we learn from Step 2?"

**DISCUSSION:** It is important to ask students what they have learned. The question encourages students to review and to clarify. You may discover they are learning more than you thought or other things than you thought. Extend the discussion by asking, "What else did you learn?" This will push the discussion past, "I learned to do a Blind Contour drawing." "What did this teach you?" or "Are there any generally useful skills or ideas?" are questions which extend the relevance of the exercises even further.

**SAY:** "Now, we are going on to Step 3, Light-Medium-Dark. It is called a value drawing. What do you think LMD stands for? Once we identify LMD, we can define the word value."

**DISCUSSION:** Students usually come up with Light, Medium and Dark. Let them guess until they do. Then, discuss how light allows us to see. Students know that if it is dark they do not see anything. However, they may not have grasped the fact that light falls on different objects in different ways or that light is both absorbed by and reflected from surfaces depending upon color, texture and condition. When students have talked about shiny and dull surfaces, white and black surfaces, wet and dry surfaces, provide, if you wish, some of the following lefthand page information. Then, define the word "chiaroscuro," and clarify the distinctions between the words value, hue, color and chroma.

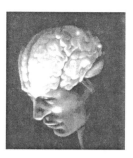

i **ADDITIONAL INFORMATION:** The perception of color is neurophysiological, electromagnetic and psychological. The human eye is designed to discriminate certain wavelengths of light called the visible spectrum. Furthermore, the brain insists on seeing an apple as red even when existing lighting and atmospheric conditions make it appear purple. The visible spectrum includes wavelengths of light between 400 and 700 millimicrons. The invisible spectrum includes gamma rays, x-rays, ultraviolet rays, infrared rays, radar, radio waves and television. Defined in this way, color, as electromagnetic vibration, represents a small portion of the electromagnetic field. Newton discovered colored light by directing a beam of light through a prism. The visible wavelengths arranged themselves into the rainbow: indigo, blue, green, yellow, orange and red. Newton joined the colors in a circle, creating the first color wheel, making the flow from tone to tone continuous, and creating purple where the first (indigo) and last (red) tone overlap. Joseph Albers, major color theorist, remarked that "color deceives continually" (Bevlin, 1963, 120). His theory of complementary colors is called simultaneous contrast. Albers reasoned that, by staring at, say red, the nerve cells in the retina responsive to red become fatigued. The eye naturally registers an afterimage of the complement of a color, in this case, green. The green is enhanced because the adjacent nerve cells for red are tired.

**ASIDE:** Blaise Pascal (1623-1662), French mathematician, physicist, profound skeptic and passionate Christian apologist and theologian remarked in *Pensées (1958)*, "When I consider the short duration of my life, swallowed up in the eternity before and after, the little space which I fill, and even can see, engulfed in the infinite immensity of spaces of which I am ignorant, and which know me not, I am frightened....The eternal silence of these infinite spaces frightens me."

We receive certain wavelengths of light from objects, people, places and creatures. We do not directly receive the objects, people, places and creatures themselves—unless we touch them. Through touch, we reassure ourselves that the distance between us and the perceptible world is bridgeable and that, in fact, contact and verification are possible.

Communication in the brain occurs in the spaces between neurons. Communication in the world happens in the spaces between people and things. Even though glial cells and interneurons fill up most of the interstitial space, we speak of being empty-headed—as if the brain included vast spaces. The artist's term for a fear of empty spaces in a work of art is *horror vacui*. We fear too much open space. It is possible to put an existential fearfulness about such spaces aside if we focus on honing our sensing devices, placing trust in them to provide accurate impressions of the world around us, and using the sense of touch whenever we can to fill the vast spaces around us with the experiences within our reach. Besides these two strategies, we can confirm and enlarge our personal experiences by talking with other people, and by examining their drawn and written records.

**SAY:** "Chiaroscuro is the formal term used to describe value drawings. The Italian word *chiaro* comes from the Latin word *clarus* for 'bright' or 'light' or 'clear.' *Oscuro* comes from *obscurus* meaning 'obscure' or 'dark.'

Distinctions exist between the terms value, hue, color and chroma. *Value* is the degree of lightness or darkness of an object. The word *hue* is interchangeable with the word *color*. *Chroma* is the particular shade or tint of a color and is determined by intensity, or the degree to which a pigment is "saturated" with color. A red apple placed in a dark corner may look blue, or black. A bright light on a red apple produces highlights which may register as brilliant white areas. The fact that an object can be black in color but look white in bright light challenges the mind. The student must resist using the color he associates with an object—say, red for an apple—and see what is actually there, given the lighting conditions.

In the LMD drawing, the student is not doing a color study. Color comes into Drawing/Writing exercises only accidentally and relates to the arbitrary choice of a colored marker. The LMD exercise focuses on *value* or the degree to which certain areas of the object are light or dark. Color may or may not affect value.

Talk to students about the advantages of squinting, followed by some more general comments about the benefits to students' minds of practicing the LMD drawings:

Squinting is an LMD drawing strategy. The LMD drawing and the squinting strategy raise several issues. You will need to decide how many of these to bring up with students. All of them are important:

- Consensual domain. Students more or less agree about where the lights and darks are on an object. There will be some differences of opinion. As with poetry, each student brings his or her life experience to bear on the interpretation. There can be general agreement about the overall subject of a poem, but opinions will differ, often radically, about what the poem means. The same holds true with the LMD drawing. There will be areas of agreement and disagreement.

- Materials. The materials used to make the objects and how those materials have been treated make a tremendous difference in how the Drawing/Writing objects react to light and how light reacts to them.

- The deliberate suppression of details as a strategy for focussing on selected items. The act of squinting suppresses details. In an LMD drawing, the only relevant details are those which describe value. Students learn through squinting to dismiss irrelevant information. It is a challenge to suppress certain details—especially color—while selecting others. The mind wants to hold on to the familiar and the easily accessible, particularly to ideas about color. The fact that apples are red is a known fact. If an apple actually appears blue in certain lights, the senses will need to battle the mind to achieve an optically correct representation that includes this new information about apples and blueness.

- Enlightenment. The use of this term in connection with a drawing exercise about light may appear ambitious, but the LMD drawing has serious implications. Students who force themselves to see what is really there, pushing away what they have believed to be true, see in a new way. The activity of squinting brings blind spots into relief. By squinting, we see more clearly. Like other truths, this is a paradox. Seeing less, we see more.

- On being closed. Squinting helps students discover the degree to which their minds are closed and how tightly we hold on to old, comfortable information—like the illusion that a black object is black no matter what the lighting situation may be.

- On understanding color. Wavelengths of light are absorbed or reflected by objects. We perceive what is reflected, or "left over," as color. A red object absorbs all wavelengths but red. Wavelengths of red light hit our retinas. A shiny object reflects all wavelengths, appearing white. White hits our retina whether the object in less dramatic lighting is blue or red or yellow. The surface property of the object and the way in which light behaves around that surface determine the color of an object. The surface of the object has properties which affect the behavior of light. We receive the results of the interaction between light and objects. We do not receive the objects themselves. This situation could be unsettling.

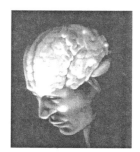

**RECORD:** Write the word *chiaroscuro* and its definition and linguistic breakdown, *claro* and *oscurus*, on the board. As usual, students will copy this information into their Drawing/Writing journals.

**DEMONSTRATE:** Provide a range of photos, drawings, paintings. Make sure some have subtle value and some have strong value. A pencil drawing and a pen and ink drawing provide a contrast in value. Ask students to identify light areas, middle areas, and dark areas. Ask students why accurate value drawings seem so real.

**SAY:** "Let's look at these. Which of these images is the strongest? I am not talking about accuracy. I am talking about contrast in value, or the distance between the lights and darks. Which works catch your eye first? Why do you think this happens?"

**DISCUSSION:** Students will notice that drawings with strong chiaroscuro, or contrast, or degree of distance between lights and darks, catch their eyes on several levels. The first effect on the brain of light/dark contrast is retinal. The second three-dimensional effect is "mental." Works strongly suggesting the illusion of three dimensions engage the mind as well as the eye.

**DEMONSTRATE:** Bring in a shiny spoon and a piece of driftwood or some kind of dull material.

**SAY:** "The word 'value' is used to describe the degree to which an object is light or dark. A shiny spoon has high value. A piece of driftwood has low value. In general, rough objects absorb light, while smooth objects reflect light. The more light-reflective an object is, the higher its value. The less light-reflective, the lower its value."

**DEMONSTRATE:** Hold up your object, turning it around. Squint at it. Talk about where it is light and dark. Do not say why it is light or dark. Go around the room and ask each student if his or her object is high or low value. Hold up your object again.

**SAY:** "My object is low value here and high value there (or whatever is appropriate). Did you notice that I am squinting at my object? If I squint, it helps me see the lights and darks. Squint at your objects. Does it help you to see the lights and darks?"

**ASK:** "Does an LMD drawing of an object with low or subtle value have to be a weak drawing? Let's complete a value drawing of our objects and see."

**SAY:** "We will keep using markers for the LMD drawing. The shapes will be clear and strong. Try to isolate the shapes of the lights, the shapes of the darks, and the shapes of the middle values. This is a Basic Shape drawing—in relation to light, not form. When changes in value are recorded on a two-dimensional surface, like a piece of paper, the result is a three-dimensional illusion. 3-D drawings are very compelling because they look real. The LMD drawing is one of the basic tricks of powerful drawing."

**DEMONSTRATE:** You may want to use a flashlight or some kind of spotlight to demonstrate value dramatically. Turn out the lights. Shine the flashlight on an object. Point out the light and dark areas. A spotlight makes the situation far easier, but that ease lessens the effect of the training, which is to teach students to make subtle as well as dramatic visual distinctions under natural, everyday conditions. A better course of action is to simplify the light source, if possible. Turn out the overhead lights, allowing natural light from one source into the room. If you can, move the students to the window wall of the room, placing their objects in front of them, close to the window so that the objects will be as brightly lit as possible. If the weather is good and time allows, take the students outside to draw their object in natural light. If you

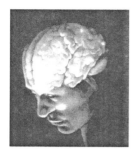

have a series of overhead lights, use just one set so that light is coming from one source rather than from all over the ceiling.

Make sure students do not mask their objects with their bodies, but place them so that light will shine directly on them. No matter how you set up this drawing exercise, the lighting will prove challenging.

**DEMONSTRATE:** (Hold up a piece of paper.)

**SAY:** "The paper has length and width. It has no depth, does it? We are drawing on a two-dimensional surface; we are not sculpting. If we were sculpting, how many dimensions would we be working in?" (Students will provide the answer "in three dimensions.")

"We are working with a two-dimensional surface, a piece of paper. Still, we can draw in ways that fool our eyes into thinking we are really looking at a 3-D object. We can create this illusion by seeing and recording light values, middle values, and dark values.

"Remember when I squinted at my object and asked you to squint? Squinting eliminates everything but value. Squinting will block out the outline, the basic shapes, and the little details. You should be able to see the lights and darks better. First, try drawing the shapes of the lightest areas. Or you might want to start with the darkest areas. Remember, we are still using markers, we are filling the page, and we are drawing completely closed shapes. The middle value shapes will be located between the lightest lights and darkest darks.

"I'll try an LMD drawing of my hammer, starting with the shapes of the lights which are the easiest for me to see. I will draw the shapes as if they were levitating in space."

**DEMONSTRATE/DO:** Put the hammer in the light. Squint at it. Start drawing the shapes of the highlights. Construct your object as you did with the Basic Shapes drawings, only this time lights and darks, not structure and volume, will determine the shapes. The shapes will be the actual shapes you see in the patterns of lights and darks, not for instance, simplified Euclidean shapes.

**TIP:** Some students will assume "shapes" means Euclidean; in the LMD drawing, "shapes" means isolating the highlights, shadows and middle values as distinct, bounded entities. The bottom two drawings "fit" the values into a pre-existing contour drawing. This is the incorrect way to do an LMD drawing. The method on the left is correct.

**SAY/DO:** "Now, I'll squint, and draw the shapes of the lightest values I see."

**DEMONSTRATE:** Squint at your object; hold that pose for several seconds; then, draw the shapes of the lightest lights you see in your object. Now, do the same with the darks. Color the dark shapes in completely.

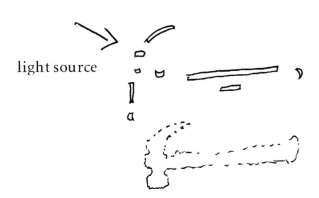

*Highlights of a hammer, with imaginary line of hammer held in the drawer's mind's eye, SRS*

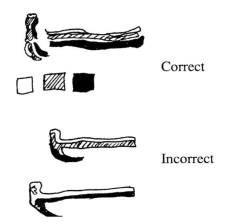

Correct

Incorrect

*The top hammer is constructed with actual shapes of light, middle and dark values*

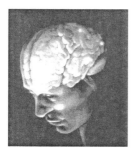

**SAY:** "The easy solution is that the shapes inbetween the darks and lights will be the middle values. The shapes of middle value can be cross-hatched or dotted, or filled with whatever consistent pattern you choose."

**ASK:** "If the lines are closer together, what kind of value results?"

**DISCUSSION:** Allow students to provide the phrase "a darker value."

**SAY:** "If the lines are farther apart?"

**DISCUSSION:** Allow students to provide the phrase "a lighter value."

*Hammer with middle values added, SRS*

**DEMONSTRATE:** Add the shapes of the middle values to your LMD drawing. Fill in the middle value shapes with parallel lines, or dots, or cross-hatching; choose a simple, consistent pattern. Indicate the light source with an arrow heading down toward the object.

**SAY:** "Watch: I am going to draw an arrow to indicate the light source. Do you see how the light source determines where the light areas will be? Generally, the area farthest from the light source will be, what?"

**DISCUSSION:** Allow students to provide the comment, "That area will be dark." This is not a false Socratic question, nor a demeaning one; it is, however, a leading question.

**SAY:** "Yes, usually the areas farthest from the light source are dark. But let me show you something called bounce light."

*The three different value patterns, boxed*

**DEMONSTRATE:** Draw an arrow going down toward the baseline of your drawing. Draw it hitting the baseline and then extend the end of the arrow, so that it zooms back up in the air. Add more arrow-lines like this, as if rain were drumming down around your object. Some of the lines that zoom back up will strike the hammer on the underside. You want to show the students that light does the same thing.

## Bounce light

**SAY:** "Let's use a drawing of a pear. Do you see that the part of the pear that is away from the light source is not always dark? When light hits a surface and bounces off it, it may strike the underside of an object which is otherwise situated away from the light. It is impossible to know where any one light ray will strike, but we can observe that some rays of light do strike the underside of the object."

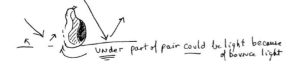

*Bounce light arrows*

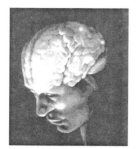

 **REMEMBER:** As the Drawing/Writing program adds complexity to the drawing exercises, the concepts and ideas become more complex, too. Drawing/Writing increases students' tolerance for attention, work, and thought. Students' increased ability to sit quietly drawing and writing will hit you with a shock. At this point in the Drawing/Writing process, the entire room may be engaged in largely silent, productive work.

**DEMONSTRATE:** Draw your hammer. Draw light striking it and the surface it rests on, bouncing all over.

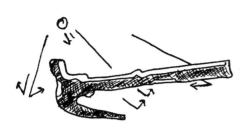

*Hammer with bounce light*

**SAY:** "If a surface on which the object rests is light-reflective, the light will strike the underside of the object. Odd things happen. Watch for light areas where you would normally expect dark ones. Your ability to see and record these spots will make your LMD drawing even more convincing."

**DEMONSTRATE:** Do more work on your LMD drawing. Make neat, overlapping, parallel strokes with the marker to fill in the shapes of the darkest darks. Careful overlapping saves the points of markers. "Scrubbing" to fill in shapes ruins the points.

**SAY/DO:** "Take a new piece of paper and put your initials, the date, and the letters LMD at the top of the page. Stay with markers. Do an LMD drawing. Fill the page.

"Be careful how you use your fat marker. Do not scrub with it when you fill in the dark shapes. Lay down overlapping, parallel lines; your work will look elegant and the marker will not be ruined."

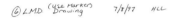

*Geode LMD drawing #1, Heather Lyons, 1997, Merrimac Education Center/Fitchburg State College Continuing Education Program*

"As usual, I will write, 'My LMD drawing tells me that my object is... because....' This piece of writing forces me to think about why the object reacts to light in certain ways. Why does it shine? Or, why doesn't it shine?"  ·

**TIP:** Just because an object is black does not mean that it is dark. A black area can have strong highlights. In the same way, just because an object is white does not mean it is light; a white object can have strong, dark shadows. Students will make these discoveries for themselves over time.

**DEMONSTRATE:** As you write, identify outloud surface characteristics of the object like "light-reflective-ness," "shininess," "dullness," "deep shadows," and so forth. Write on the board or easel pad, "My LMD drawing tells me that my hammer is made of different materials. The hammer has some highlights around the head, and highlights along the shaft. The highlights are brighter along the shaft, which is made of varnished wood. The head is made of a duller metal, which absorbs light more than it throws it off."

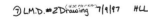

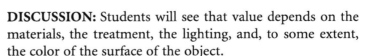

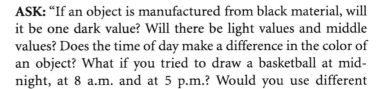

*Geode LMD drawings #2, Heather Lyons, 1997, Merrimac/Fitchburg State College*

**ASK:** "What do you think determines how light behaves around an object?"

**DISCUSSION:** Students will see that value depends on the materials, the treatment, the lighting, and, to some extent, the color of the surface of the object.

**ASK:** "If an object is manufactured from black material, will it be one dark value? Will there be light values and middle values? Does the time of day make a difference in the color of an object? What if you tried to draw a basketball at midnight, at 8 a.m. and at 5 p.m.? Would you use different colors? Different values? What do you think?"

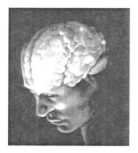

**DISCUSSION:** Allow students to think about these questions. If they have never drawn the same object at different times of day, they can still make intelligent guesses.

"Besides line and shape, what else determines how we draw an object in connection with light? The surface texture and the condition of the surface determine the degree to which light is absorbed or reflected. Highly polished surfaces or machined (metal) surfaces glint. Satin shines. Velvet glows. A pair of corduroy pants or scuffed leather shoes appear dull because the textured or rough surfaces absorb much of the light.

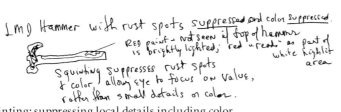

Squinting: suppressing local details including color

*LMD drawing of hammer, labeling light source, rust spots, local color, with value in some places* **overriding** *rust spots and local color. The reader must imagine color.*

"Light acts differently when it hits an area that is rough, worn, damaged or blemished or where there are rust spots or smears of paint. Let's look at our objects. Where is it going to be really hard to distinguish the values and resist being sidetracked by color? To avoid being sidetracked, we need to discuss the term "local color."

"The term 'local color' means the actual color of the object apart from conditions. The word 'local' derives from the Latin noun, locus, meaning 'place' or 'spot.' Here are some points to remember about color:

- color is a function of the actual pigment embedded in or applied to an object and the atmospheric conditions around it. An object located under a waterfall on a sunny day will assume different colors (and values) than the same object on the desert sands at dusk.

- color is a function of what part of the object we are looking at. The top of a peach in sunlight appears to be one color. The underside of the peach appears to be another.

- Color is a function of condition, including age; the ripe side of the peach is pink. The non-ripe side of the peach is yellow-green.

- an object will throw off its complementary color as its corona or shadow. This is the law of 'required change' or 'chromatic adaptation' (Zajonc, 1991, 197-8).

- "local color" as a function of place, distinguished by certain characteristics, features or customs provides an entirely different use of the term. When traveling, some tourists place "local color" at a premium. When local color is added to a play or novel, a heightened sense of realism results.

"Attention to color can heighten realism in art, or it can startle viewers. Fauve artists used color in idiosyncratic ways. Who is to say that Derain did not actually *see* violent pinks and greens in water under bridges? A non-traditional use of color may be an objective statement of what the eye of the artist is actually seeing.

"Monet's cathedrals, haystacks, water lilies and poplars reveal a wide range of colors which are accurate descriptions of the subject at a moment in time and space. Some of Monet's haystacks are pink, some are blue, some are blue and pink. Monet did not <u>feel</u> pink about haystacks. He saw haystacks as pink at a certain time of day. Some German expressionists, on the other hand, <u>felt</u> blue or red about life in general, or about the subjects they were painting and deliberately provided a visually incorrect, emotionally charged color scheme.

"Your objects will look different, too, depending upon where you place them in the room. When you do your homework with your object at home, try drawing it outside at different times of day. Take notes on how the LMD drawing changes and whether your object seems to change color. You will be using one marker only. So, your value study will not depend on *color* but on *local value*. That is, a bright red apple at noon which reveals many light values may look blue or dark in value at dusk. Some understanding of how local color and value change due to environment and time of day is useful to convincing 3-D drawings."

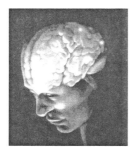

**TIP:** Through practice with the LMD drawing, students will learn to differentiate lights and darks, and they will learn to distinguish them *apart from* local color. The "local color" of a toy train may be black. Parts of the train can still be drawn as white where light strikes it. A bone may be white. The bone will still have dark areas where light does not hit it. Local color, or "true" color may or may not be important in a value drawing. An apple whose local color is red may be effectively and convincingly drawn with shades of gray. What will convince the eye is careful attention to changes in value. The outline, the shape, and the shading tell us we are looking at an apple, not color alone. Look at a range of still life paintings throughout art history. Identify the flowers and fruits. Check what color the artist chose to depict the flower or fruit. A purple apple is no less convincing than a red apple if the contour, form and value of the apple are accurately presented. On the other hand, a canvas suffused with red may have nothing to do with apples. (See Mark Rothko's purple/red color field paintings for the Rothko Chapel, Rice University, Houston, Texas.)

**SAY:** "The LMD drawing is challenging. Each time you draw, you will see value more clearly; your drawings will become more accurate in describing value and therefore more convincing as three-dimensional objects. If your drawings are so convincing they fool the viewer into thinking he can touch the object, then you have created a work described in French as 'trompe l'oeil,' or 'fool the eye.'"

**DEMONSTRATE:** Show students prints of work by Fauve artists—Derain, Vlaminck, Gauguin, Marc, Matisse. And, for instance, of American trompe l'oeil artists William Michael Harnett and John Frederick Peto.

**RECORD:** Write the phrase "local color" on the board, and the words "a blue apple is still an apple."

**DEMONSTRATE:** Go back to your value drawing on the board.

**SAY:** "Remember, we are not just drawing the contour and filling in the values. We are drawing the actual *shapes* of the values, as if they were pieces of a puzzle, arranged in space. Once you have constructed your objects from light, middle and dark building blocks, your eye will invent the outline that encloses these value shapes. You will not need to draw this imaginary line to see your object becoming three-dimensional before your eyes."

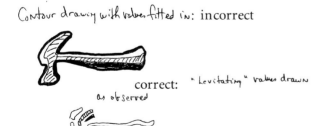

Contour drawing of a hammer with lights and values fitted in. Mark this "incorrect." This approach is incorrect because the exercise involves isolating and drawing only the shapes of the lights, middle and dark values, not the outline of the object.

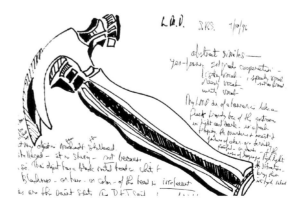

LMD hammer created by drawing the **_shapes_** of the light, medium and dark areas. Correct approach to the LMD drawing.

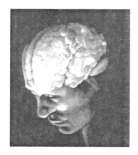

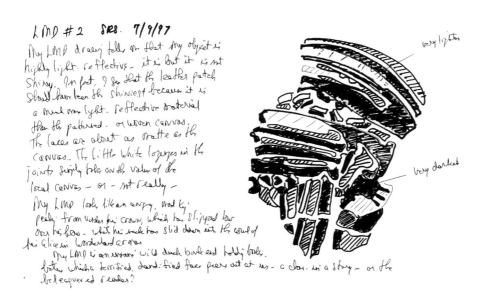

*LMD, Lacrosse Glove, SRS 97*

**SAY/DO:** "Now, let's write one simule and one metapor. Remember to use the word "because" to explain your similes and metaphors."

## SHARE AND BUILD:

**DISCUSSION:** The LMD drawing teaches students to make distinctions based on dramatic or subtle contrasts in value. This ability to filter out all information except for value encourages a greater appreciation for high drama as well as for nuance—say, for the death of Hamlet, as well as for the power of a piece of punctuation—a dash, for instance, in the poetry of Amy Clampitt or Seamus Heaney.

After students have shared their LMD drawings and writings, start a discussion about lights and darks in connection with text including literature, newspaper articles and advertising. Are some words high-contrast words? "Murder?" "Disaster?" Are some words low-contrast?

**SAY:** "How about books? What about advertising, or song lyrics? Some ideas are obvious, some are subtle, some are hidden."

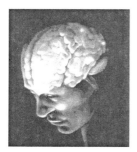

 **REMEMBER/REMINDER:** Your goal in leading these discussions is to help students transfer skills and understandings from the Drawing/Writing program to other fields of study and into their lives. Students need to apply what they learn. For this to happen, what they learn in school must be made applicable. Ideally, students will learn to think in the following way: "I have learned a piece of information which makes sense to me in this context. How has this information changed my thinking? Is any of it applicable in other situations?"

Drawing/Writing provides students with a process for analysis and inquiry. Faced with new information and new predicaments calling for judgment, decisions and action, students can apply sequential, cumulative Drawing/Writing-like strategies, learning to evaluate and modify their responses to information.

 **ASIDE:** With longer lives and increased leisure, the arts and other forms of exploratory and expressive activities will be more, not less, necessary. Many people's lives will be spent in part-time work, in short-term projects, in transitional teams, or in retirement. Teaching students to draw and write and read and wonder and speculate for self-fulfillment, as well as for academic and job success, will help determine the quality of their lives.

THE BEACH PEA  by Amy Clampitt

FOR SUSAN RICH SHERIDAN

*Photo, Amy Clampitt and Hal
Korn, London, 1991, SRS*

*Oil portrait, Amy Clampitt
and Hal Korn, 1996, SRS*

That first summer, what little
we'd learned of the geography
kept its own counsel--a vaporous
drip and sob, the whistle buoy
lowing offshore, the mittened
treacheries of ledge and tidefall,
mysteries of repose lapped and
delivered in a shawl of breakers.
Blundering through fog, late
one day, along an alder-bordered
track disclosed a meadow, at
its seaward edge a house,
its looming, boarded-up remoteness
big with soliloquy.

A decade later
we skirted that same meadow, in
daisy-freckled sunshine, to find her
kerchiefed, statuesque
among the rocks--a collie
her one companion where
the beach pea flourished
untended, garish in the midst of
such concussion and dismemberment,
tide after tide, gale after gale; the house
behind her, its now unshuttered
solitudes delivered into daylight,
and back of that the larger
solitude of alder pockets, snarled
spruce, tamarack, pincushion
plush and calico of heath plants,
rockbottom footholds of the
purple iris, the sphagnum deeps
small vivid orchids with
their feet in quicksand.

Before her,
poised at the edge--the day
was one of bone-white splendor,
a slow surf filleting the blue--
lay a view such as one comes to
be at home with, to rest in,
intimate as with the hollows of
a lover's body; needled diadem
and fractured granite centered,
as in an altarpiece with kneeling
figures, on the inverted pendant
of 'Tit Manan light, its turning
gaze above the driftwood
phased like a moon.

No sometime
visitor, by then, she'd come, drawn
by some such perception (she herself
was never so explicit) to live here;
come in fact--though we'd not, from
any hint of hers, have guessed--
to die here.

The weight of an
adieu, each summer, overhangs
the solstice--the weightier,
the more immaculate the daylight's
interfusing blue. Some throb
of sorrow, of the apprehended
and consented to, repoved
our quashed tiff (we'd been bickering
the two of us, for days) the day
we saw her last, that summer,
that serene, last,
perfect afternoon.

Word came
in January: she might just possibly
live through the spring. Midsummer,
that year, found us in Northumberland:
white midnights, gray days
of drizzle, the laburnum's
golden dross on all the sidewalks--
kin of broom and gorse, of
the acacia, the beach pea...
The beach pea!  That, in retrospect,
was the connection: tough,
ubiquitous, perennial, intimate
of granite and driftwood, of all
those ponderous displacements
at the endge: so unaspiring,
so mundame, except--
except for, looked at
up close, those tendrils,
those reaching rings
that now encircle nothing.

*Amy Clampitt's poem "The Beach Pea," commemorating the death
of my mother, Virginia Ruth Garberson Rich, who died May 31st, 1985*

**DISCUSSION:** Using books students are currently reading in school, along with their favorite ads, comics, song lyrics, television, movies, videos, discover what information is highly lit, less well lit, or hidden and how these effects are achieved visually and verbally. The student who is sensitive to value in drawing will be sensitive to emphasis in text. Students quite literally need to discriminate among a range of "values" in their lives. Direct the dialogue toward practical/philosophical speculations.

**SAY:** "What about hard-sell and soft-sell advertising? What about people? One person may be striking. Highly lit and dramatic. Or a person may be softly lit and fascinating in a subtle way."

**TIP:** With young children, you might ask, "What's a really popular toy? What does it look like? How do you know about it? Is it advertised on TV? What kinds of toys are not advertised on TV? How do you know about them? Is there a difference between the two kinds of toys?"

With older students, discussions can include the bright allure of substances or activities that might not be healthy or useful.

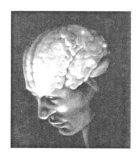

**ASK:** " What kinds of things are advertised as really exciting ? What ads make you feel you have to buy the item? Is there something especially attractive about what is hidden in shadows?"

Students' discrimination skills are challenged daily. The ability to make "value" judgments is important to their well-being and success.

**SAY:** "Let's talk about another meaning of the word 'value.' Some ideas, causes, information, careers are more worthwhile than others. They have more value to us personally or to society in general. What about deceptive values? If a very bright light hits the hammer where it is rusted, the light will bounce off, creating an area of whiteness. The hammer is not really shiny in the rusty area, but it looks shiny and new in that area because of the bright light. If we transfer this 'deception of light' to real-life situations, how could we apply the idea of false value? Does an ad with dramatic content have high value as information, or as a rule of thumb to live by, or is the value largely emotional and deceptively persuasive? What kinds of items have value in terms of real worth? How can we separate our emotional responsiveness from accurate seeing? Can emotion and reason work together?

**DISCUSSION:** Students need to think about worth or value and deception in advertising, TV, movies, videos, political propaganda, religious propaganda.

**SAY:** "Let's come up with examples of high-lit and low-lit people, movies, books, sporting events, media events, political events, world events, advertising. Do these items have real value or only the illusion of value?"

**DISCUSSION:** Students may bring up O. J. Simpson, Michael Jackson, Madonna, Leonardo di Caprio, Brad Pitt, Will Smith, Tommy Lee Jones, Paula Coles, Princess Diana. What matters is who and what *students* think are high and low visibility and why.

My L. M. D. drawing tells me that my object reflects light more strongly from the left side. It seems to get darker in the middle and the lower right side. My L. M. D. drawing is like some kind of foreign insect. Its legs are getting ready to launch itself from its surface. It looks like the skin has different tonal values. My L. M. D. drawing is an insect because it is going through some kind of metamorphosis, from an ugly insect to a pulchritudinous flying creature. The top seems to be augmenting upward and outward in a curving way. It is like the pieces are multiplying. The pieces are not clutched together and look to be placed in a fluid loose movement.

*LMD Drawing, Chair, Pamela Frigo, Continuing Education, Westfield State College, 1996*

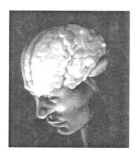

# Step Four

# THE "PERFECT" WHOLE

## or

## "WARTS 'N ALL"

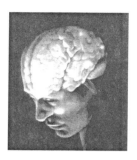

"Perfect" Whole writing, fish, Joanne Krawczyk

My "Perfect" Whole at first glance appears to be an organic being, a fish to be exact, because it is a representation of the true article. Taking a closer look, my p.w. drawing tells me that my object is merely an imitation because of its rigid plasticity. A real fish, having lain for an hour on a table, would surely relax its tail and fins, even after initially flopping and gasping for air. In spite of my imaginary antics, my p.w. drawing tells me that my drawing is an adequate illusion of a three-dimensional object on a two-dimensional surface because line, shape, value, texture and shading have joined forces to tell a more complete story of my object.

My p.w. drawing is like a person about to take their last breath because of the frozen stare of the eyes, the mute gaping mouth and the silence of its pre-cadaverous state.

My p.w. drawing is the non-voting public on election day who have forgotten the lessons of the past and underestimate their potency because they feel as powerless as a fish out of water.

*"Perfect" Whole, Fish, Joanne Krawczyk, Continuing Education, Westfield State, 1996*

# STEP FOUR

# The "Perfect" Whole
## or
## "WARTS 'N ALL"

## 4.1 The "Perfect" Whole Drawing

OBJECTIVES:

> *Drawing techniques: chiaroscruro as a soft transition between values; usefulness of
> the eraser for lift-off*
> *COMPLETENESS—NOT PERFECTION*
> *Completeness as a decision*
> *Wholeness as a decision*

MATERIALS: Pencils, objects, paper, folders. **Put the markers away**. Provide 2B and 2H pencils
with erasers.

**BACKGROUND:**

Step 4 is called the "Perfect" Whole. "Warts 'n All" is a hand-me-down phrase from my mother, indicating that this drawing will be scrupulously honest in its inclusion of all important details—from the
beautiful to the not-so-beautiful. The degree of detail required by this drawing develops students' analytical skills as well as their ability to synthesize information in a comprehensive and persuasive statement.
Students are now ready for the sustained drawing and writing exercises required by Step 4. The procedure
for Drawing/Writing has become routine and students show signs of impatience because they are capable
of more demanding work. The "Perfect" Whole drawing gives students a chance to show what they have
learned from the Contour drawings, the Basic Shapes drawings and the LMD drawing. Because they can
produce an accurate outline, expressive shape, and compelling light/dark patterns, students are now able to
produce "razzle dazzle," optically real drawing. Students who produce optically convincing drawings, so
real-seeming that the object appears touchable, experience a huge boost in confidence. This confidence
spills over into their writing. It is an exciting time to be in a classroom.

How you teach The "Perfect" Whole depends on how much class time you can devote to the exercise.
The word "whole" suggests drawing the whole object. Some students will ask whether you mean "hole" or
"whole." When they hear the term "the perfect whole," some students evidently think of some kind of hole
in the ground. This happens with adults, too. So, be prepared to clarify this by writing the words "hole" and
"whole" on the board and underlining or circling the word "whole."

If you can devote an hour to the drawing, encourage students to draw the whole object. If you can only
devote one-half hour, suggest drawing a part. Students will now be able to sustain their focus. In fact, they

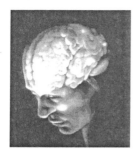

will not notice the passage of time. Providing time for students to concentrate on a self-directed task in which they will be extremely successful is of inestimable educational value. As they work on the "Perfect" Whole drawing, students will see how powerful they have become as visual artists. Their abilities to concentrate and to draw have grown in interrelated ways. An accurate, convincing drawing indicates that students have not only learned some of the tricks of drawing analogous to literary strategies—the apt metaphor, the incisive opening sentence, the powerful concluding paragraph—but strong analytical visual skills. At this point in the Drawing/Writing process, most students will produce a fully developed, impressive drawing. The room will be silent.

Students now use pencils for the first time since the completion of the Preliminary Drawing and Writing. You will notice that most students chose pencil to produce that initial sample. After a session of Drawing/Writing, students are less likely to select a pencil automatically, often choosing markers instead for their visual power. You will show them that pencils allow a soft rather than a hard-edged transition between values, and that erasers can be used for lift-off, creating brilliant highlights, as well as for correcting mistakes. Erasers can still be used for corrections, but correction will no longer be the only advantage to pencils.

In this step, the words "perfect" and "whole" are both used ironically. The quotation marks signal the fact that no drawing is ever perfect or whole because—like any piece of writing—no drawing is entirely accurate or complete. Even realistic drawings involve choice. It is impossible to include every detail. In my experience, children know this instinctively. Some teachers suggest using the words "Complete Drawing," rather than the "Perfect" Whole, reporting that irony is confusing to young students. Others say that children know that the quotation marks enclosing the word "perfect" mean that the drawing will not be perfect because "nothing is perfect" (as one second grader in Joanne Quail's class remarked). In my experience, most students understand the ironic use of the word "perfect" in the context of this exercise.

## PROCEDURE

**REHASH:**

**HOMEWORK:** Remind students that they will repeat the following exercise for homework. Remind them that you will not be writing instructions on the board and that they will not be taking their in-class portfolios home. Students will need to remember what they did in class.

**SAY/DO:** "Now, we can use pencils. Take a pencil, your object, your portfolio, fresh paper. Put your initials and the date at the top of the page. Now, write the words the 'Perfect' Whole. Why did I put quotation marks around the word 'perfect'?"

**DISCUSSION:** Make clear that a drawing is complete when it contains every bit of visual information *the student feels* is necessary. One student may choose to include certain kinds of information about an object in her drawing—for instance, she may emphasize value; another student may make very different kinds of decisions and concentrate on surface texture. It is at this point in the five-step that individual styles start to emerge. Not only will students create realistic drawings through a variety of learned tricks or strategies but they will create unique drawings. This uniqueness will be based on the critical choices the students make about the kinds of information they choose to define the object completely or accurately *for them*. Discuss the word 'perfect' and the idea of perfection until it is clear that you are talking about a complete or an accurate drawing, not about one without flaw.

**SAY:** "What do we mean by the word 'whole?' Notice how I spelled it. The word has a 'w.'"

**DISCUSSION:** Students understand quickly that a "whole" drawing is accurate or complete, not perfect.

**REMEMBER:** Do every drawing step and every writing step with students. Stay closely in touch with what your students are doing. Keep growing through your own work. Resist hovering over student work. Focus on your own. Facilitate discussions and critiques. In this way, you will encourage independence and self-reliance.

**SAY:** "We are striving for a drawing that is whole because it is complete. Because it is complete *and* accurate, it will also be realistic. You are ready to try to see *everything*—the outline, the shape, the value, the details—and put them all together."

**ASK:** "Why do you think we are going to use a pencil now?"

**TIP:** If your classroom includes students who have studied art, they will know about different hardnesses in graphite, but many people have never thought about pencil leads as softer or harder, lighter or darker. Most of us know that a Number 2 pencil is used for multiple choice tests, but otherwise we have little experience with pencil lead categories.

The "Perfect" Whole drawing requires a lead that will smudge well but is not too soft. If you have pencils with very soft leads, students will have to spray fixative on the drawings to prevent them from smudging other work in their portfolios. The cheapest unscented hair spray is an effective fixative.

**DISCUSSION: SPECIFIC:** Students know that pencils are useful for erasing. By now, they have moved to a different position on erasing. Because they are more accurate drawers, erasing is no longer a priority. They are comfortable with markers. In fact, pencils are a trade-off. Pencil drawings mean an immediate loss in visual power in terms of strong edges and contrasts, off-set by gains in subtle transitions and fine-grained detail. Bring out these points.

**SAY:** "When we move to pencils, we are going to lose some of the visual power of markers. Can you describe the advantages pencils do have over markers?"

### *Drawing One, the "Perfect" Whole*

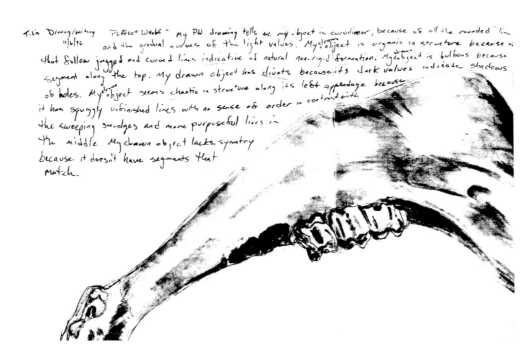

*"Perfect" Whole, Jawbone, Tim Lis, Continuing Education, Westfield State College, 1996*

**ASIDE:** Labeling the carbon in pencils is tricky because the designations are arbitrary; students must understand that <u>B</u> stands for black or degree of darkness, and <u>H</u> stands for hard, which actually means a lighter "drier" mark. By making a distinction between pencil leads, you provide information about pencils as drawing tools, also encouraging students' discriminatory skills.

 **ASIDE:** When air, or atmosphere, interposes itself between us and other things, other things become paler and fainter the farther away they are. Pencil leads allow students to take advantage of this illusionary drawing trick called atmospheric perspective.

**SAY:** "Being able to correct mistakes is important. But let me show you what pencils can do besides erase. First, pencil leads differ. Some are harder, some are softer. Softer leads produce blacker, more smudgeable lines. Harder leads produce lighter, thinner, 'drier' lines. 'B' on the pencil stands for 'black,' or soft carbon; 'H' stands for 'hard.' The higher the numbers, the harder or softer the lead. Thus a 3B pencil is softer than a 2B. And a 3H pencil is harder than a 2H. A 3B pencil will make a dark, blurred lined. A 3H pencil will make a light, precise line. A pencil labeled H/B is somewhere in between. Try it out and see what line quality and value it produces."

**DEMONSTRATE:** Start a "Perfect" Whole drawing on your paper. Tape your paper to your folder. Hold up your folder so that the students can see. Lay your pencil on its side and start shading in the values, using a sweeping approach. You do not want students to tighten up. If they choose to start with an outline, fine, but it is better if you do not. Students are now practicing artists and writers who can make informed choices about their work.

**ASK:** "What advantages does a soft pencil lead have for drawing? What advantages does a hard pencil lead have for drawing? You can use one type of lead or both for your drawing. Think about areas where the softer lead would be better. Where could that be? Where could a lighter, drier line be better?"

**DISCUSSION:** Allow students to experiment with pencils as they talk. They will discover the advantages and disadvantages of different pencil leads. Fine details may require a harder lead. Soft, rich shadowing is produced by a softer pencil lead. Introduce the concept of atmospheric perspective: a lighter, finer line may suggest a certain part of the object has receded appreciably from the viewer and is much farther back than the more strongly drawn, darker sections of the object.

**SAY/DO:** "If I turn my pencil on the side, parallel to the paper and hold it in this way, I can sweep across the paper, covering a larger area; by changing the pressure, I can move smoothly from a lighter to a darker value. Then, I can take my finger and smudge the transitions between the pencil strokes. I can also use the eraser for something called lift-off. This is useful for creating dramatic highlights. This eraser-use is called subtractive; carbon is taken away."

**DEMONSTRATE:** Hold pencil on side, sweep it across page, changing weights of line.

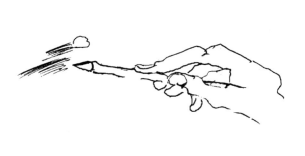

*How to hold pencil to lay on lines, SRS*

*Shoe, "Perfect" Whole drawing, Shelley Weinstein, Merrimac Education Center/Fitchburg State Continuing Education, 1997*

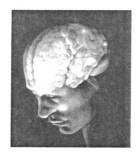

**SAY:** "By using my fingers, I can blur the transition from light to dark. We call this kind of blurring creating a 'soft' transition between values. When we used magic marker, what kind of transition between values did we create in the LMD drawing? Right, a 'hard' transition. Why was it hard? The edges were 'hard' because they were clearly defined. Do soft transitions create more convincing illusions of three-dimensions, seeming more 'perfect?'"

**DISCUSSION:** Students may decide that heightened 3-D illusions and soft transitions go together. The hard transitions in the LMD are visually compelling. But the soft penciled values are often more convincing as "the real thing."

**SAY:** "Remember, the word 'chiaroscuro' describes a value drawing. The word combines two Italian words: 'chiaro' from 'claro,' or 'light,' and 'oscuro,' or 'dark.' Think of the words 'obscure' and 'clarity.'"

**SAY/DO:** "Erasers are not only useful for correcting mistakes. Eraser can be used for 'lift-off,' creating a highlight. Carbon can be lifted off, like this."

*Sketch of lift-off*

**DEMONSTRATE:** Show lift-off by erasing a small area of pencil marks.

**SAY:** "Notice that I am not 'drawing around' a highlight? I move the pencil back and forth, creating a field of value. Then, I remove a dot of carbon from the middle of the field, creating a sudden highlight.

"Now that the values are laid down, I can draw sharp, clear contour lines and add other tiny details. These details are what I call 'warts 'n all.' 'Warts 'n all' are blemishes, bruises, chips, cracks, holes. 'Warts 'n all' are what make an object unique. These little marks are your object's history."

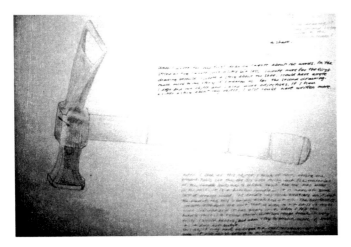

*"Perfect" Whole drawing of hammer, Jaime Babowitch, studio course, Westfield State College, 1994*

**DEMONSTRATE/DO:** Start drawing your object. Hold the pencil on the side and broadly darken in the general shape, using value. Then, raising the pencil so that only the point touches the surface of the paper, draw a fine contour line where you see it most clearly on your object, and add details. Do some smudging between values. Use the eraser to create a highlight by using lift-off.

**If time is limited to one-half hour, SAY/DO:** "We do not have time to draw the entire object. Think about drawing one part of your object. Do we ever have to choose to do part of something, instead of all of it?"

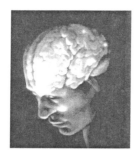

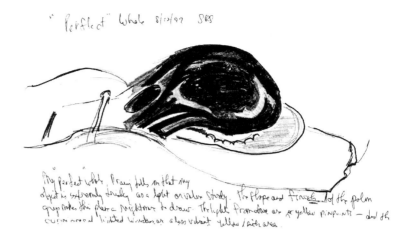

*My "perfect" whole drawing tells m that my object is extremely tricky as a light on value study. The slope and finish of the palm grey makes this place a nightmare to draw. The light from above ar. yellow pinpoints — and the curtain area lighted windows ar. a less vibrant yellow/pink area.*

*Part of a plane, handle, SRS 1997*

*7/9/99 My "perfect" whole drawing tells m that my direct pointing lens threads, pinned drawings, a combination of foam — soft & stiff — leather canvas and a kind of webbing plus the cotton of the lace with their plastic tips, plus the metal eyelets. My P.w. drawing tells m that my object is curled & zipped, contoured, they are. It looks like fingers pinching a tiny hot sandwich. The finger like structures on the top of the front of the hand is very pronounced — the glove curves, sweep, twists, turns, grabs — is sensuous "limp &*

*"Perfect" Whole drawing, lacrosse glove, SRS*

**DISCUSSION:** The need to focus on a small part of the object provides an exercise in choice. Generate a discussion about the necessity for choice when faced with a large project or a large number of options. Does life sometimes limit options, forcing you to focus on one thing?

**DEMONSTRATE:** Pick up your object and start to draw it. Select one section and draw that, big.

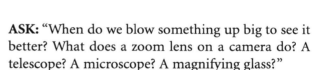

**SAY:** "We can focus on a small part by blowing it up big."

**ASK:** "When do we blow something up big to see it better? What does a zoom lens on a camera do? A telescope? A microscope? A magnifying glass?"

**TIP:** Bring in magnifying glasses, a microscope, binoculars, or a telescope. Drawing/Writing keeps the student connected with the object on macro or micro levels. The connections are your goal—as teacher and as student.

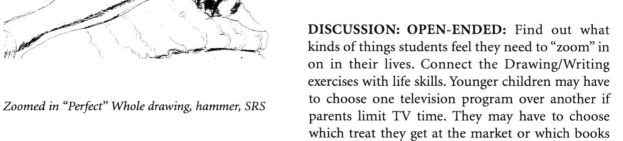

*Zoomed in "Perfect" Whole drawing, hammer, SRS*

**DISCUSSION: OPEN-ENDED:** Find out what kinds of things students feel they need to "zoom" in on in their lives. Connect the Drawing/Writing exercises with life skills. Younger children may have to choose one television program over another if parents limit TV time. They may have to choose which treat they get at the market or which books they take home from the library. Older students may have to choose to be in the band or the art club or the debating society or in athletics. They may have to focus on playing one instrument well, rather than continuing with several. Faced with college applications, juniors in high school are forced to zoom in and focus on a few.

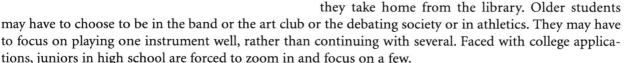

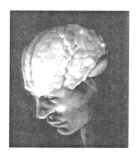

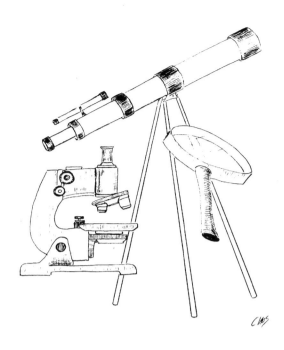

*Telescope, magnifying glass, microscope,
Claus Kormannshaus, 1997*

**SAY:** "Remember, every drawing has to fill the page. The bigger you draw, the more information you can include. Like a zoom lens on a camera or an electron microscope, when we focus on a small area and enlarge it, we can really see what we are working with. We see details that might have been invisible. Have you ever had this experience?"

**DISCUSSION:** Younger children may talk about seeing bugs when they lie down in the grass, or grains of sand on the beach. Older children may talk about electron microscope photos in their biology textbook of dust mites.

**ASK:** "Do we 'focus in' when we write? Do we ever back away when we write, 'zooming out,' so we can see the whole subject better?"

**DISCUSSION:** Ask students about story writing. What kind of zooming in makes a narrative more powerful? Encourage comments about the precise descriptions of everyday details which make people and places vivid for the reader.

**DEMONSTRATE/DO:** After developing the "Perfect" Whole drawing by broad shading, add a few fine outlines and some surface details to get students going, then let them work for forty-five minutes or so.

**SAY/DO:** "When you finish your drawing, write, 'My 'Perfect' Whole drawing tells me that my object is... because....'"

*Cecily Howell, "Perfect" Whole, Cow Skull, Merrimac Education
Center/Fitchburg State College, Continuing Education, 1997*

Cecily Howell wrote, "My Perfect Whole drawing reveals the many striations within the bony structures. They interlock with each other with a flexible cohesion. The dark, concave hollows pulsate pleasingly with the white convexities. I would have preferred the utter blackness of charcoal to express these qualities rather than every nuance of light and dark. I feel this is too fussy with details."

**PEER SHARE AND BUILD**

**ASK:** "What kind of writing is 'Perfect' Whole writing?"

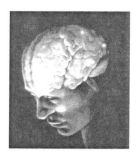

**TIP:** The three preceding steps have trained students to extract information from line, value and form in accurate observational drawings, and to translate that information into prose. Prose which describes and analyzes information is expository. Expository writing takes many forms. The expository essay is not its sole form of expression. Advice on the expository essay is provided in Part 4.

**DISCUSSION:** Students will produce many kinds of writing in response to the exercise that begins, "My 'Perfect' Whole drawing tells me that my object is...because..." including poems, songs, and cartoons. The hammer I am drawing may become the logo of a band or a tool for building shelters for the homeless. Romantic poetry is no more valuable inherently than a rap song. The appropriateness and power of word-choice is at issue, not the genre. The act of committed writing is the goal in Drawing/Writing.

**GROUP CRITIQUE**

## 4.2  The "Perfect" Whole Writing Program: PATTERNS OF PRACTICE

OBJECTIVES:

>    ***Multi-sensory writing***
>    ***Concrete and abstract comparisons***
>    ***Thinking analogically, speculatively and hypothetically***
>    ***Writing from drawing***

**BACKGROUND on writing exercises accompanying the "Perfect" Whole:**

The brain does not always visualize information first and then recode the information in text second. Many brains, in fact, are trained in school to encode information verbally first and may not receive training in translating that information into visual terms. All brains can learn to reap the benefits of translation exchanges, in either direction.

The Drawing/Writing program models neural exchanges by deliberately connecting spatial and linguistic systems through exercises in translation. The term "translation exchange" describes how the brain charges information from one mode to another. Enchanced information results when there is a deliberate translation from one mode of expression, say a drawing, to another mode, say writing. The second mode—in this case, writing—is organized by the following exercises to go beyond description to metaphorical, analogical, hypothetical levels of analyses. It is at these levels of analysis that the individuality of the human brain distinguishes itself. Some cross-modal constructions are cross-sensory. For instance, the sentence "My hammer smells like dust because it looks like an old bone" combines the sense of smell with the sense of sight. "My corkscrew smells as sharp as rain because it has repeated diagonals in the screw part which remind me of driving rain" (David Belval, 1997) combines the sense of smell with touch and the sense of touch with sight. Just as right/left hemisphere transfer extends analyses, so cross-sensory processing enriches comparisons.

Until this point in the Drawing/Writing process, the emphasis has been on visual searches, followed by verbal analyses. Now, students are asked to write first. The drawings based on written exercises in analogy, prediction, speculation and hypothesis move beyond physical description to other kinds of explanatory drawing.

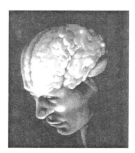

At this point in the five-step program, the reference point for the writing changes. It is no longer the drawing, it is the object itself. "Perfect" Whole drawings look so much like the object that students might as well write directly about the object. In addition, because so many of the verbal constructions are multi-sensory, the obvious source of information is the tangible object rather than a drawing of the object. The transferable skill learned is the value of going back to the original source for new information, whether this means the original text or a carburetor. For instance, I would no longer write, 'My *drawing* of the hammer is like....because....' I would write, "My hammer is...because...."

The writing exercises called Patterns of Practice teach students to use negative as well as positive constructions. It is harder to say what something is not like or why it is not "thus and so" than to say why something *is* "thus and so." For instance, it is easy to say, "My object, the jawbone of a cow, is like a pair of rose clippers because the mechanical action of the hinged parts cuts up growing things." It is harder to say, "My cow jawbone is not like rose clippers because the action of teeth is not only to cut in an up-and-down motion, but to grind in a circular motion. As a matter of fact, jaws work in more complex ways than clippers; a more complex, flexible hinging system based on ligaments allows circular action in jaws, while rose clippers are hinged by an inflexible nut and bolt-like apparatus which only allows for up-and-down cutting. The differences in hinge design for the tool versus the hinge design for an animal's jaws relate to purpose or process; jaws are designed for cutting and for mashing for digestion; jaws clip and grind, breaking food down into a more digestible form. Rose clippers are designed to cut rose stems, not to grind them." The negative comparison forced me into an extended, increasingly precise analysis.

The word "because" forces students to explain their reasoning to themselves, developing their abilities to be logical and persuasive. By taking positive similes or metaphors and rewriting them in the negative, students discover why their basis for comparison is—or is not—as valid as they thought. For instance, I might write in the positive mode, "My hammer is like talons of an eagle's claw because the section on the back of the head has two flaring hooks." If I rewrite this in a negative mode: "My hammer is not like the talons of an eagle's claw because there are only two flaring hooks, not three, and these hooks do not replicate the curve and sharpness of an eagle's talons," I may not feel the original simile was as apt as I thought.

*Skate, "Perfect" Whole drawing, Jennifer Lenfest, Merrimac Education Center/Fitchburg State College, Continuing Education, 1997*

Demands for proof are stimulating. Negative similes and metaphors, analogies, predictions, speculations and hypotheses challenge the brain. Negative comparisons also provide opportunities for impassioned peer arguments. If the other student's "because" section does not hold water, the peer is encouraged to probe the soft spot. A class becomes giddy and excited—even rowdy—with this freedom to challenge a peer's thinking. Students enjoy an intellectual field day. As long as the rules of fair play are followed, howling with laughter at logical inconsistencies is a healthy activity for growing brains. Mounting excitement and intellectual rigor, as well as humor, characterize maturing Drawing/Writing peer exchanges.

Patterns of Practice is like a good physical workout; it is sequential and repetitive, designed to build mental muscles.

As you teach the following program, you may want to share examples of student work on the Drawing/Writing worldwide web page.

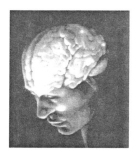

Patterns of practice include the following writing exercises:

   5 concrete sensory similes and 5 concrete metaphors, each explained by the word "because"

   5 abstract sensory similes and 5 abstract metaphors, each explained by the word "because"

   1 positive and 1 negative concrete analogy with "because"

   1 positive and 1 negative abstract analogy with "because"

   1 positive concrete and 1 positive abstract speculation with "because"

   1 negative concrete and 1 negative abstract speculation with "because"

   1 positive concrete prediction and 1 negative abstract prediction with "because"

   1 positive concrete hypothesis and 1 negative abstract hypothesis with "because"

Students are often reluctant to smell or taste their objects. There may be "yuk!" reactions. Try to overcome these aversions, especially to smell. Remind students that the olfactory bulb (which receives signals from the nose) is an important part of the brain; many of our strongest memories are encoded by smell; home and the smell of bread baking; childhood and the smell of fresh ironing; early summer and the smell of lilacs; full summer and the smell of roses and the ocean. Pheromones—chemicals received by the olfactory bulb via the nose—continue to influence our reactions. Because they receive so much information electronically rather than experientially, many students have a hard time generating sensory similes. They do not know what things feel, sound or smell like.

A note on "sounds like": it is not just listening to the object that provides sound. Some things do not have moving parts, nor any other way to provide sound. If shells are included as Drawing/Writing objects, sound will be inherent because of their spiraling interior structures; we all know that a shell held to the ear sounds like the waves of the sea. How objects sound can be determined by tapping them with a fingernail or against the table, or by dropping them—gently, if they are breakable. We know that real crystal makes a noise if you rub your finger around the rim of the glass, as does the rim of a Tibetan metal meditation bowl.

Patterns of Practice include six drawings: The "Perfect" Whole, the Concrete Sensory Simile, the Analogy, the Speculation, the Prediction, and the Hypothesis.

## PROCEDURE:

**REHASH:**

**HOMEWORK:** Remind students that they will repeat the following exercise for homework. Remind them that you will not be writing instructions on the board and that they will not be taking their in-class portfolios home. Students will need to remember what they did in class.

**SAY:** "The following writing exercises are called Patterns of Practice. The rules we use to create verbal comparisons change the way we use language and therefore the way we think. For instance, I might write this simile: 'My hammer is like a cat because it has a claw.' Or I might write, 'My hammer is a cat because the head springs into the air after striking a surface.' We may not be able to analyze exactly why the simile says what it does or why the metaphor differs, but we can observe that the two comparisons are different and that the metaphor includes action and is verb-based while the simile focuses on a noun and a shared attribute."

**DEMONSTRATE:** Write your simile on the board.

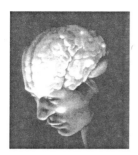

**SAY:** "To change the simile into a metaphor, I can remove the word 'like' and write, 'My hammer is a cat because it has a claw.' Or, I could explain the metaphor in a new way by writing 'because it yowls when I use it to pull out nails.'

To review: *meta* means 'above' or 'beyond.' "Phor" comes from the Greek verb *pherein,* meaning 'to bear or carry.' A metaphor carries meaning from one thing to another so that it *goes beyond* to a more elevated understanding. For instance, I might write, 'The handle of my hammer is noon because its pale color reminds me of Arizona pastures when the sun is high.' How has this metaphor *elevated* my understanding of a hammer? It lifted my understanding of a hammer to the level of Arizona pastures 5,000 feet above sea level, where the notion of a desert noon—its stillness, its heat, its bonewhite glare—color the hardware store handle of my hammer with moods and memories unavailable to other hammers."

**SAY:** "Changing the simile into a metaphor with a new 'because' clause led me—in connection with the cat claw/hammer comparison—to choose an active rather than a passive verb—'yowls' instead of a form of the verb 'to be.' Explaining the metaphor in this new way required not only a vivid verb but a metaphorical use of the verb "yowl." Hammers do not yowl. The verb 'yowl' is onomatopoetic; it sounds like the noise it describes. Looking at the hammer, I hear a cat; the hammer gains expressive power through the use of a special category of verb which sounds like its meaning."

**RECORD:** Write "active verb," "metaphorical use," "expressive power," and "onomatopoetic" on the board. To analyze and manipulate language, students must understand linguistic terms. In addition, write the parts of speech on the board. Do this in K-12, at the college level, and at the adult continuing education level. Ask students to copy these terms into their Drawing/Writing journals. Many students do not know or have forgotten or were never clear on the parts of speech. This is the ideal time to start teaching grammar. Students will need to know these terms to conduct Rescore at the end of the five-step session:

noun – the name of a person, place, thing or idea. *Girl, garden, gartersnake, grace, crack cocaine.* Proper names are capitalized and name a particular person, place, or thing. *Alice, Tuileries, The Vladimir Madonna, Sting.*

pronoun – used in place of a noun or more than one noun: *He, she, they, we.*

adjective – a word describing a person, place, thing, or idea. It modifies a noun. *Intelligent* girl.

adverb – a word that qualifies a verb, adjective, or another adverb; often ends in *-ly* or describes where. *Very* intelligent boy. *Hardly* functioning. Over *there.*

verb – an action word or state of being. Action: I hit the ball. *Hit* is an active verb. Passive, states of being acted upon using the verb *to be,* as in the phrase *I am hit* which refers to the state of being hit or *She is in the garden* which refers to a state of being.

conjunction – joins words or groups of words: *and, or, yet, so.*

preposition – shows the relationship of a noun or pronoun to some other word in the sentence. Often refers to where. *Over, under, off, on, against, toward.* The words *like* and *as* used in similes are prepositions.

**SAY/DO:** "I am going to list the parts of speech. Copy them in your journals. We cannot talk about active verbs or onomatopoetic verbs unless we know what a verb is. We cannot talk about appropriate adjectives unless we know what adjectives are. For some of you, this will be review. All of us will need to know these terms to evaluate our writing when we finish this session of Drawing/Writing. To evaluate changes, we will count numbers of verbs, nouns, adjectives and other forms of speech. Then, each of us will decide what these changes in the numbers of parts of speech mean for our own writing."

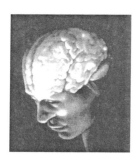

**TIP:** Never assume a term has been learned. Always review terms like simile and metaphor, analogy, verb, adjective by asking students what the term means. Repeated answers encourage understanding. A skill is powerful when it becomes automatic. If you have to think every time you shoot a basketball or drive a car, you will be hesitant shooting basketballs or driving cars. The same is true with grammar.

Writing takes a tremendous amount of conscious energy and requires ongoing practice. Writing is not like "riding a bike." "The habit of words" is just that, a habit. It can be acquired or lost. The phrase "use it or lose it" applies to drawing, writing and thinking skills.

**SAY:** "We'll write directly about the object, now, not about the drawing of the object, so that we return to direct exploration of the object using our five senses: touch, taste, smell, feel, sight, hearing."

**DEMONSTRATE:** Write on the board, "My hammer looks like a shark because...." Or, "My hammer smells like dust because...." The new sensory information we need rests with the object, not with the "Perfect" Whole drawing.

PATTERNS OF PRACTICE #1:
SENSORY SIMILES

### Five Concrete Sensory Similes

**SAY:** "Get another sheet of paper for the 'Perfect' Whole writing. Let's review the meaning of the word 'simile,' and let's review the meaning of the word 'concrete.' The word 'simile' reminds us of the word 'similar' which means 'like.' Thus, a simile connects two things because they are alike. What about the word 'concrete'? A concrete simile compares your object to some touchable thing. An abstract simile will compare your object to some non-touchable idea."

**DEMONSTRATE:** Draw the five icons shown below on the board. After the eye icon, write "My object looks like a... because... ." After the ear icon, write, "My object sounds like a... because...." "And so forth, using "smells like," "tastes like," "feels like."

*The five sensory icons*

Now, write five sensory similes.

    My hammer looks like a...because....

    My hammer tastes like a...because....

    My hammer smells like a...because....

    My hammer feels like a...because....

    My hammer sounds like a...because....

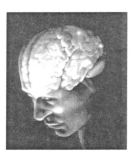

Concrete Sensory Simile Writing, Joanne Krawczyk, fish

My concrete sensory simile drawing tells me that I chose to use the organic basic shape approach to draw my object, a fish, and a bandaid because I drew the fish first and it lends itself nicely to organic shapes since it is modeled after a real organic shape. The bandaid would probably best be described with Euclidean shapes because I see rectangles and triangles.

My concrete simile of my fish tells me that although my object does, indeed, smell like a bandaid, they have few common physical denominators because one is flat and the other is three-dimensional. One object is free flowing and the other is geometric.

Yet, I now see that they both have repeating surface decoration because circles and lines are used to represent those areas. My c.s.s. drawing also tells me both of my objects have the potential to strike a vertical pose because of the way these elongated shapes are laid on the page.

Joanne Krawczyk, continuing education student and high school art teacher, wrote:

My fish looks like a lost person because of its open, yet voiceless mouth, doleful eyeball and defenseless position.

My fish tastes like the meat of a lobster claw because it feels slippery and chewy simultaneously as I press it to the roof of my mouth with my tongue.

My fish smells like a freshly opened bandaid because it blends the scent of antiseptic and plastic together.

My fish feels like a cheese grater because the repetitive embossed plastic pieces of its skin imitate the texture of the grater's open metallic pattern.

My fish sounds like an old-fashioned bellow used to fuel the flames of a fire because I hear its gusts of air breathe in and out as I squeeze it.

**SAY:** "You do not have to taste your in-class object. Save that for your at-home object. You can sniff your object. Close your eyes. What does it smell like?

"We may have to tap our objects to find out what our objects sound like, or even drop them gently."

### Drawing Two, a concrete sensory simile

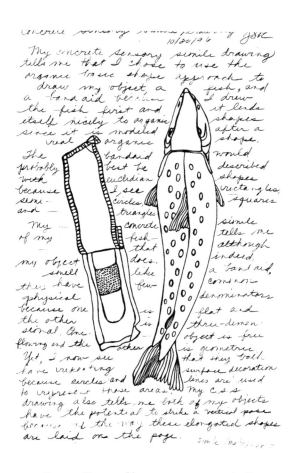

*Joanne Krawczyk's concrete sensory simile*

**DEMONSTRATE:** Generate concrete sensory similes using your object. Make sure students see you touching, sniffing, tapping your hammer. I wrote, "The wooden handle of my hammer feels like sand in a dried-up river bed because its surface is smooth, yet faintly granular." Ask students to help you complete this series of sensory similes. Then, ask students to construct their own sensory similes, using their objects.

**SHARE AND BUILD:** Ask students to read their five positive sensory similes aloud to each other.

**SAY:** "We are going to do something new. Instead of drawing first and writing second, we are going to use writing to generate a drawing.

Let's draw the concrete simile. Because my simile compared the hammer with sand in a dried up river bed, I will draw the hammer and some sand in a river bed."

**DISCUSSION:** Ask students how it feels to follow the more traditional approach of writing first and drawing second. Until they started Drawing/Writing, most students connected writing, reading and literacy—not drawing, writing, reading and literacy. They are learning that drawing provides visual information useful to writing. Now, they are asked to use writing as the more traditional stimulus to visual

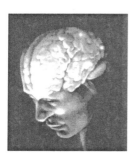

~ Concrete Sensory Similes ~

My chair looks like an old woman with bad posture because of the wrinkled fabric, folds and hunched over frame.

My chair tastes like a warm cup of herbal tea because its sweet, relaxing and has an unexpected flavor.

My chair smells like a garden of wild flowers because its fresh and beautiful.

✳ My chair feels like dry skin because it feels thick and has a reptilian, bumpy texture.

My chair sounds like a tire pump pumping air into a tire because it is making a whooping sound when you sit in it.

My chair does not look like an old woman with bad posture because it stands up straight and has no wrinkles or folds.

My chair does not taste like a warm cup of herbal tea because it is cold and stiff.

My chair does not smell like a garden of wild flowers because it is stale and hideous.

My chair does not feel like dry skin because it is smooth and moist.

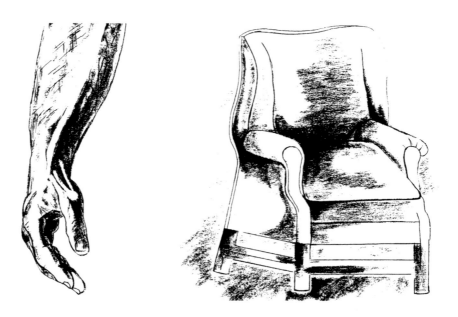

*Pamela Frigo's concrete sensory simile, chair, Continuing Education, Westfield State College, 1997*

expression. How do they feel about this change in procedure? Meta-cognition, or thinking about thinking, encourages students to be conscious of their mental strategies and to improve them.

**DEMONSTRATE:** Draw your concrete simile; then ask students to draw their concrete similes.

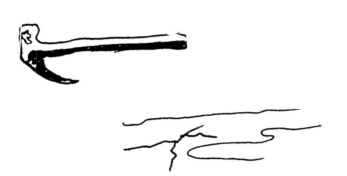

*Hammer and dried river bed.*

**SAY:** "Let's add a new piece of writing about the drawing of the simile. 'My simile comparing the hammer with a dried-up river suggests that some part of the hammer—the wooden handle—feels granular and slightly rough.' Joanne Krawczyk wrote the following about her concrete sensory simile: 'My concrete sensory simile drawing tells me that I chose to use the organic basic shape approach to draw my objects, a fish and a bandaide. I drew the fish first and it lends itself nicely to organic shapes since it is modeled after a real organic shape. The bandaide would probably best be described with Euclidean shapes because I see rectangles, semi-circles, squares and triangles. My concrete simile tells me that although my object does indeed smell like a bandaide, it has few common physical denominators because one is flat and the other is three-dimensional. One object is free flowing and the other is geometric. Yet, I now see that they both have repeating surface decoration because circles and line are used to represent those areas. My c.s.s. drawing also tells me both of my objects have the potential to strike a vertical pose because of the way these elongated shapes are laid on the page.'

Now, it's your turn to write about the drawing of your simile."

**DISCUSSION:** Where did this reflective writing take students? What new understandings were gained about the object?

**PEER SHARE AND BUILD**

**DEMONSTRATE:**

*Five Abstract Sensory Similes*

Deconstruct the word "abstract" on the board: *ab* means "away from," and *traho* means "to pull or drag." An abstraction is a characteristic or a quality that is extracted from the object. It is not a touchable, concrete thing. Although the following exercises still refer to the five senses, abstract sensory similes compare the object with an idea. Instead of comparing the feel of the hammer to sand in a dried up river, I might compare the feel of the hammer with dessication. The word "dessication" is an abstract noun. Dryness is a quality. A quality is intangible. Sand is touchable. The word "sand" is a concrete noun.

Discuss essences or qualities associated with things. For instance, "redness" is an abstract quality that can be "pulled" from an apple. Brainstorm a list of abstract terms. Make sure the abstractions include darker qualitiesand emotions. The dark side of life provides grist for the writer's mill, too. For instance, "rottenness" as an abstract noun associated with apples might provoke writing different from "redness." Include emotions like grief, sorrow, madness, and anger; include political terms like patriotism, anarchy, democracy, rebellion, wildcat strike, passive resistance.

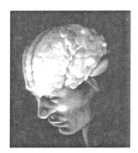

**DEMONSTRATE:** Draw the five icons for the senses again on the board. Construct your series of abstract sensory similes.

*The five sensory icons.*

 My hammer feels like freedom because...

 My hammer smells like imprisonment because...

 My hammer sounds like the end of the world because...

 My hammer looks like conquest because...

 My hammer tastes like old age because...

Joanne Krawczyk's writing:

My fish feels like pain because its skin feels like freshly skinned knees.

My fish smells like illness because it has a hospital aroma.

My fish sounds like an obscene phone call because it simulates heavy breathing when I pump its stomach.

My fish tastes like trickery because it slips and slides on my tongue.

**SAY:** "Now, it is your turn to write five abstract sensory similes. Draw the icons for the five senses. Now, write your similes."

**PEER SHARE AND BUILD**

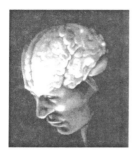

## PATTERNS OF PRACTICE #2:
## POSITIVE SENSORY CONCRETE AND ABSTRACT METAPHORS

Ask students to construct one concrete sensory metaphor and one abstract sensory metaphor by following the instructions below.

- Review the word "metaphor."

- Demonstrate by writing your own concrete sensory metaphor and abstract sensory metaphor.

- Watch for cross-modal, cross-sensory results. A former student who was both dysgraphic and dyslexic created this abstract metaphor: "My geode is like life because it is dark and hard on the outside, but has sparkling surprises on the inside." Whatever may have been true about this student's handwriting and reading abilities, his ability to construct abstract metaphors was unimpaired.

**SAY:** "Let's write one concrete sensory metaphor and one abstract sensory metaphor. For instance, I could write, 'My hammer is rifle fire because its repeated blows sound like shots from a gun. Or, I could write, 'My hammer is death because the metal of its head feels inert and cold.' Which is the concrete metaphor? Which is the abstract metaphor? Which senses did I use? Are the explanations in the 'because' clauses abstract or concrete?"

**PEER SHARE AND BUILD**

## PATTERNS OF PRACTICE #3:
## NEGATIVE CONCRETE SIMILE AND METAPHOR

Generate the following constructions, writing them on the board. Students can choose to change their simile into a metaphor by dropping the word "like," or they can generate a new metaphor. Similarly, they can take their positive similes and state them negatively, seeing what happens with the "because" clause.

**TIP:** The pragmatic approach of taking positive similes and making them negative is very useful. In this case, generating a brand new metaphor is not as useful as reexamining the original simile. Turning a positive simile into a negative one clarifies the degree to which the original simile was apt. Negative constructions with a "because" clause are hard work. There is no reason why the previous positive material can not be recycled here in negative form.

**SAY:** "'My hammer does not taste like a dried up river bed because....' can be turned into this negative concrete metaphor:

'My hammer is not a river bed because its taste is more like glue than gravel.'"

## PATTERNS OF PRACTICE #4:
## NEGATIVE ABSTRACT SIMILE AND METAPHOR

My hammer is not like death because it can be used to build structures for the living.

My hammer is not death because it is a constructive, not a destructive tool.

**PEER SHARE AND BUILD.**

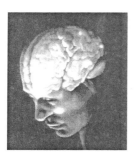

 **ASIDE:** For instance, Leonhard Euler provided the first carefully supported vibrational theory of light in 1746 by modeling light on sound because it traveled in waves. By doing so, Euler "participated in the well-established tradition of proceeding by analogies with better understood phenomena" (Zajonc, 1997, 111).

PATTERNS OF PRACTICE #5:
ANALOGY

one positive concrete analogy using "because"

one negative concrete analogy using "because"

one positive abstract analogy using "because"

one negative abstract analogy using "because"

**SAY:** "In Greek, the prefix *ana* means 'up' or 'toward.' And the word *logos* means 'word' in the sense of 'meaning.' An analogy moves us toward meaning through relationships. Analogies mean that certain admitted resemblances imply probable further similarity. Analogies are very powerful.

**SAY:** "For instance, I might write, 'As the claw is to the hammer, so the hooked section is to the beer can opener.' The claw of the hammer is curved and so is the hooked part of a beer can opener. The claws work differently: the claw of the hammer removes nails by pulling up, while the 'claw' of the beer opener pushes a wedge of metal down. Still, the hammer and the beer opener are tools which work in similar or *analogous* ways. In both instances, resistance must be overcome: the nail resists pulling and the metal resists piercing."

An analogy can be expressed in words this way: As A is to B so C is to D.

It can be expressed algebraically in this way: A:B ‖ C:D

**DEMONSTRATE:** Write on the board:

A:B ‖ C:D

Then, translate this into words: "As A is to B so C is to D."

**SAY:** "Let's construct some analogies making sure we add the word 'because.' Here's one: 'As the handle is to my cup so barbecue tongs are to sizzling meat because both provide ways to handle hot things.'

"Notice that the comparison focuses on how cups and tongs are used—on function. Keep including the word 'because' to clarify and refine your analogy. An imprecise analogy forces you to devise a better one. Since the handle of a cup encircles a finger, while tongs pinch, a better analogy might be: 'As the handle is to my cup, so a ring of fire is to campers sleeping out at night in a coyote-filled desert.' In both cases, an *encircling* element provides the protection."

**RECORD:** Write some analogies provided by students on the board.

**SAY:** "Now, let's try a negative concrete analogy. For instance, 'As the claw is to my hammer, so the hook is NOT to the can opener because the claw is for pulling and the hook is for piercing.'"

**SAY:** "Now, let's try a positive abstract analogy. Remember, an abstraction is intangible. It cannot be touched. For instance, merriment is an abstraction.

"Here is an example of a positive abstract analogy: 'As my hammer is to construction, so words and deeds are to religious worship.'"

Show students how you arrived at this analogy. "Hammers build houses. Words and deeds build the practice of worship. A practice of worship is like a spiritual house. The idea of building a house is what brought the hammer and religion together in this analogy."

**SAY:** "Let's construct one abstract analogy using the word 'because' and share it."

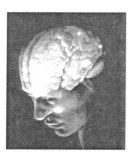

 **REMINDER:** Students must construct their understanding of negative abstract analogies by trial and error, measuring the results againt the requirements. This back and forth pattern matching lets them see where their constructions do and do not fit the "rules." The hardest job for the teacher remains not being too helpful. Examples provided by teachers often remain opaque. Students literally see what a negative abstract analogy is through their own trials and errors. Ask, don't tell. Once a teacher learns to practice this approach consistently, a classroom becomes constructivist. Students will re-learn how to ask and answer questions.

## PEER SHARE AND BUILD

**SAY:** "Now, let's try an abstract negative analogy. 'As tact is useful to a discussion, so a put-down is not useful to an argument.' I got to the word 'put-down' because a put-down acts like a hammer. It smashes the other speaker's pride. Tact allows people to speak without anger. If you say, 'That was a dumb thing to say,' the person you are talking to will probably turn away in fury, cutting off the discussion. If you say, 'Yes, I can see your point of view; that does make a lot of sense, but I look at it this way...,' the person is far more likely to continue the discussion. You have not put down or cut down that person's intelligence. Do you think the negative analogy makes the usefulness of tact clearer? Can you think of other negative abstract analogies which help to clarify either side of the analogy?"

**RECORD:** Write down students' positive and negative abstract analogies. There will be confusion at this point. Working through confusion is useful. Keep asking students to generate these positive and negative abstract analogies. Write them on the board. Examine them. Joanne Krawczyk wrote for a positive abstract analogy: "As my fish to to swimming, so a boat is to sailing because fish swim to travel around underwater just as a sail boat is used to transport people over a body of water." To make a double-sided negative abstract simile, we might write "As my fish is not to human swimming, so a walking human is not to worm locomotion: a fish does swim but it uses fins, not limbs; a human does move, but it uses legs, not an undulating body.'"

**DISCUSSION:** Do negative comparisons clarify issues? In the above case, I was forced to think about different methods for moving: fins, limbs, undulating surfaces.

## PEER SHARE

**SAY:** "Now, let's draw one of the analogies, concrete or abstract. Joanne Krawczyk wrote this positive concrete analogy: 'As the top fin is to the fish, so the rudder is to a boat because both provide ways to move through the water.' Here is her drawing"

### *Drawing Three, Analogy*

*Joanne Krawczyk's analogy drawing, Continuing Education, Westfield State College, 1996*

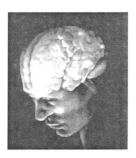

 **REMEMBER:** Clarify every Drawing/Writing exercise with examples. Go too slowly rather than too fast. Ask, don't tell. Instead of providing your own examples, encourage students to construct their own examples. Keep asking open-ended, exploratory questions. Keep waiting in a leisurely, interested way for answers.

*Pamela Frigo's hypothesis, Chair, Continuing Education, Westfield State College, 1996*

## PEER SHARE

**TIP:** The Drawing/Writing program sharpens students' abilities to think. A range of devices, including analogy, encourages students to discover similarities and differences.

In the spaces provided on the lefthand pages, enter samples of analogies generated by you and your students and share them with other Drawing/Writing teachers via the Drawing/Writing web site for field research:

> http://K12s.phast.umass.edu~sheridan

As Drawing/Writing teachers compile data, developmental benchmarks may emerge. Some of these benchmarks will be surprising. One of the assumptions behind Drawing/Writing is that students who are exposed to a range of strategies for thinking from pre-kindergarten on will be more capable thinkers *in the long run* than students who are exposed only to those strategies that have been pre-determined as age-appropriate. Our reach is only as high as our grasp. We do not know for sure the length, depth or breadth of any child's grasp. Without sufficient stimulation, opportunity and nurturing, no child can reach full potential.

### PATTERNS OF PRACTICE #5, 6 AND 7:

> #5 SPECULATION
> #6 PREDICTION
> #7 HYPOTHESIS.

**SAY:** "We have just generated analogies. Now, we'll construct speculations, predictions and hypotheses."

**DEMONSTRATE:** Write the three words on the board: speculation, prediction, hypothesis.

**ASK:** "What is a speculation? How could we write one?"

**DISCUSSION:** Students may offer words like "could" or "might" to designate speculations. These words will be used to signal a speculation.

**ASK:** "What is a prediction? How could we write one?"

**DISCUSSION:** Students may provide the word "will" for predictions. Agree that this word, "will," designates a prediction. Students may suggest that speculations are closer to guesses while predictions are based on past experience. Allow for enough discussion to distinguish between speculations and predictions from students' points of view.

**ASK:** "What is an hypothesis? How could we write one?"

**TIP:** The word "hypothesis" in Greek means "groundwork, foundation, supposition," from *hypo* meaning "under," and *tithenai,* meaning "to place under." An hypothesis is an "if...then" statement which provides the groundwork or foundation for supposition or conclusion. An hypothesis is assumed proved for the purpose of argument. Although proof-like, an hypothesis preserves an experimental or lab-like feel and is a particular type of inquiry—formalized speculation or prediction. If students are not familiar with the "if...then" construction, teach it. Then, ask students to generate hypotheses.

Pam Frigo's hypothesis is: "If I push my chair over, it will fall to the ground because of gravitational pull."

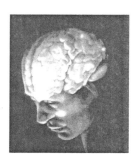

~ Speculation ~

✳ My chair might have been used for a king or queen because it is decorative and its fabric is plush and lusterous.

My chair could bring comfort because it stands for consolation and its arms and padding seem to surround you and hold you.

My chair could not be used as a lawnmower because it doesn't have controlls, blades, or a motor.

My chair might not seem abandoned if it could be placed back in my childhood.

*Pamela Frigo's speculation drawing, Chair,*
*Continuing Education, Westfield State College, 1996*

**SAY:** "SPECULATIONS use the words 'could,' and 'might.' Let's write:

      one positive concrete speculation with "because"

      one positive abstract speculation with "because"

      one negative concrete speculation with "because"

      one negative abstract speculation with "because"

Examples:

      My hammer might be used to build a tree house because I have seen my father build our house with his hammer.

      My hammer could bring happiness because it stands for renewal.

      My hammer could not be used to blow up a balloon because it does not contain air and it has no hollow passage to deliver the air, even if it did contain air.

      My hammer might not sound like destruction if it were used in a gentle manner.

Joanne wrote the following speculations:

      My fish might be used as a prop in a play because I have seen plastic models used in a theatrical set.

      My fish could give nourishment to the soul because it represents a story about Jesus from the bible.

**SAY:** "Now, your turn to write. Then, draw one of your speculations. Your speculation drawing will include your object and something else. Joanne Krawczyk's speculation was 'My fish might not seem cold and distant if it were held in an affectionate way.'"

### *Drawing Four, Speculation*

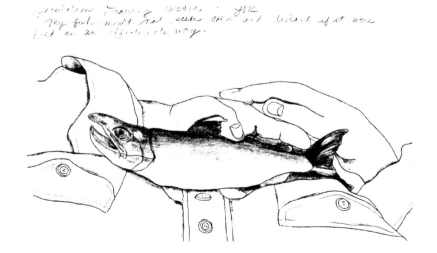

*Joanne Krawczyk's speculation drawing, Continuing Education, Westfield State College, 1996*

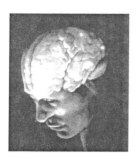

~ Prediction ~

My chair will be useful to sit and relax in because it has a comfortable back and padded seat. It is soft and cushiony.

My chair will bring peace because it brings out positive thinking and the best in people.

✱ My chair will not cut paper because it has no blades or sharp or jagged edges.

My chair will not vociferate because it is not suffering from grief & pain. It may be worn out on the outside but inside it still remains the same.

*Pamela Frigo, prediction, Chair,*
*Continuing Education, Westfield State College, 1996*

**PEER SHARE**

**SAY:** "PREDICTIONS use the word 'will.' Let's write:

    one positive concrete prediction with "because"

    one positive abstract prediction with "because"

    one negative concrete prediction with "because"

    one negative abstract prediction with "because"

Examples:

    My hammer will pound a nail because it has a flat, hard head.

    My hammer will bring justice because it can bring about urban renewal.

    My hammer will not frost a cake efficiently because the head of the hammer is heavy and does not have a large enough surface to smooth frosting over the surface of a cake.

    My hammer will not construct in the millennium because the foundation of the economy has toppled.

Joanne wrote the following predictions:

    My fish will not fall apart because it is made of a continuous, sturdy piece of plastic.

    My fish will bring happiness because it can bring back memories of fishing with grandpa.

**SAY:** "Now, it is your turn to write. Then, draw one of your predictions. Joanne Krawczyk's prediction was, 'My fish will not write or draw well because it doesn't contain any lead, ink or pigment.'"

### *Drawing Five, Prediction*

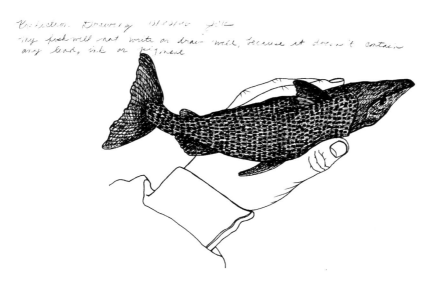

*Joanne Krawczyk's prediction drawing, Continuing Education, Westfield State College, 1996*

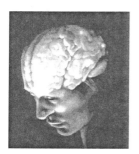

## PEER SHARE

SAY: "HYPOTHESES use this form: 'If...then ....' Let's write:

> one positive concrete hypothesis with "because"
>
> one negative concrete hypothesis with "because"
>
> one positive abstract hypothesis with "because"
>
> one negative abstract hypothesis with "because"

Examples:

> If I hit a nail squarely with my hammer, then the nail will be driven straight into the board because of the direct nature of the hit.
>
> If I do not hit the nail squarely with my hammer, then the nail will not drive straight into the board because it will go in at an angle.
>
> If the head of the hammer of justice is like a jail sentence then the claw of the hammer of justice is like a verdict of innocence; the head forces the guilty defendant into jail, while the claw removes the power of the accusing lawyers to imprison the defendant.

Joanne wrote these hypotheses:

> If I throw my fish at the wall it will fall to the ground because of gravitational pull.
>
> If I throw my fish at the wall near a table then the fish would land on the table because the fish will not go through a solid object.
>
> If the head of my fish is like the beginning of a journey, then the tail is like the end of a trip; the head anticipates unknown delights while the tail drags the traveler back to a predictable routine.

"It's your turn to write hypotheses. Then, draw one of your hypotheses."

### *Drawing Six, Hypothesis*

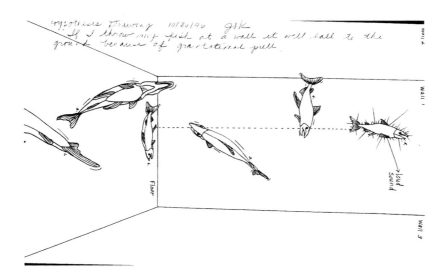

*Joanne Krawczyk's hypothesis drawing, Continuing Education, Westfield State College, 1996*

**A DEEP QUESTION and a DEEP ANSWER** may lie at the heart of this discussion. A prediction has some basis in experience. An hypothesis does not necessarily have to have a basis in experience. Some hypotheses are closer to predictions. Some are closer to experiment and inquiry. Do students feel that there is a hierarchy of degrees of difficulty for verbal/logical constructions? Do they agree on which of these forms is the most difficult? On what do they base their ordering system?

**ASK:** "Is it easier or harder to write speculations and predictions than it is to write hypotheses? Is it more interesting to write negative or positive hypotheses?" (Whatever your students answer, ask them <u>why</u>.) "Why is a prediction harder or easier to write than an hypothesis? Why is a negative—or a positive—statement easier or harder? Are analogies harder to construct than hypotheses? Find one of your analogies. Now, find one of your hypotheses. Which one was harder for you to write? Why?"

**RECORD:** Write several student analogies and hypotheses on the board. Generate a discussion around the student work.

**DISCUSSION:** Opinions about degrees of difficulty in connection with analogies, speculations, predictions and hypotheses will be based on students' direct experience with constructing them. By talking about actual experiences with verbal constructions, meta-cognition—thinking about thinking—is encouraged in a hands-on accessible way.

**TIP:** This a good time to talk about audience. Who—besides ourselves— are we writing for? Do our similes, metaphors, analogies, speculations, predictions, and hypotheses speak to others in the class? Are there ways in which we can change our writing to reach another person? Who is our audience? What is our purpose in writing?

**ASK:** "Your predictions make sense to you, but did they make sense to your peer? What if you were writing for younger—or older—students? For females, not males? For Thai students not Hispanic students? How might a piece of writing change to fit a certain audience?"

Ask a high school senior how she would write for a kindergartner. Ask a kindergartner how he would write for a grandparent. Ask everyone how they would write if they were working with someone with few English skills. Or who did not know anything about music but did know a lot about car repairs. Or who is a boy while the writer is a girl who is writing about fashion design. Or a boy writing for women about car design. See if you can debunk some stereotypes. For instance, some boys are very interested in fashion design while many women are major car consumers. How women respond to car design is taken very seriously. How men respond to clothes and grooming aids matters to many advertisers. Young children do not necessarily need "talking down to," nor do college grads require "talking up to." If language is used cleanly and accurately, it should be clear to a range of ages and experience. That has certainly been the goal in writing this book, particularly this section.

**SAY:** "Thinking about who we are writing for brings up the concept of audience. In a play, the audience is the people in the theatre who are watching and listening. As writers, our audience is our readers. We need to keep them in mind. We do not have to devote all of our energies to our audience, but we do need to be clear to ourselves and to take our readers into account."

**DISCUSSION:** Encourage students to think about instances when the reader is especially important; for instance, instructional manuals. In connection with writing directed to the reader, ask students which drawing—the LMD drawing or the "Perfect" Whole drawing—appeals to the viewer most directly. Is the hard-edged drawing more effective or is the soft-edged drawing more effective in conveying the illusion of three-dimensional realism? Some students may decide that the marker-drawn LMD version is more powerful visually and emotionally than the pencil-drawn "Perfect" Whole. By the same token, is hard-hitting writing or more gentle persuasion the best vehicle for certain kinds of written persuasion?

Strong line quality and high light/dark contrast are powerful attractors. Just because they are powerful visually does not mean that the message they convey is a useful one. For instance, a cigarette ad may have strong visual appeal. Smoking is still a deadly habit. Cigarette smoking does not guarantee the smoker a life of power, glamour, success or fun; it guarantees a life of increasing ill-health. There are also some powerful anti-smoking ads. As consumers, students need to become astute visually and verbally.

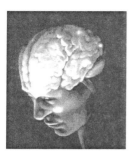

**ASIDE:** Theories of brain function, drawing, writing and thinking intersect. In this case, Walter Freeman's "phase portrait" of a perception produced by EEGs reveal that the thinking brain produces waves of excitation that look like coiled spirals. Spirals may be attractive to the brain in the visual arts and in certain forms of writing, like the acknowledged spiral form of the sestina, because spirals are intrinsic to brain activity. The brain may recognize and be drawn to recursive, self-referential patterns that reproduce the experience and "look of" its own activity. This theory about the pervasiveness and attraction of spirals is explored in the fractal section of Geometric Basic Shapes, Part Two, as well as in Part Three, "Hitchikers' Guide to Brain Science."

From a neurobiological point of view, neurons in the macula, the area of greatest concentration of cells in the retina, fire most strongly for high-contrast edges. On a neural level, drawings with strong light/dark contrast will be more excitatory to the eye, and thus to the visual cortex of the brain, than more subtle line quality. How higher levels in the brain choose to interpret the enhanced signal depends upon accompanying text or other issues. Education plays its part. An educated brain is able to interpret subtle cues as well as obvious ones. The Drawing/Writing goal is to teach students how to differentiate between strong and subtle cues in both image and text, allowing the brain to focus on relevant bits of information whether communicated directly or implied.

**DISCUSSION:** Discuss choice of drawing tool, or *mediums*. The word "mediums" is used in art vocabulary to describe materials because the word "media" as it is currently used defines a range of electronic communications. The somewhat awkward plural form, mediums, denotes the range of materials used in the art studio. As mediums, markers and pencils provide different results. Each has potential visual and expressive power.

**PEER SHARE AND BUILD**

**GROUP CRITIQUE**

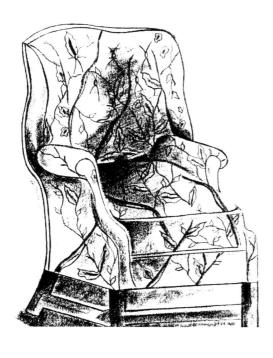

My "Perfect" Whole drawing tells me that my object is like drapery on a Hellenistic sculpture. The drapery seems to share the qualities of a liquid substance as it flows throughout the object. I feel the rhythmic grace of the design is particularly striking in the spirited movement. The folds seem to engulf you with dramatic impact. My object reflects light more on the left side and at the top. The surface of my object feels smooth but slightly granular because of the textural pattern that runs through it. When I close my eyes the smell of my object reminds me of home with its sweet smell and warm feel.

*"Perfect" Whole, Chair, Pamela Frigo, Continuing Education, Westfield State College, 1996*

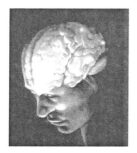

## 4.3 The "Perfect" Whole Writing Exercise: The Sestina

OBJECTIVES:

**\*The sestina as a dynamic structure\***
**\*Fractal dimensions: Drawing/Writing and poetry\***

MATERIALS: Zerox the numerical rotation for the sestina shown below along with the sestina "On the way home from Nowhere, New Year's Eve" by Miller Williams.

| 1 | 6 | 3 | 5 | 4 | 2 | 2—5 |
| 2 | 1 | 6 | 3 | 5 | 4 | 4—3 |
| 3 | 5 | 4 | 2 | 1 | 6 | 6—1 |
| 4 | 2 | 1 | 6 | 3 | 5 | |
| 5 | 4 | 2 | 1 | 6 | 3 | |
| 6 | 3 | 5 | 4 | 2 | 1 | |

**BACKGROUND**

A sestina is a long poem which does not rhyme. It has a spatial arrangement rather than an alphabetic rhyme scheme as used, for instance, by the sonnet. In a sestina, certain words are laid out on the page according to a pattern. This patterned procedure is extremely attractive to students. The six words ending the lines "spool around" the 39-line poem in a spiraling motion. This book theorizes that the visual sensation of spiraling may be what attracts the mind of the writer.

The ends of the lines of the sestina are important because they contain six words which repeat in a designated order. The sestina is said to have been invented by a poet and mathematician named Arnault Daniel in the thirteenth century. The form was popular with the troubadours of France and with the Italian poets Dante and Petrarch.

First, the writer must devise a "natural rhetorical set"; they must come up with six words. Then, the poet constructs the first six-line stanza, using one of the six words to end each line. Each end word receives the number in which it occurs. If the word "blanket" is used to end the last line of the first stanza, it becomes word #6, and it must end the first line of the second stanza. Following Daniel's number pattern for the second stanza, the word ending the fifth line of the first stanza ends the third line of the second stanza, the word ending the fourth line ends the fifth, the word ending the second line ends the fourth line, and the word ending the first line ends the second line. The poem closes with a 3-line *tornada* or envoi in which all 6 words are embedded. This is where the meaning "turns" and the "message is sent."

As complicated and long as the form is, students apply themselves diligently to the sestina. This willingness to finish a long poem is empirical evidence gathered over the past ten years about the effectiveness of combining a well-developed information base with an explicit structure. In a recent Drawing/Writing workshop, ten adults spent three full hours each on the sestina. Why? The sestina is a considerable yet manageable challenge.

The sestina is like the Drawing/Writing process itself, fractal-like—recursive and self-referential—in structure and dimension. It resonates with students' natural mental processes. Like Drawing/Writing, the sestina focuses on the object, or a visual "seed." From this visual seed, it produces six words, or the "natural rhetorical set"—a verbal seed. As I teach the sestina, one word must be the noun standing for the object, one is the pronoun "I" or "me," one is a verb, one is an adjective, one is a concrete noun and one is an abstract noun, all of which are connected closely to the object. The personal pronoun forces the poem to be autobiographical; the abstract noun forces it to be philosophical. Because students have just finished the writing-intensive fourth step, many words from a host of verbal constructions ranging from simile to hypothesis are available for this rhetorical set.

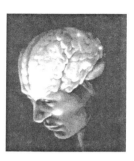

ON THE WAY HOME FROM NOWHERE, NEW YEAR'S EVE

For papers I think I need, we bump off
the street and stop. I leave the engine on,
mean to make my way to the buzzing light
above the back door, but the door is dark.
Old Main's a hulking, dull, uncertain form,
no windows and no size. Then I remember

one small truth I didn't mean to remember,
that all the lights at ten would be turned off
for somebody's purpose. I enter the hollow form,
try one time to flick the light switch on
and shrug my way into the seamless dark.
What outside seemed scattered, useless light

would be a brilliance here. Reflections. Moonlight.
Sensing my way between the walls I remember
old mythologies of daytime and the dark
spun by gods and monster movies, cast off
with ignorance. My fingers stumble on
another switch. Nothing. I feel my form

falling away into another form.
I hear the hound, look for the quick light
glancing out of his eyes and imagine my own
open, aimless, milky. I remember
what children think of when the lights are off.
Something brushing the hand. To fit the dark

I tell myself I am blind. In such a dark
I could be moving down the spaceless form
of time, a painted tunnel. I twist off
my shoes and walk in deafness. Leap. Grow light
for one slow moment, then loose parts remember
gravity. I twist the sounds back on.

I'm over a million years old and going on
thirteen. I've always been afraid of the dark.
There truly are warlocks, witches, and I remember
banshees, saints and the always shifting form
of Satan himself. I feel a fly light
and crawl across my forehead. I brush it off.

Going on, I grab some papers off
some desk in the dark and turn back toward the light
I barely remember, running, hungry for form.
    —Miller Williams

*The sestina "On the Way Home from Nowhere, New Year's Eve" by Miller Williams*

The Band

Desire to make music comes from *me*.
Who breathes toward them the breath of *inspiration?*
As toddlers, each had drum, horn, and *baton*.
Other devices could also *stimulate*.
Their base for music was truly *solid*.
But they would need more than just the right *tool*.

Each could make sounds with their favorite *tool*.
"Music?", you ask.  It was music to *me*.
A paper horn or drum that was *solid*,
The sounds they could make bred *inspiration*.
The mere sight of a tube might *stimulate*.
The child without an instrument holds the *baton*.

Magically, they all want to hold the *baton*.
"Who wants to trade yours for my *tool?*"
Though just a pencil, it holds the key to *stimulate*.
She turns to Mom, "Make him give it to *me*."
I look around, hoping for *inspiration*.
Offered a set of spoons, she stands *solid*.

Her desire to conduct, makes her stand *solid*.
Spoons follow. They don't lead like the badge of a *baton*.
She wants to be the breath of *inspiration*.
To be the wind, you need the special *tool*.
Once more she presents her burden to *me*.
I must validate her need to *stimulate*.

She wants to be the one to *stimulate*.
The others do not recognize her need to be *solid*.
Though I can see she's a lot like *me*.
There is meaning in waving the bossy *baton*.
"They make the music in response to my *tool*."
Hence, the band is ready for *inspiration*.

Where will they find *inspiration?*
The conductor is ready to *stimulate*.
The music awaits in every *tool*.
The members have made their choices quite *solid*.
With horn, drum, whistles and *baton*,
They come to the kitchen to perform for just *me*.

Inspiration walks in with steps *solid*
To stimulate the toys and *baton*
The tool band makes music for Daddy and *me*.

Colleen Stillman<br/>July 10, 1997<br/>Mother, wife, dairy farmer

*"The Band," a sestina by Colleen Stillman,*
*Merrimac Education Center/Fitchburg State College,*
*Continuing Education, 1997*

My "perfect" whole drawing tells
me that my object is of wooden
fibers. The shape has been cut
along the length of the wood
The _____ of my ____ have been cut across
the grain because the tiny dots are
evidence of cut fibers.

*Honey dipper, "Perfect" Whole drawing, Colleen Stillman, 1997*

*Photo, Colleen Stillman, SRS, 1997*

Each of the six words in the set calls itself back, six times. As the object under intensive scrutiny becomes a complex whole in Step 4 and then (as will occur in the forthcoming fifth step, the Composite Abstraction) transforms itself into something pared down, essential and new, so some verbal summation or synthesis is achieved in the last three lines, or triplet, of the sestina. The six stanzas spiral down to an intense three-line core of meaning in which all six words are densely embedded. These words, like the object, undergo intense observation and manipulation, producing a dynamic system which unfolds according to a few simple rules, and then closes down tightly on itself. Like each drawing—the Tracing, the Blind Contour, the Regular Contour, the Geometric Basic Shapes, the Light-Medium-Dark drawing, the "Perfect" Whole—each stanza pushes the meaning of the object forward. The stanzas are linked through the repeating terminal words. A feedback loop is created as the last word of the preceding stanza becomes

## Me, hammer, pterodactyl, justice, cold, pound = natural rhetorical set

Stanza 1          me             1
                  hammer         2
                  pterodactyl    3
                  justice        4
                  cold           5
                  pound          6

Stanza 2          pound          6
                  me             1
                  cold           5
                  hammer         2
                  justice        4
                  pterodactyl    3

Stanza 3          pterodactyl    3
                  pound          6
                  justice        4
                  me             1
                  hammer         2
                  cold           5

Stanza 4          cold           5
                  pterodactyl    3
                  hammer         2
                  pound          6
                  me             1
                  justice        4

Stanza 5          justice        4
                  cold           5
                  me             1
                  pterodactyl    3
                  pound          6
                  hamer          2

Stanza 6          hammer         3
                  justice        6
                  pound          4
                  cold           1
                  pterodactyl    2
                  me             1

Tornada or        hammer ........... cold              2-5
Envoi             Justice ............. pterodactyl    4-3
                  pound............... me

the last word in the first line of the next stanza. There is a litany of sound. Instead of spiraling inward forever, or imploding, the poem resolves itself, settling, like the mind after work, into a minimal energy state. Structure, process, dimension, resolution. The sestina, like the procedure for a tree, or like thought itself, is iterative, recursive, fractal in dimension, whole through its unfolding, more whole through its enfolding.

## PROCEDURE:

**SAY:** "We have been writing prose. Prose is not usually characterized by a pronounced beat—called rhythm or meter—nor does it consistently use words which sound alike, or rhyme. Some poetry uses meter and rhyme and is organized in phrases and stanzas. Some does not.

> Mary had a little lamb
> Its fleece was white as snow
> And everywhere that Mary went
> The lamb was sure to go

"Do you hear the rhyme and feel the rhythm?

> Every year in June—up here, that's the month for lilacs—
>     almost his whole front yard,
> with lobster traps stacked out in back, atop the rise
>     that overlooks the inlet
> would be a Himalayan range of peaks of bloom,
>     white or mauve violet

*Amy Clampitt, from "What the Light was Light," 1985*

"How do you sense meter and rhyme in this poem?"
    "There are true rhymes and partial rhymes and near rhymes and internal rhymes. In the sestina, we will not need to think about rhyme. We will, however, think about meter or beat. A sestina has five major beats or stresses to each line. A stress is not the same as a syllable. For instance, the word "catalog" has how many syllables? Correct, three. How many beats or stresses? Right, one strong one followed by two lesser ones: cátalog. The accent over the "a" indicates the stress. The reason we want five stresses per line is to follow the sestina model and to make the lines long enough to be interesting. If I write this line: 'I love to walk in sun and shade with you,' how many stresses are there in this line?"

**TIP:** In the sample English curriculum included in Part Four, "The Thinking Child," information on metric feet in poetry is provided. Include that here if you wish. Students confuse beats with syllables. You may have to spend some time getting them to say words aloud naturally to discover the stresses.

**SAY:** "Let's try writing a poem that does not rhyme. It is structured by a set of words numbered in a series. The form of the sestina was invented by a French mathematician, Arnault Daniel, in the thirteenth century."

Drinking from a cup of water, my father
looked ahead of him into the darkness.
We were returning from a long journey.
and heading home to our small paradise.
A thin, dark street we took for a short-cut.
A chill overtook me as we entered the road,

The absent moon, dimness dwelt in the road.
The loneliness; I prayed to our father.
On both sides of the street, the land was cut.
The moon opaque; the dead sky in darkness.
UNLIKE EDEN; this was no paradise.
I suddenly came back from mind's journey.

A SUDDEN CRASH; an end to OUR JOURNEY.
Hitting a dark, dead animal in the road
Brother looks dead; p'haps in God's paradise.
Weeping aloud I prayed to our father,
Was everything gone; eternal darkness?
Was life a mere thought; so suddenly out?

My brother outside; with clippers he cut
He's putting plants out of life's brief journey
His act is black; he's dressing in darkness
I remembered the face, dead on the road.
"Brother," I said, "Leave death to our Father"
Flowers; beauty — make up our paradise.

The world may be dark — far from paradise
People die just like flowers are cut.
Cousin's tragedy killin' of his father
My many friends put out of their journey.
A good lesson I've learned from life's long road
Lets look at the light; ignore the darkness.

We'll never get through; living in darkness.
Be brave in this life and earn paradise.
In God let's entrust th' outcome of the road
Pray to him much and ask not to be cut
from the happiness brought by life's journey
And when we die, we'll be with our Father.

Do not dwell in darkness or you will be cut
from paradise after our long journey.
Take the hard road and be with our Father.

*Sestina, Fernando Poma*

**DEMONSTRATE THE SESTINA:** Hand out the Xeroxed rotation pattern along with the sample sestina. Read Williams' poem aloud with students. Provide these instructions:

1) Make up the list of 6 words. For instance, I might make this list: me (personal pronoun), hammer (name of my Drawing/Writing object), pterodactyl (concrete noun), justice (abstract quality), cold (adjective), pound (verb).

2) Optional: Discuss iambic pentameter. *Penta* means "five." Each line has five beats. If each beat goes "da-dúh," with the stress on the second syllable, the beats are called iambs. An easy way to teach this is to say that each line needs five natural beats. That is, there must be five places in each line where a syllable or a word is stressed. Write the following on the board:

   Example: I lóve to wálk in sún and sháde with yóu.

   In this line, there are five natural beats and they happen to be iambs, or short-longs, represented in poetry as ∪ _____.

3) Write the first stanza, using one of the six words to end the first line, another to end the second, and so forth.

4) After writing the extire six-line first stanza, number the end words as they occurred; the last word of line #1 becomes word #1. Then, write these words in the prescribed order for stanzas 2–6, at the far right hand side of the page, one set below the other, providing a string of terminal words for the next five verses. Place the 6 words into the tornada, two per line, in the order designated in the "turning" triplet.

5) Write up to each terminal word, line by line and verse by verse. Because both concrete and abstract nouns have been included, the poem moves naturally from concrete description to abstract generalization. This is a powerful process.

6) Peer share. When students read their sestinas aloud, they know how powerful they have become as writers. You will feel the hair on the back of your neck rise up.

7) Ask students to illustrate their sestinas. One of their drawings from the four previous steps may be appropriate, or they may want to produce a new drawing.

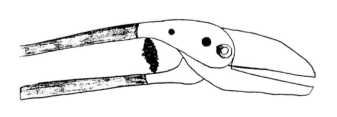

*Clippers, Fernando Poma, Deerfield Academy, 1990*

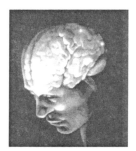

# Step Five

# THE COMPOSITE ABSTRACTION

CA#2 writing, Joanne Krawczyk, 1996

Compared to its earlier state, my Composite Abstract #2 drawing has been homogenized because the lines and shapes have evolved into an analogous group. All of the lines and forms are free flowing or organize in nature. A suggestion of depth occurs due to overlapping changes in value may also account for a sense of perspective.

My CA drawing is like the aftermath of a fuming tropical storm on the high seas because fins and watercraft alike are trying to balance on a topsy-turvy surf as the sun peeks over the horizon.

My CA drawing is a swimmer engaged in a butterfly stroke, moving through a billowy surface as the still shining sun drowns in the west because I see an arched figure in the foreground overlapping wavy lines and a distant circular shape.

*CA #2, Joanne Krawczyk, Fish, Continuing Education,*
*Westfield State College, 1996*

*CA #3, Joanne Krawczyk, Fish, Continuing Education,*
*Westfield State College, 1996*

"My CA#1 and CA#2 tell me that the following relates to my home object: a plastic fish. I tried to distill my final CA drawing to its least common denominator and the result is a totally abstract composition. Interestingly, both of my CA writings (I and II) similes and metaphors refer to the seas and words relating to it, such as mermaid, swimmer, tropical storm, watercraft, fins, surf, high seas, butterfly stroke and creature of the sea. Although I doubt my mold-injected fish is a salt water being, a real fish would live in a watery environment.

My direct descriptions relate to my object in that they use terms like free-flowing, organic and curved which might be used to describe the characteristics of a fish or fish model.

*Referential writing, Joanne Krawczyk, fish, CA #1 and CA #2,*
*Continuing Education, Westfield jState College, 1996*

# STEP FIVE

# The Composite Abstraction

### 5.1 The Composite Abstraction

### 5.2 Optional Cool-Down Exercises

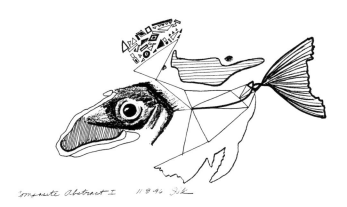

CA #1, Joanne Krawczyk, Fish, Continuing Education,
Westfield State College, 1996

CA#1 writing, Joanne Krawczyk, 1996

My Composite Abstract drawing tells me that my original object has exploded from a singular piece to an elaborate composition. I see a mixture of Euclidean, organic and free-formed shapes joining forces with an array of lines and values. My CA drawing would probably be classified as flat if not for the variation in size, plus overlapping lines and shapes. In a few areas, value might contribute to the illusion of a three-dimensional form. However, other areas seem to be colored in a scribbled fashion. There is one textured section on the curved piece that intersects a line jumping across the page, because it is filled with repeating lines and shapes.

My CA drawing is like a mermaid being visciously assaulted by a ravenous creature of the sea because I see her amputated body parts flailing in the sky while below the open jaws of death wait to chew the bit-sized pieces.

My CA drawing is a hurricane on the turbulent sea of love because I see rigid shapes of jealousy juxtaposed with smooth forgiving forms undulating on alternating waves of distrust and desire.

## 5.1  The Composite Abstraction

OBJECTIVES:

    *The New Hieroglyphics*
    *Neither too much nor too little*
    *Right relationships*
    *Acceptable differences*
    *Recombinant thinking*

MATERIALS: pencils, markers, paper, folders, the entire body of work in each student's portfolio, an art history textbook including modern art starting with the Impressionists.

BACKGROUND:

    *ab* – means "away from"

    *traho* – means "to drag"

    *co* – means "together"

    *pono* – means "to put"

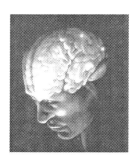

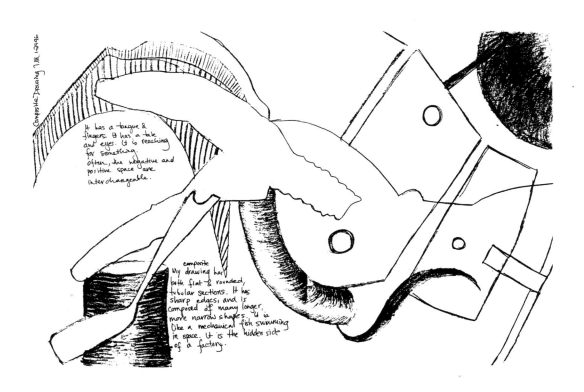

It has a tongue &
fingers. It has a tale
and eyes. It is reaching
for something.
Often, the negative and
positive space are
interchangeable.

composite
My drawing has
both flat & rounded,
tubular sections. It has
sharp edges, and is
composed of many longer,
more narrow shapes. It is
like a mechanical fish swimming
in space. It is the hidden side
of a factory.

*Teresa Mershon, CA, rose clippers, January term, Hampshire College, 1995*

The Composite Abstraction is made by *dragging* certain elements *away from* the four preceding drawings and *putting them together* in a new way. Deconstruct the term Composite Abstraction for students, using the Latin prefixes and verbs on the preceding page. Just as abstract artists focus on certain aspects of their subject matter, combining elements in new ways, so students select certain parts of their drawings, combining these elements in new ways.

In this step, students will select parts of their drawings, using self-determined bases for choice, and combine those parts in new ways, using self-determined bases for recombination, including an intuitive appreciation for pleasing or balanced or aesthetic compositions. There is one criterion: the CA must "work" or "not work" for the student: "Working" or "not working" depends upon the degree to which a drawing feels balanced or correct or integrated or "beautiful." Balance, correctness, integration, and beauty pertain to relationships between the parts of a drawing and the whole drawing. If the parts relate in a coherent, or appropriate or right or beautiful way, then the drawing expresses the aesthetic quality known as pleasingness. If the drawing is aesthetically displeasing, then the relationship of parts to whole is in some way wrong, unbalanced, unreconciled, inappropriate, or incorrect. Symmetry does not guarantee pleasingness. An asymmetrical drawing in which the two halves of the image differ may still be balanced. Students create these "felt" relationships by applying a rule: neither too much nor too little. By looking at their drawings from all angles, they decide where there is too much or too little in terms of lines, shapes, and space.

By introducing your students to ideas about balance and pleasingness, you prepare them to think about criteria for judging not only drawings but actions. Deciding where there is too much or too little in a drawing teaches students to make judicious decisions on other levels, including the moral or ethical level. In this fashion, Drawing/Writing links aesthetic training and ethical decision-making with training in drawing.

The CA is held up for the student and rotated. The student is asked to nod when he sees where the drawing has too much or too little—in terms of lines, shapes, spaces. A second CA exercise gives students a chance to add or to subtract from their first CA drawing. By adding items where there is too little and by subtracting items where there is too much, students intuitively work toward balanced compositions. One of the most powerful experiences in the Drawing/Writing program occurs during the CA group critiques. Students discover that there is consensus about where there is too much and too little in each other's work. It is at this level of discussion that the CA takes on extremely powerful implications beyond the classroom experience. On a neural/mental level aesthetics and ethical decision-making intersect not only for the individual but for members in a group.

The philosopher Plato believed that Beauty and Goodness exist apart from mind but can be accessed by reason. Drawing/Writing uses the Platonic approach to Truth through the CA: beauty or goodness in the form of "right relationships" can be apprehended through visual inquiry. Group critiques for the CA provide empirical proof that ideas about right relationships, or the Good, are shared—a point of interest for curricula including ethical behavior. In a fast-changing world, it is imperative to equip students with a working code of ethics, including practical approaches to deciding what actions are and are not correct for their lives.

When visual solutions differ radically from optically accurate drawings, students learn to expand their ideas about drawings. They ponder another concept: acceptable differences. This notion of acceptable differences, like that of right relationships, can be transferred, through discussions, from the aesthetic to the ethical domain. Practice with tolerance encourages empathy, even compassion. Tolerance is a precondition for cooperative behavior. Cooperation is the pulse of peaceful co-existence. As a tolerance for difference grows in the Drawing/Writing classroom, a tolerance for difference in a world of diversity becomes more possible.

To achieve transfer from training in right relationships and acceptable differences to students' lives, you will need to elicit experiences of actual ethical dilemmas, making a direct connection between too much and too little in a drawing and too much and too little in human behavior in students' lives.

If we should discover—as we do in group critiques about CA's—that there is agreement among students about right relationships in drawings and about acceptable human behavior, then a code of ethics can be forged, at least for a particular student group, which goes beyond the purely personal. Because the personal and the social intersect, individual and group codes for acceptable behavior may also intersect.

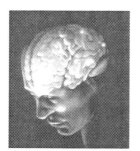

The goal of the criterion "neither too much nor too little" is a reasonable balance, not bland moderation. Group critiques in Drawing/Writing over the past ten years demonstrate that these criteria—"neither too much nor too little"—are shared *and intrinsic*. This does not mean that students always agree, but, generally, they do. In my teaching experience, disagreement about aesthetics is not culture-based. Disagreement occurs because some students are more analytical than others. As students come closer in analytical abilities, their decisions about balanced compositions become closer. Culture does play a role in *how* students apply the criteria "neither too much nor too little." One student may feel he has plenty of personal space at a crowded work table. Another student may need more space to work. These culture-based sensibilities will influence aesthetic and, possibly, ethical decisions.

Brain research shows that, although our brains are more or less alike, our experiences of space, time and motion may differ culturally. Still, we retain a common experience of gravity. Quite literally, we share a common ground. Common neural processes, or shared criteria for balanced decision-making, do not guarantee agreement among nations, but they are a place to start.

The drawings—the Geometric Shapes drawings, the LMD drawings, the "Perfect" Whole drawings—which will create the CA are not practice studies. Each work is complete and finished in itself and stands as a statement of truth about the object. A contour drawing is no more nor less than an LMD drawing. It is itself. A sensitive contour drawing is replete with meaning. As a combination of all these drawings, the CA moves beyond literal description to interpretation on a very different level—that of abstract symbolic expression—where the mind becomes most inventive. This solution, too, stands on its own as a statement of truth.

It may prove useful to refer to the educational benefits of the Composite Abstraction listed in Part 1. Beyond providing early experience and practice with abstract symbols—reading and math readiness—the CA has important remedial and even pre-ventative effects. Students at risk for writing or reading difficulties may self-remediate before the onset of serious problems by accepting writing as an advanced form of drawing. Developmentally delayed students have a chance to experiment successfully with abstract symbols as do students who lack fluency in the primary language of the classroom. Developmentally delayed children who are pressed to write and read before they are ready may acquire learning disabilities. Drawing/Writing protects a range of children from premature expectations about writing and reading while providing them with substantive training in the use of abstract symbols. Beyond its preventive and remedial advantages, the CA encourages innovative thinking.

To explore the possibility of a neural basis for shared understandings about right relationships useful in aesthetic and ethical decision-making, the material in "Hitchhikers' Guide," Part 3 of this book, will prove useful.

Composite Abstraction 1  1/10/97 DJM

This composite abstraction looks like a bird flying into a bird bath. It has strong wings and a rather plump undulating body. The bird bath is of sturdy construction. The base is thick and solid looking. There may be a cat hiding behind the bird bath waiting for the unsuspecting bird to become involved in his bath.

*Garden Fork CA, Donna Murray, 1997*
*Merrimac Education Center/Fitchburg State College,*
*Continuing Education*

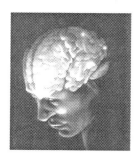

## PROCEDURE:

### REHASH HOMEWORK IN PEER PAIRS.

### ASSIGN HOMEWORK

**SAY/DO:** "Take a new piece of paper, write your initials, the date and the words 'Composite Abstraction' at the top." Review the previous four drawing exercises by asking your students to call out the names in order. As they call out the names—Preliminary Drawing and Writing, Blind Contour, Regular Contour, Euclidean Basic Shape, Fractal Basic Shape, Organic Basic Shape, LMD, the 'Perfect' Whole—write the names on the board. Draw a box below each one. Add a large empty box below this string of boxes and label that 'CA.'

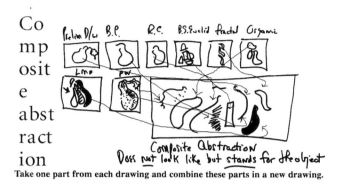

Take one part from each drawing and combine these parts in a new drawing.

*Illustration of how to do the CA using labeled boxes*

Students may want to use a pencil to copy areas that were originally done in pencil or markers for areas originally done with markers, or they may choose to work in new ways.

**SAY:** "We're going to take one part from each drawing and put those parts together in a new way. Here's the procedure for a Composite Abstraction:

- Take one part you especially like from each drawing. This part may be a line, or part of a line, a shape, or part of a shape. You can change the size of the part but otherwise you may not distort it. The piece remains a faithful copy of the piece. Like a word, you are simply using it in a different combination and context.

- Combine these parts in any way you choose to, with or without overlaps. The result should not look like the original object."

**DEMONSTRATE:** Make quick sketches in the labeled boxes; that is, sketch a Blind Contour drawing in the Blind Contour box. Then, look critically at each drawing and select one part, transferring that part to the large empty box below, labeled "CA."

**SAY:** "I am not going to draw a circle around the selected parts. I am just going to point them out. I do not want to mark up my drawings. These drawings are both working sketches and finished products. They deserve to be treated as serious work."

**ASK:** "How will we decide what parts to select?"

**DISCUSSION:** Lead the discussion toward these criteria:
- Accuracy: one part of the drawing looks especially like the object.
- Aesthetics: one part of the drawing is especially pleasing.

**ASK:** "Did the part appeal to you because of accuracy or because of aesthetics, or both?

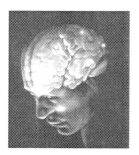

**DEMONSTRATE THE COMPOSITE ABSTRACTION:** You have sketched the visual procedure for the CA. Now, show students how to construct a Composite Abstraction. Spread your drawings out. Be surprised at the number of drawings. Students, too, will be startled and pleased by the volume of their work.

Write "CA" and your initials and the date at the top of a sheet of paper. Going from drawing to drawing, select one part and draw it on the new piece of paper, larger or smaller. Follow this procedure until you have selected and copied one part from each drawing, combining the parts as you go. Discuss how you are arranging them. Show that you are not re-drawing your object. You are making a totally new statement about it which is not recognizable as the object anymore. Make sure your drawing is "abstract" in this sense, and is not just an outline of the object with some shapes fitted inside.

*Joanne Quail, CA of a cow horn, Applewild School, 1997*

Complete your Composite Abstraction. You have already demonstrated the CA schematically, and now you have demonstrated how you will undertake the CA with your own work. If you show them more of your process, you may inhibit theirs.

Look at your own CA. Write for at least 10 minutes. Model sustained writing. In my teaching experience, writing about the CA takes the writer into unpredictable, interesting places.

**SAY:** "These are the rules for the CA:

- Choose any drawing medium; it can be the same one you used for that particular study, or not. Use both markers and pencils if you choose to.
- Choose one part from each drawing.
- Copy the selected part onto the new piece of paper; you can make the part bigger or smaller, but it must be an accurate copy.
- Copy the next selected part; place it on the paper. You can place any part in any place on the new sheet of paper, overlapping or not. Combine the parts in a pleasing or balanced way."

**ASK:** "What does 'pleasing' mean? Pleasing means that the drawing appeals to your senses: in this case, the sense of sight and, by implication, touch. Maybe you like curves. Maybe you like sharp angles or a combination of curves and angles.

A drawing that is pleasing is also balanced. When a drawing is just right, it will be pleasing. This feeling of rightness is what artists mean when they talk about a balanced composition. How can we define the word balanced? Do we mean balance as in a balanced scale with equal weights on each side? Are there other kinds of balance? Does a drawing have to be symmetrical, or identical on both sides, to be balanced? Could a large object be counterbalanced by a series of parallel lines?"

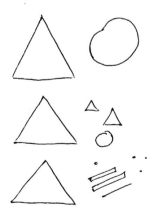

*Large triangle counterbalanced by: large circle, several triangles and squares, parallel lines and dots*

**DISCUSSION:** A balanced drawing does not have to be symmetrical. Try drawing a large triangle on the board and see what kinds and quantities of shapes or lines would counterbalance it from the students' point of view. Some students may choose one large counterbalancing shape. Some may choose several smaller shapes. Some may use a series of lines and dots.

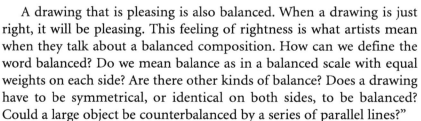

Ideas about balancing sides of a drawing paves the way for introducing a key CA concept: "right relationships." Right relationships are

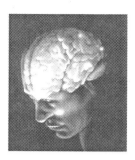

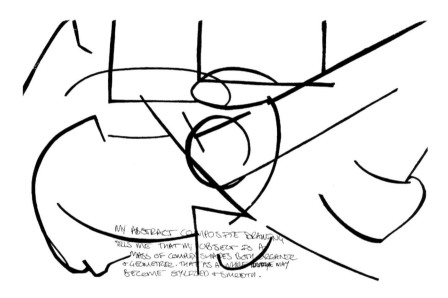

*Emily Lavelle, CA, turkey drumstick, January term, Hampshire College, 1995*

Emily writes, "My CA tells me that my object is a mass of complex shapes both organic and geometric that may become complex and smooth."

achieved intuitively in drawing but can be explained in Group Critiques. The "felt" quality in a balanced composition can be described as a high level impulse from lower levels of neural resolution. The processes for achieving low level and high level resolution must include something like "neither too much nor too little." For a nerve impulse to propagate, there must be neither too much nor too little electrochemical energy. For a drawing to balance, there must be neither too much nor too little of any compositional element.

In the context of discussing right relationships, encourage students to think about the connections between how they balance their drawings and how they construct ethical behavior. Correct ethical relationships may profitably take their cue from "neither too much nor too little," too, but here the issues will involve personal space rather than negative and positive space, or appropriate allocations of time, energy, and financial and emotional resources rather than the correct disposition of line, shape, color, and space.

**DEMONSTRATE:** The CA exercise has two parts: CA#1 and CA#2. The procedure for CA#1 has been described. The procedure for CA#2 is as follows: a student holds the first CA up for the peer to examine, rotating it until the peer nods. The nod signifies that the peer understands where there is too much or too little in the drawing and is now ready to go "back to the drawing boards," producing a second, better balanced CA.

The second CA poses questions of design. A good design is one to which you can add no more and from which you can take no more away (Bates, 1960). In the context of Drawing/Writing, this definition of a good design is expressed as "neither too much nor too little" or "right relationships."

**ASK:** "What could be considered too much or too little in connection with our own behavior or the behavior of other people?"

**DISCUSSION: OPEN-ENDED:** Encourage students to identify excessive or restrictive behavior. When this discussion has run its course, return to the procedure for the CA.

**SAY:** "Use the tables and the floor. Lay out all of the drawings in your portfolio so that you can see them."

**SAY/DO:** "When you finish drawing your CA's, write, 'My CA tells me........because...' Do not write, 'My CA tells me *that my object* is....because....' Your object is 'out of the picture' now, isn't it?

Look at your CA drawing. Let the CA take you anywhere it wants to take you as a writer. Keep looking at your CA as you write. After you finish, write one simile and one metaphor using the word 'because' as usual."

**PEER SHARE**

**GROUP CRITIQUE**

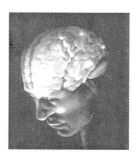

*CA, shell, maximum security prison inmate, George, 1987*

CA, shell, writing, maximum security prison inmate, George, 1987

This abstract makes me think about oriental architecture. Maybe in Japan, where it is all coastline, builders would of been inspired by shells they saw and the beauty and strength they possessed. This part was fun—to manipulate different parts of one object to make an entire different idea.

I noticed that at first [in the Preliminary Drawing and Writing] I commented on the emotional reaction the object provoked. As we continued, I spent more time on the object itself. As more and more details were observed I forgot the feelings and had to concentrate on only the object. Then at last the details I had focused on now brought forth new ideas and different observations and all new feelings.

## PROCEDURE FOR CA#2

**REHASH:**

**HOMEWORK**

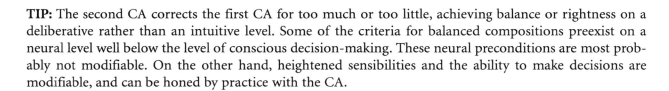

**SAY/DO:** "We are going to do a second CA. To make a second CA that is better than the first, we have to decide how we would change the first CA. Here is an easy way to decide where your drawing needs work. Look at your CA and ask yourself these two questions:

- where is there too little?
- where is there too much?

By careful looking, you will be able to figure out where there is too much or too little in your first CA. You can add color, now, making it part of the balancing procedure. Decisions about relationships among line, form, color and space achieve balance."

**TIP:** The second CA corrects the first CA for too much or too little, achieving balance or rightness on a deliberative rather than an intuitive level. Some of the criteria for balanced compositions preexist on a neural level well below the level of conscious decision-making. These neural preconditions are most probably not modifiable. On the other hand, heightened sensibilities and the ability to make decisions are modifiable, and can be honed by practice with the CA.

**DEMONSTRATE:** Hold up a CA. Ask the student who drew it to look at the drawing while you rotate it. After applying the criteria "neither too much nor too little," ask the student to nod when he/she sees what needs fixing.

**TIP:** It is a time-honored artist's trick to look at work upside down, or in a mirror, or both. Seeing work in a new way, apart from narrative or figurative content (apart from being a horse plowing a field, or a woman taking a bath), allows the artist to focus on the formal aspects of the work. The CA is already freed of subject matter as such, but it still has a "right side up" and an "upside down" aspect for the artist. Turning the work sideways and upside down helps the artist identify areas of "too much" and "too little." By resolving these areas, the student achieves a balanced composition or a good design more easily.

I am still amazed to see students nod, showing they know just what to do with their drawings, going confidently back to work. Why do a second drawing? The first CA is an exercise in recombination. The second CA is an exercise in deliberation, judgment and innovation. CA#1 is like a rough draft. CA#4 is like a polished piece of writing. Like writing, drawings can be revised. Students who learn to revise their drawings are more likely to revise their writing.

**SAY/DO:** Addressing a student who has produced a CA#1, say, "I am turning this drawing around and around so that you can see the drawing sideways and also upside down, deciding where there is too much or too little. When you nod, I will stop. Do the same for your peer. Because the drawing is being rotated, your peer must look at it in new ways: sideways and upside down, getting a fresh view. It is easy to think a drawing is balanced when it is "right side up" just because it is right side up. When we look at it upside down, suddenly we see the gaps and the crowded areas."

**DEMONSTRATE:** Continue to rotate the student's drawing until the student nods.

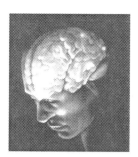

Cecily wrote, "The eye hollow has become a convex egg, cracked slightly open to reveal dark interior. The teeth fly away, no longer necessary or useful. The escaping dots of energy have gained more power and significance as they create new life and as they arrange themselves in order once more."

The writing which goes with CA 2 drawing
refers to the original object by the words I used
to instance comfortable, content, surrounded and leasure,
My CA.2 writing tells me that the following relate to
my object - mother, small girl, comfortable, warmth and
relaxation. These words surround you, cradle you and protect
you. My writing brings me back to the original object.
It brings me to the experiences I've had drawing
my object and experiences in my own life.
The writing of my object is reminiscent of the old days.
It is simplistic but tells alot. The lines and lines tell a
story of their own. My words and my drawing
bring the viewer into motion physically and
emotionally.

11/13/96   F
Referential Writing

*Pamela Frigo, Chair, referential writing, 1997*
*Continuing Education, Westfield State College*

**SAY:** "Let's add one new element. Once you have decided where there is too much or too little in your first CA, you are free to include one new element in CA#2. ( The need for one new element is a recent unanimous student decision.)

The rules for CA #2 :

- As your peer rotates your drawing, decide where there is too much and too little. When you have made your decisions, nod.

- Draw the CA#2 by taking what you like from the original drawing. You may distort, shorten, lengthen, overlap and omit what is no longer necessary.

- Add one entirely new element if you feel this is necessary."

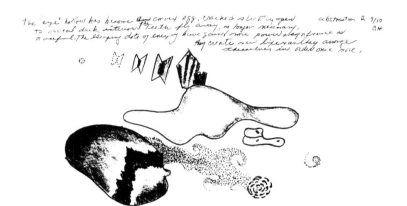

*Cow Skull, CA#2 drawing and writing, Cecily Howell, 1997
Merrimac Education Center/Fitchburg State College Continuing
Education*

**RECORD:** Write these rules on the board.

**SAY:** "Now, let's write about CA#2. First, describe how you used shapes, lines, colors, spaces. Did you use many triangles, circles, organic forms? Then, free-write. Let the drawing lead you into language about the CA#2. When you finish writing, generate one simile and one metaphor using 'because.'"

**TIP:** Because CA's fill the page, students may not want to write on the drawing, choosing to write on a separate sheet of paper. The interrelationships between drawing and writing have been established by now. Even if students use separate sheets of paper at this point for their drawings and for their writings about their drawings, they are unlikely to disassociate the two activities.

Students agree that this piece of writing springs directly from the visual stimulus and process of the CA and that it could not have been generated "cold turkey," that is, without the CA. In fact, students often agree that the drawings and writings generated by the Drawing/Writing five-step are unique to the five-step procedure.

For adult students, the CA writing becomes increasingly personal and self-revelatory.

**DEMONSTRATE: Referential Writing.** The CA writing refers back to the object, just as the CA drawings still contain hints of the original object. These hints can be examined and clarified. Hold up your second CA and read the writing aloud. Share the connections to the object you see visually and verbally. Write about these visual and verbal connections. For instance, my CA#2 writing about the hammer describes waves pounding on a shore. The verb "pound" refers to the action of a hammer.

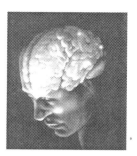

CA#2, Wood Plane:
Bobbie Jo wrote, "This drawing tells one it's colorful, wide, huge, black, white, purple, green, interesting, weird, different. Railroad track, fun looks like a playground. It has a balance beam, jungle bars, a ladder to climb, a merry-go-round, it also looks like a game on the top of TicTacToe. It looks like a building in pieces. There could be cool looking stairs and a circular window, doors, a roof half put together."

CA#2, Wrench:
Deanna Sevarino wrote, "My drawing is weird, huge, purple, green, mysterious, linear, circular, bubbly, adventurous. My drawing looks like a monster from the end of the world because no one ever saw one before unless they went to the end of the world but it is there… or it could be a purple blob of clay that you mold to whatever you feel it looks like to you. It's very strange but with your memory, it becomes one with you and to all that see it too. Green running down a child's face long and gross for your eyes as you see it but to that child it's saying just clean my face so I can go back and play. The mouth and teeth of a shark ready to attack, scared faces as death appears in their mind. Serious, huge and sharp, through your mind (be) happy, joy, sad and excited that it was just a thought… at that time."

**SAY/DO:** "Let's examine how the CA#2 writing relates to your original object. Let's call this CA#2 writing "Referential Writing" because it refers back to the object. Be specific. When you have finished this referential writing, generate a final simile and a final metaphor about CA#2."

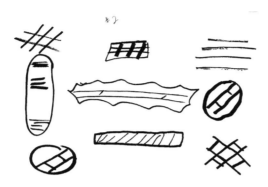

*Wood Plane, CA#2, by Bobbie Jo Dunn, student of Peggy Reidister and Brenda Ewing, GED and instructors, June 1996*

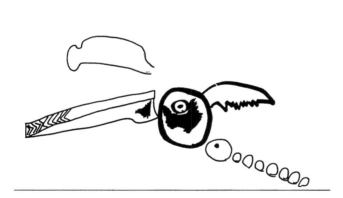

*Wrench #2, CA, by Deeana Sevarino, student of Peggy Reidister and Brenda Ewing, GED instructors, June, 1996*

**SAY/DO:** "How do the simile and metaphor refer to the object? Write about the visual and verbal connections."

**ASK:** "How do the original object, CA#2 and the simile and the metaphor connect? Identify the visual and verbal connections. Your peer may be able to help." Seeing connections and translating between them  persists as a primary Drawing/Writing strategy.

**PEER SHARE AND BUILD**

**GROUP CRITIQUE**

~ Composite Abstraction ~.

My composite abstraction drawing tells me that my drawing is diverse. I reviewed all of my pieces and picked various one's which I thought were of most interest to me. The majority of my pieces are curvilinear. My pieces occupy the majority of space on my piece of paper. It doesn't look like my object but I know it is because parts of it resemble the whole. I recognize it because of some of the shapes, lines and tonal values.

*CA#1, Pamela Frigo, chair, Continuing Education, Westfield State College, 1996*

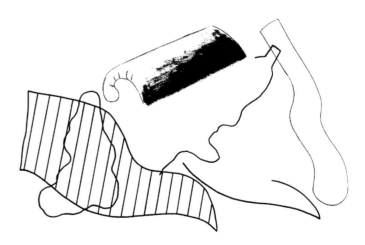

~ Composite Abstraction ~

My composite abstraction drawing tells me that my drawing has been evaluated and redefined. Now I feel there is neither too much or too little line, space or form. There are parts of my drawing that have tonal value and have outlines. The shapes represent and are symbolic of many things. You can see that some of the pieces are overlapping and others are spread apart. It looks balanced and is pleasing to the eye. My drawing takes me around it and to the center to a place where I am comfortable and content. I am surrounded by the relaxing curves. It brings me back to a time when I was a very small girl. When I used to have scary dreams and my mother would sit me down and reassure me that everything is alright and she is always here for me.

*CA#2, Pamela Frigo, chair, Continuing Education, Westfield State College, 1996*

## 5.2 Optional Cool-Down Exercises

_Advanced Drawing Problem_

Simple, Simpler, Simplest
Complex, More Complex, Most Complex

**BACKGROUND:**
Like the CA, the "double three-step" is a logical development. As the "Perfect" Whole required the  Composite Abstraction, so the CA required the double three-step known as Simple, Simpler, Simplest; Complex, More Complex, Most Complex.

Instructions:

- Draw the object as simply as possible, then, on a new sheet of paper, draw it even more simply, then, on a third sheet, most simply. Draw in any way you choose to with any materials.

- Draw the object as complex as possible, then more complex, and then most complex. Draw in any way you choose to, using any materials.

- Each time, start with a new sheet of paper. Each time, keep the object in front of you and refer directly to it through your drawing.

Training in right relationships has taught students to think about including neither too much nor too little in their drawings. In this double three-step, they will be working toward the right amount of information to express the object simply and the correct amount of information to express it in a complicated way. Both drawings—the most minimal and the most replete—will contain exactly the right amount of information to express the thing itself.

When they finish the double three-step, ask students to compare and contrast the most complex and the most simple drawings in writing. Something startling but logical—even predictable—happens as students mature as visual artists. This same thing happens to writers.

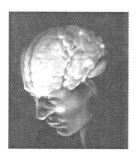

# CLOSING

# DRAWING AND WRITING:

## POST-TESTS

## and

## RESCORE

*Closing Drawing and Writing, Shell, Joanne Krawczyk, Continuing Education, Westfield State College, 1996*

My Closing Drawing tells me that I feel liberated from a prescribed assignment. I have enjoyed each exercise but now I am inclined to experiment with methods and materials rather than focusing on what can be gleaned from the immediate task because I see drawing that combines a variety of materials and my experiences as an artist. Although I don't feel pressured to describe my drawing in detail, my Closing Writing tells me that I continue to use the writing format that has become so routine to all of us. My favorite part is writing similes and metaphors. My Closing Drawing is like a fallen bee's nest that has outgrown its usefulness because I see that the familiar gray tissue is torn in several places and the shadow underneath indicates that it has fallen to the ground long after the insects left their seasonal home.

My Closing Drawing is an artist's conceptual rendition of a rotund nude posing in a reclined position because I see a bulging curving shape that calls to mind the undulations of the female form.

# Closing Drawing and Writing
# and Post-Tests

## 6.1  Closing Drawing and Writing

OBJECTIVES:

   ***New benchmarks***

MATERIALS: A new object, pencils, markers, paper, folder

**BACKGROUND:**

   The closing sample of drawing and writing functions as a post test. Tell students that this sample will be  timed just like the preliminary sample. Don't emphasize the fact that students will compare this piece of drawing and writing with the preliminary sample.

   Students will use the constructivist evaluation tool called Rescore to compare the Preliminary and Closing samples of drawing and writing. Rescore starts with the easy task of counting, moving to the more difficult task of qualitative analysis. As an assessment tool, Rescore is quantitative and qualitative. Rescore includes evalutive questions about how students' drawing and writing have changed. The answers are "felt" decisions. Students are asked to approach these decisions by counting specific parts of speech and forms of punctuation, first, thereby assessing changes in grammar and punctuation, constructing a precise under-standing of changes in their verbal strategies.

   The Rescore "grade" on the pre- and post-test samples, as well as the cumulative grade on the entire Drawing/Writing portfolio, are provided by the student. A detailed checklist helps students grade their portfolios for completeness—not for quality. Students alone know the level of their intent and investment. Grading for whether work is completed or not is a clean and fair way to structure self-assessed "grading." Some students' 100% will reflect more work than others' 100%. Since the rewards of work are intrinsic and hard to measure, and since group critiques have made all student work public, it is not necessary for teach-ers or students or parents to fret over qualitative differences between "A's." One "Perfect" Whole drawing is one "Perfect" Whole drawing. If it has not been done, the portfolio is missing one drawing. If that missing drawing costs the portfolio 5 points, then the portfolio is scored less by 5 points. It is all very simple. I have found that this straightforward approach works well. The implications of the missing drawing are the student's business.

9/4/96          Writing

                        T.W.S.

This is a Drawing of a scuba mask
This mask is used for diving
in the ocean.

Tom Sheehan, Preliminary Writing, scuba mask, 1996

This is a drawing of a scuba mask. This mask is
used for diving in the ocean.

*Preliminary Drawing and Writing*

WS
1/20/96          Closing Drawing and Writing

When I First started drawing this new object I said this should be easy.
a new object a new thing to draw and write about. So here I am babbling
about nothing because I couldn't come up with anything. all I want is
my scuba mask back. This new object has got me thinking. The old
one was easy to write about everything just came to my warped mind when I
was working with the scuba mask. I don't even know what you call my object

Tom Sheehan, Closing Writing, unknown object.

When I first started drawing this new object I said this should be easy.
A new object a new thing to draw and write about. So here I am babbling
about nothing because I couldn't come up with anything. All I want is my
scuba mask back. This new object has got me thinking. The old one was
easy to write about. Everything just came to my warped mind when I was
working with the scuba mask. I don't even know what you call my object.

*Closing Drawing and Writing*

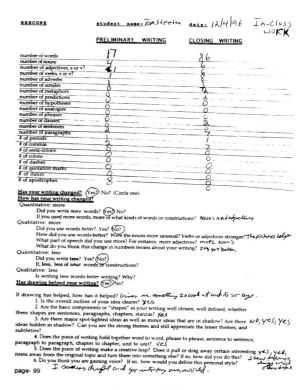

RESCORE        student name: Tom Sheehan  date: 12/4/96  In-class work

|  | PRELIMINARY WRITING | CLOSING WRITING |
| --- | --- | --- |
| number of words | 17 | 86 |
| number of nouns | 4 | 6 |
| number of adjectives, s or v? | 1 | 8 |
| number of verbs, s or v? | 1 | 6 |
| number of adverbs |  |  |
| number of similes | 0 | 0 |
| number of metaphors | 0 | 0 |
| number of predictions | 0 | 0 |
| number of hypotheses | 0 | 0 |
| number of analogies | 0 | 0 |
| number of phrases | 0 | 0 |
| number of clauses | 0 | 0 |
| number of sentences | 2 | 3 |
| number of paragraphs | 1 | 1 |
| # of periods | 2 | 1 |
| # of commas | 0 | 7 |
| # of semi-colons | 0 | 0 |
| # of colons | 0 | 0 |
| # of dashes | 0 | 0 |
| # of quotation marks | 0 | 0 |
| # of italics | 0 | 0 |
| # of apostrophes | 0 | 0 |

Has your writing changed? (Yes) No? (Circle one)
How has your writing changed?
  Quantitative: more
      Did you write *more* words? (Yes) No?
      If you used more words, more of what kinds of words or constructions? Nouns and adjectives
  Qualitative: more
      Did you use words *better*? Yes? (No?)
      How did you use words better? Were the nouns more unusual? Verbs or adjectives stronger? The pictures help
      What part of speech did you use more? For instance, more adjectives? more nouns
      What do you think this change in numbers means about your writing? It's got better
  Quantitative: less
      Did you write *less*? Yes? (No?)
      If, less, less of *what* words or constructions?
  Qualitative: less
      Is writing less words *better* writing? Why?
Has drawing helped your writing? (Yes) No?

If drawing has helped, how has it helped? gives me something to look at and to so large.
      1. Is the overall outline of your idea clearer? Yes
      2. Are the basic components or "shapes" in your writing well chosen, well defined, whether
these shapes are sentences, paragraphs, chapters, stanzas? Yes
      3. Are there major spot-lighted ideas as well as minor ideas that are in shadow? Are there No, Yes, Yes
ideas hidden in shadow? Can you see the strong themes and still appreciate the lesser themes, and
subtleties?
      4. Does the piece of writing hold together word to word, phrase to phrase, sentence to sentence,
paragraph to paragraph, chapter to chapter, unit to unit? Yes
      5. Does the piece of writing make a creative leap? Does it pull or drag away certain interesting Yes, Yes,
items away from the original topic and turn them into something else? If so, how did you do this? I saw different
      6. Do you think you are gaining voice? If so, how would you define this personal style?
page- 99    I somehow caught and go into my own world.

*Rescore, Writing*

RESCORE        student name: Tom Sheehan      date: 12/5/96

|  | Preliminary Drawing | Closing Drawing |
| --- | --- | --- |
| Use of line- tentative, bold |  |  |
|    inaccurate, accurate | Few lines | Few lines |
|    hasty, sensitive |  |  |
|    few lines, many lines |  |  |
| Use of shapes- geometric |  |  |
|    organic |  |  |
|    repeating |  |  |
|    tentative, bold | bold, inaccurate | many shapes, geometric |
|    inaccurate, accurate | Few shapes | inaccurate |
|    hasty, sensitive |  |  |
|    few shapes, many shapes |  |  |
| Use of value- subtle contrast, strong contrast | strong contrast | hard-edged transition |
|    few lights, mediums, darks | soft-edged transition |  |
|    many lights, mediums, darks |  |  |
|    soft-edged transition |  |  |
|    hard-edged transition |  |  |
| Use of detail- few, many | Few, poorly chosen | many details |
|    inaccurate, accurate |  | well chosen |
|    poorly chosen |  | descriptive |
|    well chosen |  |  |
|    distracting |  |  |
|    descriptive |  |  |

Negative space - is the space around the object thoughtfully perceived?
      Do negative and positive spaces balance each other?

Have your drawing skills changed? Yes? (No?)
Quantitative:
      Are there more or less lines in the 2nd drawing? more
      Are there more or less shapes in the 2nd drawing? Do the shapes combine several kinds more, yes (combine
of geometry? What kinds? Do any shapes repeat at different scales? Is there a yes
fractal element in the drawing?
      Are there more or less shapes for light, medium and dark areas in the 2nd drawing? more
      Are the shapes for value soft-edged or hard-edged? Is there strong contrast, or subtle hard, strong
contrast between values?
      Are there more or less details in the second drawing? more
      If there are more details, are they helpful in describing the object more fully? No
      Are there more or less lines, shapes, colors overall in the 2nd drawing? more
      Is there better use of space in the second drawing? No

      How would you rate the first drawing in terms of realism on a scale of 1-10? 5
      How would you rate the second drawing in terms of realism on a scale of 1-10? 1

Qualitative: How have your drawings changed? more imagination
      1. accuracy of contour, expressivity of contour. Are the lines stronger, surer, more
pleasing, more striking, more descriptive in an emotional way of the object? more startling   That is,
are they more expressive? yes
      2. accuracy of basic shapes, expressivity of basic shapes. Are these shapes more
      descriptive of the object? Are the shapes more emotional? yes, yes
      3. accuracy of values, expressivity of values. Is value handled more descriptively yes
page- 100

*Rescore, Drawing*

*Thomas Sheehan, Continuing Education, Westfield State College, 1996*

The self-assessment approach to grading will be new, even suspect to some parents. However, it has been my experience that once parents have looked at their children's portfolios and the Rescore sheets, they understand and appreciate this approach. They also gain respect for teachers who include student-based approaches to assessment and learning. Parents who have been reluctant to praise their children's drawing skills will see that drawing skills qualify as visual literacy, allowing parents who may have discouraged their youngsters' drawings as "doodling" to take pride in them.

Drawing/Writing portfolios provide a focus for fruitful exchanges between parents and teachers. The portfolios let parents actually see what their student's work looks like as well as to read their children's assessment of growing skills. Changes in drawing skills are easier to appreciate than changes in writing. Parents will be dazzled by their children's drawing skills. A glance at the increase in writing will reassure them. For parents who do not speak English, portfolios including a sample of writing in their native language followed by a sample of writing in English create a bridge of understanding. In such cases, drawings help enormously, too.

Teachers do not see Rescore results until they confer with students. Unless students miscount, there will be few discrepancies between the self-evaluation and the work. Students bring the critical, analytical skills they have learned in peer sharing to objective self-assessment. Teachers can accept students' self-evaluations as valid.

A copy of the evaluation tool Rescore is included at the end of this section. Copy it freely. The categories for counting are based on grammar and punctuation. If some of your students already know about grammar and punctuation, let them help each other. You will have taught some grammar already in the context of the Drawing/Writing program. Drawing/Writing provides a structure for incorporating grading and grammar into literacy education.

By using Drawing/Writing three times a year, three thorough evaluations of visual and verbal skills are provided for each student. Rescore proves especially useful to students and their parents because the terms are clear, thorough and understandable. Teachers and administrators can use numerical Rescore results in longitudinal statistical research to determine the effects of cross-modal education on literacy statistics. The scores on standardized tests for writing, reading and mathematics skills can be compared across groups: do Drawing/Writing students score higher on these nationally adminstered tests? As teacher/researcher, you can put the numerical data from the Rescore sheets through an analysis of variance to measure changes in your classroom. Or, you can find a professional—a graduate student in education at the local university—to do this. It is exciting to measure the effect of your Drawing/Writing program in this formal way. Apart from statistics, the significant aspect of the Drawing/Writing program is students' increased skills and their appreciation for these skills.

The samples of Rescore on the lefthand page shows that Tom Sheehan felt he made gains in his writing and drawing. Both sets of gains are clear to the reader at a glance.

In the sample of Rescore on the following page, Paul Gagnon observes that he wrote more: from 80, he wrote 201 words, and his writing became more descriptive. It also becomes more integrated with his drawing, actually flowing around it.

*Carol Wichler, Closing Drawing and Writing, flashlight, 1997, Merrimac Education Center/ Fitchburg State College, Continuing Education*

*Prelim Drawing & Writing 9/11/96 rg*

I shall write about this sneaker. Although well used it displays good quality merchandise useful to any child or person who may use it. True you may need both left and right foot sneaker and they both must fit your feet. Shoes and sneakers are very common every day items you will need every day as you dress, you must learn to match left and right correctly and then to lace them correctly. One sneaker is only useful for a one legged person which I assume you are not. The true mark of a great sneaker is durability.

**Preliminary Drawing and Writing, sneaker**

My Closing Drawing tells it is a water spigot on the end of a hose, really pouring water onto my lawn. It also tells me that it is a powerful force moving tons of water to make things grow. Growing grass is all around and surrounds our drawing making a green background for all to see. Curvature reminds me so much of green hose shapes that it all fits together nicely. Man am I happy that sneaker has parted company with me — Too physical. Good luck to it. Dog all other onto my lawn and visit me on their walks boy. Altogether, makes a great picture. Our omission. Sprinkler to move things around. A wheelbarrow carries things and is useful. A weeder is no less. Cultivating is important too. Garden, in mine its chore to keep away the unwanted. Perhaps, only perhaps Pearl will get me a new one.

**Closing Drawing and Writing, hose**

---

| | PRELIMINARY WRITING | CLOSING WRITING |
|---|---|---|
| number of words | 360 | 203 |
| number of nouns | | |
| number of adjectives, s or v? | | |
| number of verbs, s or v? | | |
| number of adverbs | | |
| number of similes | | |
| number of metaphors | | |
| number of predictions | | |
| number of hypotheses | | |
| number of analogies | | |
| number of phrases | | |
| number of clauses | | |
| number of sentences | 17 | 8 |
| number of paragraphs | | |
| # of periods | | |
| # of commas | | |
| # of semi-colons | | |
| # of colons | | |
| # of dashes | | |
| # of quotation marks | | |
| # of italics | | |
| # of apostrophes | | |

**Has your writing changed?** (Yes) No? (Circle one)
**How has your writing changed?**
Quantitative: more
   Did you write *more* words? (Yes) No?
   If you used more words, more of what kinds of words or constructions? MORE DESCRIPTIVE
Qualitative: more
   Did you use words *better*? (Yes) No?
   How did you use words better? Were the nouns more unusual? Verbs or adjectives stronger?
   What part of speech did you use more? For instance, more adjectives?
   What do you think this change in numbers means about your writing? MORE DESCRIPTIVE
Quantitative: less
   Did you write less? Yes? (No?)
   If, less, less of *what* words or constructions?
Qualitative: less
   Is writing less words *better* writing? Why?
**Has drawing helped your writing?** (Yes?) No?

If drawing has helped, how has it helped? CLEAR UNDERSTANDING IN IT'S STRUCTURE BETWEEN EACH PIECE OF WORK.
   1. Is the overall outline of your idea clearer? YES
   2. Are the basic components or "shapes" in your writing well chosen, well defined, whether these shapes are sentences, paragraphs, chapters, stanzas? LATER IS MY FEEL
   3. Are there major spot-lighted ideas as well as minor ideas that are in shadow? Are there ideas hidden in shadow? Can you see the strong themes and still appreciate the lesser themes, and subtleties? YES I CAN
   4. Does the piece of writing hold together word to word, phrase to phrase, sentence to sentence, paragraph to paragraph, chapter to chapter, unit to unit? WE CAN DO BETTER WITH A CREATIVE UNDERSTANDING
   5. Does the piece of writing make a creative leap? Does it pull or drag away certain interesting OF THE items away from the original topic and turn them into something else? If so, how did you do this? OBJECTIVE
   6. Do you think you are gaining voice? If so, how would you define this personal style? PURE LUCK
                TOUGH QUESTION! ASK MY SHRINK
                SELF EVALUATION IS OFTEN INACCURATE

page- 99

**Rescore**

---

*Paul Gagnon, 1997, Continuing Education, Westfield State College*

## PROCEDURE:

**SAY:** "We are going to close with one more short drawing and writing session. To do this, we need to choose a new object. Is there an object in the box you have been wanting to draw?"

**TIP:** The choice of a new object is critical to the success of the evaluation process. To measure the degree to which skills develop and transfer, students needed to work with a new object. The new object serves two purposes: it re-arouses attention, and, as a new problem, it measures transfer of skills.

**SAY/DO:** "Get a piece of paper, and your markers or pencils. Write your initials, the date, and 'Closing Drawing and Writing' on the top of your paper. Let's draw for about 10 minutes, and then let's write for about 10 minutes about this new object. Since we are not going to have much time, you may want to zoom in on one part of your object."

**TIP:** Do not stress the fact that students will be comparing this drawing and writing with the Preliminary Drawing and Writing samples. If a student notices this, acknowledge the fact that the two samples will be compared, but do not stress the pre- and post-test aspect of the exercise. The goal of the post-test is simply to measure changes in visual and verbal skills at this point in students' development. In a neuroconstructivist classroom, the assumption is that these skills will grow and change.

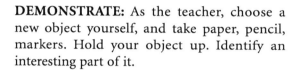

**DEMONSTRATE:** As the teacher, choose a new object yourself, and take paper, pencil, markers. Hold your object up. Identify an interesting part of it.

**SAY/DO:** "Since I only have 10 minutes to draw, I will focus on the blades of the garden shears."

**SAY/DO:** "Ten minutes is up. We need to stop drawing and start writing. The way you started the drawing is the way you would have finished. You can get back to this drawing another time if you want to. Now, write, in any way you choose to. Again, we will work for about 10 minutes."

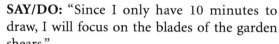

**TIP:** Your intent with the comment about the possibility of returning to the drawing is reassurance; students who know how to draw may wish to continue this work at another time. Some students will be very disappointed to stop after only ten minutes. Comfort may be in order.

As with every other step of the Drawing/Writing program, make sure you complete this Closing Drawing and Writing exercise yourself.

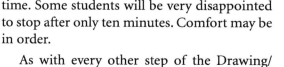

*Peter McEnaney, Closing Drawing and Writing, Garden shears, 1997, Merrimac Education Center/Fitchburg State College, Continuing Education*

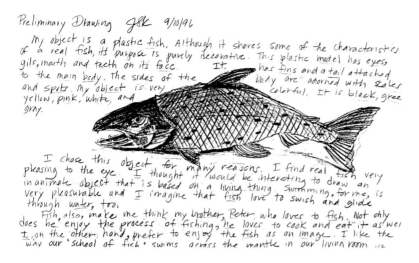

Preliminary Drawing and Writing, fish, Joanne Krawczyk

My object is a plastic fish. Although it shares some of the characteristics of a real fish, its purpose is purely decorative. This plastic model has eyes, gills, mouth and teeth on its face. It has fins and a tail attached to the main body. The sides of the body are adorned with scales and spots. My object is very colorful. It is black, green, yellow, pink, white and gray.

I chose this object for many reasons. I find real fish very pleasing to the eye. I thought it would be interesting to draw an inanimate object that is based on a living thing. Swimming, for me, is very pleasurable and I imagine that fish love to swish and glide through water, too.

Fish, also, make me think of my brother, Peter, who loves to fish. Not only does he enjoy the process of fishing, he loves to cook and eat it as well. I, on the other hand, prefer to enjoy the fish as an image. I like the way our school of fish swims across the mantel in our living room.

*Preliminary Drawing and Writing, Fish, Joanne Krawczyk, 1996*

My Closing Drawing tells me that I feel liberated from a prescribed assignment. I have enjoyed each exercise but now I am inclined to experiment with methods and materials rather than focusing on what can be gleaned from the immediate task because I see drawing that combines a variety of materials and my experiences as an artist. Although I don't feel pressured to describe my drawing in detail, my Closing Writing tells me that I continue to use the writing format that has become so routine to all of us. My favorite part is writing similes and metaphors. My Closing Drawing is like a fallen bee's nest that has outgrown its usefulness because I see that the familiar gray tissue is torn in several places and the shadow underneath indicates that it has fallen to the ground long after the insects left their seasonal home.

My Closing Drawing is an artist's conceptual rendition of a rotund nude posing in a reclined position because I see a bulging curving shape that calls to mind the undulations of the female form.

*Closing Drawing and Writing, Shell, Joanne Krawczyk, 1996*

**To the reader:** What changes do you see in these two samples of drawing and writing?

 **REMEMBER:** Seeing changes over time is exciting. A student who did very little writing a week ago who now writes 50 or 100 words will be impressed. A student who wrote no similes before and who has just written five similes is going to be impressed. On the other hand, a student who has written fewer words can look for "strong" adjectives and "strong" verbs as well as for similes, metaphors, analogies, predictions and hypotheses as indications of verbal growth that do not correlate with volume of words. A strong verb can make up for several weaker verbs. One vivid metaphor may eliminate a paragraph.

The Drawing/Writing program gives students the tools not only to become stronger writers but to be discriminating readers of their own writing, and, by extension, the writing of others.

## 6.2 Rescore

*Evaluation in a constructivist context*

OBJECTIVES:

    \*self-assessment\*
    **\*a quantitative approach to a qualitative evaluation\***
    **\*an associative approach to grammar**

MATERIALS: The Rescore sheets (zerox for students), pencils or pens and the pre- and post-test samples of drawing and writing

**BACKGROUND:**
   Not only is an instrument for self-evaluation a logical extension of constructivist teaching, but it is critical to the constructivist enterprise of self-constructed knowledge. To construct self-knowledge, students require clear criteria for self-evaluation.
   Rescore has evolved over time. It was, at first, a very simple evaluation tool. Students counted changes in numbers of words. There were no additional grammatical categories like nouns and verbs. Initially, there was no way to evaluate changes in drawing, either. Now, Rescore is exhaustive, if not exhausting! Tailor this evaluation tool to your needs.
   Although rescore has been designed specifically for the five-step Drawing/Writing program, Rescore can be used to evaluate writing in any language.

PROCEDURE:

**SAY:** "I am handing out an assessment tool called Rescore."

**ASK:** "What is assessment?"

**DISCUSSION:** Let students provide the words "grading, scoring, testing, evaluating, judging, passing, fail-  ing, excelling." Encourage students to discuss self-assessment. Many students are used to accepting grades provided by teachers and standardized tests. Self-assessment may be an unsettling idea. Once they get used to Rescore, students will appreciate the fact that tests provide benchmarks for modifiable skills. At best, IQ tests provide an indication of the intellectual potential of a student. Many students have been led astray by knowing their IQ's. The neurocontructivist approach in this book suggests that judgments about the mental powers of children are ill-advised. Children grow mentally, emotionally and physically in response to stimuli—or the lack thereof. The point to remember is this: the brain remains modifiable over a lifetime. The brain changes in response to learning as long as that brain is alive. As admonished in Part Three of this book, "Use it or lose it."

**SAY:** "Rescore is what it sounds like: a score sheet. You'll score your own drawing and writing samples. For  instance, count the number of words in the Preliminary Writing and then count the number of words in the Closing Writing and compare them. One sample may have more words than the other. Then, decide which sample is better: the one with more words or fewer words? You might decide that the Drawing/Writing program has not improved your writing. This is your decision. Only you know if your writing has improved. Just because a teacher says your writing has improved does not provide enough information. From your point of view, the teacher may be wrong."

**REMEMBER:** Counting is an easy point of departure for the challenge of self-evaluation. Rescore demonstrates that a quantitative analysis using counting can be extremely useful as a springboard into a more difficult category of qualitative analysis. Rescore proceduralizes this move. Columns provide spaces to tally items. A list of questions encourages students to interpret the meaning behind the numbers.

**REMEMBER:** I have found that the Preliminary Drawing and Writing of a student—or a student's initial entry in a Drawing/Writing journal—immediately gives me a way to appreciate students, especially the ones who lack verbal skills. Samples of student drawing and writing provide teachers with powerful tools for diagnosis and assessment. Students who draw well but who cannot write, read or speak well have a chance to show intelligence through drawing. A demonstration of skillful drawing changes a teacher's attitude, encouraging the teacher to redouble his efforts to reach these students. A teaching strategy which includes drawing protects non-verbal or reclusive students from being neglected or discarded by the educational system. Drawing also prevents students from abandoning their education themselves.

Intelligence, training, assessment and diagnosis constitute a continuum. They intersect continuously. Students build skills over time. Intelligence is developable and assessable as a dynamic entity. At this point in social and educational history, it is sound practice to assume that demonstrable intelligence and the learning environment are directly related.

[CONTINUED ON THE NEXT LEFTHAND PAGE]

**SAY/DO:** "Get two Rescore sheets. One is for classwork. One is for homework. Let's start with the writing section. Count the number of words in the Preliminary Writing. Count the words in the Closing Writing. Is there a change in overall number of words?

Now count your nouns in Preliminary Writing, now, in the Closing Writing. Do the same with verbs, adjectives, adverbs. Mark SV for strong verbs, and SA for strong adjectives. For instance, the adjectives 'pretty' or 'nice' are weak; they are over-used and imprecise. They do not tell us much. 'A calico cat' is more descriptive than 'a pretty cat.' In the same way, the verb form 'is' might not express much. 'The cat *lounges* on the couch is more descriptive than the phrase 'the cat is on the couch.'"

**DISCUSSION:** Encourage students to identify strong verbs and weak verbs, strong adjectives and weak adjectives.

**RECORD:** Write these lists on the board. Examples:

| weak verbs: | stronger verbs: | weak or imprecise adjectives: |
|---|---|---|
| relates to | connects | weird |
| has to do with | springs | cool |
| refers to | returns | pretty |

**SAY/DO:** "Take the Preliminary Drawing and Writing out of your folders and use Rescore to score it. Then take your Closing Drawing and Writing and use Rescore to score it. Fill in all of the spaces. Answer all of the questions. Share your Rescore findings with your peer."

**PEER SHARE:**

**GROUP CRITIQUE:** This critique will be especially powerful. Students will see dramatic changes in their drawing. Changes in writing may be equally dramatic but not as obvious.

The key to the power of Drawing/Writing is this: it is easy to develop powerful drawing skills. It is harder to develop powerful writing skills. It is easy to see changes in drawing skills. It is harder to see changes in writing skills. A student can easily self-evaluate when it comes to drawing. It is harder for a student to self-evaluate when it comes to writing. By using a simpler analysis to lead into a more difficult one, Drawing/Writing facilitates and enhances the process. A Drawing/Writing critique reveals changes in drawing skills and in writing skills in general ways, then in specific ways. As students take over the assessment process, their investment in drawing and writing—or literacy—rises.

This does not mean that teachers must stay mute or never provide grades. It does mean that criteria for grading must be clear and include quantitative and qualitative criteria, and that grading can largely be handled by the students themselves.

**SAY:** "Take your Preliminary Drawing and Writing and your Closing Drawing and Writing. Use the evaluation sheet called Rescore to help compare these two samples. Let's count first and analyze second. If you need help with a part of speech, ask your peer or we can open a general class discussion. Rescore will help you to see how your drawing and writing skills have changed."

**PEER SHARE:** Preliminary Drawing and Writing and Closing Drawing and Writing, and Rescore results.

**GROUP CRITIQUE:** Preliminary and Closing samples of Drawing/Writing. Every student sees every other student's gains. Mutual praise abounds.

In some student work, there is a special clarity to both drawing and writing. This combined clarity shows a highly functional mind, both logical and expressive. Some students show clarity only in their drawings. It is more rare to find a student who writes well but who has very weak drawing skills. Strong drawing and writing skills are often paired.

These are the categories I have identified:

- High visual and verbal skills: an ability to record information accurately and completely, both visually and verbally. An ability to organize information clearly is shown through accurate, expressive drawing <u>and</u> writing. Sometimes student writing—just because it is well-formed—looks more cogent than it is. A quick reading will reveal a lack of accuracy or specificity.
- Strong visual skills, weak verbal skills. In this case, the drawing is accurate but there is much less writing, and the writing itself is messy, illegible or hesitant.
- Strong verbal skills, weak visual skills. Weak drawing skills usually respond to training and can be improved quickly and dramatically by teaching the student how to pay attention.
- Scattered but bright. This kind of Drawing/Writing sample is messy; visually and verbally, it goes all over the page. Once you are able to decode what has been written and take the time to talk about the drawing with the student, it becomes clear that these students are capable; they may simply need some attentional/organizational tools. They may have a way of working that is inaccessible to you but which works for them and which may produce unusual results. The inventive quality of these images and text is one predictor. Messiness can prejudice our evaluations and obscure the actual content of the writing in particular.
- Able but LD or ADD. This student may draw well but may not be able to write much, due to attentional problems, or to what have been labeled as dysgraphic or motoric problems with writing. It is highly unlikely that a student who draws well has motoric, small muscle problems. Learning about the relationships between drawing and writing—even the near equivalency underscored by the slash used between Drawing/Writing—may remediate some language-related problems. On the other hand, the problem may relate to genuine brain-based problems with encoding and decoding languages and require long term remediation.
- Spare marks, little *detectable* effort. This kind of Drawing/Writing sample may show the "lazy" or bored or disaffected student. Or it may not. I have italicized the word "detectable" for a reason. There can be many reasons for spare, faint drawing and writing marks. Students may lack confidence, training, energy or all three. Seeming disengagement in school may have nothing to do with stupidity. If a student is relatively well nourished and emotionally sound, and is still disaffected, this student might simply need to be presented with:

    1) an engaging task that is understood to be worthwhile and relevant or
    2) an attentional strategy.

    Visual searches of interest are natural attention-getters. Many students require basic training in self-directed learning. This training can be introduced through drawing. Once interest is engaged and confidence levels rise, students will show sustained focus, effort, will and investment. It is impossible to overestimate the power of drawing to engage even the most miserable and hostile mind.
- There is one final group. An extremely capable student may turn out a series of sketchy, minimal drawings and writings in response to time constraints. You cannot assume that a capable drawing student has become lazy. They may be making judicious decisions about time and energy. The only way to find out what is going on is to ask the student directly about the apparent lack of skill in the work and to encourage them to draw smaller sections of works since you both know their skills are superior.

Besides using Rescore, students use a check-list for completeness to assess their Drawing/Writing portfolios. Make as many copies of the check-list for the in-class and at-home portfolios as you need. Students will need two copies of Rescore and two check-lists to evaluate in-class and at-home portfolios.

## 6.3 What Drawing/Writing Does

Drawing/Writing establishes ground rules for conduct where the common goal is everyone's improved literacy skills. By everyone, I mean the native English speakers and the non-native English speakers, the more attentive and the less attentive, the more visual and the less visual, the more verbal and the less verbal, athletes and intellectuals, the rich, the poor and the middle class student, the dreamer and the literal-minded, the gifted and the apparently giftless.

There are many ramifications to the Drawing/Writing program. Some are pedagogical, some are psychological, some are cognitive, some are philosophical, some are behavioral. If the goal is the development of the whole jperson, how could it be otherwise?

Be ready to be patient. The program moves slowly. Be ready to listen to student conversation. It will take time for them to learn to speak. Remain open.

At first, you may feel hesitant about teaching Drawing/Writing, apprehensive about trying this program for the first time. I wish I could be with you as I have been with so many teachers for so many years. In every step of these instructions, my good wishes go with you and I, in a sense, go with you.

Until now, I have avoided that over-worked word "empowerment," but that word describes the overall effect of Drawing/Writing. With a little bit of instruction, everyone can learn to draw well. The ability to draw well lends its energy to the task and the privilege of writing. Drawing well, writing well, thinking well require practice. Like a muscle, the brain needs exercise. Repeated sessions with Drawing/Writing provide benefits to the brain, as a good workout provides ongoing benefits to the body. Mature artists do not stop figure-drawing. Mature writers do not stop daily writing. Readers keep reading. The brain demands the equivalent of the StairMaster, the Nautilus, the daily jog, the energetic arm-swinging-walk to remain keen. If students become restive with repeated sessions of Drawing/Writing, ask, "Would you stop your physical exercise program?"

From birth, babies thrive on intelligent, engaged conversation. This exposure to a constant stream of language is crucial for future abstract reasoning skills. Increasingly, we are learning how and when children learn best. Although we still cannot see exactly what is going on in the "black box" of the brain, brain research is giving us a better picture. As teachers, parents, and other mentors, we can observe knowing nods, and confident hands. We can note increasing levels of mutual respect. We can appreciate improvements in drawing, writing, reading, and speaking skills.

Still, we can never be sure how students themselves evaluate their own mental powers. Drawing gives students a window and a mirror, clarifying their vision of themselves as literate human beings.

## 6.4 Why Teach Drawing/Writing

Because of rapid change, the distance between teachers' worlds and students' worlds is increasing. My religious experiences will not "do" for my students anymore than my experiences as a woman growing up in the world will "do" for my adult daughters. When I teach church architecture, I do not assume that my students have any experience of churches or of religion. I can describe church architecture with words and slides, I can share some feelings about my own religious experience, but, most usefully, I can show my art history students plans of subterranean Western European "womb-tombs" from 3000 b.c. e (Gimbutas, 1989, p. 253) which set the precedent for axial church layouts. Beyond comparing wombs and tombs and Western Church axial architecture, I encourage my students to describe what they consider religious experiences. For many of them, "church" and "religious experience" are associated with the wilderness, tall trees, mountaintops, or the ocean, and do not depend upon vaulted ceilings, ambulatories, radiating chapels, stained glass, or liturgy.

*Closing Drawing and Writing, Pamela Frigo, Fire bellows, Continuing Education, Westfield State, 1996*

Pamela Frigo, Closing Writing, bellows, 1996

My closing drawing is an object I feel has many beautiful shapes, variety of line and tonal value. The bellow has such charm and dignity.

My object is like a bull making a deep hollow sound. It calls out in a deep voice as it becomes angry, its nose presses together thereby drawing in air and then expelling it. The bellow is sadness, crying out loudly in anger and pain.

My object reflects light more from the top left side. It seems to become darker on the right side toward the bottom. The bellow contains few Euclidean shapes and also has a free flowingness to it. It is wide at one end and tapered more at the other.

In this closing drawing color is used freely and it contributes to making this drawing balanced. Also contributing is the light, mediums and darks.

## 6.5  How to Grade a Session of Drawing/Writing

**Note:  Rescore and portfolio checklists are provided at the end of this section.**

1) **Rescore** – each student must fill out two Rescore sheets, one for Preliminary Drawing and Writing, Closing Drawing and Writing, in-class portfolio and one for Preliminary Drawing and Writing and Closing Drawing and Writing, at-home portfolio. Count up number of items on the Rescore sheet. Students have to add up the number of items they responded to. That number over the total number of items will give them a score.

> Rescore sheet #1 for portfolio #1 = % completed
>
> Rescore sheet #2 for portfolio #2 = % completed

2) **Checklists** – ·

> **Portfolio #1** – Decide how many points per drawing and piece of writing, including the shared class vocabulary and powerful ideas recorded in Drawing/Writing notebooks. Give drawings a certain number of points. Give writing a certain number of points. Ask students whether the drawings and writings should be weighed equally? Count up number of drawings and multiply by number of points. Do the same for writing. Add the two totals.
>
> **Portfolio #2** – same as above

3) **Attendance** – Count up how many classes and decide how many points per class.

4) **Class participation** - Decide scale, say, 1-20. This means how much students participated as peers in peer pairs and in group critiques and discussions.

5) **Add up the points items 1-4 with your students.** Say the total is 500 points.

6) **Ask students to add up the points in items 1-4 for each of their portfolios, attendance and participation.**

> Say this score is 400.
>
> GRADE:  $\dfrac{400}{500}$ = 80% or a B–

**SAY:** "Here is your portfolio check list. You will need two lists: one for the in-class portfolio and one for the at-home portfolio.

Check off the work in each portfolio, using list #1 for portfolio #1. See what is missing. Do the same with portfolio #2. How many drawings are missing? Say 3. If each drawing is worth 5 points, you are down 3 x 5 = 15 points.

How many pieces of writing are missing? Say 4. If each writing is worth 5 points, then you are down 4 x 5 = 20 points.

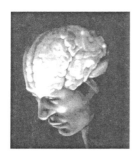

Check your Rescore sheets. Are both complete? Good.

If the total points for portfolios and Rescore sheets is 500 points, and you subtract 35 points from 500, you get 465 divided by 500 or 93%.

Now, ask students to figure out their attendance and participation. If a student came to every class and participated with his/her peer and in group critiques every day, her/his grade is 93%. She/he has earned the grade of 93%."

**TIP:** Students will slave over these lists. This scoring and grading makes sense to them. They are willing to do it to make sure it is done right. There are no arguments with the teacher after this constructivist grading. Because students decide the number of points for their portfolios, points may differ from class to class. This does not make a difference. The fact that students create and follow the agreed-upon point system on their own is the important point.

**TIP:** Scoring the drawing is as important as scoring the writing. For some teachers and students, the drawing sheet may seem irrelevant. If the overall goal is visual literacy as well as verbal literacy, both sets of skills require evaluation.

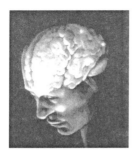

# Rescore: Writing

**Student name:** _____          **Date:** _____

<u>PRELIMINARY WRITING</u>          <u>CLOSING WRITING</u>

number of words

number of nouns

number of adjectives: Strong or weak?

number of verbs: active or passive? Strong or weak?

number of adverbs

number of similes

number of metaphors

number of predictions

number of hypotheses

number of analogies

number of phrases

number of clauses

number of sentences

number of paragraphs

# of periods

# of commas

# of semi-colons

# of colons

# of dashes

# of quotation marks

# of italics

# of apostrophes

**Has your writing changed?**   Yes?  No?  *(Circle one)*

**How has your writing changed?**

Quantitative: more

>       Did you write *more* words?   Yes?   No?

>       If you used more words, more of what kinds of words or constructions?

Qualitative: more

> Did you use words *better*?   Yes?   No?
>
> How did you use words better? Were the nouns more unusual? Verbs or adjectives stronger?
>
> What part of speech did you use more? For instance, more adjectives?
>
> What do you think this change in numbers means about your writing?

Quantitative: less

> Did you write **less**?   Yes?   No?
>
> If less, less of *what* words or constructions?

Qualitative: less

> Is writing less words better writing? Why?

**Has drawing helped your writing?**   Yes?   No?

If drawing has helped, how has it helped?

1. Is the overall outline of your idea clearer?

2. Are the basic components or "shapes" in your writing well chosen, well defined, whether these shapes are sentences, paragraphs, chapters, stanzas?

3. Are there major spotlit ideas as well as minor ideas that are in shadow? Are there ideas hidden in shadow? Can you see the strong themes and still appreciate the lesser themes, and subtleties?

4. Does the piece of writing hold together word to word, phrase to phrase, sentence to sentence, paragraph to paragraph, chapter to chapter, unit to unit?

5. Does the piece of writing make a creative leap? Does it pull or drag away certain interesting items from the original topic and turn them into something else? If so, how did you do this?

6. Do you think you are gaining voice? If so, how would you define this personal style?

# Rescore: Drawing

**Student name:** _____    **Date:** _____

                        <u>PRELIMINARY DRAWING</u>          <u>CLOSING DRAWING</u>

**Use of line**        tentative, bold
                       inaccurate, accurate
                       hasty, sensitive
                       few lines, many lines

**Use of shapes**      geometric
                       organic
                       repeating
                       tentative, bold
                       inaccurate, accurate
                       hasty, sensitive
                       few shapes, many shapes

**Use of value**       subtle contrast, strong contrast
                       few lights, mediums, darks
                       many lights, mediums, darks
                       soft-edged transition
                       hard-edged transition

**Use of detail**      few, many
                       inaccurate, accurate
                       poorly chosen
                       well chosen
                       distracting
                       descriptive

**Negative space**     Is the space around the object thoughtfully perceived?
                       Do negative and positive spaces balance each other?

**Have your drawing skills changed?**    Yes?  No?

Quantitative:

   Are there more or less lines in the 2nd drawing?

   Are there more or less shapes in the 2nd drawing? Do the shapes combine several kinds of geometry? What
      kinds? Do any shapes repeat at different scales? Is there a fractal element in the drawing?

   Are there more or less shapes for light, medium and dark areas in the 2nd drawing?

   Are the shapes for value soft-edged or hard-edged? Is there strong contrast, or subtle contrast between values?

Are there more or less details in the second drawing?

If there are more details, are they helpful in describing the object more fully?

Are there more or less lines, shapes, colors <u>overall</u> in the 2nd drawing?

Is there better use of space in the second drawing?

How would you rate the first drawing in terms of realism on a scale of 1-10?

How would you rate the second drawing in terms of realism on a scale of 1-10?

Qualitative: How have your drawings changed?

1. Accuracy of contour, expressivity of contour. Are the lines stronger, surer, more pleasing, more striking, more descriptive <u>in an emotional way</u> of the object? That is, are they more expressive?

2. Accuracy of basic shapes, expressivity of basic shapes. Are these shapes more descriptive of the object? Are the shapes more emotional?

3. Accuracy of values, expressivity of values. Is value handled more descriptively in the 2nd drawing? Is value used more emotionally? How? What emotion?

4. Accuracy of details? Are the details more descriptive? Do they carry emotion? What emotion?

5. Overall impact. Is the 2nd drawing more realistic? How?

6. Is there better integration of line, form, space, details in the second drawing?

7. If there is too much in drawing 1, where is it?

    If there is too little in drawing 1, where is it?

    If there is too much in drawing 2, where is it?

    If there is too little in drawing 2, where is it?

8. Is the second drawing better compositionally? Is it better balanced? How?

What kind of emotion, if any, do you get from your first drawing?

What kind of emotion, if any, do you get from your second drawing?

How would you describe the first drawing in terms of emotional power?

How would you describe the second drawing in terms of emotional power?

If students compare an earlier with a later CA, these questions can be answered:

1. To what degree does this CA meet the requirements "neither too much nor too little?"

How would you change this CA to meet these requirements?

2. Do any shapes overlap in this CA?

3. Do any shapes go off the format in this CA?

4. Does this CA have diagonals, horizontals, verticals? How many of each?

5. Does this CA include a combination of organic and geometric shapes?

6. Is color important in this CA? What colors do you use?

7. Is line, shape or color more important to this CA?

8. Is there a variety of line weights in this CA?

9. Is there a variety of shapes and sizes of shapes in this CA?

10. Does this CA have power, balance, variety, interest? What kind of power? Where do you see balance? Where do you see Variety? Where do you see interest? Where do you see meaning?

## OVERALL:

Do you think you are developing a personal style in drawing? How would you describe this style?

Do you think writing helped your drawing?   Yes?   No?

How did writing help your drawing? Did it help the drawing become:

more accurate

more descriptive

more metaphorical or symbolic

more realistic

more abstract

more powerful

more expressive

other?

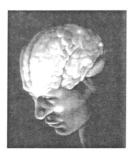

# Portfolio Checklist

1)  **Preliminary Drawing and Writing** (the roughly timed samples of drawing and writing). Labeled, dated, signed.

2)  **Step 1: THE CONTOUR DRAWING**

    a.  **Blind Contour drawing.** Labeled, dated, signed. The sentence that begins, "My Blind Contour drawing tells me that....because...." One simile using the word "because," and one metaphor using the word "because."

    b.  **Regular Contour drawing.** Labeled, dated, signed. The sentence that begins, "My Regular Contour drawing tells me that...because...." One simile using "because." One metaphor using "because."

3)  **Step 2: BASIC GEOMETRIC SHAPES**

    a.  Euclidean Basic Shape drawing. Labeled, dated, signed. The sentence that begins, "My Regular Contour drawing tells me that...because...." One simile using the word "because." One metaphor using the word "because."

    b.  Fractal Basic Shape drawing. Labeled, signed and dated. "My Fractal Basic Shape drawing tells me that...because...." One Simile, one metaphor, as above.

    c.  Organic Basic Shape drawing. Labeled, signed, dated. "My Organic Basic Shape drawing tells me that my object is ....because...." One simile using "because." One metaphor using "because."

4)  **Step 3: THE LIGHT-MEDIUM-DARK OR LMD DRAWING**

    Labeled, signed, dated. The sentence that beings, "My LMD drawing tells me that my object is...because...." One simile using the word "because." One metaphor using the word "because."

5)  **Step 4: THE "PERFECT" WHOLE**

    Patterns of Practice writing

    7 major drawings

    DRAWING #1. **The "Perfect Whole" Drawing.** Labeled, signed, dated. The sentence that begins, "My 'Perfect' Whole Drawing tells me that my object is....because...."

    **Write: SIMILE AND METAPHOR**

        Five concrete sensory similes with because:

        My object feels like...because....

        My object looks like...because....

        My object tastes like...because....

        My object sounds like...because....

        My object smells like ...because....

DRAWING #2. Draw one of the Concrete Sensory similes. Label, date, sign. Write: what does this drawing tell about the object.

**Write:**

Five abstract sensory,, similes with because

One concrete sensory metaphor with because

One abstract sensory metaphor with because

One negative concrete sensory simile with because

One negative concrete sensory metaphor with because

One negative abstract sensory simile with because

One negative abstract sensory metaphor with because

**Write: ANALOGY:**

One positive concrete analogy with because

One positive abstract analogy with because

One negative concrete analogy with because

One negative abstract analogy

DRAWING #3. Draw a concrete or an abstract positive analogy. Label, date, sign. Include both your object and the thing or relationship to which you are comparing it.

**Write: SPECULATION** – using the words *might, could*

one positive concrete speculation

one positive abstract speculation

one negative concrete speculation

one negative abstract speculation

DRAWING #4.  Draw a concrete or abstract positive speculation as above.

**Write: PREDICTION** – using the word *will*

one positive concrete prediction

one positive abstract prediction

one negative concrete prediction

one negative abstract prediction

DRAWING #5.  Draw a prediction as above

**Write: HYPOTHESIS** – using *if...then*

one positive concrete hypothesis

one positive abstract hypothesis

one negative concrete hypothesis

one negative abstract hypothesis

DRAWING #6.  Draw a hypothesis as above.

6) **Step #5: The Composite Abstraction**

   **Write: COMPOSITE ABSTRACTION**

   DRAWING #7.  CA#1

   "My CA#1 tells me that because...."

   DRAWING #8. CA#2

   Write: CA #2: "My CA#2 tells me that...because...." Write a simile and a metaphor using because.
   Write how CA#2 and simile and metaphor relate to your object ("Referential" writing).

7) **Closing Drawing and Writing.**

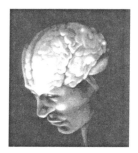

# HITCHHIKERS' GUIDE
# TO BRAIN SCIENCE

*Hitchhiking on the corpus callosal highway, Samuel Sheridan, 1997*

# PART THREE

## *Guide to the Brain: Use It or Lose It*

A thumbnail sketch of brain structure and process with tips and suggestions for WholeBrain education.

**3.1  Gross Process and Structure**
    **Evolution**

**3.2  Fine Structure and Process**
    **Development**

**3.3  The Eye**

**3.4  Language**

**3.5  The Growing Brain**
    **Educational Implications: Tips and Suggestions**
    **Health Implications:  How to Use It or Lose It**

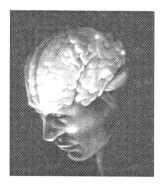

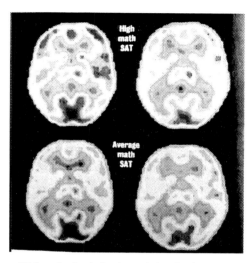

*Bi-hemispheric brain activity, brain scan*

## Objectives:

- To provide enough basic information about brain structure and process for students, parents, teachers and independent learners to appreciate brain-based strategies like Drawing/Writing and to understand the degree to which the learner is in control of the learning process.

- To provide enough information about how the brain grows and flourishes for learners to take control of the learning process. The fact that the actions and attitudes of learners themselves influence how their brains function is powerful information, particularly for students who have been under-educated or who have run up against roadblocks to learning.

- To provide an alternative approach to traditional drug-education programs by explaining what drugs do at the micro level while suggesting why natural highs achieved through communication and expression at the macro level are not only safe but satisfying.

- To encourage alternatives to loud and/or violent entertainment. If students know how their brains receive and process information, they can make better decisions about how to treat their sense receptors. For instance, they may choose to maintain their hearing by monitoring and controlling decibels of sound. Students can learn to discriminate among the stimuli they allow into their brains through their eyes, ears, mouths, noses, hands and bloodstream.

Learners who embark on the Drawing/Writing program will benefit by knowing the following:

- the brain is bilateral—structurally and procedurally (it has two sides which operate in more or less distinguishable ways).
- the brain is unified—structurally and procedurally (it is a densely interconnected unit which operates globally).
- the brain can be encouraged and trained to work more efficiently and more cooperatively.
- students can control how their brains grow by picking and choosing among learning experiences as simple organisms do.

Organisms usually move toward nutrients and away from poisons. By learning more about what happens at the synapse, we higher level organisms may be able to recognize and avoid destructive or constrictive experiences and damaging substances.

## Materials:

- A model of the brain.

You might borrow one from the biology department, but as a Drawing/Writing teacher you will need a model of the brain. You will also need a slide or a color photo of a computer-imaged brain doing work, showing bilateral and global metabolic activity. Even though the MRI[25] image above is in black and white, making its color-coded information about metabolic activity unavailable to the reader, the double-sided nature of the human brain is clear. No matter what the work—drawing, reading, writing, mathematics—the whole brain lights up. Point to matching lighted areas on each side. Remind your students that each half of the brain helps the other with its work.

---

[25] MRI: Magnetic Resonance Imaging. MRIs are non-invasive. They create fine-tuned, real-time maps of brain activity by tracking oxygenated hemoglobin in high magnetic fields. Oxygenated blood has not yet been depleted by the working brain. De-oxygenated hemoglobin has, and, like oxygenated blood, it exhibits specific magnetic properties. By mapping replete and depleted hemoglobin, MRIs show where the brain has expended energy and where it has not. Inferences about brain activity may be made from these maps (Fite, 1993).

MRIs differ from PET: Positron Emission Tomography. PET is an invasive, expensive, problematic procedure that uses radioactive agents to describe rates of glucose metabolism. Glucose is the metabolic fuel used by active cells. By determining where glucose metabolism is highest, observations can be made about the amount of work done by that part of the brain (Fite, 1993).

Because the two hemispheres specialize in their particular approaches to processing information and constructing meaning—the right hemisphere specializes in spatial processing while the left specializes in linguistic processing—the net result is a rich, blended interpretation. MRI images of brains doing work clearly demonstrate this bilateral yet global activity. The Drawing/Writing process makes this blended exchange conscious and overt for students.

Pass the brain model around the classroom so that students can feel it and take it apart. Point out the corpus callosum, a C-shaped strip above the mid-brain and below the neocortex which joins the left and right hemispheres.

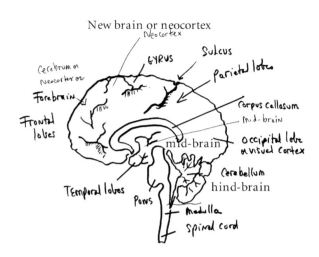

*Cross-section, tri-part, labeled with arrows indicating the corpus callosum, the hind-brain or reptilian brain, mid-brain or mammalian brain, and new brain or neocortex or forebrain or cerebrum, with gyri and sulci, SRS.*

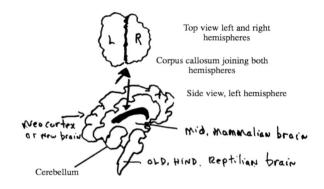

*Cross-section, left and right hemispheres with corpus callosum*

Point out the hind-brain, cerebellum, mid- and forebrain as sub-sections. In evolutionary terms, the brain stem was the first brain, controlling autonomic functions like heart rate and breathing. The mid- or mammalian brain evolved next, then, the cerebrum, including the neocortex. The densely folded cortex is the "bark" or outer layer of the brain. Gyri and sulci—hummocks and fissures, or furrowed rows like plowed fields—allow the one square metre of neocortical brain tissue to be tightly enfolded. The folding brings networks close together.

Using the information provided in the pictures on this page, discuss how the brain constructed itself over time as well as how students' own brains construct themselves over a lifetime. Copy the following drawings for students and ask them to copy them in the Drawing/Writing vocabulary and concepts journals they will use doing the five-step process.

Draw a neuron with its axon, dendrites and synapses as represented below. Ask students to copy your drawing.

Show students the David Macauley drawing of the hurley-burley of inter-synaptic space where neurons

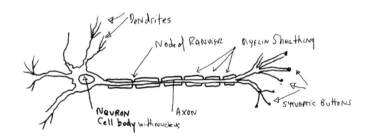

*A neuron with axon, myelin, dendrites, SRS, '97.*

*Intersynaptic space*

From: **The Amazing Brain** by Robert Ornstein, Richard Thompson and David Macaulay. Illustrations copyright (c) 1984 by David A. Macaulay. Reprinted by permission of Houghton Mifflin Co. All rights reserved.

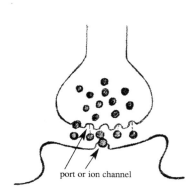

*Synapse, Tim Lis, 1997*

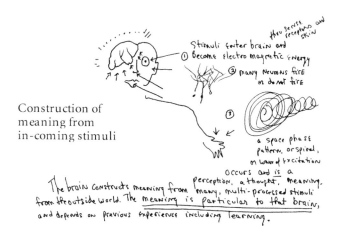

Construction of
meaning from
in-coming stimuli

*Electromagnetic process, SRS*

communicate via an avalanche of chemicals. Discuss the idea that ports, or ion channels, open and close at these points of contact between neurons, releasing and absorbing chemicals.

Now, share the following information.

## 3.1 Gross Process and Structure

### Cross-modal, electrochemical processes

Most information enters the brain through more than one sensory system. I may see your face and hear your voice at the same time. Or, I may see you and touch your shoulder at the same time. Because the human body is multi-sensory and because the brain is bihemispheric, incoming information is multi-modal the instant it enters the brain. Then, despite the form of energy in which it arrived—for instance, visual information arrives as electromagnetic energy—the brain converts the stimuli into a common coinage: electrochemical energy. Meaning is constructed only after incoming stimuli are processed many times by many brain areas, resulting in a global summing of the combined firings and non-firings of a vast array of connected neurons.

This book uses the term cross-modal to describe the exchange that occurs between the two hemispheres of the brain; this use of the term cross-modal *presupposes* that information coming into the brain is multi-sensory, or cross-sensory. Drawing/Writing deliberately models cross-modal interhemispheric exchange as training for intelligent thought by engineering a deliberate exchange of information between drawing and writing. In the case of Drawing/Writing, the common coinage of thought is a stream of sustained attention rather than a stream of ions and electrons.

### Gross structure—evolutionary

The brain is a tri-part structure which includes four major regulatory systems: the autonomic breathing/heartbeat/blood pressure system, the sleep/wake/appetite system, the emotional/sexual system, and the evaluative/reasoning system. All systems contribute to thoughts and meaning.

The human brain evolved over millennia, adding parts, like rooms to a house.

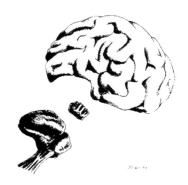

*The tri-part, segmented brain, Tim Lis, 1997*

1) The cold-blooded reptilian brain, or hind brain, or brain stem, evolved more than five hundred million years ago. The brain stem controls autonomic functions, including breathing, blood pressure, and body temperature.

   Attached to the brain stem is the cerebellum, or little brain, a structure that fine-tunes balance and movements in space. Learned actions, like tying shoelaces, are stored in the cerebellum, but it is also capable of contributing to higher-level decisions about what to do once your shoelaces are tied.

2) The mammalian brain, or mid-brain, sits on top of and enfolds the reptilian brain. It evolved about 300 million years ago; much of its informational input is olfactory, based on smell. The mammalian brain includes the diencephalon which is the locus of sleep and appetite, and the limbic system. The limbic system is the locus of sexual behavior and instinctual emotions like nurturing, rage and fear.

3) The top or outer level of the brain is the cerebrum, or the neocortex. The neocortex—or "new bark"—developed more than four million years ago. It looks like scrambled eggs and is densely enfolded. The neocortex is about one-eighth of an inch thick and, if spread out, would cover about a square yard—the size of a baby blanket or a road map. Tightly packed, convoluted folds allow the appreciable surface area of this information-processing tissue to fit into the skull, a cavity about the size of a medium saucepan.

The cerebrum includes the two hemispheres joined by a strip of tissue called the corpus callosum, or "thick body." Think of a callus on your thumb or the phrase "callow youth" or the adjective "callous," as in a callous comment—meaning unfeeling or insensitive or thick-skinned.

Each hemisphere is divided into four lobes:

- the occipital lobes or visual cortex—at the *ob caput,* or "back of" the "head"

- the temporal lobes or auditory cortex—at the temples, or forward sides of the brain

- the frontal lobes, commonly accepted as responsible for executive functions like planning, deciding, purposeful behavior—at the front of the brain

- and the parietal lobes (*paries* means "wall," or "side"), said to function as assemblers, allowing us, among other things, to put together letters in words and words in thoughts—at the sides of the brain.

The lateral (*latus* means "side" or "flank"), or two-sided, specialization of the brain occurred between one and four million years ago, creating a division of labor. The left hemisphere took over control of the right side of the body and eventually specialized in linguistic processing. The right hemisphere took over control of the left side of the body and eventually specialized in spatial processing.

Generally, the left hemisphere is somewhat larger than the right. One enlarged frontal area of the left hemisphere, especially in males, is the planum temporale. This area facilitates speech and written language and is targeted as one area where difficulties with writing and reading may occur.

If either hemisphere is damaged, the intact hemisphere may assume lost functions. This ability to assume functions usually assigned to the other hemisphere is called equipotentiality, and it diminishes over time as the brain becomes more "specialized" or "lateralized." Female brains remain equipotential longer and are, in general, less lateralized than male brains. If one side of a female brain loses function, the other side may assume lost functions more quickly and completely than in a male brain.

The cerebrum, including the neocortex, is protected by the meninges, or "envelopes" containing fluid. Like water, cerebro-spinal fluid is nearly incompressible, acting as a shock absorber, cushioning the brain. The bony layer of skull encasing the meninges provides additional protection from injury. The blood-brain barrier protects the brain internally from certain substances. However, it is not foolproof; chemicals masquerading as familiar neurotransmitters can sneak past this barrier, wreaking havoc on occasion by convincing the brain that it is beyond all society's rules, or that it hears voices giving it highly worrisome and often dangerous information, or that the body in which it is housed can fly. On the other hand, useful chemicals which adjust incorrect neurochemistry can be introduced, allowing the brain to construct more accurate representations for that particular mind.

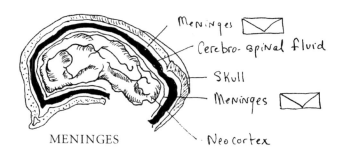

Meninges
Cerebro-spinal fluid
Skull
Meninges
Neocortex

MENINGES

*The meninges, SRS 97*

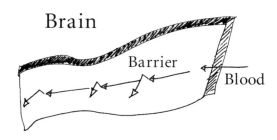

Brain

Barrier

Blood

*The blood-brain barrier, SRS 97*

## Gross process

### Interhemispheric transfer

*The Chinese Horse, Lascaux, France.*

To introduce the idea of inter-hemispheric transfer, refer to the image of "The Chinese Horse" in Part 1. The cave drawing is a unified statement: it is like an illustration with captions which allows the reader—then and now—to interpret the horse at the right level—probably as female and pregnant. The brain is organized to make unified statements, too. Ask students to point out the two different kinds of marks in this image: the drawing marks and the more abstract proto-writing marks. Discuss the fact that the brain has myriad possibilities for representing information with and beyond images and words. For instance, mathematical symbols and musical notation can be learned and used to expand and sharpen meaning.

### The bicameral brain in a bipedal body

Bicameral brain in a bipedal body

R        L

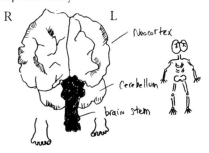

Neocortex
Cerebellum
brain stem

*The bicameral, bipedal brain, SRS*

Like the brains of other great apes, human brains evolved in response to changing circumstances. When our aboriginal ancestors exchanged leafy habitats in dense rain forests for vast, open savannahs—a momentous move occasioned by climate and curiosity—humanoid brains changed. Bipedal, upright location freed our hands (our knuckles no longer dragged on the ground and our thumbs became "opposed" for fine-tuned gripping) and vast vistas challenged our near-distance, forest eyes. All of these factors reorganized our brains.

Upright locomotion created a problem: as a result of supporting the entire weight of the body on only two legs, rather than on two legs and two leg-like arms with feet-like hands, the human pelvis thickened and the birth canal narrowed. To be born, large-brained babies had to arrive prematurely. If human babies waited for their brains to be, say, the size of a chimp's relative to an adult chimpanzee brain, they would be birthable only via Caesarean section. At birth, the brain of a chimp is nearly 50% of its adult weight while the brain of a human baby is about 25%. Consequently, baby chimps can move around like grown-up chimps while human babies are nearly helpless at birth. Human brains do most of their growing outside the uterus, subject to experience.

*Chimp*                          *Babies*

*Reprinted by permission of Dover Pictorial Archive Series (c) 1969 Dover Publication, Inc.*

The evolutionary process is conservative. Instead of throwing things away, it saves them. The hind-, mid-, and forebrains—reptilian, mammalian, and highly evolved including human—did not displace each other; they grew on top of each other, like fungus on trees. Each brain was retained for its original functions. The old reptilian brain is still used for autonomic functions like heartbeat. The middle or mammalian brain still

generates emotions and regulates sleep and waking, while the neocortex and the lobes of the cerebrum make abstract thought including language possible.

The brain is a relay system. It receives, transports, translates, and interprets information. The act of shunting information back and forth between the two hemispheres is achieved by a strip of nerve-rich tissue called the corpus callosum. The corpus callosum changes information. A larva crawling onto a leaf and flying off as a butterfly achieves a transformation no more marvelous than inter-hemispheric transfer.

*Butterfly, SRS*

What cave paintings reveal is that between 25,000 and 15,000 years ago, the two hemispheres of the brain were interacting, producing both drawing and proto-writing. The corpus callosum is not a passive conduit, like a drainage ditch; it facilitates the comparison and translatation of information. Its activity contributes to the work of an "interpretor" or "comparator, " 1980's terms for the agency of thought (Changeux, 1985; Gazzaniga, 1985). Currently, chaos theory provides another explananation. Bursts of electrical discharges, traveling in wave-like patterns, generate spirals, producing the actual physical/electrical shapes of thoughts (Freeman, 1991). These are called phase portraits (Freeman, 1991).

*Drawing from a photo of a "phase portrait" of olfactory processing in animals. "The Physiology of Perception" by Walter J. Freeman and Peter Broadhead, Scientific American, Feb. 11, 1991, p. 78.*
*Permission by author. All rights reserved.*

*Cats, Dogs, Us*

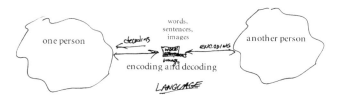

*Moving from inner speech through the tiny box of shared language, Valerie Faith.*

What makes humans distinct from other warm-blooded creatures is not just a bihemispheric brain: great apes and dogs and cats have bihemispheric brains. It is *where* the human brain is large and *how* the larger parts of the human brain are used that makes us different from other thinking creatures. Procedurally, how we use language symbolically sets us apart. We do more than create intelligent, intentional sounds, gestures and territorial marks. The range of our marks and sounds distinguish us from other creatures with eyes, bicameral brains, neo-cortices, and language systems. Most importantly, the symbolic use of language distinguishes us from other intelligent creatures.

The draw-er draws for herself. Still, her work is meant to be seen. As a writer, she speaks as if to herself, using inner speech. But, again, she means to be heard. Arduously, she translates this inner speech to a communication intended for her reader. The reader receives this information by applying her own inner code. Communication occurs in the *act* of encoding and in the *act* of decoding. When information is given and received, language systems meet and interact (Faith, 1989).

In whatever ways meaning occurs between neural nets, hemispheres, and people, communication is a mutual enterprise.

## 3.2  Fine Structure and Process

### Neural networks develop over time

**Note:** It will be useful at this point to refer back to Part 2, Step 2, Fractal Basic Shape drawings, including additional information and asides on fractal dimensions and processes and chaos theory. By doing so, the reader will be better prepared to think about the brain in terms of fractal, chaotic patterns and processes. In addition, it is useful to revisit Douglas Hofstadter's reflections on neural processes, including Strange Loops.

"My belief is that the explanations of 'emergent' phenomena in our brains—for instance, ideas, hopes, images, analogies, and finally consciousness and free will—are based on a kind of Strange Loop, an interaction between levels in which the top level reaches back down towards the bottom level and influences it, while at the same time being itself determined by the bottom level. ...The self comes into being at the moment it has the power to reflect itself.... In order to deal with the full richness of the brain/mind system, we will have to be able to slip between levels comfortably.... At the crux, then, of our understanding ourselves will come an understanding of the Tangled Hierarchy of levels inside our minds" (Douglas Hofstadter, *Gödel, Escher, Bach: The Eternal Golden Braid*, p. 709).

from inner speech to
shared, adjusted mutual
speech

*Shared, adjusted mutual speech, SRS*

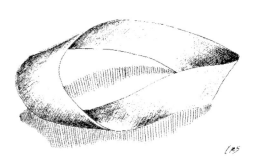

*Moebius strip, Claus Kormannshaus, 1997*

## *Mental processes: strange loops*

*Strange loops drawing, Tim Lis, 97*

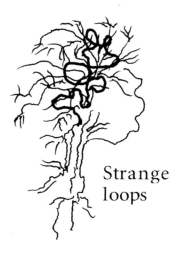

Strange
loops

*Strange loops drawing, SRS 97*

Lower levels and upper levels of the brain exchange signals constantly. The brain is a vast bundle of feedback loops. Like the Moebius strip, these processes are self-contained and continuous, infinite in the sense of being endlessly ongoing until the death of the system. Strange things happen when billions of interconnected events occur simultaneously. Even if the circuitry and action of the brain were precisely mappable, it would still be difficult if not impossible to explain thought in neural terms. There are aspects of indeterminacy and incompleteness to a theory of thought—as there are in mathematics and physics.

Fractal processes and chaos theory shed light on the strange workings of the brain. Fractal processes are self-

referential, self-organizing and self-correcting. So is the brain. Chaos theory describes systems so complex that their orderly patterns are nearly inaccessible. Such systems are extremely sensitive to very small changes, or "perturbations." A butterfly flapping its wings in Iceland occasions a hurricane off the coast of Florida. One neuron may have a momentous effect, too. Research conducted by Walter J. Freeman and his associates at the University of California at Berkley over the past twenty years demonstrates this complex but orderly, or "chaotic" profile of brain activity. Studies with sense perception, especially the sense of smell, produce EEGs, or spatial patterns of receptor activity, that look like tightly wound spirals of coiled wire. These periodic "phase portraits" are what the wave patterns of a thinking brain look like; looser, far less organized spirals describe the EEGs of the brain at rest. These loosely organized coils suddenly organize themselves into a tight, Slinky-like pattern when a smell is recognized by the brain. "The chaos is evident in the tendency of vast collections of neurons to shift abruptly and simultaneously from one complex activity pattern to another in response to the smallest of inputs.

"This changeability is a prime characteristic of many chaotic systems. It is not harmful in the brain. In fact, ... it is this very property that makes perception possible.... Chaos underlies the ability of the brain to respond flexibly to the outside world and to generate novel activity patterns, including those that are experienced as fresh ideas."[26]

Throughout history, humans have devised pictures and words to explain the agency and activity of thought: the homunculus (or little man in the brain), the "space phase sandwich," a "sieve-like" process, a logarithmic spiral like the one illustrated by the shell of the chambered nautilus, or, a holograph. If we combine a handful of descriptions, we start to appreciate the complexity of brain processes.

*Deli Sandwich, Claus Kormannshaus, 1997*

---

[26] Walter J. Freeman, "The Physiology of Perception," *Scientific American*, February, 1991, pps. 78-85.

*The Sieve, Claus Kormannshaus, 1997*

*Chambered nautilus spiral, photo, Elizabeth Nyman, 1997*

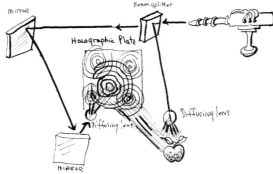

A hologram is when a single laser light is split into two separate beams. The first beam is bounced off the object to be photographed, in this case an apple. Then the second beam is allowed to collide with the reflected light of the first, and the resulting interference pattern is recorded on film. When another laser beam is shined through the film, an image of the original object re-appears. Planaria-like, any slice of a piece of holographic film generates an entire apple. Memories are stored in the brain in this overall way. Visual information is, too. Because of wave-like connectivity between branching nerve cells that send out ripple-like signals, brain function is holograph-like (Talbot, 1991, Sheridan, 1991).

*Holograph, SRS, 1997*

## The nervous system

The nervous system is composed of about one hundred billion nerve cells. Most of them are busy most of the time. Electrochemical impulses race through forests of neural nets. In hundredths of a second, neurons receive and send millions of messages. In the midst of all this physical activity, there is a mystery: "thought" occurs. Fluctuating electrochemical activity produces

descriptions, analyses, speculations and interpretations. The exact relationship between the brain and the mind is probably indeterminable. Describing mind as an "emergent property" of brain activity is not quite enough. Douglas Hofstadter's definition of consciousness as Strange Loops—as not entirely explicable neural activity—brings us closer to understanding the connections between our brains and our minds. The work of Walter Freeman brings this author closest. The spiral phase portrait would work like a Strange Loop swirling dynamically between brain layers, "reaching" between them. According to Freeman, populations of neurons fire, generate currents, and release transmitter chemicals. *Each neuron relates nonlinearly to the others.* Nonlinearity means that the input does not equal the output; that is, the same smell entering two different noses and brains will not necessarily result in the same identification of the smell or any other thoughts about it. The smell of a summer morning may be fresh ironing to some, fresh bread to another. The degree to which brain activity is nonlinear is phenomenal. Human thought is highly personal, idiosyncratic and unpredictable, even to the thinker thinking the thoughts. Freeman describes neuroactivity as the relationship between neurons and the outside world. The relationship can be described as solipsistic: brains function by actions taken in relation to the outside world and can only know what they construct within themselves.[27]

---

[27] Freeman, Walter J., interview with Jean Burns, discusses Freeman's book *Societies of Brains, Journal of Consciousness Studies 3, No. 2,* 1996, pps. 172-180.

The brain and the spinal cord comprise the CNS, or central nervous system. The rest of the neural networks in our bodies comprise the PNS, or peripheral nervous system. The PNS is accepted as "brain," too (Pert, 1993). We think with our bodies. Brain research supports a mind/body unity—not a mind/body dichotomy.

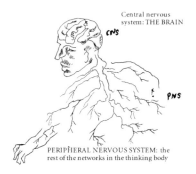

*PNS and CNS, SRS*

*Neuron*

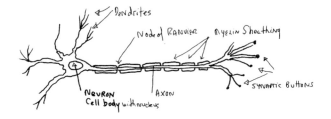

*Neuron with hilloc, mitochondria, axon, myelin, synapse et al, SRS, 97*

Neurons are special cells which send and receive electrical signals. These signals excite or inhibit them, making them fire or not fire. For cells, not firing is as important as firing.

Our brains have approximately ten to the eleventh power of neurons ($10^{11}$). Each cell communicates on average with one thousand other cells, receiving information from as many. This means a potential two thousand-fold interaction per cell at any second. When cells are firing strongly, they may fire fifteen times per second, or at about the speed of a machine gun. Some neurons are several feet long and reach from the brain down into the body; some are only millimeters in length. Nerve impulses travel about ten meters per second. However long nerve cells are, they do not actually touch; they

communicate across microscopic gaps called synapses through chemical exchanges. As many as 1,300 nerve impulses can be fired per second by one nerve cell. If one hundred billion cells fire 1,300 impulses per second, the level of neural communication is staggering. Communication is non-linear. Millions of nerve impulses—or computations—occur in parallel, interconnected systems; the outcome is unpredictable and variable, and is extremely sensitive to the action of a single neuron. The overall effect is like fire racing through a forest fanned by high winds.

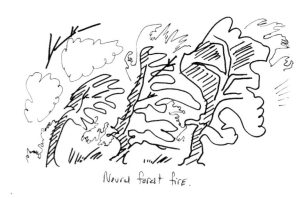

*Neural Forest Fire*

The forest is dense. Intertwined axonal and dendritic branches create a neuropil, as finely spun as babies' hair (*pilus* means "hair" in Latin). The nervous system includes neuroglia, or nerve glue. Neuroglia separate neurons from blood vessels. This interstitial material means that there is very little extracellular space in the CNS. Spaces between individual cells are no more than 20 mm wide (Carpenter & Sutin, 1983). According to Walter Freeman, "any creature with a laminated neuropil has consciousness" (1991).

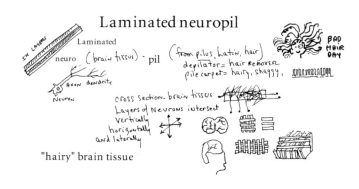

*Laminated neuropil*

Imagine a fruit like a pomegranate filled with seeds. Like pomegranates, brain tissue is packed with neurons.

"Perfect whole" Febuary 10, 1997

*Maria Grigoryeva, pomegranate, PW, 1997*

Until recently, it was thought that the human brain was born with all of its neurons and, after the age of forty, lost about 1,000 neurons per day with no chance of recouping the loss. It is now known that nerve cells, like other cells, are renewed. In particular, the experience of learning encourages the production of additional cells (Greenough, Black and Wallace, 1987; Greenough and Black, 1992; Greenough, Black and Wallace, 1992).

As the human fetus develops, there are periods of exuberant brain growth; just before birth, neurons proliferate. Right after birth, synapses, or the connections between neurons, proliferate. Then, in response to internal timetables, certain connections are pruned. Others are pruned in response to experience. Growth and pruning eventually stabilize the neural system. Some systems, like the sensory systems, become largely unmodifiable. Other systems remain dynamic, continuously making and breaking connections, especially for learning. The brain, through the sensory system, including the entire body, moves out into the environment to test for changes, achieving what Freeman describes as "multisensory integration" and "reafferent redistribution." Think of waves on a shore. They rush in and withdraw, only to rush in again. The brain reaches out for the world and the world rushes in. Waves of stimuli ebb and flow, neural waves of excitation ebb and flow, comparison and revisions occur within the very dynamics of the ebb and flow.

## Axon

Neurons grow trunks, or transmitting cables, called axons. A protein sheathing called myelin (semi-fluid and double refracting), grows over the axons like bark, acting as insulation. Myelin sheathing lets nerve impulses travel fast along the axon via contact spots, or constrictions in the myelin, called Nodes of Ranvier. As axons age, the myelin sheathing sloughs off. Nerve impulses trudge down the axon. The progation of the action potential becomes continuous; it no longer jumps from node to node. Jumping or "saltatory" conduction is due to the electrical resistance and capacitance properties of the myelin sheath (Carpenter & Sutin, 1983). Jumping is faster than trudging, yet, in the final analysis, the transmission is all. The older thinker may operate at a different speed.

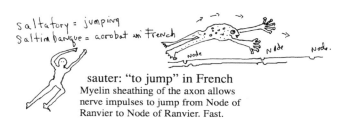

saltatory = jumping
saltin banque = acrobat in French
sauter: "to jump" in French
Myelin sheathing of the axon allows nerve impulses to jump from Node of Ranvier to Node of Ranvier. Fast.

*Nodes of Ranvier, SRS 1997*

The wealth of human experience older brains bring to problem-solving offsets myelin loss. This *quid pro quo* underscores the usefulness of a lifetime of experience. On-going learning, as well as reduced-calorie/reduced-fat diet, vitamins, exercise, close human contact, meaningful work, a positive, outgoing, curious, lively, and alert frame of mind protect us from disease and heighten the quality of the time we have.

In evolutionary terms, electrical transmission was an improvement over chemical transmission. Signals washing from one side of a cell to another, like waves lapping on distant shores, achieve a leisurely form of general communication: extend a pseudopod, move over there, and eat that. Electrical signals are much faster and a complex circuitry fine-tunes the message: get out your favorite cook book, find a recipe, buy the ingredients, prepare them, cook the dish, serve it with wine and good conversation.

*Dendrites*

*Neural Nets, SRS*

*Neural Nets #2*
*Reprinted courtesy of Dover Pictorial Archive Series*
*All rights reserved (c) 1969 Dover Public., Inc.*

Axons, the long-distance cables attached to neurons, spin out branch-like or net-like structures called dendrites. Branching cables send and receive signals. Signals jump across tiny gaps between the surface of one dendrite and another or one dendrite and the cell body of another neuron at spots called synapses, or "boutons," the French word for buttons.

EEG tracings show that thought happens in waves. Signals at synapses create waves of neuroactivity which wash across the minute spaces between neurons, forming spirals of thought. Ideas happen in extracellular space. Thoughts are currents, or waves, or bursts of activity, evidence of collective behavior from a complex background. It is not at the micro level but at this macro level that perception occurs as cooperative, "chaotic" behavior (Freeman, 1991).

*Synapse*

The synaptic gaps between nerve cells are measured in millimicrons. Synapses are visible under the electron microscope as slightly thickened, darker areas on the cell membrane. These "boutons" or "buttons" decorate dendrites like Christmas tree ornaments.

*Christmas tree ornament*

Each synapse is a little sandwich consisting of the presynaptic membrane, the gap, and the postsynaptic membrane. When a nerve cell fires, molecules tumble into this minute gap. Some of these cascading molecules lock into receiving ports, or ion channels, passing the signal on.

*The synaptic space, THE AMAZING BRAIN by Robert Ornstein, Richard Thompson and David Macaulay.*
*Image copyright (c) by David A. Macaulay. Reprinted by permission of Houghton Mifflin Co. All rights reserved.*

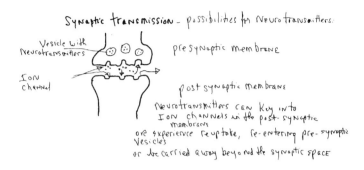

Synaptic transmission – possibilities for Neurotransmitters:

Vesicle with Neurotransmitters

Ion Channel

Pre synaptic membrane

Post synaptic membrane

Neurotransmitters can key into Ion channels in the post-synaptic membrane

ore experience reuptake, re-entering pre-synaptic vesicles

or be carried away beyond the synaptic space

*Pre- and post-synaptic space with ion channels, SRS*

## Neurotransmitters

There are twenty-six or so known chemicals called neurotransmitters which control the brain's electric signals by changing the voltage of the receiving cell. Neurotransmitters—acetylcholine, dopamine, nor-epinephrine, serotonin, glycine—are exquisitely adjusted. Too much or too little of a certain chemical messenger has appreciable results. Too little dopamine, for instance, contributes to Parkinson's disease. Too much dopamine contributes to schizophrenia. Dopamine is called the reward hormone because it produces feelings of optimism and energy. Closely related chemicals—amphetamine and cocaine—produce similar feelings including a sense of power and knowledge. Too little serotonin causes depression. Prozac is not an agonist—it does not mimic and replace serotonin—but it prolongs the effect of the already existing serotonin in the brain. Prozac is an SSRI, a selective serotonin re-uptake inhibitor. Other chemicals that exist naturally in the brain like vasopressin and oxytocin promote trust. These neurochemicals are released by the experience of falling in love, as well as by sexual intercourse and orgasm. Loving, parenting and partnering allow the solitary system to join a community larger than itself (Freeman, 1997).

Synapses are dynamic systems. Chemical messengers are released from tiny factories in the neuron called vesicles, causing messages to "go," "not go," "sort of go," or "go really powerfully." Released like ping pong balls into the gap between the pre- and post-synaptic membranes, these chemicals may open ion channels in the post-synaptic membrane and enter them or close ion channels preventing their own entry; they may experience reuptake back into the original pre-synaptic vesicles; or, they may even tumble out beyond the synaptic space where waste-disposal cells break them down and carry them away. (I pronounced the word "reuptake" *ray-uhp-táhk-ay* until I realized the verb was simply re-up-take, as in "take up these chemicals again.")

Once an electrical signal is transmitted chemically, the synaptic membranes return to resting states and the depleted vesicles manufacture more chemicals, getting ready for more in-coming signals.

Synapses are strengthened during training or learning. The responsiveness of the postsynaptic cells to excitatory input is increased by training or learning. This responsiveness increases the output of other connected neurons which have been excited by the "learning experience" of the responsive cells.[28] It is easy to appreciate the nonlinear, or "butterfly" effect of a single neuron on the entire system. A single learning experience, a flash of understanding, an identity crisis, a conversion experience, one single breakthrough in understanding can reorganize a whole brain or mental system.

## Vesicles and chemical production

Vesicles are spherical chemical factories located in neurons. Some signals make vesicles dump all of their neurotransmitters, depleting the store entirely. The post-synaptic membrane requires increasing stimulation to fire, necessitating a larger production of neurotransmitters in the vesicles in the presynaptic membrane. Eventually, the pre-synaptic vesicles are not only depleted but exhausted, requiring increasing recovery time. These production/depletion effects register on mental levels as craving, euphoria, anxiety, depression and withdrawal.

## Mitochondria and energy production

Mitochondria are a set of lozenge-shaped bodies or organelles—like vesicles—located in neurons, dendrites and axons. Mitochondria provide power for neural networks by metabolizing carbohydrates and amino acids, releasing $CO_2$, water and energy. In a carburetor, air and gas mix to make a spark; in a nerve cell, oxygen and glucose mix to make a spark. Cells breathe: the energy released transports ions across cell membranes.

---

[28] This strengthening is described by Hebb's rule: synapses between neurons that fire together become stronger, as long as the synchronous firing is accompanied by a reward. Learning *is* its own reward.

Ion-transfer creates electrical signals. Electrical signals are the brain's messengers. Mitochondrial energy also synthesizes proteins. Proteins are the building blocks of cells. The byproducts of mitochondrial activity are physical and structural, and electrical and process-related. Mitochondria are arranged either parallel to the long axis of the dendrite or in gentle swirls or spirals (Carpenter and Sutin, 1983). Dynamic systems exhibit dynamic patterns on nano-levels as well as at cosmic dimensions.

### Indeterminacy

The number of neurons—10 to the 11th power at least—and the fact that neurons are anatomically independent despite being functionally interconnected make it impossible to map exactly what is happening in the brain. The brain keeps changing, building new circuits and destroying old ones in response to experience. All is action and flux.

Brain research faces several obstacles. If nerve tissue is disconnected from other neurons for *in vitro* research, there is no neural firing to track and measure. Alternatively, the blood-brain barrier that exists between the circulatory system and the brain to protect the brain from dangerous substances makes chemical experiments on living, intact brains via injections difficult. Still, scientists can identify structures and make assumptions based on animal studies, on autopsies of human brains, and on MRIs of living brains. In addition, the effects of psychoactive drugs which mimic certain neurotransmitters can be tracked and documented. Some psychoactive drugs increase brain activity; some decrease it. Some heighten sensation; some suppress sensation. Some are corrective, restoring normal chemical levels; some are destructive, flooding or depriving the brain of necessary chemicals.

### Growth, aging, disease, trauma, disuse and abuse

Aging happens when cells die: skin cells, organ cells, brain cells die. Some brain cells die due to damaged mitochondria.[29] When free radicals, or uncombined oxygen molecules, ratchet around like pinballs inside cells, mitochondria are smashed into bits and pieces. Even more important than skin creams, "antioxidant" vitamins, like C&E, provide anti-aging health care where it really counts: the cellular level.

---

[29] "Mitochondrial DNA in Aging and Disease," by Douglas C. Wallace, *Scientific American*, August, 1997.

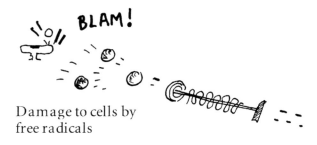

Damage to cells by free radicals

*Pinballs rachetting around in a pin ball machine, SRS*

It is possible that neural and cosmic levels intersect in some manner. Madeleine L'Engle, far-sighted author of novels for children and adults, describes the cosmic implications of mitochondrial intra-cellular sickness in *A Wind in the Door* (1974).

Growth, aging, disease, trauma, disuse and abuse register in the brain at the levels of gross structure and of fine structure. In traumatized brains, several gross systems, including the limbic system and the hypothalamus, fail to develop normally and are smaller or shriveled.

On the level of fine structure, a newborn brain and a six-year-old brain differ in degree of connectivity:

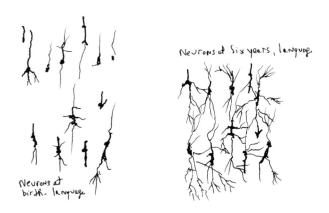

*Newborn and six-year-old brain, SRS 97*

The brain of an Alzheimer's patient differs from that of the newborn and of the six year-old and of the normal adult. An Alzheimer patient's neural nets are broken off like over-bleached hair. The thought processes are disconnected and sparse, too. A study comparing writing samples produced by nuns entering convent life found that the writing could be used predictively. Nuns whose writing was "jampacked with ideas and peregrinations" did not develop Alzheimer's disease. Nuns who wrote more simply, did. A highly developed linguistic ability may protect the brain from disease. Although scant, this research provides brain-based incentives for a lifetime of invested writing.[30]

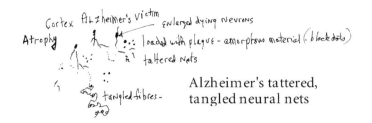

Alzheimer's tattered, tangled neural nets

*Alzheimer's tangled and tattered neural nets, SRS 97*

## Agonists

Chemicals that key in by mimicking neurotransmitters are called agonists. They are "active agents." Like natural neurotransmitters in the brain, they make things happen—or fail to happen. The word "agonist" comes from the Latin verb "ago, agere" meaning "to make or do or act."

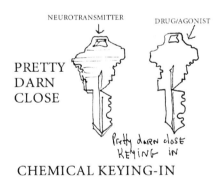

NEUROTRANSMITTER     DRUG/AGONIST

PRETTY DARN CLOSE

CHEMICAL KEYING-IN

*Chemical keying, SRS 97.*

Drugs are effective—positively and negatively—because they form molecular bonds with pre- and post-synaptic surfaces by mimicking the shape of the brain's own neurotransmitter molecules, thereby "keying" into the ion channels.

Some agonists excite the central nervous system; some inhibit it. Some suppress pain. Some cause euphoria. Psychoative drugs alter mental states, changing perceptions and sensations. Agonists which over-stimulate and then exhaust neurons create dysfunction at the synapse. Synaptic dysfunction may have global repercussions, registering throughout the brain and the body as sickness, pain, depression, anxiety, craving or withdrawal. Pronounce the word "agonist" aloud. In certain instances, physiology and psychology are related.

Like neurotransmitters, agonists have specific geometric shapes. Even though morphine, methadone, meperidine and nalorine have different chemical structures, they have similar geometric structures.

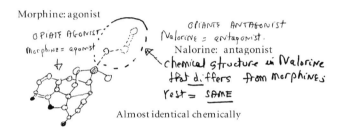

Morphine: agonist

Nalorine: antagonist

Almost identical chemically

*Chemical structures of morphine and nalorine, showing slight difference, SRS*

Because they mimic normal chemical messengers, agonists are carried past the protective blood/brain barrier by the blood stream, slipping into the brain.

Agonists sneaking into brain by keying into ion channels. There are good and not-so-good agonists, or active agents.

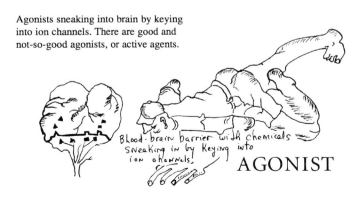

AGONIST

*Agonist as spy crawling on belly, SRS 97*

---

[30] Rogers, Adam, "The Weight of Words" *Newsweek*, Mar. 4, 1996, p. 55.

Some agonists, like heroin, trigger an avalanche of neurotransmitters, exhausting the vesicles' supply and over-stimulating the post-synaptic membrane by pouring chemicals into its receiving ports. The brain may register this intense over-activity as pleasure. A brain becomes addicted to speeded-up activity, or "rushes." Cravings for rushes take over the life of the brain which sends messages to the body to get more of these substances. Over-stimulation at the synapse results in "habituation." Depleted synapses require larger chemical inputs to function. The brain sends more insistent messages to the body: procure more of the substance any way you can.

An agonist's effect may be useful or harmful, or both. For instance, L-dopa is an agonist which mimics the effects of the neurotransmitter dopamine. In certain amounts, L-dopa remediates some symptoms of Parkinson's disease. Too much L-dopa triggers schizophrenia-like symptoms.[31]

### Oxygen starvation, excitotoxicity, and channel blocking

Stroke victims suffer brain damage because blood clots cut off neurons' oxygen supply, killing them. Neurons can also be destroyed through "excitotoxicity." Cells can self-poison by absorbing too many overactive proteins. A neurotransmitter called glutamate naturally floods the brain hours after a stroke occurs, helping to regulate the flow of charged ions in and out of cells. By closing ion channels, glutamate protects cells from toxic levels of calcium and sodium. Drugs mimicking glutamate are now used to protect the brains of stroke victims from chemical over-absorption. Blocking ion channels may also affect Alzheimer's disease, as well as epilepsy, head trauma, Huntington's disease and AIDS encephalopathy (Leutwyler, 1997).

### Distance

Certain drugs increase the distance between the pre- and post-synaptic membrane by shrinking the length and depth of the synaptic membranes. Increased distance means that neurotransmitters are more likely to fall between the cracks, failing to key-into the ion channels, interrupting transmission.

### View from the axon hilloc

The central processing unit in the neuron is called the hilloc. The summing of all incoming signals occurs at this spot, sending signals to open, close, damp-down or excite ion channels. Myriad chemical inputs to the neuron result in a single "send" or "don't send" response. Imagine receiving 1,300 telephone calls per second, sorting out the messages, and then sending or not sending one single message on. In addition, imagine that your message is limited to a 0 or a 1. Human thought is like a series of 0's and 1's which stand for sent and not-sent nerve impulses. This string of sent and not sent signals results in thoughts—like virtual bouquets sent via the Internet as interminable strings of symbols translatable into electronic flowers. Computer languages like BASIC and LOGO achieve the same symbol-to-image transformation with a press of a key.

*View from the axon hilloc,*
*a.k.a. Jessica Rich Sheridan, SRS 97*

*Windows of opportunity, SRS*

---

[31] The movie "Awakenings" with Robin Williams tells the L-dopa story.

## Early development

There are "critical periods" or "windows of opportunity" for brain development in the young of any species. Many cortical connections are made during these periods. Experience determines the quality of many other connections. For instance, if a very young child's eye is patched, or if a child is born with congenital cataracts, the neurons in the retina of the affected eye will receive no stimulation. Retinal neurons that do not fire do not compete for neural territory in the visual cortex. When the eye is unpatched or when the cataracts are removed, that eye is functionally blind. The situation is irreversible. In general, the circuitry is no longer modifiable. Research with kittens and with children with cataracts confirms these findings.

*Kitten with sutured eyes, Claus Kormannshaus, 199*

Depending upon timing, deprivation can have lifelong effects. When kittens are restrained, they do not learn to move with normal fluidity. Visual stimulation *and* active physical exploration are necessary to normal sensory-motor development—physical and mental.

Early childhood experience *matters tremendously.*

## Monkey's thumbs and remediation

*Monkey with amputated thumb, Claus Kormannshaus, 1997*

When a monkey's finger is amputated, that neural area on the sensorimotor cortex does not become a dead zone but extends its influence via neural drift to the other intact fingers. The thumb may be gone but its area of neural influence is added to the remaining fingers. Neural drift has implications for remediation and preservation of function. A functional brain area can make up for a dysfunctional brain area. This knowledge has implications for education; learning strategies which play to students' strengths may remediate weaknesses.

Infancy and the early elementary school years provide optimal periods for brain stimulation, setting the stage for how children will learn and think and act. Early and elementary school years *are* the windows of opportunity. Still, a brain deprived of adequate learning experiences in childhood can be enriched in adulthood.

## 3.3  The Eye and Visual Processing

### Vision and attention

We use our eyes more than we use almost any other sensory system. The more we learn about the eye as structure and process, the more we will know about the brain.

Vision is one of the primary mechanisms of attention. Once attention is aroused, it may be sustained. What the brain *thinks* about the original visual stimulus determines the level of interest. Seeing is much more than a mechanical operation (Zajonc, 1993).

Research with the macaque monkey, the squirrel monkey and the cat provides information on visual systems like ours. The brain organizes visual information according to categories: form, color, movement, depth, and texture. These categories are often recognized as "artistic" categories.

### The eye

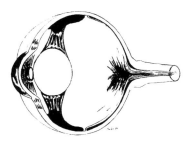

*The eye, Tim Lis, 1997*

We have two eyes which are separated by about two and one-half inches, pupil to pupil. Our brains receive two sets of information from slightly different vantage points.

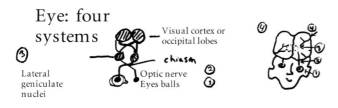

*Eye: four systems*

Four brain systems directly contribute to the act of seeing: the eye ball, the optic nerve, the lateral geniculate bodies, and the striate (or striped/layered) visual cortices. The eyeball receives visual information and starts processing it at the threefold level of retinal cells; this already processed information is passed along the optic nerves through the optic chiasm to the six-layers of the geniculate system where this information from both left and right eyes is evaluated for length, direction and weight of line, and intensity of light-dark contrast; each of the six layers receives information from only one eye.

EYE BALL

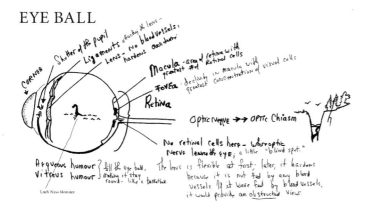

*The eyeball, the optic nerve and the visual cortex, SRS 97*

Eyeballs evolved in several ways. In some retinal systems, like that of the octopus, the photocells point toward the light with their neural connections leading backwards into the brain. In humans, the opposite is true: the photocells point away from the light and the wires leading to them point toward the light, not backwards into the brain. In whatever way retinal tissue in eyes is organized, it requires its own special parts of the

brain, or the visual cortex. Before visual information reaches the two lobes at the back of the brain, it passes through the optic chiasm, where information from both sides of each eye converge, and then diverge again into a stream of mixed and matched information, resulting in binocular (bi-ocular or two-eyed) vision. Two-eyed vision provides depth perception. (Presumably, the Cyclops lives in a flat world.)

*A cup that became a ball: how the eye developed*

*The cup that became a ball, SRS 97*

Some single-celled organisms developed a light-sensitive spot with a little pigment screen behind it. The screen shielded the spot from direct light while providing some direction for the light. In various types of worms and shellfish, the pigment-backed, light-sensitive cells grew into a little cup. Because each cell was selectively shielded from light rays coming into the little cup from its own side, this structure provided a slightly better directional focus to light. From a flat sheet of light-sensitive cells, the eye developed into a deeper cup and then into a hollow ball. Each additional degree of curvature resulted in an optical improvement. A closed cup with a tiny hole became a lensless pinhole camera.

*The pinhole camera, SRS 97*

Like the pinhole camera, primordial eyeballs were able to form images; the smaller the hole, the sharper but dimmer the image. The larger the pinhole, the brighter but fuzzier the image. The advantage to an eyeball with a lens is the projection of an image which is both sharp and bright.

## The camera metaphor

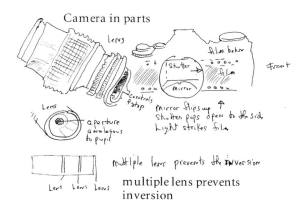

Camera in parts

multiple lens prevents
inversion

*The camera, in parts, SRS 97*

"When you have a cup for an eye, almost any vaguely convex, vaguely transparent or even translucent material over its opening will constitute an improvement. The lens-like properties collect light over its area and concentrate it on the smaller area of the retina" (Dawkins, 1986, p. 86).

The eye is an optical instrument like a camera. Light passes through the cornea, a transparent protective cover. The cornea is more than a rigid glass cover; it is an initially pliant, refractive system which bends and focusses light, directing it through the pupil. The pupil is an aperture in the iris like a camera shutter. Like the shutter, the iris is diaphragm-like. Instead of being made of sliding metal plates, it is made of smooth muscles which control the size of the pupil, allowing the iris to function like the f-stop on a camera, letting more or less light into the eye. On entering the eye through the cornea and the pupil, light next passes through the lens, a transparent disc suspended by ligaments just inside the eye, beyond the pupil. As light passes through the lens, it becomes highly focused. Then, light strikes a photographic film-like area at the back of the eye called the retina. The most sensitive film emulsions require exposure to 25 times more light than the retina requires to detect a point of light.

## Organizing wavelengths

To maintain an accurate image, the exact organization of the wavelengths coming into the eye from the object has to be maintained. A diffuse striking of wavelengths all over the back of the eye produces meaningless signals. The mechanism achieving this precise organization is the lens. Because it cannot be nourished by veins, the transparent structure of the lens becomes inflexible over time, creating problems with vision. If images are focussed

either before or "behind" the retina (the "behind" is metaphorical—there is no place "behind" the retina), the image becomes distorted; vision is then described as near- or far-sighted.

Unlike the camera, our eyes are equipped to filter out the light source. Color remains constant despite changes in the light source. Artists learn to ignore this filter and see an object under the sun and under a tungsten light very differently in terms of color, recognizing and recording "local color." An orange may truly look blue under certain lighting conditions. The artist who records the orange as blue is not being whimsical; she is being accurate.

## A rotation explanation for upside-down images

EYEBALL; UPSIDE-DOWN
IMAGE: one lens

*Upside-down image, SRS 97*

The image projected by the lens on the retina is "upside down." The biophysiology of the eye/brain may require a rotation of the image as it approaches the retina. The last stage of this rotation may be an "upside down" image. As Harvard professor of psychology Stephen Kosslyn writes, "Images show a strong inclination to obey the laws of physics.... There is little reason to expect objects in images to behave like real objects. Yet, mental rotation of an image as if it were a thing is what brains do" (Kosslyn, 1983, 104, 105). Automatic rotation may be the first step in the mental examination process. Flipping the image upside down via the lens and sending it on through the refractive, watery interior of the eye may help preserve exact relationships between wavelengths coming off objects into the eye.

## The retina

The retina is a mosaic of 125 million light detectors called rods and cones. These light receptors make synaptic contact with two other layers of nerve cells in the retina. The third layer of retinal cells bundles its axons into a dense cable called the optic nerve. Each retinal cell is very fussy about which information it processes. The receptive field of each cell is limited to about 1 millimeter in diameter. Some receptive fields are designed to see either a light line on a dark background, a dark line on a light background, or an edge between light and dark (Hubel, 1988, in Layzer, 1995, 125, 126).

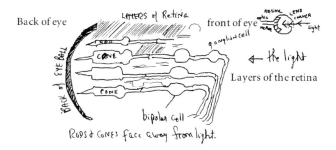

*The retina with its layers of cells, SRS 97*

The circular form of the retina is determined in part by the cup-like way cells grew to catch light during the evolutionary history of the eye. Spherical suns may require ball-like eyes and circular light-sensitive tissue.

The retina experiences exuberant cell growth after birth, followed by pruning, like the rest of the brain. About half of the retinal cells whose nerve fibers grew to the incorrect side of the brain die. If these cells lived, their nerve fibers would produce confusing patterns of impulses, resulting in impaired sight.

### *The fovea*

A declivity, or dip, in the cells in the middle of the retina is called the fovea. This area contains the greatest concentration of visual cells; in turn, that concentrated area is called the macula. In most people, foveal vision is the center of gaze; it is here that vision is sharpest. Macular degeneration signals cell death in the fovea, making this area less acute visually. In the center of the fovea is a blind spot; this is where the optic nerve exits the eyeball.

Many animals do not have a fovea in their retina; they rely on head-movements to control their gaze. Babies, too, evolve from afoveate vision towards foveal vision. At first they must rely on head movements to place an object in their visual field (Roucoux, 1983). Later, children swivel their eyes, placing the fovea, or center-of-gaze, where they wish to concentrate vision.

As soon as we open our eyes, neurons in the retina compete for territory in the visual cortex. A bright light "compels the reaction" (Arnheim, 1969, 24). At first, the stimulus *is* the response.

### *A vision-based explanation for dyslexia*

One vision-based explanation for dyslexia is that the fovea in students with reading problems have less retinal cells than normal. The theory is that these dyslexic students would read better if they did so parafoveally, relying on a peripheral approach rather than on an inadequate "center of gaze" strategy. A method for reading off-the-center-of-gaze has been effective for some dyslexic readers (Geiger & Lettvin, 1987). Another vision-based explanation suggests that dyslexic readers' eyes scramble wavelengths. Colored glasses have helped some dyslexic students to read (Irlen, 1991). Depending upon the eyes, lenses of a certain color keep words from jumping around or appearing incomplete. The mother of one second grade student who wears light purply-blue glasses reports that the doctor fitting her son for these glasses said they were for writing, reading and all computer work. Drawing was not mentioned. Was this an oversight or is drawing a different visual task? The boy does not need these colored glasses to draw. The mother commented that she is an artist and, although reading was troublesome for her (even art history texts in which she was very interested), she never had problems with drawing. This anecdotal information suggests that either the lens of the eye organizes wavelengths differently depending upon whether the information coming through the pupil is drawing or writing, or the brain works with information somewhere past the retina in different ways depending upon whether it is understood to be image or text. Or, something else is going on. An informal experiment could be devised with Drawing/Writing to determine whether sustained drawing affects how children's brains organize wavelengths visually for writing and reading.

*Parafoveal vision*

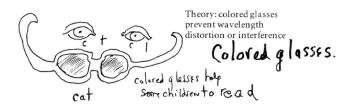

*Colored glasses, SRS 97*

## Visual processing

### Cross-modal and mixed

Each eye splits the visual field in half. The right half of the retina of the right eye and the right half of the retina of the left eye send information to the right visual cortex; the left half of the right eye and the left half of the left eye send information to the left visual cortex. The left hemisphere gets information from both eyes about the right half of the visual world, and the right hemisphere gets information from both eyes about the left half of the visual world. Connections between hemispheres mix this matched information. This highly complex, mixed and matched process characterizes brain activity in general.

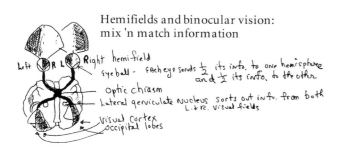

*Hemifields, SRS*

### Serial and parallel

The visual system, like other brain processes, functions not only serially in a linear manner, but in a non-linear manner via parallel, interconnected systems.

*"Cereal" and parallel, SRS 97*

Like other brain processes, serial and parallel visual processes are connected by interneural loops.

## Sight, touch and the blind

*Icons for hand and eye,*
*Sam Sheridan, Claus Kormannshaus*

The visual cortices located at the back of the brain are highly active brain areas. Much of the activity is produced by the inner act of visualizing rather than by the "outer" act of looking at things in the external world. Blindfolded rats running complicated mazes register activity in their visual cortices. As they run, they are able to visualize the twists and turns (Rozenweig and Bennett, 1978). Using internal "seeing," we visualize, imagine, fantasize, and theorize.

Vision as sight is a first level of abstraction in an extremely complex system of mental abstractions. We start at one remove from the object and quickly move from it to other levels of understanding. The sensory system called sight is informed by the sense of touch. In like manner, the sense of touch is extended by the act of sight. Sight allows us to touch at a distance (Arnheim, 1969).

We do not know exactly how the congenitally blind form internal images through touch but we do know they learn to navigate in the world of objects, people and text by constructing mental maps, primarily by using the sense of touch. Drawings made by blind people are like those of sighted people in terms of strategies for perspective: they use foreshortening and converging lines to indicate depth (Kennedy, 1997). The blind may be born knowing how to draw, like sighted children. They can learn to read and write through touch. Touch not only informs sight; it can compensate for lost sight.

### A mathematical explanation

The mind responds to information from the eyes in a variety of ways producing picture-like, word-like, or map-like representations. These mental images are far less like photos, than they are like mathematical computations (Kosslyn, 1983; Churchland, 1986). The eye and the brain achieve extraordinary feats of translation; beams of light are reorganized as people, places, and things. We see reflections off the surfaces of objects and equate these reflections with the things themselves (Crick, 1984). We perform mental gymnastics with words, too. We read them or hear them and equate them with what they stand for. Wavelengths and words are simulacra; they provide evidence, suggestions, hints for things but they are not those things. They are themselves—energy and marks, requiring translation and interpretation. Mathematical-like computations (vector and frequency analyses, tensor transformations, and matrix multiplication) are responsible for these interpretations (Changeux, 1985; Churchill, 1986). Other languages layer themselves on top of these computations. How did we lose track of this understanding about the relationship of mathematics-like operations to thought?

## 3.4 Language

### Language development

No one knows exactly how babies learn language, but very young children learn to talk, urged on by parental babble. The pitch, tone, inflection, rhythms of the maternal tongue structure babies' brains for that particular language. This phenomenal ability to learn a language is scaffolded on eons of human experience with visual/spatial processing. Sight, sound, and touch continue to be related in writing and reading.

The sooner sighted or blind or deaf children learn to speak, the easier it is for them to acquire spoken language. Sometime after the age of six, nine or twelve years, spoken language becomes extremely difficult to acquire. Although writing and reading can be acquired later in life, speech becomes much harder. Spoken languages are best learned young.

### Language dysfunction

*A neurobiological processing link, SRS 97*

### Remedial links: self-correction

People who suffer left-hemisphere damage can regain language. It may take a long time and a lot of work, but the patient can learn to speak, write and read again. Three phenomena are responsible: redundancy, neural drift and equipotentiality. All three phenomena create additional processing links. Extra neurons, net-casting neurons, and adaptive brain tissue allow the brain to self-correct. Like self-construction, self-correction is an important capability for dynamic systems.

Although the left side of the brain specializes in language, this does not mean that the left hemisphere cannot process spatial information or that the right hemisphere cannot process language. Brain tissue is flexible and adaptive, although this adaptability diminishes over time. In general, the female brain is more adaptable than the male brain due, in part, to its equipotentiality, or lack of specialization. In instances when a male brain might use one specific section to process information—for instance, sounding out a word or doing a math problem—a female brain uses the corresponding part on the other side, too. This double-sided, or global approach is described as being "balanced bilaterally." The balanced bilateral brain recovers faster and more completely from brain trauma than more lateralized brains. Strategies that encourage balanced bilateral processing will be remedial. This is an important tip for educators.

### Structural anomolies

Some brains with structural anomalies exhibit problems with language. Some dyslexic male brains have a larger left planum temporale (Galaburda, 1987). On the other hand, many male dyslexics demonstrate enhanced spatial skills. Larger left plana may correlate with spatial skills, language dysfunction or both. The developing brain grows according to chemically delivered, coded instructions. We know that neurochemical imbalances are responsible for attention deficits and for imbalances in mood and perception and that sustained neurochemical imbalances have structural effects. Emotionally abused limbic systems are smaller. They are less capable of emotion and less able to control emotions like rage. Childhood abuse changes the anatomy of the brain; trauma floods the brain with a hormone called cortisol which eats away the brain's hippocampus, where memories are organized and stored. Violent criminals lose personal memories along with memories of their crimes. Childhood abuse is also detectable in a smaller, less myelinated corpus callosum. From what we know of the structural and procedural centrality of the corpus callosum, this information is deeply distressing and significant. We can appreciate the ramifications of a slow, smaller connector/transformer. A diminished corpus callosum means that signals between the hemispheres pass more slowly and less efficiently. In particular, connections with the left hemisphere are affected. Language and logic suffer. Less interhemispheric connectivity results in dissociated behavior, in polarized attitudes, and in irrational, extreme mood swings. The parallels between morphology, function and behavior are startlingly close.

### Learning activities and the regulation of neurochemical imbalances

Drugs like Prozac adjust serotonin levels and, thus, states of mind. Homeopathic remedies like St. John's Wort are routinely prescribed in Europe for depression and appear to have less side effects than synthetic drugs. Many drugs serve important psychoactive or mental functions. Ritalin adds chemicals to understimulated brains, bringing them "up to speed" attentionally.

The term "hyperactive" has caused confusion about children with attention deficits. Children may be overactive physically—their thoughts and actions impulsive and scattered—but this is not because their brains are overstimulated. Their brains are understimulated. They lack the correct amount of certain neurotransmitters, including norepinephrine. This deficit reduces their ability to focus, or to pay sustained attention.

Like hyperactivity, dyslexia is also sometimes misunderstood. MRIs show that dyslexic brains work harder than brains which read easily. Dyslexic brains are not lazy; they overwork because their decoding strategies are ineffective. It takes much longer to do something inefficiently and the results are poorer. Dyslexic brains need strategies for easier processing. Brain scans of very bright mathematics students show that the most efficient brains work less.

Research suggests that the least lateralized, most equipotential brains work most efficiently. The question is whether educational activities can regulate neurochemistry. Other activities change brain chemistry—for instance, physical exercise releases the brain's natural opiates called endorphins. Educational activities can, too.

A safe, happy childhood produces larger limbic systems than traumatized childhoods. Good feelings have neurochemical ramifications including the ability to control rage and to preserve memories. Educational strategies designed to promote feelings of safety and success encourage brains to grow. Physical cross-training is effective for athletes. Mental cross-training is effective for thinkers—on the same grounds: exercise of all the parts in a connected system enhances the performance of the system. If the educational strategy focuses on drawing, writing, and speaking, the brain is not only tuned up attentionally, but it is trained specifically for literacy. Because of neural drift, it is logical to expect training in drawing to remediate difficulties with writing and reading. Bilateral brain training will develop both visual and verbal skills in more flexible ways.

The activity called Drawing/Writing was designed to create neurobiological processing links between the abilities to draw, write, and read. These drawing-based processing links strengthen visual and verbal skills, increasing the brain's capacity for work.

### Visual processing as the basis for language

The rationale for the Drawing/Writing program rests on brain science in general and on visual processing in particular. Visual processing precedes verbal processing phylogenetically and ontogenetically. Children watch and listen before they speak. They scribble and draw before they write and read. In general, human beings are visual learners before they become verbal learners. By repeating this pattern in Drawing/Writing, we model the development and process of intelligent thought.

### Comparing and translating representations

The child is a learning system. The system learns by creating multi-sensory representations of the world, and then comparing them and translating them. Drawing/Writing models intelligent thought by recreating this process.

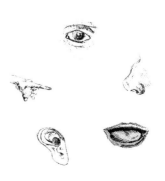

*The five of the sensory icons in a circle*

## 3.5 The Growing Brain

### Educational implications: Tips and suggestions

 13 tips for a better brain.

If learners keep these tips in mind, thinking skills will be maximized. These tips provide practical, useful information about the brain. Read them aloud with students and discuss them.

### 1—The brain builds itself.

The brain builds neural assemblies. Some of the neural assemblies, like the ones for vision, are time-sensitive and become hard-wired. Some remain modifiable over a lifetime, like those for learning. The brain's neural assemblies are blueprinted by genetics and realized by experience.

The brain's capacity for self-construction, integration and self-correction distinguishes these neural assemblies. Individual learning styles bring the brain's self-regulatory abilities into high relief. For individual learning styles to emerge, the learning environment must be flexible and rich, providing a range of sensory experiences, including visual, tactile and verbal exploration.

Brains require nutrients and stimulation to grow and flourish. By studying brain science and other fields connected with physical and mental growth, we can determine what experiences and substances are most likely to contribute to healthy brains. Cross-modal learning creates more connected and efficient brains. Cross-modal learning increases feelings of success and control. Feelings of success and control increase the amounts of natural substances in brains that make them feel good and increases the brain's tolerance for sustained, productive work. "Natural highs" provide alternatives to other approaches to stimulation which may damage important brain connections.

### 2—Each brain is different.

Each brain self-constructs, using inherited blueprints and experience. Although the blueprints for the wiring plan may be more or less alike in human brains, the wiring pattern of each brain is unique for several reasons: one is the indeterminability of the exact path any neuron will take as it burrows through brain tissue; another is the result of individual human experiences, especially with people and language in the world.

Each brain has more neurons than the Milky Way has stars, or hundreds of billions. As each neuron noses its way through brain tissue, "sniffing out" its proper site, a random function associated with the growth-cone at the tip of the neuron insures the fact that no two brains can be wired exactly the same, even in identical twins. This characteristic of the central nervous system is called "irreproducability" (Changeux, 1985; Rosenfield, 1988). The sheer number of neurons, along with the random function, creates individuality at the neural level. Experience, including educational experience, creates individuality on a mental/emotional level thereafter.

Each individual brain not only functions differently from every other brain, but, at any moment, that brain can change its own approaches to thinking, dramatically changing its own metabolic profile as well as its neural nets and their level of connectivity. The extraordinary point emphasized by this book is the degree to which the variability of the brain remains in the control of the learner for a lifetime.

### 3—There are critical periods for brain growth.

Just before birth, the brain makes more neurons than it needs. Soon after birth, the brain makes more connections than it needs. A continual rhythmic firing literally constructs the brain. Exuberant synaptogenesis subsides; connections are pruned in response to experience and learning. The brain's wiring systems for vision, language, attention, emotion, and motor skills stabilize. Many of the most significant connections are forged for life by the age of three years—some, by six months.

The brain's wiring remains modifiable for learning; but there is a Catch-22: the feedback loop. The quality of the learning determines the quality of the wiring, and non-modifiable wiring systems determine some of the brain's future learning capabilities. If a baby is born with cataracts and they are not removed, the baby's ability to see as an adult will be limited. Because visual networks stabilize when children are young and because visual learning remains so important, the quality of children's visual stimulation at the pre-school and elementary levels of education is very important. Other early experiences persist, too, including attitudes about other people and the world.

## 4–The brain grows in stages.

Some brain systems mature and stabilize before others can mature and stabilize. The timing between two interdependent systems is sometimes so close that several systems develop almost simultaneously. The exact timing or order of multiple maturations is indeterminable. No two brains grow in exactly the same way at the same time. Classroom expectations for "developmental milestones" must be flexible.

## 5–Exploratory problem-solving helps the brain to grow.

Physical exploration using all of the senses, particularly touch, encourages brain growth.

The more physically the brain approaches a problem, the more clearly formed and fully dimensional the solution to that problem will be. Exploratory problem-solving not only streamlines neural assemblies (Greenough et al, 1987, 1992), it also increases the production of myelin, the fast-axon insulator.[32] A better wiring system for problem solving is pared-down, densely associative, and very fast. The brain needs the explorations of the body to grow.

## 6–Feelings of control help the brain to grow.

Feelings of well-being and brain growth correlate. A child who feels helpless and victimized may grow up with an underdeveloped limbic system. The adult may experience problems with controlling rage.

A sense of control encourages the growth of the limbic system which makes a broad range of controllable emotions possible. Educational strategies which play to children's strengths—like drawing—increase feelings of success and control.

## 7–Experience affects the brain's potential and keeps modifying the brain for learning.

Brains deprived of sufficient stimulation or abused by injury or trauma can be 20% to 30% smaller than average. The brain thrives on activity; it atrophies from disuse. An under-used or abused brain develops poorly and works poorly. For the human brain to grow, the body needs cuddling and play, and the mind requires personal, direct, interesting conversation. Language experience is particularly important.

Experience modifies neural networks. Although many systems in the brain stabilize, becoming largely unmodifiable, neural changes in response to learning occur over a lifetime. It is possible to construct a better brain at any time. It is most effective to lay down patterns for effective thinking skills early in childhood, just as it is most effective to learn to ski, ride a bike or speak a foreign language when we are young.

As a self-correcting system, the brain can repair itself by using old areas in new ways, new areas in old ways, and new areas in new ways. Because of a phenomenon described as "neural drift," a functional brain area is able to infiltrate and remediate a dysfunctional area. This information is especially relevant for remedial education. A strength helps a weakness. For instance, left hemisphere damage is compensated for by right hemispheric strengths. By inference, the " drawing part" of the brain should be able to substitute for the "writing part." All students can take advantage of the brain's repairability and flexibility by determining their own special strengths through experimentation. To do so, the learning environment must be informed and flexible. Then, students can use their strengths to their best advantage.

## 8–Bodily experience helps the brain to construct mental maps including language.

Spatial understanding helps direct actions of the eyes, hands, and feet. The geometry of physically experienced space becomes a frame of reference for the brain's sensorimotor maps. This spatial understanding precedes and undergirds multiple levels of linguistic understanding. Educators are apt to dichotomize non-linguistic and linguistic systems of representation—like art and language. Language systems are continuous with each other and depend upon each other for structure and information. The premise of this book is that writing, reading and mathematics skills benefit from training in drawing. Neural systems for representing meaning are scaffolded. This means that drawing, writing and mathematics are interconnected systems and can and should be taught integratively.

## 9–The brain is redundant.

Brains have more processing power than is necessary, making recovery from damage and compensation for damage possible. The fact that the brain is equipped with a margin for error insures its repairability, recoverability, and modifiability—in short, its resourcefulness. This is important and useful information.

---

[32] Studies with rats running interesting mazes show increased myelin production, wider, deeper synapses and greater neural connectivity (Rosenzweig & Bennett, 1978).

## 10–Visual searches help the brain grow.

An innate predisposition toward order described in this book as "deep grammar," or the Form of the form, stimulates visual searches. Visual searches organize the brain for language. A "grammar for intelligent thought" organizes incoming stimuli. This spatial grammatical system extends itself to the brain's linguistic systems. Exposure to language triggers language. Then, specific cultural codes or grammars for mother tongues become influential.

With no previous exposure to or training in visual searches, babies conduct visual/physical searches. The flailing of arms and legs and the instinctual motions of the eyes quickly become purposeful and informative. New information organizes the brain in new ways. Visual searches and brain growth constitute a feedback loop.

As the brain's visual system matures, the brain's ability to make distinctions sharpens. The visual system becomes adept at determining the edges of things. Once the brain is able to determine where one thing stops and another begins, the brain can make comparisons. By comparing and contrasting information, the brain determines similarities and differences, providing the basis for analysis.

The way the brain learns to conduct visual searches profoundly influences the brain's mental and emotional growth. The visual system, the emotional or limbic system, and the ability to form attachments are interconnected. The early visual ability to make distinctions between light and dark, between edges of objects and surrounding space, lays the cognitive foundation for more general abilities, like recognizing a person's face as familiar or appealing, or, as the child matures, choosing between two alternatives.

Drawing trains the brain's visual system to search for and to identify and to recognize distinctions, to make comparisons and, ultimately, to make value judgments among alternatives in preparation for forming intelligent attachments. This training establishes a grammar of intelligent thought , or a procedure for order.

## 11–Storing memories in more than one way creates stronger, more accessible memories.

The same information can be stored and accessed in different ways. A child can create and access information about an object—like a bird's wing—by drawing it, talking about it, writing about it, reading about it, dancing about it, remembering stories about it, making metaphors and similes, analogies, predictions and hypotheses about it. With this broad knowledge base in place, a child can access the bird's wing by selecting the mental directory labeled "bird" or "wing" or any of a host of other personal associations.

## 12–Comparisons help the brain to organize and categorize, or recognize, information.

Some of the templates for comparison are determined by the senses. Spoken and written languages use similar strategies as do spatial information systems including vision. "Saccades"(sah-cáhds) describe the infinitesimal, back-and-forth scanning motion of the eyes. This scanning movement "refreshes" an image by re-stimulating the visual cells in the retina. On a mental level, saccades may provide the neural basis for comparing and constrasting information.

One thing may be darker or lighter than another, more or less defined at the edges, larger or smaller, stiller or more in motion. At linguistic levels, one object may be more or less important than another or more or less interesting. The deliberate use of comparative strategies including simile, metaphor and analogy contribute to the grammer of intelligent thought. Comparative strategies can become saccade-like if they are practiced until they become automatic.

## 13–Language is central to thought.

Dynamic systems exhibit orderly behavior. Apparent chaos or messiness is an aspect of highly organized systems and is intrinsic to their complexity.

The brain executes numerous processes simultaneously. How the brain mobilizes organizational strategies determines the quality and usefulness of its highly complex processes. This book maintains that a systematic parts-to-whole, concrete to abstract, visual to verbal strategy is brain-like and teachable, and describes this cumulative strategy as an orderly system, or "grammar of intelligent thought." The five-step program outlined in Part 2 demonstrates that this dual language system can be established through consistent training in integrative cross-modal processes like Drawing/Writing.

Currently, many brains receive waves of visual stimuli passively, indiscriminately, uncritically. To protect itself from unresolved messiness—to organize and assess this information—the brain requires tools, most especially language. Language is a major organizational tool.

## Health implications

### The vulnerable brain

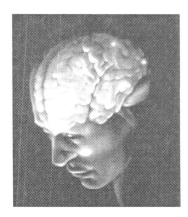

*Brain*

Certain substances alter consciousness, feelings and behavior; some of these substances are useful, some are harmful or even lethal. Alcohol, nicotine, and cocaine reduce oxygen supplies to the brain, kill cells and cause addiction. Noise can damage the brain as well. Exposure to too many decibels of sound destroys nerve cells in the outer ear. Like war veterans, many teenagers have lost 20% or more of their hearing.

What we see, hear, smell, touch, and eat makes us who we are. What we fail to do with our bodies also registers in our brains. The brain is a complicated, finely woven web of connections. Synapses shrink and close over from lack of stimulation. An inactive brain is less connected.

Certain diseases, like Alzheimer's and schizophrenia, shred neural connections like confetti. Exploratory, successful, complicated activities weave neural connections like tapestries. If we learn about our brains, we will be less likely to damage them.

### The invulnerable brain

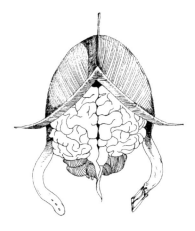

*Helmeted brain, Sam Sheridan, 1997*

The brain is protected from blows and dangerous chemicals by the hard bones of the skull, the tough envelope of the meninges containing a liquid cushion of cerebro-spinal fluid, and the blood-brain barrier which excludes certain chemicals from the brain. Still, foreign chemicals invade the brain disguised as recognizeable molecules. Dangerous learning experiences can enter the brain, too, through the eyes and ears far more easily than masquerading molecules. The more we know about how we think, the better able we will be to provide our brains with healthy experiences.

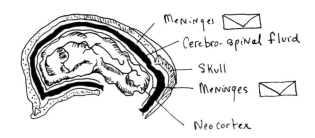

*Cross-section: skull, meninges, cerebro-spinal fluid, cortex, SRS*

### TIPS ON HOW TO LOSE IT

*Searching for the lost brain, Sam Sheridan, 1997*

**"Now, where did I put my brain?"**

### Failure to practice thinking

Certain drugs encourage brains to "space out," lessening motivation for action including problem solving. Eventually, through disuse, the synapses for purposeful action and analytical thinking thin out, shorten up, and close over, like dimples in dough. The neural nets can be rewoven and the synapses recreated. But it takes time and work.

*Minute changes*

The brain is a mass of excitable cells intricately emmeshed in circuitry (the "laminated neuropil"). Minute changes in brain chemistry and structure have large-scale effects (chaotic behavior). Educational strategies can capitalize on this information. Drug dealers depend on it. The transmitter theory of substance addiction targets the synapse as the receptor site for psychoactive drugs (Heynman, 1996).

*Active self-destruction*

Some brains on drugs think they can fly, which is not true. Some drugged brains damage themselves through seizures or violent physical action. Some drugged brains cut off their own oxygen supply, causing massive cellular death resulting in shut-down of the entire system—brain and body.

### Unhealthy brains and unnatural highs: Information usually provided by school-based drug education programs

*Spray cans and tubes, SRS 97*

*Skull, Tim Lis, 1997*

*Face with hypodermic, Claus Kormannshaus, 1997*

School-based drug education programs generally provide the following information:

**Common inhalants:** fast-drying glues and cements; paints, lacquers, varnishes, thinners and removers; lighter and dry cleaning fluids; kerosene and lantern and stove fuel; fingernail, shoe and furniture polish; typewriter correction fluids; felt-tip marking pens; aerosol cans. symptoms of use include lack of coordination, lack of inhibitions, nausea, vomiting, violent behavior. Effects range from mild dizziness to total unconsciousness, even death. Symptoms of overdose include brain damage, abnormalities in liver and kidney, damage to the stomach lining and to bone marrow activity, permanent damage to muscles and nerve cells leading to difficulties with balance, walking and even sitting, suffocation, coma, even death.

**Narcotics** are opiates—including cocaine, heroin, morphine, codeine, opium. They are used therapeutically as pain killers. Because they are powerfully addictive, narcotics they have a high potential for abuse. Narcotics provide sensations of euphoria; overdoses result in pulmonary edema (lungs filling up with water), respiratory arrest, convulsions, coma, possible death. Symptoms of withdrawal include diarrhea, tremors, chills, shakes, muscle jerks, cramps, nodding sleep.

**Depressants, or "downers,"** include barbituates (Seconal, Nembutal), Benzodiazepines (Valium, Librium) and alcohol. These drugs are sedatives and tranquilizers. They depress the central nervous system producing a calming effect or sleep. They are highly addictive. Symptoms of use include relaxation, loss of inhibition, lack of concentration, slurred speech, staggering, confusion. Symptoms of overdose include hypertension, coma, possible death. Alcohol kills neurons in the brain. Symptoms of withdrawal include severe anxiety, agitation, hallucination, tremors, shakes, delirium, convulsions, even death.

**Stimulants** include amphetamines, phenmetrazine (Preludin), and methylphenidate (Ritalin). Symptoms of use include agitation, excessive activity, argumentativeness, euphoria, insomnia, loss of appetite, foul breath, hallucinations. Symptoms of overdose include cardiac arrhythmia, convulsions, coma, possible death. Symptoms of withdrawal include voracious hunger, muscular aches, abdominal pain, chills, tremors, prolonged sleep, exhaustion, depression.

**Hallucinogens** include LSD, PCP, STP, mescaline, and psilocybin. Symptoms of use are visual hallucination, confusion, paranoid delusions, euphoria, anxiety, panic. Symptoms of overdose include extreme hyperactivity, violence, psychosis, convulsions, possible death. Symptoms of withdrawal are minimal and may include flashbacks.

**Tobacco:** Besides depositing tar in the lungs, tobacco is a vaso-constrictor. It cuts off oxygen to the brain, and can cause anoxia, black-outs or fainting.

**Alcohol:** Medical consequences of alcoholism include liver damage, heart damage, esophageal bleeding and tearing, gastritis or swelling of the lining of the stomach, and stomach ulcers. Brain damage includes degeneration of the cerebellum which controls for coordinated movement. This damage is not reversible. Athletes run the risk of losing these skills permanently. Alcohol raises blood pressure which can result in strokes (brain damage caused by burst blood vessels in the brain). Because alcohol causes violent behavior and lessened coordination, the brain may suffer from secondary causes, like damage from a bullet, or spinal cord damage from a car accident. Cancer risks may increase for breasts, the larynx, the esophagus, the lungs. Alcohol raises the risk for lung cancer because heavy drinkers often smoke heavily, too.

*Alcohol, SRS*

*Cannabis, SRS 97*

**"I do not think those tomato plants are going to bloom this spring."**

**Marijuana** is a difficult drug to classify. Some users experience it as a mild hallucinogen, some as a sedative. It is used by doctors as an anodyne and as a mild tranquilizer for everything from menstrual cramps to migraine headaches. It is a difficult drug for doctors to gauge. It cannot be injected but it can be ingested and smoked. When smoking marijuana, it is difficult to tell how much is being inhaled and absorbed. It decreases interocular pressure in glaucoma sufferers; it decreases nausea and increases appetite in AIDS and cancer patients; it lowers blood pressure; it increases the heart rate moderately; it dilates vessels in the eyes causing the reddening of the eyes; it mitigates epileptic seizures.

The psychoactive effects of marijuana are subtle and include a sense of well-being which is heavily dependent on the situation and expectations of the user. Marijuana heightens sensations of color, sounds, patterns and textures, distorts time and space, slows the passage of time, and often creates a dream-like or fantasy state. "Mellow" is a word often used by marijuana users to describe the state it produces. Positive symptoms of use: relaxation, talkativeness, appetite. Negative symptoms: loss of concentration, loss of motivation. Symptoms of overdose: fatigue, paranoia, hallucinations, possible psychosis.

***Damage to the lungs:*** Because the smoke is held in the lungs, one marijuana joint puts five times the tar of a cigarette in the lungs. One hundred of the 421 chemicals in marijuana are irritating to the lungs and can cause severe bronchitis. Inflammation of the bronchial tubes causes thickening of the tubes and a loss of hair cells that sweep congestion out of the lungs. Mucus builds up, causing difficult breathing, chest pain, fever and coughing. Marijuana smoke also contains 150 complex hydrocarbons, some of which cause precancerous growths. Marijuana often contains mold and other disease-carrying organisms, like salmonella. These germs go deep in the lungs and cause infection, even death.

**Damage to the heart:** Increased heart rate puts stress on blood vessels and the heart. Dilated blood vessels may cause a drop in blood pressure. Marijuana users have bloodshot eyes because the tiny blood vessels in the whites of their eyes dilate. Many users wear dark glasses to hide this.

**Damage to the brain:** Chemicals in marijuana widen the synapses between nerve cells, making synaptic communication difficult. These chemicals cause dense material to build up, clogging synapses. Clogging causes packets of neurotransmitters to clump up and become inactive, hampering activity inside cells, especially the synthesis of protein. Interference with protein production interferes with thinking, making it difficult to learn anything or remember what happened the day before.

**Damage to males:** Marijuana reduces testosterone necessary for boys to sexually mature into men. It may sustain or it may inhibit erections and lower sperm count, making it difficult or impossible to father children. Marijuana-damaged sperm may produce males with birth defects. If boys start using marijuana at age 10, often they may be smaller, less able to grow a beard, have reduced drive, and show poorer muscle development.

**Damage to females:** Marijuana elevates testosterone levels, causing dark body hair, facial hair, acne; it disrupts the menstrual cycle and may interfere with ovulation. Eggs and the developing fetus are vulnerable to the active ingredients in marijuana. Fetuses may exhibit the same effects as FAS, or Fetal Alcohol Syndrome including attention deficits and learning disabilities. Marijuana increases chances of miscarriage; it causes lower birth weight, and it may result in male babies with deformed genitals. Marijuana's influence is on-going, since it will pass to the baby through the mother's milk.

**Suppression of immune system:** Marijuana weakens the immune system, opening the body to infection, especially lung infections, and extending the period necessary for recovery from bronchitis, flu or colds.

Marijuana is called a "gateway drug" because it may lead users to try other drugs.

In combination with alcohol or street drugs, marijuana may cause such bodily slowing that the user stops breathing.

**Influences behavior, performance and personality:** Physical appearance becomes sloppy; workdays are skipped; there is a backing away from family and friends;

reactions slow, which makes driving hazardous. Job skills slip. Panic attacks occur. Judgment and confidence slip away.

An actual or potential marijuana user must consider all of these options carefully and balance certain kinds of pleasure against certain kinds of liabilities or damage.

Harvard is currently conducting a five-year study on marijuana use.

## Healthy brains and natural highs: New information for school-based drug education programs

There is no evidence that activities like drawing, writing or analytical thinking cause body-organ damage or brain damage. In fact, the contrary is true. There is direct scientific evidence from animal enrichment studies that challenging activities—mental and physical—organized around visual searches of interest, or through internal visualizing, result in enhanced brain connectivity.

*Thinking Children, Claus Kormannshaus, 1997*

*Girl thinking, Claus Kormannshaus, 1997*

## Hooked the natural way

*Hooked on the arts, SRS 97*

A healthy brain requires adequate oxygen, glucose, neurotransmitters, visual searches of interest, challenging but not too challenging problems, verbal stimulation, close, nurturing human contact, and a physically fit body. Being physically fit, feeling interested, smart and capable may be enough for our brains, but it is evidently not enough for our minds. We need to feel loved and we need to feel really good. We crave "highs." Or, as my nineteen year old daughter, Sarah, commented, "We need to transcend."

"Self-directed, cross-modal learning" may sound like a pretty pedantic term for a set of combined drawing and writing exercises. But self-directed, cross-modal learning is, in fact, an exciting proposition, and, properly implemented, lays the foundations for feelings of extraordinary well-being including those rare and precious moments of transcendence and joy.

## Natural highs

*Football player reaching for ball, Claus Kormannshaus, 1997*

Physical exercise releases the brain's natural opiates. The release of natural endorphins is addictive. Runners get hooked on running because it makes them feel good. Meditation and the arts provide heightened states of alertness and peacefulness. People practice both for the same reason: feeling good. The renowned alpha wave characterizes the brain waves of painters and meditators. We can feel good after we run, and we can feel good while we are painting and meditating. We have other agendas for running, painting

and meditating, but part of the impulse is the in-the-moment at-oneness we experience during such activities. These states signal heightened neural/mental events. Neurally, transcendence may correlate with resolution, or settling into minimal energy states. Mentally, transcendence is ecstatic peace or "feeling good."

There are many routes to heightened attention and a sense of profound well-being. Athletics, the arts and brain science point the way. Pleasure and education can go hand in hand. Beyond cognitive benefits, there are social and ethical benefits to a pleasurable education.

*Singing*

*Dancing, Sam Sheridan, 1997*

*Loving*

*Partnering*

*Caring*

*Painting*

*Parenting*

## Opening the black box

For many years, the brain remained a "black box." It was closed and its sides were opaque. At last, the black box of the brain is opening, and we glimpse a treasure chest.

In 1996, the magazine *Newsweek* featured the child's brain twice as cover story news. It did so again in 1997 (Begley). *Time* magazine featured babies' brains, too, early in 1997 (Nash). *The New Yorker* featured an article on brains and violent behavior in the early spring of 1997 (Gladwell)..

*Top off the black box, Sam Sheridan, 1997*

*Treasure chest brain, SRS 97*

It is not new that learning takes practice. What is new is this: the mind can practice so that it develops fast, integrative parallel processing, focused attention, broadly retrievable information bases including memories, and an array of all-purpose, transferable logical operations; or, the mind can practice and practice and not learn anything.

By learning one simple strategy—how to sustain attention—considerable emotional and cognitive reserves become accessible. In fact, attentional/integrative activities constitute the neurobiology of an intelligent mechanism. It is this mechanism which Drawing/Writing sets in motion.

## The brain and the Self

The following quote from an article by Walter J. Freeman, Professor of Physiology and Anatomy at the University of California, Berkeley provides closure to this section on neurobiology: "Wholeness refers to progressive growth of the self, from embryo to fetus to birth, childhood, adulthood and into old age. The self has a certain potential in this trajectory, which may or may not be realized. But the intent in this process of stretching forth is to realize the maximum potential, and the purpose of the striving of individuals is to achieve their maximal state of being.

"Each new insight creates a change that involves everything. One of the best pieces of evidence for the global nature of the learning process involves a release of hormones—norepinephrine, dopamine, acetlylcholine, histamine, serotonin and uncounted neuropeptides—and the systems that release these hormones are global ones that project throughout the cerebrum. When hormones are released, they soak the brain, they drench it. So a learning experience involves the entirety of both hemispheres.

"The intentional structure is a synaptic web which is drenched in neuro modulators, and which is a continual process of reaching out into the environment to incorporate new input. The dynamical systems have two aspects. One is the external aspect in which the animal or person is engaged in activity. That is the self which is doing things. The other aspect is the internal monitoring of the system, and that's consciousness."[33]

Each of us must reach out into the world, as we can, creating of that external world what we can. As we reach out, we monitor and modify our constructions against previous ideas and experiences. We also encounter other people's thinking, adjusting ours to theirs when required. To some degree, our perceptions and those of the people we live and work with must tally. Pictures and words help us to express, adjust and share our worlds.

This reaching out and this monitoring is called "intentionality": our will to know and be known, our will to communicate and to understand, our will to act and to interact—these are our intentions. Childhood, early education and on-going education determine, in part, the degree to which we maximize our mental potential. Our brains and our selves are up to us. Words and images are two sets of tools for our self-creation.

---

[33] Walter J. Freeman, "Happiness Doesn't Come on Bottles", *Journal of Consciousness Studies* 4 No. 1, 1997, pp. 67-70.

# Drawing, writing and therapy

*Staircase, reflection, little water, Greg Albert, 1997*

Self-creation and self-knowledge go hand in hand. The therapeutic uses of drawing and writing are well-known. Many therapists use drawing and writing in their practices. Greg Albert, a twenty-nine year old Continuing Education student in early childhood education has climbed the staircase out of his past through drawing and writing. For Greg, writing opened the "shadowy box" of "stuffed down" feelings.

*Stackable boxes, shadowed, Greg Albert, 1997*

Greg was taught by an art therapist to draw boxes in perspective. Journals became a routine part of his recovery when another therapist asked him to write down his memories and thoughts. In the past seven years, Greg has filled 15 journals. Recently, he has added "diamonds" to the boxes and is "stacking" the boxes. In addition, he is drawing dynamic spirals.

*Box with diamond. Saturn, Greg Albert, 1997*

The fact that Greg draws the dynamic spiral of life and writes poems courageous enough to express the ambiguous reality of family love attest to his growth. Greg's example supports the therapeutic usefulness of drawing and writing to the survival of the human mind and body. In the following poem, the phrase "knows no boundaries" does not mean that love is limitless in the usual sense, but that hurtful family love recognizes no boundaries between family members.

*Family poem, parts 1 and 2, Greg Albert, 1997*

Therapy is a lifelong process. It is the on-going business of the self. Like the brain, the self constructs itself over and over again. To do so, it requires tools for self-reflection, like Greg's "small water." The activities of drawing and writing are integral to this business. Diaries are not the exclusive property of young girls. In the eighteenth and nineteenth centuries, men as well as women kept journals, especially travelogues which often included drawing and watercolor sketches. Drawing/Writing journals persist as companions to those who intended to live an examined life.

### Lighting the black box

In many ways, the brain still remains a "black box." In 1986, the pioneering work by David Andrews, professor of psychology at Keene State College, pointed the way toward educational applications of brain science. Andrews used EEG's of dyslexic boys' adolescent brains to encourage these students to experiment with their brain processes. Until MRIs become routine diagnostic procedures in the classroom, we cannot peek into students' brains to catalog developmental delays or damage, underworked or overworked brain areas, mono- or bilateral strategies, gifts or genius. We can, however, appreciate the fact that every brain is a renewable, modifiable, extraordinary resource, and we can do everything in our power to maximize learning experiences for children's brains. We can observe attentive, excited faces;

we can gauge the success of our tactics by observing demonstrable changes in drawing, writing, reading and speaking skills.

This book provides a strategy based on brain research for solving the conundrum of the "black box." Without referring to brain scans, students' brains can be remediated and enriched in demonstrable ways that are clear to both teachers and students. After a session of Drawing/Writing, the drawings and writings of talented and gifted students show gains, as do the drawings and writings of students with deficits or delays, as well as those of the "average" student. In fact, these categories no longer remain distinct. In a Drawing/Writing classroom, descriptions like gifted, limited, or average are far less useful than words like attentive, engaged, productive, and literate. The telling evidence of growth, the real indications of caliber of mind are the selectivity, integration, and innovation demonstrated by students' drawing and writings, and by their increased thoughtfulness, expressivity, judiciousness, and tolerance. Even if the box of the brain remains shadowy, the area around it can shine with light. In a neuroconstructivist classroom, teachers and students are this light.

*Boxed brain shining with light, SRS 97*

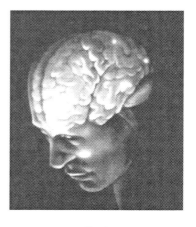

*Brain*

# THE THINKING CHILD: TRAINING TO TRANSFER

*Claus Kormannshaus, 1997*

"If the **brain** is cross-modal by nature, education should be cross-modal by design"

*– SR Sheridan, 1991*

# PART FOUR

## *The Thinking Child*

### A WholeBrain Curriculum Guide

**Cross-modal teaching and learning strategies
for a Neuroconstructivist classroom
including sample materials:**

- **A Drawing/Writing-based English curriculum**
- **A Drawing/Writing-based Studio Arts curriculum**
- **A Drawing/Writing-based Art Survey curriculum**
- **Sample Drawing/Writing syllabi, quizzes and final exams**

"All of the research and theory indicate that learning has nothing to do with speed."

*Ethan Micheaux Hazzard-Watkins, during his Harvard/Radcliffe interview
when he was a senior at Amherst High School, 1996*

"We must be flexible as adults and teachers, aware that our perceptions of the world around us
are clouded by what we think we know."

*Claus Kormannshaus, artist, teacher, biker, MAT student, in conversation, summer, 1997*

# To the Reader

I am an artist and a writer. It is logical for me to design a translation exchange between drawing and writing. The deliberate exchange of information between two modes of representation defines a cross-modal teaching strategy. In this case, the exchange reflects the basic left brain/right brain, verbal/visual capabilities of the mind. Thus, this exchange makes general neurobiological sense. As a teacher, you will devise your own cross-modal exercises. I am simply providing the guidelines, a sample method, and several sample curricula to illustrate Neuroconstructivist teaching and learning in the context of the two disciplines with which I am most familiar.

The first part of this book is a persuasive essay designed to demonstrate that the activities of drawing and writing are related and should be connected. The second part of the book shows how to implement the program called Drawing/Writing, providing evidence of its success through illustrations. The third part of the book offers information on brain structure and process and provides specific teaching tips and suggestions for brain-based education.

The fourth part of this book is a curriculum guide to a drawing-based approach to writing across the curriculum. In terms of the evolution of the human brain, and in terms of everyday life, writing remains a *spatial* activity, as does reading. Making decisions about the layout or the format or the pattern of words on the page is one of the first steps in the mental organization in writing and reading. In general, we organize the marks we call writing—as we organize the marks we call arithmetic or geometric proofs or calculus or figure drawing—in certain ways. A glance at the layout of the marks on a page will not tell us whether the marks are fiction or non-fiction, narrative or biography or an essay, but a glance will tell us that the marks are writing, not drawing or mathematics, and that the writing is probably meant to be poetry, even a specific verse form.

Writing and reading are multi-level tasks; a preliminary task is spatial pattern recognition, like recognizing a face. Successive analyses move toward linguistic analysis. Not only did written language develop out of a spatial location system by adding the "what is it?" to the "where is it?" questions asked by the brain, but written language endures as an act of spatial recognition. After that first decision—from this layout of words on the page, this is probably poetry or prose—reading progresses to content and meaning. Unless the writer sits down deliberately to write, say, a sestina, there is often a simultaneity to layout and meaning. Form and content are mutually generative.

Training in drawing teaches students to be alert and attentive to the spatial implications and *requirements* of text. The spatial implications of words on a page are powerful. Font, size of type, length of sentence, inclusion or absence of punctuation, inclusion or absence of images engage the brain through the eyes. The charmed eye reads on.

The following Neuroconstructivist guidelines for teaching do more than demonstrate how to combine drawing with writing in your field. A Neuroconstructivist teacher in any field, including English, realizes that how material presents itself to the brain through the eyes, or through appealing to the brain's ability to visualize, is of primary importance to introducing the material, to studying it, to understanding it, to learning it, and to using it.

The relationship between spatial and linguistic information processing is so embedded that the exact moment or the exact brain location where spatial understanding gives way to language—where visual meets verbal—is difficult to pinpoint, anecdotally or scientifically. It makes the most sense educationally to emphasize the continuities rather than the discontinuities, teaching writing and reading in the context of training in drawing.

# The Thinking Child

Guidelines for teaching and learning are provided by studying the brain. Specific tips for WholeBrain teaching and learning are located in Part 3, "Hitchhikers' Guide." By combining these tips and the following guidelines, the Neuroconstructivist student or teacher can devise effective teaching and learning strategies.

The general Neuroconstructivist guidelines are these:

- use a spatial or visual approach to information, first
- use a linguistic or verbal approach, second
- then, deliberately connect the spatial and the linguistic tasks in a translation exchange exercise.

The translation exchange exercise in Drawing/ Writing, for instance, is achieved by the sentence, "My Contour drawing tells me that my object is....because...." The implication is that the drawing contains accessible, identifiable information which can be described with words. A sample Neuroconstructivist English curriculum follows. Sample Fine Arts Neuroconstructivist curricula are provided, as well. A WholeBrain guide to Drawing/Writing in Spanish is in progress, as is an elementary school language arts and mathematics curriculum called "Rainbow Noodles and Zebra Trees."

*Rohit Sangal , Fractal Basic Shape, feather, second grade, Applewild School, 1997*

*Kate Snyder, Closing Drawing and Writing, cow jaw bone, second grade, Applewild School, 1997*

## The Neuroconstructivist classroom: A dynamic system

To see clearly, to draw accurately and powerfully, to write responsively and abundantly, to work independently with full attention, to work cooperatively with others, to have confidence in decisions, to communicate with increasing clarity, to be brave enough to try to restructure the world through language, the mind requires an education tailored to its nature and its needs. A Neuroconstructivist, or WholeBrain, approach provides an education geared to comprehensive meaning-making. Like the brain's connections, the Neuroconstructivist classroom is dynamic, responsive and complex.

Phylogenetically and ontogenetically the human brain begins its meaning-making adventure with visual information. In a similar fashion, this Neuroconstructivist literacy curriculum initiates meaning-making through a visual approach, drawing. In each of the following writing exercises, drawing provides the first level of information; then, writing extracts that information. Far too powerful to be relegated to "pre-writing," the act of drawing connects the thinker directly with experience, memory and emotion. Drawing acts as an *aide memoire*, as well as an in-the-present activity for recording current information, illuminating writers—sometimes in startling ways.

## A Neuroconstructivist curriculum: The child as thinker

This curriculum focuses on students as thinkers. More definitive than age, gender, race, culture or socio-economic class, the act of thinking characterizes students. The richer the learning environment, the denser the neural connections; the more powerful the thinking skills, and the broader the range of mental strategies. Students *learn* to think. The Neuroconstructivist approach aligns with popular classroom practices honoring student learning and adds another dimension; students not only learn how to think; they construct their brains in the process.

Intelligence: *inter* means "between" or "among," and *legere* means "to gather, pick or choose." Thinking involves choosing and gathering.

## Training to transfer: The theoretical bases

The theoretical foundation for "The Thinking Child" is provided by six conclusions distilled from educational and neurobiological research (Sheridan, 1991). These conclusions place curricular focus on the thinking child as a dynamic, delicate system designed for receiving, exchanging, transferring and transforming information:

1) Intelligence is dynamic and modifiable; it is developable or retardable.

2) Information stored in more than one way is remembered more strongly and is more broadly accessible than information stored in just one way. Connected information bases are more flexible and versatile than bases without connections.

3) Effective abstract thought is based on a graphic and concrete (highly tactile, visual, multi-sensory) understanding of things.

4) The role of the involved observer is critical for students as thinkers. The act of observation not only determines what is learned (or according to physics, what actually happens), but the quality of the act of observation determines the accuracy, completeness and comprehensiveness of what is learned.

5) Intelligent thought accepts as givens these two premises: every symbol system is approximate; several symbol systems, linked in parallel mode, provide a more complete—if still approximate—explanation.

6) Intelligence tests should do several things: they should measure spatial as well as linguistic intelligence; they should be administered promptly after a training program which has been designed to promote the kinds of intelligence being tested for. In addition, they should be administered by the test-takers themselves, allowing students to evaluate their own skills, hereby growing in meta-cognition—or the ability to think about thinking—which in and of itself encourages richer thought. Finally, intelligence tests should be given in the spirit of providing temporary benchmarks in a lifetime of broadening and deepening mental skills.

## A position on language

The Neuroconstructivist position on language is that the quality of language training determines not only what mental objects students' minds construct but the ways in which their minds will go about constructing mental objects thereafter. The relationship of mental objects to modes of thought is like the relationship of the chicken to the egg: the mutuality poses a conundrum. Still, education must start somewhere. This program starts with visual language instruction, using that training to establish the preconditions for how the mind will view and manipulate mental objects framed with language. Students benefit by learning how to adjust and negotiate meaning, appreciating the fact that their own use of language will grow and change, and can become increasingly rich and precise.

Not only how language is acquired but what specific language is acquired influences the shape and quality of thought. A mother tongue may encourage and allow certain kinds of thinking. A language like mathematics encourages logical operations, speculations and intuitions in universal ways, as do the languages of the arts. Like other brain processes, the capacity for language in connection with a mother tongue is given—an accident of birth—and yet constructed, word by word. Each new word extends the scope of thought.

Not only do we learn to speak, and thus to think, in French or Spanish, Khmer or Chinese, we learn to speak the language of the arts, sciences, histories or mathematics. Whatever our accident of birth in terms of a mother tongue, we can share the eye and tongue of the artist or the geologist. Additional "eyes" bring us closer together as linguists. Harvard professor David Layzer writes, "We *learn* to see in certain ways. A landscape painter doesn't see the same scene as a non-painter, even though the patterns of light impinging on their retinas may be nearly identical" (Layzer, 256). Similarly, Amherst College physics professor Arthur Zajonc writes about the relationship of language use to an appreciation of rocks in *Catching the Light* (1993): "Standing with a geologist before an outcropping of rock, he sees more than I who stand next to him. I make a few distinctions, he a hundred, and each one tells a story to him of which I know nothing: glaciation, a lake bed, or volcanic lava flow; he finds the fossil under my foot. I feel not only illiterate but blind. Not only does the geologist interpret phenomena more fully, he sees things I miss utterly" (204). The more languages we know—the language of the geologist, the language of the artist—the more we will see and the more we can share. If we learn to draw, write, and read and if we are raised in the habit of learning, we can acquire as many languages for seeing and knowing as time and energy allow.

## Two general curricular categories: visual studies and verbal studies

In a Neuroconstructivist curriculum, two broad categories subsume content areas: Visual Studies and Verbal Studies. No content area is taught without reference to the relevant thinking skills in both broad categories. A student might major in painting, or Visual Studies, but he would also study art history texts and literacy criticism about painting, as well as the physics of color theory, the chemistry of pigments, and the lives of individual painters who particularly interest or influence him. Similarly, a student might major in Medieval literature, or Verbal Studies, but also study the art, music, and dance of the times.

In this book, the words "visual" and "verbal" are used in the broadest sense, aligning visual information processing with spatial intelligence and verbal information processing with linguistic intelligence. The categorization of a content area is quite arbitrary. Mathematics, for instance, might fall under the general category of language; still, geometry, one of its subsystems, requires spatial understanding, and, in fact, spatial skills are currently recognized as fundamental to mathematical understanding and are posited as one of the reasons why boys do better than girls with mathematics. Similarly, the applied and performing arts might be classified as visual studies, although dance is one of the body's languages, as drawing is one of the eye's languages. The advantage to cross-modal or spatial/linguistic curricular design is that it is not necessary to fight to the death over classifications; specific content areas, as well as visual intelligence, verbal intelligence, logico-mathematical, musical, bodily-kinaesthetic, personal and social intelligences[34] are subsumed under these two categories. By making sure students attend to the visual and verbal aspects of any subject they study, a range of spatial and linguistic intelligences are exercised in an evenhanded manner, training the whole brain to conduct comprehensive explorations in any discipline or content area. Brain science supports the meta-classification of content areas and mental skills.

How do we devise Neuroconstructivist curricula? We do so by asking two questions: what spatial exercises are relevant to a specific content areas? What linguistic exercises are appropriate to that specific content area? These questions extend beyond academics to athletics or any other course of study, including technical/vocational education. For instance, after asking herself these questions, a basketball coach might decide that the relevant spatial training in her field includes shooting baskets and passing to a teammate. Additional relevant spatial/linguistic training might include the physics of space, time, motion and the dimensions of a basketball. To add these dimensions to her coaching, she might have to do some boning up on physics. The coach can engage players in a linguistic dialogue that relates to the spatial dialogue called basketball. Because reading is a general skill, the coach has the necessary skills to devise her own cross-modal approach to teaching basketball. Her teaching will automatically be Neuroconstructivist if she encourages students to draw and write about the game. An English teacher must discover the spatial/visual dimensions for his field—from how words are arranged on a page to visualizing plot or character. As for the maths and sciences, these fields already make use of graphing calculators and illustrated lab reports. If tactile, exploratory approaches are not already in place, three-dimensional models and direct field exploration can be added to all fields. In technical/vocational curricula, the linguistic element may require greater emphasis, including more mathematics and increased writing and reading. The invaluable element—spatial/visual, hands-on training—is already in place.

A Neuroconstructivist approach simply integrates spatial and linguistic training—on any terms available to the teacher or coach. The athlete trained via a Neuroconstructivist mode will not only dribble, run, shoot and pass, but will be able to express and refine these activities using words, diagrams, and formulae, increasing her awareness of the relationships on the court as well as the relationships between playing basketball and other physical and mental activities. This awareness, in turn, reinforces the principles involved, making them more broadly useful. An awareness of the skills and principles in basketball allows that sport to enrich other areas of study like mathematics, physics, and human physiology. In a Neuroconstructivist athletic program, the sport becomes the study of the applicability and transfer of skills and concepts, besides playing a game. The Neuroconstructivist focus blurs the distinction between academics and athletics, as it does between the

---

[34] The theory of multiple intelligences has been developed by Harvard educational theorist Howard Gardner in *Frames of Mind* (1983), and in *The Mind's New Science* (1985).

arts and academics. The human endeavor of thought takes center stage. *Mens sana in corpore sano.* Our brains are housed in bodies designed to absorb and express meaning. The health of the body influences the health of the mind, and vice versa. Neurobiological research brings mind and body ever closer.

## Visual searches of interest

Before considering content, that is, before deciding whether to teach the legend of Beowulf or the legend of Gilgamesh, two connected issues require attention in curricular design. First, what inherently interests students must be identified. Then, using this activity or content area as a hook, persistent work can be encouraged by teaching students the basic habit of mind necessary to all substantive mental endeavors: sustained attention. Because what is attended to becomes interesting, habits of attention are the preconditions for work with new material. Attention and content constitute a feedback loop.

The activity of drawing is inherently interesting to children. They are born wanting to draw and able to draw. Like a shiny object, the act of drawing attracts children's bodies and minds. As children grow, training in drawing can be used to encourage them to pay sustained attention. With time, training in drawing can be used to

teach minds to visualize and construct mental models in a variety of ways. The complexity and accuracy of the models the mind constructs will depend upon the brain's training in visualization. The five-step drawing program provided in this book trains the mind to pay attention, to conduct sustained visual searches, and to construct accurate and comprehensive mental models using contour line, several approaches to geometry, optically accurate three-dimensional rendering, and recombinant, balanced, abstract representations. Drawing scores triply as a valuable learning activity.

Visualization enhances mathematical understanding. Graphing calculators have become standard equipment for many students. Drawing is commonly used as a tool for understanding and learning information in the physical and biological sciences. Computer modeling provides enhanced understanding in the maths and the sciences, as well as in the field of design. To understand complex systems, a variety of representations are required; each sheds light on an aspect of the system. Traditionally, drawing has been reserved for academic subjects of considerable rigor—or drawing has been relegated to the non-academic play of very young children. Children's writing develops into adult writing. By logical extension, the drawings of children develop into adult powers of visualization, extending the possibilities for intellectual exploration inherent in the brain's design.

# A Course in Composition

<u>Objectives:</u> The objectives of the course are:

- To increase students' writing and reading skills by teaching them to pay attention to visual detail and to recognize and appreciate the spatial layout and effects of written language through their own drawing, then through their own writing, and then through the modeling and analysis of texts of others.
- To teach students that writing is as accessible as drawing. Students who create Composite Abstractions know that dense text—whether complicated prose or the intense distillation of poetry—will give way to their probing scrutiny.

<u>Materials:</u> The Drawing/Writing supplies listed in Part 2, including Drawing/Writing journals, as well as your usual composition and literature program.

## BACKGROUND:

Engaging students in writing and reading is a challenge. Brain-based strategies meet this challenge. The following exercises are translation exercises. To enter the experience of writing, students recall direct experiences through drawing, and then translate that drawing into writing. As the curriculum progresses, the translation exercises require certain layouts for words: prose-like layouts, poetry-like layouts, a playwriting layout. Eventually, specific samples of writing are introduced for students to model and analyze. Using a certain verbal layout—say, the specific grammatical organization Paul Gallico used in the first part of *The Snow Goose*—students learn to participate in and to appreciate text as structure. By translating their own personal narrative into a certain structure, they participate directly in that spatial arrangement. They see and they feel the pattern, learning that the formal arrangement of words on a page strongly influences the organization of content, and, thus, of meaning. Certain visual layouts, like the 39-line verse form called the sestina, in which 6 words repeat in a mathematical order, create spatial connections between words and ideas. The look and feel of language on a page enhance and even determine meaning. These formatting or layout-occasioned events, these Strange Loops, are sometimes called inspiration, or, the Muse.

A sentence, a paragraph, a short story, a poem, a play, an instructional manual—all of these pieces of writing are layout problems, or visual tasks. A series of translation exercises and layout problems follow. By practicing them, students will learn that the distinctions between poetry and prose are arbitrary, organizational and intentional. They will experience writing directly, as a natural, possible, compelling and important action of the mind in which choice of format is a basic element. They will learn that composition is just that: composing words on a page in certain ways for certain reasons and effects. Like organizing line, form, color and space in a drawing, words, too, require right relationships; neither too much nor too little provides a useful strategy for composing text as well as images.

Competent writing, reading and thinking skills are the primary goals of an English teacher. To meet these goals, Drawing/Writing uses training in drawing to introduce students to analytical and inferential thought processes. Initially, some students will mistrust drawing as a "baby activity." Students who have been identified as learning disabled may jump to the conclusion that the teacher has given up on them as students. Many students mistrust drawing in connection with English, even though they may accept drawing as a legitimate activity in the biology lab. For many students and teachers, drawing and writing only go together in the younger grades when children are encouraged to illustrate stories. After grammar school, story illustration no longer figures prominently in literature programs, and training in drawing is not a usual preparation for the study of grammar or style. In general, as students move up through the educational system, drawing becomes increasingly foreign in connection with most content areas except the maths and sciences.

One session with Drawing/Writing gives students the neurobiological background (you, as a Drawing/Writing teacher, are invited to share the material in Part 3, "Hitchhikers' Guide") as well as the direct experience necessary to understand cross-modal processes. One session also allows students to appreciate drawing as a legitimate intellectual activity connected to language-learning. An understanding begins to grow: cross-modal training helps build better brains. Students learn, in addition, the importance of attentive and accurate visualization to effective writing.

As a purely practical matter, Drawing/Writing students rarely wonder what to write about. The drawn object provides subject matter for poems, plays, essays and stories. Self-portraits and figure drawings supply material for character studies. The self-evaluation tool, Rescore, supplies direct experiences with grammar and punctuation, encouraging the skills and sensibilities necessary to the growth of voice and style.

After two weeks of Drawing/Writing, students become more attentive, more self-directed, and more cohesive as a group. Analytical drawing combined with reflective writing allows brains to blossom and flourish. This experience of growth, along with training in attention and self-expression, makes it unlikely that students will return to less effective habits of thought.

Procedure: Fit Drawing/Writing in when it is possible— say, at the beginning, middle, and end of the academic year. After using the object, you might try the self-portrait, and then the figure study as outlined in Part 2 of this book. Otherwise, follow your English curriculum (or other curriculum), adding any of the drawing-based writing exercises described below that fit your needs. The rule of thumb is to teach prose in the context of students' prose, poetry in the context of students' poetry, formal

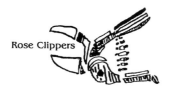

Rose Clippers

Step one: the first thing we did was to write about the five senses, using my object; the garden clippers looked like the mouth of a bird; they tasted like salt; they were heavy. When you squeezed them, they sounded like a duck, and they smelled like old dust in a desert.

Step two was to write about the line quality of my drawing; the yellow part is smooth like a little kitten. It's rough like rocks on the mountain. My contour looks like a bird mouth. The lines that I used to draw it look like a continuous road.

Step three was to write about value: my object is light like a bright angel, because you can see the shape of it. My object is medium in value as if you are standing in the middle of the pit because the light comes in the sides. My object is dark in value as if you were inside a cage and you cannot see anything.

Step four was to write about geometry: the triangular part looks like a piece of cheesecake. The rectangular part looks like a street under construction; the circular part looks like a basketball; the trapezoidal part looks like the shape of a bridge and the rhomboid part looks like a weird door or like a drop of falling, heavy oil.

To finish, the inorganic part looks like an eroded part; it looks like a squared "o."

by Jorge Fiallos, Form V

*Jorge Fiallos, Rose Clippers, ninth grade, Eaglebrook School, 1990*

Untitled

One day, Mrs. Sheridan brought a bag of objects in the class; then, she told us to take one of them from the bag; I took a toy firetruck. She told us to write about our objects using our five senses—sight, hear, smell, touch and taste; then she told us to use our five senses and feel it in the class. When I touched it, I felt that it was cold like ice, but the cold shine made it look as hot as the sun. There was a bell in the truck; it was silver. When it rings, it sounds like a coin dropping into an empty glass. I smelled it. It smelled like an old iron. It tasted salty. There was a place for hoses at the back, but there were no hoses there, so there was lots of space around the back. There were discharge valves at the rear. When I tried to force it, it didn't move; I thought that this was an old toy.

In Hong Kong—where I come from—the fire trucks are different. I think they are bigger; at the back, there is a very big box for storing water, and there is a long ladder for saving peoples lives from the windows.

The next day, we drew the contour of our objects, and wrote about the quality of the line in the contour drawing, then I drew my toy firetruck and wrote about the lines. The quality of the line was smooth like the surface of a desk. Smooth suggests that my object was light-reflective like a mirror; the side line of the wheels are bumpy like the surface of infirmary field in the winter. The line is simple like a rectangle. The side line of the bell curves like a soup bowl turned over and the side lines are curved like a big, rectangular rubbish bin, tipped over.

The next time, we used different kinds of geometry to draw our object, and used similes to write about it. The wheel wells were trapezoidal like the roof of a house. The bell was semi-circular like a compass. The wheels were circular like a hanging circle pan in the kitchen. The whole shape of the toy fire truck's cab

6

was rhomboid like how a little boy draws a square. The wheels of the truck were organic like a diver's path through the air, but the whole drawing is inorganic like a huge rock.

The last drawing of the toy firetruck was called LMD; it meant Light, Medium, and Dark. My object was light in value like the moon because it reflects light in the same ways as the moon, and it was light in value like freedom because light can reflect freely. It was medium in value like dust because its color was grey and it looks a little bit dirty; and it was medium in value like sadness because it was not bright. It was dark in value like carbon because its color is black and it looks very dirty; it was dark in value like deadness because it was as dark as the place of death.

I have learned lots of things in writing because Mrs. Sheridan chose drawing and writing for us; I think this is a good way to learn English.

by Tom Yeung, Form V

*Tom Yeung, Untitled, ninth grade, Eaglebrook School, 1990*

structures, like the expository essay, in the context of previously generated student writing.

**PEER SHARE:** Not only do students show their drawings to their peers and read their writing aloud in a Drawing/Writing English curriculum, but students exchange pieces of writing, doing peer-editing. As peer readers gain practice and skill with editing, they provide specific suggestions for spelling, punctuation and grammar. As peer mentors, students shoulder work traditionally done by the teacher. Peer-sharing encourages mutual teaching and learning, enabling initially weaker students to discover startling analytical and directive strengths, gaining confidence. Increasing confidence allows the mind to relax and absorb new material, including the technical details of grammar, punctuation, spelling, and formal systems like the sonnet. The natural desire in human beings to take control, to correct, and to improve is given soil, rain, air and light, allowing the growth of a luxuriant interest in the structure of language. Some of the least likely students grow into fierce and bushy grammarians.

There is a saying: "A gentleman is never unintentionally rude." The same can be said of a literate person, "She is never unintentionally ungrammatical." The more words and grammatical constructions students share, the better they will communicate. This does not mean that students must always use standard English. Editing provides challenges beyond asking questions in the margin or identifying specific spelling or grammar errors. The distinction between an error and emerging voice can be a very fine line. The only way to distinguish between error and voice is to ask the writer if he knows whether the construction is ungrammatical and whether he is using it deliberately. Some grammatical constructions may be technically "wrong," yet "right" for the tone of the writer. Editing requires keen sensibilities and judgment and time. Peer-to-peer editing provides the one-on-one attention most teachers simply cannot provide. And, in the final analysis, who needs to be the grammarian: the writer or the teacher?

Peer-editing can be assigned as homework. To preserve valuable classroom time, the peer-edited work can be shared in mini, peer-to-peer conferences scheduled by the students for out-of-class time. It is in this intense one-on-one, discursive context that learning about language as structure occurs. Optimally, mini-conferencing between students should occur during class time so that general principles of good writing discovered by students can be shared with the group.

Students need to work out a system for editing each other's work, including abbreviations like "sp" for spelling, and symbols for questions about grammar, punctuation, organization, audience, voice. Questioned usage—apart from specific suggestions—allows the writer rather than the reader to do the correcting. The peer need not necessarily know the answer to the question he or she raises in the margins of a peer's paper. A "felt" question is as useful to the writer as a specific suggestion—in fact, if we stay aligned with the constructivist mode—more so.

**DISCUSSION:** Teachers of Drawing/Writing-based curricula like the one that follows repeatedly ask students in class discussions to describe how drawing affects their writing as well as how each translation exercise extends their writing. As students become practicing poets, playwrights, and prose writers, their ability to critique literature increases. Informed experience as writers gives readers a foothold on literary criticism; they speak from personal knowledge. In a Neuroconstructivist classroom, direct experience with a literary mode precedes the study of literature in that mode. Then, modeling published writing in that mode, striving for word-for-word correspondence, students feel the bones of an author's writing. Knowing the bones, they appreciate the flesh.

### The First two-week session with Drawing/Writing using the object

Note: This will be followed by a second Drawing/Writing session with the self-portrait and a third with the figure, if time allows.

**Blind Contour, Regular Contour**
**Basic Shapes Euclidean, fractal, organic**
**Light-Medium-Dark**

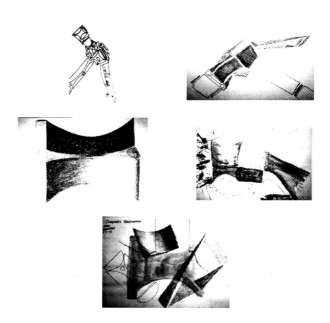

*The object by Jaime Babowitch; hammer, Euclidean, hammer LMD, hammer PW zoom in, Hammer CA#1 and #2, Westfield State studio course, 1994*

*Dave Wesniak, LMD drawing, Central High School, Springfield, MA, 1997: student of Holly Tuttle*

### The "Perfect" Whole

*Melissa Donovan, self-portrait, Westfield State studio course, 1994*

*Chad Roberts, self portrait, Westfield State studio course, 1994*

## The Composite Abstraction

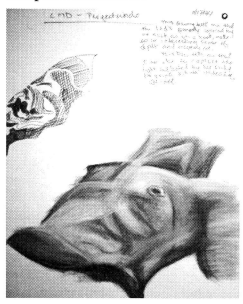

*Dawn Kruzewski, figure study (2). LMD, Westfield State studio course, 1994*

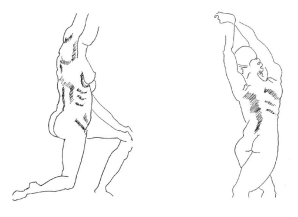

*SRS, Figure studies, 1995*

### Exercise 1:

### A walk from the doorway. Translating from personal experience to drawing to writing.

Procedure: Ask students to imagine themselves taking a walk from the doorway of the place they live. Ask them to close their eyes and see, taste, smell, feel, hear everything that happens on the walk.

*The five sensory icons*

Then ask students to do the following:

- Draw this walk. Include every detail sensed in the mind.
- Now, look at the drawing.
- Write about the walk by looking at every detail in the drawing.
- Write about the direction of the walk. Why did the student go right, for instance, and not left?
- Is the direction the student took on the mental walk important? Why?

**PEER SHARE:** The first time students peer share as editors, the teacher will have to take time out to ask them to devise an editing procedure and set of abbreviations.

**GROUP DISCUSSION:** Allow the group to devise editing procedures and abbreviations.

**DEMONSTRATE:** After students have drawn and written "The Walk" and peer-edited this piece, hand out a favorite piece of writing about place. By asking students to read this piece aloud, sentence by sentence, student by student, all of the students will stay alert and engaged and every one will get practice with reading aloud. Reading aloud is important even at the college level.

**DISCUSSION:** How the published writing about place resembles and differs from students' writing about place provides starting places for discussion in which student opinion is informed by personal experience with the genre.

## Exercise 2:

### Preparation for poetry: Translating the prose walk into students' conception of poetry

<u>Procedure:</u> The brain is organized to translate from one mode of representation to another. Translation exercises encourage optimum brain function. After translating a prose description into poetry, students will appreciate the fact that ideas can be expressed in different ways, and that different modes of expression have different advantages.

Students have definite ideas about poetry. Some students think that the last words of lines have to rhyme, and must do so in couplets. Some students believe that there need be no rhyme structure. Some say poetry is hard to understand. Some say it is easy. By writing these opinions down as if they were rules, students construct a system for poetry before studying poetry formally. These rules and "Walk from the Doorway" poems written by the rules can then be compared with forms like the sonnet, as well as with specific sonnets, like those by Shakespeare.

Like drawing, poetry comes naturally to children. By encouraging students to write poetry, the teacher brings them into a closer, more natural relationship with writing.

**PEER SHARE:**

## Exercise 3:

### Translating student poems into sonnets

*A Wave*
*from a Dr/Wr session with a pair of swim goggles*

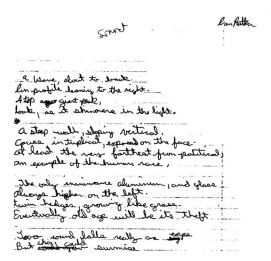

*Sonnet, Ian Rutka, "A Wave," eighth grade,*
*Eaglebrook School, 1990*

*A wave, about to break.*
*In profile leaning to the right*
*Atop a giant peak,*
*Look, as it shimmers in the light.*

*A steep wall, sloping vertical,*
*Caves in triplicate, exposed on the face.*
*At least, the very farthest from political,*
*An example of the human race.*

*The only inanimance aluminum and glass*
*Always higher on the left*
*Twin hedges, growing like grass.*
*Eventually old age will be its theft.*

*Two round balls really are eyes.*
*But who could surmise.*

*Ian Rutka, self portrait #1, #2 and #3, eighth and ninth grade,*
*Eaglebrook School, 1989-1990*

<u>Procedure:</u> After students have written their own poems following their own rules, they will be more receptive to the formal aspects of poetry. Write the rhyme scheme and metric pattern for the Elizabethan, or Shakespearean, and for the Petrarchan, or Italian sonnet on the board. Teach metric feet as an immediately useful tool, not as an academic abstraction. Sonnets are usually written in iambic pentameter: there are five iambs per line, or "short-long" units—as in the word "remárk." Invite the class to call out lines to a nonsense poem using both rhyme schemes. The rhyme scheme for the English sonnet is abab, cdcd, efef, gg. The rhyme scheme for the Italian sonnet is abbaabba

cdcdcd or cdecde. This scheme appeals to the ear, first, more than to the eye. (The sestina, on the other hand, appeals to the eye, first, and then to the ear. The visual/pattern appeal of the sestina may be one of the reasons for its popularity with students. The mind also thrives on complexity and ingenuity which the sestina also provides.) Write these "poems" down as students call out the lines. (This is usually an uproarious experience.)

Ask students to choose one of the two sonnet forms and to translate their poem version of the original prose walk into a sonnet.

*The metric feet and their syllabic symbols*

After students have written their sonnets, read the following poems aloud. Which is the English, or Elizabethan sonnet and which is the Italian, or Petrarchan sonnet?

**THAT TIME OF YEAR**

That time of year thou mayst in me behold
When yellow leaves, or none, or few, do hang
Upon those boughs which shake against the cold,
Bare ruined choirs where late the sweet birds sang.
In me thou see'st the twilight of such day
As after sunset fadeth in the west,
Which by and by black night doth take away,
Death's second self, that seals up all in rest.
In me thou see'st the glowing of such fire,
That on the ashes of his youth doth lie
As the deathbed whereon it must expire,
Consumed with that which it was nourished by.
 This thou perceivest, which makes thy love more strong,
 To love that well which thou must leave ere long.

*William Shakespeare (1564–1616)*

*"That Time of Year" by William Shakespeare*

**ON FIRST LOOKING INTO CHAPMAN'S HOMER**

Much have I travelled in the realms of gold,
 And many goodly states and kingdoms seen;
 Round many western islands have I been
Which bards in fealty to Apollo hold.
Oft of one wide expanse had I been told          5
 That deep-browed Homer ruled as his demesne;
 Yet did I never breathe its pure serene
Till I heard Chapman speak out loud and bold:
Then felt I like some watcher of the skies
 When a new planet swims into his ken;
Or like stout Cortez when with eagle eyes
 He stared at the Pacific – and all his men
Looked at each other with a wild surmise –
 Silent, upon a peak in Darien.

*John Keats (1795–1821)*

*John Keats "On First Looking into Chapman's Homer"*

**PEER SHARE:** Include peer-editing.

Procedure:

1) Hand out sonnets written by Shakespeare and other poets, and ask students to read them aloud, line by line, going around the class. This procedure not only forces the group to pay attention and to practice oral reading skills, but encourages a shared cadence and the ability to work as a single voice.

2) Now that students are practitioners of poetry, ask them to evaluate the sonnet as a literary form.

3) Write their comments on the board. Compare these comments with the students' initial definitions of poetry, including the list of student "rules." How are the lists alike? How are they different?

4) List these conclusions on the board. Again, the goal is metacognition, or thinking about thinking in the context of poetry, rather than coming up with an ironclad code for poetry.

5) Ask students to translate their writing into the formal structure of the sonnet. Provide celebrated examples of that formal structure, like Shakespeare's sonnets, inviting comments from students about the success or non-success of the celebrated example from their new point of view as practitioners of the sonnet. This approach allows budding expert knowledge to inform student discussions,

encouraging learning and critical thinking, rather than parroting. When students have decided why and how Shakespeare is any good, ask them to model one of his sonnets grammatically, using their own words.

This order of events persists in a Neuroconstructivist English curriculum: ask students to write in response to a drawing exercise aimed at a certain goal, say, description, or narrative; teach a genre of writing, say, poetry, and then a specific form of writing in the context of student writing, like the sonnet, and present a celebrated example. Then ask students to model that celebrated example, using their own words, but strictly copying the example grammatically, noun for noun, comma for comma.

After writing a poem of one's own, it is easier to appreciate Emily Dickinson. After writing a sonnet of one's own, it is easier to be impressed by Shakespeare.

**DISCUSSION:** Ask your students how their first poems relate to their sonnets? How are they alike? How are they different? Where is each poem effective? Where is it not? Was the formal structure of the sonnet constraining or liberating? Discuss the possibility of freedom within a strict system of rules. Ruminate with your students about the extent to which rules and freedom can co-exist? Generalize from the sonnet to life.

## Exercise 4:

### Poetry in earnest

Presenting poetry as an esoteric form of writing runs contrary to observations about children's writing. As children's natural mark-making includes drawing, so children's natural writing patterns include poetry. Once students have written what they call poetry as well as what the world identifies as poetry, they are ready to discuss the work of recognized poets. Having laid this groundwork through the foregoing exercises, a series of poetry-writing exercises can be introduced, including modeling. The mystery poem, persona poem, dream poem, Elder poem follow. There is no particular order to these categories, only range—although subject matter progresses from things to people just as it does in the Drawing/Writing program.

Students who read poems aloud cannot escape the music of poetry any more than youngsters who repeat rap lyrics can escape the rap beat. My twenty-two-year-old son bursts into these verbal incantations spontaneously on city sidewalks. Their cadences are apparently in his blood. Wallace Steven's "Sunday Morning" perseveres as the beat in my blood:

### Sunday Morning
#### by Wallace Stevens

*Complacencies of the peignoir, and late*
*Coffee and oranges in a sunny chair,*
*And the green freedom of a cockatoo*
*Upon a rug mingle to dissipate*
*The holy hush of ancient sacrifice.*

Stevens' inspired oxymoron "mingle to dissipate" demonstrates the power of poetry.

Repeated practice with a sport develops certain muscles and skills. Practice with the sound and look of good writing develops certain mental muscles and skills. In athletics and writing, skill mastery only comes with practice. Writing exercises requiring grammatical modeling train the brain grammatically. To model a phrase word for word, students must be able to recognize nouns, adjectives and verbs as well as forms of punctuation. For this reason, grammatical modeling is brain-training in the context of poetry just as it will be below in the context of prose. I use models of poetry produced by elementary school children.[35]

To teach this section, discuss poetry as a craft.[36] Introduce aspects of sound including rhythm, assonance, alliteration, feminine endings and masculine endings, internal rhyme, terminal rhyme, and near-rhyme. Discuss aspects of form: the couplet, triplet, quatrain, sestet, and sestina. Discuss the terms image, symbol, and allusion. Students record all of this information in their Drawing/Writing journals, creating their own poetry reference books. Ask students to read poems aloud which illustrate the formal aspects of poetry. Then, let students write as they choose, peer-sharing after each venture into poetry. Students will take what they need from the formal aspects of poetry.

---

[35] Elizabeth McKim and Judith Steinberg's book <u>Beyond Words: Writing Poetry with Children</u> (Wampeter Press, Green Harbour, ME 02041, 1983). Other models I use are "Dulce et Decorum Est" by Wilfred Owen, and "What the Light Was Like" by Amy Clampitt. Poems by children as well as by older published poets may be used for grammatical modeling.

[36] Laurence Perrine's <u>Sound and Sense</u> (1956), Harcourt Brace Jovanovitch, Inc.

In this series of poetry exercises, students are asked to identify with the subjects of their poems. Recent research in child development shows that emotional intelligence in children, including their abilities to empathize and to exhibit compassion, is established by the age of three. Practice with identification through imaginative participation in poetry channels attention away from the self to others.

In the book *I/Thou,* the German theologian Martin Buber describes the importance of subject-to-subject rather than subject-to-object relationships. The act of drawing allows the recorder to join, or merge with the recorded event. Artists and writers learn to blur or eliminate distinctions between self and the other through attention. The removal of boundaries between self and other achieved through prayer or meditation is a similar attentional procedure. Art is, in this sense, devotional.

Students who take on the persona of a rabbit or describe a mystery in words participate in other modes of being.

<u>Mystery poem procedure:</u> Ask students to draw a picture of a mystery and to write a mystery poem. A mystery poem is a verbal puzzle. The subject is described in equivocal ways. I use Emily Dickinson's poem "I like to see it lap the miles." In the Dickinson poem, the mysterious subject turns out to be a train. Ask students to model the chosen mystery poem grammatically, word for word, as a follow-up exercise.

Drawing of a train, Neil Kohnke, Eaglebrook School, 1991

Mystery poem by J. J. (Jennifer) Heaton, Navajo, 1990, Las Cruces, Native American Preparatory Middle School, a Cushing Academy program, Cushing Academy, Ashburnham, MA Her ambition: Airforce pilot.

**DISCUSSION:** Was it hard to describe something in misleading ways? Was it freeing or constraining to model the Dickinson poem?

**PEER SHARE:**

I like to see it lap the miles,
And lick the valleys up,
And stop to feed itself at tanks,
And then, prodigious, step

Around a pile of mountains,
And, supercilious, peer
In shanties by the sides of roads,
And then a quarry pare

To fit its sides, and crawl between,
Complaining all the while
In horrid, hooting stanza,
Then chase itself down hill

And neigh like Boanerges—
Then, punctual as a star,
Stop—docile and omnipotent—
At its own stable door.

*"I like to see it lap the miles" by Emily Dickinson*

*Mare and foal, Claus Kormannshaus, 1997*

*Horse, after the sketch books of Da Vinci,*
*Sam Sheridan, 1990, Deerfield Academy*

Dream Poem Procedure: Discuss dreams and then ask students to draw a dream and to write about it. Hand out a student dream poem and read it aloud with the class. Discuss that poem in the context of other dream poems produced by your students.

Dreams are wishful thoughts -
they are mysterious and
exciting to us as human beings.
Sometimes they frighten us
and sometimes they fascinate us.
Dreams help us make our
own world subconsciously.     ad.
Dreams help us think of
why things work.
Dreams make us happy
when we're low.
Dreams help us find the
many different possibilities
and challenges of our
life.

Metaphor
Dreams are said, "to come true"!
But they don't.
People say dreams are supposed
to be happy.
Those people I envy, because I
only receive only nightmares.
Are these glimpses of my past,
present or my future life.
Are they going to happen or
did I eat something that
upsetted my stomach.
Are these dreams going
to affect me in anyway
Oh! Why! Oh! Why! is
this happening to me

**Animal poem procedure:** Ask students to draw a favorite animal and then to write about it in the Animal/Persona poem. The word "persona" means "very being." To assume the animal's very being, the writer must research the habits, habitats, looks, sounds, peculiarities, myths and lore associated with the animal.[37]

"A Lone again"
I, a lonely pond swimmer
with no companion
makes his sadness seem
brighter, full of cheer and happiness
And his eyes show gloom and emptiness.
but loneliness, kindness and sadness.
Isn't he just like me?
He is gentle, strong,
but cunning and skillful
He faces obstacles
that make him feel unwanted
and rejected
For he has no companion. no mate,
and no flock to fly with. He lives
but barely. It is his loneliness,
his sadness, his kindness and
his emptiness. that makes me
feel pity and love for him.
I can say again
Isn't he just like me?

*"Alone Again," Mary Abeita, Santo Domingo Pueblo,*
*middle school summer session, Native American Preparatory*
*School, 1990*

**DISCUSS AND PEER SHARE**

*Dream Poems, Phillip Russell, Navajo, middle school summer*
*session, Native American Preparatory School, 1990*

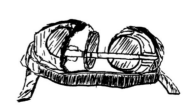

My object looks like a
mysterical world with
tiny people. The sound
also is very symmetrical
and simple. It shows
or tells me it is mis-
shapen but my object
is still useful.

*Phillip Russell, swim goggles, 1990*

**DISCUSS AND PEER SHARE:**

---

[37] Some of the following work was generated by a Drawing/Writing based English curriculum used by Massachusetts-based Cushing Academy's summer school for talented and gifted middle school Native American students in a program called NAPS. The work was first presented in NAPS Summer School Publications or is reprinted here by permission provided by the students to Dr. Sheridan during those sessions in Las Cruces, New Mexico in 1990.

Close Friend Poem: Ask students to pick a friend and sketch him or her. To acquire biographical information necessary to the writing, devise an interview sheet. The student-devised sheet facilitates and standardizes the information exchange. After students have written their Friend poems, provide a professionally published example and discuss it in the context of student friend poems.

*Friends, sketches, SRS*

Poem of Address: Write a poem of address, or an ode, to a close friend. Discuss direct address. Provide students with examples of odes. Proceed as above.

Murmur to a Girl

Listen, girl; listen to the storm-tide fog-groan --
That hoarse rumble of a voice over somersault water,
That gurgled dead-man's croon to an adopted daughter --
It's a warning, girl, from white-swirl chill-to-the-bone.
Take heed of what your daddy says as you stand there alone,
On that jagged shore of sometimes; ready or not or
Maybe just the salt-foam, girl naked where lost wind caught her.
Listen, girl; it's a secret no man can own.

What's it saying, girl, that tired moan of a voice?
What's it whispering in your homely, foolish ear?
Age warns as it beckons, silly girl; your dreams pay a price
As they're plunged into the fog where a bouy-face leers --
An echo of someone's yesterday can tumble you in, it's your choice --
Still child, chilled child-girl, in the mist with your fear.

*"Murmur to a Girl," Jessica Sheridan,*
*Phillips Andover Academy, 1987*

*Girl, Sarah Sheridan, 1993, Northfield Mount Herman School*

Elder Poem: Draw a favorite elder. Translate that drawing into a poem. I use Peter Blue Cloud's "To My Aunt" and I ask my students to model this poem grammatically for their Elder poem. The exercise has proved successful.

*The Elder, a drawing after a photo of Geronimo*
*by Claus Kormannshaus, 1997*

Frail feline
why are you mute
how can I penetrate your densel head
your refined coat reeks
yet you do not care to clean it
your eye is glazed
yet you have no other freakish qualities
your home is habitable
yet it is hardly a tranquil environment
you're not a stray
yet your family has not congregated recently
frail feline do not hide.
I cannot comprehend why you are anonymous
you are notable however
frail feline do not be scared.

*"Frail Feline," Dan Demaine, eighth grade,*
*Eaglebrook School, 1990*

PETER BLUE CLOUD
(1935- )

To-ta Ti-om

for an aunt

my aunt was an herb doctor, one-eyed with crooked yellow
    teeth
    The Christians called her pagan witch
  and their children taunted her
  or ran in fear of their bible lives
    at her approach,
her house of barn lumber leaned into the wind as if toppling
  in winter it grew squat with snow
  and bright sparks from the wood stove
  hissed the snowflakes into steam
    icing the roof,
"when my body dies it will be in winter just in time to see
    the spring"
  she told this while rolling leaves
  to powder between her boney hands
  for duty as a medicine person
    was to cure,
in early summer grandfather and i would begin planting
  the corn and beans and squash
  just behind my aunt's house
  and she'd hobble over to help
    plant the tobacco,
as the first green shoots emerged into sunlight
  she would sit on the steps
  grating dried roots into a bowl
  stopping every so often to gaze
    at the garden,
when the time of tobacco curing came she'd be there
  feeling and smelling and tasting
  and every season she would approve
  then later sit by the woodstove
    smoking her pipe,
"Come," she would stay to me, "the time for onanoron is
  here,"
  and she would walk to the pond
  and she would point out strong plants
  for me to wade to and slowly pull
    those medicine roots,
we strung the roots of twisted brown above the woodstove
  to preserve their sacred power
  to be released as needed
  by those who had need
    of such strength,
tiny bundles were made of the roots with bits of string
  then she named the persons
  i was to take onanoron to
  and tied all in a blue bandana

and said, "go,"
this is for Kaienwaktatse and this for Kaerine
  Lives Close to Town
  and She Bends the Boughs
  a penny or two and bread and jam
    I shyly ate,
the pennies slowly filled the glass jar on the table
  until my aunt went to the store
  a block of salt pork one finger square
  a nutmeg, salt and four candies
    just for me,
sitting there by the woodstove I would steal a glance
  at her tired wrinkled face
  and I'd want to shout loud
  feeling a tightening in my throat
    and maybe cry
"she was sitting at her table with a bowl in her lap
  and it was just turning Spring,"
  my grandfather wrote this to me
  and i went somewhere to be alone
    and just sat,
it's planting time again and all done except tobacco
  grandfather leaning on the hoe
  and looking at my aunt's house
  then he smiles and I smile back
    lonely, like crying.

*"To my Aunt" by Peter Blue Cloud*

**for an uncle**
(Excerpted)

  My uncle works at a plant, tall mustached
  and wears a cowboy hat.
  His relations call him cowboy
  and his children have blonde hair
  and they read the Bible as they are taught by him.
  His house is at the top of a hill
  in the winter there is snow all around
  and the brightly lit stars light the snow up
  and the snowflakes dance among themselves
  on the icy frozen ground.
  "When my horse has itscolt, it will
  be here just in time to see the spring."
  he told this while watching her
  and cleaning the barn
  for his duty as a cowboy was to make sure
  she colted all right.

      ---*Kevin Charboneau (Turtle Mountain Chippewa)*

*"For an Uncle, " Kevin Charbonneau, Turtle Mountain
Chippewa, high school, summer session, 1990,
Native American Preparatory School*

## Issue of Concern Poem: Wilfred Owens' poem "Dulce
et Decorum Est Pro Patria Mori" provides an example of
a poem of concern expressed with bitter irony. Owens
died in World War I at the age of twenty-five. The Latin
title, recalling hortatory titles of the Roman poets Cicero

and Virgil, states: "It is sweet and proper to die for your
country." The poem anticipates Owens' death, while presenting his attitude about war. The title is ironic: Owens
makes clear that it is neither sweet nor proper to die for
one's country. Ask students to model the ironic title as
well as the rest of the poem grammatically, word for
word, including identical punctuation.

DULCE ET DECORUM EST

Bent double, like old beggars under sacks,
Knock-kneed, coughing like hags, we cursed through sludge,
Till on the haunting flares we turned our backs,
And towards our distant rest began to trudge.
Men marched asleep. Many had lost their boots,     5
But limped on, blood-shod. All went lame, all blind;
Drunk with fatigue; deaf even to the hoots
Of gas-shells dropping softly behind.

Gas! GAS! Quick, boys! – An ecstasy of fumbling,
Fitting the clumsy helmets just in time,     10
But someone still was yelling out and stumbling
And flound'ring like a man in fire or lime. –
Dim through the misty panes and thick green light,
As under a green sea, I saw him drowning.

In all my dreams before my helpless sight     15
He plunges at me, guttering, choking, drowning.

If in some smothering dreams, you too could pace
Behind the wagon that we flung him in,
And watch the white eyes writhing in his face,
His hanging face, like a devil's sick of sin,     20
If you could hear, at every jolt, the blood
Come gargling from the froth-corrupted lungs
Bitter as the cud
Of vile, incurable sores on innocent tongues, –
My friend, you would not tell with such high zest     25
To children ardent for some desperate glory,
The old lie: *Dulce et decorum est*
*Pro patria mori.*

               *Wilfred Owen (1893–1918)*

*"Dulce et Decorum Est Pro Patria Mori" by Wilfred Owens*

It's Easy to get in secondary school

Hige Worry, like the evil twine around

Di-Ta-Di-Ta, Time travel just like you have already lit the
bomb

My parents pay lots of money; it's hard work just like hiking to
the Himalaya MTN. That kind of hard.

I'm a E.S.L Student who is like a mute-Deaf and Dumb
in America.

It's like there's a fire around me, and I don't know what
I have to do.

SSAT's are like poison; when you touch them, you get dead

The grade is like a shrapnel bomb in the air which blow
apart my head

Friends measure up like inch worms; they eat your skin and
gnaw you insides; that's kind scary,

School, I've decided is like being lost in the jungle
If you are lost, you got to Dead.

getting into secondary school is a terrible task

It's an old lie: It's easy to get into secondary
school

Hurrah

*Jack Liang's model of "Dulce," Eaglebrook School, eighth grade,
1991, see typed version that follows. Jack began his education at
Eaglebrook School as an ESL student from Taiwan.*

### It's Easy to Get into Secondary School

*Huge worry, like the evil twine around*
*Di-Ta-Di-Ta, time travel just like you have already*
*    lit the bomb*
*My parents pay lots of money, it's hard work just*
*    like hiking to the Himalaya MTN. That kind of*
*    hard.*
*I'm a E.S.L. student who is like a mute-Deaf and*
*    Dumb in America.*
*It's like there's a fire around me, and I don't know*
*    what I have to do.*
*SSAT's are like posion: when you touch them, you*
*    get dead.*
*The grade is like a shrapnel bomb in the air which*
*    blows apart head*
*Friends measure up like inch worms; they eat your*
*    skin and gnaw you insides; that's kind scary.*
*School, I've decided is like being lost in the jungle.*
*If you are lost, you get to dead.*
*Getting into secondary school is a terrible task*
*It's an old lie: It's easy to get into secondary school.*

* * * * * * * * * * * *

### Mourir avec la dignite, c'est en l'esprit de la paix

*Wide-eyed, like someone who has felt a shot*
*Arch-backed, drooling like a baby, I sweat under the*
*    covers*
*Squirming, like somone whose soul the devil has*
*    bought*
*At the thought of death I flinch and my blood does*
*    clot*
*I think, awake. I clutch the side of the bed*
*I think more, weak. All became quiet, but thoughts*
*    still collide*
*Trembling with fear; deaf even to what is being said*
*By a car passing switfly outside.*

*Light, LIGHT quick - a choatic movement of*
*    rustling*
*Throwing the heavy burden over my head just in*
*    time, just by chance*
*But something was still out in the cold, bustling*
*and freezing, like a nude man in an avalanche*
*Bright through the translucent covers and thick*
*    black night*
*As under a pale blue light I saw my foot thawing.*

*In all of my dreams before my dimmed sight*
*My foot is whisked inside and begins melting,*
*    flowing, thawing.*

*If in some odd way, you too could see*
*Under the covers in the pale blue light*
*The fearful look on my face, fearful even to me*
*Almost as if I had been through many a fight*
*If you could hear at every hiss my breath*
*Come rasping from heavy lungs*
*At the thought of death*
*Of evil, deathly sores on innocent tongues*
*You would not tell with such high sanctite*
*To children innocent, young and gay*
*The old lie: Mourir avec la dignite*
*c'est en l'esprit de la paix.*

*Ben Block, 1990, Eaglebrook School, eighth grade*

<u>The sestina</u>: Even if you have assigned the sestina as described in Part 2, assign it here. The form is complex enough yet accessible enough from elementary school on to provide a substantive boost to students as writers. Part 2, Fractal Basic Shape background section, offers information on the sestina as a spiral form, particularly suited to recursive, self-referential brain processes. As an Optional Exercise in Part 2 located at the end of Step 4 (the "Perfect" Whole), this 39-line verse form is described in detail.

<u>Procedure</u>: Explain a sestina: a sestina is a long poem which does not rhyme. The ends of the lines are important because they contain six words which repeat over and over again, in a certain designated order. The sestina contains six verses of six lines each, closing with 3 additional lines called the *tornada*, or 39 lines in all. First, a "rhetorical set" must be provided by the writer, or six words which will be used to end the first 36 lines, and

*Dale Sharbaugh, drawing, hockey glove, sestina,*
*ninth grade, Eaglebrook School, 1990*

My Hockey Glove

It is filled with power, darkness, and is my hockey glove.
I wear it for grip as well as for my protection,
and the aroma fills me with spirit, like old leather.
It is new, unused, ready for action. Like a bat, stiff
until broken in. Dark, such a solid dark, the pure black
color causes a glare, like a glazed black. It gives me the feeling of
death.

In contests, I wear it to drive the feeling of death
into the mind of the opponent. A weapon is what the hockey
glove
resembles. It captures something, the sight of my black
pupil because of its sheer elegance. It glances back, promising
protection
if I protect it. It'll remain as hard as possible, stiff,
like a new pair of skis, if I treat it like gold wrapped leather.

If you bend it in uncommon directions, it screeches like a leather
whip, cracking against a man being punished by the Reaper of
Death.

When you grasp the stick, the leather will tighten up as stiff
as your hand squeezes, allowing no chance of the hockey glove
to slip, causing a lapse in the full promise of protection,
giving your hand no chance to receive bruises of black.

The darkness of the glove resembles the extravagant darkness of space. It is one, held together by the means of leather,
like the earth holds its orbit because of the sun. Protection
is given to the user of it. If the possibility of death
is near, the special glove, the only glove, the hockey glove
will protect you from being transformed into a stiff.

It can give a person a blow producing a stiff
back, but only if the owner ignores the man in black.
It is capable of destroying itself, another hockey glove,
if the mind sends a signal to power its leather
towards the other. Sometimes it loves to drive death
into the adversary. It does this also for my protection.

When the game is on ice, it is used for my protection,
grasping anything that is wished, as stiff
as a vice. A man may receive a dreadful death
or a flash of blackness, or even a screen of black
if the potential of the glove is issued. It is the leather
and the black that makes up this weapon, my hockey glove.

Protection helps the owner plus the pads of black.
Stiff as a piece of maple is the superior leather.
Death, instant death, shielded away by the black hockey glove.

by Dale Sharbaugh, Form VI

*Dale Sharbaugh, sestina, ninth grade, Eaglebrook School, 1990*

*Alex Taylor, self portrait, ninth grade,*
*Eaglebrook School, 1990*

which will be included, 2 per line, in the last 3 lines. Each line has five beats or stresses, using the metric foot called the iamb. I ask students to create the set of six terminal words by listing the name of their Drawing/Writing object, a verb, an adjective, one concrete and one abstract noun from a simile or metaphor about the object, and the pronoun "me" or "I." After writing the initial sestet using the six words to end the six lines, these words are numbered as they occur; the word used to end line one becomes word #1. Then, the writer follows the numerical scheme for the sestina, in effect, "writing up to" each terminal word, closing with the 6 words as indicated in the instructions for the *tornada* or *envoi*. The triplet that ends the poem is where the poem "turns" and the "message is sent."

A Vision

To the world of pain, we are swiftly sucked into the dark,
Within the boundaries of a faceless madman, he is enticing and
seductive.
Yet I wish to venture forward, for the pinholed light makes me
curious.
Down this corridor of distorted uncertainty, my encasings thick
but hollow.
I don't know which way I'm looking, but the hall swims far and
deep.
Beyond, and past the source of light, there is a thunder that
keeps rumbling.
Now I lay closer to the light, yet my surroundings breathe more
dark.
I'm beginning to lose my bearings, and am stumbling into this
whirlwind from deep.
I feel as though I'm small, in a great world of power and seduc-
tion.
Is the light big or small? I let my hand drift, yet all is hollow.
My heart is beginning to pound, for this light source is brave
and curious.
I take another step, then another, for I am unconscious of my
curious.
I can't tell if it's my chest, or the light source that keeps rum-
bling.
I can't tell if I have a chest, for all I hear and feel is hollow.
I stop to take a breath and think, so I don't get lost in the dark.
Out of the dots in the night forms a knowing, sly face of
seduction.
But I just blink my eyes, and it disembodies full and deep.

I feel as though I'm looking the wrong way into the solar depths
of infinity. I wish I had a ship to the light that makes me
curious.
I am a fool to go forward, yet I am always taken in by weaker
seduction.
Now my heart is beating smooth, but my blood seems to be
rumbling.
A cloud just covered the light, a reckless cloud with no mind, for
it is dark.
Yet the star now prevails, being a different colour, for it is
hollow.

It begins to sway and dance, and my head is swollen and hollow.
My legs now carry no weight, and I fall far and deep.
I open my opened eyes, and before me lies an eye, then dark.
Where is my star? Where is the otter, hungry and curious?
My need spins to the light, then it runs away silent with a
rumbling.
A madman, an empty-eyed madman. So seductive.
I can't help myself, I run. I'm witlessly reeled in. So seductive.
Out of the deep night, forms a box; no, a door. A strong door,
tall and hollow.
I stop and stare at the knob. Far beyond the dark wall, I hear a
terrifying rumbling.
I look over my shoulders to see how far I've come; it's been long
and deep.
I have to open this door, for the light beyond drives me to be
curious.
I reach for the door. I let my hand fly through the dark.
At last, I open the door of seduction, to a world growing silent,
far and deep.
There is a candle beyond the hollow, gazing on me
frightened and curious.
Behind the candle are hollow eyes, then a face, whiskered and
rough, then whoosh, all is dark.

by Alex Taylor, Form VI

*Alex Taylor, "A Vision," sestina, ninth grade,*
*Eaglebrook School, 1990*

**PEER SHARE:** Include peer editing.

Read a sestina aloud. If the six words from the Drawing/Writing session with an object are used, the sestina will develop around the object and the self, moving the poem's message from description of the concrete object to thoughts on the abstraction associated with it. A summing-up inevitably occurs in the last three lines, providing a satisfactory and often illuminating resolution to the poem's meaning

Marc Drew
Mrs. Sheridan
2/3/90
English

### THE BONE

I was on a camping trip, long ago when the world was not so <u>old</u>.
We were trekking across the open plains, and I saw it lying there on the <u>ground</u>.
It reminded me of another poor, untimely <u>death</u>.
A sudden feeling came over me, it was a feeling of <u>pity</u>.
For the one who had all the answers in life, and now her own was <u>gone</u>.
The thing was strange to me, though I knew it was some kind of <u>bone</u>.

It lay there still, growing in my mind, but I can not tell why my thoughts of a loved one were brought back by a <u>bone</u>.
It had happened so long ago, I could almost not remember, and it made me feel <u>old</u>.
I remember wishing that at the time these thoughts could forever be <u>gone</u>.
In just that short time, the life of a loved one passed in front of me, almost knocking me to the <u>ground</u>.
She left me so quickly, no one could understand what had happened. no one came to give me <u>pity</u>.
It was because there was no one for me, that I almost brought about my own <u>death</u>.

Then I thought about the animal, that had died to have this bone be here and what had brought upon its <u>death</u>.
I wondered upon what means of transport, had moved this single solitary <u>bone</u>.
I felt sorry for the animal, and also for myself. Though now that I look back I relize that it was not sorrow but <u>pity</u>.
I knew that I could not run from my thoughts, but only sit and eventually become <u>old</u>.
Then what of me, an old crippled man, what would happen to me, especially my final resting place. Where? and upon what <u>ground</u>.
After I am laid to rest, who shall remember me? for no children had we, and now she is <u>gone</u>.

All that we had ever dreamed together was now forever <u>gone</u>.
would anybody know, or would anybody care if it was here that I finally sucumèd to <u>death</u>.
I thought about the hills, and the wind whistling through the trees, But eventually returned my attention to the object on the <u>ground</u>.
How could this be happening to me? the want of my own death, just because of a <u>bone</u>.
I had other visions of me when I was older, not lively and happy, but sad and <u>old</u>.
"STOP IT" "STOP IT" I found myself yelling, Why was this happening to me, "Oh god please have <u>pity</u>."

No I could prove these visions untrue, and I could do it without anyone's despair and <u>pity</u>.
People didn't care anyway, for all they cared I could be forever <u>gone</u>.
This was all because of her, she left me like this so alone so distraught, eventually to die or become <u>old</u>.
Is this right? Is it right that one persons life should be ruined by her <u>death</u>.
These memories, how could they be brought back, when I hoped I had forgotten, and all by a <u>bone</u>.
I look up, nervous that anybody could be watching me bet again my eyes return to the <u>ground</u>.

I couldn't stop myself, it seamed crazy as I bent down and picked the bone from the <u>ground</u>.
As if something was telling me to keep it. A great weight lifted when I held it close, and no longer did I feel the <u>pity</u>.
There was no reason or logic to what had happened, but I knew that forever I would keep this <u>bone</u>.
I ran back to camp, and I was for the first time, glad that for the while everybody was <u>gone</u>.
Nothing could hurt me now; Nothing could take away the feeling of joy, not even <u>death</u>.
I knew that it would happen, but I thought of all the things that I could do before I got <u>old</u>.

Now that I am on my death bed and soon to be buried in the <u>ground</u>, and when I am <u>gone</u>.
I hope that no one has to <u>pity</u> me the I did her., because now I am not afraid of <u>death</u>.
As for the <u>bone</u>, it shall be buried with me, and together we will both grow <u>old</u>.

*Marc Drew, sestina, ninth grade, Eaglebrook School, 1990.*

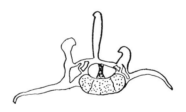

*Marc Drew, Drawing/Writing object, ninth grade, Eaglebrook School, 1990*

The sestina has proved as successful with Elderhostel students as it has with younger students. Sandra and Richard Glessner teach medical ethics in Elderhostel classes, and Sandra has used the Drawing/Writing approach in composition courses she has taught. In 1989, the Glessners studied Drawing/Writing in an Elderhostel program at Deerfield Academy in Deerfield, Massachusetts.

A mystery surrounds the rust-brown sphere
Which launches my Deerfield journey.
A seashell speaking with secret voice,
A boring vessel, taking time to wave
Sets my stressful mind free
And invites me to hear its timeless call.

The mentor urges me to heed its call,
To trust her introduction to the sphere,
To allow my expressions to be free,
To just submerge myself within the journey.
I agree with a reluctant tiny wave
And hear a mumbled acceptance in my voice.

Encouraged by the seashell's patient voice,
No longer shutting out its ancient call,
I grant the still-strange lump a second wave,
Wrap my sweaty palms around its sphere,
Ask it to join me on an unknown journey,
Revealing that its service must be free.

Seeming to know my power to make it free,
It remained silent, waiting for my voice
To reveal the steps and guidelines of our journey
Now clarifying themselves in mentor's call.
Blindly I sketched the uneven contours of the sphere,
Finally squinting to see more clearly, the whorling of the wave.

I came to know the power of ocean wave
Which thrusts to shore its children to be free,
And yet I wrestled troubled thoughts about my sphere
Agonizing on paper and to the mentor with a voice
Distressed over my inability to grasp the surviving call
Which was insisting that I become the boss of our journey.

So a mere shell joins a non-artist for a journey.
The shell sits— a hard breast, a fat rump, an indolent wave.
I do take charge, demanding that Euclid perform at my call,
That fractal, LMD, and the "perfect whole" set me free.
The shell becomes a cave of birth where my now fertile voice
Flings abstract lines of triumph to liberate my sphere.

My Deerfield journey has set me free.
A wave of joy fills my happy voice.
I call fondly, " Thanks, O dearest mentor, dearest sphere."

Sandra J. Glessner
August 3, 1989
Deerfield Academy Elderhostel

*Sandra Glessner, sestina, Deerfield Academy Elderhostel, 1989*

1. The horn falls on my soft-inquiring eye
   made yet more puzzling by the driving rain.
   I lift its craggy form, damp from the grass,
   and pass my fingers past its jagged edge
   to contemplate it's wailing mystery:
   "How moves its inner darkness to the sky?"

2. The storm's retreating now. A spotted sky
   displays itself to my uplifted eye.
   The cow's horn still holds, curled, its mystery;
   with subtle coil, it grips me yet in rain,
   trumpets to me to peer beyond its edge
   to view its prairies wide, its waving grass.

3. Drawn to its call, I kneel upon the grass
   and taste with warmth a far and foreign sky
   within the horn, and halfway from its edge
   I find its secret means by which to eye
   the prairie dog, the ambling bear, the rain,
   the calm: the horn's most guarded mystery.

4. O kindly horn, to share your mystery,
   your prairie feast, however thin the grass,
   your summer cool when falls the scarcest rain,
   your pointed darkness easing toward the sky.
   It is your self-illuminating eye
   that finds infinity beyond your edge.

5. Now closer to its inner core I edge,
   enthralled to comprehend the mystery:
   that in this piece of bone resides an Eye,
   a sightful organ, holding bygone grass
   with piercing vision, finds a widening sky
   to prove that sun-parched air can fall in rain.

6. Stand tall, my heart, in drought or flashing rain;
   capricious Chance may push you to the edge.
   Remember how you found a piece of sky
   enshrined within the horn's dark mystery,
   and there, halfway mid predator and grass,
   the horn held all, within its ample eye.

7. Hear, Sky, no longer broods that mystery;
   no darkening rain creeps now o'er mountains' edge!
   I paused in grass. The horn gave me its eye!

*Richard Glessner, "Eye of the Horn," Deerfield Academy Elderhostel, 1989*

*Sandra Glessner, LMD shell, 1989*

*Richard Glessner, PW horn, 1989*

# Conduct the second two-week session with Drawing/Writing, using the self-portrait

*Dawn Kruzewski, self portrait, "Perfect" Whole (PW), Westfield State Dr/Wr studio course, 1994*

*SRS, self portrait as totem mask, 1985*

*Michelle DeFilippo, self portrait, LMD, Westfield State Dr/Wr studio course, 1994*

<u>Procedure</u>: Follow the five steps in Part 2 used for the object, applying them to the self-portrait. Then, launch into your regular composition course, using drawing exercises before every writing exercise. Introduce published prose after students have written their own version of the genre. Then, ask students to model a sample of the published prose in that genre. Following this grammatical, syntactical modeling exercise, ask students to critique the published sample as well as their own word-for-word substitution, or translation.

*Tate Wright, self portrait, PW, ninth grade, Eaglebrook School, 1989*

*Javier Creel, self portrait, Euclidean BS, ninth grade, Eaglebrook School, 1990*

*Beth Stevens, self-portrait, Organic Basic Shape, Drawing/Writing, Westfield State College, studio drawing course, 1994*

*Anne Charron, self portrait, PW, Drawing/Writing
studio course, Westfield State, 1994*

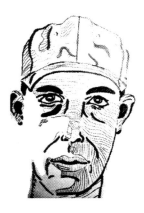

*Dan Simson, self portrait, LMD, Westfield State
studio course, 1994*

*Allison McCarthy, two self portraits, both PW, Westfield State
studio course, 1994*

## Exercise 5:

**Translate the sonnet about the walk or the
sestina about the object into journalism or
advertizing.**

<u>Procedure</u>: In journalism and in advertising, text and
image are succinct and persuasive.

Students will need to find a photograph to go with the
newspaper or magazine article and a visually compelling
image for the ad. If students take the photo themselves or
create the visuals for the ad, so much the better.

**PEER SHARE:** Include peer-editing.

**DISCUSSION:** Ask students to bring in newspaper articles and magazine ads. In peer pairs, discuss the
successful features of the articles and ads. Take a poll and
write these features on the board. How much of the effect
is visual? Identify and define these visual effects. How
much of the effect is verbal? Identify and define these
verbal effects. How might students alter their original
drawing of a walk from their doorway to make it more
effective visually? Students may want to incorporate one
of the images generated by the Drawing/Writing five-step
with their object.

**PEER SHARE:** Share reworked drawings, student articles
and ads.

**DISCUSSION:** How do the students' versions of newspaper articles and ads resemble the professional newspaper
articles and the ads? How do they differ? List the similarities and differences from the students' point of view.
Come to conclusions, stimulating meta-cognition, and
providing new standards for student writing.

## Exercise 6:

**Translate the newspaper article or the advertise-
ment into a short story or a one-act play**

<u>Procedure</u>: Ask students to define a short story and a
one-act play from their point of view. List these criteria
on the board. Students will have definite ideas about stories and plays. Ask students to choose one genre and
write about their walk using that form, using student-
generated criteria.

**PEER SHARE:** Include peer-editing.

Procedure: Choose a short story on a one-act play and assign it as homework. If time allows, break the class into small reading-aloud groups to cover the short stories and plays in this shared way. Discuss what make the short story and the play effective from the students' point of view. List these items on board. Compare the list for the short story with the list for the play. How are they alike? How are they different? Come to conclusions. Compare the new list for the play with the students' former list. Do the same for a short story. Because students have been exposed to fine writing in both instances, their criteria for effective short stories and plays will be enlarged and refined. By establishing new criteria, students create new standards for their own writing.

DISCUSSION: This is a good time to discuss differences between poetry and prose from your students' points of view. Because students are increasingly able to make fine distinctions, they have a fair idea about what constitutes poetry and what constitutes prose and can consider where a line between them might be drawn.

## Exercise 7:

### Draw a person you know very well.

Procedure: Ask your students to think about a person they know well. They might think about a person who upsets them—who frightens, bothers, or worries them. Difficult situations provide grist for the mind's mill. The subject matter presented by an English curriculum is not, after all, unremittingly cheery, nor are students' lives. In addition, adolescents feel emotions strongly. As a practical matter, worrisome or frightening people can provide more vivid language and images than comfy people. Earlier in this curriculum, students have been asked to write about an esteemed elder, who has had a strong positive influence in their lives.

Start by brainstorming a range of "darker" emotions: fear, anger, rage, anxiety, stress, depression. Ask students to think of a time when they felt one of these dark emotions strongly. Ask students to draw this situation, including location, people, objects, action, and, if possible, the look of the emotion. By looking at the drawing, students will be able to identify the upsetting person. They can then write about this person, including the significance of visual details they might not have noted when they were drawing—hands, face, hair, clothes. Accoutrements, the items that go with and define this person—like a cane, or a special hat—should be

included. What people or creatures does this person associate with? Should any of them be included? Where is the person often found? Watching and listening to my children and their friends play "Dungeons and Dragons" years ago has led me to ask my students to think about describing character in "D&D" terms. Thus, I ask students to think about the person's beliefs, charisma level, moral attitude, personality quirks, fears, eccentricities, hopes, desires, needs. Can any of these characteristics be suggested by the drawing before the student starts to write? Arrows and labels can indicate where specific items or characteristics are located in the drawing.

PEER SHARE: include peer-editing.

## Exercise 8:

### A familiar activity.

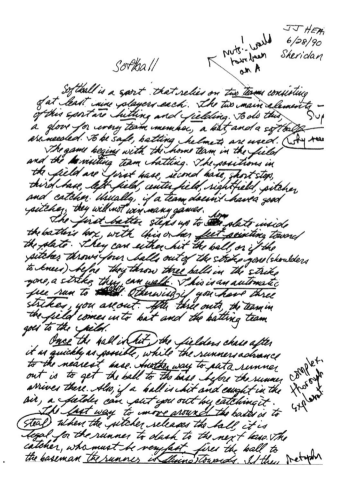

*Softball by J. J. Heaton, Navajo, middle school summer session, Native American Preparatory School, 1990*

Procedure: Ask students to choose a familiar activity, like changing the tire on a car, tuning a carburetor, doing a layup in basketball, spiking or braiding hair, installing a car stereo, cooking, shopping, playing an instrument, taping a mix. Students must explain the activity visually and verbally. Ask them to sketch all the necessary tools, equipment and supplies and to show through drawing exactly how the activity is done, step by step. Students must then describe each tool, supply, and piece of equipment in writing, making no assumptions about the knowledge of the reader. The challenge is to draw and write as if the reader has no experience whatsoever with the activity. Ask students to include comments on why they chose to describe this particular activity.

DISCUSSION: In the book *Mind Storms* (1980), MIT LOGO inventor Seymour Papert explains the computer language LOGO in terms of procedural knowledge. If children can break a procedure down into its parts—for instance, the procedure for drawing a square: TO SQUARE: REPEAT 4 (FD 10 RT 90)—they understand a square. This Drawing/Writing exercise focuses on visual and verbal procedural knowledge. Acquaint students with the term "procedural knowledge" in the context of The Familiar Activity Exercise. Later, when you teach the expository essay, students will already have an essay including precedural knowledge under their belt. Like the descriptions of character and place and incident above—mini essays which inform or explain—the how-to essay will make the formal expository essay more familiar.

PEER SHARE: including peer-editing.

## Exercise 9:

### A difficult time

Procedure: The same principle holds true for this exercise as with the "Person You Know Well" exercise: difficult situations provide grist for the mind's mill. Follow the same brainstorming procedure about dark emotions. Identify a dark time; draw the location, people, objects and, if possible, the shape of the dark emotion. Troublesome subject matter requires expression, examination, and explanation before resolution is possible. As students' visual and verbal skills increase, they will be increasingly able to resolve some of these situations themselves through drawing and writing.

PEER SHARE: including peer-editing.

## Exercise 10:

### Translate the Difficult Times writing into a formal essay presenting an Issue of Concern

*Jack Liang, drawing, issue of concern, Eaglebrook School, ninth grade, ESL student from Taiwan, 1991*

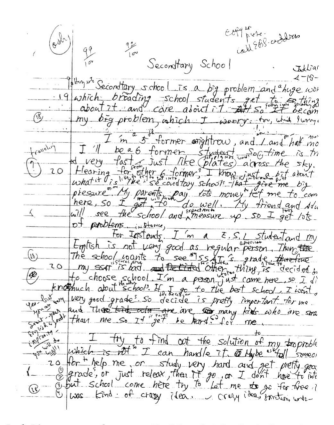

*Jack Liang, essay of concern, Eaglebrook School, ninth grade, 1991*

Procedure: The Difficult Times writing often brings issues of deep concern to the surface. Encourage students to identify general issues of worry or concern in group discussions. List these items on the board. The middle school Native American students I worked with in the summer of 1990 raised these issues: teenage pregnancy, substance abuse, and pollution. In 1991, during the Gulf

War, my male ninth-grade students were concerned with war and death. They also expressed fears about their parents' deaths .

*Expository Essay:*

By this point in the writing program, students have produced many pieces of invested writing. The imposition of formal structure is unlikely to turn them away from writing. Write the term "opening paragraph" on the board and explain that the opening paragraph often includes a thesis statement including the subject of the essay and the main idea expressed in the essay about that subject. The thesis statement includes information and may include an attitude toward this information. After crafting the thesis sentence, the writer adds a sentence connecting the issue and the attitude to the next paragraph, signaling the direction of the essay. Paragraphs #2 and #3 provide instances of this issue of concern. Paragraph #4 documents solutions or responses to the problem, including the students' own solutions. Encourage inventive, even radical, paradoxical or fanciful solutions—like turning trash into tofu using polymer science. Paragraph #5 concludes the essay by "wrapping up" its major points. I explain this paragraph by saying: "Tell 'em what you told 'em" by restating the preceding four paragraphs, briefly. Though formulaic, even tedious, this scrupulous recapitulation produces a sound concluding paragraph. More importantly, the conditions are set for a breakthrough solution to the issue of concern. The simple act of restating often elicits a brand new idea.

The concluding paragraph of the essay can be used as the introductory paragraph of a second expository essay. As the second Composite Abstraction refines and extends the first Composite Abstraction, the second essay refines and extends the first. Students who appreciate the value of a second CA may be willing to revise their expository essay by writing a new one, using this strategy.

## Exercise 11:

## Introducing the prose grammatical model

<u>Procedure</u>: Art students learn by copying museum pieces. Writers can learn the same way. The following grammatical modeling exercises allow students to feel the structural bones of an established writer's work, experiencing effective writing from the inside out.

After your students have drawn and written about an issue of concern, hand out a favorite passage describing a person, event or issue and ask students to read it aloud.

Then, ask students to rewrite their piece modeling the structure of the sample. If the sample starts with an indefinite article like "a" or "an," the student will start with an indefinite article. If an adjective comes next, the student will use one of his own adjectives. Grammar resurfaces as a major writing tool when students experience a professional writer's prose on a formal basis.

## The Gallico model:  a word-form for word-form approach

The Snow Goose
by
Paul Gallico

The great marsh lies on the Essex coast between the village of Chelmbury and the ancient Saxon oyster-fishing hamlet of Wickaeldroth.  It is one of the last of the wild places of England, a low, far-reaching expanse of grass and reeds and half-submerged meadowlands ending in the great saltings and mud flats and tidal pools near the restless sea.

Tidal creeks and estuaries and the crooked, meandering arms of many little rivers whose mouths lap at the edge of the ocean cut through the sodden land that seems to rise and fall and breathe with the recurrence of the daily tides.  It is desolate, utterly lonely, and made lonelier by the calls and cries of the wildfowl that make their homes in the marshlands and saltings--the wild geese and the gulls, the teal and the widgeon, the redshanks and curlews that pick their way through the tidal pools.  Of human habitants there are none, and none are seen, with the occasional exception of a wild-fowler or native oyster-fisherman, who still ply a trade already ancient when the Normans came to Hastings.

Grays and blues and soft greens are the colors, for when the skies are dark in the long winters, the many waters of the beaches and marshes reflect the cold and somber color.  But sometimes, with sunrise and sunset, sky and land are aflame with red and golden fire.

Hard by one of the winding arms of the little River Aelder runs the embankment of an old sea wall, smooth and solid, without a break, a bulwark to the land against the encroaching sea.  Deep into a salting some three miles from the North Sea it runs, and there turns north.  At that corner its face is gouged, broken and shattered.  It has been breached, and at the breach the hungry sea has already entered and taken for its own the land, the wall, and all that stood there.

At low water the blackened and ruptured stones of the ruins of an abandoned lighthouse show above the surface, with here and there, like buoy markers, the top of a sagging fence-post.  Once this lighthouse abutted on the sea and was a beacon on the Essex coast.  Time shifted land and water, and its usefulness came to an end.

Lately it served again as a human habitation.  In it there lived a lonely man.  His body was warped, but his heart was filled with love for wild and hunted things.  He was ugly to look upon, but he created great beauty.  It is about him, and a child who came to know him and see beyond the grotesque form that housed him to what lay within, that this story is told.

It is not a story that falls easily and smoothly into sequence.  It has been garnered from many sources and from many people.  Some of it comes in the form of fragments from men who looked upon strange and violent scenes.  For the sea has claimed its own and spreads its rippled blanket over the site, and the great white bird with the black-tipped pinions that saw it all from the beginning to the end has returned to the dark, frozen silences of the northlands whence it came.

*The Snow Goose, Claus Kormannshaus, 1997*

<u>Procedure</u>: With your students, read aloud the first chapter of Paul Gallico's *The Snow Goose*. Then, ask students to model the first section (pages 3-7 in the 1988 Alfred A. Knopf edition, or about 640 words) starting, "The great marsh" and ending "frozen silences of the northlands from when it came." the exercise to to model this section grammatically, substituting students' own location and animal/bird of choice.

11/14/88
Englesh

Booth Bay

Booth Bay slices deeply into Maine's vast East coast, it lies between Portland and the lobster-fishing harbor of Christmas Cove. It is one of the last remaining sanctuary for nature left in New England, a low, far-reaching coast of rocky beaches and dense forest beyond which is the vast expanse of the Atlantic Ocean.

Roaring rivers and trickling streams, They cut neatly through the land engraving a permanent path for others to follow to the open sea. It is cool, quiet and peaceful, made more so by the soft breeze carried inland by the sea, and by the distant roar of the waves pounding brutally against the rocks of the shore. Black-tip goals glide smoothly almost effortlessly through the air. Booth Bay is settled mainly by fisherman and lobstermen collecting their traps, combing the sea for fish and shrimp like their fathers and their father's fathers.

The hazy gray and dull blues blend smoothly together with the rocky beaches and restless ocean. But sometimes, with sunrise and sunset, the sky becomes alive with a red flame outlines the distant horizon.

Near one of the swerving arms of the Ryle River stands a rocky cliff, rough and solid, warding off the harsh beating of the heaving ocean. The riverwings deep into the heart of the coastland branching out into little streams, and covered the land with a maze of rivers and streams. It has been eroded by the beating of the bitter winds and harsh storms cutting deeply into the surface of the rock wall.

At low tide the rocks that where once part of the cliff and had crumbled down upon the beach below shown above the crashing waves in its last defiance against the swelling sea. Above the face of the cliff stood a house observing this battle between land and sea. Times changed but the house still stands there fighting off the realization of its ultimate defeat.

Now an old man lived there, sheltered from the biting cold of the November air. His body was old, but his mind was full with love for the land and the sea. He was aged and wrinkled, but he created an air of enchantment. It is about him and his grandson who came to know him and look beyond his aged form that this story is told.

It is not a story that is placed neatly into sequence. It has been pieced together from many people and places. The patchwork of this story comes from men who looked upon this strange and odd man almost contemptuously. For the ocean has claimed its own and spread a thick blanket over the sight, and over the great black bird with its long wings covering the sky like a black cloud that saw it all to the end has returned to the cold, frozen silence of Northern Canada from whence it came.

*"The White Crane" by Tom Pulliam, Eaglebrook School, 1988*
*Modeling first section of The Snow Goose by Paul Gallico*

*"Boothbay" by John Royall, ninth grade, Eaglebrook School, 1988*
*Modeling first chapter of The Snow Goose by Paul Gallico*

POTATOES

The vast fields lie in Northern Maine between the Canadian border and the authentic Maine lobster-fishing village of Jonesport. It is one of the few directly Irish Potato counties of the U.S., an intense, never-ending expanse of hills and trees and dirt-covered fields ending in the forests and lakes and rivers of Northwest Maine.

Flowing brooks and streams and the curled, twisting body of the great river whose arms penetrate the heart of the timberland sweep through the dehydrated soil that seems to live and bloom and animate with the recurrence of the yearly seasons. It is remote, partially abandoned, and made more abandoned by the calls and hoots of the loons that make their homes on the lakes and streams- the fox and the moose, the bear and the deer, the perch and the chub that weave their way through the many lakes. Of human habitants they are few, and few are seen, with the occasional exception of a trout-fisherman or native lumberjack, who still exercise a livelihood already ancient when the Vikings came to Greenland.

Blues and browns and tempered greens are the colors, for when the sun is shining in the prolonged summer, the many leaves of the trees and fields reflect the warm and glowing color. But many times with fall and winter the sky and land are lifeless with gray and smothered fires.

Close by the twisting torso of the big River Aroostok lies the embankment of an old river, lined and cracked, without a flat plane, a bulwark to the town against the rising river. Deep into a town some five-hundred miles from Bangor it runs, and there flows straight. At that point it's face is gouged, fractured, and smashed. It has not been breached, and everywhere the river has never entered nor taken for it's own the town.

At high harvest the greened and velvet leaves of the fields of man rise above the surface with here and there like mean-reminders, the blossom of a mustard weed. Once these plants flourished on the land and where a source of pride in Aroostok County. Chemicals changed land and water and it's bounty came to an end.

Presently the plant serves again as a human source of pride. In the county there lives a wise professor. His body is wrinkled but inside he is filled with knowledge for the dry and wasted land. He is not beautiful to look upon but he creates great relief. It is about him and the men who came to know him and see beyond the ugly skin that protects him to what lay within, that this story is told.

It is not a tale that flows freely and polished in continuity. It has been harvested from many fields and from many people. Some of it comes in the form of fragments of stories from men who gaze upon the insane and unneeded landscapes. For the land has captured for it's own and strewn

its shattered window over the scene, and the small brown vegetable with opaque-white insides that watched everything from the beginning has returned to the bright, frozen Northlands whence it came.

by: THAD CAMPBELL

*"Potatoes" by Thad Campbell, ninth grade,*
*Eaglebrook School, 1988*
*Modeling the first section of The Snow Goose by Paul Gallico*

The precept "neither too much nor too little" used in Part 2 to define a balanced drawing, also guides the writer. *The Snow Goose* provides an example of parsimonious, elegant prose. By copying its "bones," students flesh out a well-proportioned body. As the Golden Ratio organizes the relationship of parts to wholes in the facade of the Parthenon, so "neither too much nor too little" provides a felt or instinctive ratio of parts to wholes in text.

**PEER GRADING:** A new element may be added to the constructivist classroom: peer-grading.

Students grade a peer's writing-to-a-model for grammatical accuracy in this way: as the peer reads his work aloud, the student follows the Gallico text with his eyes.

At the same time, the student listens to the peer reading the model of the Gallico aloud. The grader is pattern-matching, cross-modally. His eyes check what his ears hear for grammatical equivalence. This pattern-matching provides a humdinger of a cognitive task. If I had not assigned this exercise successfully with middle school students, I would have doubted that simultaneous cross-modal pattern matching were possible. Not only is it possible, students love it. Like the Composite Abstraction and the Double Three-Step, cross-modal pattern matching occurred to me, directly and intuitively—in this instance, as a necessary and natural way to conclude the modeling/translating exercises. Like the CA and the Double Three-Step, it is attractive to students and it allows them to perform a substantive mental feat.

As he follows the Gallico text with his eyes and listens to the peer reading the peer's own text aloud, the grader decides the degree to which the peer's writing matches Gallico using these criteria: "exactly," "closely," "loosely." Then, as homework, the peer grader evaluates his partner's writing word for word against the Gallico model. This scrupulous pattern matching increases a working knowledge of grammar. This word for word evaluation is challenging, but not nearly as difficult as the in-class cross-modal simultaneous translation task. The fact that children's brains love to do this cross-modal translation supports the theory behind the Drawing/Writing program; human brains have evolved to make meaning by making comparisons and translations among and between several systems of representation. Education should include training and practice in the operations the human brain has evolved to perform best: to translate, fast, between systems of representation.

## The Flannery O'Connor model: a more general, Gestält approach.

Ask your students to read Flannery O'Connor's "Enoch and the Gorilla" as homework, and then ask them to model the general shape of the entire short story, paragraph for paragraph, staying as close to the action in each paragraph as possible. This Gestält exercise moves the writer beyond exact imitation to more general modeling, focusing on meaning and intent rather than form. Students will be ready for this, already trained in precise analysis and translation. If presented with this more general exercise first, students run the risk of foundering on the broader demands for analysis and inference required by this task.

* W. ll Haffner
Chris Fritz
English
Mrs. Sheridan
10/29/90

### George and the Star

George Davis borrowed his father's 50 year old track shoes. When he
tried to put them on, they felt like they had been through World War II.

The inside of the shoe was like a big flatland with five craters where the toes
had been. When he finally got both of his feet inside, he wiggled his toes
around and noticed that the shoe's toe-craters didn't fit his feet.

The shoes were one's that his father had stopped using when he had
gotten in a car accident and broke both of his legs. His injuries made it so he
wouldn't be able to run track again. As soon as he started to run the
shoelaces broke and he went tumbling down on the ground. He got up and,
luckily for him, the show lace broke close enough to the end so he could tie
them up again. He started running again and every few seconds he would
get a sharp pain in his foot, like when this is a rock in your shoe. Finally, he
stopped in front of a store and loosened the shoe laces as best he could. As
he was looking down the street, he saw a crowd, so he started out down the
street to see what the big attraction was. It was a Saturday and there were
a lot of older men standing in a big, mobbed crowd.

George was not very fond of older people, but they always looked at
him in an awkward way. The crowd turned and looked at him and seemed
to be inspecting his outfit. His shoes looked awkward with what he was
wearing. They looked like when someone is wearing snow boots with shorts
on. He had on a pair of old dress pants with a t-shirt and track shoes. All of
the men started laughing at him. He turned around and found himself facing
a big, life-size color poster of a world class sprinter in track and field. Beside

*(margin notes: "Plot"; "Setting Character"; "Conflict Character")*

*Chris Fritz, "George and the Star," ninth grade,
Eaglebrook School, 1990; page 1 of 8 pages Gestält modeling
"Enoch and the Gorilla."*

The peer grader, Will Haffner, counted 6 similes and
7 metaphors in Chris' writing. He gave him a score of
9/10 for sim/met use. Will gave Chris a score of 8/10 for
labeling each paragraph as a model of Flannery
O'Connor's in connection with plot, character, setting,
conflict, foreshadowing, climax, theme. Chris got a 10/10
for closeness to the model. Total score for closeness to
model, labeling of each paragraph, and simile and
metaphor use was 27/30. Haffner wrote, "Very well done.
Followed the story well. No punctuation problems. A few
wording problems but otherwise very good."

Another eighth grader had this to say about a peer's
modeling of the short story "Enoch and the Gorilla";
"Your story was quite confusing. Did you know what you
were going to say before you said it? I had trouble understanding your words sometimes. Your similes and
metaphors were OK, but some of them did not make

sense. I think you need to proofread more on your
papers. Overall your story was very interesting. I did not
understand how this story had any type of accoutrement
that would make your character noticeable and get attention. In 'Enoch and the Gorilla' the ape suit is supposed
to make Enoch more noticeable and different. Your character does not have this. Your story has a considerable
amount of conflicts. This is basically what I have to say.

Your grade is  B+ to B- (crossed out)

A- to B+ ( crossed out)

B+ to B."

*Garrison Francis, Eaglebrook School, 1990*

### A third session of Drawing/Writing with the figure study

Follow the five-steps with figure-study as you did
with the object and with the self-portrait. A final session
with Drawing/Writing provides experience with figure
drawing. A third sample of Rescore gives each student
three sets of benchmarks for visual and verbal literacy
skills for the academic year. Students should see appreciable changes over a year's work.

*Michelle DiFilippo, figure study, 1994, Westfield State College*

*Nicole Bernet, figure study, 1994, Westfield State College*

*Allison McCarthy, figure study, 1994, Westfield State College*

## Exercise 12:

## Playwriting.

The play is a good way to end the academic year when interest and energy may flag. Allow several weeks for this. After students have written their own plays, introduce them to a favorite professional play by reading it aloud. Because acting is social and active, playwriting provides an upbeat, energizing end to the school year.

The following Drawing/Writing exercises create characters and settings. With this groundwork done, the plays almost write themselves. Ask your students to share their playwriting homework at the beginning of each class period in groups of four. The author takes one part, assigning the others. The group conducts "dramatic readings" of the plays-in-progress. Along with additional Drawing/Writing exercises, each day's reading-aloud encourages the next night's writing.

Drawing/Writing lets the plays evolve character-by-character and scene-by-scene. A plot is not devised beforehand. Changes in character and scene drive the development. The cumulative visual and verbal content of the preliminary exercises make the playwriting seem effortless. The plays grow organically.

The following exercises bring one actor on stage at a time. When two or more characters are on stage, the writer, in effect, listens to them talk, writing down what they say. Like soap operas, the action is episodic; it could go on and on. A monologue or a soliloquy ends the play with a flourish.

## Procedure:

Explain what the following words mean: character, set, scene, flats, props, scrim, special effects, action, plot, dialogue, business, blocking. For instance, instructions for action are called "blocking." Smaller actions, like taking off a hat or adjusting a necktie, are described as "business." As well as providing dialogue and scene changes, playwrights may describe business including some blocking. Generally, directors provide blocking instructions.

Define the French word "didascalie" (die-dass-coll-lee). The word sounds like "didactic." Didascalie are written instructions for blocking and business and are italicized in the script. The playwrights Eugene O'Neill and Tennessee Williams provided abundant didascalie.

_Preparation for Scene One:_

- Draw two characters in full detail. Students must draw all features, hair, clothes, accoutrements.
- Describe these two characters using writing, including personality quirks, charisma, beliefs, likes, dislikes by looking carefully at all of the visual details, making inferences from them. If a character has a certain kind of haircut, what does this mean?
- Describe the setting for the first scene—flats, props, scrim, furniture, sound effects, lighting.

_Writing Scene One:_

- Bring one character on stage. Have that character say or do something. Then, bring the second character on stage. Have that character say or do something. Then, get the two characters to interact and start talking.
- Draw a third character. Describe this character in writing as above.
- Bring this character on stage. Have one of the others leave. Describe what the two remaining characters are doing and saying or not saying.
- Continue to work with these three characters for a day or so.

_Preparation for Scene Two:_

- Draw a new setting. Describe it in writing as above.

_Writing Scene Two:_

- Have one or two of the characters already on stage in the new setting. Let them talk. Bring the third on eventually. Let him or her talk. Describe what each character does and says.
- Continue in this manner until the concluding monologue or soliloquy, adding or taking away a character, or keeping the number fixed, until five scenes have been written.

**MONOLOGUE OR SOLILOQUY:** Close the play with a monologue or a soliloquy. Both forms offer chances for impassioned writing. The word "solo" means "alone;" in a soliloquy, an actor is alone on stage. "Mono" means "one" and "logos" means "word;" in a monologue, the actor is the only one speaking on stage although the stage may be full of people.

_Dale Sharbaugh, self portrait, ninth grade Eaglebrook School, 1990_

Dale Sharbaugh sets the scene for a soliloquy: "Granite sits dripping with mud and his eyes are relieved to see the moonlight instead of the mud he had escaped from. He is able to move freely now, the rain has washed out most of the mud and pebbles that were trapped in his skin. He sits alone, for Rampage has left because of his fear of death."

Granite: Here I sit all alone with nothing to think about, just to be scared. I waited all those years for a magician to free me from my frozen state and finally it happened and I just almost lost everything, just for a thrill. Why did I have to become so selfish? I never cared for anybody excepy myself, only myself. I hate it, I hate everything. For the first time in my life I am sad. I've killed over two hundred people in this year alone and finally, I experienced the fear and suffering involved. That one moment was the most frightening and damaging thing that has ever happened to my in my life. I'm not even alive, I should still be standing before Mangar's Tower as a monument, unmovable, like how I was when I was drowning in that mound of mud. I've never helped anybody in my life. I've only helped myself. I can't believe that I actually took a family's supply of food and money. I even took a gold necklace. Now, while I sit hear alone, I noticed how much pain the kid and his family went through. I ruined their lives completely. I walked off jumping and signing to myself not even thinking what I had done. All I could think about was killing and stealing from other people. Well, there is nothing that can be done. I'd be better off going in that mud again. I am worthless to myself and everybody around me, just plain worthless.

_Soliloquy, Dale Sharbaugh, 1990, Eaglebrook School from his play about Rampage the Dwarf and Granite the Giant._

Marc Drew, commenting on Dale's play, ninth grade, 1990, Eaglebrook School, writes, "I have read your play and I think it is very good. I have a couple of things that I think need improvement. First I thought that it was very hard to read your handwriting, but I suppose that I can't complain as mine is worse. I also think that the way it is set up is hard to understand. This I don't think is your fault, but I think that you should have all the characters at the beginning, so you wouldn't have to keep interrupting the story.

I think the plot is very interesting, especially how at the end the stone giant decides to kill himself because he has hurt so many people for no reason. In fact, this story could almost have a moral at the very end. I thought that the settings were very descriptive and well written, so I felt like I was right beside that person. The only other thing that was hard to understand was the dialogue. It was hard to follow at times because there were no ' ' marks around the people's speech. Over all it was a good play and if you do not understand anything talk to me in class. Your peer, Marc Drew."

Marc Drew
Mrs. Sheriden
English
4/2/90

### Sevarker Saxe

Sevarks, as everybody calls him, is an ugly man, with an unshaven beard, and a pointy face. His eyes burn with an inner fire.he is a tall thin man , almost like a weasel. Around people, he is very quiet, he just sits and takes in everything that is going on near him. He also has the disgusting habit of smoking long thin cigarettes. He belongs to the street gang called the brushnells, this gangs main interests are theft, murder, and rape. And no matter how much violence they get, it is never enough, because recently their small town of Serbia has been taken over by the Austrians. This man, of only seventeen and the rest of his gang, have a plot to kill the heir to the Austrian thrown, Frans Ferdinand.

### Frans Fredinand

This is the type of man, who at the present age of thirty-nine has been pampered all his life. He has a regale air about him that has been ground into him since he was born, and the many servants following him around also tend to add to his appearance. He is the person who has everything about him as perfect as it could possibly be.He is neither fat or thin, he is just the right height, and it could be even said that he has an unblemished face. His wife Sophie follows him everywhere, almost more like a servant than his wife.He is taking a goodwill tour to Serbia on which the brushnells plan to kill him as he is driving through the streets in his open-roofed car.

### The Place

there is a fair to be held For Frans Fredinand, much to the peoples dislike. The fair is all set to travel down a certain route, and the Brushnells are set and ready, all in their positions. Then, just before the cavalcade is about to set out, word is brought to the Emperors guards about the plot on Ferdinands life. Instead of canceling the Parade, He decides to send his police to find the Brushnells, as he and Sophie continue down another street. It is only in vane, because they see the police coming and scatter down different streets.....

*Marc Drew, three character sketches for a play, Eaglebrook School, 1990*

Marc Drew
Mrs. Sheridan
2/27/90
English

### MONOLOGUE

Behind Tom now the house is steadily burning, and the Fire trucks can be heard coming with their sirens blaring. Tom is just walking down the road almost in a daze. "Why?" "Why did I kill her?" "She was young, and had everything going for her, she was beautiful, she looked life a normal person under the mask of the S.S." "I'm a killer now, and the Germans are going to be even more out to get me. What's the use of living if You are just going to be hunted all your life."

He walks a little more then needs to sit down, he is old now, and gets tired easily, the burning house can not be seen,but the light that it is emitting and the yells and shouting can be heard all over the neighborhood. He crawls onto a park bench and almost falls asleep, Near where he is sitting, there is a slight rustle in the bushes, and he turns around to see another S.S. agent coming out of the bushes with a gun pointed at Tom's head

I'm too old to fight anymore," says Tom in a tired moan   didn't want to kill her, but she came at me and when I had her tied down I just got so angry I couldn't stop myself.....You understand don't you?"

The S.S. soldier shook his head, and put a puzzled look on his face. Then a look of anger crossed his face he raises his gun and fires five shots into Toms chest. Tom falls to the ground and is still. Carefully he walks over to Tom, and raises his gun to finish him off, He looks away momentarily and Tom uses all his strength grabs the soldier's legs and pulling him to the ground. Tom pulls the pin on the other grenade, looks at the panicked face of the soldier, and is gone in a sudden explosion of fire.

*Marc Drew, Monologue, play, Eaglebrook School, ninth grade, 1990*

### Preparation for the Monologue or Soliloquy:

Choose the character who will deliver the speech. Decide on which form of the speech the character will deliver. Draw the scene. Draw how the character now looks.

### Writing the end of the play:

Pose the character. Let him or her talk. Write down what the character says. Lower the lights. Close the curtains. Listen to the applause.

## Exercise 13:

## The cartoon-frame bubble quote

- Ask students to draw cartoon-like frames including " bubble quotes" to describe the main points in the piece of literature you are studying. The comic book-like series written by American physicist Joseph Schwartz and illustrated by the British artist Michael McGuinness, featuring booklets like *Einstein for Beginners*, provides an excellent example of this educational genre in which highly complex material is presented in a visual, accessible format. The comic book format provides an easy way for students to select and express the main points in the chapter, poem, essay, period of history. This approach works well with a range of students.

*"On Shark's Tooth Beach" by E.L. Konigsburg,*[38] *bubble quote descriptions by Tom Yeung , ninth grade, Eaglebrook School, 1989*

***The Baked Bean Supper Murders** by Virginia Rich, bubble quote description by Jorge Fiallos, ninth grade, Eaglebrook School, 1989*

- Ask your students to "five-frame" the conflict or the climax or the major symbolic content in a story, using direct quotes from the text placed in the "bubble quotes" in each frame.

This can be fascinating assignment. What a student identifies as the major symbolic content and what you identify as the major symbolic content may differ. Make sure the student knows what symbolic is and proceed from there.

As a Drawing/Writing teacher, complete the same writing assignments you give your students. Not only will you improve your own writing, but you will learn how long your assignments actually take.

## Exercise 14:
## Free writing and punctuation

- Let students write about any subject in any way for fifteen minutes or so. Ask students to include and circle as many of the 17 forms of punctuation as they know. Instruct them to circle the form of punctuation the first time it occurs only. This exercise encourages students to use a range of punctuation marks.

## Exercise 15:
## Student-provided homework , pop quizzes, and grades.

Offer students a chance to teach the class, including figuring out the homework and devising means for its "correction," or "grading." This is very fertile territory. As soon as I hear complaints in a class about hard assignments or hard homework or unfair grading, I hand the class right over to the students and suggest we all work it out together. I learn and they learn. They usually find me fair—fairer than they. They also find out that teaching is work.

---

**The Crucible**                        Name:
                                        Date:
                                        Course:

Directions:
Answer all questions about half a page or more (except ones with asterix next to them) in complete sentences on a separate sheet.

1. Why was Mary Warrin in Salem? Who let her go and why? Why was Mr. Proctor upset that Mary went to Salem?

*2. In Act One what town does it take place in? What year? Where, what room? Describe it.

3. Why is Parris worried that Beth is possessed besides that she is sick? What is Beth's state of sickness?

4. What does Tituba do that causes the girls to be possesed?

5. What do you think that witchcraft is?

Vocabulary
Directions: write a couple of words on the definition

1.Predilection:
2.Paradox:
3.Heathen:
4.Vindictive:
5.Diametrically:

*Jake Robards, quiz, The Crucible, Eaglebrook School, ninth grade, 1988*

---

[38] "On Shark's Tooth Beach" from the book of short stories, *Throwing Shadows* by E.L. Konigsburg, 1979, Colliers Books, New York.

JAKE ROBARDS
10-13-88
English Mrs. Sheridan

Method of grading:
19 points for each essay - MAX
1 point for each vocabulary word

    I asked the questions I did
because I wanted to know wether the reader
was really paying attention. I am trying
to find out if the person who read
understood what he read and what thoughts
were going on inside his brain. I included
the vocabulary because I wanted to see
if the reader looked up words he
didn't know or just bypassed them.
My main reason for having this quiz is to see
what the readers' reading comprehension
skill is and help improve it.

*Jake Robards, comment on his quiz, ninth grade,
Eaglebrook School, 1988*

      Quiz         John Royall
choose five out of the 8 questions  10/14/88
given. Answer in complete or
incomplete questions. You will
be graded on the amount of
facts given. Write on seperate page.

① Tell us about the relationship between
Elizabeth and John Proctor, give some
examples of this relationship.

② What was Hale's beliefe in witch craft
and what where some of his ways of
finding it?

③ For what reason did Hale come to
see mr. and mrs. Proctor and what
went on between them?

④ What caused Marry Warren to be treated
so respectively and leaninfly by the
Proctors?

⑤ What is the change of manner in Abigale
from when she was accused and when
Tituba walks into the room?

*John Royall, quiz, The Crucible, Eaglebrook School,
ninth grade, 1988*

## For teachers and student-teachers: illustrate your verbal instructions with drawings

- Draw pictures of your writing assignments on the board. Then, transcribe that picture into words. Illustrated homework assignments are much easier to understand than purely text based ones. As you will note, the final exams I give in art history at the college level include pictures of the writing assignments.

## Students and pop quizzes

- Ask students to suggest questions for pop (or unscheduled) quizzes on literature as a homework assignment. Then, give these quizzes in a "round-robin" fashion. Students place all of their questions on one sheet of paper, in a list, leaving space below each question for an answer. Xerox this sheet, providing one for each student. After answering the first question, the sheet goes back to that question-provider who grades the answer according to his or her version of the

Part IV- Recombitant Drawing.
Choose 3 images from the entire text that interest you, which you have not yet drawn.
Name all 3, defining with all six categories. Do not draw the images.

Choose one section from each of the three plates.
Enlarge it and draw it.
Combine all 3 sections chosen from the 3 works in a new drawing. You can overlap.
You can distort. Use color and collage. If you need to add some elements, add them.
Indicate additions with arrows. Label, "addition of.........(your name)."

Look at what you have created. Using arrows and labels, identify at least 6 areas
strongly characteristic of 3 different styles of art studied this semester.

Example:

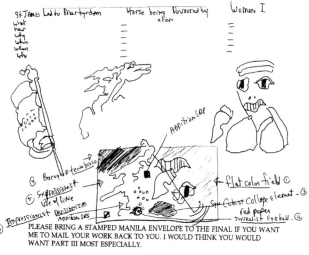

PLEASE BRING A STAMPED MANILA ENVELOPE TO THE FINAL IF YOU WANT
ME TO MAIL YOUR WORK BACK TO YOU. I WOULD THINK YOU WOULD
WANT PART III MOST ESPECIALLY.

HAPPIEST HOLIDAYS
GOOD WORK! GOOD LUCK!

*Drawing, Part IV of an art survey exam, Westfield State College*

answer and so on, back and forth. (The classroom becomes pleasantly "chaotic" in behavior.) If students disagree about the answers, let them hash this out after the quiz. Disagreement encourages close textural analysis. I let students use open books for these pop quizzes in literature. Students become adept at finding the perfect supporting quote in response to a quiz question. The closer students stay to the text, the more familiar they become with it.

## Exercise 16:

### Deep Wisdom

*Identifying deep wisdom*

- Invite students to identify deep wisdom—or truth, in stories. This assignment worked well with the collection of Native American short stories called *The Sun is Not Merciful,* by Anna Lee Walters[39]. The phrase "deep wisdom" interests students. Make sure you choose work that contains deep wisdom! This can become tricky;

what you think is deep wisdom may be of no interest to your students. Choose texts with them in mind, or ask students to suggest them.

*Amanda Lynne Braden, LMD self portrait, studio course, Westfield State College, 1994*

---

[39] Walters, Anna Lee, *The Sun Is Not Merciful*. Ithaca, NY: Firebrand Books, 1985.

# DRAWING/WRITING and the Fine Arts
## Studio Arts and Art Survey

## Guidelines

It is said that we generally teach as we were taught, and not as innovators. This is one of the reasons why education takes so long to change. If we were taught in a text-based way, we will probably teach this way. If we were taught by imposition, we will probably impose information on students, rather than allowing them to discover and construct it.

In the past, it was feasible to teach the visual arts apart from literacy. It is no longer feasible for several reasons:

- a technological society requires visual literacy skills

- a student population less interested and practiced in reading and writing require the highly visual, hands-on stimulus of the arts to bolster attention and to sustain interest.

The popularity of some technical/vocational schools is high enough to necessitate entrance requirements. The physical plant, financial resources, curricular latitude, and pupil-teacher ratio are better in many technical/ vocational schools than in other high schools. If we sift out the components which distinguish technical/ vocational education, characteristics emerge which align with cues from brain science about how the brain learns best. Highly visual, exploratory, practically relevant, hands-on learning is engaging and effective. By adding a strong writing component and exercises in abstract thinking, vocational education becomes as literate as it is technical and practical. Seeing, doing, making things that can be tested against certain standards of form and function: these activities provide bases for writing and reading and computing. Wiring can short-circuit. Plumbing can leak. A joist can weaken. These problems can be experienced, analyzed and fixed. So can drawings and writings. There is no such thing as a wrong drawing, although there are inaccurate or incomplete drawings. There is no such thing as a wrong sentence, although there are inaccurate or incomplete sentences, or sentences trapped in "inner speech" (Faith, 1989). If the habit of crafting objects is established, writing can also be constructed and crafted.

As well as training in trades like plumbing, wiring, carpentry, food preparation, and hairdressing, the studio arts and art history can increase students' practical and technical skills, too. If art departments include courses on practical design problems, as well as on visual literacy, reframing existing courses with these emphases in mind, art departments will draw larger numbers of general education students as well as a bigger part of the budget.

The Drawing/Writing English curriculum outlined above presents a course of study enriched by drawing. The Drawing/Writing Fine Arts curricula outlined below present courses enriched by writing. These courses have been taught at the middle, high school and college levels—some once, some twice a semester for five years, some for seventeen years.

### STUDIO ARTS

**Basic Design** and the Drawing/Writing five-step with:
> the object
> the self-portrait
> figure studies
> Simple, simpler, simplest
> Complex, more complex, most complex

**Basic Drawing, Painting, Print-making, Ceramics, Sculpture,** and the Drawing/Writing five-step as subject matter for painting
> the object
> the self portrait
> figure studies

**Composition:**
> Drawing/Writing and Right Relationships in connection with drawing, painting, print-making.

**Color Theory:**
> Drawing/Writing and Right Relationships in connection with complementary colors and adjusted hues.

*The self portrait, LMD, Jessamyn Smith, studio course, Westfield State College, 1994*

*Figures, Allison McCarthy, Westfield State College studio course, 1994*

*The self portrait by Jaime Babowitch, series, Dr/Wr studio course, Westfield State College, 1994*

*The self portrait, Organic and Fractal, Jaime Babowitch, Dr/Wr studio course, Westfield State College, 1994*

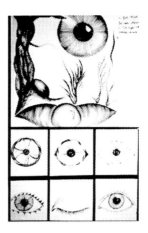

*Combined CA using the object, self portrait and figure studies, plus a drawing of a transformation, Nicole Bernet, Westfield State College, Dr/Wr studio arts drawing program, 1994*

*James Barbere, figure, Dr/Wr studio course, Westfield State, 1994*

Whether you are teaching basic drawing or design or painting or print-making, start the course with the five-step using the object, then the self-portrait, and then the figure. Once the Drawing/Writing exercises have been done, teach basic painting techniques and then ask students to paint from their object drawings or from the self-portrait drawings or from the figure drawings. Students might choose to paint the "Perfect" whole version of their face, or the Composite Abstraction. Or, as a painting teacher, you might require the "Perfect" whole first, and then the CA.

In the same way, after an introductory session with the five-step, the instructor can move briskly into issues of design. In this way, the basic skills required by artists, writers, and readers, as well as the habits of rigorous thinkers in any field, are established first. Exposure to a specific art form or period in art history follows naturally, receiving a trained and receptive audience.

## ART HISTORY
## THE DRAWING/WRITING WAY

### Drawing/Writing journals as aides to learning

### The Drawing/Writing approach to lecture notes, new vocabulary and concepts, quizzes and exams.[40]

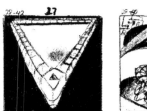

*Quiz. Rebecca Parco, drawings of slides, Westfield State Art Survey, 1995*

*Dr/Wr journals, Jean Whitlock, 1994, Westfield State, "Bull Jumping", Knossos*

*Dr/Wr journals, Rich Strolis, Westfield State, 1995, St. Sernin*

*Dr/Wr journals, Rich Strolis, Westfield State, 1995, "Pantocrator"*

*Dr/Wr journals, Karen Whitney, 1994-5, "Grande Odalesque", Ingres*

Ideally, art history courses are taught in conjunction with studio courses so that students approach art history as practitioners of art. It is easier to appreciate an Impressionist artist after practicing Impressionist brush strokes and approaches to light, atmosphere, color and form. Some colleges have taken this hands-on approach to art history. The Neuroconstructivist approach to the art history lecture gives students a taste of this hands-approach through Drawing/Writing journals. Although the journals are no substitute for actually practicing Impressionism, they create a closer bond with art work than glancing through a text.

---

[40] Sample Drawing/Writing syllabi, quizzes and exams are included at the end of this section.

## THE DRAWING/WRITING JOURNAL

Large lecture courses preclude teaching the actual five-step Drawing/Writing program. The amount of material that has to be covered by the course, the number of students, the lecture hall set-up make the five-step impracticable. Still, Drawing/Writing journals can be used to heighten attention, and to engage students' visual and verbal skills. Be forewarned; if you decide to use Drawing/Writing journals, they will create additional work for everyone. TA's can be trained to respond to Drawing/Writing journals. The professor must continue to work with the TA's to keep in touch with student work and to provide support for the TA's. The professor should continue to comment on journals, too, moving to a new set of students for each round of quizzes and journal-grading.

It is of critical importance to reassure students that their drawings will not be graded. If the drawing is done, it receives an "A" as a drawing that has been completed. The same holds true with the writing assignment; if it is done, it receives credit. Over time, the professor may make comments designed to spur the drawer/writer to more substantive efforts. This can only be done if the commentator knows that student's work. In general, comments in the margins provide praise for strong draw-ers and encouragement and tips for weaker draw-ers. Reassure students that the more they draw, the better their drawing skills will become.

By copying images from their art history text into a journal, students establish a direct, hands-on relationship with a piece of work. By writing about these images, students clarify their relationship to the work and their understanding of it. Sketching an indifferent black and white photograph provides a closer link with a work of art than glancing at an image in a text.

Drawing/Writing journals provide practice not only with drawing—or, with seeing—but with writing, a skill often neglected in art courses except for a paper or two. A common method for grading art survey lectures is by electronically-scanned multiple choice exams. These exams do not encourage students' writing abilities.

## LECTURE AS DISCUSSION

It is possible to turn a large lecture hall into a discussion group if you are willing to make a seating chart. Ask students to continue to sit in the same seats. Because you have asked them to form peer pairs for the sake of sharing their Drawing/Writing journals at the beginning of each lecture, students are usually willing to maintain the

seating plan. A seating chart makes students feel known. It also makes them accountable. They can be questioned by name. Their opinions can be solicited. I start a course by giving over one whole lecture to a general discussion called "What is Art?" I bring in a small hooked rug made by my grandmother, a sketch done by Sam Sheridan of a horse's head after Da Vinci, a sketch Sarah Sheridan did from a magazine photo of a woman's head, a piece of stained glass, a Coke can, a Native American squash blossom necklace, a patchwork vest made in South America, stiffened with newspaper and appliqued with frogs and ginkos. Students discuss, in pairs, whether each item is art or is not art and if so, why and if not so, why. I insist on conversation between peers in the decision-making process. It takes time to encourage some students to talk and think freely. The question "What is Art?" is a thorny one. There are no absolute answers. We eventually produce some thoughts on the power of the intent of the art-maker, and the judgment of history, and the decisions of museums and galleries.

## OVERHEAD PROJECTION

Overhead projection of assignments, terms, styles, concepts, vocabulary and powerful ideas makes these items clear to students. I show slides as I project the terms and concepts. Then, I start the formal slide show, addressing students by name and teaching to the terms. The student must immediately use the appropriate term or concept. If the student has not been listening, this is apparent. If there is a general misunderstanding, this is apparent, too. I have learned that what I think is crystal-clear may not be clear to students. By copying these items in their Drawing/Writing journals, students take ownership of terms in ways handouts can not provide. The actual process of slide-showing and "lecturing" becomes an interactive exchange. This personalized approach keeps a lecture course alert, lively, and well-attended.

The pun connected with "attended" is intended. Teachers are responsible for attendance and attention. Especially at this point in educational history when students are used to the high-level visual and aural stimulation of videos, movies, television and computer programs, teachers are responsible for helping students to be alert, present, *and there*. To do so, the teacher must be alert, present, and there. One way to "be there"—for professor and students—in a lecture situation is the seating chart. The chart shows students that the teacher knows and cares who they are and that they are there. Naming is one of the single most important acts of recognition a teacher performs. Naming signals a mutually attentive attitude, and typifies Neuroconstructivist teaching. Naming aligns with Robert Kegan's convictions that it is both the privilege and the responsibility of educators to "attend on the child" (1982).

Art history provides one of the most effective ways to engage students in the new literacy. The following art history program develops this new visual and verbal literacy by training students to draw and then to write in response to six questions about every work of art they elect to study as part of their weekly Drawing/Writing assignments. After drawing two works of art in their journals, students ask themselves these questions, answering them in writing in their journals:

- what is it? (category: is this a basket, statue, building, piece of jewelry)
- how was it made? (materials, style)
- why was it made? (intent of the artist, requirements of society)
- where was it made? (location or provenance)
- when was it made? (relative or absolute dating)
- who made it? (attribution: name of the artist, group, school)

Much of the preparation for quizzes and finals in Drawing/Writing-based art survey courses is "open-book," assigned as homework and done ahead of time. A great deal is drawing-based. For instance, to learn the slides, students draw them ahead of time and bring the drawings of the slides into the exam. All they need to do is label them. This allows students to work at their own pace during the exam; they do not have to wait for the slide to appear on a screen. Additionally, they must provide a textbook-based image to go with each vocabulary term and bring that drawing with the term into an exam, providing the written definition by looking at the drawing. Or, they must choose an object and draw it in the style of a Renaissance artist, Impressionist, Expressionist, Cubist, Futurist, Dada, and Abstract Expressionist artist, explaining exactly how their image fulfills the requirements for a particular style of art. The following work illustrates that series, using Nintendo as subject matter.

Part III of every quiz and exam requires drawing three images and describing them using the six categories, then analyzing them through comparing and contrasting all three images across all six categories, and then making inferences about the three works in two fully developed conclusions about sameness and

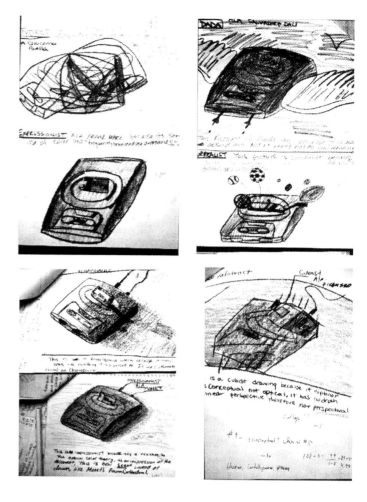

*Exam, Nintendo game rendered Renaissance through Modern, Westfield State College, 1996*

difference using the word "because." This format recapitulates the triple goal in Drawing/Writing: to teach students to describe information, to analyze information, and to make inferences about information—on their own terms.

*Cynthia Olson, Drawing/Writing journals, Westfield State art survey course, 1993*

The amount of work students will do for assured grades is phenomenal, particularly if that work involves drawing. This ahead-of-time, open-book drawing and writing approach lowers test anxiety, reduces rote memorization, and promotes pride as well as understanding. Students come into the testing situation with most of the work done. In addition, they come into the testing situation equipped with a set of visual, mnemonic devices in the form of drawings to cue definitions of pre-assigned terms. If students draw each assigned slide ahead of time, they can work through names, titles, dates and styles at their own speed, and go on to the next section without waiting for a slide projector. This approach encourages self-regulatory test-taking behavior. In addition, students get extra credit for drawings of slides, offsetting a missed date or two. (Other drawings are required; if students skip them, they lose points.) The extra points earned by drawing slides also offset problems in other sections of the quiz. A student can earn more than 100 points per quiz. One over-achieved quiz compensates for a botched quiz or lets a student skip one section of the final. A hard-working student can earn an "A" in the course in spite of occasional lapses. In this way, students learn to manage their abilities, time and grades intelligently. The level of personal control in a Drawing/Writing lecture course, as well as the hands-on approach to learning, characterizes Neuroconstructivist programs, providing mental and emotional benefits as well as knowledge.

Students report that the observational skills acquired in a Drawing/Writing art survey course are useful in other fields, including criminal justice. In my experience, about one-fifth of the students in each Drawing/Writing art survey course change majors, registering for Fine Arts. It is not unusual for students to flock into the art department as their major after a Drawing/Writing-based lecture course, nor for Criminal Justice majors to sign up for other art courses. The benefits of a personal, drawing-and-writing-based approach to art survey courses are increased levels in student attendance, engagement, output and learning. Drawing/Writing students tend to take additional courses taught in this way. Some start to question other teaching approaches, creating little pockets of inquiry.

It is important to present the study of art history as training in visual literacy. Students who approach art history as draw-ers and writers increase their abilities to decode and encode visual information in general. In a personal, hands-on way, they join the fundamental human enterprise of visual/spatial meaning-making. This Neuroconstructivist approach appeals strongly to special needs students, foreign students, disaffected students and gifted students. Neuroconstructivist guidelines help instructors tailor their delivery of the content area so that it reaches a broad range of student needs, abilities, skills, and backgrounds.

Cynthia Olson, Drawing/Writing final exam, vocabulary words with mnemonic drawings, Westfield State College art survey course, 1993

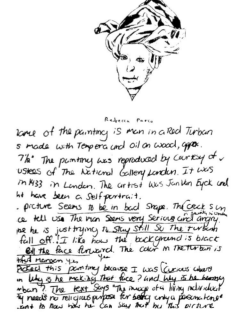

Rebecca Parco, Drawing/Writing journal, Westfield State College art survey course, 1995

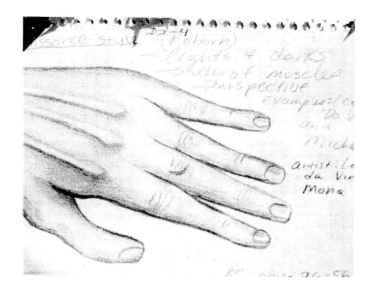

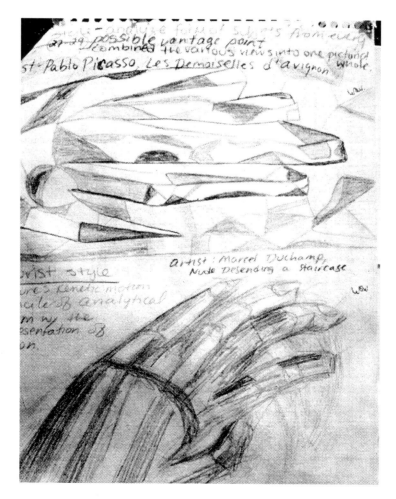

*Nancy Hay, Drawing/Writing final exam, Renaissance hand, Impressionist hand, Cubist hand, Futurist hand, Westfield State College, 1996*

# Sample syllabi, quizzes and exams

**Syllabus**
ART DEPARTMENT
WESTFIELD STATE COLLEGE
Studio Drawing Course
Fall, 1994

**COURSE TITLE:** DRAWING 1 - ART0103-002

**INSTRUCTOR:** DR. SUSAN SHERIDAN

*LMD, self portrait, Beth Stevens, studio course, Westfield State College, 1994*

**COURSE DESCRIPTION:** The point of this course (which should be the aim of any course in any field of study) is to develop a range of all-purpose thinking skills. There is visual literacy and there is verbal literacy. Words can be used effectively to draw pictures in the mind. A picture, or a drawing, on the other hand, can be worth, as they say, a million words. This drawing course takes an innovative approach by redefining training in drawing as training in visual literacy, combining this approach to visual literacy with connected writing exercises. The product will be "Drawing/Writing" portfolios. Your drawing skills will improve dramatically. Your writing skills should, too. So should your ability to describe, to analyze and to infer.

**CLASS HOURS:** Tuesday/Thursday, 8:30-11:10 a.m.

**CLASS CONDUCT:** 3 sessions of the five-step Drawing/Writing program using:

1) an object
2) the self portrait
3) figure or life studies

**MEDIUMS** to be explored in each of the 3 areas of study:

1) markers
2) pencil
3) pastel and/or charcoal
4) water colors
5) water color and pen in ink.

*PW, Self portrait, Nicole Bernet, studio course, Westfield State College, 1994,*

**SUPPLIES:**

A small dormitory-size mirror, about 10″ by 12″, for the self-portrait. Or any size you can get ahold of from Caldor's etc.. Make-up size is probably too small. **Do not rip** off the dorm mirrors, but do ask maintenance if they have any extras handy.

A portfolio for your work, size 18″ by 24″; 2 sheets of heavy manila paper taped closed to form a large portfolio OK.

A fishing tackle box with:

A set of $1.99 finetip magic markers

Several H and HB pencils—that is hard graphite and soft graphite-with erasers

A set of pastels- and fixative or hair spray

*"Judith and Maid Servant with the Head of Holofernes" by Artemisia Gentileschi, Drawing/Writing journal,*
*Isaac Flores, Art Survey, Westfield State College, 1996*

A gum or lift-off eraser.

Some sticks of charcoal—and fixative or hair spray

A dimestore set of water colors, and brushes and a water pot of some kind.

Some drawing pens, several nib sizes—thick, fine. Or an old fashioned drawing pen, with nibs, and a bottle of permanent black ink.

A large sketch pad, inexpensive white paper—NOT NEWSPRINT. Get the most for the least, size 18″ by 24″.

**GRADES:** There will be 16 grades; one for each of the 3 subject areas (the object, the self portrait, the figure study), in each of the 5 media (3x5=15). The 16th grade is for attendance, which will be scrupulously recorded and graded. Grades are cumulative. Attendance counts for 10 points. Each of the 15 assignments count 6 points each, for a total of 90 points. 90+10=100.

We will conduct group critiques. Your input vis-a-vis others' work is important and graded as occurring or not occurring.

**GROUP CRITIQUES:** Let's see if we can identify quality work, and then, by analyzing it verbally, winnow out the specific qualities making good art work effective.

**ASSIGNMENTS:** You will receive regular assignments.

**OFFICE HOURS:** 11:30-12:00, Tuesdays and Thursdays, room 208B, Parenzo Hall (up one flight from Art Office, glass door on immediate left before the big double doors).

*"St. James led to martyrdom" by Andrea Mantegna, Drawing/Writing journal,*
*Isaac Flores, art survey, Westfield State College, 1996*

# COURSE OUTLINE – STUDIO ARTS

## THE OBJECT, THE SELF PORTRAIT, THE FIGURE STUDY

1) **First drawing/writing**, circa 15 min. each, choice of media, exactly as described in Part 2 of this book.

2) **The Drawing/Writing five-step exercises** as described in Part 2 of this book. Each drawing is accompanied by reflective writing following the usual Drawing/Writing format: "My ... drawing tells me that ... because...." Students share class work daily in peer pairs, just as they share the assigned work at the beginning of the next class. In this way, a studio arts class provides training in verbal communication skills, often neglected in art courses, giving art students a reputation as visual but not as verbal communicators. Self-promotion is critical to marketplace success, whether the student becomes an artist or as the more usual model provided by this book— the visual literacy or graphics specialist.

3) As outlined in Part 2, the steps and materials follow this progression:

    Blind Contour: marker

    Regular Contour: marker

    Basic shapes - Euclidean, fractal, organic: marker

    LMD: marker

    The Perfect Whole - media

    2-3 hour pencil study.

    charcoal

    pastel

    watercolor and ink

    Experiment with 3/4 or other view.

    Write a Petrarchan or Elizabethan sonnet about the "Perfect" Whole

    The Composite Abstraction, 18″ by 24″, mixed media.

*LMD Figure,*
*Allison McCarthy, 1994*

4) After 3 consecutive two-week sessions with the object, the self portrait and the figure, a transformation study is introduced: in 3 steps or more, transform the object into the self portrait or into the figure study. 18″ by 24″, choice of media. Write about the transformation.

5) The double three-step called *Simple, Simpler, Simplest and Complex, More Complex, Most Complex* follows. See end of Part 2.

6) After completing each 2-week session, and before completing the transformation exercise and the double two-step, students complete Rescore sheets, identifying and analyzing growth in technical skills, expressivity, and style, visually and verbally, placing these sheets in their portfolios.

7) Students are graded on the completeness, not the quality of the portfolio, and on the completeness of the Rescore sheets, as well as on the completeness of the transformation and double two-step exercises. In addition, students receive a grade for attendance and one for class participation as demonstrated through peer pair sharing and group critiques. This grading system for the portfolio is provided at the end of Part 2.

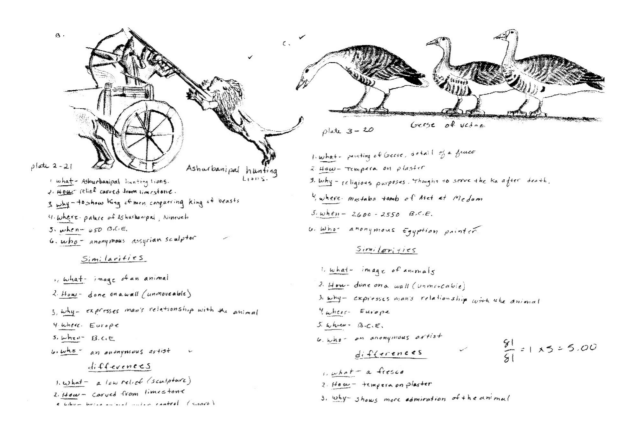

B.

C.

plate 2-21

Asharbanipal hunting lions.

1. what - Asharbanipal hunting lions.
2. How - relief carved from limestone.
3. why - to show King of men conquering king of beasts
4. where - palace of Asharbanipal, Nineveh
5. when - 650 B.C.E.
6. who - anonymous Assyrian sculptor

Similarities

1. what - image of an animal
2. How - done on a wall (unmoveable)
3. why - expresses man's relationship with the animal
4. where - Europe
5. when - B.C.E
6. who - an anonymous artist

differences

1. what - a low relief (sculpture)
2. How - carved from limestone

plate 3-20          Geese of Medne

1. what - painting of Geese, detail of a fresco
2. How - Tempera on plaster
3. why - religious purposes. Thought to serve the Ka after death.
4. where - mastaba tomb of Atet at Medum
5. when - 2600 - 2550 B.C.E.
6. who - anonymous Egyptian painter

Similarities

1. what - image of animals
2. How - done on a wall (unmoveable)
3. why - expresses man's relationship with the animal
4. where - Europe
5. when - B.C.E.
6. who - an anonymous artist

differences

1. what - a fresco
2. How - tempera on plaster
3. why - shows more admiration of the animal

$$\frac{81}{81} = 1 \times 5 = 5.00$$

*Part III, Quiz, Ancient Near Eastern and Egyptian art, Jennifer Coughlin,*
*Art Survey, Westfield State College, 1997*

# Art Survey Syllabi including:

## First Assignment • Sample Journal Entries • Sample Quizzes • Sample Final

\* \* \* \* \* \* \* \* \* \* \* \* \* \*

ART DEPARTMENT
WESTFIELD STATE COLLEGE
**FALL 1996**
**COURSE TITLE:** ART SURVEY II - ART 0I07-001 AND 002
**INSTRUCTOR:** DR. SUSAN SHERIDAN

**COURSE DESCRIPTION:** Major works of Western art and architecture from THE RENAISSANCE through MODERN ART. The art will be presented through six practical questions: what? how? why? where? when? who? Students will also be introduced to art terms and to aesthetic and philosophical principles and considerations. The class will be highly participatory.

**CLASS HOURS:** TUESDAY AND THURSDAY
  SECTION 1 12:45-2
  SECTION II 2:10-3:25

*Rodin's Thinker, Jennifer Coughlin,
Art Survey, Westfield State College, 1997*

**CLASS CONDUCT:** Use of overhead projector to introduce vocabulary and concepts.
  Lectures and slides
  Class discussion and partnering.

   Be ready to draw and write. Don't worry; you will learn to draw better and to write better and to think better in this MODIFIED LECTURE APPROACH. The ways in which work is assigned and graded make it easy to achieve at a high level on a cumulative basis in this class.

**GRADES:** There will be **eight** components to your final grade. A "drawing/writing" journal will be graded 3 times; there will be 3 major quizzes plus 1 cumulative final; attendance will be scrupulously recorded and graded.

**ASSIGNMENTS:** You will receive regular reading assignments in the text, as well as regular assignments for your drawing/writing journal. You must keep up with both the reading and the drawing and writing. The drawing/writing assignments make it easy to keep up with the reading. You will be responsible for all class discussion and for all overhead projections of vocabulary and concepts. Coming to class will make this easy. Not coming to class will make this impossible.

**TEXT:** <u>Art through the Ages</u>, Volume 11 Renaissance and Modern Art by Helen Gardner, 10th edition Harcourt, Brace and Jovanovich, publishers.

**Drawing/Writing journal:** students must bring the textbook and a drawing sketchbooks, spiral bound, to class. This sketchbooks will be your "drawing/writing" journal.

**OFFICE HOURS:**  11:30-12:30 a.m. – Tuesdays and Thursdays – lobby Wilson, outside of lecture hall B.

**QUIZ and EXAM DATES:** to be determined.

*Note:* **This is the kind of art survey course not to take if you plan to "bag" it. The design of the course makes it impossible to take it in a "hit or miss" way.**

**Explanation, Drawing/Writing journal:**

This course is about thinking. The goal of the course is that, by studying art history, you will become a more <u>critical visual thinker in general</u>. Drawing, as well as writing, is a powerful way to think. Since we will be doing a lot of writing, your verbal strengths should increase, too.

Interactive learning, where you do some of the work , is more effective than my talking to you for 1 and 1/2 hours. The journal is one place to do this work. Another place is sharing this journal with your peer partner in class. A third is through group discussions during the course of the lecture itself.

**Supplies:**

As well as a **lecture notebook** (where you take down your own reading notes, and lecture notes) , and the **textbook**, you will need to bring a **second spiral bound sketch pad** to class or your Drawing/Writing journal. This is where you will do assigned drawings and writings and keep class vocabulary and ideas. You will be graded on this drawing/writing journal 3 times during the semester. **Everything shown on the overhead projector goes into this journal—vocabulary, drawings, ideas.**

## FIRST ASSIGNMENT

1)   READ INTRO. to the text book.

2)   CHOSE ONE IMAGE in the intro. AND DRAW IT IN YOUR JOURNAL.

3)   THEN, WRITE IN YOUR JOURNAL about this image.

WRITE ABOUT EACH OF THESE FOUR POINTS:

WHY did the image GET YOUR ATTENTION?

WHAT MEANING DOES IT HAVE PERSONALLY FOR YOU?

WHY DO YOU THINK YOU CHOSE IT?

What seems strong or powerful about the image?

4)   Draw anything you want to in your house, dorm room, ect. Then write in response to these questions:
   a.   Is the object "art?" Yes, no, and why.
   b.   Is your drawing of the object "art?" Yes, no and why.

**Today. Choose a partner.** This partner will stay constant throughout the course. This is your peer partner.

Take a sheet of paper. Decide the following together, taking notes. WHICH OF THE FOLLOWING OBJECTS IS ART? Yes, No, WHY? WHY NOT? Answer all 4 questions, each item, in writing, with your peer. You will need to discuss each item with your peer.

1)   hand-made, newspaper-stuffed, cotton vest
2)   stained glass
3)   small hooked rug
4)   Native American silver and turquoise necklace
5)   sketch horse head, pen and ink
6)   girl's head, pencil sketch
7)   found object
8)   manuscript, ink on vellum
9)   cup, ceramic
10)  a doll, cloth

*Teapot, Drawing/Writing journal, Jennifer Coughlin, Art Survey, Westfield State College, 1997*

**Conclusions after voting on the art or non-art status of each object:**

How did you vote? Why did you vote this way?

What were your criteria—your reasons for making a judgment about each object? That is, paintings and drawings are art, sewing is not?

**Some questions:**

Do some **materials** make art, some not.

Is any sketch, art? Any piece of sewing, not?

Is **good design** necessary? What is good design? Neither too much nor too little? Do things that are not art have good design? What? Planes, snowflakes.

**Aesthetic experience?** Enjoying for own sake. Is this what art has to do with? If so, what is enjoying? Is a good photo of starving Somalian kids art?

Is the attitude or mood of the **viewer** important to art? Are your attitudes or moods reliable? Do you like x one day and hate it the next?

Is the **knowledge** of the viewer about the artist/maker important to determining what is art? If I know Van Gogh painted it, is it art? If I know a four-year-old painted it, is it not?

**Is the attitude or INTENT of the artist important to identifying what is art? The philosophy of art considers the "intentionality." If the artist intends to create art, does the intention determine whether we view it as art or not art. What do I mean when I say I intend that this thing I have made to be a work of art?**

Is there any absolute method for determining what is and what is not a work of art?

**Idea:** Margaret Mead—art was originally something someone made as well as they could for some purpose.

Let's think about this.

**WHAT ABOUT a text book in which all work is presented about the same size in terms of format, whether it is a coin or a statue or a building?**

**THE SIX CATEGORIES AS A WAY TO GET A HANDLE ON A PIECE OF ART.**

As we walk, run, race through Art Survey 1—let's START with the facts:

THE SIX CATEGORIES are a way to get at the facts.

> **WHAT IS IT? IDENTIFY THE THING. WHAT THE HECK IS THIS THING?**
>
> **HOW WAS IT MADE ? MATERIALS, STYLE.**
>
> **WHY WAS IT MADE? FUNCTION, PURPOSE.**
>
> **WHEN WAS IT MADE? CHRONOLOGY.**
>
> **WHERE WAS IT MADE? LOCATION or PROVENANCE.**
>
> **WHO MADE IT? ARTIST, ARTISAN, ARCHITECT, OR ATTRIBUTION.**

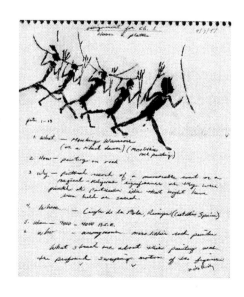

*Marching Warriers, Drawing/Writing Journal, Jennifer Coughlin, Art Survey, Westfield State College, 1997*

<u>EXAMPLE:</u>

**What:** x is a .....painting, sculpture, construction, building, ruined remains of, drawing, print, event or happening, floor plan, schematic drawing of....., reconstruction of.....

**How:** x was made by doing this to that, and looks a lot like other examples in the style of.....

**Why:** the purpose of x was to.......... do magic, shelter a person, inspire a person, present the portrait of a person, essentialize........whatever, criticize x, celebrate x, x seems to be suggesting that........ means that.......conveys that.......(ART IS SOMEONE'S ATTEMPT TO SAY SOMETHING OF IMPORTANCE ABOUT SOMETHING). That is, what was the guy's intent (read for"guy" female or male artist).

**Who:** x is clearly the work of..... ( name of the artist). Or nobody knows.

**When, where:** x. seems to be an example of work done in the .....period .....in the country of......

**O.K. Let's say it is art; how can we deconstruct it - that is, break it down?**

LINES—descriptive, expressive, abstract, outline (cartoon), contour, hatching, implied, edges, horizontal, vertical, lines of sight, idea of closure—true or implied.

FORM suggestive, closed, open (allowing shapes to penetrate)—geometric, organic.

MASSES, open, closed. Additive, subtractive.

SPACE—positive, negative. Bounded, unbounded. Finite, infinite.

Dimension: 2-d 3-d. Vanishing point, horizon line. One point perspective, two point perspective, multiple points, reverse perspective.

TEXTURE

MOVEMENT

VALUE—light, medium, dark. Chiaroscuro.

COLOR, hue, chroma.
    additive (lights) and subtractive (pigments) color
    saturation.
    complementary, analogous or adjacent, monochromatic, expressive (red means grief in Africa, so be careful!)

DESIGN.

STYLE—realistic or representational or figurative.
    abstract or non-representation or non- figurative.
    by artist, school, period, location.

GENRE—as category
    as everyday scene.

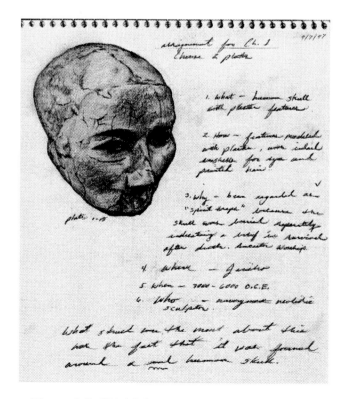

*Plastered Skull/Spirit house, Drawing/Writing journal, Jennifer Coughlin, Westfield State College, 1997*

## Quiz chaps. 19, 20, 21, 22 in the 9th edition of Gardner's Art through the Ages, Harcourt, Brace Jovanovich College Publishers, 1991.

### 3 parts, each worth 5 points. Bonus section worth 2 extra points.

**Part One**

**SLIDE IDENTIFICATION.** <u>Memorize title, artist, period, and one piece of specific</u> information about <u>each</u> work.

<u>Extra credit</u>, 1 point /drawing of slide.

| Title, artist | Style or Period | One salient comment |
|---|---|---|
| 1. Lamentation over the Dead Christ, Giotto | 14th c.proto-Ren.S.It | turned backs create continuous space |
| 2. The Annunciation, Simone Martini | | |
| 3. The Merode Altarpiece, Robert Campin | | |
| 4. Giovanni Arnolfini & his Bride, Jan van Eyck | | |
| 5. The Escorial Deposition, Rogier van der Weyden | | |
| 6. The Adoration of the Shepherds, Portinari Altarpiece, Hugo van der Goes | | |
| 7. Garden of Earthly Delights, Hieronymus Bosch | | |
| 8. Isaac & his sons, Bronze Doors, Baptistry, Florence, Lorenzo Ghiberti | | |
| 9. The Trinity, Mosaccio | | |
| 10. David, Donatello | | |
| 11. The Expulsion of Adam and Eve, Mosaccio | | |
| 12. The Battle of San Romano, Uccello | | |
| 13. The Annunciation, Fra Angelico | | |
| 14. The Birth of Venus, Sandro Botticelli | | |
| 15. The Dead Christ, Andrea Mantegna | | |
| 16. The Virgin of the Rocks-Leonardo Da Vinci | | |
| 17. The Last Supper- Leonardo Da Vinci | | |
| 18. Madonna with the Goldfinch-Raphael | | |
| 19. The School of Athens-Raphael | | |
| 20. David-Michelangelo | | |
| 22. The Creation of Adam,Sistine Chapel, Michelangelo. | | |
| 23. The Last Judgment-Michelangelo. | | |
| 24. Dome of the Florence Cathedral, Filippo Brunelleschi | | |
| 25. Villa Rotonda, Andrea Palladio | | |

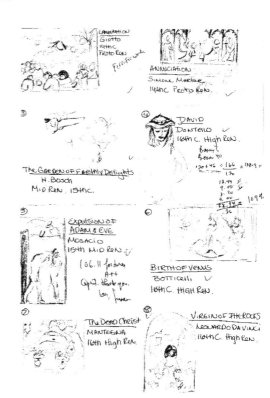

*Quiz 1, April Johnson, Art Survey,*
*Westfield State College, 1996*

## Part Two

### VOCABULARY.

**Take-home part requires a <u>text</u>-specific drawing FOR EACH WORD; come to quiz with each word listed with a drawing beside it. In quiz, write verbal definition beside the drawing. Do <u>not</u> use this sheet. Use blank, unlined paper provided in the lecture hall. Leave room to write def. beside drawing.**

1. chiaroscuro (List this word; draw a picture from text; be ready to write definition during quiz.)
2. continuous space
3. hierarchical or adjusted scale
4. Linear PERSPECTIVE
5. spatial instability
6. rational pictorial space
7. SCHIACCIATO
8. CONTINUOUS NARRATION
9. FORESHORTENING
10. GENRE
11. SYMBOL
12. DONOR
13. PATHOS
14. PROTO
15. POLYPTYCH
16. STIGMATA
17. RENAISSANCE
18. contrapposto
19. PRIMACY OF THE WALL
20. DI SOTTO IN SU
21. sfumato- (an extension of atmospheric perspective)
22. uomo universale
23. terribilitá

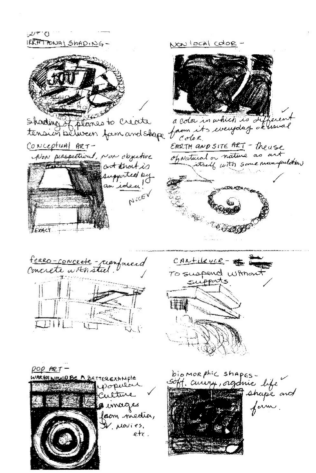

*Vocabulary #1 with mnemonic drawings quiz,*
*April Johnson, Westfield State College, 1996*

## Part Three

### ESSAY, TOTALLY TAKE -HOME.

CHOSE 2 PLATES FROM CHAPTERS 19, 20, 21, or 22. Do not choose two from the same chapter.
Do <u>not</u> choose plates included on in the SLIDE I.D. section, PART I.
CHOOSE ONES YOU HAVE <u>NOT</u> DRAWN BEFORE. <u>DO NOT RIP</u> A DRAWING OUT OF YOUR JOURNAL (You
will lose credit in your journal if you rip a drawing out, so why do it?)

1. DRAW EACH PLATE AND DEFINE EACH PLATE, USING ALL 6 CATEGORIES in LIST FORM
2. COMPARE, across ALL 6 CATEGORIES, USING A LIST-LIKE FORMAT.
3. CONTRAST, across ALL 6 CATEGORIES, USING A LIST-LIKE FORMAT.

COME TO <u>TWO</u> OVERALL CONCLUSIONS ABOUT THE 2 WORKS, USING THE WORD **"BECAUSE"** TO
PROVIDE SUPPORT . Try to interest yourself in these conclusions. INCLUDE THE TITLES OF BOTH WORKS AS
YOU BEGIN YOUR CONCLUSION.

FOR EXAMPLE, The mid-Renaissance fresco the "Birth of Venus" by Sandro Botticelli and the High Renaissance oil
painting "The Virgin of the Rocks" by Leonardo Da Vinci differ in technique and intent. The linear quality of the
Botticelli presents the clean lines of the non-physical, pure soul, wafted to shore as a giant, serene goddess by the winds
of creation, while the sfumato technique used by Leonardo presents a corporeal mystery, a holy baby in the grotto of
mystery who will live to redeem men's souls. Because both men use very different techniques, their intent is clarified;
Botticelli to present the clear lines of the pure soul; Leonardo to present the smoky, mysterious outlines of a divine family whose main character crossed the boundaries of behavior for a man or a god.

IN FACT, for my second conclusion, ... I HAVE JUST DISCOVERED THAT Leonardo's masterful use both of
descriptive line and of sfumato, as well as of chiaroscuro make "The Virgin of the Rocks" a more convincing story for
the contemporary viewer. **BECAUSE of the number of techniques he was able to use in his work. In contrast, the
Botticelli painting seems flat. The painting has loveliness and elegance,** but because its primary intent is a statement
about an idea rather than the representation of a real-life scene, it communicates an idealness rather than realness.
Granted, Leonardo's realness presents a mystery, but it is a mystery about a real baby who grew up to be a real
historical man.

Let the first conclusion drive the second. This will happen naturally if you are being precise and rigorous in the
compare and contrast list sections above. If you generalize in the compare and contrast parts, your conclusions
will be general, boring and wishy washy. **It is really
important that you interest yourself in what you are
writing. YOU REAP THE REWARDS OF HOW YOU
DRAW AND WRITE, NOT ME! I am just your cheering
section.**

**UNDERLINE WORD "BECAUSE" TO MAKE IT EASY
TO SEE AND GRADE.**
**Make the two conclus. clear in the same way BY USING
THE WORD "BECAUSE."**

**Picture of essay:**

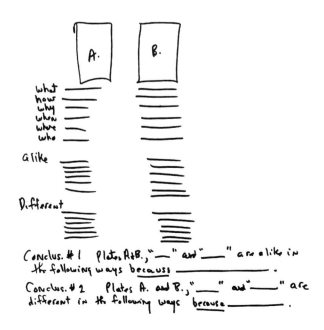

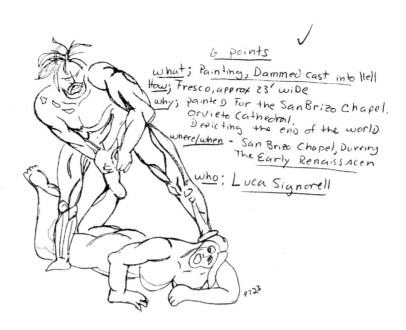

*"Damned Cast into Hell" by Luca Signorelli, Drawing/Writing journal,*
*Isaac Flores, Art Survey, Westfield State College, 1996*

# Quiz chaps. 22.23.24, Gardner text.

### 3 parts, each worth 5 points. Bonus section worth 2 extra points.

## Part One

**SLIDE IDENTIFICATION** - **Memorize title, artist, period, one salient comment. or distinguishing characteristic. Extra credit,** 1 point /drawing.

| Title, artist | Style ,Century | One salient comment |
|---|---|---|
| 1. Madonna of the Long Neck | Mannerist, 16th c. | Spatial instability; tiny prophet. (Or) Elegant elongation of Madonna's neck. |
| 2. Descent from the Cross, Pontormo | | |
| 3. Concert Champetre-Giorgione | | |
| 4. Venus or Urbino, Titian | | |
| 5. The Last Supper - Tintoretto | | |
| 6. The Isenheim Altarpiece-Mathias Grunewald | | |
| 7. Knight, Death and the Devil-Albrecht Durer | | |
| 8. The French Ambassadors, Hans Holbein the Younger | | |
| 9. Hunters in the Snow-Peter Bruegel the Elder | | |
| 10. Burial of Count Orgaz-El Greco | | |
| 11. Ecstasy of St. Theresa- Gianlorenzo Bernini | | |
| 12. Conversion of St. Paul - Caravaggio | | |
| 13. Las Meninas -Diego Velasquez | | |
| 14. Elevation of the Cross- Peter Paul Rubens | | |
| 15. Archers of St. Hadrian- Frans Hals | | |
| 16. Self Portrait - Rembrandt. | | |
| 17. Woman with a Water Jug - Jan Vermeer | | |
| 18. The Death of Marat -Jacques-Louis David | | |
| 19. Grand Odalisque -Jean-August-Dominique Ingres | | |
| 20. The Third of May -Francisco Goya | | |
| 21. Raft of the Medusa -Theodore Gericault | | |
| 22. Liberty Leading the People -Eugene Delacroix | | |
| 23. The Slave Ship - J.M.W. Turner | | |
| 24. The Hay Wain - John Constable | | |
| 25. The Ox Bow - Thomas Cole | | |
| 26. Burial at Ornans -Gustave Courbet | | |
| 27. The Fox Hunt - Winslow Homer | | |
| 28. Handspring -Eadweard Muybridge | | |
| 29. Dejeuner Sur L'Herbe or Luncheon on the Grass-Edouard Manet | | |

*Karen Whitney, Grand Odalisque, Westfield State College, Art Survey, 1995*

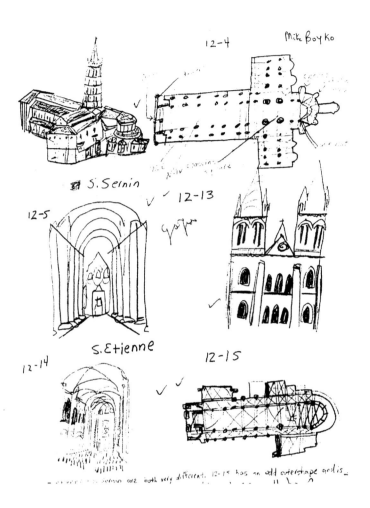

*Mike Boyco, Art Suvey Quiz, Westfield State College, 1995*

*Part Two*

VOCABULARY.
Do a <u>text</u>-specific drawing FOR EACH WORD ; come to quiz with each word listed with a drawing beside it.
In quiz, write verbal definition beside the drawing.

Arcadian landscape

concert or fête champetre

pendant or balancing figure

anamorphic image

cosmographical landscape

Baroque theatricality

tenebrism

torsion

unseen or invisible complement

unstable pyramidal composition

memento mori or vanitas

psychology of light

alla prima style

camera obscura

complementary after-image

optical realism

*Quiz, Michelle Luongo, Vocabulary with drawings,*
*Westfield State College, 1996*

*Shelly Green, Dead Christ by Mantegna, Drawing/Writing journal,*
*Art Survey, Westfield State College, 1996*

## Part Three

**Take Home. TWO PARTS**

1) **Drawing/Writing #1**
   **The move from the High Renaissance and Mannerism to the Baroque**

   a.  Choose one plate that is High Renaissance or Mannerist that anticipates 2 elements in Baroque art.

   b.  **Draw** the High Renaissance or Mannerist plate

   c.  **Define** all 6 categories

   d.  Choose a Baroque work that incorporates these two "theatrical" elements from the High Renaissance or Mannerist plate

   e.  **Draw** the Baroque plate

   f.  **Define,** all six categories.

   g.  **Write:** Describe the two "baroque" aspects in plate 1 – be specific. Show how these two elements are reflected in plate two. Be specific.

                    * * * * * * * * * * * * * * * * * * * *

2) **Drawing/Writing #2**
   **THE CHALLENGE OF PHOTOGRAPHY; THE RESPONSE OF THE PAINTER**

   a.  **Reread** pages 958-962.

   b.  With what you learn in lectures about photography, think about the challenges posed by photography for painters.

   c.  Reread pages 981-1017

   d.  Draw one of the photographic images pages 958-962

   e.  **List** two advantages photography has over painting.

   f.  **List** two possibilities painting has that photography did not have at that time. (Contemporary photographic possibilities allow this form of expression enormous freedom.)

   g.  **Do a black and white or color drawing** that shows two ways in which artists—faced with competition from photography—might have proceeded.

   h.  **Write briefly about** the two advantages or avenues of exploration painting could offer artists which photography did not.

This exercise is intended to get you ready for understanding "modern" art. We will not get past Manet in lectures. By finishing chapter 26, you will have read ahead on your own, "constructing" (as they say in education) your own understanding of the challenges facing the artist in the mid-to-late 1800's.

*Kristina Pellerin, art survey, Drawing/Writing journal, Westfield State College, 1995*

*Riace Warrior (detail of head) bronze, Kristina Pellerin, art survey, Westfield State College, 1995*

# Final Exam

Art Survey

worth 36 points. 4 sections, each worth 9 points.

Bonus 1 point per drawing, slide section.

Vocab. drawings <u>must be from the text or count zero. No stick figures or schematic drawings.</u>

## *Part One*

**Slides: Title, Artist, Period <u>or</u> Style.** Only 3 pieces of information.

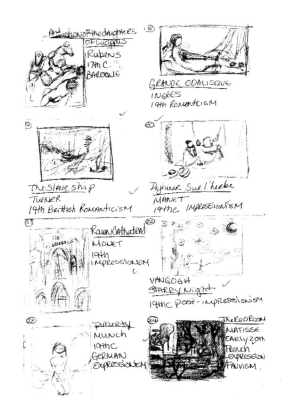

*Art Survey Final, April Johnson,
Westfield State College, 1996*

1) Lamentation, Giotto

2) Annunciation, Simone Martini

3) Garden of Earthly Delights, H. Bosch

4) David, Donatello

5) The Expulsion of Adam and Eve, Mosaccio

6) Birth of Venus, Botticelli

7) Dead Christ, Mantegna

8) Virgin of the Rocks, Leonardo Da Vinci

9) Creation of Adam, Sistine Chapel, Michelangelo

10) Madonna with the Long Neck, Parmigiano

11) Pastoral Symphony (Concert Champetre), Giorgione

12) Isenheim Altar Piece, Grunewald

13) Hunters in the Snow, Bruegel

14) Conversion of St. Paul, Caravaggio

15) Woman with a Water Jug, Vermeer

16) Ecstasy of St. Theresa, Bernini

17) Abduction of the Daughters of Leucippus, or The Raising of the Cross, Rubens

18) Grande Odalesque - Ingres

19) The Slave Ship, Turner

20) Dejeuner sur L'Herbe, Manet

21) Rouen Cathedral, Manet

22) Starry Night, Van Gogh

23) Puberty, Munch

24) Red Room, Matisse

25) Demoiselles D'Avignon, Picasso

26) The Portuguese, Braque.

27) Nude Descending a Stair Case, Duchamps.

28) Le Viol, the Rape or Ceci n'est pas une Pipe, Magritte

29) Guernica, Picasso

*Young Man, Sandro Boticelli, Drawing/Writing Journal,*
*Karen Whitney, 1995*

*The Merode Altarpiece, Robert Campin, Drawing/Writing*
*Journal, Karen Whitney, 1995*

30) Painting, Francis Bacon

31) Lucifer, Jackson Pollock

32) Woman I, Willem de Kooning

33) Vir Heroicus Sublimis, Barnett Newmann

34) Surrounded Islands, Christo

35) Target with Four Faces, Jasper Johns

36) Marilyn Diptych, Andy Warhol

37) The Dinner Party, Judy Chicago

38) Supermarket Shopper, Duane Hanson

39) Falling Water, Frank Lloyd Wright

40) Notre Dame du Haut, Le Corbusier

41) Vietnam Veterans' War Memorial, Maya Ling Lin.

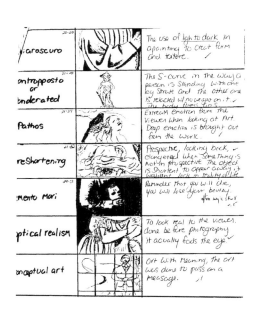

*Rebecca Parco, Westfield State College Art Survey quiz, 1995*

## Part Two

**Vocabulary** – do **text drawing** at home; do definition in quiz.
<u>No credit</u> for stick fig. non-text drawing.

| | |
|---|---|
| irrational shading | pop art |
| non-local color | biomorphic shapes |
| conceptual art | color field |
| earth and site art | mixed media |
| ferro-concrete | action painting |
| cantilever | op art |

**THANKSGIVING ASSIGNMENT: DOUBLES AS _PART THREE_ FINAL.** The feedback you get when I hand journals back on Dec. 5 will allow you to perfect this assignment as Part III Take home part of final

### _Choose an object and draw it in the following ways:_

1) In the Renaissance manner, in the specific style of _(name the artist);_ cite and label 2 Ren. stylistic devices.

2) in the Impressionst manner, as above

3) In the Post-Impressionist manner, as above

4) In the Expressionist manner, as above—include color

5) In the Cubist manner, as above—adding an element of collage

6) in the Futurist manner, as above

7) in the Surrealist manner, as above

8) In the Abstract Expressionist style, as above.

See illustrations on final for how this looks as an assignment.

### Part Three

**Refine** the Thanksgiving assignment. If what you handed in with your journal is perfect, attach that to your final exam as Part Three. Put your address on the final exam and I will mail it back to you.

**If that work was never done, or needs revision, work accordingly.**

**Part Three is your drawings of an object done in the style of artists representative of all 8 following styles, labeled for that artist, as well as for two characteristics of that style.**

Renaissance, Impressionist (with color), Post-Impressionist (with color), Expressionist (with Fauve use of color), Cubist (with element of collage), Futurist, Surrealist, Non-Objective (including Abstract Expressionist).

Example:

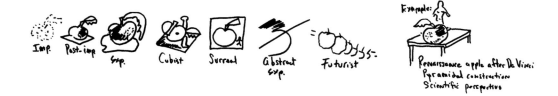

### Part Four

**Recombinant Drawing.**

Choose 3 images from the entire text that interest you, which you have not yet drawn.
Name all 3, defining with all six categories. Do not draw the images.

Choose one section from each of the three plates.
**Enlarge it and draw it.**
Combine all 3 sections chosen from the 3 works in a new drawing. You can overlap. You can distort. Use color and collage. If you need to add some elements, add them. Indicate additions with arrows. Label, "addition of........(your name)."

Look at what you have created. Using arrows and labels, identify at least 6 areas strongly characteristic of 3 different styles of art studied this semester.

EXPLANATORY SKETCH:

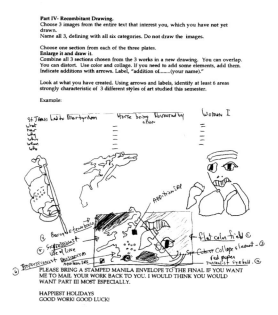

2nd EXAMPLE:

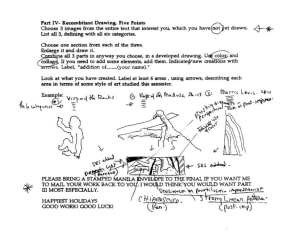

## Sample DRAWING/WRITING Journal entries for Art Survey course.

### Extra credit if you drew two plates in intro.

**Chapter 19**

Draw 2 plates or "figures" in chapter 19.

Answer these questions for each plate:

1. Why did the plate get your attention?
2. What meaning does the image have personally for you?
3. Why do you think you chose it?
4. What seems strong or powerful about the image?

Draw an object in your dorm or at home.

Write about the following:

1. Is the object you drew a piece of art?

   If yes, then why?

   If no, then why?

2. Is your drawing art?

   If yes, why?

   If not, why?

*Peaceful City, Lorenzetti, April Johnson, Drawing/Writing journal, Westfield State College, 1996*

*Perfume Bottle, April Johnson, Drawing/Writing journal, Art Survey, Westfield State College, 1996*

**Chapter 20**

1. Draw 2 plates
2. Define each using the 6 categories in list form.
3. Come up with one argument with the text, cite page, quote text, rebut and use "because"
4. Come up with one question with the text, cite page, quote text, speculate your own answer, using "because"
5. Draw two more plates

   Define in list form, all 6 categories

   Compare, list from, across all six categories

   Contrast, list form, across all six categories

   Come to two conclusions, citing names of plates; back up using word "because"

**Chapter 21**

Draw 2 plates

Define, all 6 categories

One question with text

One argument with text.

One pithy observation.

*Mary Magdalene, Donatello, April Johnson, 1996*

JOURNAL ENTRIES CHAPTERS 22, 23, 24.
HAND JOURNALS IN ON QUIZ DATE NOV. 9

Chapter 22 and 23 journals assignments:

For each chapter:

1) Draw two plates

2)  Define each plate listing the 6 categories

3) Write why you chose each plate

4) Write what interested you about each plate before you read the text.

5) What did the text write about the plate that interested you, and why did it interest you? It is not enough to say, "The text says that the painting is organized on 3 levels. You need to write about why this bit of info. was interesting to you.

*Galatea by Raphael, Drawing/Writing Journal, April Johnson. Westfield State College, 1996*

Chapter 24 journal assignment:

1) Write a paragraph defining Baroque Art. Look over chapter 24 and see if by looking at the plates you can identify some of the characteristics. List them. Then read the text and see how close you got. Then write the pargraph, referring specifcially to 5 works in the chapter by name, artist, and specific Baroque characteristics. Discuss at least <u>3</u> characteristics of Baroque art in the context of these <u>5</u> works.

2) Compare and contrast two works in chap. 22 or 23 and 24 in this way:
   a. Choose one High Renaissance (Italian, chap. 22, or N. European, chap. 23) ) or High Mannerist work (chapter 23) that to your mind **leads** to the Baroque—that is, **has** some Baroque qualities. ˙
   b. Draw it.
   c. Choose a Baroque work in chap. 24 that demonstrates one of the strong Baroque characteristics.
   d. Draw it.
   e. Compare a. with c. in terms of at least 2 Baroque characteristics. Be specific.


Journal Assignment for Thurs. Nov. 2

Compare and contrast **The Isenheim Altarpiece**, the central panel by Mathias Grunewald, 1510-1515 with **Elevation of the Cross** by Peter Paul Rubens, 1610:

Draw each plate

Define each plate using the six categories

Compare across all six categories, using a list form, being specific

Contrast across all six categories, list form, being specific.

Write one strong conclusion having to do with how the two works are specifically **alike IN TWO WAYS** using "because."

Write one strong conclusions having to do with how the two works are specifically **different IN TWO WAYS** using "because."

**Journal entries due Tuesday, Dec. 3 after Thanksgiving.**

After that 1/2 credit only if bona fide excuse for missing the last two classes in which journals being due on Dec. 3rd was made clear. This due date was also mentioned at the time of the last quiz.

**Chapter 26**

Copy 1 Impressionist work

Define all six

Write how the work is Impressionist; hit 2 items, plus because...

Copy 1 Post-Impressionist work

Define all 6

Write about 2 Post-Impr. items, using work because

**Chapter 27**

Look at the work of Derain, Matisse, Kirchner, Marc, Kandinsky

<u>BEFORE reading</u> chap. 17:

Copy 2 plates

Define all 6 categories

Write how plate #1 uses line, form, color, space in new ways from your point of view. Do not quote the text.

Write how plate #2 uses line, form, color, space in new ways from your point of view. Do not quote text.

**ASIDE:** by asking students to draw, write and think before reading the chapter, you insure that they bring their own intelligence to the task. Furthermore, many students will not read the text. This approach forces them to think.

Copy 1  Fauve work—

may focus on one section

define all 6; **use color**

Write what is Fauve about this work- one item

Copy 1  German Expressionist work

     as above

     write about two items

Copy 1  Cubist work

     as above

     write about two items.

*Bather, Jacques Lipchitz, Drawing/Writing Journal,*
*Karen Whitney, Westfield State College, 1995*

# HOW I GOT HERE

*SRS painting, The Farm, Addison, Maine, summer 1995*
*Photo by Priscilla Drucker of Amherst, MA*

In the summers when I was young, my brother, John, and I played in a slapped-together, sun-bleached, sand-scoured house built from drift-wood. We kept purple garter snakes in jars with pierced lids and swore faithfulness to our club. We signed a contract in blood, pricking our wrists with pins. Raised on Kenneth Graham's *Wind in the Willows*, we called our fort Mole Fort. Our war cry was, "A mole! A mole!"

*The author in front of Mole Fort*

*The Swiss Family Robinson, The Narnia Chronicles, Huckleberry Finn,* and *Treasure Island:* these were only a fraction of the books Mother read aloud to John and me at suppertime. I grew up believing the things I needed in life would come to me. If I needed rubber, then, like the Swiss Family Robinson, I would discover a caoutchouc tree. This is how Drawing/Writing came to me. It was a necessary gift provided by the needs and searchings of my personal and professional life.

*Photo of Sam Sheridan with his grandmother's paint box, 1995-6, The Carpenter Center, Harvard University, by SRS*

When I was ten, my mother gave me her wooden paint box and her oil paints and her canvas boards. It was then that I began to paint. My son now has that box. He, too, is a painter. If my son gives that box to a child of his, it will become like a blood memory. I loved painting from the moment I opened that wooden box. I loved the smell of oils, linseed oil, turpentine. My heart beats faster when I smell them now.

*Mom's paint box*

Like many children of my time, I was a serious writer. One of my works was a play called "The Day the Doctor Got Sick." I wrote, directed and acted in it. My brother and I put it on in the airy attic of our Philadelphia house using a silk parachute my Dad brought back from the war as the curtain. I think it was my Grandmother Rich who gave me my first journal. It was one of those small diaries with a floral cover and a pretend-brass lock and a tiny key. I wrote and painted to record and to understand my life. I have never stopped.

The color of the blue sky above the long, purling shore of Long Beach Island on the New Jersey Shore smote me. I painted the beach, the water (very difficult), and flowers. I painted my beagle, Cannifer Flips (an approximation of the name for the antiseptic we put on bug bites called Campho-Phenique). My mother's constant letter writing, her reading aloud, her talking to us about books taught me the pull and the importance, the magic and the necessity of language.

Our mother read, wrote, talked, and thought *a good deal.* We did not have television until I was twelve. By then, I was a dedicated reader and a writer—not so unusual for a child born in 1942: Many people think that children who write and paint have special talents. They do not. Given encouragement and exposure, children are by nature artists and writers.

*Sam, drawing for this book, summer, 1997, SRS*

My mother did everything to encourage me. She let me paint over a mural of an Arcadian landscape in our formal dining room. I replaced languid shepherdesses and filmy trees with starkly geometric shapes. I was allowed to make art; I had the paints, the time, the encouragement, and the *walls.*

Like many children, I was always constructing things: paper dolls with curvy figures, dioramas of King Arthur's court complete with stand-ups of mice scurrying off with hunks of cheese and dogs battling for bones in the shredded paper straw. I Scotch-taped scraps of satin to the walls to give the eye a feel for tapestries. My mother approved another request: she let me work with clay in my bedroom. The bust I sculpted is still where my mother put it in southern Arizona thirty-five years ago.

I spent hours in my room. In high school, it was routine to spend five hours a night on homework. I continued to write in my journals. When I applied to college, my one question was whether I could get a single room. I needed a place to work—a room of my own. By that time I was writing eight or nine hours at a stretch in my journals.

*Self-portrait, Cambridge, 1961*

At Radcliffe, I majored in Classics and English and studied painting with Theodore Lux Feininger, Lionel Feininger's son. The main thing I remember TLF saying was, "Paint more." I had the time, the space, and a permissive presence. In those days, the studio courses at Harvard were located in the attic of the Fogg Art Museum—where the print library is now. My son sculpts and paints in the Carpenter Center designed by Le Corbusier—a whole building set aside for Visual and Environmental Studies. It did not take me long to

complete the studio courses offered at that time. The German theologian, Paul Tillich, was at Harvard. I signed up for his courses to fill the vacuum, and was privileged to experience Tillich's "Harvard years."

In college, I fell into a rhythm of painting half the year and writing half the year. I would paint until I had no more to say as a painter, and then I would start to write again. I studied poetry writing with Robert Lowell. I gave readings at Lamont library. Throughout it all, I kept my journals.

Doll

I painted her in a corner.
I painted my plaster mourner in the attic light
That barred the walls and striped the metal play-stove
To her left upon the fear-white table, to my right.

I didn't see she was afraid until I'd finished.
I didn't see until the light diminished on the walls
And crawled around the round point of her chin
Beneath the black-blue, upside down "u" of her mouth that falls.

Her brows were hair-fine, child-fine worryings, hair-thin.
One eye was larger than the other, staring down.
The other seemed to wander out and in.
One chipped fist gestured at her throat,
The plaster belly groped,
Her seated feet splayed awkward, out and in.
Both soles were little loaves or baked potatoes in the skin.
Each seemed to weigh a pound.

She cradled like a child of mine, or kin.
She fit, and better fits as I grew older,
Knowing how the shape should feel as it curves out and in.
I left her with a careless seal upon her forehead.
I left her in the storeroom,
Underneath a blanket, tucked her in
Where bats drop droppings on the newspaper around the door
                    that lets them out and in,
And rats roll pellets of melasses on the floor, like boulders.

Natural diaspora has emptied the attic,
The place where I sat them, the slanted room
That wanted rearrangement of the stuffed ones, and the new synthetic ones
                    that did not nick.
I climbed up every Christmas, guilty with neglect,
Buttoning small dresses up the back where fingerprints collect.

Heads roll and holes appear when witches prick.
Elderly collectors shut them up in cases where the hinges stick
And all the air is gone, and even dust won't bloom.

She sits alone inhabiting the gloom of our lean attic.
Green ruffles limp and yellow on her skin.
Her skin is ageless.  She has no tongue and no one movement is erratic.
She won't distract the children moving out and in.

*Poem "The Doll," 1962 the first poem in my own voice according to Robert Lowell.*

After college, a traveling fellowship took me to Europe for a year of drawing and writing. I wrote and illustrated a book called *Chez Les Autres.* Then, I married a Harvard man and we had three children.

*Self Portrait with Sarah, 1979*

*Death Portrait, VGR, 1985*

economics and journalism major at the University of Iowa at Ames. In her books, food or food-related items are the culprit, like sharp dicing knives. I had always known she should write. At last, she was taking time for her work. Each book was place-specific, allowing her to record her memories of Iowa, Maine, Nantucket and Arizona.

As my mother lay dying, I started my first novel, *All Saints*. It, too, is place specific, and describes life in a tiny town in Western Massachusetts which I call "Never-never land." It was about this time that I started teaching. I became an art teacher. Five years later, I switched to teaching English.

*Portrait of Jessica, Samuel and Sarah, c. 1991*

*Self Portrait, Eaglebrook years, 1991*

We spent summers on the coast of Maine. I wrote a musical about those summers. I wrote a book of poetry for my mother's sixty-fourth birthday which we all celebrated in Maine. After that, I stopped writing except for letters. I continued to paint at night—in the basement, in the kitchen, in the garage.

My mother died of cancer. Before she died, she survived two open heart surgeries. Sometime after the first and before the second surgery, she began to write culinary murder mysteries. Mother had been a home

I entered an MAT program and it was at this point that I developed the drawing half of the Drawing/Writing program as a teaching assistant in Basic Drawing and Design. A doctorate was the next logical step. To prepare for it, I talked to people in the fields of medicine, neurobiology, and education—Maxine Greene, Lucy Calkins, David Perkins, Seymour Papert, and Rodolpho Llinas. I corresponded with Albert Galaburda, Michael Gazzaniga, Candace Pert, Stephen Kosslyn, and Howard Gardner. At New York University Hospital, I computer-researched two fields—learning disabilities and mental illness—to determine whether there were sufficient reasons to spend the next few years, or maybe the rest of my life, promoting the educational usefulness of drawing to writing.

Why was I driven? I knew some children whose early learning experiences were negative and repressive. These children were ready to greet the world with open arms and minds and the world rebuffed them. These children became uncertain, fearful even, about learning. I felt a passionate concern. How could I help? I looked at my own life and at my teaching. I knew that the arts were among the most direct ways to develop identity and mind. I also knew that the arts required redefinition if they were to be regarded as central to education. The evidence must lie in an obvious place: brain science. I began taking courses in undergraduate neurobiology. I read widely in the field. My university professor, Dr. Katherine Fite, agreed to sit on my comprehensives committee. By studying neurobiology, linguistics, education, psychology, computer science, and artificial intelligence—the field described as cognitive science—I found some of the answers I was searching for.

My doctoral research concentrated on three questions:

- Are drawing and writing a rare double talent, or are drawing and writing natural forms of expression for human beings?

- Are the skills of drawing and writing interconnected?

- If drawing and writing are deliberately taught as interconnected forms of inquiry and expression, could some learning disabilities be remediated and could some aspects of the looming literacy crisis be averted?

Applying to the Breadloaf School of English at Middlebury College, Oxford, I spent the summer of 1992 at a keyboard at Lincoln College, rewriting my dissertation. The result was *Drawing/Writing: The Magic Mirror. A handbook for teachers.*

At this time, I started down several new and uncertain paths: single parenthood, a new community, a search for a new home and a new job. I became an adjunct college professor, teaching art history.

*Tony Burgess, professor, Institute of Education, London University and visiting professor and my tutor, Lincoln College, Oxford, U.K., 1992, SRS*

In 1995, I chaired and presented a session called "Drawing and Writing: Connections and Implications" at the College Art Association conference in San Antonio, Texas. Eighty art educators asked for a guide to Drawing/Writing. I hired a freelance editor and built a mini-team to rewrite the book again, this time as a highly visual text. Two and one-half years later, I am self-publishing the book. It is now called *Drawing/Writing and the new literacy.* I am still a painter and a writer. I am still a mother. I have also become an empassioned teacher with one goal: encouraging and developing intelligence through drawing and writing.

*Self Portrait, after Vézelay, 1993*

# Mothers and self-belief

**VIRGINIA RICH divides her time between a ranch in Arizona and a home in Maine. This is the first in a series of culinary crimes.**

*Photo, Virginia Rich*
*From her book jacket, **The Cooking School Murders***
*Author's photo copyright (c) 1982 W.M. Sommerville,*
*E.P. Dutton, Inc., New York*

I have told you about my childhood so that you will understand that there was one person in my life who loved me very much. She taught me to write by her example of writing. She taught me to read by her example of reading. She listened to my papers. She looked at my drawings and paintings. She let me work with red clay in my bedroom. She let me paint on the walls of the dining room. She talked with me about people and ideas. She *laughed* with me. My mother taught me this: if you have to write to get along in life, or if you have to paint, then you are a writer, you are a painter. Being either has nothing to do with how good or how famous you are.

You can probably name someone who did the same thing for you as my mother did for me. Maybe it was your mother or your father, aunt or uncle, grandmother or grandfather—or a neighbor or a teacher. Someone let you do the things you had to do to find out who you were. These people are the helpers.

As teachers, we may choose to help through art or English, through history or science or math or music, but what we are really doing is helping students *to be*. As teachers, we are encouraging language, thought, and being.

Mathematics, music, the sciences, and the arts are languages. We all can learn to speak several of them. I believe that drawing is a lovely arching bridge with giant heroic figures beckoning us over into language: "Come over! Come over!"

The conviction that drives this book is the recognition that I am not unique. A new generation of children has the same potential I had. They, too, can learn the two languages of drawing and writing.

I feel whole and connected when I write or paint. I feel most at peace and "right with the world" when I lift a brush and move it toward a canvas. This action—so introductory, so tentative—eases my mind in some deep way. I am starting to understand the complex nature of this peace. The Latin verb "creo, creare" means to "to make," or "to do." Having been raised in the Episcopal Church, I associate how I feel when I paint with the "peace which passeth understanding"—that state of spirit achieved by the action of creation which means so much and which is impossible to say aloud without lisping.

I pass my understanding on to you; writing and drawing achieve wholeness and connection in a world of fragments and missed connections.

We are *all* artists and writers.

*My chop brought from China*
*by Dr. Claire W. Carlson*

# Cover Notes

The cover shows a brain working with a cross-modal strategy. The visual/verbal work unfolds in a dynamic spiral, "uttered" by the thinker.

The illustration of the lighted brain is taken from the textbook **Mind, Brain and Behavior** by Bloom, Lazerson, Hofstadter (c) 1985 by Educational Broadcasting Corporation and is reprinted with permission from W.H. Freeman and Company, publishers.

The reader will be interested in the writing featured on the cover. It was produced by a student at Hampshire College in Amherst, MA in a January term course titled "Art History the Drawing/Writing way."

Desiree Dubois's work has been taken for the work of Leonardo Da Vinci. This association reinforces the artist/writer/scientist role promoted by the Drawing/Writing program. It is natural, as well as being in the best Renaissance humanistic tradition, to encourage minds to use image and text—or function as what this book describes as a balanced bilateral mind.

Starting with the image closest to the face and progressing to the top of the brain, Desiree's writing is as follows:

**Blind Contour writing:** "Hand-like protrusions, long, slim offshoots, tear drop shapes. Looks like a manta ray or skate. Hand-eye coordination needs work. Brain doesn't quite process eye to hand movement. Someone wearing a ghost costume or a flying, wind-blown cloak with big puffy mittens on."

**Regular Contour writing:** "Tells me that I don't like contour drawing—the outside line and the exterior can not quite convey the object in full...looks beaky, like it has eyes and short legs and stick-like wings...cute. I am finding it hard to take this seriously."

**Basic Shapes writing:** "This object is...broken into geometric shapes with spots of organic circular shapes. A robot coming to grab you, has wheels for feet. Looks like some sort of video game monster, exploding ghosts."

**Light-Medium-Dark writing:** "My object is very complex and organic. Light is suffused across its planes with sharp divisions at the axial top (symmetrical) and in small curling connections.
Reminds me of a horned, screaming bat or gargoyle with outstretched wings, big eyes, gaping mouth and stocky tail. Little back feet like a bat."

**The "Perfect" Whole writing:** This drawing tells me that my object is very organic, has smooth and rough textures, rounded. First time it doesn't look like a little monster immediately. It looks as if it is not resting on the ground, but.... I am used to this little thing but that does not mean that I know it. Every time I've turned it I find a whole new aspect of it—each time is just as difficult. I have not used an eraser though it may help to bring out the lightest areas."

**The Composite Abstraction #1 writing:** "Has dark, womb-y spaces in a spiral that draws you in and thrusts you out into the world again. From organic to geometric and back again."

# Terms and Powerful Ideas

*Blue Heron, SR Sheridan good luck bird, pen and ink drawing, 1997*

Some of the terms used in this book are new; some are used in particular ways. Some information is so relevant to education that it is described as Powerful Ideas.

## TERMS:

### WholeBrain:

The terms "whole brain" and "whole mind" are existing terms used to describe educational strategies informed by brain science which take into account the fact that the child exhibits distinct intelligences—spatial, logical-mathematical, and so forth (Gardner, 1983), and that these intelligences are best developed in integrative, cross-disciplinary ways.

**WholeBrain is a new term. WholeBrain education categorizes intelligence under two general categories: spatial and linguistic.** These two broad categories are informed by a grammar of intelligent thought that is natural to the brain and also learnable. WholeBrain education focuses on the development of mental powers in the context of these two general categories in mutually reflective exercises. The goal is encouraging learning that is brain-like, or interhemispheric.

WholeBrain education begins with the fact that students have a right hemisphere and a left hemisphere—as well as other corresponding brain parts—which work together. WholeBrain education recognizes that the bihemispheric brain has evolved to make translations between systems of representation—most particularly, between the visual and the verbal. Image and text developed syncretically. Education can teach drawing and writing in the same co-creative manner.

**WholeBrain education is cross-modal;** it deliberately encourages an exchange of information between visual and verbal brain processes. These exchanges, or cross-translations, extend understanding. **Translation exchanges are the bihemispheric brain's particular strength.**

Educational strategies which provide training with translation exchanges are Neuroconstructivist. Constructivism is an existing term which focusses on the student as the knower and the learner. **Neuroconstructivism is a new term.**

**Student's not only construct knowledge, but their brains.** The brain is a highly modifiable, complex organ. The environment and more especially, how the learner responds to the environment, strongly influences how the brain grows and functions. The ways in which the brain learns to connect information determines the quality of its neural networks, and, by extension, the usability of that information.

The goal of WholeBrain education is well-developed, well-connected visual and verbal observational, analytical and inferential thinking skills. Brains educated in this way will be astute about meta-messages embedded in advertising—political, commercial, and otherwise—and will also be skilled at producing messages designed to communicate precisely where verbal meets visual, or where text and image intersect. These brains will be equipped to navigate effectively in an historic period described as the Age of Technology, or the Age of Information. In addition, brains trained by humanistic/Neuroconstructivist strategies like Drawing/Writing, will be adept at balancing options and accepting differences—two mandatory skills in a complex, increasingly global society. And, most importantly, such brains will be multi-lingual. They will speak the language of drawing, the language of writing, and the several languages of the classroom, from a highly examined argot to a shared, more formal language based on a classroom-generated vocabulary informed by the arts, mathematics, grammar, philosophy, science, and Latin and Greek prefixes, suffixes and roots. Such brains will be equipped to and expect to move between languages.

The brain is predisposed to think intelligently. But, like language, intelligence requires triggering and training, and, like language, intelligence is developable or retardable. Neuroconstructivist education focuses on language as central to thought and provides experiences designed to produce brains interested in and skilled with language.

## Extended definitions

### The cross-modal translation exchange:

A cross-modal teaching strategy requires a transfer of information from one mode of representation to another. For instance, in Drawing/Writing, a deliberate transfer of information is achieved from drawing to writing. The sentence, "My drawing tells me that my object is...because...." achieves this transfer. The goal of the transfer is inter-influence: each mode of representation intends to extend the other. The result of the transfer is a transformation, or a new kind or level of information or understanding. **The term cross-modal translation exchange is new** and describes the Drawing/Writing program in particular and Neuroconstructivist programs in general.

The terms "cross-modal," or "cross-domain transfer" are existing terms used to describe the ways in which the spatial and linguistic capabilities of the brain cross-cue and complement each other. It is useful to appreciate the four ways in which the term cross-modal is already in use as a descriptor of brain function beyond the fifth, specialized use described above—the cross-modal translation exchange:

1.     The term cross-modal means "multi-sensory." Multi-sensory thought is intrinsic to all organisms with sensory systems. We access information about the world through our eyes, ears, noses, mouths, and fingers, as well as through the entire surface of the skin of our bodies. In addition, there is a sixth sense described as proprioception: this is our ability to know, as if we were a gyroscope, where and how and at what attitude or angle we exist physically in the world of physical phenomena. In the form of multi-sensory processing, cross-modal thought happens in the routine course of adaptive behavior in intact sensorimotor systems.

"My hammer smells like dust because it looks like an old bone" combines the sense of smell with the sense of sight. "My corkscrew smells as sharp as rain because it has repeated diagonals in the screw part which remind me of driving rain" (David Belval, Drawing/Writing student, 1997) combines the sense of smell with touch and the sense of touch with sight. Multi-sensory processing enriches comparisons.

2.     The term cross-modal means "inter-hemispheric," or spatial/linguistic. In the intact human central nervous system, the entire brain, including both hemispheres, contribute to thought. Brain scans clarify the fact that every act of thought is both spatial and linguistic.

Spatial and linguistic processes are associated with one hemisphere or the other. Generally, the left hemisphere specializes in language, while the right hemisphere assumes spatial tasks. Although initially equipotential, each hemisphere eventually suppresses the other for the ability it assumes. Suppression of function, or delegation of tasks, maximizes the capability of the brain for specialized operations. Thus, brains become "lateralized." We speak about the right hemisphere as a spatial information processor and the left as a language processor, but we must keep firmly in mind that such distinctions are themselves linguistic; a spatial/visual mental operation like drawing is linguistic: it is visual language, and linguistic/verbal mental operations like writing and reading are spatial: they include and often start with a visual analysis of the patterns of marks on a page.

**3.** Cross-modal processing is global operations and global operations are cross-modal processing. Multiple brain scans of the same individual can be combined with averaged scans of other brains using a tracer chemical, oxygen 15. These averaged scans demonstrate metabolic activity all over the brain, as well as in both hemispheres, for either a visual or a verbal task.

**4.** Cross-modal thought is both concrete and abstract or practical/theoretical. As a brain's problem solving skills become more powerful, the mind is capable of thinking about things and ideas in equally rigorous ways. In fact, the brain manipulates ideas and things in similar ways (Minsky, 1988).

Doing something to a thing, having an idea about a thing, and having an idea about an idea about a thing are so interrelated in effective problem solving that making a distinction between these ways of thinking becomes meaningless or, at least, counterproductive. The point to hold to is the enduring usefulness of the back-and-forth rhythm between concrete and abstract processes in language-based thought.

A letter of application from my second cousin, John Bannister, written in 1996 after his sophomore year at Reed College, to Columbia University about qualifying for a summer physics program, describes such a moment of recognition about the intimate and important relationship between practical and theoretical thought:

"During the last two years, while occasionally struggling my way through Reed's notoriously theoretical physics classes, I have asked myself this question, 'Why am I bothering with all this theory?'

"I came to Reed College for a number of reasons, a burning desire to study physics not being one of them. I thought, at the time, that I might possibly like to become an engineer, and physics seemed a logical stepping stone.... Predictably, I began to be frustrated with the theoretical emphasis of Reed's first-year physics class. I didn't want to learn the theory. I wanted to learn how to build things!

"Working over the summer as a computer repair technician, I began to consider computers with the insight I had gained during my first year of college physics. Surprising myself, I realized that I could conceptualize a basic theory and how the various computer components worked. It gave me a thrill and boosted my confidence considerably when I did some basic research and discovered that many of my theories were more or less correct. With this small success, I began to examine other things around me and realized that I could apply the physics I had learned to many situations. This was much more fun that solving word problems in the book. Being able to apply my knowledge to real life situations was far more gratifying. Also, while I had been an able computer repairman before, able to follow installation and repair instructions well enough, I felt that I was becoming a better one; I was now able to grasp more fundamentally what I was actually doing (Before, it might have been simply, 'Don't put your disks near a magnet.' Now it was, 'Here's why you shouldn't put your disks by a magnet...').

"More importantly, at least for myself, is the fact that an understanding of the underlying physics allows me to look at things at a new level, and to see beauty and simplicity where before I saw nothing. My understanding of physics, even as rudimentary as it is at the moment, allows me to see not only the spinning top, for instance, but to understand and appreciate the forces and interactions which keep it upright. To quote Richard Feynman: 'I can appreciate the beauty of a flower. But at the same time, I can see much more of the flower. I can imagine the cells inside, which also have beauty. There's beauty not just at the dimension of one centimeter, there's also beauty at a smaller dimension.'

"I've modified my career goals; I don't see how I could ever have considered a career in engineering without wanting to learn the theory behind what I was doing. An understanding of the theoretical foundations is what makes engineering and science (especially physics in my opinion) such elegant and interesting subjects. No matter what I choose to do, I believe that I will do it better, and derive a greater satisfaction from it because I will understand the physical principles behind it " John Bannister, 1996. John majored in physics at Reed.

5.    Cross-modal operations provide cross-domain cues. Cross-domain cues are responsible for linking or integrating codes, triggering the combination of several modes of representation. Cross-domain cues also have the power to unleash additional processing capabilities for the second or subsequent mental operation. Should the second mental operation be the more difficult or challenging one, as might be the case with writing, or mathematics, that mental operation profits by this boost in processing power. This is the observed effect of the relationship of drawing to writing in a deliberate cross-domain cueing situation called Drawing/Writing.

Cross-domain cueing happens in the course of our daily lives: we hear a dog and a mental image of a dog, or of the many dogs in our experience, are cued as well as our emotional responses to dogs, and, in addition, the word "dog" or the names of specific dogs may be cued. When language is cued, a high-level code comes into play; through this code we are able to tag and describe the barking dog through a wide range of characteristics, relationships, stories, works of art, poems, associations, emotions, allusions and inferences.

Cross-modal, multi-sensory, interhemispheric, spatial/linguistic, globally-distributed, concrete/abstract thought is intrinsic to the human mind. It is in particular the spatial/lingusitic, or visual/verbal aspect of cross-modal thought that the Drawing/Writing process emphasizes.

## Neuroconstructivism:

**Neuroconstructivism is a new term.** Neuroconstructivism places the emphasis on the child's brain as the active agent in learning. It shares with Piagetian and Vygotskian thought the understanding that the mind of the child is qualitatively different from that of older children and adults, and that knowlege, intelligence and morality spring from the child's actions, and that this "child-action" has the quality of being playful and experimental.

Children not only construct knowledge, intelligence and morality but they construct their brains on neural levels through thought and action. The point to remember as parents and educators is that the networks children construct determine present and future capabilities for thought and action.

The brain is alone and would be very nearly inert or at least quiescent—a shut-in—were it not for its body's sensory systems. Each brain constructs its world from experience. That world may be like or very unlike other brains' constructions. The position of the atheist existentialist is relevant to Neuroconstructivism: all things are allowed. Still, if we accept the atheist existentialist position, each brain's moral or ethical decisions must be made in the context of the common weal, or the good of all. This paradoxical freedom is like that of the Christian existentialist who worships a god "in whose service is perfect freedom." In a society comprised of many cultures, belief systems, and codes of behavior, when it is unclear what behaviors are and are not allowable, a strategy for determining right action based on compositions in drawing provides a practical approach to ethical decision-making .

The mind might fragment in despair were it not for integrative activities. Dance and song and painting—the applied and performing arts—allow the human spirit to feel as if it were one with creation. Human interaction, on the other hand—communal worship, collaborative productions, parenting and partnering—allows the human spirit to feel as if it were at one with humanity. The brain's aloneness is its protection and its vulnerability, its joy and its sorrow, its pleasure and its pain. The more lively, the more attentive, the more efficient the brain becomes in its searches, the more expressive it becomes in its outreachings, the more integrated that brain will be within itself, and within the context of the world it constructs for itself.

"The world is infinitely complex, and an individual brain can only know the little that it can create within itself. It turns out that this view is well known to philosophers.... Now neurodynamicists can show experimentally that it is true.... As existentialist philosophers from Kierkegaard to Heidegger and Sartre have concluded, each of us constructs our self by our own actions, and we know our self as it is revealed to us in our actions" (Freeman, 1997, 69).

## The Thinking Child:

**The Thinking Child is the name of a new educational theory and practice which focus on the child as a self-constructing thinker.** The program is informed by both brain science and by constructivist educational practice. Neuroconstructivist curricula are appropriate to thinking children because they are cross-modal, modeling brain processes.

## Grace periods and educational lag time:

WholeBrain approaches to thinking skills take into account periods of grace. One child's brain grows differently from another child's brain. Each brain grows differently from day to day. Robert Kegan's advice—"attend upon the child"—means that educators and other caregivers must provide patient support for the child as a thinker. Some children are ready to read in the first grade. Some are not. In the meantime, students can create cognitively useful abstract drawings, like Composite Abstractions, even if they are not yet ready to read or write. The CA provides a grace period in the literacy process.

With the current overemphasis on visual stimulation and underemphasis on verbal stimulation, expectations about writing, reading and speaking skills should be flexible. In classrooms where primary languages differ, grace periods are required.

## The new literacy:

The brain shunts information between systems. The shunting is so continuous that the process is best described as spatial/linguistic, or visual/verbal. Language instruction should mirror and mine this relationship. Classroom practices which disconnect drawing from writing, or writing from reading, parse brain functions, interrupting the continuum and isolating mental endeavors. Brain-like educational practices have optimal effects: efficient networking on neural levels; rich syntheses on mental levels.

The deliberately syncretic, or co-creative integration of visual and verbal modes of expression constitutes the new literacy. The new literacy is the ability to "read" and to "write" these combined, complex communications. Images developed in connection with text and text developed in connection with images, allow each mode to be read at certain levels. It is precisely "where verbal meets visual"—where two information systems converge—that the meta-message occurs. It is the combined effect of several systems that increases the possibilities for precise communication, and, for good or for ill, influence.

The new literacy takes into account the fact that students may need to be fluent in informal as well as formal versions of their mother tongue, and, for many, in a second language—the language of the classroom which, for many Americans, is English. Slang or argot as languages are not necessarily less precise than more formal language. The group that uses the argot knows exactly what is meant. Generally, argot is appreciably informed by glance, gesture, inflection, tone and particular group usage. Problems occur when one group's informal language or slang or argot is unintelligible to another group or identifies them prejudicially or simply proves inadequate socially or professionally when they move beyond the group. It is here that training in translation exchanges proves useful. Students who are used to translating between drawing and writing, and who are trained in critical yet supportive peer exchanges, and who are used to constructing and explaining drawings and writings including Composite Abstractions in group critiques, know that clear communication in any language requires work and negotiation. These students know that several languages facilitate communication. A well-placed word in argot may be effective if the group understands it. Beyond the group, additional words shared across domains may be necessary.

## Balanced bilateral brain:

A brain that uses both hemispheres in a less lateralized or less specialized manner is described as balanced bilaterally. Research shows that the female brain is naturally less lateralized for some tasks than male brains, using corresponding spots on both sides to solve certain kinds of problems faster and with less expenditure of energy. The female brain also remains equipotential longer than the male brain; its capacity for recovering functions usually located on one side or the other after trauma is higher initially and remains so for a longer period. When combined image and text dominate as the favored method of communication, it makes sense to train brains for balanced bilateral processing and production.

# POWERFUL IDEAS:

## Redundancy:

The brain is redundant. It has more connections than it needs. Educational strategies should be redundant, too, allowing repeated practice with connected, richly experiential, reflective activities.

## The Arts as knowledge informed by touch:

If the arts are redefined as knowledge informed by touch, it becomes clear that the arts are neither frills nor the pursuit of the elite nor the exclusive activity of the very young but that they are the everyday business of the body/brain.

## Dynamic nonlinear system:

The human brain, the Drawing/Writing process, and the neuroconstructivist classroom are nonlinear systems. The output from each system has the possibility of being phenomenally different from the input. The child's ability to think, as well as brain-like teaching and learning strategies and classrooms conducted in a neuroconstuctivist manner, produce unpredictable, nonlinear outcomes.

The highly variable aspects of dynamic, nonlinear systems like the brain and the classroom mean that small changes can have large effects. This is a message of hope for over-stressed school systems. The introduction of a neuroconstructivist program like Drawing/Writing and the training it provides in the new literacy have substantial, observable effects on behavior and performance in the classroom, most especially in connection with increased attention, self-direction, and visual and verbal skills.

## Embeddedness:

The quality of nestedness—of being fit inside itself in increasingly small, cloned models, like Russian dolls—is responsible for the self-referential aspects of human thought, including language. In the brain, layers and columns of brain tissue interwoven like the Ardebil tapestry with hundreds of neural knots per square inch achieve parallel and simultaneously interconnected transmissions. The organization of brain tissue for feedback loops provides the physical/procedural basis for iterative, recursive human thought.

Like the relationship of energy to matter, the relationship of thought to language is reciprocal. Educational strategies which nest language activities within each other—like Drawing/Writing—mirror brain activity, encouraging cooperative, transformational exchanges between modes of representation. Cross-modal exchanges, particularly visual/verbal exchanges, can be used iteratively and recursively, calling themselves back over and over in operations described as translation exchanges. By making use of a simple command—draw and then write reflectively about the drawing—the Drawing/Writing program calls back one procedure over and over again throughout an expanding system. That iterated command models the bihemispheric brain's own command relayed by the corpus callosum: translate and extend this visual information verbally, and translate and extend this verbal information visually.

## Fractals:

Fractal objects and procedures describe complicated systems. Fractals have changed the way we understand the word chaos. Complex systems whose orderly patterns repeat so infrequently that only a vast string of computations reveal the system behind the behavior is described as a chaotic system. It is only apparently indescribably messy. A single event can occasion a global change in a chaotic system. This hypersensitive perturbability is a characteristic of chaotic systems, including brains. The complexity and the modifiability of the brain make it a prime candidate for fractal models and explanations.

## Holographs:

The brain also lends itself to holographic modeling and explanation. A hologram is produced when a laser beam is split in two. One beam hits the object—say, an onion—and bounces off; the other beam collides with this bounced light. The collision creates an interference pattern. Like dropping two pebbles in a pond which send out two sets of concentric ripples which intersect, a holographic image is created by interference patterns. The complex configuration of troughs and crests from the colliding ripples creates intersecting, concentric rings. This interference pattern is recorded on a piece of film. When another laser beam is shined through the film, an image of the original object—the onion—re-appears. The observer can walk around this object but can not touch it. The object/image is perceptible but immaterial.

There are curious qualities to holographs. They are self-generative. Shine a laser on a small piece of the holographic film and the whole onion is generated. Cut off a slice of the holographic film containing the laser-imprinted image of an onion, and, planaria-like, any slice of that piece of holographic film regenerates the entire onion. Memories in the brain are stored in this overall way: they are not localized, as researchers once thought, and yet certain aspects of a memory—smell, sound—can be triggered locally via a carefully inserted electrode. Visual information is stored in the brain in overall ways, too. The wave-like connectivity between the branching dendrites of nerve cells creates wave or ripple-like electrical signals. These waves intersect, causing patterns of interference which we recognize as thoughts. On several levels, brain function is holograph-like (Talbot, 1991; Freeman, 1991; Sheridan, 1991).

According to the holographic model, not only brain function but reality is the result of waves of interference in a now-you-see-it-now-you-don't mode. The observer makes the difference. Look, and you see an onion. Look away from the onion, and the intersecting ripple pattern on the holographic film returns. When you are not looking, the interference pattern is all there is. This point of view is akin to experiments in quantum mechanics; how the observer sets up the experiment determines what happens, including the appearance and behavior of an individual photon. All that exists by itself—apart from any observer—is an unbroken wholeness (David Bohm in Zukov, 1979, 95). Holographic theory means that the world is interference patterns—unless there is an observer. The eye of the observer achieves a laser-like transformation (using, perhaps, a Fourier-like calculation: Changeux, 1985; Churchland, 1986; Talbot, 1991), which translates interference patterns into things or people, as we believe things and people exist.

For educators, the point of holographic theory, as is the point with quantum physics, is that the observer makes a difference. More particularly, the mental acuity of the observer determines how the interference patterns are translated by that particular observer, including their sharpness and completeness. Acuity is trainable—from the most direct level of looking at objects and drawing them—to writing about objects using categorized and embedded language systems. The holographic model underscores the radical individuality of perception, as well as its variability and its embeddedness. The holographic model (as does the fractal model) also emphasizes the mathematical aspects of human thought. Research with Warlpiri (contemporary seminomadic hunter/gatherer Central Australian aborigines) who create sand songs and site path designs suggest that preliterate symbolic communication has a grammar and that this iconography is a form of mathematics with visual components that interact like notational components in algebra. This field of study is described as ethnomathematics. In communications like the sand songs (marks drawn in sand like petroglyhs are carved in rocks, only sand songs, like Native American sand paintings, are evanescent: the wind blows the marks away) "mathematics provides a means for individuals to explain and control complex situations of the natural and of the artificial environment and to communicate about those situations. On the other hand, mathematics is a system of concepts, algorithms and rules, *embodied in us,* in our thinking and doing; *we are subject to* this system, it determines parts of our identity" (Roland Fischer, *Mathematics as a means and as a system* in Restivo, Sal; van Bendegem, Jean Paul; and Roland Fischer, *Eds. Math Worlds: Philosophical and Social Studies of Mathematics and Mathematics Education,* Albany: State University of New York Press, 1993, pp.113-133 cited in the article "Sand Songs: The Formal Language of the Warlpiri Iconography" by James R. Rauff, Humanistic Networks Journal #15, p.26, July 1997).

<u>Note</u>: Italics under "embodied in us" and "we are suject to" were added by the author to underscore the intimate relationship between our brains, our thinking, and mathematics.

If the implications of the holographic model are to be taken seriously, it is critical to train the mind to work with abstract and intangible patterns matter-of-factly and concretely. It is also extremely important educationally to make connections between mathematics and other languages, like the ones we speak and write and read.

## The Form of the form

**The Form of the form is a new term** to describe the structure and process (fractal, holographic, and mathematical) underlying and responsible for the brain's operations. Like religious terminology or systems of geometry, the term can only be an approximation but it provides an attempt to describe hierarchically something which operates, for all intents and purposes, globally and simultaneously.

The predisposition toward language is a form of this Form. Languages—spoken, written, mathematical, musical—are specific manifestations of one—the linguistic—form of many forms of the Form. The predisposition toward language is variously called deep or innate grammar. This grammar allows very young children to construct strings of well-formed sentences. Overheard language triggers and operationalizes innate grammar. Another manifestation of the form of the Form is drawing. No trigger is necessary for children to mobilize this visual grammatical system.

The Form (fractal, holographic) organizes stimuli in waves and patterns via neural-based, mathematics-like operations. A nerve fires when there is neither too much nor too little electro-chemical energy. A wave of excitation floods the brain as a result of millions of right relationships, achieving a pattern of tightly spiraled energy recognized as a perception or a thought.

In a drawing, right relationships are felt, first, but are capable of analysis. A student who creates right relationships between line, form, and space in a CA through thoughtful, largely non-verbal contemplation of the work from all angles is able to analyze these relationships verbally, bringing them to a conscious, communicable level. Right relationships in abstract drawings depend upon something like Praxitelian symmetria—the chiastic, "crossed," asymmetrical balance expressed in the contrapposto stance of the Greek sculpture "Doryphoros." Right relationships in the brain occur neurally and globally, and are felt on some level as resolution, and may include not only perceptions and thoughts, but provide the basis for decisions and conclusions. Having come to a conclusion after struggling with a dilemma is often felt as relief, or peace. That sensation, too, can be examined verbally: why do I feel so relieved as I drive away from that situation? I feel relieved because I see that I have decided to leave that situation behind. Mathematical problems often yield to intuitive, felt solutions, first. These solutions are capable of backward analysis, providing a logical, spelt-out proof, or explanation. As we become increasingly sensitive to brain processes, the same should be true, to some extent, of our understanding of our own thinking through the use of images and words.

## Bihemispheric brain processes can be described as employing three formal sub-systems:

1. a meta or over-arching rightbrain/leftbrain, spatial/linguistic system
2. a visual system
3. a verbal system.

The brain spoke the language of the senses, first, a "where is it/what's it doing?" locational language. When humans started naming, the brain added a categorical "what is it?" word-based capability. The spatial/linguistic system became visual and then it became verbal. Pictures, words, mathematical and musical notation developed as specialized sub-sub-systems.

**A set of mathematical operations and/or syntactic rules organize incoming stimuli in accordance with relationships recognized in some manner by the brain as coherent or balanced or resolved.** Research in neurobiology supports the existence of innate syntactic rules which operate at levels well below and above verbal language. The fact that students in group critiques agree about "too much or too little" in each other's drawings supports the existence of innate sensibilities, or spatial/syntactic rules for rightness, or pleasingness, or balance.

Drawing/Writing provides practice with right relationships. These exercises work from the simple to the complex, from the concrete to the abstract, and from the visual to the verbal. The specific instructions or rules or syntax are:

- Select visual information, express it visually, and then express it verbally.
- Combine visual information in one coherent presentation and then express it verbally.
- Take the visual statement and break it back down into parts, producing a new visual statement; then, express that new statement verbally.
- Take verbal statements about visual information in simile, metaphor, analogy, prediction and hypothesis, and translate these in visual terms.
- Include neither too much nor too little in the visual and in the verbal translations.
- After every translation exercise, explain the translation exchange using the word "because."

In Drawing/Writing, visual processing begins with the distinction between figure and ground—or what is and what is not the subject under consideration. This distinction is made by drawing the outline of the object. The informational search moves on to form, continues to value, and culminates with a wealth of additional information including texture and relevant details. This resulting drawing is optically accurate. It is followed by an abstract, recombinant drawing which no longer looks like the object but stands for it. This process of selection, accumulation and transformation of visual information provides an overall shape or form or grammar of intelligent visual thought.

In Drawing/Writing, verbal information begins with physical description and works toward analysis, then inference through the use of declarative sentences, simile, metaphor, analogy, speculation, prediction and hypothesis. This process of description, analysis and inference provides an overall shape or form or grammar of intelligent verbal thought. When used deliberately in parallel and interconnected modes, this visual grammar and this verbal grammar enhance and extend thought. This extension and enhancement demonstrate and develop human thought as naturally and optimally spatial/linguistic, or visual/verbal—as a combined, cooperative enterprise.

We inherit a mother tongue and either do or do not acquire other spoken and written languages. The specific grammars and syntaxes or rules for organizing words in strings called sentences influence how we think, as does the depth and breadth of our command of the vocabulary in that language. As the contemporary British author A.S. Byatt observed in one of her earliest books (it may be noted that she uses the language of geometry), all Western philosophical studies—as far as the philosopher Nietzsche was concerned—are variations on the same problems in recurring circles because all ideas are "unconsciously dominated and directed by simple grammatical functions which are in the end physiological" (*Shadow of the Sun,* 1993, 187).

This book supports the position that the grammars we use to organize spoken and written language are, at base, physiological. Great circles occur in many geometries and structure many philosophies because they are inherent in the organization of mind/body. The question is whether a syntax or grammar or form of intelligent thought can be designed and taught which takes its design cues from brain science and other disciplines within the combined field of cognitive science which will allow any mind using any mother tongue to use its brain optimally despite any peculiar grammatical constraints placed on that brain by that language's sentence structure or vocabulary. This book suggests that the answer is yes—any language can be used in optimal, brain-like ways—and a five-step program called Drawing/Writing provides one such syntax for intelligent visual and verbal thought.

## A non-pharmacological approach to optimal brain performance:

The arts provide natural ways to normalize certain aspects of neurochemistry because of their high attentional, motivational, emotional and cognitive benefits. The normalization of brain function in connection with the arts is self-regulatory. Artists, writers, dancers, musicians learn how to initiate, sustain and regulate attention. When action and attention provide a self-regulatory neurochemical feedback loop, brains produce their best work, achieving, as a dividend, states like peace, satisfaction, happiness, euphoria and joy. Since the brain requires heightened experience, it makes sense to devise methods for providing heightened experiences that do not damage brain function.

## Strange Loops:

Solutions to complex problems are not strictly trackable—logically or neurally. Douglas Hofstadter used the term "Strange Loops" in *Gödel, Escher, Bach: The Eternal Golden Braid* to describe the non-explainable aspects of powerful systems, including the brain. In mathematics, Strange Loops are accounted for by Gödel's Theorem as they are in physics by Heisenberg's Uncertainty Principle. In brain science, a theory like Neuroconstructivism and a practice like The Thinking Child recognize and champion the nonlinear aspects of children's learning, predicting the unpredictability of WholeBrain classroom practice. Inexplicable events are inherent in complicated systems.

## A unified duality:

The brain functions discretely and globally. This "right-left hemisphere complementarity" (Rucker, 1987) is like the "wave/particleness" of light described by Arthur Zajonc, Amherst College physics professor (*Catching the Light,* 1993), or like this book's definition of geometry as the study of shapes-in-space—another dyad—or this book's presentation of a teaching and learning strategy called Drawing/Writing. Paradoxical complementarity is a way of explaining the nature of our minds, our actions, and our realities. A unified duality describes productive classrooms in which teachers and students constitute a nonlinear, complex feedback loop.

*Blue Heron, oil painting, unified male/female, standing and in flight, SRS 1975*

# Works Cited

Abbott, Edwin A. (1884) <u>Flatland</u>. New York: Signet Classic, 1984.

Abelson, Harold and Andrea diSessa, Andrea. <u>Turtle Geometry</u>. Cambridge, MA: MIT Press, 1980.

Andrews, David Bruce, "The half-silvered mirror: brain assessment and learning skills improvement. A demonstration project with 8th graders." Dissertation. The Ohio State University, DA 8625177, 1986.

Arnheim, Rudolph. <u>Visual Thinking</u>. Los Angeles, Calif.: University of California Press, 1969.

Ashton-Warner, Sylvia. <u>Teacher</u>. New York:Simon & Shuster, 1963.

Barthes, Roland. <u>The Responsibility of Forms: Critical Essays on Music, Art, and Representation</u>. Berkeley, Calif.: University of California Press, 1985.

Bates, Kenneth F. <u>Basic Design. Principles and Practice</u>. New York: Barnes & Noble Books, 1960.

Begley, Sharon, "Your Child's Brain: How Kids are Wired for Music, Math and Emotions." *Newsweek.* Feb. 19, 1996, pps. 55-58.

"Uncovering Secrets, Big and Small." *Newsweek.* Jan. 27, 1997, pps. 63-69.

Blakeslee, Sandra, "Studies Show Talking with Infants Shapes Ability to Think," *The New York Times,*. April 17, 1997, Section D, p. 21.

Bloom, Floyd E., Arlyne Lazerson, & Laura Hofstadter, eds. *Brain, Mind, and Behavior.* New York: W.H. Freeman & Co., 1985.

Bevlin, Marjorie Elliot. (1963). *Design through Discovery.* New York: Harcourt Brace College Publishers, 1993.

Bonnefoy, Yves, compiler. *American, African, and Old European Mythologies* by Honigsblum, Gerald et al. Chicago: University of Chicago Press, 1993.

Bowen, Ron. *Drawing Master Class.* Toronto, Canada: Bulfinch Press, Little Brown & Co, 1992.

Buber, Martin. *I/Thou.* New York: Charles Scribner's Sons, 1958.

Bullock, James O., "Literacy in the Language of Mathematics." *The American Mathematical Monthly* Vol. 101, No. 8, October, 1994, pps. 735-743.

Burton, Daniel M. <u>The History of Mathematics. An Introduction</u>. Newton, MA: Allyn and Bacon, Inc., 1985.

Byatt, A.S. (1993) Shadow of the Sun. New York: Harcourt Brace and Co.

Carpenter, Malcolm B., and Sutin, Jerome. <u>Human Neuroanatomy</u>. Baltimore/London: Willaims & Wilkins, 1983.

Changeux, Jean Pierre. <u>Neuronal Man</u>. London: Oxford University Press, 1985.

Churchland, Patricia Smith. <u>Neurophilosophy</u>. Cambridge, Mass.: MIT Press, 1986.

Chomsky, Noam. (1980). Rules and Representations. New York: Columbia University Press.

    (1973) Language and Cognition. New York: McGraw-Hill, Inc.

    (1968). <u>Language and Mind</u>. New York: Harcourt Brace Jovanovich, Inc., 1972.

    (1965) Aspects of the Theory of Syntax. Cambridge, Mass.: MIT Press.

Cook, Theodore Andrea (1917) The Curves of Life. New York: Dover Publications, Inc., 1979.

Crick, F.H.C., "Thinking about the brain." *Scientific American.* 1984.

David, Lloyd. "Massachusetts Employer Survey Incumbernt Worker Training." *Massachusetts Coaliton for Adult Education Network* October, 1995.

Dawkins, Richard. <u>The Blind Watchmaker.</u> New York: W.W. Norton &Co., 1986.

Dendel, Esther Warner. <u>Designing from Nature</u>. New York: Taplinger Publication Co., 1978.

Edwards, Betty. <u>Drawing on the Right Side of the Brain</u>. Los Angeles: J.B. Tarcher, 1979.

Faith, Valerie, "Kinetic Grammar." Center for Study of Teaching of Writing, Towson State University, Towson, MD. Oct. 1989.

Ferreiro, Emilia & Teberosky, Ana. <u>Literacy Before Schooling</u>. Portsmouth, N.H.: Heinemann, 1979.

Fite, Katherine V., " Television and the Brain: A Review," commissioned by the Children's Television Workshop," June 15, 1993.

Freeman, Norman. <u>Visual Order</u>. Cambridge: CambridgeUniv. Press, 1985.

    <u>StrategiesZ  of Representation in Young Children</u>. London: Academic Press, 1976.

Freeman, Walter J., "Happiness Doesn't Come in Bottles" <u>Journal of Consciousness Studies 4, No.1</u>, 1997, pps. 67-70.

    "Societies of Brains." <u>Journal of Consciousness Studies 3 No.2</u>, 1996, pps. 172-180.

    <u>Societies of Brains</u>. New Jersey: Lawrence Erlbaum Associates, Inc., 1995.

    "The Physiology of Perception." *Scientic American,* Feb., 1991, pps. 78-85.

Galaburda, Albert M., Joan Corsiglia, Glenn D. Rosen, Gordon F. Sherman. "Planum temporale asymmetry, reappaisal since Geschwind and Levitsky." <u>Neuropsychologia</u> 25 (1987) : 853-868.

Gardner, Howard. <u>The Mind's New Science</u>. New York: Basic Books, Inc., 1985.

    <u>Frames of Mind</u>. New York: Basic Books/Harper Collins Publishers, 1983.

Gazzaniga, Michael. <u>Mind Matters</u>. Boston: Houghton Mifflin Company, 1988.

    <u>The Social Brain</u>. New York: Basic Books, 1985.

Geiger, Gad, & Lettvin, Jerome Y., "Perpherial vision in people with dyslexia." <u>The New England Journal of Medicine</u>, <u>316</u>, 1987, pps. 1238-1243.

Gimbutas, Marija. <u>The Language of the Goddess</u>. San Francisco: HarperCollins Publishers. 1989.

   <u>The Goddesses and Gods of Old Europe. Mythis and Cult Images</u>. Berkeley: University of California Press, 1974.

Gilmore, Timothy M., "Overview of the Tomatic Method." <u>About the Tomatis Method</u>. Amherst, MA: Listening Centre Press, 1989.

Gladwell, Malcolm, "Damaged." *The New Yorker,* Feb. 24 and Mar. 3, 1997, pps. 132-147.

   "The Tipping Point." *The New Yorker.* June 3, 1996, pps. 32-38.

Gleick, James. <u>Chaos</u>. New York: Penguin Books, 1987.

Gombrich, E.H. (1985). <u>The Story of Art</u>. Englewood Cliffs, N.J.: Prentice Hall, 1995.

   <u>Art and Illusion</u>. Princeton, N.J.: Princeton University Press, 1956.

Goodnow, Jacqueline. <u>Children Drawing</u>. Cambridge, Mass.: Harvard University Press, 1977.

Gordon, Elizabeth Scott. <u>The Transitive Vampire: A Handbook of Grammar for the Innocent, the Eager, and the Doomed</u>. New York: Times Books, 1984.

   <u>The Well-Tempered Sentence. A Handbook of Punctuation for the Innocent, Eager and the Doomed</u>. New York: Times Books, 1983.

Gould, Stephen Jay, "The Shape of Life." *The Art Journal* Spring, <u>Vol 55 No.1</u>, 1996, pps. 44-46.

Greenough, W.T. and J. E. Black, "Introduction of brain structure by experience: Substrates for cognitive development." In Gunnar, M. and C. Nelson, eds. *Developmental Behavioral Neuroscience* <u>24</u>, 1992, pps. 155-200.

Greenough, W.T., J.E. Black, and C.S. Wallace, "Expereince and brain development." In Joynson, M.H., ed. <u>Brain Development and Cognition: A Reader</u>. Cambridge: Blackwell Publishers, 1992, pps. 290-319.

   "Experience and brain development." *Child Development* 58, 1987, pps. 539-559.

Greenough, William T., "What's special about development? Thoughts on the bases of experience-sensitive synaptic plasticity." <u>Developmental Psychology</u>. New York: Academic Press, 1986.

Hall, James E. "Tilings through Art and Science." *Humanistic Mathematics Network.* October 12, 1995, pps. 7-17.

Hancock, LynNell, Pat Wingert, Mary Hager, Claudia Kalb, Karen Springer, Dante Chinni, " Mother's Little Helper." *Newsweek.* March 18, 1996, pps. 51-56.

Harb, Mary B., "Letters." *Newsweek* March, 1996, p. 15.

Hawkes, Terence. <u>Structuralism and Semiotics</u>. Berkeley, CA: University of California Press, 1977.

Hernstein, J. and Charles Murray. <u>The Bell Curve</u>. New York: Free Press, 1994.

Heynman, Gene, "Resolving the contradictions of addiction." *Behavioral and Brain Sciences,* #19, 1996, pps. 561-610.

Hofstadter, Douglas R. Gödel, Escher, Bach: The Eternal Golden Braid. New York: Vintage Books, 1985.

Honigsblum, Gerald et al. American, African, and Old European Mythologies. Compiled by Yves Bonnefoy. Chicago: University of Chicago Press, 1993.

Horgan, John, "Group Think." *The Scientific American,* July 1996, pps. 19-20..

"The New Social Darwinists." *The Scientific American,* October 199, pps. 174-181.

Hubel, David H., "Eye, Brain and Vision." Scientific American Library series number 22. New York: Scientific American Library, 1988.

"Vision and the Brain." (1988). Space, Time and Motion editted by David Layzer, Harvard Course Science A-18, 995.

Hughes, Robert. The Shock of the New. New York: Alfred A. Knopf, 1980.

Irlen, Helen. Reading by the Colors. The Irlen Method. California: Avery Press. 1991.

Kegan, Robert. The Evolving Self: Problem and Process in Human Development. Cambridge, Mass.: Harvard University Press, 1982.

Keller, Helen. (1908) The Story of My Life. New York: Bantam Books, 1990.

Kempermann, Gerd, H. Georg Kuhn and Fred H. Gage, "More hippocampal neurons in adult mice living in an enriched environment." *Nature* Vol. 386/Issue 6624. Apr. 3, 1997, pps. 493-95.

Kennedy, John M., "How the Blind Draw." *Scientific American.* Jan. 1997, pps. 76-81.

Kolata, Gina, " Men and women use brain differently, study discovers." *New York Times,* Feb. 16 1995, A1+. (Kolata reports on study by Drs. Sally E. and Bennett A. Shaywitz and colleagues at Yale University School of Medicine.)

Korzybski, Alfred. Science and Sanity: An Introduction to Non-Aristotelian Systems and General Semantics. Englewood, New Jersey: Institute of General Semantics, 1933.

Kosslyn, Stephen Michael. Ghosts in the Mind's Machine. New York: W.W. Norton and Co., 1983.

Kozol, Jonathan. Savage Inequalities. New York: Crown Publishers, Inc., 1991.

Lane, Harlan. Wild Boy of Aveyron. Cambridge, Mass: Harvard Univ. Press, 1976.

Landini, Gabriel, "Pathology in Geometry and Geometry in Pathology." Fractal Horizons. The Future Use of Fractals ed. Clifford A. Pickover. New York: St. Martin's Press, 1996, pps. 252-261.

Layzer, David. Space, Time and Motion. Cambridge: Harvard University Publication, Science A-18, 1995.

L'Engle, Madeleine. A Wind in the Door. New York: FSG Arrar Strauss & Giroux, 1974.

Leutwyler, Kristin. "Blocking Stroke Ion Channels." *Scientific American* April 1997, p. 26-28.

Lewis, C.S. (1950) The Lion, the Witch and the Wardrobe. First published by Geoffrey Bles.

Llinas, Rodolpho, " 'Mindness' as a functional state of the brain." Unpublished when given to researcher. New York: New York University Hospital, 1986.

   "Calcium in synaptic transmission." Scientific American, Oct. 1982, pps. 3-11.

   "The cortex of the cerebellum." Scientific American, 232, 1, 1975, pps. 56-71.

Lipschutz-Yevick, Miriam, " The Questionable Probability Theory Behind the Strange Story of the Bell Curve's Bell Curve." *Humanistic Mathematics Network* Journal #12, Oct. 1995, pps. 22-27.

Luria, A.R. The Making of Mind. Cambridge, Mass.: Harvard University Press, 1979.

Luston, Ellen & J. Abbott Miller. Design Writing Research: Writing on Graphic Design. New York: Princeton Architectural Press, 1996.

Mandelbrot, Benoit B. The Fractal Geometry of Nature, New York: W. H. Freeman and Co., 1977.

Martineau, Lavan. The Rocks Begin to Speak. Las Vegas, Nevada: KC Publications, 1973.

McKim, Elizabeth and Judith Steinberg. Beyond Words: Writing Poetry with Children. Green Harbour, Me: Wampeter Press, 1983.

Minsky, Marvin. Mind in Society. New York: Simon & Shuster, 1985.

Montessori, Maria. (1912). The Montessori Method. Cambridge, Mass.: Robert Bentley, Inc., 1964.

Motherwell, Robert. The Collecting Writings of Robert Motherwell, Oxford: Oxford University Press, 1992.

Nash, Madeleine, "Fertile Minds." *Time Magazine.* Feb. 3. 1997, pps. 49-56.

Ornstein, Robert & Richard F. Thompson. The Amazing Brain, Boston: Houghton Mifflin Company, 1984.

Pascal, Blaise. (1958) Pensees. New York: E.P. Dutton.

Pappano, Laura, "Getting from A to B." *The Boston Globe Magazine* Nov. 26, 1995, pps. 28-30,45-52.

Papert, Seymour. Mind Storms. New York: Basic Books, 1980.

Papert, Seymour & Daniel Dennett, "Letters." *Newsweek,* 1966 p.15.

Perkins, David. "Creativity by design." Educational Leadership, Sept. 1984, pps. 18-25.

   The Mind's Best Work. Cambridge, Mass.: Harvard University Press, 1981.

Perrine, Laurence. Sound and Sense, 5th edition, New York: Harcourt Brace, Jovanovich, Inc., 1977.

Pert, Candace, "The Chemical Communicators." Healing and the Mind by Bill Moyers, New York: Doubleday, 1993.

Piaget, Jean.(1955). Thought and Language in the Child. New York: Meridien Books, 1959.

Pickover, Clifford A. Fractal Horizons. New York: St. Martin's Press, 1996.
    Computers: Pattern, Chaos and Beauty. New York: St. Martin's Press, 1990.

Pinker, Steven How the Mind Works, New York: W.W. Norton, 1997.
    The Language Instinct, New York: Harper Collins, 1994.

Poincare, Henri. Science and Hypothesis, 1952, pp. 35-72 in Space, Time, and Motion by David Layzer, Science A-18, Harvard University, Fall, 1995.

Rauff, James V. (1977) "Sand Songs: The Formal Languages of the Warlpiri Iconography," *Humanistic Mathematics Network,* #15, July 1997.

Root-Bernstein, Robert, *The Art Journal* Spring Vol. 55 No. 1, 1996.

Rosenfield, Israel. The Invention of Memory. New York: Basic Books, Inc., 1988.

Rosenzweig, Mark R. & Bennett, Edward L., "Experiential influences on brain anatomy and brain chemistry in rodents." In Gilbert Gottlieb ed. Early Influences. New York: New Academy Press, 1978, 289-323.

Roucoux, A., Culee, C., & Roucoux, M., "Development of fixation and pursuit eye movements in human infants." Developmental Brain Research, 10, 1983, pps. 133-139.

Rubin, John, "Mind meets brain." Technology Review, 92, 1, 1989, pps. 13-14.

Rucker, Rudy. Mind Tools. Boston: Houghton, Mifflin, 1987.

Sacks, Oliver. Migraine. University of California Press: Berkeley, 1992.

Schroeder, Manfred, " Fractals in Music." Fractal Horizons. The Future Use of Fractals. Ed. Clifford A. Pickover. New York: St. Martin's Press, 1996, pps. 207-224.

Schwartz, Joseph & Michael McGuinness. (1979) Einstein for Beginners. New York: Pantheon Books.

Scinto, Leonard R.M. Written Language and Psychological Development. New York: Academic Press, 1986.

Shaywitz, Sally E., & Bennett A., "Sex difference in the functional organization of the brain for language." *Nature,* Vol. 373, 16, Feb. 1995, pps. 607-609.
    "Evaluation and treatment of children with attention deficit disorders." Pediatrics in Review, 6, 1984, pps. 99-108.

Shaywitz, Sally E., "Dyslexia." *Scientific American* Nov. 1996, pps. 98-104.

Shearer, Rhonda Roland, " Real or Ideal? DNA Iconography in a New Fractal Age." *The Art Journal,* Spring Vol. 55, 1996 pps. 64-69.

Sheridan, Susan, "The Rescore method of evaluating descriptive and inferential thinking skills in children's writing." Unpublished. 1989.

"The Bill Budge Pin-Ball Machine and Douglas MacLeod: An Empirical Study." Unpublished, 1990.

Drawing/Writing: a brain research-based writing program designed to develop descriptive, analytical and inferential thinking skills at the elementary level. Dissertation, U. Mass: Amherst, 1991.

Smith, David A. (1994) "Trends in Calculus Reform." Conference Preceedings, Preparing for a New Calculus, Anita Solow, Ed. Mathematical Association of America, notes #36.

Talbot, Michael. The Holographic Universe. New York: HarperCollins, 1991.

Tillich, Paul. The Courage to Be. New Haven: Yale University Press, 1952.

Vygotsky, Lev. (1934, 1962) Thought and Language. Cambridge, Mass.: MIT Press, 1986, 1987.

Elementary Mathematics. Collets: London, 1979.

"The prehistory of writing." The Mind In Society. Cambridge, Mass: Harvard University Press, 1978.

Wallace, Douglas C., "Mitochondrial DNA in Aging and Disease." *Scientific American,* Aug. 1997, pps.40-47

Walsh, Jill Paxton. Knowledge of Angels. New York: Bantam Books, 1995.

Walters, Anna Lee. (1985) The Sun is not Merciful. Ithaca, New York: Firebrand Books.

White, Alvin, "Humanistic Mathematics Network, Journals 5-12." Claremont, Calif.: Harvey Mudd College Press, 1990-1995.

Williams, Miller. Patterns of Poetry. Baton Rouge: Louisiana State University, 1986.

Winner, Ellen. Invented Worlds. Cambridge, Mass.: Harvard University Press, 1982.

Wolkomir, Richard. "Making up for Lost time: the rewards of reading at last," *The Smithsonian,* August, 1996, pps. 82-91.

Yevick, also under Miriam Lipschutz-Yevick, "The Questionable Probability Thoery Behind the Strange Story of the Bell Curve's Bell Curve." *Humanistic Mathematics Network,* Journal #12, Oct. 1995, pps. 22-27.

Zajonc, Arthur. Catching the Light, New York: Oxford University Press, 1993.

Zukov, Gary. The Dancing Wu Li Masters, New York: William Morrow and Co., 1979.

# Extended Bibliography

Adler, Mortimer. (1984) The Paideia Program. New York: MacMillan Publishing Co.

Allport, D.A., S.P. Tipper, & N.R.J. Chmiel, N.R.J., "Perceptual integration and postcategorical filtering." Attention and Performance, Michael I. Posner and Oscar S.M. Marin eds. Hillsdale, N.J.: Lawrence Erlbaum, Assoc., 1984, pps. 108-110.

Arnheim, Rudolph. (1969) Visual Thinking. Los Angeles, Calif.: University of California Press.

Ashton-Warner, S. (1964) Bell Call. New York: Simon & Schuster, 1964.

Ayres, A. Jean. (1974) The Development of Sensory Integrative Theory and Practice. Dubuque, Iowa: Kendall/Hunt Publishing Co..

"Cluster analyses of measures of sensory integration." American Journal of Occupational Therapy, 31, 1977, pps. 362-371.

Bakhtin, Mikhail. (1986) Speech Genres and other Late Essays, Caryl Emerson & Michael Holquist eds. Transl. by Vern W. McGee. Austin, Texas: University of Texas.

Barrs, Myra, "Drawing a Story." (1988) The Word for Teaching is Learning: Essays for James Britton, Martin Lightfoot and Nancy Martin, eds. London: Heinemann Educational Books.

Barthes, Roland. (1978) A Lover's Discourse: Fragments. New York: Hill & Wang.

Elements of Semiology. (1964) New York: Hill & Wang.

Bates, Kenneth F. (1960) Basic Design. Principles and Practice, New York: Barnes & Noble Books.

Belenky, Mary Field, Blythe McVicker Clinchy, Nancy Rule Goldberger, Jill Mattuck Tarule. (1986) Women's Ways of Knowing: The Development of Self, Voice, and Mind. New York: Basic Books.

Bellak, Leopold. (1954) The T.A.T., C.A.T. and S.A.T. in Clinical Use. New York: Grune & Stratton, 1971.

Benton, Arthur L., "Dyslexia: Evolution of a concept." (November, 1979) Annual Conference of the Orton Society, Indianapolis.

Blakemore, Colin. (1977) Mechanics of the mind. Cambridge: Cambridge University Press.

Bloom, Floyd E., Arlyne Laserson, & Laura Hofstadter. (1985) Brain, mind, and behavior. New York: W. H. Freeman and Company.

Brazelton, T. Berry. (1969) Infants and Mothers. Differences in Development. New York: Delacorte Press.

Toddlers and Parents. (1974) New York: Delacorte Press.

Brigham, Don L., "Visual Art in Interdisciplinary Learning." Program of Promise, A. Hurwitz ed. New York: Harcourt Brace. 1974, pps. 75-86.

Britten, James. (1982) <u>Prospect and Retrospect</u>. London: Heinemann Educational Books.

    <u>Language and Learning</u>. (1970) London: Penguin Books.

Britten, James & Tony Burgess, Nancy Martin, Alex McLeod, Harold Rosen. (1975) <u>The Development of Writing Abilities (11-18)</u>. London: McMillan Education.

Bruner, Jerome. (1986) <u>Actual Minds, Possible Worlds</u>. Cambridge, MA: Harvard University Press.

Bruner, Jerome. (1983) <u>In Search of Mind</u>. New York: Harper Colophon Books.

Calkins, Lucy M. (1986) <u>The Art of Teaching Writing</u>. Portsmouth, N.H.: Heinmann Co..

Calvin, William. (1986) <u>The River that Flows Uphill</u>. San Francisco: Sierra Club Books.

    <u>The Throwing Madonna</u>. (1983) New York: McGraw Hill.

Calvin, William H., & Ojemann, George A. (1980) <u>Inside the Brain</u>. New York: New American Library.

Carpenter, Malcolm B. & Jerome Sutin, Jerome. (1983) <u>Human Neuroanatomy</u>. ( 8th ed.). Baltimore/London: Williams and Wilkins.

Chamberlin, Robert W., "Developmental Assessment and early intervention programs for young children: lessons learned from longitudinal research." <u>Pediatrics in Review, 8</u>, 1987, pps. 237-247.

Chance, Paul, "The remedial thinker." <u>Psychology Today</u>. Oct. 1981, pps. 63-73.

Coleman, J. Michael. Neuroscience of Learning Symposium, Cleveland Clinic, 1988.

Cowey, A., "Aspects of cortical organization related to selective attention and selective impairments of visual perception: a tutorial view." <u>Attention and Performance</u>, Michael S. Posner and Oscar S.M. Marin eds. Hillsdale, N.J.: Lawrence Erlbaum Associates, 1985, pps. 41-58.

CTB/McGraw-Hill. <u>CAT Writing Assessment System</u>. Monterey: California, 1986.

David, Lloyd. "Massachusetts Employer Survey Incumbernt Worker Training," *Massachusetts Coaliton for Adult Education Network* Oct. 1995

Davies, D.R., D.M. Jones, & Anne Taylor, "Selective-and sustained-attention tasks: individual and group differences." <u>Varieties of Attention</u>, Raja Parasuraman & D.R. Davies eds. Orlando, Florida: Academic Press, 1984, pps. 402-433.

De Bono, Edward. (1972) <u>Children Solve Problems</u>. New York: Harper & Row.

Denckla, Martha, "Mental health aspects of learning disabilities and their sequelae." Lecture, Orton Society Medical Symposium, May 5, NYC, 1988.

Denhoff, Eric, "Current status of infant stimulation or enrichment programs for children with developmental disabilities." <u>Pediatrics, 67</u>, 1981, pps. 32-41.

Devries, Rheta, & Lawrence Kohlberg, Lawrence. (1987) <u>Programs of Early Education</u>. New York: Longman.

Diamond, M.C., A.B. Scheibel, & L.M. Elson. (1985) <u>Human brain coloring book</u>. New York: Barnes and Noble.

Diamond, Marion. Lecture, Cleveland Clinic, 1988.

Donaldson, Margaret, "The mismatch between school and children's minds." <u>Human Nature</u>, 1979, pps. 60-67

Drexler, Eric. (1986) <u>Engines of Creation. The Coming Era of Nanotechnology</u>, New York: Anchor Press/Doubleday.

Duckworth, Jane C., & Wayne T. Anderson. (1986) <u>MMPI Interpretation Manual for Counselors and Clinicians</u>. Indiana: Accelerated Development, Inc..

Eccles, John C. (1973) The <u>Understanding of the Brain</u>. New York: McGraw-Hill Book Company, 1977.

Elberger, Andrea J., "The functional role of the corpus callosum in the developing visual system: a review." <u>Progress in Neurobiology, 18</u>, 1982, pps.15-79.

Elbow, Peter. (1990) <u>What is English?</u> New York: The Modern Language Association of America.

Elkind, David. (1974). <u>Children and Adolescents. Intepretative Essays on Piaget</u>. New York: Oxford University Press.

Eisner, Eliot, "Mind as Cultural Achievement." <u>Educational Leadership, 38</u>, 1981.

Eisner, Eliot W. (1982) <u>Cognition and Curriculum</u>. New York: Longman Press.

Elkind, David. (1971) <u>Children and Adolescents. Interpretative Essays on Jean Piaget</u>. New York: Oxford University Press.

Farah, M.J., M. S. Gazzaniga, J.D. Holtzman, & M. Kosslyn, " A left hemisphere basis for visual mental imagery?" <u>Neuropsychologia, 23</u>, 1985, pps. 115-8.

Feldman, Edmund Burke. (1970) <u>Becoming Human Through Art</u>. New Jersey: Prentice-Hall, Inc.

Feuerstein, Reuven, Ronald Miller, Ya'acov Rand, Mogens Reimer Jensen, "Can evolving techniques better measure cognitive change?" <u>The Journal of Special Education, 15</u>, 1981, pps. 201-219.

Forman, George E.,& Catherine Twomey Fosnot, "The use of Piaget's constructivism in early educational programs." <u>Research in Early Childhood Education</u>, B. Spodek ed. New York: Collier Macmillan, 1982, pps. 85-211.

"The value of kinetic print in computer graphics for young children." <u>Children and Computers</u>, June 1985, pps.19-34.

Fox, Jeffrey L., "The brain's dynamic way of keeping in touch." <u>Science, 225</u>, 1984, pps. 820-821.

Fox, Jeffrey. (1988) Lecture, Cleveland Clinic.

Franck, Frederick. (1973) <u>The Zen of Seeing</u>, New York: Vintage Books.

Freeman, Norman H. (1976) <u>Strategies of Representation in Young Children</u>. London: Academic Press.

Freire, Paolo. (1921) The Politics of Education. MA: Bergin and Garvey Publications, Inc., 1985.

Pedagogy of the Oppressed. N.Y.: Continuum, 1970.

Cultural Action for Freedom. Cambridge, MA.: Harvard Educational Review and the Center for the Study of Development and Social Change, 1970.

Gardner, Howard. (1980) <u>Artful Scribbles</u>. New York: Basic Books/Harper Collins Publishers.

"Promising Paths Toward Artistic Knowledge; A Report from Harvard Project Zero." *The Journal of Aesthetic Education,* <u>10</u>, Oct. 1976, pps. 201-207.

The <u>Shattered Mind</u>. New York: Vintage Books, 1974.

Garey, Lawrence J., "Development of visual system: comparison of monkey and man." <u>Acta Morphologica Hungarica,</u> 31, 1983, pps. 27-38.

Gazzaniga, M.S., J.J. Sidtis, T. Volpe, C. Smylie, J. Holtzman, & D. Wilson, "Evidence for paracallosal verbal transfer after callosal section. A possible consequence of bilateral language organization." <u>Brain, 105,</u> (Pt. l) 1982, pps. 53-63.

"Our 'two brains': facts and myths." Article later incorporated in <u>The Social Brain</u>. New York: Basic Books, 1985.

& Holtzman, J.D., "Enhanced dual task performance following corupus commissurotomy in humans." <u>Neuropsychologia, 23</u>, 1985, pps. 315-321.

"Perceptual and attentional processes following callosal section in humans." <u>Neuropsychologia, 25</u>, 1987, pps. 19-33.

& J.D. Holtzman, C.S. Smylie, "Speech without conscious awareness." <u>Neurology, 4</u>, 1987, pps. 682-5.

Graham, Norma, Patricia Kramer, & Nancy Haber, "Attending to the spatial frequency and spatial position of new-threshold visual patterns." <u>Attention and Performance</u>, Michael I. Posner & Oscar S.M. Marin eds.Hillsdale, N.J., Lawrence Erlbaum Associates, 1985, pps. 269-271.

Graves, Donald. (1983) <u>Writing: Teachers and Child at Work</u>. Portsmouth, N.H.: Heinemann Educational Books.

Geschwind, Norman, "Why Orton was Right." <u>Annals of Dyslexia, 32</u>, 1982, pps. 13-32

Gooch, Stan, "Right brain, left brain." <u>New Scientist</u>, II, 1980, pps. 790- 792.

Gottlieb, Gilbert ed. (1978) <u>Early Influences</u>. New York: Academic Press.

Gould, Stephen Jay. (1980) <u>The Panda's Thumb</u>. New York: W.W. Norton & Co.

Gould, Stephen Jay. (1977) <u>Ontogeny and Phylogeny</u>. Cambridge Mass.: Harvard University Press.

Graves, Donald. (1983) <u>Writing: Teachers and Children at Work</u>. Portsmouth, N.H.: Heinemann Educational Books.

Grinnell, Paula C., & Nancy A. Burris, "Drawing and writing: the emerging graphic communication process." <u>Topics in Learning & Learning Disabilities</u>, 3:3, 1983, pps. 21-29.

Grusser, O.J., T. Selke, & B. Zynda, "A developmental study of face recognition in children and adolescents." <u>Human Neurobiology, 4</u>, 1985, pps. 33-39.

Harter, M. Russell, & Cheryl J. Aine, " Brain mechanisms of visual selective attention." <u>Varieties of Attention</u>, Raja Parasuraman & D.R. Davies eds. New York: Academic Press, 1984, pps. 293-317.

Harwerth, Ronald, Earl L. Smith III, Gary C. Duncan, M.L. J. Crawford, Guner K. von Noorden, "Multiple sensitive periods in the development of the primate visual system." <u>Science</u>, 232, 1986, pps. 235-238.

Haskins, Ron, Neal W. Finkelstein, Donald J. Stedman, "Infant-Stimulation programs and their effects." <u>Pediatric Annals</u>, 7:2, pps. 99-123.

Hellerstein, David, "Plotting a theory of the brain." <u>The New York Times Magazine</u>, May 1988, pps. 16-19.

Hockey, Robert, "Varieties of Attentional State." <u>Varieties of Attention</u>, Rajar Parasuraman and D.R. Davies eds. Orlando, Florida: Academic Press, 1984, pps. 463-466.

Holtsman, Jeffrey D., Bruce T. Volpe, & Michael S. Gazzaniga, Michael S., "Spatial orientation following commissural section." <u>Varieties of Attention</u>, Raja Parasuraman & D.R. Davies eds. Orlando, Florida: Academic Press, 1984, pps. 375-386.

Holt, John. (1967) <u>How Children Learn</u>. New York: Selta/Seymour Lawrence.

Hubel, David, & Weisel, Torsten. (1962) <u>Early Influences</u>. Gilbert Gottlieb ed. New York: Academic Press.

Huttenlocher, P.R., & Ch. de Courten, "The development of synapses in striate cortex of man." <u>Human Neurobiology, 6</u>, 1987, pps.1-9.

Jansson, H.W. ( 1962) <u>History of Art</u>. New Jersey: Prentice-Hall, 1977.

Johnson, George, "Scientists identify 'gate' in brain as crucial to memory." <u>The New York Times</u>, May 10, 1988 C-1.

Kahneman, Daniel, Anne Treisman, Anne, "Changing Views of Attention and Automaticity." <u>Varieties of Attention</u>, Raja Parasuraman & D.R. Davies eds. Orlando, Florida: Academic Press, Inc., 1984, pps. 29-57.

Kasner, Joan F., "Theoretical support for and use of original drawings and associative cues in vocabulary acquisition by children with severe reading disorders." <u>Journal of Learning Disabilities, 18</u>, 1985, pps. 395-399.

Kauffman, Stuart, "At Home in the Universe." London: Oxford University Press, 1995.

Kinsbourne, Marcel, & Mark Byrd, "Work load and visual hemifield shape recognition: priming and interference effects." <u>Attention and Performance</u>, Michael I. Posner & Oscar S.M. Marin eds. Hillsdale, N.J.: Lawrence Erlbaum Assoc., 1985, p. 529.

Kirsner, Kim, & John Dunn, "The perceptual record: a common factor in repetitive priming and attribute retention?" <u>Attention and Performance</u>, Michael I. Posner & Oscar S.M. Marin eds. Hillsdale, N.J.: Lawrence Erlbaum Assoc., 1984.

Kowler, Eileen, & Caroline Zingale, "Smooth eye movements as indicators of selective attention." <u>Attention and Performance</u>, Michael I. Posner & Oscar S.M. Marin eds. Hillsdale, N.J.: Lawrence Erlbaum Associates, 1985, p. 285.

Kellog, R. (1970) "Analyzing children's art." National Press, Palo Alto.

Keogh, Barbara K. (1988) "The Neuroscience of Learning." Cleveland Conference.

Kemp, Fred, "Getting smart with computers: computer-aided heuristics for student writers." <u>Writing Center Journal,</u> <u>8</u>, 1987, pps. 3-10.

Kosslyn, Stephen. (May, 1988) Lecture, Cognitive Sciences Group, U. Mass., Amherst, Mass.

Kosslyn, Stephen M., Rita S. Berndt, Timothy I. Doyle, "Imagery and language processing: a neuropsychological approach." <u>Varieties of Attention</u>, Raja Pararsuraman & D.R. Davies eds. New York: New Academy Press, 1984, pps. 319-321.

    & Rita S. Berndt, Timothy I. Doyle, Timothy J., "Imagery and language processing: a neuropsychological approach." <u>Varieties of Attention</u>, Raja Pararsuraman & D.R. Davies eds. New York: New Academy Press, 1984, pps. 319-321.

Kuhn, Deanna, "The application of Piaget's theory of cognitive development to education." <u>Harvard Educational Review, 49</u>, 1979, pps. 340-360.

Greene, Maxine. (1978) <u>Landscapes of Learning</u>. New York: Teachers College Press.

Greene, Maxine. (1973) <u>Teacher as Stranger</u>. Belmont, Calif.: Wadsworth Press.

Harb, Mary B., "Letters," *Newsweek,* March, 1996, p. 15.

Hawkes, Terence. (1977). <u>Structuralism and Semiotics</u>, Berkeley, CA: University of California Press.

Heath, Shirley Brice. (1983) <u>Ways with Words</u>. Cambridge: Cambridge University Press.

Horgan, John. "Group Think." *Scientific American,* July, 1996, pps. 19-20.

Howard, Vernon A., "Harvard Project Zero: A fresh look at education." <u>The Journal of Aesthetic Education</u>. 1971.

Hughes, Robert. (1980) <u>The Shock of the New</u>, New York: Alfred A. Knopf

Ives & Rakow. (1980) Project Zero. Harvard.

Kegan, Robert. (1994) <u>In Over Our Heads: The Mental Demands of Modern Life</u>, Cambridge, Mass.: Harvard University Press.

Kozol, Jonathan. (1995) <u>Amazing Grace</u>. New York: Crown Publishers, Inc.

Lehrer, Warren. (1983) <u>I mean you know</u>. New York: Visual Studies Workshop.

Levine, Melvin D., Judith S.Palfrey, George A. Lamb, Herbert I. Weisberg, & Anthony S. Bryk, Anthony S., "Infants in a public school system: the indicators of early health and educational need." <u>Pediatrics, 60</u>, 1977, pps. 80-586.

Levine, Melvin D., & Nancy C. Jordan, "Learning disorders: the neurodevelopmental underpinnings." <u>Contemporary Pediatrics, 4</u>, 1987, pps. 16-43.

Levy, Jerre, "Research synthesis on right and left hemispheres: we think with both sides of the brain." <u>Educational Leadership</u>, 1979, pps. 66-71.

"Right brain, left brain: fact and fiction." <u>Psychology Today</u>, 1985, pps. 38-77.

Lightfoot, David. (1986) <u>The Language Lottery</u>. Cambridge, Massachusetts: MIT Press.

Lightfoot, Martin & Nancy Martin. (1988). <u>The Word for Teaching is Learning: Essays for James Britten</u>. London: Heinemann Educational Books.

Llinas, Rodolpho, "Calcium in synaptic transmission." <u>Scientific American, 247</u>, 1982, pps. 56-65.

Lowenfeld, V. (1964) <u>Creative and mental growth</u>. (4th edition compiled by W.L. Brittian). London: Collier-MacMillan.

Maloney, Michael P., Michael P. Ward. (1976) <u>Psychological Assessment</u>. New York: Oxford University Press.

Marg, Elwin, "Prentice Memorial lecture: is the animal mode for stimulus deprivation amblyopia in children valid or useful?" <u>American Journal of Optometry and Physiological Optics, 59</u>, 1982, pps. 451-456.

Malaguzzi, Loris, director of the Reggio Emilia preschool system, Italy. Lectures, December 2-3, 1988, U. Mass.

Martin, Nancy. (1983) <u>Mostly about Writing. Selected Essays</u>, Upper Montclair, N.J.: Boynton/Cook Publishers.

McCorduck, Pamela. (1979) <u>Machines Who Think</u>. San Francisco: W.H. Freeman & Co.

McDonald, Mary Alice, Marian Sigman, & Judy A. Ungerer, "Intelligence and behavior problems in 5-year-olds in relation to representational abilities in the second year of life." <u>Developmental and Behavioral Pediatrics, 10</u>, 1989, pps. 86-91.

Mistretta, Charlotte M., & Robert M. Bradley, "Effects of early sensory experience on brain and behavioral development." <u>Early Influences</u>, Gilbert Gottlieb ed. (pp. 215-241). New York: Academic Press, 1984, pps. 215-241.

Morgan, W.P., "A case of congenital word-blindness." <u>British Medical Journal, 2</u>, (1896): 1378.

Motherwell, Robert. (1992) <u>The Collecting Writings of Robert Motherwell</u>, Oxford: Oxford University Press.

Othanian, Susan. (1993) <u>Garbage pizza, patchwork quilts, and math magic</u>, N.Y.: W.H. Freeman and Company.

Ottenbacher, K.J., L. Muller, D. Brandt, Hojem Heintzelman, & P. Sharpe, "The effectiveness of tactile stimulation as a form of early intervention; a quantitative evaluation." Journal of Developmental Behavior, Pediatrics, April 8 (2), 1987, pps. 68-76.

Ottenbacher, K.J., P. Petersen, "The efficacy of vestibular stimulation as a form of specific sensory enrichment." Clinical Pediatrics, Aug 23(8), 1984, pps. 428-33.

Orton, Samuel. (1937) Reading, Writing and Speech Problems in Children. New York: W.W. Norton.

Ozman, Howard A. & Samuel M. Carver. (1976) Philosophical Foundations of Education. Columbus, Ohio: Merrill Publishing Co.

Parasuraman, Raja, & D.R. Davies eds. (1984) Varieties of Attention. Orlando, Florida: Academy Press, pps. 251-259.

Pauls, David L. (1988) Neuroscience of Learning Symposium, Cleveland Clinic.

Penrose, Roger. (1989) The Emperor's New Clothes. Oxford: Oxford University Press.

Petrovski, Henry. (1996) Invention by Design, Cambridge, MA: Harvard University Press.

Piaget, Jean. (1962) Play, Dreams and Imitation in Childhood. New York: W.W. Norton & Co.

Piaget, Jean. (1960) The Psychology of Intelligence. Totowa, New Jersey: Littlefield, Adams & Co.

Polatajko, H. J., "Visual-ocular control of normal and learning-disabled children." Developmental Medicine and Child Neurology, 29, 1987, pps. 477-485.

Polanyi, Michael. (1958) Personal Knowledge. Towards a Post Critical Philosophy. London and Henley: Routledge & Kegan Paul.

Posner, Michael I., & Oscar S. M. Marin eds. (1985) Attention and Performance XI. Hillsdale, New Jersey: Lawrence Erlbaum Associates, Publishers.

Pradl, Gordon M. ed. (1982) Prospect and Retrospect: Selected Essays of James Britton. Montclair, N.Y.: Boynton/Cook Publishers.

Rabbitt, Patrick, "The control of attention in visual search." Varieties of Attention, Raja Pararsuraman & D.R. Davies eds. Orlando, Florida: Academic Press, 1984, pps. 273-287.

Rohrbaugh, John W., "The orienting reflex." Varieties of Attention, Pararsuraman & D.R. Davies eds. Orlando, Florida: Academic Press, 1984, pps. 323-342.

Roucoux, A., C. Culee, & M. Roucoux, "Development of Fixation and pursuit eye movements in human enfants." Developmental Brain Research. 10, 1983, pps. 133-139.

Read, Herbert. (1956) Education through Art. New York: Pantheon Books.

Rucker, Rudolf v. B. (1977) <u>Geometry, Relativity and the Fourth Dimension</u>. New York: Dover Publications.

    <u>Infinity and the Mind</u>. (1982) New York: Bantam Books.

Sandler, Kathe, film maker. "A Question of Color: Healing Racism's Hidden Wounds." 1993. The film lasts 56 minutes, and can be rented for $75 or bought for $195 through Resolution, Inc./California Newsreel. 149 Ninth Street/420; San Francisco, CA 94103; 415-621-6169

Schachter, Steven C., & Albert M. Galaburda, Albert M., "Development and biological associations of cerebral dominance: review and possible mechanisms." <u>Journal of the American Academy of Child Psychiatry, 25</u>, 1986, pps. 741- 750.

Schickedanz, Judith A. (1986) More Than ABCs. Washington, D.C.: National Association for the Education of Young Children.

Schneider, Walter, "Toward a model of attention and the development of automatic processing." Attention and Performance, Michael I. Posner, & Oscar S.M. Marin eds. Hillsdale, N.J: Lawrence Erlbaum Associates, 1985, pps. 475-477.

Singh, Jagit. (1959) <u>Great Ideas of Modern Mathematics: Their Nature and Use</u>. New York: Dover Publications.

Shimojo, Shinsuke, Eileen E. Birch, Jane Gwiazda, & Richard Held, "Development of vernier acuity in infants." <u>Vision Research, 24</u>, 1983, pps. 721-728.

Shonkoff, Jack P., & Penny Hauser-Cram, Penny, "Early intervention for disabled infants and their families: a quantitative analysis." <u>Pediatrics, 80</u>, 1987, pps. 650-658.

Smith, Frank. (1982) <u>Writing and the Writer</u>. London: Heinemann Educational Books, Ltd.

Smolucha, Larry. (1996) <u>The Visual Arts Companion</u>. New Jersey: Prentice-Hall.

Snider, Vicki E.,& Sara G. Tarver, Sara G., "The effect of early reading failure on acquisition of knowledge among students with learning disabilities." <u>Journal of Learning Disabilities, 20</u>, 1987, pps. 351-356.

Sperling, George. (1984). Attention and signal detection. <u>Varieties of Attention</u>, Pararsuraman & D.R. Davies eds. Orlando, Florida: Academic Press, 1984, p. 172.

Spitzer, H.F. (1961) <u>The Teaching of Arithmetic</u>. Boston: Houghton Mifflin.

Springer, Sally P., & Deutsch, Georg. (1981,1985) <u>Left Brain, Right Brain</u>. New York: W.H. Freeman and Company.

Suchman, J.R. (1962) <u>The Elementary Training Program in Scientific Inquiry</u>. Urbana: University of Illinois.

Tredennick, Hugh. (1959) Plato, <u>The last Days of Socrates</u>. Baltimore, Md.: Penquin Classics.

Van Essen, David C., & John H.R. Maunsell, "Hierarchical organization and functional streams in the visual cortex." <u>Trends in Neuroscience, 6</u>, 1983, pps. 370-377.

van Glasersfeld, Ernst. (1995) <u>Radical Constructivism</u>. London: Falmer Press.

Weir, Sylvia, "The Computer as an Creative Educational Tool." <u>American Annals of the Deaf, 127</u>, 1982, pps.690-692.

"Logo and the Exceptional Child." <u>Microcomputing</u>, Sept. 1981, pps. 78-83.

<u>Logo as an Information Prosthetic for the Handicapped</u>. Cambridge: MIT Press, 1981.

& Watt, Daniel. <u>LOGO: A computer Environment for Learning-Disabled Children</u>. Cambridge, Mass.: LOGO Group, MIT, May 1980.

Weisel, T.N., "Postnatal development of the visual cortex and the influence of the environment." <u>Nature, 229</u>, 1982, pps. 583-592.

Wertsch, James. V. (1985) <u>Vygosky and the Social Formation of Mind</u>. Cambridge, Mass.: Harvard University Press.

White, Alvin. (1990-1995) *Humanistic Mathematics Network, Journals* 5-12, Claremont, Calif.: Harvey Mudd College Press.

Winograd, Terry, & Fernando Flores. (1986) <u>Understanding Computers and Cognition</u>. Norwood, N.J.: Ablex Publishing Co.

Wolf, Dennis, Lyle Davidson, Martha David, Joseph Walters, Matthew Hodges, & Larry Scripp, "Beyond A, B, and C: a broader and deeper view of literacy." Project Zero, Harvard, 1988.

Wolf, Dennie, & Sharon Hya Grollman, "Ways of playing: individual differences in imaginative style." Contr. Hum. Dev. 6/7 Spalte l T&B, 1982.

Wolf, W.C., "Systematic communication of educational innovation: a synoptic history of research and practice." <u>Viewpoints in Teaching and Learning</u>, 54, 2, 1978, pps. 57-70.

"Change agent strategies in perspective." <u>Specialist Continuing Education</u>. Northfield, Il.: Cooperative Educational Research Laboratory, Inc., 1969.

Yaroshevsky, Mikhail. (1989) <u>Lev Vygotsky</u>. Moscow: Progress Publishers.

Zinsser, William. (1988) <u>Writing to Learn</u>. New York: Harper & Row.

Photo by Carl Allen, Allen Photography, Shelburne, Mass.

Dr. Susan Rich Sheridan is a teacher, an artist and a writer. She received her BA in Classics and English from Harvard College and her MAT and doctorate from the University of Massachusetts at Amherst.

Dr. Sheridan currently teaches art history, design fundamentals and continuing education courses in Drawing/Writing at Westfield State College. Over the past ten years, Drawing/Writing has reached a range of students including middle school English, art, biology and ESL students, special education students including LDD and ADD students, talented and gifted middle school Native American students, high school English, art and philosophy students, Elderhostlers, prison inmates, college level art educators, college level regular education and art education majors, K-12 school teachers, principals and superintendents, and job skills trainees.

The book *Drawing/Writing and the new literacy* establishes Dr. Sheridan as a pioneer in the field of brain-based teaching and learning.

# DRAWING/WRITING and the new literacy
### BY SUSAN RICH SHERIDAN, 1997
*An illustrated guide to a brain-based literacy program*
*including "Hitchhikers' Guide to Brain Science" and "The Thinking Child"*

Cost per book: $29.95
Shipping & handling: $4.00 per book
Shipping & handling: $3.00 per book thereafter
Europe (surface mail): Additional $5.00 per book

| # of Items | Price Each | Total Price |
|---|---|---|
| _____ | _____ | _____ |

Merchandise total: _____

Shipping & handling: _____

ORDER TOTAL: _____

*Method of payment:*   ❑ MasterCard   ❑ Visa   ❑ Check

CREDIT CARD NUMBER

☐☐☐☐☐☐☐☐☐☐☐☐☐☐☐☐   Exp. Date_____

( )

Authorized Signature                    Daytime Phone

**Susan Rich Sheridan, Ed.D.**
*Drawing/Writing*
**68 Maplewood Drive**
**Amherst, MA 01002**
**sheridan@k12.oit.umass.edu**

**Ship to:**

☐

Name: _____

Home Address: _____ Apt. # _____

City: _____ State: _____ Zip: _____

Home telephone number and/or FAX: _____

**OR**

☐

Business or Institution _____ Dept. or Title_____

Address: _____

City: _____ State: _____ Zip: _____

Business telephone number and/or FAX:_____

## About the Book:

*Drawing/Writing and the new literacy* opens with the background and rationale for a brain-based literacy program called Drawing/Writing. The book then provides step by step instruction in the five-step Drawing/Writing process, fully illustrating each step with student work. Two supplemental sections follow: a thumbnail sketch of neurobiology called "Hitchhikers' Guide to Brain Science: Use it or Lose it," and "The Thinking Child," a guide to cross-modal curriculum design including sample English and Arts curricula appropriate at the elementary, middle, high school and college levels.

The bi-hemispheric brain integrates visual and verbal information. Drawing/Writing models this process, deliberately connecting drawing with writing to increase overall literacy abilities. Students are more ready and more able to write, read and think when they receive substantive training in drawing. Being able to "write" and "read" images as well as words is *the new literacy*. A technological society requires *the new literacy*.

Brain-based teaching and learning is cover-story news. Children's brains grow and change over time. To grow and change, children's brains require appropriate teaching and learning strategies. Drawing/Writing provides an appropriate strategy. Because the activity of drawing encourages attention, self-esteem, self-directed learning and group cohesiveness, this literacy program has relevance for today's diverse classrooms. Experience this five-step program through the book *Drawing/Writing and the new literacy*. Teach and learn directly from your experience. No prior drawing skills necessary.

**Susan Rich Sheridan, Ed.D.**
*Drawing/Writing*
**68 Maplewood Drive**
**Amherst, MA 01002**

Photo by Carl Allen, Allen Photography, Shelburne, Mass.

Dr. Susan Rich Sheridan is a teacher, an artist and a writer. She received her BA in Classics and English from Harvard College and her MAT and doctorate from the University of Massachusetts at Amherst.

Dr. Sheridan currently teaches art history, design fundamentals and continuing education courses in Drawing/Writing at Westfield State College. Over the past ten years, Drawing/Writing has reached a range of students including middle school English, art, biology and ESL students, special education students including LDD and ADD students, talented and gifted middle school Native American students, high school English, art and philosophy students, Elderhostlers, prison inmates, college level art educators, college level regular education and art education majors, K-12 school teachers, principals and superintendents, and job skills trainees.

The book *Drawing/Writing and the new literacy* establishes Dr. Sheridan as a pioneer in the field of brain-based teaching and learning.

# DRAWING/WRITING and the new literacy

BY SUSAN RICH SHERIDAN, 1997

*An illustrated guide to a brain-based literacy program*
*including "Hitchhikers' Guide to Brain Science" and "The Thinking Child"*

| Cost per book: | $29.95 |
| Shipping & handling: | $4.00 per book |
| Shipping & handling: | $3.00 per book thereafter |
| Europe (surface mail): | Additional $5.00 per book |

| # of Items | Price Each | Total Price |
| --- | --- | --- |
| _____ | _____ | _____ |

Merchandise total: _____

Shipping & handling: _____

ORDER TOTAL: _____

*Method of payment:*  ❏ MasterCard  ❏ Visa  ❏ Check

CREDIT CARD NUMBER

▢▢▢▢▢▢▢▢▢▢▢▢▢▢▢▢  Exp. Date_____

( )

_____
Authorized Signature                     Daytime Phone

**Susan Rich Sheridan, Ed.D.**
*Drawing/Writing*
**68 Maplewood Drive**
**Amherst, MA 01002**
sheridan@k12.oit.umass.edu

**Ship to:**  ❏

Name: _____

Home Address: _____ Apt. # _____

City: _____ State: _____ Zip: _____

Home telephone number and/or FAX: _____

**OR**  ❏

Business or Institution _____ Dept. or Title_____

Address: _____

City: _____ State: _____ Zip: _____

Business telephone number and/or FAX: _____

## About the Book:

*Drawing/Writing and the new literacy* opens with the background and rationale for a brain-based literacy program called Drawing/Writing. The book then provides step by step instruction in the five-step Drawing/Writing process, fully illustrating each step with student work. Two supplemental sections follow: a thumbnail sketch of neurobiology called "Hitchhikers' Guide to Brain Science: Use it or Lose it," and "The Thinking Child," a guide to cross-modal curriculum design including sample English and Arts curricula appropriate at the elementary, middle, high school and college levels.

The bi-hemispheric brain integrates visual and verbal information. Drawing/Writing models this process, deliberately connecting drawing with writing to increase overall literacy abilities. Students are more ready and more able to write, read and think when they receive substantive training in drawing. Being able to "write" and "read" images as well as words is *the new literacy*. A technological society requires *the new literacy*.

Brain-based teaching and learning is cover-story news. Children's brains grow and change over time. To grow and change, children's brains require appropriate teaching and learning strategies. Drawing/Writing provides an appropriate strategy. Because the activity of drawing encourages attention, self-esteem, self-directed learning and group cohesiveness, this literacy program has relevance for today's diverse classrooms. Experience this five-step program through the book *Drawing/Writing and the new literacy*. Teach and learn directly from your experience. No prior drawing skills necessary.

**Susan Rich Sheridan, Ed.D.**
*Drawing/Writing*
**68 Maplewood Drive**
**Amherst, MA 01002**